RELG: World, 4e
Robert E. Van Voorst

Senior Vice President, Higher Ed Product, Content, and Market Development: Erin Joyner

Product Manager: Kori Alexander

Content Manager: Samantha Rundle

Learning Designer: Emma Guiton

Product Assistant: Hannah Ells

Marketing Manager: Laura Kuhlman

Marketing Coordinator: Kelsey Grau

Sr. Art Director: Bethany Bourgeois

Text Designer: Tippy McIntosh

Cover Designer: Lisa Kuhn, Curio Press, LCC/Chris Miller, Cmiller Design

Cover Image: Natali_Mis via Getty Image

Intellectual Property Analyst: Diane Garrity

Intellectual Property Project Manager: Nick Barrows

Production Service/Composition: SPi Global

For product information and technology assistance, contact us at **Cengage Customer & Sales Support, 1-800-354-9706 or support.cengage.com.**

For permission to use material from this text or product, submit all requests online at **www.cengage.com/permissions**.

Library of Congress Control Number: 2017952269

Student Edition ISBN: 978-1-337-40505-8
Student Edition with MindTap ISBN: 978-1-337-40504-1

Cengage
20 Channel Center Street
Boston, MA 02210
USA

Cengage is a leading provider of customized learning solutions with employees residing in nearly 40 different countries and sales in more than 125 countries around the world. Find your local representative at **www.cengage.com**.

Cengage products are represented in Canada by Nelson Education, Ltd.

To learn more about Cengage platforms and services, register or access your online learning solution, or purchase materials for your course, visit **www.cengage.com**.

Printed in the United States of America
Print Number: 03   Print Year: 2020

VAN VOORST
RELG⁴ Brief Contents

Contents

LOOPS7/EIMAGES; BONNIE VAN VOORST © CENGAGE LEARNING; BONNIE VAN VOORST © CENGAGE LEARNING

AMMIT JACK/SHUTTERSTOCK

LEARNT, LOVE, LOST BUT FOUND. AN AMAZING ADVENTURE/GETTY IMAGES; BONNIE VAN VOORST © CENGAGE LEARNING

3 Encountering Hinduism: Many Paths to Liberation 60

Your Visit to Varanasi, India 61

4 Encountering Jainism: The Austere Way to Liberation 92

Your Visit with Jain Nuns 93

NINA LISCHUK/SHUTTERSTOCK.COM

5 Encountering Buddhism: The Middle Path to Liberation   108
Your Visit to a Zen Retreat Center   109

EFESENKO/SHUTTERSTOCK.COM

SOLOVIOV VADYM/SHUTTERSTOCK.COM

SHAN_SHAN/SHUTTERSTOCK.COM

8 Encountering Shinto: The Way of the Kami 186

Your Visit to the Tsubaki Shinto Shrine in Granite Falls, Washington 187

PK289/SHUTTERSTOCK.COM

9 Encountering Zoroastrianism: The Way of the One Wise Lord 204

Your Visit to Yazd, Iran 205

10 Encountering Judaism: The Way of God's People 222

Your Visit to the Western Wall in Jerusalem 223

KUNI TAKAHASHI/GETTY IMAGES

SERGEI25/SHUTTERSTOCK.COM

AUDIOSCIENCE/SHUTTERSTOCK.COM

ZOUZOU/SHUTTERSTOCK.COM

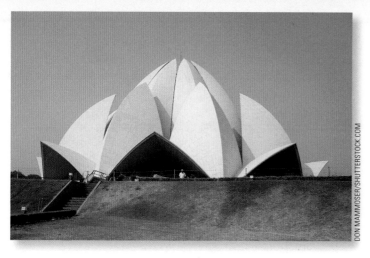

DON MAMMOSER/SHUTTERSTOCK.COM

1

Beginning Your Study of World Religions

LOOPS7/EIMAGES; BONNIE VAN VOORST © CENGAGE LEARNING; BONNIE VAN VOORST © CENGAGE LEARNING

LEARNING OUTCOMES

After studying this chapter, you will be able to do the following:

1-1 State and explain your own preunderstanding of religion.

1-2 State and explain the definition of *religion* used in this book.

1-3 Give your own answer to the question: Why study religion?

1-4 List and describe the six different dimensions of religion.

1-5 Discuss how the various academic disciplines contribute to the study of religion.

1-6 Explain the special issues involved in the study of religion today.

VIACHESLAV/SHUTTERSTOCK

Your Visit to the Hsi Lai Temple in Southern California

Imagine that you're walking up the broad flight of stone steps to the Hsi Lai (shee LAI) Buddhist temple in Hacienda Heights, California, just east of Los Angeles. Hsi Lai claims to be the largest Buddhist temple in North America, and it certainly looks like it from where you stand! When you get inside, you look around and realize that this is a religious building complex like none other you have ever seen. No large-group ceremonies are going on, at least not right now. Instead, small groups of worshipers and tourists come and go, doing their own thing. Some offer incense, a few are carrying flowers to leave in the temple, others are praying and meditating in front of statues, and out in the courtyard people are doing meditative exercises.

The families coming to this temple do not seem to reflect deeply on their faith while here. Nobody is reading Buddhist religious texts, and the monks are not teaching or preaching to a group. Rather, people come here just to sense something of the sacred and be in its presence. Their minds are calmed by the familiar architecture, the many statues of the Buddha, and by the smell of incense. They engage in quiet, low-key activities.

©LE DO/SHUTTERSTOCK.COM

A part of the Hsi Lai Buddhist Temple complex in Southern California

The new perspective of Earth from space has helped to stimulate global thinking on religions. The continent of Asia visible here is where most of the religions treated in this book originated, including Judaism, Christianity, and Islam.

You notice people who aren't doing traditional Buddhist worship. You wonder if this means that they might come from other religious traditions. Some people you see are just tourists; a few of them are only interested in the vegetarian buffet lunch served every day. But perhaps they too have come to absorb the beauty of this place, and at least a bit of its religious meaning. This temple was founded not only to bridge the differences between different groups of Buddhists, but also to be a bridge between Eastern and Western religions and ways of life.

As you are introduced to the academic study of religion, you may find yourself bewildered by the varieties of religion, by the different academic methods used to study religions, and by hot topics such as religion and gender, ecology, and violence. You may have questions about matters of fact and value: Is one religion true, are different religions true, or are none of them true? What might it all mean for *you*?

These issues may occur to you as well:

- Formal "separation of church and state" is strong in the United States and Canada, but religion and politics are mixed in powerful ways here and around the world. The government of China's continuous pressure on Buddhism in Tibet is just one example.

- Most people in North America affirm the importance of religion for their lives, but fewer actually practice it. For example, nearly 90 percent of all North Americans believe in the existence of God or gods, but only about half regularly participate in religious services or other religious practices such as prayer, meditation, or giving to those in need.

- Despite a high level of religious belief in the United States, the majority of Americans have surprisingly little knowledge of religion, even their own. Stephen Prothero (PROTH-er-oh), a professor of religion at Boston University who has appeared on *The Daily Show*, says that Americans—even those who attend services regularly—are often "religious illiterates." As Laurie Goodstein of *The New York Times* wrote while summarizing a 2010 study of religious knowledge in the United States, "Americans are by all measures a deeply religious people, but they are also deeply ignorant about religion."[1] In Western Europe, most people don't hold formally to a religion, but they know a good deal about religion, because it is often a required academic subject in schools.

- Is religion in the world shrinking, or is it growing? Actually, the answer is both. Although Christianity is shrinking in Europe and North America, in other parts of the world it is growing; Islam and Buddhism are also growing. The number of people in North America who formally adhere to no religion at all is also growing, but certain religious practices, such as prayer, are as strong as ever.

- Nearly all of the major religions of the world come from ancient times. However, every decade of the past two hundred years has seen new religious movements (NRMs) born around the world; some of them are now powerful, and some are controversial. You might wonder why we still get new religions—don't we have enough already?

- Religion has evoked the best and the worst among humans. Love, care for others, and social reforms have arisen from religion. It has inspired great music, art, and architecture and has uplifted human life in countless ways. However, it has also been the source of much destruction.

> "Americans are by all measures a deeply religious people, but they are also deeply ignorant about religion."
>
> —Laurie Goodstein

1-1 Coming to Grips with Your Preunderstanding of Religion

Imagine for a moment that a good friend tells you, "I've met and talked with an alien visitor from another planet." You might say to yourself, amid all the thoughts and emotions that you might have when you hear something strange or upsetting, "I don't believe in space aliens!" But then you might think, "Are there alien visitors to Earth after all? Maybe they're real, and maybe my friend *has* been talking with them."

preunderstanding
State of one's understanding of reality, with which one makes sense of one's new experiences

You might think this, but probably not. Instead, your mind automatically begins to sift through your knowledge for an explanation consistent with what you already hold to be true. Only people who are already convinced, or seriously entertaining the idea, that a set of things is true—there is life on other planets, beings from these places travel to Earth, and they talk with humans—will easily accept your friend's comment. Given your prior understanding that such things probably aren't factual, you won't likely entertain these theories as a serious possibility.

1-1a What Is Preunderstanding?

We interpret all of our experience in just this way, because, as psychologists tell us, this is the way the human mind operates. Our understanding of new experiences is interpreted in the light of previous experiences. **Preunderstanding** is the state of one's understanding of reality, with which one makes sense of one's new experiences. It describes what we already know, whether that knowledge is correct or not. Even if a new experience corrects our old knowledge—let's say that, in this case, you actually do meet a space alien with your friend—it is always understood on the basis of old knowledge. This new knowledge is then integrated into old understandings, and our preunderstanding grows. In other words, the term *preunderstanding* describes the existing state of our understanding before a new experience calls for interpretation. Our preunderstanding changes as we alter our knowledge, beliefs, and convictions over time.

1-1b Your Preunderstanding of Religion

All this raises the question: What elements of your preunderstanding of religion might influence your study of world religions? Each person must examine and answer this question individually. With each encounter with new people and new ideas, our knowledge of ourselves and our knowledge of others are connected and influence each other. You should first think through your own past encounters with religion, pro and con. Here are several short but thought-provoking questions

Like all human thinking, knowing about one's preunderstanding of religion is a process.

DOCSTOCKMEDIA/SHUTTERSTOCK

to consider as you think of your own preunderstanding of religion and religions:

1. Do I have an unprejudiced view of what religion in general is? Or am I biased for or against it?

2. Can I "suspend my disbelief" or "suspend my belief" to encounter religions objectively?

3. If I hold a religious belief, can I study other religions without feeling threatened in my own?

4. Can I encounter practices that seem unusual to me without getting too upset?

5. Can I be humble and provisional in my conclusions?

6. Can I postpone any personal judgment on a religion until I've learned more about it?

You are now poised to begin your study of the world's leading religions, beginning with the question: "What is religion?" During your journey in understanding, you will encounter the lives and religions of other people. In this process, you will learn more about yourself as well.

1-2 What Is Religion?

Religion is found in all cultures today and throughout history. Evidence from early human remains shows signs of religion, including veneration of animal spirits in art and human burials that suggest belief in a life beyond death. Anthropologists today have concluded that Neanderthal humans who lived around

40,000 years ago may have had religious beliefs and practices, and that modern humans (who began to emerge around 35,000 years ago) definitely had religion. From the dawn of human civilizations to today, religion has shaped all human cultures.

1-2a Defining Religion

But this talk of the prevalence of religion leads us to ask: What exactly is religion? Many people have something interesting to say about what religion is. Grappling with this question involves both careful, objective, academic thinking and personal engagement. John Bowker remarks, "We all know what [religion] is until someone asks us to tell them."[2] If pressed for an answer, people in the Western world would typically say that religion is based on belief in and obedience to God. However, do they mean the God followed in a particular religion or something more general, such as gods? A few major religions—certain branches of Hinduism and Buddhism, for example—have relatively little teaching about gods. Jainism has no gods at all.

Some people around the world would answer that religion is a system of morality. On first reflection, this might seem to be a more all-encompassing definition than the previous one. Karen Armstrong, a former Roman Catholic nun and now a popular writer on world religions, wrote that "Religion starts with the perception that something is wrong," and that the value systems in religions deal with that wrong.[3] The three main Western religions—Judaism, Christianity, and Islam—have strong moral teachings. Confucianism is so centered on morality that the issue of whether it is a social philosophy or a religion is often debated. However, a few religions, such as Shinto, have little or no developed teaching about morality. All this shows how our prior perceptions color our answer to the question, "What is religion?" Despite the difficulties of this question, many scholars from various academic fields have attempted to answer it in as objective a manner as possible.

Those who define religion in a positive way often associate it with light. They see light as a symbol of knowledge, power, and warmth.

KOSMOS111/SHUTTERSTOCK

1-2b Notable Definitions of *Religion*

Another way of studying the issue of what *religion* means is by looking at definitions that have been offered in the past and have had an influence on the discussion. Here is a sampling of how *religion* has been defined in the Western world, by scholars and others. Religion is . . .

- "The feeling of absolute dependence"—Friedrich Schleiermacher, Christian theologian (1799)
- "The opiate of the people"—Karl Marx, founder of communism (1843)
- "A set of things which the average man thinks he believes and wishes he was certain of"—Mark Twain, American writer (1879)
- "A unified system of beliefs and practices . . . which unite into one single moral community"—Émile Durkheim, French sociologist of religion (1915)
- "What grows out of, and gives expression to, experience of the holy in its various aspects"—Rudolf Otto, German scholar of religion (1917)

religion Pattern of beliefs and practices that expresses and enacts what a community regards as sacred and/or ultimate about life

- "All bunk"—Thomas Edison, American inventor (ca. 1925)
- "An illusion deriving its strength from the fact that it falls in with our instinctual desires"—Sigmund Freud, Austrian psychiatrist (1932)
- "The state of being grasped by an ultimate concern . . . which itself contains the answer to the question of the meaning of our life"—Paul Tillich, Christian theologian (1957)
- "A set of symbolic forms and acts which relate man to the ultimate conditions of his existence"—Robert Bellah, American sociologist (1964)
- "Feeling warmer in our hearts, more connected to others, more connected to something greater, and having a sense of peace"—Goldie Hawn, American film actress (2005)

1-2c The Definition Used in This Book

You will have to wrestle with defining *religion*, because scholarship isn't settled on any one definition, and defining it involves some subjectivity. Here's the definition used in this book: **Religion** is a pattern of beliefs and practices that expresses and enacts what a community regards as sacred and/or ultimate about life.

Let's unpack this definition. First, religion is *a pattern of beliefs and practices*. All religions believe certain things about the ultimate reality in or beyond the world. They answer existential questions that humans have such as:

- Why am I here?
- What does it mean to be human?
- How can what is wrong in the world—and in me—be corrected?
- Where am I—and the world—going?

They answer these questions in different ways. Different religions believe in one God (**monotheism**) or many gods (**polytheism**). They believe in a world soul in Hinduism, in Nirvana in Buddhism, and in a cosmic Way in both Daoism (Taoism) and Confucianism. They practice these beliefs in certain ways: in worship, rituals at various points of the individual life cycle, meditation, and ordinary actions in daily life. Each religion, whether monotheist, polytheist, or with no gods at all, has its own way of arranging these beliefs and practices into a distinctive pattern.

Second, this pattern *expresses and enacts what is sacred. Sacred* refers to what is considered most holy and important, whether in this world, in a supernatural world that transcends this one, or both. Religions draw on their experience of the sacred; express the sacred in all of its aspects; and enact it by continuing to make it real for believers. Because common Western notions of the sacred often entail a belief in a holy God, we add this further phrase to our definition: *ultimate about life.* This "ultimate" may be a principle, an impersonal force, or a spiritual power, hidden in the world or beyond it. Sacredness or "the ultimate" in world religions is wider than a divine being.

Third, note that it is a *community* of like-minded people that forms a religion. Religions sometimes begin with an individual (Buddha, Confucius, Jesus, Muhammad), but they soon become social communities of shared belief and practice. They persist through history as communities of religion. Not all religions try to grow throughout the world, but all of them are concerned with passing themselves from generation to generation, thus becoming traditions.

The meaning of *religion* is typically traced to the ancient Latin word *religio* (ree-LIG-ee-oh), derived from the verb *religere*, "to bind/tie fast." Of course, the meaning of a word today can't be limited to what it meant thousands of years ago, but this ancient meaning of *religion* illustrates nicely the different parts of our definition. First, it meant a supernatural constraint on behavior, doing what is good, and especially avoiding evil. It "bound" people to what was right. Second, it entailed a holy awe for the gods and sacred power in general. Third, *religio* meant a system of life that bound people together in a group and oriented them to the gods. Finally, it entailed the practices of rites and ceremonies by which the Roman people expressed and enacted their religion.[4]

> "We all know what [religion] is until someone asks us to tell them."
>
> —John Bowker

Different religions of the world call themselves by different names, many of them not using the word *religion* at all. For example, Daoism is "the Way" to most Daoists; they don't refer to it as "the Daoist religion." Many Hindus call their religion "the Eternal Teaching"; Buddhists often call theirs a "school." Many Jews, Christians, and Muslims prefer the term *faith* instead of *religion.* But no matter what they call themselves, they are in fact *religions* as that term is used in scholarship and teaching.

How does the definition given previously exclude things that *aren't* religion? Here are two examples. First, the definition speaks of religion as a system based on the sacred or on ultimate value; other systems that do not view themselves as religions do not usually speak about the sacred or ultimate. This is true of political ideologies and parties, such as Democrats and Republicans, systems of popular psychology or "life coaching" such as that of Tony Robbins, and so on. (This isn't meant to devalue these other groups; many people find a great deal of meaning and inspiration in them.) Therefore, people who belong to nonreligious groups can also practice a variety of religions or no religion at all. Second, a pattern of belief held by only one person can't be a religion as we define it here. Such do-it-yourself religion may be popular in Europe and North America, and it is usually sincere and important to the person who holds it, but it doesn't bring with it a social bond. Some scholars refer to this as **private religion**, but others question whether private religion is really religion at all.

1-3 Why Study Religion?

At first, the question, "Why study religion?" may seem pointless to you. You might say, "I'm taking the course, aren't I?" You may go on to give your reasons for taking this course: to get course credit, to fulfill a cultural studies requirement at your school and maybe pick up some knowledge and skills along the way, and ultimately to get an academic degree that will lead to a good job. But let's explore a bit further why students today should study religion.

monotheism Belief in one God

polytheism Belief in many gods

private religion Pattern of belief held by only one person

A Closer Look

Is *Religion* a Dirty Word?

To some religious people, *religion* is, if not a dirty word, at least a derogatory one. Some Christians, Jews, and Muslims think that religion is a bad thing. Many religious people want to have a strong connection with God/ultimate reality/cosmic power, but not a "religion." They call their own beliefs a faith, teaching, school, spirituality, or something similar, but they often call other people's belief systems, somewhat pejoratively, "religion." In his best-selling book, *The Shack*, written for Christians and released as a Hollywood film in 2017, William Young even has Jesus say, "I'm not too big on religion."

People who don't like any religion at all also use *religion* in a negative way. A growing number of people in North America and Europe say, "I'm spiritual, but I'm not religious." Spirituality is a growing feature of life in North America and Europe; it is a broad term, but when used in the expression "spiritual, not religious" it usually connotes

a personal interest in religious ideas and values without the social commitments that go with religion. A 2008 documentary film, featuring comic and social critic Bill Maher, was titled not *Religious*, but *Religulous*, Maher's unflattering combination of *religion* and *ridiculous*.

> ### "I'm not too big on religion."
> —Jesus, in *The Shack*

To study world religions well, you have to put aside the prejudices you might have about the term *religion*, whether pro or con. All scholars of religion use *religion* as an academic, neutral, descriptive term, and you should too, regardless of your own personal stance on religious belief and practice. To use an analogy, many people today, including students, often use the word *politics* prejudicially. But in order to study the academic field of political science, one must put aside prejudice about the term *politics*. The same is true with *religion* in the study of religion.

1-3a Studying the Persistence of Religion in the Modern World

Religion should be studied—among other reasons—to understand its persistence in the modern world, which in many ways is not hospitable to religious belief and practice. The rise of **secularism**, or life without religion, particularly in the public sphere, has challenged most religions for the past two hundred years. (A second, lesser-used definition of secularism or secularization is the shift of social institutions such as government, schools, and the rest from religious to civil authority.) Today, the secular approach to life rejects religion for the perceived evils of extremism ("Look what happened on 9/11!" is commonly heard); the inappropriateness of religious training for children ("Children should be allowed to decide for themselves when they are older"); and the better view on life offered by science ("Religion is false, because we know about evolution"). Secularism has led to a lessening of religious belief and practice, and in North America to widespread

secularism Life without religion

illiteracy about religion. Many people, including about half of all Europeans and a growing number of North Americans, are neither especially religious nor completely irreligious; they are "in the middle" between them. They combine aspects of secular life with aspects of religious life.

Secularism has led to the rise of the "nones," people with no religious affiliation. The nones are attracting attention by scholars as their numbers and influence grow in many Western societies and especially in Asia. Scholars are now researching questions like these: Are the nones significantly different as a group from religious people? Should public officials who sometimes encounter religious issues and people be aware of the nones and be prepared to deal with them respectfully? What sorts of religious beliefs might they have, despite being formally unaffiliated with any religion? As examples of this new research, two recent books stand out: Joseph Baker and Buster Smith's *American Secularism: Cultural Contours of Nonreligious Belief Systems* and Christel Manning's *Losing Our Religion: How Unaffiliated Parents Are Raising Their Children*.[5]

Despite the rise of the nones, religion is still a powerful force in the world. This means that reports of the death of religion are mistaken. The **secularization hypothesis**, widely held in the twentieth century, said that science and education would diminish or end religion in the modern world. For instance, British philosopher Bertrand Russell said in 1952 that religion "will fade away as we adopt reason and science as our guidelines." But the secularization hypothesis has now been largely discredited. Religion is strong today even as science and secularism have become more widespread. The nones are prominent, but more than three-quarters of the world's people identify with one or more religions. We still find religion everywhere in high culture, as well as in popular culture (e.g., the TV series *The Americans*, in which Russian spies in the United States have a daughter who complicates their work by converting to Christianity; *Vikings*, in which Christianity slowly challenges a brutal Scandinavian society; and the rock band U2), and in everyday life in North America and around the world. The religions of the world are now present in North America, and nearly every religion is as close as one's keyboard, on the Internet. In the Soviet Union and China—which tried with Communist fervor in the twentieth century to suppress and even extinguish all religion—religion has come back vigorously. Only one in eight people in China now call themselves atheists, and the government of China is bringing back Confucian texts and teachings to counteract the "money-first" mentality among so many young people there. At the beginning of the twenty-first century, religion is at or near the center of global issues and cultural conflict. It has an increasingly visible role in national and even international politics. One simply can't understand many of the conflicts in our world without a basic knowledge of religion. Religion is emerging as one of the main markers of human identity in the twenty-first century, along with gender, class, and ethnicity.[6]

Why does religion keep on thriving? First, despite the challenges to religion, it continues to be a powerful resource for everyday life all around the world. Religion still provides meaning, strength, and joy to many. Another reason is that religious traditions have proven themselves adaptable to the ever-changing situations of human life. They've changed over the thousands of years that many of them have existed, and the study of these changes forms a large part of the study of religion.

The rise of secularism has challenged most religions for the past two hundred years.

KARLOWAC/ISTOCK/GETTY IMAGES PLUS/GETTY IMAGES

(If religions can't or don't change, they usually die out.) Many religions even have some room for skepticism and for the secular, which gives them strength in our rapidly changing world. In many places, especially in central and southern Africa, indigenous religions tied to local cultures are fading, but universal religions such as Christianity and Islam have taken their place. If you want to understand the world today, understanding religion is an important part of it.

The study of religion is also a persistent part of the academic scene. Around 750,000 undergraduates each year in the United States take a religion course. Enrollment in world religion courses in the United States has grown rapidly since the religiously connected attacks on this country on September 11, 2001. A number of students decide to make the study of religion their major or minor. Religion is taught in the vast majority of liberal arts colleges, as well as in private and state universities. Leading universities that didn't have a religious studies program in the past because of a more secular orientation established one in the twentieth century—among them are Harvard, Princeton, Cornell, and Stanford. In 2009 the American Historical Association reported that more historians in the United States now specialize in religious issues than in any others. Even the government of China, which is officially atheistic, is setting up graduate degree programs in religious studies in several of its selective universities. What's more, the study of religion in U.S. K–12 public schools is growing, with some schools using new guidelines from the American Academy of Religion, an association of religion professors.[7] In sum, the academic study of religion is alive and well.

1-3b What the Academic Study of Religion Can Offer You

The opportunity to shape one's knowledge and values is one of the advantages of being a student, but most students today are rightly concerned about how studying religion will help them earn a living in today's economy. A small proportion of students in religion courses choose to make a professional career in religion, as the leader of a religious

secularization hypothesis Idea that science and education diminish or end religion in the modern world

community (such as a rabbi, priest, or minister), an editor of religious publications, or a professor of religion. Some students take a world religions course to clarify or strengthen their own religious knowledge and values. They realize the truth in the proverb first uttered by Max Müller, "Those who know only one religion know none."

> "Those who know only one religion know none."
> —Max Müller

Students taking a world religion course learn more about an important aspect of the world today. This study offers students training in a unique combination of academic and everyday skills such as:

- The ability to understand how religious thought and practice are related to everyday life, especially important today in careers such as teaching, health care, social work, and business.

- The ability to understand the religious dimensions of conflicts within and between nations.

- An appreciation of the complexities of religious language and values.

- An ability to understand and explain important texts both critically and empathetically.

- **Cultural intelligence** or "cross-cultural competence," the ability to understand and deal with people of other cultures. The ability to deal with people of other religions is also a part of cultural intelligence.

Few academic fields bring together so many different forms of analysis as religion does. The study of religion is interdisciplinary in a time when the value of interdisciplinary study is increasingly recognized in higher education. With this broad liberal arts background, many religion majors or minors go on to study law, business, education, and medicine in graduate school.[8] In short, the study of religion offers a foundation for a successful and fulfilling career in many fields, in addition to growth in personal knowledge and satisfaction.

1-4 Dimensions of Religion

As we examine the varieties of religious experience, all sorts of human beliefs and practices come into view. Religion seems to be as wide as human life itself. This was illustrated in one American publishing company's poster, which read: "Books about religion are also about love,

cultural intelligence
Ability to understand, respect, and deal with people of other cultures and religions

sex, politics, AIDS, war, peace, justice, ecology, philosophy, addiction, recovery, ethics, race, gender, dissent, technology, old age, New Age, faith, heavy metal, morality, beauty, God, psychology, money, dogma, freedom, history, death, and life." To get a grip on this complexity, various scholars have organized the dimensions of religion in different ways. These dimensions are somewhat artificial, and they cannot fully describe the meaning and value that believers see in their religion. However, they're helpful in grasping the mass of information available about religions. Prominent scholar of comparative religion, Ninian Smart, first laid out five dimensions in the 1960s, but by the 1990s he had come to think there were nine. Rodney Stark and Charles Glock have systematized the various interlocking aspects of religion in the following six dimensions (see Figure 1.1).[9]

1-4a The Cognitive Dimension

Religions have cognitive (thinking) dimensions that teach their followers what is necessary to know. Most religions teach about their gods and founders, often in stories. They teach about the creation of the world, the meaning of life, and ways to overcome death. They teach about human identity, both individual and social: gender,

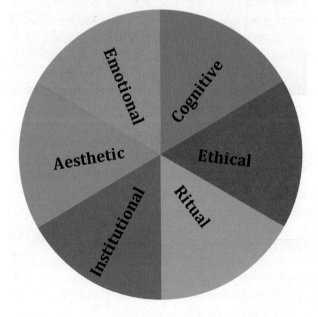

Figure 1.1 Dimensions of Religion

Emotional · Cognitive · Ethical · Ritual · Institutional · Aesthetic

ROBERT VAN VOORST © CENGAGE LEARNING

class, ethnicity, and other aspects of human identity. They provide ways of understanding what the world is and what it should be. Often, the history of religion itself is explained so that followers can know that they stand in a great tradition. The cognitive dimension of religion entails analyzing and systematizing knowledge, as well as learning it and passing it on. Its teachings are framed in stories; in short statements that summarize beliefs (e.g., the Four Noble Truths of Buddhism); and in songs, proverbs, laws, and many other forms. The cognitive dimensions of religion typically grow so comprehensive that religions usually contain an entire worldview. However, we must keep in mind that there is often a significant gap between official religious teachings and what is believed and practiced by ordinary members.

1-4b The Ethical Dimension

Ethics are important in almost all religions, because, as we saw previously, religions seek to correct what they perceive to be wrong in the world. Personal ethics are found in religions, but the emphasis is most often on social ethics. All religions have moral expectations for marriage, families, religious societies or congregations, social classes, and even whole nations. We may think of religious ethics as "rules" more negative than positive, but most religions have a balance of both "do this" and "don't do that." These systems of social ethics can become the law of the nation where religion

is not separated from the state, as is the case with Shari'a, religion-based law in some officially Muslim countries. Values, norms, and patterns of behavior in religions are internalized with the help of moral rules. Different people and activities serve to shape religious behavior: living specialist models, such as people who lead a religion (clergy, monks, gurus, and the like); celebrated models, such as saviors, saints, and immortals; and ordinary models, such as other people in one's religion. When social morality based on religion is constantly and carefully practiced, religion becomes a way of life.

1-4c The Ritual Dimension

(handwritten: moral dimension or belonging to)

Ritual is symbolic action in worship, meditation, or other religious activities. It's symbolic and often abstract, but meant to achieve very practical goals. When most people in North America today think of religion, they think of the ritual ceremonies of worship. But ritual also includes formal and informal prayer, sacrifice, chanting of scriptures, public processions, and even travel. **Pilgrimage**—travel to a special destination to increase one's devotion and/or improve one's religious status—doesn't often come to the minds of modern North Americans as a religious ritual, but in 2015 millions of people worldwide went on a pilgrimage and spent the equivalent of U.S. $19 billion on it. Ritual can be long, elaborate ceremonies performed by religious specialists or simple daily acts such as a short prayer before eating a meal or going to sleep. Rituals are directed to one God, many gods, spirits, or deceased ancestors. Ritual is not only symbolic but also effective; it helps to reenact and reapply the deep truths of a religion to people in the present. Mircea Eliade (MUHR-chuh eh-lee-AH-deh, 1907–1986) advanced his influential theory of "eternal return" around **myths**, stories that relate the basic truths of a religion. (We often use *myth* today to mean an untrue story, but religions use it in an opposite way.) This theory holds that rituals do not simply commemorate myths but actually participate in them and bring believers to

NADINA/SHUTTERSTOCK

Ethical and ritual dimensions come together in a Hindu wedding in Ahmedabad, India, where a priest offers a sacrifice for the well-being of the married couple.

ritual Symbolic action in worship, meditation, or other religious activities

pilgrimage Travel to a special destination to increase one's devotion and/or improve one's religious status

myths Stories that relate basic truths of a religion

God/the gods. In a few religions, the sacrifice of food or drink is thought to feed the gods or deceased ancestors and make them happy with those who offer sacrifices to them.

Within religions there is often a mixed attachment to ritual. For example, in Christianity some Protestants minimize formal rituals, but most Roman Catholics and the Eastern Orthodox have some elaborate rituals. Sufi Muslims emphasize pilgrimage to God "in the heart," in part to contrast with other Muslims who view the pilgrimage to Mecca as the highlight of their life. Some Hindus give up the rituals of the home and temple to seek salvation in solitary meditation. Although ritual may be downplayed, it never completely disappears from religion.

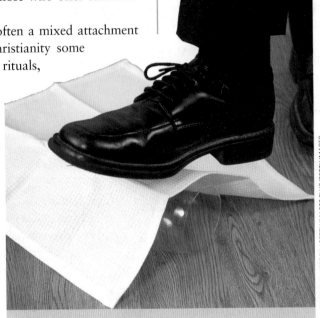

Groom breaking a wineglass at a Jewish wedding, a ritual remembering the destruction of the Jerusalem temple in 70 C.E.

1-4d The Institutional Dimension

Because religions are social more than personal, they give an organizational structure to their religious community and (usually) the wider society. Moreover, many religions are internally diverse, with different institutional structures for each internal group. Most religions come from ancient, traditional societies, so they aren't democratic organizations; power in religious institutions tends to flow from the top down. This is also true of **new religious movements (NRMs)**, religious groups that have arisen since the nineteenth century and now have sufficient size to merit study. Typically, one charismatic leader founds an NRM and wields great power; an example is L. Ron Hubbard of the Scientology movement. Religions make a valid distinction between specialists (religious healers, priests, and monks) who lead the religions and the main body of people who practice a religion, typically called **laity**. This

new religious movements (NRMs) Religious groups that have arisen since the nineteenth century and now have sufficient size to merit study

laity Main body of people who practice a religion

institutional dimension is so important that people often speak of "organized religion."

1-4e The Aesthetic Dimension

The aesthetic (beauty) dimension is the sensory element of religion. Beauty appeals to the rational mind but has a special appeal to human emotions. This dimension encompasses religion's sounds and smells, spaces, holy places, and landscapes. It also includes its main symbols (for instance, Judaism's six-pointed Star of David, and Buddhism's wheel), devotional images and statuary, and all the religious items of material culture. Islamic religious art tends to be abstract, because of strong prohibitions of anything that could enable the worship of other gods. Most Hindu art, on the other hand, is fully representational, at times even sensual. The aesthetic dimension encompasses the architecture and decoration of religious buildings, as well as works of music, poetry, and hymns. It also includes ritual gestures: hand gestures in yoga, bodies kneeling in prayer, hands pressed together in Hindu greeting and Christian prayer, and many others.

1-4f The Emotional Dimension

This dimension includes the particular emotions and wider moods experienced in religion. They include senses of awe, fear, and love. They also include some religions' hope for life after death or other religions' hope for no more life after death. The emotional dimension includes confidence received to cope with death, suffering, and evil. The emotional self-confidence and sense of purpose that religion brings are so notable that "losing my religion" or "getting religion" are common expressions. The emotional dimension includes the emotions that come with belonging and personal identity, as well as with concern for others.

EMYERSON/ISTOCK / GETTY IMAGES PLUS/GETTY IMAGES

It also includes extraordinary feelings and experiences such as isolation, union with an ultimate reality or divine being(s), and hallucinations. The emotional dimension of religion looms large today in the Western world, where belief for many is primarily a matter of emotion. In the words of the 1981 hit song by the rock group Journey, put to more recent use by such television shows as *Family Guy* and *Big Brother*, "Don't stop believing, hold on to that feeling."

To conclude this section, let us consider that sometimes people reduce religion to one or two of these dimensions. For example, they may suppose that religion is primarily an ethical system, a system of teaching about the divine, an institution, or even a feel-good emotion. This reduction is to be expected, but it's wrong. Almost all religions are multidimensional. That the many dimensions of religion are closely related to one another was suggested by British philosopher Alfred North Whitehead, who wrote that the power of religion lies in its grasp of this truth: "The order of the world, the depth of reality of the world, the value of the world in its whole and in its parts, the beauty of the world, the zest for life, the peace of life, and the mastery of evil, are all bound together."[10]

Sensual art put to spiritual use: a Hindu goddess

©MACIEJ MEDYNSKI/SHUTTERSTOCK.COM

1-5 Ways of Studying Religion

The study of religion is pursued today with a wide variety of methods. These center largely on six different academic disciplines, some of which you may be studying. We'll consider these methods and the work of prominent scholars who have influenced the rise of religious studies as an academic discipline by contributing to these methods. Along the way, we'll encounter different theories of the origin and purpose of religion. Before we discuss these methods, however, we should deal with the important matter of the difference between theology and religious studies.

1-5a Theology and Religious Studies

The study of religion in America today is pursued in two main ways. **Theology** is the study of a religion based on a religious commitment to it, in order to promote it. It is a study from the "inside." Christian theology has been an important part of the Western university since the oldest universities were founded in thirteenth-century Europe. Theology is pursued today at many American schools, especially those with religious affiliations. As the eleventh-century Christian theologian Anselm (AHN-sehlm) said, theology is "faith seeking understanding." This statement is true of theological study in other religions as well, in both Eastern and Western religions. The university thought to be the oldest still existing today—at the Al-Azhar (al-ah-ZAHR) Mosque in Cairo, Egypt—was founded for theological study. Theology is older in Buddhism and Hinduism than it is in Christianity or Islam. These religions have typically relied closely on philosophy and textual studies to carry out their theological work.

The second branch is called **religious studies**, a relatively new field of academic study of religion that aims to understand all religious traditions objectively, in a religiously neutral way, from the "outside." Religious studies doesn't ask students to make religious commitments or even require students to reflect on those they have. In the Enlightenment (ca. 1650–1800), the independence and separation of human reason from religion had developed to the extent that a scholarly treatment of religion independent from theology could begin. Reason, not faith, was now seeking understanding of religion. A recent book by Guy Stroumsa, *A New Science: The Discovery of Religion in the Age of Reason*, describes how Roman Catholic and Protestant scholars in Europe forged this new area of study in early modern times. Stroumsa writes that three major events from 1500 to 1800 laid the foundation for the birth of the study of religion: the rise of European colonial empires, which gave birth to curiosity about other cultures; the Reformation, which permanently altered Christianity; and the new academic study of world languages and literature.

theology Study of a religion based on a religious commitment to it, in order to promote it

religious studies Academic study of religion that aims to understand all religious traditions objectively, in a religiously neutral way

By about 1875, religious studies was emerging as an academic field.[11] Now using academic methods from many disciplines in the humanities and sciences, religious studies has a broad intellectual interest in different world religions. It offers a nonthreatening opportunity for students to encounter important issues about religion, different world religions, and life itself.

1-5b History

History is the scholarly study of the past, whether that past is remote (e.g., the beginnings of human civilization) or recent (the events of last year). It seeks to find out what really happened and why. This task is important because, as historian Philip Jenkins has written about religion, "Virtually everybody uses the past in everyday discourse, but the historical record on which they draw is littered with myths, half-truths, and folk-history."[12] When history is applied to religion, rich and important knowledge emerges, because religions come from the past, both remote and recent. The formal method scholars have developed is called the **historical-critical method**, the study of the past using careful scholarly analysis, such as archaeology and the study of texts in their original languages. History studies the process of a religion's beginnings, growth, diversity, decline, and so on. An example is a recent book titled *Sacred Schisms: How Religions Divide*, which carefully studies internal splits in a dozen religions and draws conclusions about the process of religious splits.[13] History has almost always been a main method in the study of religion.

Al-Azhar University in Cairo, founded in 972 C.E.

©AMR HASSANEIN/SHUTTERSTOCK.COM

Oxford historian of Indian culture Max Müller (1823–1900), whom we met earlier, is one of the founders of religious studies—some would say *the* founder. He edited a fifty-volume collection of ancient sacred scriptures from the main Asian religions, translated for the first time into reliable English editions (the Sacred Books of the East series, 1879–1910), a foundational contribution to research and teaching in religious history. He promoted a scholarly discussion on developmental and evolutionary patterns in religious history and on the relation of myth, ritual, and magic to religion in the past. In his *Introduction to the Science of Religion* (1873), Müller argued that religious scholarship can be fully scientific in its methods and results. It can collect, classify, and compare religious texts just as scientifically as a botanist collects and studies plants.

By the end of the 1800s, the notion of near-steady, almost evolutionary progress often assumed in these studies (and in much of European and North American higher learning and culture at that time) started to fade, and the surprising horrors of the First World War (1914–1918) ended assumptions of automatic progress in religion and culture. Müller's work in religious history was largely text based, especially in scriptures. This was a necessary first step, but the field of religious history would widen in the twentieth century to include popular history, the history of material culture, and additional areas. It would also become less naïve about the ability of historians to be "scientifically" objective about their work.

> The surprising horrors of the First World War (1914–1918) ended assumptions of automatic progress.

historical-critical method Study of the past using careful, scholarly analysis

One particular approach taken by a number of historians of religions is the **history of religions school**. The history of religions school began the formal study of religion as a social and cultural phenomenon. It saw religion as evolving with human culture, from "primitive" polytheism to ethical monotheism. It divided world religions into steps of evolution from polytheistic to monotheistic and from informal to formal. Despite the faults of such an approach, it contributed to a sharp increase in our knowledge about other religions. For the first time, an accurate "map" of the different religions of the world emerged (see Map 1.1).

1-5c Psychology

Psychology deals with the structure and activity of the human mind. It is the scientific study of individual behavior, including emotions and other thoughts. Psychology has an interest in religion because of religion's role in shaping human behavior—for example, in coping with life-cycle changes and death. Psychology also focuses on how religions understand the human self, including gender. It has been particularly concerned with research in conversion, mysticism, and meditation.

Psychology sought at first to explain the origins of religion in terms of the subconscious mind. Sigmund Freud (froid) and Carl Gustav Jung (yoong), the founders of psychoanalysis, sought in opposing ways to trace the origins from the strongest, most basic human needs and drives. Freud (1856–1939) and his school regarded religion as a neurotic condition that needed therapy when it persisted into adulthood. (See his definition of religion in Section 1-2b.) He held that religion, particularly a belief in God, derives from a need for a divine father figure when children gradually separate from their human fathers. These ideas can be found in his books *The Future of an Illusion*, in which the "illusion" is religion, and *Moses and Monotheism*. Freud finally admitted that a person could experience religion as a valid "oceanic feeling," but later Freudians would continue to be mostly negative toward religion until about the 1980s, when some change toward a more positive view began.

Freud's pupil Jung (1875–1961), on the other hand, was appreciative of religion. In his books *Modern Man in Search of a Soul* and *Memories, Dreams, Reflections*, he held that conceptions of the divine, whether of god(s) or another form of ultimate reality, were related to an ancient archetypal pattern that resides in the subconscious of all human minds. Religion enables each developing person to bring out and employ this archetype as the individual personality grows and achieves what Jung called "individuation," or personal maturity and wholeness. The notion of individuation would become important in the human potential/humanistic branch of American psychology. This positive archetype is found in all societies, Jung argued, and his theory also became important for many researchers in the academic discipline of cultural anthropology.

William James (1842–1910), a professor at Harvard, was an American founder of the field of psychology. In his still-important book *The Varieties of Religious Experience*, James advanced a more pragmatic and positive view of religion than did either Freud or Jung. He maintained that the religious experience of individuals, not religious institutions, should be the primary focus of the psychology of religion and of religion itself. Intense types of religious experience in particular should be studied by psychologists, because they are the closest thing to a "microscope" into the mind. Individuals must develop certain "over-beliefs" that, while they cannot be proven, help humans live purposefully and in "harmony with the universe." After James, the psychological study of religion went into something of a decline, and scientific research into religious behavior faded.

Since the 1980s, the psychological study of religion has been revived and advanced by neuroscience, particularly with regard to research on the human brain. (Here the psychology of religion comes very close to biology, which we will discuss in Section 1-5g.) A prominent researcher in this field is Andrew Newberg of Thomas Jefferson University in Philadelphia. He measures what happens in the brains of subjects while they meditate or pray—in a way, providing the "microscope into the mind" that William James sought. Newberg's research uses brain imaging to study Tibetan Buddhists in meditation and Roman Catholic nuns in prayer. He has found that during intense sessions of these activities, areas of the brain associated with concentration and emotion become more active and areas associated with the sense of self become less active. Newberg hypothesizes that this may explain the sense of "otherness" and "oneness with God or ultimate

history of religions school The first academic method to study religion as a social and cultural phenomenon

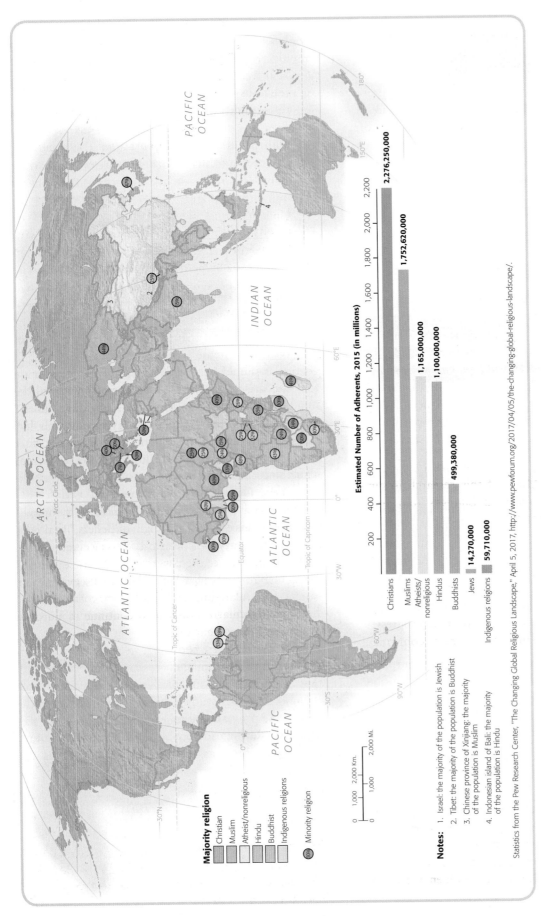

Map 1.1

Distribution of World Religions Today

Christianity has the most believers in the world today and is the dominant faith in the Americas, Oceania, Europe, Russia, and central and southern Africa. Most people in the northern half of Africa, western Asia, and central Asia embrace Islam. Hindus are concentrated in India and Buddhists in East and Southeast Asia. Although China has been largely atheistic or nonreligious under Communist rule, its main religions—Daoism, Confucianism, Buddhism, Islam, and Christianity—are growing, and are now espoused by about 25 percent of the population.

Statistics from the Pew Research Center, "The Changing Global Religious Landscape," April 5, 2017, http://www.pewforum.org/2017/04/05/the-changing-global-religious-landscape/.

Meditating in a simple yoga position

Current debates in the sociology of religion have centered on issues such as the pace of secularization, **civil religion** (the dominant religion of a nation or culture that typically involves a religious conviction about that nation or culture), and the cohesiveness of religions and religious practice in the challenges of globalization, multiculturalism, and pluralism. The sociology of religion based on empirical research is an influential tradition in the United States, and its flagship outlet is the *Journal for the Scientific Study of Religion*. Sociological studies have contributed greatly to our knowledge of religion, for example, on current issues such as NRMs and "fundamentalisms" in world religions.

> "God is society, writ large."
>
> —Durkheim

Émile Durkheim (1858–1917), a founder of sociology, came from a long line of Jewish rabbis but studied religion from the "religious studies" approach. Many scholars today have concluded that the sociology of religion, and perhaps sociology itself, began with Durkheim's 1897 book *Suicide*, which studied, among other things, the rates of suicide occurrence among Catholic, Protestant, and Jewish populations in Western Europe. Durkheim theorized, especially in his essay "The Origin of Beliefs," that religion was necessary for a healthy society: Religion binds societies together. It creates group identity and reinforces common moral values. This is true even when society is secularizing, and Durkheim correctly predicted that secularization would continue in Europe. Durkheim argued that the relationship between people and God mirrors the relationship between individuals and society. His memorable proverb in this regard is "God is society, writ large."

reality" described by people who have had intense religious experiences. Much of this research is summarized in his book *How God Changes Your Brain* (2010). Newberg argues that the physical and emotional benefits of meditation grow over years of practice, but even new practitioners get "healthier brains." After meditating twelve minutes a day for two months, most subjects who have just learned meditation gain significant improvement in memory, and their anxiety and anger decrease. As research in this field progresses, rigorous scientific experiments are now confirming Newberg's conclusions.

1-5d Sociology

Sociology, the scientific study of groups and group behavior, explains religion's role in society. Sociologists studying religion are concerned with the mutual relationship between religion and society, how each shapes the other. They examine, by both qualitative and quantitative research, the practices of religions. Sociologists are interested in beliefs mainly as the backgrounds of social practices and behaviors. They also study the various groups within different religions, including gender (see box, "A Closer Look: Why Are Women More Religious than Men?").

1-5e Cultural Anthropology

Cultural anthropology is the scientific study of human life focused on concrete human settings. It arose in

sociology Scientific study of groups and group behavior

civil religion Dominant religion of a nation or culture that typically involves some religious conviction about that nation or culture

cultural anthropology Scientific study of human life focused on concrete human settings

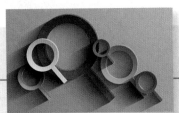

A Closer Look

Why Are Women More Religious than Men?

A recent book examines the fascinating question, *Why Are Women More Religious than Men?*[13] Despite being barred from many leadership positions in most religions, women around the world are significantly more likely to pray, meditate, worship, and otherwise practice their religion than men are. They are also much more likely to say that their faith is important to them. In other words, on average, women are more religious than men in both belief and practice. A 2016 study by the Pew Research Center, "The Gender Gap in Religion Around the World," available online, confirms this fact. Why is this so?

The authors of this book, Marta Trzebiatowska and Steve Bruce, both sociologists, conclude that the difference between the religious intensity of men and women is due not to biological differences between females and males but to differences in social roles. Giving birth, raising children, and dealing with the death of their husbands (who typically die first in developed societies) incline them to greater religious experience and commitment. Women also have attitudes toward their bodies and physical health that are associated with greater religiousness. The authors show that as women's lives become more similar to men's and indifference to religion grows, the gender gap in religiousness shrinks over a few generations, and this gap between men and women is less pronounced.

---

the nineteenth century, and soon after its birth it was applied to religions of the world, especially in tribal cultures. Cultural anthropology uncovers the underlying values of cultures, and their answer to the question, "Why are we here?" It studies such broad cultural dynamics as honor and shame, the role of kinship, and so on. It explores the roles of symbols, culture, and the natural environment; the making of social boundaries; how sex is understood and gender roles are constructed; and rituals. A special focus of anthropology has been the **shaman**, a religious specialist in an indigenous society who acts as a medium between this visible world and the spirit world, usually for healing and telling the future. Since

shaman [SHAH-muhn]
Religious specialist in an indigenous society who acts as a medium between this visible world and the spirit world

life-cycle rituals
Ceremony to mark an important point in life such as birth, becoming an adult, weddings, and funerals

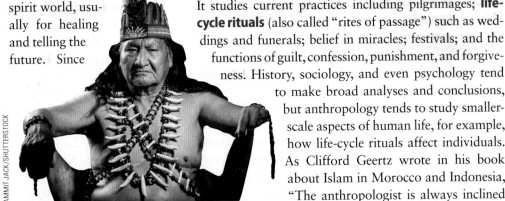

AMMIT JACK/SHUTTERSTOCK

Amazonian shaman in Ecuador, 2015

the 1960s, the formal use of cultural anthropology has become more prominent in religious studies.

Cultural anthropology can study the past, especially texts, art, and other artifacts. Almost all world religions with sacred writings have had those writings subjected to some form of anthropological study. For example, in a study of early Christianity, Bruce Malina of Creighton University in Omaha, an anthropologist and New Testament scholar, has applied this method to several books of the New Testament, especially in his *The New Testament World: Insights from Cultural Anthropology*.[14] This is often called "historical anthropology." However, cultural anthropology deals predominantly with living religions. It studies current practices including pilgrimages; **life-cycle rituals** (also called "rites of passage") such as weddings and funerals; belief in miracles; festivals; and the functions of guilt, confession, punishment, and forgiveness. History, sociology, and even psychology tend to make broad analyses and conclusions, but anthropology tends to study smaller-scale aspects of human life, for example, how life-cycle rituals affect individuals. As Clifford Geertz wrote in his book about Islam in Morocco and Indonesia, "The anthropologist is always inclined to turn toward the concrete, the particular, the microscopic. . . . We hope to find in the little what eludes us in the large, to stumble upon general truths while sorting through special cases."[15] For example, although historians made large studies about ancient Hindu sacred texts in the "dead language" of Sanskrit, anthropologists spent long periods of time in fieldwork in India to study the living use of contemporary oral traditions in other Indian languages.

Victor Turner (1920–1983), still an influential cultural anthropologist, developed a powerful theory of ritual that drew the attention of scholars to religious behaviors. His conception of rituals was shaped during his fieldwork in the 1950s with the Ndembu tribe, in what today is Zambia. His personal background in Roman Catholic Christianity also forms a background for his work on ritual. He was interested in the "social drama" of ritual presentations, especially life-cycle rituals. Ritual creates the social breaks Turner called "marginality" and the thresholds of new kinds of life that he termed "liminality."

Two Masai women prepare the roof of their mud house.

1-5f Women's Studies

When **feminism**, the movement for women's equality, came in to full bloom in the United States in the 1970s, the academic field of women's or gender studies quickly developed. It studies the social pressures, expectations, and opportunities of both genders but focuses on women, with the purpose of promoting their full equality and liberation. Feminism, thus, has both a descriptive and a prescriptive aspect. Gender studies is flourishing in North America but is not yet strong in Europe or other parts of the world. The rise of the #MeToo movement has added new urgency to the field of feminist studies in religion.

Feminist scholars of religion have pointed to religion as one explanation of the nearly worldwide subordination of women to men. They argue, correctly, that all religions stem from—and most uphold today to some extent—**patriarchy** (male domination of a society). In religions that have both male and female gods, the male gods nearly always predominate, and patriarchy prevails. Women's identification with female gods—for example, the new goddess Santoshi Ma in Hinduism—does provide religious strength, but this is qualified by male dominance among divine beings themselves. Predominantly masculine language is used to describe and address most gods, especially the one God of monotheistic religions.

Women's roles as professional religious specialists have been limited, even in the relatively few religious organizations that profess women's equality with men. (This limitation is sometimes called in the Western world the "stained-glass ceiling.") Their ambitions have often been constrained by the idea that their primary religious duty is to obey their husbands and raise their children. A number of feminists have argued that a "Mother Goddess" religion centered on the Earth and on women is the earliest form of human religion, but this is contested. Women of many religions have made different responses to the pressure of patriarchy. For example, they press for wider roles as religious specialists, trying to break the stained-glass ceiling or at least push it higher. They look for wider opportunities in the world of work, often adapting this to their religious duties in the home. And they continue to be active in their religious life, typically more active than men, as we saw in Section 1-5d.[16]

1-5g Biology

Until recently, biology (the scientific study of all life) didn't contribute much to the study of religion, aside from religious studies

feminism Movement for women's equality

patriarchy Male-domination of society

BRITTA KASHOLM-TENGVE/GETTY IMAGES

scholars' uncritical application of evolutionary theory to religion. Now, with the ability to study the human genome, or gene system, new possibilities are opening up for understanding complex human issues in the realm of religion. Many scientists are now seeking to explain religion in genetic terms, or at least to find the genetic connections of religion. Rapidly increasing knowledge of the human genome has made this possible. Some writers have suggested that the pervasiveness of religious beliefs is due to our genetic makeup.

The controversial theory advanced in Dean Hamer's *The God Gene: How Faith Is Hardwired into Our Genes* (2005) claims that religion is made possible by a genetic adaptation. Hamer even pointed to one gene, called *VMAT2* by the Human Genome Project, as the "God gene."[17] However, most scientists hypothesize that the genetic background of any complex human behavior, such as religion, probably flows from a combination of several genes. More generally accepted is the hypothesis by some biologists and anthropologists that the development of religious belief in prehistoric peoples may have been a key factor in the development of higher-order cognitive skills: A number of humans became capable of transcending themselves in thought and action, and this was passed on by natural selection.

Venus (or Woman) of Willendorf, Austria, the world's oldest religious statuette (22,000 B.C.E.)

MICHAL BOUBIN/GETTY IMAGES

{ *The development of religious belief in prehistoric peoples may have been a key factor in the development of higher-order cognitive skills.* }

religious studies is a human, not a divine, way of knowing. Religion itself can bring divine or sacred knowledge, but our academic study of it is method related and time bound. This means that religion scholars, similar to other academic experts, are part of the "concrete epistemology" (ways of knowing) of current scholarly and cultural interests and current assumptions that different generations have about life. Religion scholars' (*and* beginning students') personal development, education, and individual religious experiences, as well as their generation-specific attitudes, all affect how they adopt and use a particular method of studying religion. Religious studies is conditioned in each generation by time, a fact that is often appreciated only by a later generation for whom temporal distance allows a better view. As we sometimes say with slight exaggeration, "Hindsight is twenty-twenty."

This conditioning can be traced through time from the beginning of religious studies to today. Religious studies first went along with nineteenth-century optimism about the progressive evolution of human religion. Then, a Protestant bias crept into religious studies from the hidden values of scholars in the field, who were predominantly Protestant Christian: the privileging of sacred texts over oral traditions; the privileging of doctrine over ritual; and the belief in the primacy of private religious experience over received traditions—all crucial elements of Protestantism. Next, the scholars in the **phenomenology of religion** movement of the 1920s, after the spiritual and intellectual crisis of the First World War, searched for the so-called essence of religion by studying its observable practices ("phenomena"). Then, the baby-boomer generation of scholars in the 1960s through 1990s was driven by the experience and values of an alternative culture to pose provocative questions that challenged traditional methods in religious studies.

1-5h Conclusions about Methods of Studying Religion

We'll conclude our treatment of methods with two observations. First, it's obvious that the study of religion, similar to many other branches of scholarship, is multidisciplinary. It has no "religious method" all its own, but draws from many other methods. Second,

phenomenology of religion Study of religion through its observable practices

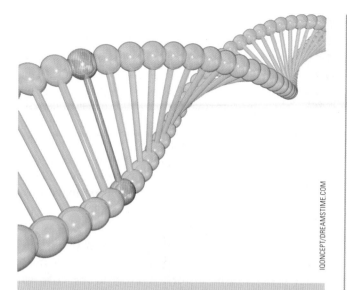

One human gene is probably not the basis for religion, but it may have a wider genetic basis.

IDONCEPT/DREAMSTIME.COM

The realization that each generation of scholars has characteristic limitations, which it typically cannot see, need not diminish the value of religious studies. Indeed, knowing the limits and biases of knowledge makes our knowledge more certain.

1-6 Special Issues in the Study of Religion Today

1-6a Tolerance and Intolerance

In Cambridge, Massachusetts, a controversy breaks out in the blogosphere and then in the print media over Harvard College's decision to reserve six hours a week for women only in the college's central gymnasium. The Harvard Islamic Society petitioned for the special hours, arguing that observant female Muslim students needed these special hours in order to observe Muslim rules about modesty and coverings for women. Although many Muslim women had exercised in the gymnasium during open hours, dressed in sweat suits and head scarves, the Harvard Islamic Society says that having hours restricted to women enables them to exercise better, in athletic shirts and shorts, without fear of male students "checking them out." Some argue that this is a reasonable toleration of another's faith; others say that this gives Harvard's approval to practices that reinforce intolerance toward women.

A handful of current advocates of **atheism**—the conviction that there is no God and that religion is mostly mistaken—are making sharp public attacks on religion. Those who make these attacks are known as the **New Atheists**. Their convictions are not new, but their practice of sharp public attack is new. (**Agnostics**, a related term, are those who do not know if a God or gods exist; agnostics are not always antireligious, and rarely combative against religion.) Christopher Hitchens wrote that religion is "violent, irrational, intolerant, allied to racism and tribalism and bigotry, invested in ignorance and hostile to free inquiry, contemptuous of women and coercive toward children."[18] The eminent biologist Richard Dawkins is also among the New Atheists. A few prominent atheists have recently pushed back against this extreme view. Edward O. Wilson argues in *The Social Conquest of Earth* that religion brought social order to early humans, giving them an evolutionary advantage.[19] Alain de Botton, in *Religion for Atheists*, says that atheists can learn a great deal from religions about meaning and beauty in human life.[20] And a noted advocate for secularism, Jacques Berlinerblau, has written *The Secular Bible: Why Non-Believers Must Take Religion Seriously*.[21] Nevertheless, Hitchens and other New Atheists articulate a strongly negative view of religion that many people share.

Tolerance means putting up with the views and actions of others that are opposed to one's own, usually for the common good. We begin our discussion of tolerance and intolerance with the Western world. The modern Western idea of religious tolerance developed in Europe after brutal wars between Protestant and Roman Catholic Christians in the sixteenth and seventeenth centuries, and has gradually been extended to people of other religions. (The murderous violence between Protestants and Roman Catholics in Northern Ireland from about 1960 to 1998 serves to remind the modern world what was gained at the end of the seventeenth century.) The First Amendment to the U.S. Constitution guarantees tolerance in "freedom of religion." The state cannot interfere with basic religious rights and must actively protect them from restriction in law or policy. In the twentieth century, the Universal Declaration of Human Rights first

atheism Conviction that there is no God

New Atheists Group of current atheists who have made sharp public attacks on religion

agnostics Those who do not know if a God or gods exist

tolerance Putting up with the views and actions of others that are opposed to one's own

Have you seen this popular bumper sticker?

"Religion is violent, irrational, intolerant, allied to racism and tribalism and bigotry, . . . contemptuous of women and coercive toward children."

—Christopher Hitchens

advocated freedom of religion for all people. Since the Enlightenment, the fostering of tolerance, religious or otherwise, has been regarded as a duty of government. Tolerance and intolerance are public, social things, but they are personal and individual as well. People of one religion can be intolerant toward people of other religions, and people outside religion can be intolerant of all or some religious people and groups.

The history of world religions reveals different ideas of tolerance. In ancient China, native religions were generally tolerated, but non-Chinese religions were admitted only by government consent; this is still true of China today. Ancient Judaism was at times welcoming to other religions in its territory, at other times not. In the ancient Roman Empire, non-Roman religious groups were generally tolerated as long as they did not undermine the religious underpinnings of Roman imperial rule. Christianity, during the thousand years since it became the Roman state religion until at least the Protestant Reformation, tended toward religious intolerance. (Compare the maxim from Roman Catholic history "Error has no rights." The Roman Catholic Church did not formally accept religious tolerance until the Second Vatican Council in the 1960s, but now is a steady advocate for it.) Islam usually granted toleration of conquered peoples of certain other religions—as a rule, but not always in practice. This toleration did not extend to Arab polytheism, which was extinguished; and over time, even tolerated religions were dramatically reduced

in Muslim lands. Mob violence against Coptic Christians in Egypt continues to reduce their numbers and influence.

Hinduism has been generally tolerant to other religions but has preferred to integrate them into its own system. Hindu relations with Muslims on the Indian subcontinent have been uneasy for centuries, and mass conversions of Hindus to Christianity and Buddhism can provoke a violent reaction. The regular, religiously motivated violence between Hindus and Muslims that has occurred since the division of India and Pakistan in 1947, and the occasional Hindu violence against Sikhs, means that Hinduism is not as tolerant as many people think. Buddhism, which teaches tolerance, has seen intolerant periods in its history, recently in the civil war carried on by armed Buddhists in Sri Lanka, in the violently repressive Buddhist government in Myanmar (Burma) against Rohingya Muslims living in camps there, and on a much smaller scale in bitter struggles between different Tibetan monastic groups. In sum, achieving and maintaining tolerance is no easy matter for religions.

> People today don't like to be called "intolerant," but few people can be equally tolerant of all opposing ideas.

A difficult question involves the limits of tolerance. People in the world today don't like to be called "intolerant," but few people can be equally tolerant of all opposing ideas and actions. If they try, difficult questions arise. For example, can a religious group that is itself intolerant be tolerated in the public sector? In North America, with its legal tradition of granting a maximum of freedom to religious groups both tolerant and intolerant, this isn't so much of an issue. But should a religion be tolerated by another if it grows big enough to take over a society and perhaps impose its own intolerance? In general, private religious *views* are tolerated in Western nations, provided that they do not lead to *actions* that could challenge a majority consensus on public life. The line between private belief and public action isn't always easy to see, however. A good example is a continuing controversy in France involving Muslim women's attire in public. Legislation bans head scarves that cover the face and/or full-body veils, which the government views as a threat to the state and its secular nature. In 2016, many French cities on the Mediterranean coast even tried to ban "burkinis," body-covering swimwear for Muslim women. The Church of Scientology is under government pressure in Germany, in part because the post-World War II German constitution forbids "totalitarian movements," which the government suspects that Scientology is. And in China, the Falun Gong (FAH-luhn GONG) meditational movement is strongly repressed by the Chinese government as a "dangerous cult" that supposedly threatens public order and the health of its followers. These examples show that struggles over tolerance continue today all around the world.

Muslims protest violence against other Muslims in Myanmar outside that nation's embassy in Malaysia, in 2016.

AIZUDDIN SAAD/SHUTTERSTOCK

1-6b Violence

In Rome, Pope Francis I approved in 2015 the creation of a special church court for judging bishops accused of covering up or failing to act in cases of known child sexual abuse by priests under their authority. This step had long been demanded by sex-abuse victims in the more than thirty years that the Roman Catholic Church has dealt with the scandal. Until now, bishops could be disciplined only directly by the pope, but no pope had yet publicly confronted or demoted any bishop for this conduct. Francis' move will get the attention of bishops around the world (most of whom are likely innocent of such dereliction of duty) as awareness of sexual abuse and calls for bishops' accountability spread. Many observers saw an immediate effect in the resignation of the archbishop of Minneapolis and St. Paul, whose archdiocese had been formally charged by Minnesota state prosecutors with covering up sexual abuse by some priests. The problem of sexual violence among religious leaders isn't unique to Roman Catholics, of course, or even to Christianity.

Violence is a difficult topic to grapple with, both emotionally and intellectually. However, this grappling is necessary. Violence is the intentional use of physical force to injure or kill people, to damage or destroy their property, or both. It is motivated by a variety of factors—political, economic, national, and tribal. Religiously motivated violence includes all events in which a follower of a religion is the perpetrator or the recipient of violent behavior or both. As with other kinds of violence, religious violence can be carried out by individuals or groups. It can be by direct attack, or by indirect means such as inducing famine.

It includes violence of any kind by members of one religion against people of another religion (the Crusades by medieval Christians against Islam, Muslim holy war, and occasional violence between Sikhs and Hindus), between different groups in a religion (Sunni and Shi'a Muslims, occasional violence between different Hindu castes in India), and crimes by powerful people in a religion against those with less or no power. It also includes persecution of one religion by another or by the state against its people, as in the Holocaust directed at Jews, in the current Chinese prosecution of the new Falun Gong religious movement, or in the practice of the "Islamic State" (IS) of taking women and girls from religious minority groups as sex slaves. It also includes violence against explicitly religious objects, as in attacks on religious buildings or sites or burning of holy books. Because religions have cultural, political, and other aspects, different motivations often lie behind what may appear to be purely religious violence. Sometimes violence can be inflicted on a public target in order to induce terror in a populace.

Religious violence committed by groups must be understood in its cultural context—not to excuse it, but to understand it. In particular, not all religious violence is the same. Some religions tend to be nonviolent, but others approve of violence in certain situations. A few religions began as explicitly nonviolent movements—Christianity and Sikhism, for example—but changed over time. Religious violence often tends to place differing emphases on its symbolic aspects. For example, sometimes violence is understood as a religiously

Thousands of girls like these bravely attend school in Afghanistan despite religiously motivated violence against females, which the United Nations calls "widespread and systemic."

approach to coaching. His teams didn't play seasons; they went on "sacred quests," as in Native American religion. Jackson taught his players short Buddhist meditations to use before they shot free throws. He called their strategy on offense "five-man tai chi," and their locker room was filled with Native American religious objects. His 1995 autobiography is called *Sacred Hoops*. Raised by devout Christian parents who taught him both religious earnestness and compassion, he calls himself a "Zen Christian."

significant act with ritual aspects. In the 1990s, Taliban Muslims dynamited ancient statues of the Buddha to remove "idolatry" from Afghanistan, and today they attack government schools for girls. The Boko Haram ("Western Education Is Evil") Muslim group in Nigeria does the same. Ritual violence may be directed against victims, as in human sacrifice, or it may be more or less voluntarily self-inflicted, as in self-flagellation with a whip. It may be a part of monastic practice, as when head monks in certain sects of Zen Buddhism beat their subordinates with rods to discipline them or try to induce sudden enlightenment. So-called "honor killings," in which family members kill another member of their family (usually female) in order to "preserve the family's honor," often have some religious motivation, although other factors are at work there too.

1-6c Pluralism

Phil Jackson, the most successful of all coaches in professional sports, wasn't a typical basketball coach. He rarely stood on the sideline and shouted at his players. Instead, he sat so serenely that he was called "Buddha on the bench" and "Zen master," terms that apply as well to his religious

pluralism Recognition of religious differences and dealing with them constructively

Nonviolent relations between religions, and between cultures and nations with different religions, are based first on toleration. Religious **pluralism**, the recognition of religious differences and dealing with them constructively, goes beyond toleration. Religious pluralism owes a great deal to the American and European experience of religious diversity. Chris Beneke, in his *Beyond Toleration: The Religious Origins of American Pluralism*, distinguishes carefully between tolerance and pluralism. By the 1730s, religious toleration toward minority religions was practiced in British colonies in North America. Toleration ended physical punishments and financial burdens on religious minorities, but it did not end prejudice and exclusion. Those "tolerated" were usually barred from holding government and military positions and from universities. The worst features of religious persecution had ended, but religious discrimination had not. However, the colonies gradually expanded religious toleration, and religious liberty for all was achieved by 1790.[22] This was not primarily a compromise with rising Enlightenment secularism in America; it was an achievement of early American religious groups themselves. The different Protestant Christian groups—Episcopalians, Methodists, Quakers, Presbyterians, Baptists, Lutherans, and others—saw religious liberty for everyone as in their own best interests, and for the common good. When a new national constitution was adopted at the end of the eighteenth century, the Bill of Rights was added almost immediately, with freedom of religion in the first amendment. The strength of religious freedom in the United States has greatly influenced the course of religious freedom in the world.

Pluralism at work: a room for multi-faith prayer and meditation in Heathrow Airport, London, was formerly called a chapel.

partial knowledge of the truth. At the far extreme, believers with a completely exclusivist mindset—that only their religion leads to the truth—prefer to convert, not converse with, people of other religions. In between full inclusivism and full exclusivism is a wide range of attitudes, where most believers today live.

1-6d Religion and Ecological Crisis

At Windsor Castle, just outside London, representatives of nine of the world's largest religions gathered in November 2009 to discuss the ecological crisis. They'd been summoned by Prince Philip of the United Kingdom and United Nations Secretary-General Ban Ki-moon. In words addressed to the Christians in the delegation, but applicable to many (but not all) of the other delegates, Prince Philip remarked, "If you believe in God . . . then you should feel a responsibility to care for God's creation."

Religion and environmentalism has emerged in the past generation as an important topic in religious studies. This isn't only because people everywhere realize that climate change is threatening life on earth. It's also because, as the Muslim scholar Seyyed Nasr explains, "The environmental crisis is fundamentally a crisis of values."[25] Because they shape the values of cultures, religions are deeply involved in how humans treat their environment. For example, the current prime minister of India, Narendra Modi, has made cleaning up the sacred Ganges River a main environmental objective.

Historian Lynn White Jr. argued in 1967 that Western Christianity, with its view of nature as under human control and direction, bears a substantial responsibility for the modern environmental crisis.[26] White's essay provoked strong reactions ranging from complete denial of his argument to complete agreement with it. By the 1990s, many scholars of religion began to analyze how nature is viewed in the world's religions. An increasing number of courses on religion and the environment are offered in colleges and

{ *Different religions exist because religions are different.* }

Religious pluralism demands interfaith dialogue and significant cooperation. Interfaith dialogue is conversation between members of different religions to reduce conflicts between them and to achieve mutually desirable goals. Dialogue calls for care to be taken with the ideas of others, without necessarily agreeing with them or assuming (as many people think) that all religions are essentially the same or could be made the same. The subtitle of Stephen Prothero's thought-provoking book *God Is Not One* points to the significance of these differences: *The Eight Rival Religions That Run the World—and Why Their Differences Matter.*[23] To put it another way: Different religions exist because religions are different. These differences make dialogue between religions possible, and they make dialogue important if conflict between religions and between the cultures they shape is to be avoided. Dialogue is easier if a religion's members hold to inclusivism, a belief that other religions may lead to salvation or at least have a significant but

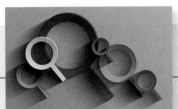

A Closer Look

DIANA ECK, AT HTTP://WWW.PLURALISM.ORG/PAGES/PLURALISM/WHAT_IS_PLURALISM. ACCESSED 7/17/10.

Statement on Pluralism by Harvard University's Pluralism Project

First, pluralism is not diversity alone, but *the energetic engagement with diversity*.... Today, religious diversity is a given, but pluralism ... is an achievement. Mere diversity without real encounter and relationship will yield increasing tensions in our societies.

Second, pluralism is not just tolerance, but *the active seeking of understanding across lines of difference*. Tolerance is a necessary public virtue, but it does not require Christians and Muslims, Hindus, Jews, and ardent secularists to know anything about one another....

Third, pluralism is not relativism, but *the encounter of commitments*. Pluralism does not require us to leave our identities and our commitments behind, for pluralism is the encounter of commitments. It means holding our deepest differences ... not in isolation, but in relationship to one another.

Fourth, pluralism is *based on dialogue*. Dialogue ... reveals both common understandings and real differences. Dialogue does not mean everyone ... will agree with one another.[24] (To learn more about Harvard University's Pluralism Project, go to its webpage: http://www.pluralism.org/. To see an example of a local interfaith organization, one in which the author of the present book participates, go to http://www.gvsu.edu/interfaith/.)

universities around the world. This topic needs careful study, because the world's religions sometimes have different beliefs about the origin, nature, and value of the physical world. (For an example of how Chinese religions can work for a greener world, see Prasenjit Duara's recent book *Crisis of Global Modernity: Asian Traditions and a Sustainable Future*.[27]) But it's probably safe to say that all religions view the world around us as significant and would view the loss of a viable home for humanity as a tragedy.

Religion united to nature: the Eternal Spring Temple in Taroko National Park, Taiwan. This Buddhist and Daoist temple commemorates those who died constructing a highway through this mountainous park.

1-6e New Religious Movements

Outside a movie premiere in Utah, crowds gather, waiting for the director, producers, and actors to arrive. Although the scene is similar to that of other premieres, the film is not. It is a feature-film adaptation of the main Mormon scripture, the Book of Mormon, and has been officially sanctioned by the Mormon Church, formally known as the Church of Jesus Christ of Latter-day Saints. Along with its general release to theaters and then to video rental outlets, the movie would be used in the missionary activities of the church. From the birth of the Latter-day Saint Church in the 1800s, its use of the Book of Mormon in missionary efforts has been a key factor in making this church probably the fastest-growing religious organization in the world.

New religious movements (NRMs), as we saw earlier, are a widely accepted area in the field of religious studies. NRMs are religious groups that have arisen since the start of the nineteenth century and now have sufficient size, longevity, and cultural impact to merit academic study. We will deal with NRMs more fully in Chapter 13, but we should consider them initially here.

New religious movements is preferable in some ways to other recent terms such as *alternative religious movements* and *marginal religious movements*. It's also clearly preferable to the older terms *sects* and *cults*. Although these terms still have some validity—especially in sociology, where scholars use them objectively—they have become so loaded with value judgments that religion scholars no longer use them for NRMs. To judge by the dimensions of religion discussed earlier, there is usually little difference between a religion and a sect or a cult. All of them have doctrines and ethics, rituals, social structures, and an aesthetic dimension, and their members typically describe powerful emotional religious experiences. The term *cult* has been used to describe many smaller, nontraditional religious groups. These groups often have new or innovative beliefs that set them apart from the prevailing religious worldviews, especially those of the religions from which they emerge. In recent times, *cult* has become rather derogatory, applied to groups that are deemed to be beyond commonly accepted bounds of social behavior. If they stay alive, sects go on to become recognized groups within the "parent" religion. The Protestant churches can be described as Christian sects that gained mainstream acceptance, as did the Hare Krishna (HAHR-ee KRISH-nah) movement (The International Society for Krishna Consciousness, or ISKCON) in Hinduism. Despite the intensity of its beliefs and actions that can make it look like a "cult" to some in the Western world, the latter is an authentically Hindu group.

Thousands of groups around the world today are NRMs, for instance, Falun Gong, Baha'i, the Nation of

"I'm a failure in the eyes of the prophet," celebrity Scientologist Tom Cruise said to Stan, a *South Park* character. Cruise believed Stan was the reincarnation of Scientology founder L. Ron Hubbard, so Cruise was shocked to hear him say the following about his acting ability, "You're not, like, as good as Leonardo DiCaprio . . . but you're OK."

Islam, the Church of Jesus Christ of Latter-day Saints, the Christian Science Church, the Unification Church, and the Church of Scientology. Each year sees the birth of others. These and other movements called NRMs often don't see themselves as NRMs at all, but instead as the true continuing body from an older religion now gone bad. Although scholars use the term "*new religious movements,*" we must note that NRMs usually branch off from older religions. Falun Gong is an adaptation mostly of Mahayana Buddhism and a lesser amount of Daoism. Baha'i arose in the nineteenth century from Shi'a Islam and sees itself as the successor of Islam. The Church of Jesus Christ of Latter-day Saints, the Christian Science Church, and the Unification Church see themselves as Christian, and experts in comparative religions view this labeling as basically correct. However, one shouldn't assume that all organizations that call themselves a church self-identify as Christian. For example, the Church of Scientology uses *church* to mean "religious organization"; so does the Buddhist Churches of America, a Japanese Buddhist organization with sixty "churches" in North America.

Some of these NRMs are highly controversial. Many were persecuted or prosecuted in their early years by religious and civil authorities, and a few still are today. However, other faiths examined in this book were also controversial when they were new. NRMs can change, sometimes dramatically, and often much more quickly than older religions do. This typically occurs when their founder dies, but later change is possible as well.

The 1960s through 1990s saw the rise of a number of new religious movements in North America. Since around 2000, however, many experts have thought that NRMs are on the wane, and some have even provocatively asked, "Where have all the cultists gone?" The public presence of NRMs and public controversy about them have receded, with perhaps a few exceptions like Scientology. Philip Jenkins has pointed to this possible explanation: increasing secularization in North American society has led to less attention to the "fringes" of religion that NRMs represent to most people.[28]

Careful students of religion will want to form judgments about NRMs that take account of what believers say about themselves in their writings and in life. As always, our learning about a religion, whether that religion is new or old, should precede any judgment concerning it.

STUDY TOOLS 1

READY TO STUDY?
ONLINE ON MINDTAP, YOU CAN:

☐ Download the Chapter Review Card, which includes key terms and chapter summaries.

☐ Learn more about preunderstanding and take a quiz.

☐ Watch a video interview with Madeleine Albright about religion being used for either peace or conflict.

☐ Interact with figures from the text to check your understanding.

☐ Prepare for tests with quizzes.

☐ Review the key terms with Flash Cards.

BONNIE VAN VOORST © CENGAGE LEARNING

2

Encountering Indigenous Religions: Ways to Tribal Life

AMMIT JACK/SHUTTERSTOCK

LEARNING OUTCOMES

After studying this chapter, you will be able to do the following:

2-1 State and evaluate the different names for indigenous religions.

2-2 Explain in your own words the challenges to the study of indigenous religions.

2-3 Discuss the common features of indigenous religions.

2-4 State and explain the main features of Lakota religion.

2-5 State and explain the main features of Yoruba religion.

2-6 State and explain the main features of Vodou religion.

Your Visit to the Petroglyph National Monument, New Mexico

Past and present: the Petroglyph National Monument now sits alongside a housing development in Albuquerque, New Mexico.

On a visit to Albuquerque, New Mexico, a friend suggests that you visit the Petroglyph National Monument. This area on a wind-swept rise just outside the city is famous for its rock carvings made by Pueblo Indian tribes. "Get an orientation at the Visitor Center before you begin, because there are several trails to choose from," she says. "And bring a bottle of drinking water."

The first trail takes fifteen minutes with continuous walking. Signs warning about rattlesnakes greet you; this gives you pause, but your walk will end without seeing or hearing one. This trail has more than a hundred glyphs (pictures) carved into hard, black rock created by volcanic lava flows. That these rocks are so hard means that carving them is not a simple process, but it also means that the resulting pictures have lasted for hundreds of years—some for perhaps a thousand. A few pictures look like they were carved yesterday, but you know they are very old. Making stops to look at the petroglyphs—impossible not to do—makes this particular trail a half-hour walk.

The carvings are typically of some kind of animal. Birds, snakes, and other wild animals make up most of the pictures, but occasionally there are pictures of humans. All of them seem to exude life and energy. But you begin to wonder—why are all these carvings (more than 20,000) in this one relatively small area? Native Americans still living near this area say that the petroglyphs speak a message about human life to those whose spirits enable them to listen.

As you begin formal study of indigenous religions, some questions about them will occur to you. Here are some things that students often wonder about:

- Why are there so many different names for this type of religion?

- Why are they so striking in both their similarities and their differences?

An Amazonian shaman blows cleansing smoke on a participant in a ritual that goes back to ancient times.

- Why are so many of their practices becoming popular among people of other religions?

- Why do they have so little emphasis on teaching and focus so much on rituals?

- How much have they changed, and how much have they stayed the same, in modern times?

Because of the large numbers of religions that are discussed here, this chapter has a special organization that differs from most other chapters. First, we will discuss the variety of names scholars have given to this overall type of religion and then explain why this book calls them *indigenous* religions. Second, we'll deal with the typical challenges to the academic study of these religions, especially the kinds of challenges that students face when they begin this study. Third, we'll draw out the common characteristics of these religions. In this section, we'll deal with history, teaching, ritual, and so on. Fourth, we'll take a closer look at three indigenous religions: the religion of the Lakota tribes of North America, the religion of the Yoruba tribe of Africa, and the Vodou (more widely known as *Voodoo*) religion of African–Caribbean peoples.

2-1 Names for This Type of Religion

Naming the overall type of religions that we are dealing with can be a challenge. But why is it necessary to name this group of religions at all if such a comprehensive name may well distort or obscure their beliefs? The answer is that religious studies itself has seen this as

SEAN LEMA/SHUTTERSTOCK

important, so we must grapple with the issue here. This section will deal with generic names, suggesting what is strong and weak about each one, and then we'll discuss the term settled on in this book: *indigenous religions*.

2-1a Traditional Religion

Traditional religion correctly implies that religions were present in various societies around the world before European and American expansion. They are *traditional* compared with newer, imported religions. However, as we saw in Chapter 1, all religions are traditions, because they are comprehensive ways of life that come from the past. It has even become common in scholarship to refer to Hinduism, Islam, and the rest as *traditions* as well as *religions*. Labeling only one type of religion as *traditional* is misleading and potentially confusing.

> { Indigenous religions are often just as complex as other world religions. }

2-1b Primitive Religion

Primitive religion or **primal religion** were more popular in the past, especially among cultural anthropologists, who used them in a nonjudgmental way. These terms mostly describe religions that are not derived from other religions, and this is a helpful distinction. However, they can also imply that these religions are undeveloped, unchanging, outmoded, or simple. Research into primitive religions has confirmed just the opposite: They are often just as complex as other world religions. Today, religious studies scholars generally avoid *primitive* but occasionally use *primal*.

2-1c Animism and Totemism

Animism and *totemism* are popular as labels for religions in some circles today. **Animism** (from the Latin *anima*, "soul, spirit") is the belief that individual spirits exist not only in people, but

primitive religion Religion that is not derived from other religions; also called *primal religion*

animism Belief that individual spirits exist not only in people, but also in all things in nature

totemism [TOHT-em-iz-uhm] Religion based on the idea that the spirit of one primary source in nature provides the basis of tribal life

manaism [MAH-nah-iz-uhm] Belief in an impersonal spiritual power that permeates the world as a whole

also in all things in nature, whether they appear to be alive or not: individual animals; plants, rocks, thunder, and lightning and mountains, lakes, and rivers. In many religions, the spirits of deceased humans keep a close relationship with the living, so that they are part of myth and ritual. The appearance of the sacred in dreams and visions is a key element of animism. Edward B. Tylor, a founder of the field of anthropology, argued in his 1871 book *Primitive Culture* that all religion began in animism.[1] **Totemism** is a religion based on the idea that the spirit of one primary source in nature—the land itself, a particular species of animal, or ancestors—provides the basis of life in one's tribe. (See "A Closer Look: Totemism in the *Twilight* Series.") Totemism is found in the Native American tribes of the Northwest coast, with their totem poles, and in the beliefs of the Aborigines of Australia. It fits these totemic religions well as a comprehensive name, but it doesn't fit the other religions in this chapter.

2-1d Manaism

Some cultural anthropologists hold that the first stage of all religion was **manaism**, a belief in an impersonal spiritual power that permeates the world as a whole. Many religions, they argue, are still based on mana. Manaism is preanimistic, because it does not connect power to spirits in individual natural things (animism) or species/groups of things (totemism). "Manaism" is drawn from the Polynesian term *mana*, "spiritual power." The Yoruban idea of a general spiritual power that infuses the universe is an example of mana. In the early 1900s, those who advocated manaism and those who advocated animism disagreed sharply with each other. Today this disagreement is largely a thing of the past.

©2009FOTOFRIENDS/SHUTTERSTOCK.COM
Totem poles

2-1e Shamanism

A shaman is a tribal member with special abilities and the authority to act as an intermediary between the people and the world of gods and spirits (both good and evil). He or, rarely, she, is known by different names in different tribes; the most common are *holy man*, *medicine man*, and *healer*. (The older term "witch doctor" is occasionally still found today, but it is so prejudicial a term that most religious studies scholars don't use it.) Shamans are so common in this type of religion that some scholars have called this system **shamanism**. But this is controversial today, especially among some cultural anthropologists. For example, Alice Kehoe, in her 2000 book, *Shamans and Religion*, argues sharply that shamans are unique to their cultures and cannot be generalized into a global type of religion called "shamanism."[2] Many indigenous peoples around the world, particularly with Native American tribes, also reject this term as misleading when applied to themselves.

A Zulu shaman in South Africa leans over a mat on which he has just thrown small bones; by reading their layout, he receives messages from dead ancestors to pass on to the living.

2-1f Small-Scale Religions

The term **small-scale religion**, taken from cultural anthropology, accurately implies that some of the religions to which it refers are held by relatively small societies. However, other so-called small-scale religions are actually practiced by more people than Judaism, Sikhism, Jainism, and Shinto. Other than the relative size of *some* of them—and there were indigenous empires in the Americas and in Africa with empire-wide religions, we must remember—there is nothing small about these religions.

2-1g Nature Religion

The term **nature religion** correctly suggests that indigenous religions can have a stronger connection to the natural environment than do other world religions. But there is much more to the religions in this chapter than a connection to the natural environment. Moreover, "nature" itself is a Western concept that many other societies, especially those we discuss here, do not share. These groups of people usually do not make a strong distinction between the natural and the supernatural, which Westerners may think is implied by the term *nature religion*. Nor do they see human beings as so superior to the rest of the world that they almost stand above and apart from nature. Catherine Albanese, in her book, *Nature Religion in America*, argues that the term *nature religion* fits a whole range of American beliefs, from precolonial Native American religions to the contemporary "New Age" movement.[3]

2-1h Indigenous Religions

In this book, we'll use the term **indigenous religion**. *Indigenous* means "native, intrinsic to an area," especially in the sense of peoples who originate and belong to a specific area. (Students should avoid a common confusion with *indigent*, which means "poor.") As we'll see shortly, *indigenous* imply a strong sense of belonging religiously to a certain place, in a way that *native* alone might not. In current usage, *indigenous* implies religions and cultures that were present in a given place for centuries, and usually millennia, before the arrival of other cultures with different religions. When used in this way, for example, it says more than the ambiguous term *Native American*. Strictly speaking, everyone born in North America is a "native American," but the vast majority of people born in North America don't belong to continuing indigenous groups of "Native Americans." Today, *indigenous* often implies a lack of political power within wider society, especially in a context where other groups of people have taken over the lands of indigenous peoples.

shamanism
[SHAH-mun-iz-um]
Religion based on the work of shamans

small-scale religion
Religions held by relatively small societies

nature religion
Religions that have a stronger connection to the natural environment than other religions

indigenous religion
Religion of the people, usually a tribe, original to an area

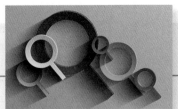

A Closer Look

Totemism in the *Twilight* Series

The leader of the Quileute (KWILL-yoot) Nation of Native Americans in northwest Washington first heard about the *Twilight Saga* novels from its readers, who wanted to know more about the place where the blockbuster vampires and werewolves tale of teenage love was set. When the novels were made into films, interest in Quileutes exploded. "Their interest in our tribe was a good surprise," tribal president Anna Rose Counsell-Geyer said to the press. "People are going to actually get to know the Quileute and we are going to be recognized as a people."

The Quileute's reservation on the Olympic Peninsula serves as the scenic backdrop to author Stephenie Meyer's fantasy novels, a place of thick woods, with rocks and

REINHARDT, DREAMSTIME.COM

The wolf is a powerful totem in many coastal Native American/First Nations tribes.

cliffs rising along the Pacific Ocean. The reservation spans only one square mile. The wolf theme of *Twilight* draws on the Quileutes' own creation story, which features the transformation of an ancient wolf pack into people who became the Quileute tribe. Since that transformation, the wolf has been the tribe's totem.

In the *Twilight* film, the Quileute creation story is used to explain the Wolf Pack, a group of young Quileute men joined by Jacob Black (played in the film by Taylor Lautner), who shape-shift into large, powerful wolves to guard the reservation from marauding vampires. The present-day *Twilight Saga* marks a departure from Hollywood's long tradition of portraying the past, not the present, of Native Americans. It also departs from Quileute religion, which does not feature tribal members who can shape-shift into wolves. This particular element is not a part of totemism, but instead draws on European werewolf legends.

When considering the names for individual indigenous groups, we should ask, What names do the individual groups use, and what names are given to them by others? The European colonizers of Africa and the Americas played a large role in giving them names, which Westerners now know them by, so we will begin here. In general, European names for indigenous peoples and their religions have been inaccurate. Europeans did not listen carefully to what other cultures called themselves, but instead adapted the indigenous peoples' names to European languages. This reflects a colonialist mentality. In recent times, there has been a movement to restore the original sound and spelling of Native American names: *Odawa* for "Ottawa" and *Algonkian* for "Algonquin," for example.

The common European name for indigenous peoples is the historic Western term for peoples who inhabited the Western Hemisphere: *Indians*. In 1492, Christopher Columbus supposed that he had reached the islands off China called at the time the Indies. However, he unknowingly had come upon a land mass between Europe and Asia that would become known to Europeans as the *New World*. The name Indians persisted even when it became obvious that it was wrong, and it was soon used by the English and French as well. To call the indigenous peoples of the Americas Indians was one of the biggest geography bloopers of all time, but it has endured for centuries.

However, ideas about names do change, and sometimes in unpredictable ways. Today, many native peoples in the United States happily call themselves Indians, not Native Americans. The latest Census Bureau survey of terminology, done in 1995, showed that 49 percent of native peoples preferred being called American Indian, 37 percent preferred Native American, and only about 9 percent either preferred another term or had no preference. *Indians* grew in approval among Native Americans at the same time as it became incorrect in wider North American culture. For example, in his highly praised memoir, *The Names*, Kiowa writer N. Scott Momaday speaks about how his mother embraced this name: "[S]he began to see herself as an 'Indian'. That dim native heritage became a fascination and a cause for her."[4]

In general, indigenous peoples of North America prefer their local group name as rendered in their language, not an English-language label or a traditional name recognized by whites. Sioux Nation Indians prefer to be known by the main name of Lakota, Dakota, or Nakota (each designating groupings within the same culture). They use Sioux as a name for themselves when speaking to outsiders, but inside their group they use Lakota or its variants. In the 2000 U.S. Census, fully 75 percent of people who identified their ethnic group as "American Indian" also identified their main tribal or national group. Sometimes political differences within a tribe or nation lead to competing preferences for different names in the same group—for example, Navajos or *Diné* (Earth People). In Canada, the broad official designation **First Nations** (note the plural) is widely accepted as a general term by native groups and wider Canadian society, but the individual tribes still use their own names. In Australia and New Zealand, **Aboriginals** (peoples there "from the origin") is commonly accepted as an ethnic label, but this term is falling out of favor, and the specific names of Aboriginal groups are preferred.

(2-2) Challenges to Study

In Chapter 1, we dealt with some challenges to the study of religion in general. When we encounter indigenous religions, some special challenges emerge that don't apply to most other religions we will deal with in this book. We will list and explain them briefly here.

2-2a Lack of Written Sources

Because the cultures in which these religions are based are predominantly oral, their religions—with only a few exceptions—have not written down their stories, beliefs, or rituals. Where these features of religious life do exist in writing today, they have typically been recorded by anthropologists. Nor do we have as much archaeological evidence for indigenous peoples as we do

> { To call the indigenous peoples of the Americas "Indians" was one of the biggest geography bloopers of all time. }

for other world religions. Some Native American and African tribes, along with their particular religions, disappeared long before the coming of Europeans—the victims of disease, famine, and intertribal warfare—and we know little about them. In the first chapter of this book, we noted the importance of history as a method of studying religion, but the use of history to study indigenous peoples is limited. This restricts the depth of study.

2-2b Difficulty Discerning Continuity and Discontinuity

By the time scholars began to study native groups in the Americas, Africa, and Australia, it was hundreds of years after the natives' first contact with European cultures and religion. Sometimes this contact led to significant changes in indigenous belief and practices, and at other times it didn't. As a result, scholars of indigenous religions are uncertain about how far back some beliefs and practices go: Are they precontact or postcontact? For example, some have argued that in Yoruba religion in west Africa, the high god developed as a reaction to Christian and Muslim missionaries who proclaimed a religion of one God. Others dispute this, arguing that indigenous religions often have belief in one high deity without any Western religious influence.

2-2c Mainstream Guilt

Indigenous peoples have been treated brutally during the whole sweep of human history and even prehistory, whenever one group came into the territory of another group and tried to take over. Treatment that was intended to reduce their numbers and end their cultures is nothing short of **genocide**, the killing of an entire racial/ethnic/religious group of people. North Americans today are rightly ashamed of the past treatment of Native Americans: broken treaties; stolen lands; killing of Native-American non-combatants; and forced relocations, like

First Nations Indigenous peoples in Canada

Aboriginals [AB-oh-RIHJ-ih-nuhls] Indigenous peoples there "from the origin" of Australia and New Zealand

genocide Killing of an entire racial/ethnic/ religious group

John Gast's 1872 painting *American Progress*, widely distributed as a print, shows an allegorical female figure of America leading pioneers westward, as Native Americans flee from them (left). This westward movement would lead to the severe reduction of Native American life that many call a genocide.

as *Dances with Wolves* and *Avatar* have portrayed indigenous tribes as habitually moral, master ecologists, or even **noble savages**. This last idea was an influential theme in the work of Jean-Jacques Rousseau (1712–1778), who held that indigenous peoples were naturally good but that contact with so-called civilization corrupts them. Such an idealized view of indigenous peoples is based on superficial knowledge; if they were in fact so noble, they would not need practices to deal with misdeeds, social disorder, and outright crimes.

On the other hand, Hollywood has depicted some religions as dangerously exotic in order to

the 1830s Trail of Tears, in which the Cherokee nation was driven from its lands in the southeast United States into the Indian territory of Oklahoma, a journey in which thousands died. Today, people think that people of European origin should have avoided such genocide at all costs. However, the ethos of the times, which allowed this to happen, was significantly different. Many of their descendants today are ashamed of the actions of their ancestors and the continued bitter legacy of prejudice and discrimination. This is probably as it should be, but sometimes guilt—powerful emotion that it is—gets in the way of understanding. Guilt can distort the careful study of indigenous cultures and their religions. People should regret the wrongs of the past, but a careful understanding of the past is a key part of knowing what to do in the present.

amuse or frighten audiences, as in *Apocalypto* or the hundreds of films made about the white settlement of the American West. Negative portrayals have seeped down into the life of North American children, among whom playing games of "cowboys and Indians" has been popular for generations—if historically incorrect, because cowboys rarely fought Indians. Africa has frequently been depicted in film as a place of more

2-2d Misrepresentations in Popular Culture

noble savages
Rousseau's term for indigenous peoples, who, he held, are naturally good

Popular culture—especially Hollywood film, which is influential in shaping attitudes today—has distorted indigenous religions. On the one hand, films such

Avatar, directed by James Cameron, is set in the twenty-second century.

savagery than nobility, with religions that are little more than superstitions. Popular culture's portrayal of Afro–Caribbean religions, Vodou in particular, is probably the worst of all. The 1973 James Bond film *Live and Let Die*, and the more frightening *Angel Heart*, portrayed Vodou as violent and dangerous. The popular film, *Night of the Living Dead*, originally from 1968 and remade in 1990, removed zombie lore from its Vodou context. Zombies have become increasingly popular ever since, as illustrated by the hit television show *The Walking Dead* and its imitators. These misrepresentations of indigenous religions have affected how we understand them, and make it harder to study them today.

Indigenous empire: Mayan temple, Chichen Itza, Mexico

2-2e Misuse of Indigenous Rituals

In today's religious climate in North America and Europe, some people freely combine elements of indigenous religions with their own religions or other beliefs. It has become popular in some circles, for example, to use sacred objects of North American indigenous religions such as the stone pipe, medicine bundles, peyote, and sweat lodges in new religious ceremonies in non-Native American religions. This removes indigenous rituals from their deeply embedded cultural context and gives them a new meaning. Some indigenous groups are offended by this and view it as detrimental to their long-term spiritual and cultural health. For instance, some Lakota leaders opposed this misuse in a controversial 1993 resolution, "Declaration of War against Exploiters of Lakota Spirituality." In 2012, Navajo authorities sued the Urban Outfitters company for its use of a Navajo symbol and name in a new line of clothing.

Now that the challenges in studying indigenous religions are in plain view, we can turn to a discussion of these religions, beginning with their most important common features.

2-3 Common Features of Indigenous Religions

In this section, we will discuss the common key characteristics of indigenous religions (see also "A Closer Look: Movements toward Indigenous Unity"). But we must realize up front that there are many significant differences among them. They are as diverse as the cultures and times from which they come. Africa has had over three thousand ethnic and language groups, with social organizations from small tribes to large empires. Africa today has more than forty nations (see Map 2.1). In the Americas there have been more than two thousand tribes, some of them organized in large nations or even empires such as those of the Aztecs and Mayans. Each of the world religions that we'll consider in later chapters has some shared idea of sacred history—of the tradition's founders, sacred texts, rituals, and the like—that gives it unity. For indigenous religions around the world, diversity is the rule. Despite the terms *Native American religion, African religion*, and *Aboriginal religion*, on the whole, no such specific things ever existed. No single system of belief or ritual unites all indigenous African, American, or Aboriginal religions. In this chapter, we present the basics of indigenous religions, but this doesn't imply that all indigenous religions are the same. Nor does it imply that indigenous peoples think of their religions as the same.

2-3a The Importance of Place

Anthropologists typically hold that the human race (*Homo sapiens*) gradually spread from one area of Africa across much of the globe beginning more than 100,000 years ago (see Map 2.2). Many groups of humans have been on the move ever since, carrying their indigenous religions with them. This common origin and subsequent travel helps to explain how modern humans are similar genetically but have had some further genetic and cultural adaptations to their new

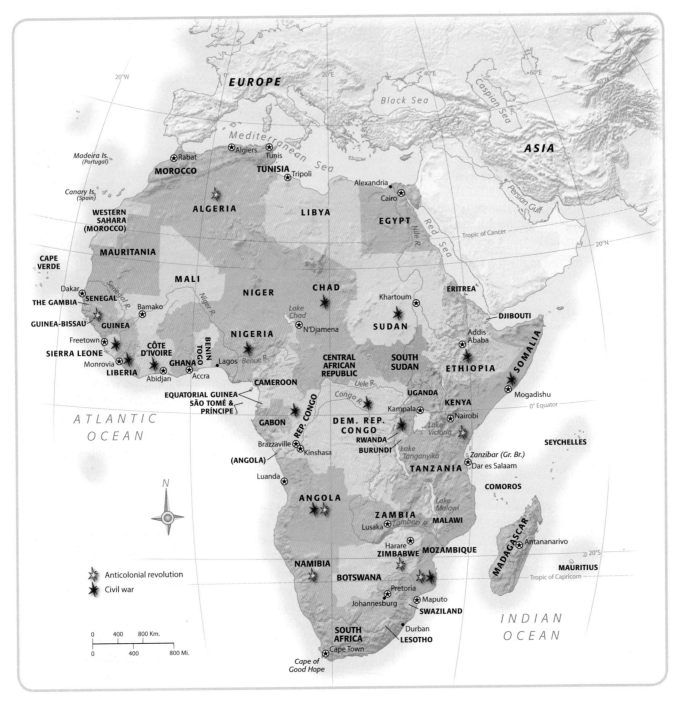

Map 2.1

Contemporary Africa

Africa contains more than forty nations. Six sub-Saharan African nations and Algeria in North Africa experienced anti-colonial revolutions, and a dozen sub-Saharan nations have been racked by civil wars since independence. In 2011, Libya, Tunisia, and Egypt experienced revolts against oppressive regimes in the "Arab Spring."

environments. Despite all this movement, indigenous peoples are deeply rooted in a place. Moreover, they usually see themselves as created in or from that place, despite what modern anthropologists think about all humans originating in Africa. For them, *place* is much more than simply a location or even a type of geography such as forest, desert, plains, and so on. Instead, it is a matter of tribal and personal identity. What Vine Deloria Jr. says about Native American religion is true of all other indigenous religions: "The sacredness of lands on which previous generations have lived and died is the foundation of all other sentiments."[5]

A Closer Look

Movements toward Indigenous Unity

A recent development brings a surprising "twist" to diversity within indigenous religions. Indigenous peoples around the world are realizing that they are in a common situation with regard to their dominant cultures and are beginning to act on this in ways that draw indigenous peoples and cultures together.

For example, a **Pan-Indian movement** began in the early 1900s and is now prominent in North America. This movement is based on indigenous American peoples' realization that they share many social and religious concerns today. One example of this is the American Indian Movement (AIM) organization. Cross-tribal memberships, powwow (intertribal gatherings, especially of leaders) networks among tribes, and national lobbying groups are found in contemporary Pan-Indianism. Increasingly, rituals have been shared among the tribes. Their lives have become more Pan-Indian, with wider use of ritual pipe

Native American drumming circle at an intertribal powwow

smoking, sweat lodges, vision quests, sun dancing, and peyote. Pan-Indianism is also found in universities, prisons, military forces, and urban settings, where general Native American identity is more important than one's specific tribal identity. The Pan-Indian movement tries to respect local tribal identities and traditions, but some tribes object to the sharing of rituals.

Stories about the land deal with myths of tribal origins, rituals, and patterns of everyday life. Because indigenous religions are typically rich in traditions that deal with their particular places, they often speak of being created not just from Mother Earth, but also for example from the earth "here in this valley." They communicate with spirits not just all around them, but "in a mountain cave over there," or revere in particular a sacred animal "in our rain forest." Sacred place has a personal status in indigenous religions. For example, at their annual intertribal gatherings in the Sweet Grass Hills of Montana, the Chippewa-Cree people pray that owners of the mines in their sacred hills will see that "these hills are just as alive as anybody, and they want to live too." People and their places are meant to live together in a harmonious balance. The struggle of the Standing Rock Sioux Tribe over the oil pipeline, which is set

{ *The current struggles over an oil pipeline set to run through traditional Lakota areas are an example of the importance of place.* }

to run through traditional Native American areas, is an example of the importance of place. Other religions we will encounter in this book all have holy places, but they are typically not connected to specific places in the ways that indigenous religions are.

2-3b Global Distribution

Indigenous religions are found around the globe today, not just in North America and Africa. In Africa, indigenous religions are spread throughout the continent south of the Sahara Desert. In general, more traditional forms of indigenous religions are found in central Africa; in the northern and southern thirds of Africa, indigenous religions have largely been

Pan-Indian movement Begun in the early 1900s to bring more unity to North American tribes

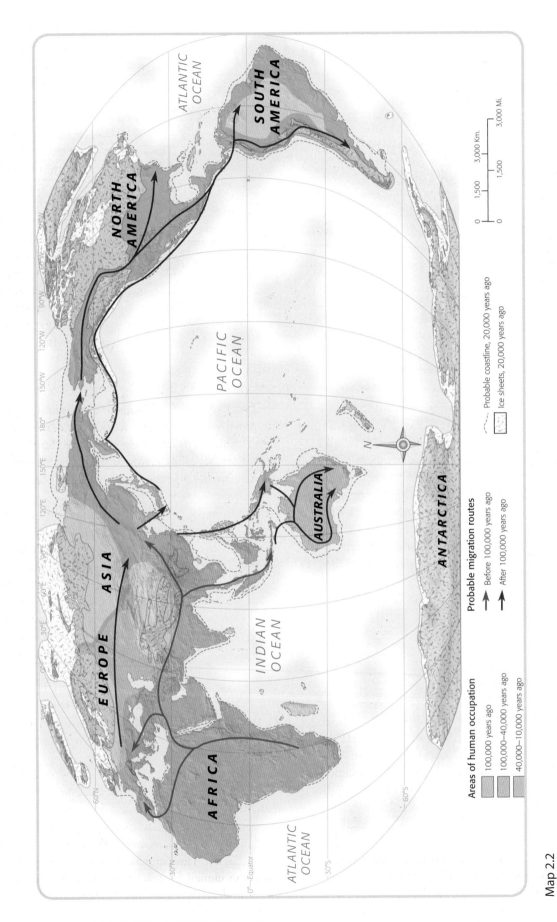

Areas of human occupation

100,000 years ago

100,000–40,000 years ago

40,000–10,000 years ago

Probable migration routes

Before 100,000 years ago

After 100,000 years ago

Probable coastline, 20,000 years ago

Ice sheets, 20,000 years ago

0   1,500   3,000 Km.

0   1,500   3,000 Mi.

Map 2.2
Spread of Humans around the Globe in Current Anthropological Understanding

©JIM PARKIN/SHUTTERSTOCK.COM

View of the Black Hills, South Dakota, the holiest place for the Lakota tribe of Native Americans

marked the end of pre-Islamic Arab indigenous religion, but other indigenous religions have been incorporated to a degree in some areas where Islam has spread. In Australia and New Zealand, original forms of Aboriginal religions exist alongside Christianity, although the majority of Aboriginal people self-identify as Christians today. In Europe, Christianity gradually overwhelmed indigenous religions, in part by absorbing some indigenous practices such as rituals to counteract evil elves and the still-practiced tradition of bringing evergreens into homes in winter.

blended into Islam and Christianity, respectively. In the Americas, indigenous religions are also widespread: Native peoples, with their distinctive religions, inhabit the hemisphere from the Arctic to the southern tip of Chile. Many indigenous peoples in the Americas today combine their indigenous religions with Christianity, in Central and South America particularly with Roman Catholic Christianity.

In Asia, the picture is complex. Indigenous religion persists almost undisturbed in some remote islands in south Asia, especially in Indonesia and Borneo. Polynesian and Micronesian cultures and religions have spread widely, so that today they are found from Hawaii to Taiwan and southward. (In fact, native Hawaiian religion has begun to assert its continuing vitality, as we will see in "A Closer Look: Polynesian Religion in Hawaii.") In Tibet, the ancient indigenous Bön religion persists inside, and occasionally outside, Tibetan Buddhism, despite persecution in the past by the Buddhist government of Tibet. Folk religions emphasizing local spirits and gods have been common for millennia in China; sometimes these divine beings have become Daoist divinities. Japan's indigenous religion of Shinto has played such a large role in modern world history that it is often treated separately, as this book will do in Chapter 8. The birth of Islam

> { Indigenous religions are found around the globe today, not just in North America and Africa. }

2-3c Many Gods and Spirits

A distinctive feature of indigenous religions, especially compared with some other world religions, is that they aren't typically focused on one deity. Some African indigenous religions claim to tend toward monotheism, usually because they have one high god, but most believe in a number of gods. High deities seldom figure into everyday religious life. Instead, they are remote gods, as we'll see in our treatment of Lakota and Yoruba religion. Moreover, as we saw previously, when high deities are regularly invoked, some scholars suspect influence from other world religions. For example, many Native American tribes believe in a high god such as the Great Spirit but don't talk about him on a regular basis or have rituals addressed to him. Where there is more frequent talk of the Great Spirit, and where this Spirit is seen as a single, personal Being, it may well be due to Native American accommodation to Christianity.

Deities or spirits are not worshiped in a detached way; they are ritually invoked and engaged as inhabitants and agents of the world itself. Some indigenous religions remember individuals from their past who were influential leaders, but none is seen as a founder of the religion. This emphasizes that native religions are less about human figures, or even gods and rituals, than they are about relationships. Relationships are shaped by prominent humans and deities and guided by morals, myth, and rituals, but they are ultimately about the people's connection to one another and the group's connection to the world around it.

2-3d Influenced by Other Cultures

Many world religions have had to deal with competition and conflict with other religions, but almost all indigenous religions have had to deal with being surrounded and suppressed by alien nation-states with alien religions. In Africa, for example, centuries of colonial rule by Europeans, and the Christian missionary efforts that went with it, changed some elements of many African indigenous religions. New gods came forth, as well as new rituals for worshiping them. Contemporary scholarship acknowledges that culture-contact changes are central to understanding indigenous cultures and their religions today. Indigenous religions *as they exist today* are worthy of study and appreciation. Scholars have little data about the past of indigenous religions that are free from nonnative influence, so trying to get back to precontact religion is problematic. Indigenous religions themselves often erase any evidence that suggests that some of their beliefs and practices are products of a particular place and time.

2-3e Based on Orality, Story, and Myth

Indigenous religious traditions are oral, not written, because the cultures in which they are based are oral cultures. Orality can open up more room for adaptive change in religion because of not being bound in a book. Orality entails skilled, compelling storytelling. As all skilled storytellers know, audiences must be "brought into the story." In indigenous religions, this is done not just as entertainment. In the religion's stories, each person's life enters a larger group story, even a cosmic story that reaches backward and forward in time. Myths and their accompanying rituals have a critical role in maintaining good relationships between all sacred beings in the universe—human, divine, animal, and even plant.

Scholars have classified different myths according to their form and function. **Cosmogonic myths** about creation explain the origin of existence. They tell how the whole world was created ("cosmogonic") especially how the particular tribe telling a myth was created. An **etiological myth** is one that explains how things have come to be as they are now (from the Greek word for "cause"), covering topics as large as why the sun travels in the sky or as small as why the beaver has no hair on its tail. The **semihistorical myth** is the elaboration of an event, usually involving a tribal hero from history such as the nineteenth-century Lakota leader Sitting Bull. Telling these myths and stories is a means of communication between humans and other beings. The religious specialist of the indigenous society is often the keeper of these stories and can perform them with power. Animals, ancestors, spirits, and gods all compose stories, and people understand the beings through the stories. Narrative is the mode that brings these indigenous traditions to life, through songs, chants, prayers, ritual dances, folktales, and genealogies. Oral tradition has not been erased by modernity and literacy, though it has taken new forms as storytellers have found modern means (including YouTube) for its expression.

cosmogonic myth
Story about creation that explains the origin of existence

etiological myth Story that explains how things have come to be as they are now

semihistorical myth Elaboration of an event usually involving a tribal hero

Aboriginal rock art, Kakadu National Park, Australia

©SAM DCRUZ/SHUTTERSTOCK.COM

2-3f Oriented More toward Practice Than to Belief

Indigenous traditions are not based on beliefs. Belief in gods and spirits is traditional and assumed as a part of the fabric of life. These beliefs are "more caught than taught," and they are reinforced in initiation rituals as children become adults. The emphasis is on practices. Indigenous religions around the world are dedicated to maintaining personal, group, and cosmic balance through ritual actions. The purpose of this balance is that the group may thrive. The scope of rituals in indigenous religions is vast. Some mark life-cycle changes at birth, the beginning of adulthood, marriage, and death. Others are designed to bless people at trying times, heal them of diseases of the mind or body, attract rain, or produce a good hunt or crops. Still others are for purposes of putting curses on people (sometimes called *witching*) and counteracting curses (*unwitching*). The purpose of most indigenous ritual is to control the power of the world—to attract good power and turn away dangerous power.

> Indigenous religions maintain the balance of life so that the group as a whole can thrive in the world.

2-3g In-Group Based

Indigenous traditions around the world are commonly in-group based. Few indigenous religions seek converts or even allow full entry by people not of their group. As we saw previously, they often don't appreciate how others have recently adopted some of their beliefs and rituals, or have come as "seekers" to explore their ways of life. This attitude can come as a surprise, even a shock, to well-intentioned outsiders who are on spiritual journeys that they believe lead to indigenous religions. (American popular culture sometimes portrays indigenous societies as open to be joined by outsiders, as, for example, in the film *Dances with Wolves*.) Unlike religions that seek converts, however, indigenous religions are ethnicity based. Either one is culturally a part of the group, or one is not. If a person is inside the group, then the religion of the group pertains to that person, because his or her place in the community and the world depends on it.

In indigenous societies, extensive life-cycle rituals are employed for bringing children into fully initiated membership in the group. Apart from this initiation, the group is closed to outsiders, and much of its religious knowledge is secret, sometimes even to members of the tribe. For instance, the Dogon (DOH-guhn) people of Mali, West Africa, have many rituals that are done in masks, but the meaning of the masks is known only to those initiated into a society of specialists. (For an example of a west African ritual mask, see Figure 2.1.) Tribal members may regard others outside the tribe as sincere, but they will not typically make them members of the community and give them easy access to religious secrets. The long oppression of indigenous peoples by others has made them even more wary of outsiders' actions and intentions.

2-3h The Goodness of the World

Indigenous peoples believe that each and every part of nature has a spiritual aspect that makes it live and gives direction to its life. All things in the world are related to humans in a cosmic natural balance. American and African indigenous cultures often see this balance as a circle. The Sioux lived in this balance by setting up their camps in circles, by gathering in circles for councils and rituals, and by erecting circular tepees. Therefore, these traditions do not deal with a concept such as salvation, enlightenment, or even eternal life. Means of transcending this world aren't important here, because

Figure 2.1   West African ritual mask

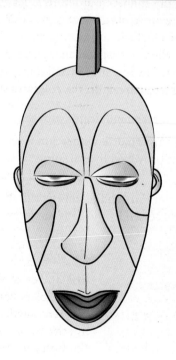

BONNIE VAN VOORST © CENGAGE LEARNING

the world does not need escaping. Its natural harmony needs only to be preserved and lived in. Likewise, these traditions aren't typically future oriented with a belief that this world is heading toward some large goal. Rather, indigenous peoples value the past because it contains the model for identity and behavior in the present and the future. This desire to make the idealized past ever present makes these religions deeply traditional. Indigenous religions maintain the balance of life so that the group as a whole can thrive in the world.

2-3i The Role of Religious Specialists

Indigenous societies have religious specialists of some sort—people selected or trained to do a variety of religious tasks at a higher level than others. They are known by a variety of names: holy men, medicine men, healers, priest/priestesses, and others. **Tricksters** are gods, spirits, humans, or wily animals (often a coyote in North American lore) that play tricks on people or otherwise act in unconventional ways often for the good of others. The most notable religious specialist is the shaman, an intermediary linking the human and spirit worlds. Many types of shamans exist throughout the world, although scholars have found the main model for shamans in Siberian tribes. They are the "spiritual leaders" of their tribes. Mircea Eliade identified their main features as follows:

- The shaman communicates with the spirit world.

- The shaman can deal with sickness or other problems provoked by evil spirits.

- The shaman can leave his body and go to the spirit realm surrounding this world, or his body can be possessed by the gods or spirits.

- The shaman evokes animal spirits as message bearers to other spirits.

- The shaman can tell the future by various forms of divination.[6]

tricksters God, spirit, human, or wily animal that acts in unconventional ways often for the good of others

Painted tepee of Plains Indians, a circular celebration of the goodness of the world

2-3j Continuing Vitality

In the past, many observers predicted the imminent death of indigenous religions. If we consider the dire straits of many of these religions a century ago, we can understand why many thought that native traditions were dying out. However, more than a few indigenous religions can now say, with the American humorist Mark Twain, when told that his death had been announced in a newspaper, "The reports of my death are greatly exaggerated." Not only have a number of native cultures and their religions survived against great pressures over the past five centuries, but also some are now thriving in ways that would have been unthinkable until recently. Native peoples' numbers and cultural influence have risen dramatically in recent generations in many, but not all, parts of the world. Improved standards of living have helped, but more

Shaman emerging from a forest in a trance after an initiation ritual, 1914

importantly being indigenous is shifting in many places from a liability to a point of pride. (A friend of mine from southern Mexico proudly calls himself not Latino, but indigenous.)

We can point to ways in which indigenous religions have flourished over the past half-century. In North America, many native ceremonies that were banned in earlier times are now protected by law. Native peoples have fought hard for these protections and continue to do so, and the wider society has seen the wisdom in preserving them. These include the protection of peyote consumption, the use of eagle feathers in rituals, burial in traditional places, and rights to fish and hunt. They also include the return of human remains and traditional cultural objects now in museums and in private collections. Various African–Caribbean religions that combine Christianity and native African religions are regaining their voice: Santería in Cuba, Candomblé in Brazil, Rastafarianism in Jamaica, and Vodou in Haiti. In Africa, a number of indigenous religions are more prominent today than in the past two hundred years, but many continue to be hard pressed by Christianity and Islam. Native African churches that combine Christianity with key aspects of indigenous religions are thriving, so aspects of indigenous African religions survive within Christianity. The increased freedom of religion in China has led to the widespread rebirth and flourishing of suppressed folk religions that seem to have gone underground for more than fifty years.

2-4 A Native American Religion: Lakota

More than a hundred different Native American tribes are found in North America today. The one offered here for study, the Lakota (lah-KOH-tah) group, which figures large in the past and present, is meant to provide a more extensive look into the religious life of this particular tribe and also provides a more definite description of what indigenous religion is.

2-4a Name and Location

The word *Sioux* (soo) applies today to seven tribal groups organized into three main political units. It dates back to the 1600s C.E., when the people were living in the western Great Lakes area (see Map 2.3). The Ojibwa (oh-JIHB-way) tribes called the neighboring Lakota *Nadouwesou*, meaning "poisonous snakes." This term, shortened by French traders to its last syllable,

became *Sioux*. They called themselves the Seven Fire Places People. French Roman Catholic missionary Jean Nicolet first recorded the term *Sioux* in 1640. Wars with the Chippewas and the Crees resulted in the reduction of the eastern Sioux and gradual displacement of other Sioux. The western Lakota were the first Sioux to arrive on the plains. Horses transformed Lakota life, and the Oglala Sioux obtained them around 1750. They were not native to North America, but were introduced by the Spanish and later obtained by the Plains tribes.

2-4b Basic Features of Lakota Religion

The Black Hills is the Lakota's sacred place of creation and life. A story says that the hills are like a reclining woman whose breasts provided life-giving power. They are a mother to the Lakota, the "heart of everything that exists." The Sioux people were created in particular from the Bear Butte in the Black Hills of South Dakota, where the Creator first taught them his ways. Both Sioux and Cheyenne come there annually for ceremonies. The spirits of the Lakota dead are often said to rest in the Black Hills.

The spirit world of the Lakota is called **Wakan Tanka**, which means "all that is mysterious, sacred." This is a generic, not a personal name. Wakan Tanka is eternal. It both created the universe and, paradoxically, is the universe. The sun, the moon, the stars, and the earth and everything on it (including humans) are all within Wakan Tanka. This term has often been translated as "the Great Spirit" but must not be understood as the one God of monotheistic religions. Wakan Tanka is remote and unapproachable, and rituals are not often performed for it. Included in Wakan Tanka are individual gods and spirits called **Wakanpi** who exercise power and control over everything. Wakanpi are incomprehensible to ordinary humans, but they enable shamans to know them and deal with them. They obtain their knowledge through direct contact with the gods and spirits in dreams and visions. Wakanpi act as intermediaries through which the power of Wakan Tanka can flow. (For an example of a Lakota symbol for the spiritual power of Wakan Tanka, see the image of the medicine wheel in Figure 2.2.)

Wakan Tanka [WAHK-ahn THAHN-kuh] "All that is mysterious, sacred"; the spirit world of the Lakota that created the universe

Wakanpi [wah-KAHN-pee] Individual gods and spirits who exercise power and control over everything

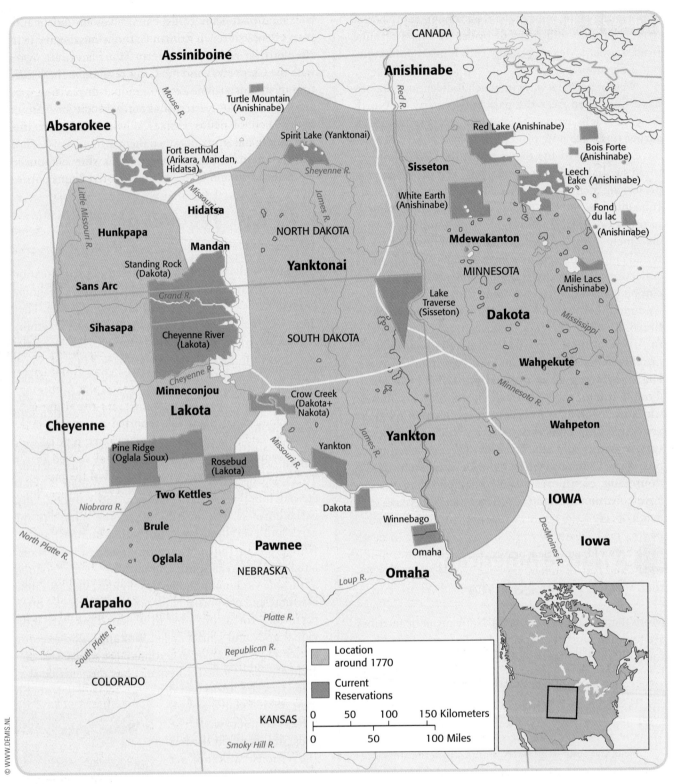

Map 2.3
Traditional Location of Sioux Tribes around 1770 and Reservations Today

The Sioux pass down their religion to each new generation in story form. Tribal history is also passed along orally, but it has always been guided by myths of origin so that the recent past doesn't contradict the deep past. Elders often gather the young around the fire to impart important tales. Some of these tales, such as the stories of the White Buffalo Calf Woman, can take up to seven evenings to tell and traditionally can only be told when the moon is shining.

Figure 2.2 Lakota medicine wheel

BONNIE VAN VOORST © CENGAGE LEARNING

The Sioux look on death and the afterlife in the spirit world as a natural part of life. Death is painful in close-knit indigenous societies, but funeral rituals help mourners cope with the pain of loss. Human souls are immortal; they come from Wakan Tanka at birth and return to Wakan Tanka at death. Because these spirits are one with Wakan Tanka, they are everywhere and in everything, even at the grave for a period after death. Before battle, Sioux warriors embraced their possible death openly—thus their famous saying "Today is a good day to die." Death in warfare was preferable to death caused by old age. Their bravery in battle has continued today, and Native Americans have been, for nearly a century, a highly decorated group in the U.S. Armed Forces.

2-4c Lakota Rituals

As with other religions, the Lakota believe that their rituals came to them from the gods. Lakota myths tell of spirits such as the White Buffalo Calf Woman, who gave her people the sacred pipe and taught them its ritual use. Holy men received other rituals during trance-like states. We now discuss Lakota rituals that are still regularly held.

Near the time of puberty, Sioux boys, and on occasion girls, go on a ritual of passage to adulthood called a **vision quest**, through which they undergo a symbolic death and rebirth and experience their personal guardian spirit. Through the vision quest, each Lakota gains a personal religious vision

GILL ANDREA©/ISTOCK / GETTY IMAGES PLUS/GETTY IMAGES

Ceremonial pipe

that supplements the group-based religious understandings of the tribe. On returning from the vision quest, the vision seeker typically integrates his or her vision into the life of the community by performing it ritually in public. This integration of one's personal vision with the socially regimented roles of tribal societies helps to make a better balance between individual and group life among the Lakota.

The modern healing ceremony is shortened from the traditional form. Prayer is still offered to the spirit of the stones, and spirit stones protect against danger or illness. This signifies a belief in a spiritual force in all forms of Creation. It isn't unusual to see a sacred stone at the bedside of sick or hospitalized Lakota even today.

The **sacred pipe** continues to be used to forge a ritual connection between Wakan Tanka and humankind, reinforcing the kinship ties of the people with all spirits in the world. It has become so important as a symbol that it now unofficially stands for the whole of Lakota life—indeed, it has become a Pan-Indian ritual implement. (Sometimes it is called a "peace pipe"; although it was used for peace ceremonies, its ritual use goes far beyond this.) Black Elk reported a common belief when he said that the red stone the sacred pipe is made from symbolizes the earth; an animal carved in the stone represents all animals; the wood of the pipe stem symbolizes all growing things; and the feathers on it represents all birds, especially the eagle. All creatures in the natural world "send their voices" to Wakan Tanka when the pipe is smoked.[7]

The **sweat lodge** is a ritual sauna meant to cleanse participants' spirits. (It isn't done, as our saunas today, for muscle relaxation or cleansing of the skin.) It can be a domed hut or a hole dug into the ground and covered with planks or tree trunks. Stones are heated in an outside fire and then placed in a pit inside the lodge. Ritual activities inside and around the sweat lodge include prayers, drumming and singing, and offerings to the spirits.

vision quest Ritual of passage to adulthood through which one undergoes a symbolic death and rebirth and gains a guardian spirit

sacred pipe Pipe ritually used to forge a connection between Wakan Tanka and humankind

sweat lodge Ritual sauna to cleanse participants' spirits

Modern Miwok tribe sweat lodge near Pioneer, California

a cleansing of their spirits and, occasionally, some healing of their bodies. The peyote movement was one factor in the rise of the **Native American Church**, a blend of indigenous North American religions and Christianity that is still strong today. This group has successfully fought the U.S. legal system for permission to use the cactus-derived drug, which is generally illegal. Use of peyote began to decline in about 2009, because it has been poorly grown and over-harvested during recent years.

The use of **peyote**, a mildly hallucinogenic, non-addictive drug made from a cactus bud, goes back for centuries among Native Americans in the Southwest. Peyote was used as a medicine in healing ceremonies before its more modern ceremonial use. It spread beyond the Southwest at the beginning of the twentieth century, when Native American culture was stressed, and some Lakota today continue the practice. Participants reported

peyote [pay-YOHT-ee] Mildly hallucinogenic cactus bud used in rituals

Native American Church Church mainly composed of Native Americans, featuring a blend of indigenous American religions and Christianity

sun dance Main festival ceremony of Plains tribes

Cactus used in making peyote

Finally, the **sun dance** ceremony is still practiced in almost twenty different North American tribes. It features dancing, singing and drumming, blowing on eagle-bone whistles, visions, and fasting. Some brave men known as *sun dance pledgers* come to the festival having already taken a vow to offer their bodies as a painful sacrifice to Wakan Tanka for the benefit of their tribe. The sacrifice usually takes the form of being attached to a pole by hide thongs, which pierce one's body in the chest with a metal hook. Each tribe holds the sun dance once a year, at the height of summer when the sun is the hottest, from four to eight days. It ritually enacts continuity between life and death, and renews the life of the tribe as connected to the earth. The sun dance continues to be an important ritual festival for the Plains tribes.

2-4d Lakota Culture and Religion: Decline and Signs of Revival

The buffalo holds a key place in Lakota life and history. From its hide they made clothing, ropes, snowshoes, and the round, moveable homes called *tipi* (also phonetically spelled *tepee*, the Lakota word for "dwelling"). The horns provided spoons, weapons, and ritual articles. The buffalo's sinew was used for bowstrings and sewing thread. The buffalo was the main friend of the Sun, and even controlled all affairs of love. Its spirit cares for the family, for the young of all beings, and for growing plants. Given the place of the buffalo in the life and beliefs of the Lakota, its extermination proved deadly for their traditional culture. Around 1800 there were possibly 60 million buffalo on the Plains; by 1884 the slaughter by hunters—encouraged by the federal government, in part to break the power of the Plains tribes—led to less than one hundred buffalo being left. The Lakota Sioux, along with other Plains tribes, were reduced to dependence on government rations on various reservations of small size and few resources.

Extermination of the buffalo proved deadly for traditional Lakota culture.

The sad story of the gradual reduction of Native American life continued. Confinement to reservations was soon followed by a government policy to "civilize" Indian peoples by **assimilation** into mainstream culture—by coercion if necessary. (Voluntary assimilation happened as well, but on a smaller scale.) Rapid white expansion into western North America meant that Indian conflicts had to end, and, therefore, much of the land granted to them by treaties was taken from them. Hiram Price, U.S. Commissioner of Indian Affairs in 1881, said history shows that "Savage and civilized life cannot prosper on the same ground."[8] This was a conviction widely held among European Americans, and by the mid-nineteenth century it was allied to a racist theory of white superiority and the belief that it was America's Manifest Destiny to occupy all the lands from the Atlantic to the Pacific. Because European Americans as a group assumed that they were superior to indigenous Americans, they knew what was best for them. This portended the rapid destruction of Native American cultures, and their religions as well.

Much of the forced assimilation was targeted at children, because they were more changeable than their parents. In schools, Indian children were prohibited from speaking their own language, living out their own culture, or having a tribal identity. Children in both the United States and Canada were separated from their families and sent far off to boarding schools if their family's influence was viewed as negative. Some government officials had second thoughts about this. For example, in his Indian commissioner's report for 1934, John Collier urged an end to this assault on native culture. But this was not to become a widespread policy until the 1960s.

Violent conflict continued into the late 1800s. In the Sioux Wars of the 1870s, the Sioux and their allies battled with the U.S. Army in the Black Hills. This culminated on June 25–26, 1876, with a battle at **Little Big Horn** in eastern Montana. Hundreds of Sioux and Cheyenne warriors under the command of Sitting Bull, a Sioux chief and holy man, met the Seventh Cavalry Regiment of the U.S. Army, commanded by General George Custer. Sitting Bull quickly destroyed Custer's forces. Although Little Big Horn bolstered Native American morale, this did not last long. The federal military presence continued, as did increasing white settlement in the West, even on Native American reservations. In response to this worsening situation, the **ghost dance** movement arose in the late 1880s. It would be the last militant attempt in the 1800s to preserve the cultural life and independence of Native Americans. The ghost dance movement was inspired by the vision of the Paiute leader Wovoka (also known by his "white" name, Jack Wilson). Wovoka's vision spread and reached the Sioux late in 1889. It spoke of dead native warriors (ghosts) coming back to life; the restoration of youth to the living; the return of the buffalo, elk, and other game; and the departure of whites.

After the U.S. Army learned that the Sioux were armed, wearing their ghost shirts, and defying government agents, troops arrived at the Pine Ridge reservation on November 20, 1890, and at other Sioux areas as well. Sitting Bull was arrested on December 15 and killed in the process, and his followers fled. Alarmed at Sitting Bull's death and anxious at the troops' presence on their reservation, the Big Foot band of Lakota, numbering about 350, headed for Pine Ridge to confront the army. Intercepted by troops, they surrendered and were kept

assimilation Entry into mainstream culture, either voluntary or forced

Little Big Horn 1876 Battle in Montana, in which Sioux and Cheyenne warriors defeated a U.S. Army regiment

ghost dance Movement in the 1880s looking for the restoration of Indian life and the departure of whites

at Wounded Knee. On December 29, as troops tried to confiscate the weapons that some Lakota still possessed, a rifle discharged and shooting immediately broke out on both sides. Historians conclude that what began as an accident quickly turned into what has become known as the **Massacre at Wounded Knee**. Of the U.S. Army troops, twenty-five were killed; of the Lakota, eighty-four men and boys and sixty-two women and girls were killed—almost half of the prisoners. The ghost dance movement ended with the Massacre at Wounded Knee. The ghost shirts worn by the Big Foot band had failed to protect them as it was believed they would. To use the words of Black Elk, "the dream died."

Native Americans then settled down to a long period of slow decline on the reservations in the United States and Canada, but over time most left the reservations to assimilate with wider American culture. In the early 1970s, a social and political protest movement arose among Native Americans. At Wounded Knee, traditional Indians and members of the American Indian Movement (AIM) protested the appalling economic and social conditions on Pine Ridge reservation, which is today the poorest area in the United States. Wounded Knee was chosen for the protest because it showed a continuity of the suffering of those who died there in 1890.

To conclude this section, let's sum up our discussion. It is important in the Lakota culture to live in a healthy, life-giving relationship with the tribe and the land. As we have seen, this relationship has been seriously damaged by military conquest, forced assimilation, relocations, and government policies made under a U.S. Bureau of Indian Affairs, which is widely recognized as incompetent. Also, high unemployment (up to an astounding 90 percent), poverty, domestic violence, and alcohol and drug abuse continue to take a toll on the reservations.

Some signs of hope are appearing: Tribal identities are growing, religious rituals are practiced and taught to new generations, tribal casino gambling recognized by state and federal governments is bringing in financial resources for tribal use (although some

Massacre at Wounded Knee Killing of about 150 Lakota prisoners of war by the U.S. Army in 1890

Sioux Ghost Dance shirt, circa 1890

WERNER FOREMAN/GETTY IMAGES

consider casinos a mixed blessing), and social ills are being more seriously attended to. Indian tribes are realizing that if improvement in their condition is to come, they must bring it themselves. Many Lakota organizations are dedicated to the continuation of traditional ways. The Lakota continue the struggle to hold on to the Black Hills, even refusing in 1980 a $100 million offer in return for giving up their claim to the Hills. This refusal is an indication of Sioux commitment to their traditional culture. The reestablishment of traditional Lakota ways of life requires no less than the rebuilding of the community from the family up.

This struggle to maintain indigenous identity in the face of opposition is shared by others. For an example, "A Closer Look" in section 2-5 examines Hawaiian religion and its struggle to adapt to Christianity.

2-5 An African Religion: Yoruba

To take a closer look at African indigenous religions, we will examine the Yoruba (YOHR-uh-buh) religion of west-central Africa. Not only is the Yoruba religion important in Africa today, but it is also important in the Western Hemisphere, because many Yoruba taken into slavery to the Americas were instrumental in the founding of new Afro–Caribbean religions. Like indigenous religions that cover a wide area, the religions of the Yoruba peoples vary significantly in different parts of west-central Africa today, especially in Nigeria. For example, the name of a god often has variations, or the same deity may be female in one town and male in the next, and the rituals to worship them may vary as well.

Despite this internal variety, all Yoruba religion shares a similar structure and purpose. A supreme but remote god rules the world, along with hundreds of lower deities actively worshiped, each of whom has a specific area of rule. These gods guide believers to find their destiny in life, one that was determined at the moment of reincarnation of one's soul into a new life but then forgotten. The rituals of the Yoruba identify this destiny for the individual, and this blesses the life of the Yoruba people as a whole.

2-5a High God and Other Gods

The Yoruba all have a high god, usually called **Olorun** (Ruler of the Sky) or *Olodumare* (oh-loh-DOOM-ah-reh, All-powerful One), but is occasionally called by a number of other names. They don't worship Olorun or make sacrifices to him, and he has no priests and no places of worship. He is a remote god. Although the Yoruba believe that he is the creator and continual giver of life, almighty and all knowing, the Yoruba ignore him in their daily lives. He is invoked only at times of extreme need, and even then with difficulty. Some scholars argue that Olorun developed as a postcontact deity through the influence of Muslim and Christian missionaries as an imitation of their God, but one that could not be integrated into other Yoruba beliefs or rituals. However, belief in Olorun is widespread among the Yoruba, both in those tribes that have not had much contact with Muslims and Christians as well as those that have. Moreover, other African tribes and nations also have remote high gods.

The main Yoruba deities that control relations between the earth and the high god are known as **orisha**. They are the gods with whom humans have contact with through myth and rituals. The numbers, relationships, and names of the orisha are exceedingly complex; they form a vast group of supernatural beings numbering between 401 and 601. Some Yoruba myths have a pair of gods, Orishala (also known as Obatala and Orisanla) and Odudua, his wife, as the gods who created the world. This association with the creator and high god Olorun gives them a higher status than that of the other orisha. In one myth, Olorun creates most of the world and then has Obatala and Odudua finish it. Obatala is often portrayed as a divine sculptor, especially of individual human bodies. The Yoruba regard physically different humans to be either Obatala's special servants or the victims of his displeasure, leaving some room for interpretation.

A doll with bananas, both tied with red ribbon, as offerings to Shango

© ISTOCKPHOTO/KIMBERLY CUBERO

The Yoruba see **Ogun** as the highest orisha. His status as the chief god of war, hunting, and ironworking makes him the patron of warriors, blacksmiths, and all others who use metals. Yoruba religion has a high regard for metal as a combination of earth, wind, and fire. Ogun also is the god of business deals and contracts. In courts in Yoruba areas of Nigeria, Yorubans take their oath to tell the truth by kissing a knife. Ogun is fearsome in his revenge; if one breaks an agreement after invoking his name, swift punishment will follow. One myth that illustrates Ogun's importance tells of several orisha making a road through a dense jungle. Ogun was the only one with the right tools for the task and so won the right to rule the orisha. When he did not want the position, it went to Obatala. (For a geometric symbol of Ogun suggesting metalwork, which is commonly used in his worship, see Figure 2.3.)

Shango the storm god occupies an important place among these orisha. A myth told about Shango provides a basis for his worship. When he was human and a king of an ancient Yoruba kingdom, he had power to create lightning, but he accidentally killed his entire family with it. He then killed himself in sorrow and became deified when he entered the spirit world. At that point he gained more power over lightning, as well as over thunder, wind, and hail. Scholars generally conclude that Shango's popularity among the Yoruba peoples results from a need to avert the violent storms that often strike western Africa. (These storms are

Olorun [OHL-oh-ruhn] "Ruler of the Sky," Yoruba high god

orisha [ohr-EE-shuh] Yoruba gods who control relations between the earth and Olorun, and with whom humans have contact with through myth and rituals

Ogun [OH-guhn] Highest orisha, the chief god of war, hunting, and ironworking

A Closer Look

Polynesian Religion in Hawaii

Hawaiian indigenous religion centers on the gods in and behind natural forces. For example, Lono is the god of rain and the fertility it brings, Kane (KAH-nay) is the god of sky and creation, and Kanaloa (KAN-uh-LOH-ah) is the ocean god. These and other deities are known by way of myth and ritual. The *Kumulipo* (KOO-muh-LEE-poh) song tells the creation myth in 1,200 lines of verse. In it, light overcame darkness, and the world was then created over several nights. The sea and life in it were created first; then land and its creatures; afterward the gods of earth, sky, and sea; and finally humans. The recital of these verses is traditionally led by the **kahuna**, a type of shaman who is both a cultural and religious leader, as a chant during a special festival to celebrate and renew the creation.

The main goal of Hawaiian indigenous religion is to maintain a balanced relationship with nature and society in which people can flourish. Gods, lesser spirits, and spirits of the ancestors all have a role in this relationship. Some kahunas have the power to communicate with the gods, using their abilities to treat the sick. Most illnesses are thought to be the result of evil forces and spirits that invade the body. The ability to heal and the healing itself derive from the kahuna's connection to the deities, and is often simply a matter of speaking to the gods about the sick person.

Prayer is an integral part of Hawaiian traditional life. For example, one prays during the process of building a house or a boat. Prayer is offered to a specific god (usually not a high deity), depending on one's needs. Prayers are spoken before eating, drinking, traveling, and sleeping. Hawaiians typically sit for prayer and look up during it. Prayers can also be said in small temples, in front of shrines, and at other sacred places, and they accompany all sacrifices and offerings to the gods.

Specific cultural laws known as the **kapu**—a word related to the Polynesian term *taboo* or *tapu*—refer to strictly forbidden acts. These ensure ritual and moral purity by forbidding one to cross certain lines of behavior;

The Pu'uhonua o Honaunau religious sanctuary. Those who had broken kapu laws could flee here for safety and cleansing, but entry was arduous, even dangerous.

©GALYNA ANDRUSHKO/SHUTTERSTOCK.COM

even today, *kapu* is seen on doors in Hawaii to forbid entry. A priest from Tahiti introduced this system to the islands around 1200 C.E. It regulated one's actions regarding social status and gender. Breaking these laws was punishable by death. Some examples: Women and children had to eat their meals in a separate place from men. Women could not enter religious shrines, temples, or the homes of their chief, and they were kept apart during menstruation. Members of a tribe could not touch their chiefs or even stand too close to them.

The kapu system was first dealt a blow by Hawaiians themselves before the coming of Christianity, who chafed under its restrictions. They burned wooden statues of the gods and destroyed some of their stone temples. In 1831 the idols were banned, and Christianity was made the only permitted faith. The hula dance performances, chanting of songs with religious overtones, and other practices were outlawed and went underground. Some traditional aspects of Hawaiian religion outlasted the influence of the Christian missionaries, however. Beginning around 1960, Hawaiian indigenous religion has come back into the light and experienced a rebirth of sorts. Hawaiian indigenous believers, some of whom combine native beliefs with Christianity or Buddhism, are now bringing back old rites and beliefs—without many of the restrictive kapus. In sum, like many indigenous religions around the world, Hawaiian religion has made an uneasy but creative adaption to new times and cultures.

kahuna [kah-HOO-nuh]
Leader in Hawaiian indigenous religion

kapu [KAH-poo]
Hawaiian laws forbidding moral and ritual impurities

Figure 2.3 **Symbol of Ogun**

BONNIE VAN VOORST © CENGAGE LEARNING

so powerful that they sometimes move over the Atlantic Ocean, form into hurricanes, and strike the Caribbean and the southern United States.)

Shango came to the New World with newly enslaved Africans. In Annapolis, Maryland, a clay bundle about the size and shape of an American football was unearthed by University of Maryland and University of London archaeologists at an old crossroads. Dated to around 1700, it was filled with about three hundred pieces of metal and had a stone axe sticking out through the clay. Archaeologists quickly identified it as African in origin and used in the worship of Shango by African slaves recently brought to America. Although almost all slaves were baptized into Christianity, they continued to observe, in secret, some Yoruban "spirit practices" in healing and in the worship of their ancestors.

Trickster gods can blur the line between good and evil in Yoruba religion. One myth dealing with the god Eshu (EH-shoo) illustrates his trickiness. Pretending to be a merchant, Eshu sold expensive items to a man's two wives, sparking a desire in each to outdo the other in purchasing. The battle for the husband's favor after this buying spree tore the family apart. This story is told as a cautionary tale against the evils of greed and ambition. Eshu is also, but not in his trickster role, the divine guardian of houses and villages. The relationship between Eshu and many Yorubans is so close that they call him *Baba* ("father") in worship. Because tricksters often blur the lines of good and evil, Islamic and Christian missionaries among the Yorubans attacked Eshu as a demonic figure. This of course betrays a misunderstanding of a trickster's overall role to promote morality, not undermine it.

The history of Shokpona (shock-POH-nuh), the god of smallpox, is an interesting story at the intersection of religion and medicine. Shokpona became important during the smallpox plagues that arose during intertribal wars in west Africa. The Yoruba also saw Shokpona's wrath in other diseases that have similar symptoms. Shokpona's wrath is so terrifying that the Yoruba are often afraid to speak his name. Instead, they use expressions such as "Hot Earth," referring to high fever, and "One whose name must not be spoken in the dry season." Priests of Shokpona had great power; they could inflict smallpox on their enemies, especially by making a ritual potion from the powdered scabs and dry skin of those who had died from smallpox. They would then spread this potion in an enemy's area. Although this indirect contact with smallpox was less deadly than contact with living people infected by it, it worked well enough. However, because smallpox has been eradicated worldwide since about 1980, the worship of Shokpona has all but vanished, and his priests with it.

African religious practice had a role at a key moment in American history. When a growing smallpox epidemic threatened the American revolutionary army encamped at Valley Forge, Pennsylvania in 1777, George Washington ordered inoculations based on an account by a famous Christian minister in Massachusetts, Cotton Mather (1663–1728). Mather detailed how his African slave named Onesimus (oh-NESS-ih-muss) had been protected from smallpox by vaccination, probably in a religious ritual of body marking connected with the worship of Shokpona. A small bit of smallpox scab had been put on his cuts so that, as Mather later wrote, Onesimus "had smallpox and then did not have it." Mather himself had successfully inoculated his sons with this procedure, minus the Yoruban religious elements, of course. Mather then urged this inoculation technique for Boston in 1721, when a smallpox outbreak occurred. The method was also a success at Valley Forge, and the American army was saved from smallpox.

2-5b Religious Specialists

Priests divine the future, offering advice for how to meet it. Male priests are known as a **babalawo**, "father of secrets," and females as an **iyalawo**, "mother of secrets." They help people to understand the destinies they chose in the spirit world but lost when they came to Earth. A babalawo or iyalawo also gives people power and guidance to make their destinies come true. Seeking a priest to help with one's future is a common

babalawo [BUB-uh-LAH-woh] "Father of secrets," the Yoruba male priest

iyalawo [EE-yah-LAH-woh] "Mother of secrets," the Yoruba female priest

occurrence throughout life, but faithful Yorubas take their child to a diviner soon after birth so that the child's destiny can be made clear from the very start.

The process of divination varies by priest and region, but following is the most common method. The believer, usually under some sort of duress, makes her or his way to a diviner. Contrary to many other systems of divination and fortune-telling, the believer doesn't tell the diviner what the problem is. Instead, the diviner summons the gods and then casts sixteen separate palm nuts or a chain of sixteen shells onto a divination board. Depending on the results, the diviner then chants a group of poems called **Ifa** verses, presided over by a god of the same name. The collection of Ifa verses is vast, and diviners often know several hundred of them by heart. These poems recount short stories about the gods and usually tell of some sacrifice, gift, or action the believer must take. It is then up to the believer to discern which of the poems and prescribed actions are correct in her or his situation. The Yoruba believer is very active in this process; it's not just a matter of telling one's problems to a priest and then getting some quick advice. This system of divination has worked for centuries, probably millennia, and even today many Yoruba consult an expert in the Ifa before making any important decisions. A recent book by Velma Love, *Divining the Self*, shows how Ifa divination is practiced in African American communities in Oyotunji Village, South Carolina and in New York City.[9]

2-5c Spirits of the Ancestors

The Yoruba venerate their dead ancestors, which is typical of indigenous societies. Some Yoruba groups believe that their dead ancestors become semidivine figures. This is related to another aspect of the Yoruba faith: possession of one's body by the gods. During these possessions, priests acting as mediums take on the individual characteristics of the deities. The behavioral patterns of how each god takes possession of a medium are so entrenched that many mediums as far away as the Caribbean move their heads and legs just as mediums of Shango do in west Africa.

Ivory wand or tapper used in Yoruba Ifa divination practice, Nigeria. The diviner taps an Ifa board with the point of the tapper repeatedly to summon the attention of the gods.

HIP/ART RESOURCE, NY

Ifa [EE-fuh] Poetic verses used in Yoruba divination

2-6 An Afro–Caribbean Religion: Vodou

Those who follow the Afro–Caribbean religion of Vodou (VOH-doo) currently number an estimated 5 to 7 million people. Vodou is widely referred to in North America today, but with much misunderstanding, especially in American popular culture. In this section, we'll put this religion in its African and New World contexts and try to shed some light on its significance for today. An important part of our study of Vodou will be to rehabilitate the name of this religion, so that it doesn't always stir up negative emotions and misleading opinions. Although Vodou is not, strictly speaking, indigenous to Haiti, the centuries of its combination with Roman Catholicism in the setting of the New World qualify it as a North American indigenous religion.

2-6a Location and Name

Similar to the Brazilian religions Candomblé and Umbanda, Cuban Santería, or Jamaican Rastafarianism, the Vodou religion is based on an African indigenous religion. An estimated 9 to 12 million Africans were brought as slaves to the New World between 1500 and 1850, most of them to Brazil and the Caribbean islands, and they brought their religions with them. Similar to other indigenous religions, Vodou is concerned mainly with bringing its followers into harmony with the gods that control the natural world, so that in this harmony their lives can be happy and blessed. These religions were brought to the New World by enslaved members of west African tribes, and there underwent an independent development to become Afro–Caribbean.

The word *Vodou* (or the lesser-used *Hoodoo*, which is often used on a popular level for the magical practices of Vodou) is from the Haitian Creole-French language. It is also spelled *Voudon* or *Vodun* in scholarship today. You probably know it as *Voodoo*. Until recently, this was the accepted spelling of the word, but many Haitians and modern scholars now acknowledge *Vodou* as the preferred spelling, because it is phonetically closer to the original African word. It originated in the language of the Ewe Fon west African peoples brought to Haiti as slaves from present-day Benin and Togo. Specifically, it is from *vodú*, the Ewe Fon word for both "god" and "worship." Beginning in the seventeenth century, *Voodoo* was used in the missionary literature about the Ewe people

Another Call from Africa by Haitian artist Turgo Bastien has African–Caribbean religious themes.

TURGO BASTIEN

Ronald Reagan were competing in 1980 for the Republican nomination for president, Bush called Reagan's economic plan "Voodoo economics." Other uses of Vodou center on the current popularity of zombies, especially "zombie walks." Observers of American popular culture say that in 2009 zombies replaced vampires as the leading symbol of unnatural threats. This interest in zombies distorts and demeans the Vodou religion.

2-6b Divinities

Similar to other Afro–Caribbean religions, Haitian Vodou has authentic African traits. Vodou is a typical example of a religion centered on different groups of gods. These deities are called **loas**, meaning "divinities" or "mysteries." They are also commonly called "saints," in the sense of "holy ones." In Fon myth, there are three regions of the world, and various loas reign in each one: the sky, the earth, and, in between these, the clouds. The creator god (Yoruba, *Olorun*; Creole, *Bon Dieu Bon*—literally "Good God Good") lives in the remote sky. Because he isn't involved with everyday life, he isn't honored in everyday rituals. Through the influence of Roman Catholicism, Vodou believers also worship the Christian God. It's not uncommon for them to worship in a Catholic church on Sunday morning and in a Vodou sanctuary on Sunday evening. They also venerate two other kinds of spiritual beings who live between the sky and the earth: souls of dead humans that have become spirits and spirits that have never been directly tied to matter. Vodou gods live on the earth—in the sea, in waterfalls, in springs, in forests, at intersections of roads, in cemeteries, and in piles of stones. Many earth gods of Vodou correspond to Catholic saints, on whose feast days the Vodou deities are also celebrated. The recognition and worship of these gods helps to bless the lives of people on earth, so that they can be happy, peaceful, and productive.

in Africa, who called a newly initiated member of their religion a *vodúnsi* or *hunsi*, a "bride of the deity." But the use of *Voodoo* has prejudicial and exotic overtones in the Western world today. In general, Vodou in Africa is an African indigenous religion, not combined with Roman Catholic Christianity as it is in the Americas.

In the Western Hemisphere, *Vodou* means various things. It often refers to an Afro–Catholic religion that is widespread on the Caribbean island of Hispaniola, especially in Haiti. It can also be applied to persons—for example, spell-workers are often called "hoodoo doctors" in the southern United States. In Haiti, Vodou is applied as an umbrella term to a large number of Haitian religious groups with roots in African religion rather than Roman Catholic Christianity. In mainstream American usage, it has become a common pejorative for "deceptive nonsense," usually with no connection to religion. For instance, when George H. W. Bush and

{ *In 2009 zombies replaced vampires as the leading symbol of unnatural threats.* }

2-6c Groups

Gods and rites are divided into groups according to the geographical regions of their origin. The two main groups are the *Rada* and the *Petro*, who are found especially in urban areas. *Rada* derives from the old kingdom of Arada in Africa. *Petro*, more

loas [LOH-uh] "Divinity" or "mystery"; in west African and Vodou religions, a god or group of gods

oriented to the indigenous Creoles, comes from the name of a Vodou priest, Don Pedro, who introduced a variant of the Vodou trance dance in the eighteenth century. (The Petro group is named after him, but he did not found it.) Petro gods and spirits are invoked especially for magical or counter-magical actions that we will consider in the following section. Vodou priests may support both groups, and a believer is usually either Rada or Petro but may likewise take part in ceremonies of the other type.

2-6d Worship

As with Candomblé in Brazil and Santería in Cuba, North American Vodou is a fusion of African religions with Catholicism. Some traces of Caribbean Indian religion can also be found in it. The religion of Vodou refers not to a body of beliefs, creeds, sacred scriptures, or other elements of religion, but to ritual practice. Vodou is often described as a **possession cult** in which the gods inhabit people and speak through them, usually during rituals. Rituals of animal sacrifice as well as trance dances forge and maintain possession by the deities. The rites are practiced by initiated members called *hunsi*, "brides of the gods," presided over by priests and priestesses called *hugan* and *mambo*, respectively. Initiates are introduced into the group by a complicated and spectacular ritual. Worship is held in sacred cabins or city temples, all with an altar for the sacrifice of animals and other offerings. They have a central post that enables the loas to descend to believers and "ride" them like "horses" in a state of trance.

A few Vodou rituals tap into the power of the spirits of the dead, and cemeteries have become important places of Vodou gatherings for worship. The head loa in the cult of the dead is **Baron Samedi**, the "Lord of the Dead." His depiction and name vary, but he often wears a top hat, a black tuxedo, and cotton plugs in his nostrils, all of which are found on a corpse prepared in a Haitian style for burial. Baron Samedi has a white, skull-like face and is regarded by all as a fearsome presence. Although dead, he is very much alive. He is charged with sexual energy and is frequently represented by phallic symbols. Baron Samedi is known for obscenity and debauchery, and he enjoys tobacco and rum. He is worshiped and celebrated in order to keep him at bay, so that he won't disturb the living.

Also connected to death—and the African experience of deadly slavery in Haiti—is the figure of the zombie. As we saw previously, Yoruba religion has a large role for the spirits of the dead, and Vodou further blurs the distinction between the living and the dead. It believes that a human body can be revived by an especially powerful magician after the spirit of the dead has departed, and then used as a slave for the magician's purposes. These bodies are the ultimate slaves, the worst possible kind of "life" for Afro–Haitian people. Zombies remain under the control of the sorcerer because they have no will, mind, or soul of their own. This is why in popular culture, zombies are usually depicted as mindless, almost robotic figures that shuffle around. However, the notion that zombies eat human flesh, thus making other people into zombies, is a mistaken view that taps into a revulsion against cannibalism.

PHOTOS 12 / ARCHIVES DU 7E ART/ALAMY

Vodou has so entered the popular imagination that even animated Disney films for children can feature (and exploit) it. In *The Princess and the Frog*, the Vodou character known as Dr. Facilier resembles Baron Samedi, dressed in tails and a top hat with a sign of death on it.

possession cult
Religion in which the gods inhabit people and speak through them, usually during rituals

Baron Samedi
[sah-MEHD-ee] "Lord of the Dead," head loa in the Vodou cult of the dead

2-6e Spell and Counter-Spell Rituals

Similar to some of the world's largest religions, Vodou has a place for magical practices, and, also similar to other religions, this is found more often on a popular, not an official, level. Magic is the preferred form of Vodou practice of the lowest social class in Haiti—the small farmers, the urban working poor, and the masses of unemployed—although today some members of the upper class are also drawn to it. People use magic to seek deliverance from all the difficulties of life, which for the lower classes in Haiti are many. Diseases, poverty, and other difficulties are seen as the effect of demonic spells, which need to be countered with magic. Probably the magical practice best known in the West is the one performed with a small doll, a practice that is seen as being able to harm someone's health or even cause death.

Also used are **gris-gris**, originally images of the gods in the shape of little dolls but now small cloth bags containing herbs, oils, pebbles, bits of bone, hair, finger- or toenails, and pieces of sweat-soaked cloth. These are gathered and bagged to protect the owner from harm. Legends of the most famous Vodou practitioner in the United States, New Orleans "Vodou Queen" Marie Laveau (1794–1881), say that her gris-gris contained bone, colored pebbles, cemetery soil, salt, and red pepper. In addition to protective uses, gris-gris are for gaining money and love, insuring good health, and for accomplishing other similar purposes. The ingredients are always an odd number of items, and are chosen to fit the purpose of the gris-gris.

Curse rituals, services of worship in cemeteries, the use of snakes in worship, and zombies have made the Vodou religion a favorite subject of **exoticism**, distorting something in another culture by portraying it as strange or exciting. Ever since Spenser St. John's 1884 adventure account about Haiti, *Hayita or the Black Republic*, exoticism around Vodou has continually sprung up. The Vodou religion, by way of Hollywood, became an important part of the horror

A shop selling Vodou supplies in the French Quarter of New Orleans

JSF 306

film genre. Filmmakers have found that exotic presentations of Vodou can easily frighten and entertain audiences.

2-6f Political Influence in Haiti

Haitian Vodou has, at times, had an important political and social role. Its faithful were able to mobilize forces against the French colonialist rulers at the close of the 1700s; this led to the abolition of slavery and the country's independence from France in 1804. Through the years, Vodou believers opposed various Haitian regimes that were devoted to their own power even as the gap between the rich and the poor masses grew. The last instance of such resistance was to dictator "Papa Doc" Duvalier, who ruled from 1957 to 1971. After the devastation of Haiti in the earthquake of 2010, Vodou remains powerful on a popular level.

Rural and urban forms of Vodou differ in Haiti. In rural areas, worship and belief are oriented to small farmers and are supported by extensive family alliances. Involvement with

gris-gris [gree-gree] In Vodou, small cloth bags containing items gathered under the direction of a god for the protection of the owner

exoticism [egg-ZOT-uh-siz-uhm] Distorting something in another culture by portraying it as strange or exciting

ancestors and ritual practices to bring about successful farming are the center of religious practice. Vodou believers in the cities have adapted their practice to urban relationships. They find a "second family" in the temple communities. This urban adaptation of Vodou has found its way to mainland North America.

Widespread continuous poverty and political instability in Haiti have led to the need for a religion that can help the poor cope with their problems. Vodou offers this help; the other main religion of Haiti, Christianity, is tied in the minds of many Haitians to the social elites who oppress the common people. This dismal situation in Haiti has led to the emigration of Haitians to mainland North America. They have taken the Vodou religion along with them to New York City, Miami, and Montreal, and especially to New Orleans, where today there is a museum of Vodou and a thriving trade in Vodou objects. Vodou is starting to get a foothold in some countries of Europe, but mainly as a practice adapted for those who are not initiates in the religion.

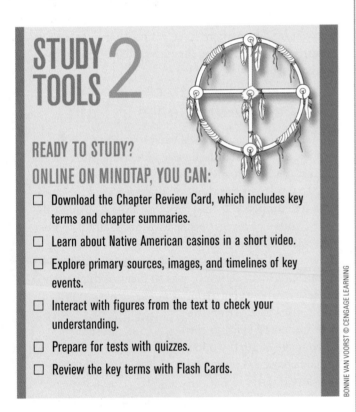

STUDY TOOLS 2

READY TO STUDY?
ONLINE ON MINDTAP, YOU CAN:

- ☐ Download the Chapter Review Card, which includes key terms and chapter summaries.
- ☐ Learn about Native American casinos in a short video.
- ☐ Explore primary sources, images, and timelines of key events.
- ☐ Interact with figures from the text to check your understanding.
- ☐ Prepare for tests with quizzes.
- ☐ Review the key terms with Flash Cards.

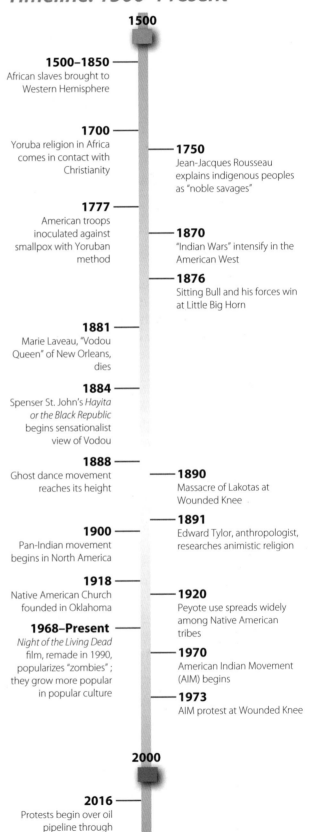

Indigenous Religions Timeline: 1500–Present

1500

1500–1850
African slaves brought to Western Hemisphere

1700
Yoruba religion in Africa comes in contact with Christianity

1750
Jean-Jacques Rousseau explains indigenous peoples as "noble savages"

1777
American troops inoculated against smallpox with Yoruban method

1870
"Indian Wars" intensify in the American West

1876
Sitting Bull and his forces win at Little Big Horn

1881
Marie Laveau, "Vodou Queen" of New Orleans, dies

1884
Spenser St. John's *Hayita or the Black Republic* begins sensationalist view of Vodou

1888
Ghost dance movement reaches its height

1890
Massacre of Lakotas at Wounded Knee

1891
Edward Tylor, anthropologist, researches animistic religion

1900
Pan-Indian movement begins in North America

1918
Native American Church founded in Oklahoma

1920
Peyote use spreads widely among Native American tribes

1968–Present
Night of the Living Dead film, remade in 1990, popularizes "zombies"; they grow more popular in popular culture

1970
American Indian Movement (AIM) begins

1973
AIM protest at Wounded Knee

2000

2016
Protests begin over oil pipeline through Sioux areas

BONNIE VAN VOORST © CENGAGE LEARNING

3

Encountering Hinduism: Many Paths to Liberation

LEARNT, LOVE, LOST BUT FOUND, AN AMAZING ADVENTURE/GETTY IMAGES; BONNIE KAY DEARSE/CENGAGE LEARNING

LEARNING OUTCOMES

After studying this chapter, you will be able to do the following:

3-1 Explain what *Hinduism* means and its strengths and weaknesses as a name.

3-2 Explain how the main periods of Hinduism's history have shaped its present, especially its unity and diversity.

3-3 Outline the essentials of Hindu teachings in your own words.

3-4 Relate Hindu ethics to essential Hindu teachings.

3-5 Outline the ways Hindus worship, at home and in temples.

3-6 State the main aspects of Hindu life around the world today, especially in North America.

Encountering Hinduism is like a visit to an Indian restaurant. You can't sample everything, but if you choose a variety you'll have a good introduction.

Your Visit to Varanasi, India

Imagine that you're on a visit to the city of Varanasi (vuh-RAH-nuh-see). You know that Varanasi, located on the Ganges (GAN-jeez) River, is unique among the cities of the world, but nothing can quite prepare you for its sights, sounds, and smells.

Your visit begins with a dawn boat ride on the Ganges. You see Hindu pilgrims on the western shore of the river descending the wide steps—two miles of them at Varanasi—leading down to the water. They wash themselves physically and spiritually, and pray toward the rising sun. After the boat ride, you walk to the Golden Temple, the most sacred of the city's many shrines dedicated to Shiva (SHIH-vuh), the patron deity of Varanasi. There you see Hindus making offerings of flowers to the black stone emblem of Shiva.

As you walk with your group through the narrow, twisting streets down to the river, you notice many small temples and even smaller shrines that seem to be everywhere. You also notice many old, frail people, some in the doorways of hostels and others living on the street, who have come to die and be cremated in Varanasi in the hope of achieving liberation from the cycle of endless rebirth and death. Occasionally, you see human bodies, wrapped and propped up on rickshaws, on their way to the water. As you get close to the Ganges, you notice three men with wild hair, squatting on a stone platform overlooking the river. You can't tell if they are wearing anything at all, because their bodies are smeared with ash and dried cow dung. On the right is a group of women bathing fully clothed in the water near the steps, and men in Indian loincloths. Both the men and women have come to wash away their sins, and, perhaps, even the necessity of rebirth. The river seems polluted to you, but this means nothing to the thousands of Hindus who worship in it.

As you keep walking up the river, you notice a cluster of large fires and hundreds of large logs stacked up behind them, and you realize, with a bit of a shock, that you've reached Varanasi's open-air cremation area. In a scene that you'll remember, you see the steps of the Hindu funeral: members of the Dom group piling wood into a pyre and laying on it a body that has been dipped into the Ganges, a son lighting a pyre, priests intoning ancient scriptures as a body begins to burn, Doms tending a body for three hours to burn it as fully as possible and then pushing the cremated remains into the river. Your group must stand respectfully at the top of the steps, where you have a better view.

In the evening, you come to the shore of the Ganges to witness the happy Aarti ceremony that is part of the evening religious devotions to Shiva. You enjoy music and dancing, and you see small candles lit on miniature "boats" and put into the river to memorialize the dead.

< This image in a Varanasi temple of the god Nandi, who represents the god Shiva, has received worship with flower garlands.

Varanasi's open-air cremation area

REUTERS

If this is your first encounter with the Hindu religion, you may be bewildered by all its varied beliefs and practices. Calling something a religion usually implies a unified system of belief and practice, but Hinduism has little obvious unity. It has no human founder, defined core beliefs, standardized worship practice, or central authority. This diversity has led to what you may consider contradictions. For example:

- Hinduism has literally millions of gods, but many Hindus typically see one god behind them all, and some see only an impersonal Oneness in and beyond the universe.

- Hindus often control their bodies to pursue a hidden spiritual reality behind all physical things, seeking liberation from the endless cycle of rebirth of the soul after death and pursuing the peace that liberation brings here and now. Other Hindus joyously affirm bodily existence with a striking affirmation of sexuality.

- Many Hindus are strict vegetarians for religious reasons, but others eat meat on occasion, and some even sacrifice animals at Hindu temples.

In Varanasi, India, a Hindu man bathes and makes offerings in the Ganges River.

- Hinduism teaches personal duties tied to one's place in a rather rigid social structure, but allows some people to "drop out" of ordinary life completely to pursue individual religious goals.

- Hindus number around 900 million today in India, a number that includes some 220 million Indian "outcastes." The modern Indian state now considers them Hindus, but they are not considered as such by most other Hindus.

In light of all this obvious diversity, is there a hidden unity of Hinduism that binds it together? Scholars have argued about this for more than one hundred years. Some of them say that Hinduism is so diverse we should only speak about different Hinduisms. The most common answer is this: Hindus have a reverence for the ancient Hindu scriptures called the *Vedas*, and they perform their caste duties. But this may seem a bit vague to you, and you should keep the question open as you study this chapter. In sum, encountering Hinduism is a bit like going to an Indian restaurant for the first time. When you see a wide variety of dishes on the menu, or even if you go to an Indian buffet, you realize that you can't taste them all. But at the end of the meal, you know that your experience in the restaurant gave you a good introduction to Indian cuisine.

> *"Hinduism" is an umbrella term gradually imposed on Hindus, and then accepted by them.*

3-1 The Name *Hinduism*

Similar to the names of some other world religions, the formal name of *Hinduism* came from outside the faith. *Hindu* first appears around 500 B.C.E. as the ancient Persian word for the Indus River and the inhabitants of its valley. From the 1300s C.E., invading Muslim rulers of northern India used "Hindu" for all non-Muslim Indians, whatever religion they practiced, to distinguish them from Indian converts to Islam. Beginning in the 1500s, European colonizers coming to India used it in its current sense to mean the members of the supposedly single religion to which all Indians, other than groups such as Muslims, Christians, and Zoroastrians, belonged. From about 1800 on, *Hinduism* gradually became accepted by most

Hindus in India as a valid name for their religion, especially to distinguish their religion from others. Thus, *Hinduism* is an umbrella term gradually imposed on Hindus, and then accepted by them.

The approximately 2.3 million Hindus living in North America and the sizeable Hindu communities in other parts of south Asia (especially Bali, Indonesia), a few parts of Africa, and Great Britain also embrace this name. However, upper-class Hindus in India often refer to their religion as the "eternal teaching" or "eternal way of life." Some scholars of religion also question the adequacy of *Hinduism* as a name, preferring to speak of "Hinduisms." On the whole, it is fitting that a vague term such as *Hinduism* be used today for a religious tradition that has so much internal diversity. (This diversity is also reflected in the symbols of Hinduism; see "A Closer Look: The Symbols of Hinduism.")

> *Hindus don't usually think of their religion in historical terms, but look to eternal spiritual truths.*

3-2 The Hindu Present as Shaped by Its Past

Throughout India, yoga became a political matter in 2016. Prime Minister Narendra Modi (MOH-dee) promoted an "International Day of Yoga," in which 175 countries participated. On the last Sunday in June at 7:00 a.m., millions of Indians did yoga at more than 50,000 locations in that nation. Modi claims that yoga is a secular activity, but not everyone agrees. Some Muslim leaders charged that this celebration was being used to spread Hinduism throughout the nation. Similar controversies about yoga, whether it can or should be done in a non-Hindu way, have broken out in many parts of the world, including the United States.

History is an important tool for those who study today's religions from a Western academic standpoint. We understand the present of religions by way of their past. Although Hinduism must be understood historically as well, history itself is not an important concept in Hinduism. Hindus don't usually think of their religion in historical terms, but look to eternal spiritual truths beyond historical events. They often look to cycles of change for individuals (e.g., death and rebirth of the soul) and for the universe itself (repeated creation and dissolution), not to the kind of linear developmental process that the word *history* implies to Westerners.

Nevertheless, studying Hinduism's past is valid and helpful, particularly because in Hinduism new developments reinterpret and update past practices rather than end them. In Hinduism today, we can see important beliefs and practices taken from the entire sweep of Indian history.

3-2a The Vedic Period (1500–600 B.C.E.)

Around 2500 B.C.E., an **Indus Valley civilization** thrived in northwest India, in what is now the nation of Pakistan (see Map 3.1). It centered around two city-states on the Indus River, Harappa (huh-RAHP-uh) and Mohenjo-Daro (moh-HEN-joh-DAHR-oh). The Indus Valley inhabitants were a dark-skinned people whom many scholars connect with today's Indians called **Dravidians**, but this is a controversial idea. (About 25 percent of Indians today are Dravidians.) This civilization traded internationally and had a high material culture. Harappa and Mohenjo-Daro were carefully planned and even had a sewage system connected to private houses. The religion of the Indus Valley civilization is largely unknown to us. Archaeologists have found many female deity figurines, so it is thought that the Indus Valley people probably worshiped goddesses of fertility in connection with their farming. The cows on their official seals, a variety of stone objects probably used in worship, and sculptures of people in seated meditation may suggest religious practices that influenced Hinduism. But until much more is known about the Indus Valley religion, its effect on Hinduism must remain uncertain.

The Indus Valley civilization was in decline around 1500 B.C.E., when nomadic tribes who called themselves **Aryans**, or "noble ones," migrated into northwest India from their home between the Black Sea and the Caspian Sea. These Aryans must be distinguished

Indus Valley civilization Culture of northwest India before the coming of the Aryans

Dravidians [druh-VIH-dee-uhnz] Dark-skinned peoples who now live mostly in south India, perhaps descended from the Indus Valley civilization

Aryans [AIR-ee-uhnz] "Noble ones," Indo-European peoples who migrated into India

A Closer Look

The Symbols of Hinduism

Although Hinduism has no official symbol, the common religious symbol sacred to Hindus is the mystical syllable **Om** (Figure 3.1). Although as a syllable it has no literal meaning, Om symbolizes the fundamental hidden reality of the universe and is the basic spiritual sound the universe makes, particularly the sound of the world soul. Om is often pronounced at the beginning of religious readings or meditation. Many Hindus wear this symbol in jewelry, and it is found in family shrines and in temples. Pronounced in a deep, lengthy way, it can resonate throughout the body so that the sound of Brahman can penetrate to one's center of being.

You may be surprised, even shocked, to encounter the swastika (Figure 3.2) as a common, ancient symbol in Hinduism, Buddhism, and Jainism. *Swastika* is an ancient Indian word meaning "sign of good fortune." The

BONNIE VAN VOORST © CENGAGE LEARNING

Figure 3.1 Om

swastika has crooked arms facing in a clockwise or counterclockwise direction (both directions are common in Asia). This feature of the arms extending in all directions suggests to Hindus the universal presence of the world soul. It is continually rotating like the wheel it resembles, symbolizing the eternal nature of ultimate truth. This symbol is often found on Hindu, Jain, and Buddhist temples, and it is worn on neck pendants as a good-luck charm.

In 1935, the Nazi Party of Germany adopted the swastika as its symbol of the party and the nation with no intent to endorse Hindu teachings. It is still used today by some neo-Nazi groups. So we have an odd situation: For many Asian people, the swastika is a much-loved symbol; for people in the Western world, the swastika is much despised.

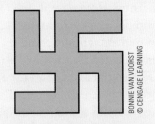

BONNIE VAN VOORST © CENGAGE LEARNING

Figure 3.2 The Swastika

---

from the modern Nazi misuse of this term, which identifies the Nordic-Germanic people as a superior race. Moreover, some Hindus dispute the notion of an Aryan migration/invasion, unattested as it is in Hindu scripture and lore, so they call it the "Aryan Invasion Theory," and note, correctly, that it was developed by Western scholars, not Indians. Nevertheless, it is widely accepted that the Aryans were light-skinned cattle herders and warriors with horse-drawn chariots. They were a part of the migration from central Asia into both India and Europe; hence the term *Indo-Europeans* is much more common than *Aryans*. They soon took control of the Indus Valley peoples.

These Indo-Europeans spoke Sanskrit, a language related to most European languages. They had oral collections called the **Vedas**, which form the foundation of Hinduism. The *Vedas* represent a diversified and continuous oral tradition from around 1200 to 800 B.C.E.; they were written down much later. The earliest *Vedas*, four in number, were "books of knowledge" consisting of hymns to deities (the *Rig Veda*), instructions for sacrifice (the *Yajur Veda*), songs for sacrifice (the *Sama Veda*), and spells to bring blessings and avert evil (the *Atharva Veda*).

The heart of Vedic religion was sacrifice by means of fire, accompanied by sung praises and requests to the gods. Vedic gods living in the skies or in heaven play a role in human life as forces of nature, forces that can be influenced by sacrifice. In general, Vedic sacrificial rituals aim at aiding and strengthening deities, who then strengthen the world, so that those who offer sacrifice may prosper. In this worldview the gods and humans are partners in a "circle of life" that maintains the

Om [OHM] Spoken syllable symbolizing the fundamental hidden reality of the universe

swastika [SWAHS-tee-kuh] Indian symbol of good luck

Vedas [VAY-duhs] Hindu "books of knowledge" consisting of *Rig, Yajur, Sama*, and *Atharva Vedas*

ongoing creative processes of the world. Both need each other to thrive. The Vedic stage of Hinduism affirms the world, accepting the physical aspects of the world as good and proper. At the daily and domestic level, the simple **Agnihotra** ritual to the sun was performed by the heads of households three times each day and is still common in India. Even given its adaptations over time, the Agnihotra is arguably the oldest continually practiced ritual in the world. Agni (AHG-nee), the god of fire, carried the sacrificial offerings to Indra, the king of the gods and both a war god and a thunder god; to Varuna (VUH-roo-nuh), the god guaranteeing moral order; and to Brahma (BRAH-muh), the god of creation. Many other Vedic deities, mostly male and some female, are also associated with the physical and spiritual forces of nature.

A key person of Vedic times was the **rishi**, or "seer" of the divine, a priest who was able to commune directly with the gods. The rishis achieved an altered state of consciousness in which they could see and hear the gods. To reach this state, they drank a hallucinogenic drug called soma, pressed out perhaps from a mushroom. When the rishi drank soma as a part of Vedic sacrifice, he took a trip to the realm of the deities and experienced their hidden truth. He then composed hymns in their praise, hymns that came into the *Rig Veda*. Soma even became a god, so powerful were its effects. This quest for a direct individual encounter with ultimate, hidden truth has persisted in the Hindu tradition to this day, although the encounter itself has changed. No longer is it an encounter with all the gods, but a discovery of an ultimate reality hidden in one's soul or an ecstatic devotion to one's chosen god. The means of achieving it have also changed (now with intense meditation rather than with a drug), as have those who can achieve it (no longer limited to soma drinkers, but now open to all).

The Indus Valley people's official seals featured the cows still venerated today in Hinduism.

"The sun would not rise if the priests did not sacrifice."
—Famous saying at the end of Vedic times

Near the end of the Vedic period, the Vedic system of sacrifice grew into a dominant power in Aryan society. The power of sacrifice ceased to be dependent on the gods' favor as influenced by the humble prayer and household sacrifices of ordinary Aryans; now what was important was the faultless priestly performance of increasingly more elaborate sacrificial rituals. At least sixteen priests, and many more assistants, were needed for the regular sacrifices. Sacrifice became a requirement for the maintenance of the world itself rather than just a means of attaining blessings for things such as children, long life, and prosperity. A famous saying of the time claimed that "the sun would not rise if the priest did not sacrifice" (*Satapatha Brahmana* 1.3.1). Religious and social power was consolidated in the hands of one type of priest among the many, those who called themselves Brahmins. The books detailing sacrifice and its power are called the *Brahmanas*, "Brahmin books." This concentration of power in the hands of the Brahmin priesthood, perhaps combined with other factors, such as the influence of surviving indigenous Indus Valley religious practices, would spark change for Hinduism in its next period of history. Furthermore, this change would catalyze the birth of a new religion, Buddhism, which would change religion in virtually all of ancient Asia and, in modern times, the world.

3-2b The Upanishadic Period (600–400 B.C.E.)

In the first millennium B.C.E., Hindus added another dimension that has endured to this day. This is the quest for knowledge so deep and sacred that to know it is to bring eternal freedom from this world

Agnihotra [AHG-nee-HOH-trah] Ancient Hindu prayer to the sun

rishi [REE-shee] "Seer" of the divine and writer of the *Vedas*

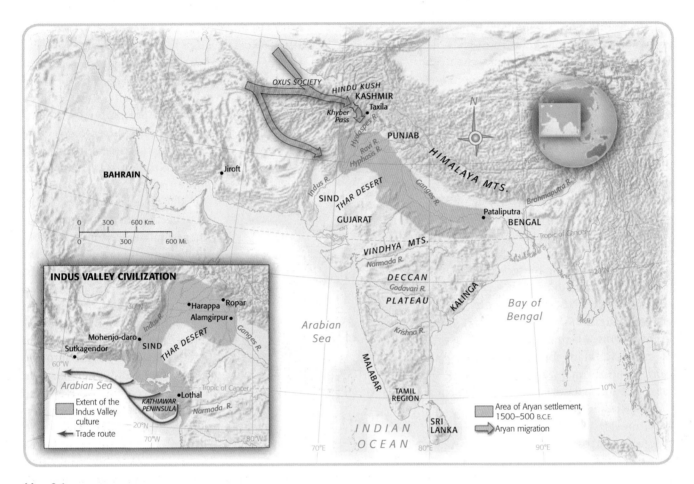

Map 3.1

Indus Valley Civilization and Aryan Migrations

The Indus Valley culture emerged in the city-states of the Indus River basin. It was in decline when the Aryan (Indo-European) peoples began migrating into India around 1500 B.C.E.

of appearances and constant change. The **Upanishads**, philosophical Hindu scriptures from this period, are primarily dialogues between teachers and young students who seek this sacred knowledge through a withdrawal from ordinary life. These teachers and students renounced the Vedic value put on ordinary life and pursued extraordinary truths. They criticized the Vedic rituals as unnecessary, and they rejected the rising social and economic power of the Brahmin priesthood. Their criticism of Vedic sacrifice was so effective that its main remnants surviving today are the relatively simple ones often incorporated into newer rites, especially weddings, funerals, other traditional rites of passage, and basic daily sacrifices. (This criticism of sacrifice continues today, for example, when in 2014 a judge in northern India controversially banned all animal sacrifice in Hindu temples. This ruling was overturned in 2015 by the Indian Supreme Court in a judgment that said that the judiciary could not stop centuries-old traditions of sacrificing animals by different religions.) The *Upanishads* urge physical and mental rigors that became increasingly important for Hindu practice. Buddhism and Jainism, which will be considered in later chapters, arose at this time in India to teach a single way to enlightenment, but each one denied key Hindu teachings and practices. Most Hindus gradually rejected these new movements in favor of Hinduism's inclusive approach.

The *Upanishads* teach that underlying reality is a spiritual essence called **Brahman**, a single "world soul" that is the foundation of all physical matter, energy, time, space, and being itself—in short, of everything in and beyond this universe. (This term should not be confused with the Vedic creator god Brahma or the Brahmin priests.) Although it is

Upanishads [oo-PAHN-ih-shahds] Philosophical scriptures at the end of the Vedic period

Brahman [BRAH-muhn] "World soul," the foundation of all physical matter, energy, time, space, and being itself

cosmic, Brahman is present in all people in the form of the **atman**, a person's innermost self or soul. In other words, each person's atman is the one world soul. For most (but not all) Hindus, Brahman is not a personal being, as "world soul" might imply; it is spiritual, but it is not *a* spirit. The religious quest in the *Upanishads* involves understanding that Brahman and one's atman are one and the same. The realization of this truth, which is the deepest form of self-understanding, brings freedom from ignorance and misery, and liberation from the endless cycle of **reincarnation** of one's atman. Unlike the Vedic hymns, the *Upanishads* do not affirm the physical world as real and good, but rather aim at transcending it.

This goal of liberating one's soul by perfect knowledge of it, and the use of physical and meditational techniques to achieve this knowledge, became important aspects of Hinduism that endure through today. These techniques gradually coalesced into a system called **yoga**, Sanskrit for "yoke." Yoga is an ancient practice that yokes the body and mind for religious deliverance. (You may know it as an exercise and meditation system, but it is much more than that for most Hindus.) Yoga aims at removing humans from the overwhelming mental flow of the material world, if only momentarily, in order to recapture their original spiritual purity.

DINODIA PHOTOS/GETTY IMAGES

Statue in Bangalore, India, of the god Shiva meditating in the lotus yoga position.

3-2c The Classical Period (400 B.C.E.–600 C.E.)

A growing number of conversions to Buddhism and Jainism was a threat to Hinduism. The Mauryan (MOHR-yuhn) dynasty that governed north India was pro-Buddhist, and its famous king, Ashoka (ah-SHOH-kuh), extended Aryan rule and Buddhist influence into all of India. Hindus dealt with this threat in a way that has become typical of Hinduism even today, by integrating foreign elements into the broader Hindu tradition. The new teachings of the *Upanishads* were seen as compatible with the earlier *Vedas* and accepted into the Vedic body of scripture.

In addition, Hindus incorporated a variety of religious practices of lower, non-Aryan populations that were converting to new religions such as Buddhism. To put it another way, the Sanskrit tradition of the *Vedas*—for the educated upper classes and the "high" gods—took in and controlled the tradition of the non-Aryan lower classes and the "low gods" of local village and tribal deities. As a result, local deities became a part of the village shrines and temples. The local deities were identified with the older gods, or regarded as their incarnations, or became one of their "family members." Non-Aryan people were taken into this system, some into the lower castes and others into the "outcastes." This development solidified Brahmin power and religious teachings, and eventually stemmed the conversions of non-Aryans to other religions. However, conversions to Buddhism and Christianity in particular are still a difficult issue when they occur today among lower classes in India.

Around 400 B.C.E., as the wandering Aryans finally settled into towns and cities, they built permanent homes for themselves and temples for their gods. Before that, all sacrifice was done outdoors, with sacrifice as nomadic as the Aryan tribes themselves. During the Classical period the two great Hindu epics still popular today were written: the *Mahabharata* (MAH-huh-BAH-rah-tuh) and the *Ramayana* (rah-MAH-yah-nuh). (To give an indication of the size of these epics, a recent poetic translation of the *Mahabharata* by Carole Satyamurti runs to 888 pages!) Both relate royal rivalries, perhaps reflecting political turmoil during this period as different Aryan clans struggled for territorial power in the areas where they settled. They feature a tension between the aim of upholding the world

atman [AHT-muhn] Person's innermost self or soul

reincarnation Cycle of rebirth of one's atman after death

yoga [YOH-guh] Ancient practice that yokes the body and mind for religious deliverance

found in the *Vedas* and that of isolating a person from society in order to achieve individual liberation found in the newer Upanishadic tradition. Both epics emphasize that social and moral obligation must be maintained, and that rulers acting in the Hindu tradition have a key role in maintaining it. However, many characters in these epics have renounced the world, live alone in forests or in small settlements, and are said to possess extraordinary powers to bless or to curse. The epics' heroes almost always treat these world renouncers, or **sadhus**—of whom we will speak more in the following section—with respect and learn much from them.

Another solution to this tension is found in the part of the *Mahabharata* known by the separate title of ***Bhagavad Gita***, "Song of Heaven" or "Song of the Lord." In the *Gita*, the god Krishna appears to the warrior-class leader Arjuna (AR-joo-nuh), to convince him to do his caste duty of fighting, but in a way in which he understands and controls its effect on him. The *Gita*'s solution is a masterful blend of world-affirming action and world-denying detachment from the results of one's actions. True renunciation does not involve giving up socially responsible actions. Rather, it involves cutting off a desire for the results of actions even as one fulfills one's social duty. For example, this means for Arjuna that he must fight well but not care about whether he wins or loses. Selfless action without desire for reward is true renunciation for the *Gita*. The *Gita* recognizes that this is difficult and that people must use yoga and other disciplines to accomplish it. This ingenious approach has contributed to the *Bhagavad Gita*'s status as the best-loved of Hindu scriptures today.

Goddess sculpture at a temple in Mathura, northern India

A different genre of literature also concerned with society arose at this time, the law codes—particularly the single most important code, the ***Laws of Manu***. What epics do in a literary way to balance social responsibility and individual liberation, the law codes do in a formally legal way. They carefully restrict renunciation of the world to older males. One must earn the right to renounce the world by first being in the world as a good student, then as a husband and father. Opting out of ordinary life can only be done after one has successfully engaged in it. Underlying the *Laws of Manu* is the strong Hindu affirmation that doing one's duty for an orderly, stable society is necessary for this world and after one's death leads to better reincarnation. This social order involves the proper functioning of the main social-religious classes that arose in Vedic times, as well as the proper observance of interaction within and among these classes. Women belong to the various classes even though their social roles are not as determined by their class as their husbands' roles are. We will consider these classes more fully in Section 3-4a.

> True renunciation does not involve giving up socially responsible action.

3-2d The Devotional Period (600 C.E.–Present)

The next period in Hinduism is characterized by three developments: the rise of devotional movements, especially those devoted to Shiva, Vishnu (VISH-new), and the Goddess; Tantrism; and the rise of Hindu reform movements. Of these developments, the first is so influential that it has given its name to the entire period.

sadhus [SAH-doos] Renunciants, also known as "holy men"

Bhagavad Gita [BAH-guh-vahd GEE-tuh] "Song of the Lord"; a poem on duty in the *Mahabharata*

Laws of Manu [MAH-new] Main Hindu law code

Actors in traditional clothing and makeup perform part of an Indian epic.

F9PHOTOS/SHUTTERSTOCK

The *Tantras*, the basis of the second major development of this period, are hundreds of writings based on practices that arose outside the elite Brahmin tradition. Many Westerners today associate Tantrism with exotic sexual practices, but it is much broader than that. The *Tantras* often criticize the religious "establishment," especially the Brahmins. However, the *Tantras* can also affirm traditional Hindu teachings. For example, an individual is a microcosm of the universe, and by knowing the sacred "geography" and life forces of one's body one may, using yoga, reach liberation from reincarnation. The *Tantras* speak of a right-handed path that all Hindus can take, one that employs **mantras** (short sacred words or sounds used widely in prayer or meditation, not just in Tantrism), sacred diagrams called *mandalas*, and ritual techniques based on body geography. The left-handed path, appropriate for those with an especially adventurous, fearless temperament, centers on ritual actions strictly forbidden in mainstream Hinduism, gaining liberation by transcending the tension between good and evil. For instance, by having emotionally detached sexual intercourse with a forbidden woman, a man may seek to overcome lust. Left-handed Tantrism is highly controversial among many Hindus, but right-handed Tantrism is commonly approved.

We turn now to the next topic in the Devotional period: Hindu reform or revisionism. Hinduism was not, on the whole, so affected by Islam during Muslim rule in India that it had to make adaptive changes. However, with the arrival of European colonizers and Christian missionaries in the nineteenth century, their interaction with Hindus led to Hindu movements for change. Attempts were made to change Hinduism spiritually and socially, ending practices that the majority of Hindu reformers found objectionable: the harshest features of the caste system, "superstitions" such as Vedic

Devotion to one's chosen god is a main way of being Hindu. Devotion, or **bhakti**, enters the Hindu tradition as early as the *Bhagavad Gita*, where devotion to Krishna brings a cognitive mental discipline to guide action in the world. Around the sixth century C.E. in southern India, advocates of bhakti praised Shiva and Vishnu in emotional poetry and song. This devotional experience involves often-uncontrollable joy in one's god, sometimes with fainting, frenzy, weeping, and ecstatic speech. By the seventeenth century, bhakti had spread into most Hindu traditions, where it remains. The devotional movement gradually coalesced into three movements, one each for Shiva, Vishnu, and Shakti (SHAHK-tee), the Goddess.

Devotion is typically described in its poetry and song as deep love for one's god. Devotees will sacrifice anything to revel with their god in divine happiness. A well-known example is the followers of the cowherd Krishna: women who abandon their husbands to frolic in the forest with Krishna. Women have played an important role in the rise of devotional movements. Two famous women devotees, Mahadeviyakka (MAH-huh-DEH-vee-YAHK-uh) and Mirabai (MEER-uh-bigh), were both unhappy in traditional marriages and eventually left their husbands to devote themselves entirely to a god. Despite this practice, Hinduism finds a way to balance devotion to a god and renunciation of the world.

bhakti [BAHK-tee]
Devotion, particularly in a devotional movement or group

Tantras [TAHN-truhs]
Writings in the Tantric movement of Hinduism

mantra [MAHN-truh]
Short sacred formula used in prayer or meditation

astrology, popular blessings and curses, the worship of images, and the like. Here are the most important reform movements:

- Rammohan (RAHM-moh-hahn) Roy (1774–1833), perhaps the world's first scholar of comparative religion, had watched in shock as his sister burned to death on the funeral pyre of her husband (a practice we will discuss in Section 3-4d). He was dismayed at what he saw as the harmful effects of caste divisions. He founded the Society of Brahmanism in 1828. Roy claimed that the *Upanishads* reveal the one God of all people. The One was to be worshiped through meditation, quiet worship, and a moral life, not by the emotions of devotional Hinduism.

- Dayananda Sarasvati (DAH-yuh-NAN-duh SAH-rahs-VAH-tee) founded the "Noble Society" in 1875. Dayananda found the pure, original essence of Hinduism in the *Vedas* as centering on monotheism and a reasoned morality. He opposed much of devotional Hinduism and also rejected Islam and Christianity. His movement, along with Ram Roy's, gained little steady acceptance from Hindus.

- Ramakrishna (RAH-muh-KRISH-nah), who lived from 1836 to 1886, taught traditional Hindu beliefs and spiritual techniques. He was a devoted temple priest of the goddess Kali, but he worshiped other Hindu deities as well—even the God of Christians and Muslims. He incorporated selected Western ideas and religions into a Hindu context and did not attempt to change Hinduism by making it conform to Western ideas of religion or rationalism. This program was widely effective and led to Ramakrishna's lasting fame in Hinduism.

The twentieth-century Indian movement for religious reform and independence from the British Empire—particularly its religious and political leader, Mohandas K. Gandhi (moh-HAHN-dahs GAHN-dee; 1869–1948)—shows again the persistence and adaptability of Hinduism. Gandhi is widely known by his honorific name, Mahatma ("great soul"), and he certainly was one of the great figures of the twentieth century. The civil rights movement in the United States and South Africa is heavily indebted to him for nonviolent resistance as a religious–political program. Although Gandhi drew on different religious

traditions, especially nonviolence in Jainism (*ahimsa*, found to a lesser extent in Hinduism) and Christianity (the teaching of Jesus on forgiving one's enemies while refusing to cooperate with them in evil), he was thoroughly Hindu. He emphasized Hindu teachings and practices that the masses could appreciate—such as devotion, prayer, and trust in divine grace—and combined this with strong moral reasoning and action. His favorite book was the *Bhagavad Gita*, which provided the religious foundation for his system of "persisting in the truth." This approach involves expressing the truth in every action, no matter what the result and regardless of possible rewards. Gandhi read the *Gita* as a text urging nonviolence, not war. He forbade violence as a tool in his political campaigns; instead, he urged self-control, negotiation and tactical compromises, and even self-sacrifice.

Gandhi's lifestyle drew on the renouncer tradition in Hinduism. At middle age he practiced strict poverty and later in life took a vow of celibacy. He wore little clothing and lived on a bare minimum of food, becoming very thin. Gandhi believed that this austere lifestyle built spiritual strength in him for his task of liberating Hindus from caste hatred, colonialism, and widespread poverty. The nonviolent movement Gandhi led secured independence from Great Britain in 1947, but to his sorrow this independence resulted in not one nation but two: India and the officially Muslim nation of Pakistan, to which many Indian Muslims migrated. He was assassinated by a Hindu in 1948, after rising complaints that he was too much of a pluralist and too accommodating to Muslims. Some Hindus had even mocked him as "Mohammed Gandhi." Unfortunately, his murder

NILESH BHANGE/GETTY IMAGES

Gandhi's image is known to most Indians today through their currency—ironic in view of Gandhi's self-imposed poverty.

The Taj Mahal, built in the 1600s as a Muslim tomb, has become the architectural symbol of India and is widely considered one of the most beautiful buildings in the world.

increased the tension between Hindus and Muslims—something that challenges the whole Indian subcontinent even today—but his positive legacy continues in India and throughout the world.

The government of modern India has tolerated all religions and has brought some significant improvement to the lives of the lower classes and the outcastes. This has provoked a religious–political reaction widely but controversially referred to as "Hindu fundamentalism." For the members of Hindu fundamentalist groups, Hinduism is just as much a symbol of national political identity as a religion. The main group of this type is the Indian People's Party, often known by its Hindi-language initials, BJP. The principal concern of members is the perceived danger to the Hindu majority by conversions among untouchables and other Hindus, which they see as a threat to what they call the "Hindu-ness," **Hindutva**, of India. They have enacted laws restricting efforts at conversion by Muslims and Christians, and sometimes they have looked the other way when Hindus commit violence against Muslims. In 1992, a Muslim mosque in the city of Ayodhya was destroyed by a mob of militant Hindus, and then

rioting by Muslims and Hindus killed more than a thousand people.

From 1998 to 2004, the BJP was in control of the Indian government, with a leader of the BJP as prime minister. During this time India openly deployed nuclear weapons, prompting Pakistan to do the same. In 2014 they regained leadership in the national government, led by the powerful Hindu politician Narendra Modi. Modi has moderated his pro-Hindu policies somewhat, but many of his followers still promote Hindutva. For example, they have urged the Indian Parliament to adopt the *Bhagavad Gita* as the official scripture of India, a move the Parliament has so far rejected. Hindus typically see Hindu fundamentalism as contrary to the generally inclusive, tolerant spirit of Hinduism. Moreover, many progressive Indians view continued caste structures as hindering social and economic reforms.

3-3 Essential Hindu Teachings

In central India, a woman offers prayer and a sacrifice of food in a temple dedicated to Santoshi Ma (san-TOH-shee mah), or "Mother of Satisfaction." Santoshi Ma is a goddess of prosperity—especially the wife's prosperity, including modern appliances in her home—and the woman in the temple is asking for a more bearable load of housework. Santoshi Ma was unknown until a few devout Hindus discerned her existence in the 1960s. A few temples were then built in her honor, and in 1975 she was featured in a blockbuster Hindi-language film, *Hail Santoshi Ma*. The film presented a mythology for Santoshi Ma's divine birth and growth as the daughter of Ganesha, and featured a simple devotional ritual to gain her blessing. Santoshi Ma became an important, much-loved goddess practically overnight, the first time that modern mass media have influenced the rise of a deity. Because the establishment of new deities has a strong precedent in Hinduism, Santoshi

Hindutva [hihn-DOO-tvuh] "Hindu-ness" of India as promoted by the BJP

Ma is now well integrated into the pantheon of Hindu deities, and her many devotees see her as one with all the other goddesses.

In this section, we will discuss the main beliefs of Hindus about the world, human society, and the individual. We begin with a treatment of the main deities in the three devotional movements we encountered in the previous section.

3-3a Main Deities in the Three Devotional Movements

Shiva. Shiva is the god who meditates in his home in the Himalayas. He is a fearsome deity with tangled hair and an ash-covered body. Animal skins are his clothing, and he carries snakes and human skulls. He repeatedly burns the god of love to ashes when she tries to distract him. In the cosmic cycle of creation, destruction, and re-creation, Shiva guides and empowers destruction. However, Shiva devotees today view this destruction positively, as a symbol of the removal of obstacles to salvation; destruction is a necessary part of re-creation. The destructive side of Shiva is depicted in the popular bronze statue called Shiva Nataraja (NAH-tuh-RAHJ-uh), "Shiva the Lord of the Dance." In this statue Shiva is surrounded by a circle of fire, which destroys in order to purify. He embodies the world-renouncing side of Hinduism and provides a model for this aspect of the tradition.

Shiva is often portrayed as the Lord of the Dance.

The sons and consorts of Shiva are particularly appealing. Much of Shiva's mythology tells of his marriage to the goddess Parvati (PAHR-vah-tee), stories in which a feminine, life-affirming side of Shiva emerges. His other consorts are Durga, the goddess of death, and Kali, the frightening destroyer of evil. His son Ganesha (or simply Ganesh), the elephant-headed god who clears away obstacles to success, is one of the best-loved Hindu divinities. Ganesha's image

lingam [LING-gahm] Symbol in Shiva's shrines probably of erect phallus

is found in nearly every Hindu shop, restaurant, and office around the world. Shiva's special image in his temples is the **lingam** ("sign"). The meaning of the lingam is disputed; it may depict the erect phallus, which celebrates Shiva's power, but for Hindus this meaning is not important. Shaivites often worship Shiva by pouring milk over the lingam. Another main symbol of Shiva is the bull Nandi, whose statue is often found, and venerated, outside his temples (see the photo of Nandi in the opening of this chapter). Shiva is also represented by the trident, and his followers often wear horizontal stripes painted on their forehead and display a trident.

Vishnu. Vishnu is a cosmic king who supervises universal order and prosperity, protecting and preserving the world. When needed, he descends to the world in various incarnations to defeat enemies—both humans and deities. Vishnu is a gracious god, revered by his devotees with loving loyalty. His female counterpart is Lakshmi (LAHK-shmee), the much-loved goddess of fortune and wealth. Vishnu is often depicted with blue skin, because he once killed a five-headed snake; the snake's venom that he took into himself turned his skin blue. To his followers, this blue color is a symbol of his power. Vishnu's familiar incarnations are Rama, hero of the *Ramayana*, and Krishna, hero of the *Bhagavad Gita*. Both Rama and Krishna are today among the best-loved Hindu gods. This has ironically led to Vishnu himself being seen as too remote to intervene directly on behalf of an individual in trouble. Devotees of Vishnu who have renounced the world typically wear two vertical markings on the forehead that come together on the bridge of the nose.

Shakti as the Goddess. The worship of Shakti as the feminine side of the divine originates in the *Vedas*. The *Rig Veda* portrays Shakti as the powerful upholder of the universe. She is the sister of Krishna and is also Shiva's wife. Shakti is worshiped as Devi (DEH-vee), "the Goddess," who is one with Brahman. The literature of Shaktism is found in the *Tantras*; they sometimes, but not uniformly, have a high view

Shakti (standing) and Shiva in a mural in a temple in Hyderabad, India

universe is powered by a combination of the male and the female.

With Hinduism's millions of deities—traditionally put at 330 million!—and even with these three more focused devotional movements, how do Hindus put it all together in a way that makes everyday sense for them? Whether a Hindu honors Vishnu, Shiva, or Shakti, that particular deity is for her or him the sole and the highest god, whereas other Hindu gods are lower forms. Thus, one god is thought to appear at various levels. At the "top" is a nonpersonal absolute, Brahman, the world soul that cannot be described. Brahman is so comprehensive that some Hindu scriptures describe it as encompassing everything that exists. Brahman manifests itself in various personal high divinities that create the world (Brahma), maintain it (Vishnu), and destroy it again (Shiva). In practice, however, followers of one deity will attribute all three functions to him or her, as our previous treatment suggests. They see all other gods as standing under their god or as further manifestations of that deity. Although the teaching of the ultimate world soul plays little or no role in the religious everyday life— it's hard to pray, sacrifice, or express emotion to something that is unknowable—it leads to most Hindus seeing no problem in acknowledging other Hindu traditions, and sometimes even other religions, as authentic paths to the divine.

of women and oppose ways in which the caste system holds down women. In some regions of India, the Great Goddess (*Mahadevi*) is revered as the supreme divinity. Female power in the Goddess alone is seen as the ultimate cause of the creation, preservation, and end of the world.

Similar to Shiva, the Goddess is venerated both in her gentle, motherly aspects and in her cruel, dangerous, and erotic aspects. Accordingly, she is honored under a wide variety of divine forms. The best known are Lakshmi, the goddess of wealth and consort of Vishnu; the black goddess Kali ("dark one"), riding on a lion; and the demon-slaying Durga, the goddess of death. The **yoni**, probably a stone representation of the human female genitalia, is a symbol of the feminine power of the cosmos. The lingam is often set within the yoni to suggest that the

Lingam set in a yoni, receiving worship to Shiva.

yoni [YOH-nee]
Symbol probably of the human female genitalia representing the feminine power of the cosmos

3-3b Hindu Doctrinal Concepts

Dharma is the foundational concept in Hinduism, a wide-ranging term for righteousness, law, duty, moral teachings, religion itself, or the order in the universe. Dharma is also the god who embodies and promotes right order and living. The ancient *Vedas* emphasize the order of the cosmos, and dharma builds on it by emphasizing the correct ordering of human life. Dharma is more than a set of cosmic-order ideas applying in the same way to all Hindus. It's specific to one's place in the world: one's social position, caste membership, stage of life, and gender. The dharma of a member of the warrior class is distinct from that of a laborer; the dharma of a youth differs from that of the father of a family, and a husband's dharma differs from his wife's.

A Hindu must conform primarily to his or her class and caste dharma. Hindu scripture teaches this, and it is a particular theme in the *Bhagavad Gita*. Following the social and religious rules of one's caste leads to better reincarnation; neglecting it leads to a lesser reincarnation. For a man to leave his caste for a higher one is unthinkable. Opposing the caste system itself leads to a bad reincarnation. One could find oneself an outcaste, a lower animal, or an insect in one's next life. This has led to a remarkably conservative social structure and explains why, even today, traditional Hindu values often frustrate attempts at social change for women, the lower castes, and outcastes. Hinduism divides life into four stages, each with its own particular dharma—what is seen as right for each stage. These four stages will be dealt with in more detail in Section 3-4b.

Samsara is the cycle of reincarnation, endured as a hardship by the spiritual essence of all living things. The **jiva** (individual soul) is subject to reincarnation, because it is only the jiva that earns reward or punishment in the next reincarnation (see the upcoming discussion of karma). One's atman, the deeper soul identical with Brahman, is not subject to karma, but it goes along with the jiva. It travels with the jiva in samsara but is beyond it. Because actions in life involve choices, at every moment an individual is capable of making the choices to ensure a good situation in the next life. The *Brihadaranyaka* (BREE-hahd-uh-RUN-yah-kuh)

A soul, symbolized by a ray of light, travels to enlightenment through seven different lives.

DINODIA / THE IMAGE WORKS

> "Just as a caterpillar gets its front feet firmly on the next leaf before it leaves the one it is on, a soul creates its next life before it departs the present one."
>
> —Brihadaranyaka Upanishad

Upanishad 4.4.3 describes this liberation from samsara well: "Just as a caterpillar gets its front feet firmly on the next leaf before it leaves the one it is on, a soul creates its next life before it departs the present one." This leads us to a fuller consideration of karma.

Karma is derived from the Sanskrit for "deeds" and is related to one's behavior in preceding lives. After a person's death, her or his spiritual essence is reborn in another life if any karma is attached to it. Whether one

dharma [DAHR-muh] Righteousness, law, duty, moral teaching, order in the universe

samsara [sahm-SAH-ruh] Cycle of reincarnation

jiva [JEE-vuh] Individual, personal soul that collects karma and is subject to reincarnation

karma [KAHR-muh] Deeds or acts that influence reincarnation

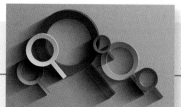

A Closer Look

Popular Misunderstandings of Karma, Mantra, Guru, and Avatar

Karma is not fate, as we often hear today in North America and Europe. Fate is a random, uncontrollable power that determines human actions and events. Karma is the *opposite* of what fate means in the Western world. In karma, each person generates her or his own reward or punishment, which comes in one's condition after reincarnation. Also, one hears muddled talk about group karma—for example, Hollywood actress Sharon Stone's suggestion that the 2008 earthquake in China that killed seventy thousand ordinary people was some sort of karmic retribution for the Chinese government's violent crackdown on dissent in Tibet. Stone said, "And then all this earthquake and all this stuff happened, and I thought, is that karma—when you're not nice that bad things happen to you?"

A mantra is not a slogan or "words to live by," such as "Her mantra is to enjoy life to the fullest" or "The candidate's mantra of change was very powerful." Rather, a mantra is a short mystical utterance of great sacred power, as illustrated by the greatest of all mantras, Om.

A guru is not anyone who acquires followers in any sort of movement, or a person who has wide authority because of his or her secular knowledge or skills. On the contrary, a guru is a private teacher of transcendent religious truth; a guru leads the student to full knowledge and release.

An avatar is not only a computer user's self-representation in a three-dimensional model for computer games or a two-dimensional icon for Internet communities. In Hinduism, an avatar is an incarnation (different, human form) of a god, as, for example, Krishna is an avatar of Vishnu. This understanding of avatar was adapted by film director James Cameron in his 2009 blockbuster film by that name, in which a human mind is projected into the body of a human-like being.

---

is rich or poor, healthy or sick, male or female, intelligent or not, talented or untalented, a member of a high or low caste, a Hindu or not, and endowed with many other life-defining traits depends on the karma inherited from the lives that have gone before. Karma explains all human inequalities. Although the conditions of an individual's current life are determined in advance by her or his deeds in previous lives, individuals must assume personal responsibility for their present actions and the associated consequences. (See "A Closer Look: Popular Misunderstandings of Karma, Mantra, Guru, and Avatar.")

Moksha means the "liberation" from rebirth that comes with the entry of the individual soul (atman) into the highest reality (Brahman). The idea of reincarnating endlessly is abhorrent to Hindus. The ultimate goal is to merge one's atman with Brahman, like a drop of water enters the Indian Ocean. To achieve moksha, one must be rid not only of bad karma, but also of good karma; any karma at all causes rebirth after death. Although actions take place, if the self that does them is not egoistic, karmic results cannot attach to them. Paradoxically, one must even give up the desire to achieve liberation

in order to reach it. (To illustrate this from everyday life, if you've ever had trouble falling asleep at night, you may have found that to fall asleep you must give up trying to fall asleep or must even try to stay awake.) Many Hindus, however, find that moksha is difficult to achieve, especially in a time when many Hindus believe that their religion is in decline. They are content to collect good karma and be reincarnated to a better life.

Three main paths lead to moksha, whether one finds it or not. There is a tendency among Hindus to see one chosen path as the best, but the paths are often combined as well. The way of active, obedient life—called the *path of deeds* (karma)—is doing ritual actions of worship and meditation, as well as carrying out daily conduct according to one's own dharma, but without a selfish intent that causes bad karma. Second, those on the *path of knowledge* see the central problem with human beings as their inability to realize that they are living in an unreal world and that the only thing real is the spirit. The path of knowledge brings personal merging with the ultimate

moksha [MOHK-shuh]
Liberation from rebirth and samsara

The path of devotion: Garlands for the gods for sale outside a Hindu temple.

unity behind the visible things of the world, particularly knowledge of the unity of the individual soul and the world soul through yoga and meditation. Third, the *path of devotion* is a loving surrender and service to one's main deity. Some who follow this path see their deity as a manifestation of the impersonal Brahman, but others see their god or goddess as the Supreme Being, with no Brahman above him or her.

3-4 Hindu Ethics and Ways of Life

Krishnan, a thirty-year-old computer engineer in Illinois, logs onto shaadi.com to begin the process of finding a wife. This Indian website bills itself as the "world's largest matrimonial service." Some of Krishnan's friends have used it and have urged him to try it, because his parents' efforts at matchmaking haven't succeeded. He enters the search terms "Hindu" for his religion, "Brahmin" for his social–religious class, and also his birthday (for a "Vedic astrology horoscope" used

caste [kast] System of social organization

varna [VAHR-nuh] "Color," a system of classification of people into four main classes

> Hindus often say that Hinduism is more a way of life than a religion.

in traditional Hindu matchmaking). In his personal statement for the website, he writes that he is looking for a traditional Hindu young woman who can grow to love him after they are married. His parents will always come first in his life, he says, then his wife, and then his brothers and other relatives.

Hindus often say that Hinduism is more a way of life than a religion. For observant Hindus today, everyday life and religious life are not separated, because Hindu ethics traditionally plays a leading role in everyday life: caste and class, marriage and children, career and retirement.

3-4a The Caste System

You've probably heard about the Hindu **caste** system, which divides people in society into economic and social groups, giving all people their occupations, level of income, and particular pattern of religious duties. The foundation of the caste system was laid in Vedic times, but it grew into its present form in classical times, especially with the writing of the *Laws of Manu*. India today has more than six thousand castes and subcastes, and scholars have long debated the roles of color, economics, and power in the caste system. Hinduism has produced some opposition to the caste system—and there are many activists working to change it today— but for the most part it has endured as one of the main features of Hinduism. Two words are used in Hindu society to refer to this social system: *varna* and *jati*.

Varna means "color" (it is related to our word *varnish*). Varna is a system dating back to Vedic times that groups Hindu society into four classes (see Figure 3.3). Some scholars have theorized that social classes are based on varna, with the lightest at the top and the darkest on the bottom. This is probably an oversimplification, and it is controversial in Hinduism, but even today in India there is a general cultural preference (e.g., in films) for the lighter skin tones found in the upper varnas. (Skin-lightening creams are often best-selling items in Indian drugstores.) Also, class is generally related to economic standing: The lower one's class, the lower one's income. But there are many exceptions to this;

Figure 3.3 The Hindu Varna System and the Dalits

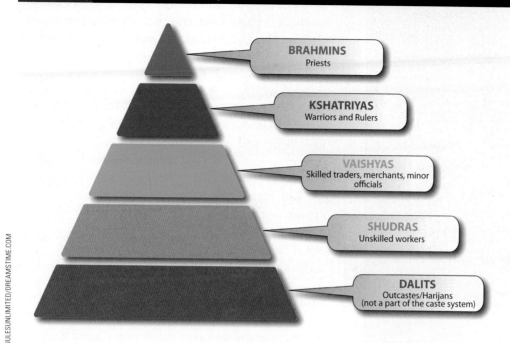

BRAHMINS
Priests

KSHATRIYAS
Warriors and Rulers

VAISHYAS
Skilled traders, merchants, minor officials

SHUDRAS
Unskilled workers

DALITS
Outcastes/Harijans
(not a part of the caste system)

The thighs of Purusha form the large varna of the common people, the **Vaishyas**, who provide the necessary semiskilled labor for society. Vaishyas are merchants, small farmers, and artisans. Finally, the **Shudras** are servants or peasants born from the feet of Purusha. The task of the Shudras, people in the fourth varna, is to support the higher castes by lowly service. Only men in the top three varna are "twice-born," receiving the sacred thread to wear on their body when they are ritually initiated into the formal stages of Hindu life. Shudra men and women, and women of the top three varnas, are thought not to have the personal qualities to be twice-born Hindus. But Shudras can do well economically, and women (not men) are allowed to marry a person one social step above them. If Shudras follow their dharma well, they can be reincarnated into a higher social class.

some upper-caste Brahmins are of modest means, and one can find members of the common-people Vaishya class who are wealthy merchants.

A well-known hymn in the *Rig Veda* (10.90) tells of how the four main classes arose from the sacrifice of Purusha (POOR-oo-shuh), a man as large as the universe. "The Brahmin was made from his mouth; his arms were made into the Prince; his thighs became the common people; and from his feet the servants were born." The **Brahmin** priests spring from Purusha's mouth so that they can chant the songs for sacrifice. When the Aryans came into India, their ritual lore was controlled by the Brahmins, who claimed to be the only class able to learn and enact them with ritual correctness. Correctness was needed to perform effective ceremonies that mediated between humans and the gods, bringing blessing to both.

This hymn also relates that the arms of Purusha were made into the "Prince." This is the class of **Kshatriyas**, who are kings and government officials. Because being a ruler entails defending and enlarging one's kingdom, the Kshatriyas are also warriors who lead in battle. The strong arms of Purusha lead to action, so the hymn says that it is the dharma of this class to defend others. Brahmins or Vaishyas cannot be rulers or warriors, because they would not have the right parts of Purusha to be Kshatriyas. (However, Brahmins have often been advisors to rulers.)

Below and outside the class system are the **outcastes**, a term not legally accepted in India today. (Note that outcastes means "those outside of the caste system," not "those cast out.") The Indian government calls them "scheduled classes," but others call them Harijans (HAHR-ee-jahns), "Children of God," a term popularized by Mohandas Gandhi with an unfortunate negative connotation in that "Harijans" is also an Indian euphemism for illegitimate children. They reject these terms, and prefer to call themselves **Dalits**, "oppressed ones."

Brahmin [BRAH-minz]
The top priestly class in the varna system

Kshatriyas [kshuh-TREE-yuhz] The warrior and princely varna class

Vaishyas [VIGH-shuhs]
Third varna class, the "common people"

Shudras [SHOO-druhs]
Fourth varna class, "servants"

outcastes Members of the lowest social class, outside the caste system; also called "Dalits"

Dalits [DAHL-its]
"Oppressed ones," the outcastes below the four Hindu castes

HINDU ETHICS AND WAYS OF LIFE **77**

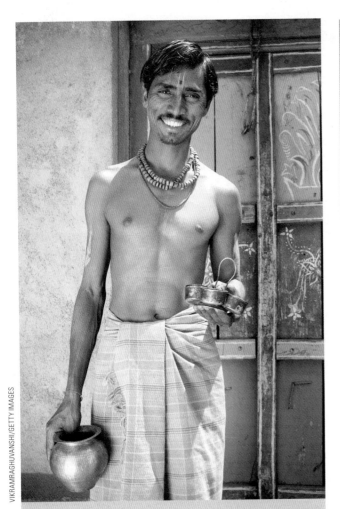

VIKRAMRAGHUVANSHI/GETTY IMAGES

A member of the Brahmin caste

by the government; their attempt was met with rioting by other Hindus. The vast majority of Dalits are still confined to menial, ritually polluting jobs such as street cleaning, manual scavenging, and handling bodies of dead animals or humans. They cannot drink from the same water pumps as the twice-born castes or eat in restaurants with them. In some villages, occasional violence is used to keep Dalits "in their place." Hindus of the four main classes do not consider them to be Hindus, and their rights and political status have been problematic in modern India. They are today the poorest of Indians, existing on the equivalent of only a few dollars a day.

Jati means "birth," and this birth caste is more important than varna for Hindus because it affects so many aspects of daily life. (Modern scholars disagree about how to translate *varna* and *jati*. Here we render *varna* as "class" and *jati* as "caste." Together, they comprise the caste system.) Although there are only four varnas in Hinduism, there are thousands of jatis. Caste is not a religious institution as the varna system is, but is economic and geographical in origin, now combined with varna into an overall religious system. Hindus today refer to jati when they talk of caste, and it is one's jati that really dictates the life of the average Hindu. Each jati has its own rules about food, jobs, marriage, contact with other jatis, and the like. From each caste come a number of subcastes, making the whole system even more complicated. Castes may often be occupational, but this does not preclude a member of one caste working at the occupation of another, for example, in agriculture—an added complexity. The Brahmin class is subdivided into many castes, just as there are many castes in the Kshatriya, Vaisya, and Shudra classes, and even among Dalits. Just

Their sheer numbers—an estimated 160,000,000—mean that they can wield considerable political power in elections. Some rise to political fame, and a number of cabinet ministers and even one prime minister have come from the Dalit class. Despite affirmative action programs for Dalits that provide a higher education and well-paid government jobs for some, strong discrimination against Dalits persists. In June of 2007, a group of Shudra shepherds petitioned to be downgraded into the Dalit class, hoping to gain access to preferential treatment afforded

jati [JAH-tee] Caste into which one is born

Dalits in northern India protesting the caste system, 2009

MUNISH SHARMA/REUTERS

as the four varnas are hierarchically organized, so are the various castes within a particular varna. A male is obligated to marry within his jati. Expulsion from the family and caste as a whole is likely to result should this obligation be broken, but if this and other caste obligations are kept, the individual is provided a strong network of support and protection.

Indian wedding ceremonial plate with a variety of foods and spices

3-4b The Four Stages of a Man's Life

The life of a Hindu male is traditionally divided into four stages of time. In modern India, fewer people observe the system completely and formally than in previous centuries, but even today it is an influential pattern for a man's life. However, Shudras, Dalits, and women of all four classes rarely follow these stages. Most Hindu males do not go through the four stages; many never advance beyond the second. Hindus who do complete all four stages sustain this world and pursue ultimate liberation from it.

The first period of life is the **student stage**. A male is taught by his family's elders from childhood, sometimes by a guru as well. His education will not only fit him for a future profession appropriate to his caste, but will also equip him for family, social, and religious life in a way appropriate to his varna and jati. In older times, this period could last for twenty years or more, but today the student stage has shrunk to between twelve and fifteen years, except for those few who obtain higher education in a university.

The second period is the **householder stage**, in which the Hindu male must marry and raise a family. Marriages are often arranged by parents while their children are still young—marriage is much too important to family and society to leave it up to young people! Since about 2010, both parents and young people increasingly use Internet matrimonial sites for Hindus, leading to marriages often called "semi-arranged." In villages child marriages often occur, but after the marriage, the child bride and child groom are separated until puberty sets in. On average, a young man is

> On average, a young man is around twenty-three at the time of marriage, a young woman around eighteen.

around twenty-three at the time of marriage, a young woman around eighteen. Hindus have always placed a high value on raising a family, and even poor Hindu couples will keep having children until a boy or two are born. During the householder stage a man works at a trade or profession appropriate to his caste, primarily for his family, but also for his community. He also engages in public and private religious duties derived from his caste.

The third stage of life is that of *retirement*, traditionally called the **forest-dweller stage**. When a man's children have grown up, when he sees signs of aging such as gray hair and wrinkles, his duty as a householder can end. In this forest-dweller stage—if he lives to see it, which in much of Hindu history isn't a given—the man is expected to retire not only from his job, but also from family and social life and much (but not all) of his wealth and possessions. Sometimes a man in this stage retreats to the forest to live a more spiritual life, either alone or in a small group of retirees, but this is rarer today than in the past. He gives up pleasures and comforts. His life is that of a celibate recluse. In view of the hardships that this partial renunciation brings, it's easy to see why this stage has become obsolete for all but a few.

The fourth stage is that of the "renouncer" or **sannyasin**, when a Hindu renounces the world and his previous life completely. This stage traditionally does not necessarily follow retirement; a man can become a sannyasin directly from the householder stage. All cares

student stage First period of life, in which a Hindu male gains knowledge for caste duties

householder stage Second period of life, in which a Hindu man marries and raises a family

forest-dweller stage Third period of life, in which a Hindu man retires

sannyasin [sahn-YAH-sin] **stage** Fourth period of life, in which a Hindu man becomes a renunciant

HUNG CHUNG CHIH/SHUTTERSTOCK

A renouncer in Nepal, with typical sadhu appearance: gathered-up hair, devotional face paint, untrimmed beard, and dried cow dung powder on his torso.

stages of life. The first goal of life, dharma, a term we saw previously, is a comprehensive concept that governs all stages of life. A good Hindu must know the dharma of Hinduism, particularly the truth that relates to his or her caste status, and practice it. This practice includes both social morality and ritual duties. Without this first goal, the others cannot be met, and spiritual practices such as yoga will fail.

The second goal of life is **artha**, material success and prosperity. This is pursued for the sake of one's family and the wider good of society. A householder is expected to become as prosperous as possible, while observing the bounds of proper dharma. Artha ties into the world-affirming side of Hindu tradition, and it makes Hinduism one of the few religions in the world to make financial prosperity an important religious goal. It also helps to explain the entrepreneurial drive and economic success of many Indians in modern times. One's dress reflects, among other things, the level of prosperity one has achieved (see "A Closer Look: Hindu Dress").

The third goal of life is **kama**, aesthetic pleasure both of the mind and the body, obviously also world-affirming. This goal is restricted to the householder stage. *Kama* is a comprehensive term for all types of pleasures: spiritual, intellectual, artistic, and physical. The *Kama Sutra* (SOO-trah), or *Scripture on Pleasure*, is often seen as a sex manual, but both kama and the *Kama Sutra* are much more than that. Hinduism is unique in teaching that the pursuit of pleasure is a valid and important religious goal.

The fourth goal of life is moksha, which we defined previously. It means "release" from life, particularly from the continuous cycle of death and rebirth. This goal is best practiced in the retirement and renouncer stages of life, although moksha can be sought in all the stages, particularly in the two paths of deeds and devotion that are thought to lead to release.

and pleasures of life are abandoned, and his concentration is devoted to achieving moksha before he dies. The sannyasin engages in intense study and meditation, typically with yoga and rigors such as solitude and a sparse diet. He is treated with the greatest respect in Hindu lands. But this respect is mingled with a certain degree of fear and skepticism, because some holy men can be hostile, even ferocious, in their words, and a few can be frauds. Upon taking up the life of the sannyasin, he will often burn an effigy of his body to show that he has died to the world. When a renouncer who has achieved moksha dies, his fellow renouncers tie stones onto his body and throw it in a river. He needs no funeral with cremation, for the soul has already been released from the dreaded cycle of reincarnation.

> The *Kama Sutra*, or *Scripture on Pleasure*, is often seen as a sex manual, but both kama and the *Kama Sutra* are much more than that.

artha [AHR-thuh] Material prosperity, the second goal of life in Hinduism

kama [KAH-muh] Spiritual, mental, and physical pleasure, the third goal of Hindu life

3-4c The Four Goals of Life

Hindus hold to four main goals in life and connect them roughly with the

3-4d The Lives of Hindu Women

The vast majority of young Hindu women get married. The Hindu wife bears children, raises them, and runs the home. Motherhood is so important that a woman is considered a failure if she is without children, especially a son; this is true even of modern Hindu women who

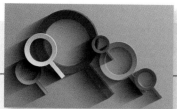

A Closer Look

Hindu Dress

Hinduism requires no particular type of clothing, as you might expect, and regional styles in India vary considerably. The traditional dress for most Indian women (Figure 3.4) is the sari, a piece of cloth five or six meters long that is wrapped and pleated around the waist and then drawn around over the shoulder so that the free end is loose. Underneath the sari are a short blouse and a long skirt, often leaving the midriff bare. In northern India, women prefer light, baggy trousers called "pyjamas" (from which we get our term) and a long, loose-fitting shirt. In mixed company outside the home or when worshiping in the home or temple, women usually cover their hair with the free end of their saris. This is a sign of respect to the gods and to other people, women as well as men.

Figure 3.4 Woman in sari, with bindi on her forehead

BONNIE VAN VOORST © CENGAGE LEARNING

Indian women of all classes typically love jewelry. Long earlobes are an ancient Indian sign of nobility, so women use heavy earrings to stretch their earlobes. The distinctive decorative mark of a married woman is the **bindi** ("little drop") on her forehead. The bindi may be a circle of colored paste, or of felt with an adhesive backing, which can more easily be put on and decorated with sequins. Unmarried women and young girls often have a small black spot on their forehead; it is not a bindi, but rather a protection against the "evil eye."

Although Hindu women often dress in traditional Indian ways, Hindu men very often wear Western clothing, especially in cities. Men in Indian villages traditionally dress in the *dhoti* (Figure 3.5). This single, large piece of fabric is wrapped around the waist and tucked up around the thighs. The *kurta* (called a "panjabi" in the United Kingdom and Canada) is a long, loose shirt coat falling to the knees and is worn by both men and women. It can be worn with a dhoti or with pants, and is both casual and formal. Turbans are usually connected with observant Sikh men (see Chapter 6), but in India some Hindu men also wear one. The most important item worn is the sacred thread, a thin cotton cord worn on the body by men of the upper three classes, symbolizing full Hindu status. It is given in a special ceremony near the age of ten. The traditional garb of Hindu men, long disdained by the Indian upper classes in favor of more-Western-style clothing, is now making a strong comeback in some social circles and in fashion design.

Holy men have a distinctive but not uniform look. (See the photo in Section 3-4b.) Their hair is often wildly matted, and they sometimes cover their body in light-colored dust or powdered cow dung, giving them the look of death. Some go around only in a thong or at times nude, to symbolize their full control of the senses and bodily desire. They can sometimes be seen with their sacred thread, but not wearing one shows that they have left the distinctions of once-born and twice-born behind.

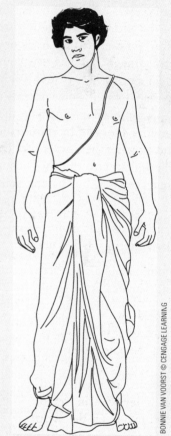

Figure 3.5 Man in dhoti and sacred thread

BONNIE VAN VOORST © CENGAGE LEARNING

bindi [BIHN-dee] Forehead mark of a married Hindu woman

may work outside the home. On the other hand, being a mother of sons brings great pride and auspiciousness. The wife performs worship in the home at the household shrine, often leading worship there. However, no woman who is menstruating is traditionally allowed at the shrine or in the kitchen. She is considered ritually unclean, and her husband will not touch her during this time. After ritual bathing at the end of her menstrual period, a woman resumes normal life in the home.

Despite the value placed on motherhood, abortion is legal and frequent in India, even among Hindus. Prenatal testing by ultrasound is now used widely to ascertain the sex of a fetus in the womb, even though this has been outlawed in India since 1994; if it is a female, it is often aborted. Some parents think it better to abort a female than to support a second or third daughter and pay for her expensive dowry. The Indian government encourages contraception, but having sons is necessary for economic support in one's old age because India has no national pension system. One also needs a son to perform one's funeral rites. The use of selective abortion to obtain sons has led, in some parts of India, to an ominous imbalance between the proportion of males and females. As a result, in 2007 the Indian government and private agencies launched a "Save the Girl Child" campaign which is still in full operation.

Divorce is difficult for a woman to obtain, especially for women of the higher classes, despite the Hindu Marriage Act of 1955 that ostensibly made it possible for any woman to get a divorce. Although divorce and remarriage are quite common among the lower castes, there is still a general feeling in villages that a wife is to blame if divorce occurs or even if the husband dies before she does. Family and friends are liable to regard a divorced or widowed woman as "unlucky," so life can be difficult for her. Widows rarely remarry and are often socially ostracized. The suicide rate for widows is high, even if **suttee**, "widow burning," is now illegal and almost unheard of. In suttee, widows would climb onto their dead husband's funeral pyre to go to heaven with him, an act of great merit.

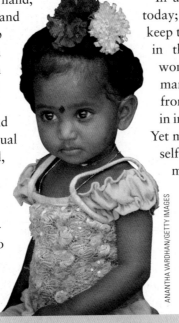

In 2007 the Indian government and private agencies launched a "Save the Girl Child" campaign.

ANANTHA VARDHAN/GETTY IMAGES

In urban areas women do have more status today; for example, they can now own property, keep their own salary, and open bank accounts in their own name. Many young Hindu women go to college, get a job, and delay marriage. Even unmarried young women from villages go to the big cities to find jobs in industries that are actively recruiting them. Yet marriage is still important, and a woman's self-esteem and social standing still have much to do with her husband. By serving him faithfully, just as she serves a god, good karma will come to her.

3-5 Hindu Ritual and Meditation

The Hindu temple in Omaha, Nebraska reflects the diversity of Hinduism. Temples in India are dedicated to one god, but this temple has twelve separate holy areas with altars, each with a statue of a different deity. All Hindus, no matter what god they worship, can feel comfortable in the Omaha temple. This temple was built as a center of worship, teaching, and Indian cultural life for people from India who live in Nebraska and Iowa. It is open for Hindu festivals, for a main weekly service on Sunday morning—an adaptation to American religion—and for traditional ceremonies marking the life stages of Hindus, from birth to death.

As you might expect, worship and meditation in Hinduism are diverse. Worship is a daily event for observant Hindus, whether performed at home, at a temple, at an outdoor shrine, or on a pilgrimage. Worship is called **puja**, a word for "honor" and "veneration." Ritual is important to Hindus, and much of it is ancient, although with regional and devotional-group variations. We will look now at several aspects of Hindu puja and meditation.

3-5a Images

Hinduism has many gods, all of them represented by images. Westerners, especially Protestant Christians who look upon images of the divine as objects that encourage false worship, often use the term *idol*, but *image* is more appropriate. *Idol* suggests that it is the statue or picture alone that is worshiped, and it is generally a pejorative term, although one will hear Hindus

suttee [suh-TEE] Burning of a widow on the funeral pyre of her husband

puja [POO-juh] Devotional actions of worshiping a god or venerating a human

A clay statute of a Hindu female god awaits painting in an art studio.

Temples large and small are found all over India, from great pilgrimage centers to humble side streets. At some of these temples more than one god is venerated in words and deeds. Usually the deity and the temple belong to one of three strands within the Hindu pantheon—Shaivite, Vaishnavite, and Shakta, including all their avatars and family members.

The deity, represented by a statue, picture, or other symbol, is the central part of the temple. The god is considered to be an honored guest and is treated with adoration, attention, and even amusements. Purification is essential before doing puja, and one usually bathes in running water and sips a little water three times. Washing the murti is essential but often symbolic—a flower or a small piece of cotton is used to touch the deity. Dressing the deity is also important, and the clothes chosen are bright and beautiful. Ornaments are placed on the murti, as well as flower garlands, perfumes, and oils. Because the deity remains at a temple, it is both woken up in the morning and put to rest at night. At many temples, sculptures help to teach about the gods and their stories, and they both shape and direct devotion. Larger temples will have priests who act as teachers.

The offering of food is also important—usually cooked rice, fruit and vegetables, liquefied butter, and sugar. The deity receives the essence of the food, and the "leftovers," called *prasad* (PRAH-sahd), are given back to those who brought them. Whatever the edible offering, both the gods and the worshipers eat the food and benefit from its richness. Fragrance and light are also offered the deity—fragrance in the form of incense sticks and light in the form of a burning lamp usually made from a burning wick placed in clarified butter,

using it happily. *Image* suggests something beyond the visible form that receives the worship offered to the visible form. Hindus use the term **murti** for the image of a deity, whether three-dimensional (as in a statue) or two-dimensional (as in a picture or poster). A murti is a representation of the deity, rather like a photograph represents a person. It draws the mind of the devotee to the gods themselves. However, an image can be more than just a symbol. The power or essence of the deity is believed to be in the murti, either temporarily, as for some festivals, or permanently, as in the case of some temple images that are treated as the deities themselves, with the god thought to reside inside the statue.

Shiva can be seen in a human-like form in an image as well as in the powerful symbols of the lingam and the trident (see the images in Sections 3-2b and 3-3a). The female side of the divine, the Goddess, is represented by the yoni, the symbol of creative female power that is the counterpart to the lingam. Hindus of the lower castes and those Hindus outside caste do not worship the "high" gods of Hinduism, but rather the "low gods," especially village and city deities. The high gods such as Vishnu and Shiva are generally considered to be uninterested in the daily events of the ordinary man or woman; their avatars and related lower deities do that duty for them.

murti [MUHR-tee] Image of a deity

which is waved before the deity. By applying a *tilak* (TEE-lahk)—a mark made with crushed flowers sometimes mixed with another substance—to the forehead between the eyebrows of the deity, the worshiper indicates awareness of the spiritual purity and power of the god. This in turn is passed to the worshiper. The worshiper may also entertain the deity with hymns that offer praise and of course increase the devotion of the worshipers. Groups of men can be seen singing hymns informally on the temple verandas in the evening. Sometimes women also sing near the temples, but they sit apart from the men.

Bowing is the traditional way of showing respect to someone in India. The more respect one wishes to show, the lower one bows. In the case of a god or a royal person, lying flat on one's face is in order. Bringing the palms together and raising them to the forehead are actions normally used in greeting in India, and they are used to greet the gods as well. The Hindi word *namaste* (NAHM-ahs-tay) or its equivalent in other Indian languages, "I bow to you," is spoken as this is done. Because famous gurus are also honored with puja, people might touch the guru's feet in respect or remove by hand the dust from his feet before touching their own head, indicating that the dusty feet of the guru are holier than the head of the one paying respect.

Worship in the home has long been an important part of Hinduism. Nearly every

Worship at a home shrine, where women and children have a prominent role

DINODIA PHOTOS/GETTY IMAGES

Hindu household has a home shrine, frequently in a special devotional room or in the kitchen, which is considered ritually pure. In this shrine, the family god—as well as the gods and goddesses honored by individual family members—have center stage, in the form of images done in brass; often, photographs of a guru or saint and the family ancestors are also in the shrine. To begin daily worship in the home, the believer purifies himself or herself by bathing. Then, with the help of mantras, the place of ritual is purified, and any evil spirits lurking to interfere with the puja are driven away. A small bell is rung to honor the deities and get their attention as the ritual begins. On occasion the gods are washed, clothed, fed, and given gifts, but worshipers always stand reverently with palms joined. At the climax of the ritual, a small lamp is swung before the shrine; the divinity resides in the fire, and the faithful receive it within themselves by holding the palms of their hands over the flames for an instant and then touching their eyes.

3-5c Pilgrimage

Pilgrimage is an aspect of ritual life important for many Hindus, although few of them have the time or money to engage in it. The destination of a pilgrimage is often a river, the ocean, or a spring. But temples built on sacred mountains or in sacred cities are also places of pilgrimage. Doing puja in a place with a strong connection to the divine brings purification from sin and ritual impurity, gains merit, fulfills vows, leads to the betterment of one's next lives in this world, and even brings deliverance from the cycle of rebirth. Millions of pilgrims go to Varanasi on the Ganges River every year to wash their sins away in the water. The largest pilgrimage event in the world is the **Kumbh Mela**, a festival held once every twelve years in Allahabad (the most recent held in 2015), when tens

Kumbh Mela [KOOM-buh MEHL-uh] Festival held every twelve years in Allahabad, India

An Indian boy with the colors of Holi splashed on him

© INTELLISTUDIES/SHUTTERSTOCK.COM

of millions of pilgrims gather where the two sacred rivers—the Ganges and the Yamuna—merge. As it is with all religions of the world, pilgrimage in Hinduism is "big business" in the cities that host it.

3-5d Festivals and Holidays

With the size and diversity of Hinduism, you would expect that its festivals and holidays would be diverse as well—and you would be correct. Estimates range from roughly one holiday per day to thousands per year, especially when regional festivals are considered. Hindu holidays tend to be based on the cycle of nature. They indicate the change of seasons, celebrate harvests, and promote fertility of animals and crops. Others are dedicated to a god or goddess and celebrate their deeds. Still other popular holidays mark events in the Indian epics, such as the *Bhagavad Gita*.

Festivals observed by most Hindus, and sometimes by other Indians, include the following, in chronological order:

- *Shiva Ratri* Festival for Shiva (February or March)
- *Holi* Festival of colors, which are applied to the body, marking the coming of spring (February or March)
- *Rama Navami* Birthday of the god Rama (April)
- *Krishna Jayanti* Birthday of Krishna (July or August)
- *Raksabandhana* Festival to renew family bonds (July or August)
- *Ganesha Chaturthi* Festival for Ganesh (August or September)
- *Dassera* Rama's victory over Ravana, the king of evil (September or October)
- *Diwali* Festival of lights, celebrated by most Indians, whatever their religion (October or November)

3-5e Funerals

Despite all the emphasis in Hinduism on karma and reincarnation, its death rites still emphasize the deceased happily joining dead ancestors rather than achieving a good reincarnation or release from all moksha. (A period of refreshment in heaven is often thought of as a prelude to being reincarnated.) Death is considered so ritually polluting and inauspicious that the images of deities in the home shrine are removed while the body is in the house. Unlike Western funerals, no one partakes of food or drink in any part of a Hindu funeral ritual.

The body of the deceased is washed soon after death, wrapped in a new cloth—white for men and red for women—and carried on a stretcher from the home to the cremation ground in a procession led by the eldest son. (Of course, funerals are held all over India, not just at the cities on the Ganges River, such as Varanasi.) Cremation on a wood fire is the traditional Indian method of disposing of human remains. Cremation is thought to separate the immortal soul from the body in a good way, resembling a fire sacrifice. At the funeral ground, Dalits of the Dom caste handle the body and incur the ritual pollution of burning it. Fresh, flowing water is usually near the cremation grounds, and the body is dipped in it for ritual purification. The body is then placed on the wood, with the feet facing south toward the home of the god who rules the dead. It is covered with a layer of wood followed by clarified butter, and scriptures are chanted over the body by a priest as the family circles the deceased. The eldest son then lights the funeral pyre, which will burn for two to three hours. After cremation begins, the youngest son leads the procession home.

The Doms tend the fire for several hours to keep it burning hot, occasionally turning the body with long poles to ensure that it is consumed more fully. The ashes and remaining bones (the larger and denser bones of the human body cannot be disposed of by a natural cremation alone) are finally put by the Doms into flowing water and left there, for a cooling and purifying effect. When the period of death rites is over, a Dalit is given all the household linen to wash. On the twelfth day, four balls of rice are offered to the gods to symbolize the happy union of the deceased with his or her forebears, which is the point of the funeral rites. Only when the house has been thoroughly cleaned can the household deities be returned.

Although cremation is the desired method of disposal of the dead, whole-body burial is not uncommon. The poorer classes usually practice burial because it is cheaper. Children of most castes who die young are buried, or sometimes put into a flowing river, rather than cremated. In the cities of India, cremation in modern crematoriums is now the norm, with ashes scattered later in sacred rivers.

3-5f Yoga

Yoga, with its emphasis on joining the body and mind, has become a main tool for achieving liberation, or at least the mental discipline that can lead to liberation. Buddhists, Christians, and people of no formal faith have adapted yogic methods to help them on their own paths to peace and freedom, or just to physical fitness. As explained previously, *yoga* means "yoke." This refers to the path of union with, or yoking to, a god or Brahman. The most popular type of yoga in India and the West is *hatha yoga*, which emphasizes breathing and physical posture as a way to ultimate knowledge of Brahman in one's atman; *karma yoga* is the path of active service that breathing and postures assist; *jnana yoga* is reflective, philosophical yoga; and *bhakti yoga* is the path of devotion to a god. Bhakti yoga is the simplest form, using repeated chanting of a mantra in a fixed posture to focus on a deity and offer one's life to a god.

> The most popular type of yoga in India and the West is *hatha yoga*.

Yogic practices draw, at least in significant measure, on the following eight steps:

1. Following five guidelines on behavior toward others: avoiding violence, untruthfulness, stealing, lust, and covetousness.

2. Following guidelines on behavior toward oneself: cleanliness of body and mind, contentment, sustained practice, self-knowledge, study, and surrender to God.

3. Learning and using formal yoga postures.

4. Performing breathing exercises, coordinated with physical postures.

5. Withdrawal of the senses, so that the exterior world is no longer a distraction from discovering the world within oneself, particularly the atman.

6. Concentration, so that one can focus on a single thing without distractions.

7. Meditation that moves beyond concentration, so that one's awareness is all-encompassing.

8. Finally, achieving *samadhi*, or "bliss." The self transcends itself through meditation and discovery of the atman, which brings one to Brahman.

Although yoga has been an important part of Hinduism for thousands of years, its use in the West has grown increasingly, and increasingly controversial in the past twenty years or so. Some Hindus have charged that yoga has been co-opted, even corrupted, for non-religious and profit-making purposes. Yoga is big business; it was estimated to be at $10 billion in 2016 in the United States alone. In her 2014 book, *Selling Yoga*, Andrea Jain shows the reasons for this controversy. Until recently, Hindus used yoga for a variety of aims, all of them religious: to turn inward in quest of one's true self and deliverance, to turn outward to devotional union with the divine, or to create and channel energy for sexual pleasure (kama, as we saw previously, is an important part of Hinduism). In contrast, today, yoga is widely used in North America, and increasingly in India, as a method for physical and spiritual fitness. This popularization of yoga is shaped, Jain writes, by modern ideas of human nature and health. She argues that this popularized yoga should not be dismissed as a distortion, because it has a variety of valid religious meanings and functions, even if they are shaped by non-Hindu ideas.[1]

Yoga classes in the West tend to emphasize the physical and emotional benefits of yoga over the religious benefits, and appeal to a wide variety of cultures. Here, women practice the "cobra" pose.

ANTONIODIAZ/SHUTTERSTOCK

3-6 Hinduism around the World Today

Shortly before the 2008 release of the Hollywood film *The Love Guru*, written by and starring Mike Myers, self-styled North American Hindu leader Rajan Zed complained about it to mass-media outlets. Zed charged that its portrayal of Hinduism is inaccurate and insulting. The potential for damage to Hindus is great, Zed argued, because Hinduism is not widely understood outside of India. Despite Zed's efforts, the consensus among Hindus in the West seems to be that they feel comfortable laughing at themselves and even laugh at stereotypes such as Apu the convenience-store merchant on television's *The Simpsons*. However, some portrayals of Hinduism in the mass media—such as in the 1984 film *Indiana Jones and the Temple of Doom*, with its false, brutal depiction of worship of the Hindu goddess Kali—have caused concern to many Hindus. Any disquiet over *The Love Guru*, however, fades rapidly as it was harshly reviewed in the press and failed miserably at the box office.

In this final section, we will consider briefly the current spread of Hinduism in the world, with a particular focus on North America.

3-6a Hinduism in South Asia and Africa

Sometimes Indian military conquests brought along with them the main aspects of Hindu culture and belief. This is how Hinduism came to Nepal and Sri Lanka. Although Hinduism moved beyond its own borders before the modern period, this was primarily a result of Indian emigration to other countries, and the resulting expansion of Hindu culture in such places as Nepal, Sri Lanka, and Bali. In the 1800s, the heyday of the British Empire, Indians moved freely to many parts of the world controlled by Great Britain, especially to south Asia and Africa. Hindus in these areas engaged in trade and other businesses, and practiced their religion; they were predominantly of the Vaishya class. Today there are almost 2 million Hindus in sub-Saharan Africa. In general, Hinduism has been the religion of only the Indian people, and formally converting other peoples has not been undertaken. This is true both in India and in the Hindu dispersion, and is one reason why Hindus are so remarkably concentrated—less than 1 percent of all Hindus live outside South Asia and the South Pacific. However, in the past two centuries various Hindus have indeed sought to spread Hinduism outside of India, particularly in North America.

Hindu women in Bali carry offerings to a temple.

KLAUS HOLLITZER/GETTY IMAGES

Distinctive ritual practices developed in Hinduism as it spread through Asia. For example, the Hindu women of Bali, Indonesia, make elaborate pyramids of food that they carry to the temple on their head as a sacrificial offering to the deity. The wealthier the family is, the higher the pyramids. A cooked chicken may be put in the pyramid, surrounded by rice dishes and many kinds of fruit. (See also "A Closer Look: Hindu Faith and Indian Food.")

3-6b Hinduism in the West

Hinduism has been viewed in widely differing ways in the West during the past two centuries. Customs such as widow burning (rarely done these days) and a caste system that resists reform have made many North Americans resistant to Hinduism until more recently. However, some Westerners were attracted by Hindu ideas of physical and spiritual life in harmony with nature. Vegetarianism and Hindu philosophy, particularly Vedanta, have also attracted Westerners

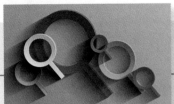

A Closer Look

Hindu Faith and Indian Food

India has considerable regional variations in food, many of which have gone into the wide Hindu diaspora, but the important aspect is a preference for vegetarianism. Because all animals are sacred to Hindus due to a general reverence for life, and particularly for the souls incarnated in animals, it is considered wrong to kill animals for food. Vegetarianism is believed to benefit the body, the mind, and the soul. Even so, many Hindus are not strict vegetarians, and those who can afford it will eat meat occasionally. The sacrifice and subsequent eating of animals, the goat in particular, is common enough in India and Nepal. Brahmin priests are rarely involved in such sacrifices, which are performed by lower-caste priests and mainly in the smaller village temples.

The cow is the most sacred of all animals to Hindus, and no observant Hindu would ever eat beef. (You should never look for a beef dish at any self-respecting Indian restaurant!) Although meat from a cow is forbidden, cow's milk and the products made from it are considered very healthy. To put it in modern Western terms, vegetarianism is common, but a vegan diet that excludes all animal products would be unthinkable to observant Hindus.

Foods high in protein are important in a vegetarian diet, and *dal*, a lentil dish, is popular throughout the world wherever Indian cuisine is found. The *Bhagavad Gita* (17:8–10) teaches that healthy foods are "tasty, soothing, and nourishing." It describes unhealthy food as things that

Indian food is widely regarded as one of the most colorful and tasty cuisines in the world.

are "acidic, sour, and excessively hot." (The spices in Indian food often make Westerners' eyes water, but of course what makes food excessively hot is a matter of acculturation. The *Gita* means foods that will give an Indian indigestion.) The particular balance of having both hot and cool foods in a meal is also important for bodily and spiritual health.

The males of the family traditionally eat first and separately from the women, and then the females eat what remains. Because all food in Hindu sacrifice is first offered to the deities and then received back by the worshiper, the practice of eating the males' leftovers as a sort of sacrificial food enables the wife to pay honor to her husband. This custom is still maintained in traditional India today, though it is not so common among Hindus living in the Western world.

to Hinduism, especially in the more intellectual echelons of North America. Hinduism came to Great Britain in the 1800s with Indian migration there. Around 817,000 people in the United Kingdom called themselves Hindus in the 2011 census, but other estimates have put the figure as high as 1.5 million. Most Hindus in the United Kingdom live in England, with half living in London alone. However, Hindus in Great Britain did not have a traditional, stand-alone temple until 1981. In all of Europe today, about 1.3 million Hindus can be found.

Hindu customs are slightly different in the West. In funeral practice, for example, the body will be washed and dressed in new clothes, placed in a coffin, and surrounded by flowers. Cremation cannot be immediate as in India, but has to take place a day or two after death because of the necessary legal arrangements. At the crematorium the priest will talk about the life of the person, and prayers are said for the departed soul in front of the sacred fire or household shrine upon returning to the home after cremation has begun. The ashes of the deceased would preferably be sent to a relative in India to be scattered in the Ganges, sent to one of the businesses recently set up for that purpose, or, if that is not possible, cast into a fast-flowing river nearby.

In the past century or so, varied expressions of Hinduism have found their way to the West in movements led by Hindu gurus. Vivekananda (VIH-veh-kah-NAHN-duh; 1863–1902) was the first successful Hindu missionary to the West. In 1893, he addressed the first World Parliament of Religions at Chicago; he was enthusiastically received there and in his other travels throughout the United States. Vivekananda established the first Hindu temple in North America in San Francisco. He returned to India as a national hero. The Hinduism of Vivekananda was much less devotional than Ramakrishna's own piety and stressed the philosophical teachings of the *Upanishads*. He was one of the world's first advocates of religious pluralism.

The Self-Realization Fellowship of North America was founded by Paramahansa Yogananda (PAR-uh-mah-HAN-suh yo-guh-NAN-duh) in 1920 and was based in Los Angeles, where it still has its headquarters. It teaches a form of yoga to enable members to realize "the god within." The Self-Realization Fellowship has more than one hundred local meeting places in the United States and Canada today, and one hundred more in Europe.

One recent guru who gained wide popularity in North America was Maharishi Mahesh Yogi (MAH-ha-REE-shee MAH-hesh YOH-gee; 1911–2008), founder of the Spiritual Regeneration Movement better known as **Transcendental Meditation (TM)**. TM is based on Vedanta, which emphasizes each person's inner divine essence and the liberating powers that may be harnessed when one knows one's true identity. Yogic meditation, practiced in the morning and evening, is the way to tap into the transcendent and its calming, directing power. When the English musical group, the Beatles, took continued instruction in Great Britain and in India from the Maharishi in the late 1960s, TM became even more popular. The popularity of yogic meditation today in North America, severed from its deep religious connections, is due in large part to the TM movement. (For more on TM as a New Religious Movement, see Chapter 13, Section 13-3b.)

{ *Some Hindu parents send their children to a summer camp that provides teaching and experience in Hindu life.* }

3-6c Hindu Migration and Life in North America

In the past few decades, especially since the liberalization of immigration laws in the 1960s, an increasing number of Indians who practice Hinduism have moved to the United States and Canada. This Hindu **diaspora**, a "spreading" from its native land, has brought hundreds of thousands of Hindus to North American cities, especially on the East and West Coasts. Some of these more recent immigrants are merchants, but many of them are highly skilled professionals who are eager to integrate into North American civic life. A 2016 Pew Research Center study found that diaspora Hindus in North America are "highly educated," with ten more years of formal schooling than Hindus in India. They tend to have more schooling than other religious groups in North America.[2] They also want to preserve basic Hindu beliefs and behaviors in an environment not conducive to them. Every home of observant Hindus has a shrine to the god(s) the family serves, and worship is conducted at the shrine a few times a day. In 2001, the American Museum of Natural History in New York City opened an exhibit, *Meeting God*, that documented the home and business shrines of several Hindus in the New York area.

Many Hindus join cultural organizations to keep traditions, such as music and cuisine, alive. Some Hindu parents send their children to summer camp that provides teaching and experience in Hindu life. North American Hindus also build temples in which Hindus worship, and sometimes, workers come from India to build them in an authentic way. Finding Brahmin priests from India to staff these temples is difficult, so activities, such as singing devotional songs that can be practiced by all Hindus, become even more important than in India. The 2014 survey of Hindu life in the United States by the Institute of

Transcendental Meditation (TM)
Meditational system, popularized by the Maharishi Mahesh Yogi, emphasizing knowing one's divine identity

diaspora [dee-ASS-pohr-uh] "Spreading," in this case of Hinduism outside of India

American Religion found 1,600 temples and centers with an estimated 600,000 practicing Hindus affiliated with them. If all those who self-identify as Hindus are included, the number rises to an estimated 1.2 million.

Hindus typically view marriage within one's caste as a necessity. Because marriages are often still arranged to some extent, Hindu parents may network for suitable spouses living in North America or even in India. As with other immigrant groups in North America, intergenerational tension often springs up as young second- and third-generation Hindu people take on the values and practices of their non-Hindu peers. Dating and mating are often difficult for Hindu young people with Western ways; this is the theme of several films, such as Mira Nair's excellent *Monsoon Wedding*, *The Namesake*, and the more recent *Meet the Patels* directed by and starring Geeta and Ravi Patel. Over time, Hindus, similar to other religious groups, will probably reach a workable, if sometimes uneasy, compromise between their religion and their life in North America.

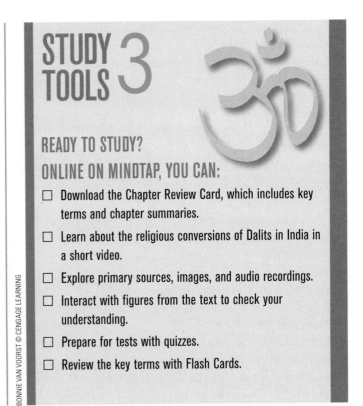

STUDY TOOLS 3

READY TO STUDY?
ONLINE ON MINDTAP, YOU CAN:

- ☐ Download the Chapter Review Card, which includes key terms and chapter summaries.
- ☐ Learn about the religious conversions of Dalits in India in a short video.
- ☐ Explore primary sources, images, and audio recordings.
- ☐ Interact with figures from the text to check your understanding.
- ☐ Prepare for tests with quizzes.
- ☐ Review the key terms with Flash Cards.

BONNIE VAN VOORST © CENGAGE LEARNING

Hinduism Timeline: 3000 B.C.E.–Present

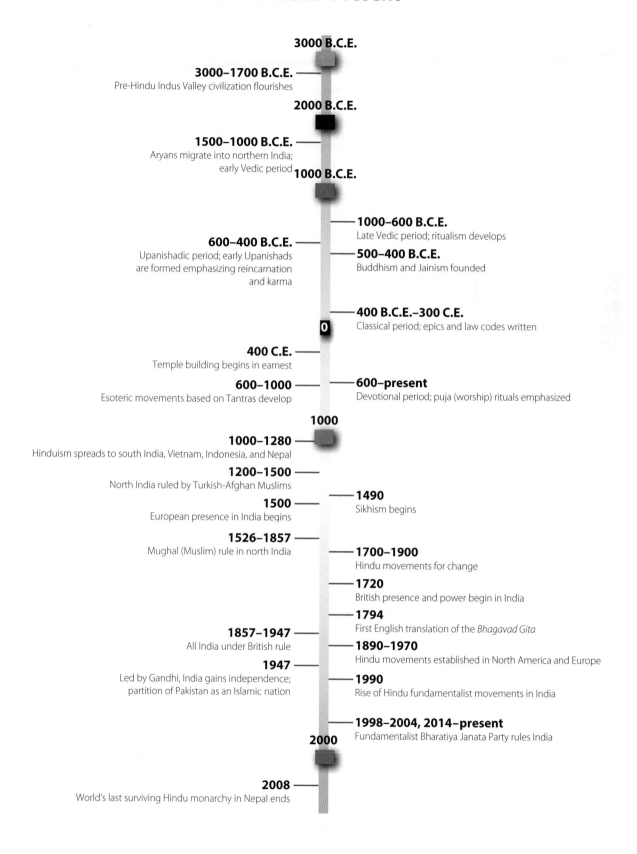

3000 B.C.E.

3000–1700 B.C.E. ——
Pre-Hindu Indus Valley civilization flourishes

2000 B.C.E.

1500–1000 B.C.E. ——
Aryans migrate into northern India;
early Vedic period **1000 B.C.E.**

—— **1000–600 B.C.E.**
Late Vedic period; ritualism develops

600–400 B.C.E. ——
Upanishadic period; early Upanishads
are formed emphasizing reincarnation
and karma

—— **500–400 B.C.E.**
Buddhism and Jainism founded

—— **400 B.C.E.–300 C.E.**
Classical period; epics and law codes written

0

400 C.E. ——
Temple building begins in earnest

600–1000 ——
Esoteric movements based on Tantras develop

—— **600–present**
Devotional period; puja (worship) rituals emphasized

1000

1000–1280 ——
Hinduism spreads to south India, Vietnam, Indonesia, and Nepal

1200–1500 ——
North India ruled by Turkish-Afghan Muslims

—— **1490**
Sikhism begins

1500 ——
European presence in India begins

1526–1857 ——
Mughal (Muslim) rule in north India

—— **1700–1900**
Hindu movements for change

—— **1720**
British presence and power begin in India

—— **1794**
First English translation of the *Bhagavad Gita*

1857–1947 ——
All India under British rule

—— **1890–1970**
Hindu movements established in North America and Europe

1947 ——
Led by Gandhi, India gains independence;
partition of Pakistan as an Islamic nation

—— **1990**
Rise of Hindu fundamentalist movements in India

—— **1998–2004, 2014–present**
Fundamentalist Bharatiya Janata Party rules India

2000

2008 ——
World's last surviving Hindu monarchy in Nepal ends

4

Encountering Jainism: The Austere Way to Liberation

NINA BSURGI/SHUTTERSTOCK.COM

LEARNING OUTCOMES

After studying this chapter, you will be able to do the following:

4-1 Explain the meaning of *Jainism* and related terms.

4-2 Summarize how the main periods of Jainism's history have shaped its present.

4-3 Outline the essential Jain teachings in your own words.

4-4 State the main ethical precepts of Jainism for monks/nuns and laity, and relate them to Jain teachings.

4-5 Outline the way Jains worship and practice other rituals.

4-6 Explain the main aspects of Jain life around the world today, especially in North America.

"Do no harm; let all creatures help each other." —The motto of Jainism.

Your Visit with Jain Nuns

Imagine that you're traveling through northern India and come across a group of three Jain nuns. Like you, they're walking on the outskirts of a small town, but they walk much more slowly and deliberately than you. They're dressed all in white and have a whisk slung across the shoulder that they occasionally take down and use gently on the road in front of them.

After you greet them respectfully, they invite you to the ashram where they're currently living. You hesitate, thinking, "Should I visit with nuns in their house? Is that proper?" You try to hide your expression, but they're so perceptive that it makes you feel like they can read your mind. They assure you that it's okay, that they are able to receive visitors and know how to conduct themselves properly with them. So you accompany them, keeping a respectful distance behind them as they walk.

At their house, you meet five other nuns. Led by their teacher, who is clearly in charge, they are walking around to different towns and villages in the area. A man next door is fixing their evening meal in a way that is approved by Jains, which is to do as little harm as possible to insects and other small beings, all of which have a soul. Soon women of the town start to gather in the ashram. They greet the teacher, and she conducts a short service of prayer and meditation for them. It ends with the saying "May you attain spiritual prosperity."

After sleeping in another building, you rejoin the nuns very early the next day. They stop at a Jain temple for prayer and meditation, and you wait for them there. Then you all leave to walk to the next town. The progress is slow, because the nuns must watch where they walk and some of them have been fasting and have diminished physical strength. When you arrive at the end of the day, you are about to leave, when one of them startles you with the question, "Why don't you become a monastic?"

Jainism is an ancient religion of India that follows a path of doing no harm to any living being. During your introduction to Jainism, you will soon encounter these unique features:

- Jainism is similar in many ways to Buddhism but has been a distinct Indian religion for more than two thousand years.

- Jainism shares much vocabulary (karma, nirvana, and other terms) with Hinduism and Buddhism, but the Jain nuance of these words is different.

- Jainism teaches self-effort to bring one's soul to release from constant reincarnation. However, this goal can be accomplished only by monks or nuns; other Jains have lesser goals.

- Jains have a challenging and restrictive diet, but in general they are remarkably healthy.

- With an estimated 5 to 6 million followers, Jainism is among the smallest of the faiths typically called "world religions." However, the contribution of Jainism is much more significant than what might be expected from its small numbers.

< A woman explains the meaning of the rice she has laid out in the Jain temple of Koch, India.

Jain nuns traveling by foot in India.

ALEXANDER MAZURKEVICH/SHUTTERSTOCK

4-1 The Name *Jainism*

Jainism (JINE-ism) is commonly traced to the Sanskrit word for "conquer." This conquering refers to the battle Jains wage within themselves to gain the full knowledge that leads to enlightenment. The person who has achieved Jain enlightenment is called a **Jina**, or "Conqueror," and all who follow this religion are called **Jains**, followers of the Conquerors. In particular, Jains are followers of the Jina who founded Jainism, **Mahavira**, but the religion was never named after him. Mahavira is the main model of how to achieve enlightenment, but he himself does not enlighten people or rescue them from error. The name *Jain* is so important to its followers that they have done something unique in the religions of the world—many of them have proudly taken the name of their religion as their family name. For more on how Jainism understands itself, see "A Closer Look: The Symbol of Jainism."

Jina [JEE-nuh] "Conqueror," a Jain who has achieved enlightenment

Jains [jines] Followers of the Conquerors

Mahavira [MAH-hah-VEER-uh] The twenty-fourth and last Tirthankara of this age and the founder of Jainism

asceticism [ah-SET-uh-SIHZ-uhm] Physical denial and mental self-discipline to achieve liberation

reincarnation Unhappy passage of the soul at death to another body

Parshvanatha [parsh-VAHN-ah-thuh] Reformer in the 600s B.C.E. regarded by Jains as the twenty-third Tirthankara

Tirthankaras [tuhr-TAHN-kah-ruhz] "Ford Finders" who lead the way across the rivers of constant reincarnation

4-2 The Jain Present as Shaped by Its Past

For thirty years, the Jain monk Gurudev Shree Chitrabhanu (CHIT-ruh-BAHN-oo) was a spiritual leader for Jains in India. He walked more than 30,000 miles there, barefoot. Deciding to give up his monastic vows, he left India in 1970 to attend conferences in Switzerland and in Boston. He did so at first to raise funds and recruit volunteers to help Indians impacted by famines and floods. Then Chitrabhanu began writing educational materials from Jain scriptures that he said could apply to Jains and non-Jains alike, and he began to interact with people of other religions in ways that were unusual for a Jain. Eventually, he settled in New York City, where he married, took up the life of a householder, and founded the Jain Meditation Center. In several ways, Chitrabhanu embodies the tension between the historic values of an ancient religion and the challenges of modern life, especially in North America.

Jains believe that their religion has no founder and no early history. For them, Jainism is eternal, even though it goes through long cycles of decline and reform just as the world does. Historians of what Jains consider their present cycle can trace out the main lines of Jain history and point to moments of its founding, growth, and change. These benchmarks help us to explain how Jainism got to be the way it is today.

4-2a Founding and the First Thousand Years (600 B.C.E.–ca. 400 C.E.)

Jainism arose during the seventh century B.C.E. in the Ganges River valley of northeastern India—a time and place of intense religious activity and reform. Jains opposed the dominant Hindu priestly groups who emphasized salvation by the sacrifices that their priests performed and interpreted. The new religious perspectives promoted **asceticism**: physical denial and mental self-discipline to achieve liberation. Jains abandoned the practice of sacrificial rituals in order to pursue an enlightenment based on asceticism that would bring freedom from **reincarnation**. Jainism began as a reform movement within Hinduism, but over time it grew into a distinct religion.

Jains believe that the present era has had a series of twenty-four religious leaders. The first Jain leader of whom we know something historically reliable about is the twenty-third, **Parshvanatha**, a religious reformer who lived in the 600s B.C.E. He rejected Hindu sacrifices and taught the abandonment of worldly attachments. Jains regard Parshvanatha as the twenty-third of the twenty-four **Tirthankaras**, "Ford Finders" who lead the way across the rivers of constant reincarnation. Tirthankaras are not gods, but rather enlightened humans whose stories and teachings point the way for others.

Vardhamana (VAHR-duh-MAHN-uh), who is known more commonly as Mahavira, was the twenty-fourth and last Tirthankara of this age. He is seen as the last and perfect teacher of true knowledge and practice, but Jains do not call him the founder of their religion, because it has always existed. Mahavira is said to have lived from 599 to 527 B.C.E., although some put him in the 400s B.C.E. Mahavira's life is written down in the Jain scripture, but these accounts are filled with later,

A Closer Look

The Symbol of Jainism

Until recently, the common symbol of Jainism has been the *swastika*, an ancient and wide-spread Asian religious symbol with none of the racist overtones that the *swastika* has for Westerners today. The Jain swastika is often seen with four dots in it. (See Chapter 3, Section 3-1, for more on the swastika.)

In 1975, Jain representatives, at a meeting to commemorate the 2,500th anniversary of Mahavira's death, drew up an image as an official symbol for the Jain religion. Since then, its symbol has become widely accepted and used. One sees it in almost all official Jain publications, religious magazines, and even in greeting cards and wedding announcements.

The overall shape of the image is modeled on the human torso, a shape Jains believe the universe shares. The small arc at the top symbolizes a realm above heaven. All liberated souls reside there as individual beings, forever in a blessed state, freed from the recycling of souls through life and death. The three dots just below

Figure 4.1 Symbol of Jainism

the zone of liberation stand for the three jewels: right belief, right knowledge, and right conduct. By gaining these three jewels, one can achieve the liberated zone.

Below this is a swastika, which has several different meanings. As a wheel, it suggests the eternal nature of the material world. It represents the four parts of the Jain community: monks, nuns, male laity, and female laity. It also represents the four infinite characteristics of the soul: knowledge, perception, happiness, and energy. (Some North American and European Jains substitute a different symbol for the swastika.)

The symbol of the human right hand in the lower portion shows openness and fearlessness. The circle in the palm of the hand is a wheel. The word in the circle is *ahimsa*: doing no harm toward all the living things in this world. Ahimsa is the key to liberating oneself from the cycle of reincarnation. A phrase at the bottom does not always appear in this symbol (and is not found in Figure 4.1). Sometimes it is translated as "Live and let live," but this is a cliché in contemporary English. It's better to translate it as "Let all creatures help one another."

legendary material. They also vary in content, depending on which of the two main Jain groups is writing his story. Despite these historical challenges, the scriptures provide an adequate basis for our historical understanding of his life and the early Jain movement.

Similar to the Buddha, Mahavira was born in northeast India into the Kshatriya class of rulers and warriors. When he was around thirty years old, he renounced his privileged status and took up an ascetic life. Mahavira spent the next twelve years in strict asceticism, punishing his body in order to free his soul. After pushing himself to the point of death several times, he experienced a sudden flash of enlightenment that gave him omniscience, or full knowledge of everything in the universe. He then converted eleven male disciples as the nucleus of his movement and formed a monastic community with them. They had no permanent home, but instead wandered as monks from place to place.

Mahavira taught his followers extensively, but many Jains believe that after his enlightenment he communicated through a divine sound that emanated from his body, which his followers could interpret into human words. He was no longer hungry, thirsty, or tired, nor did he age. Unlike the Buddha, who found a middle way between intense self-denial and ordinary life, Mahavira and his followers taught the path of radical asceticism. After more than thirty years of activity, and after starving himself at the end of his life, Mahavira's body died and his soul reached full eternal blessing, never to be reincarnated again. Two of his original eleven disciples, Indrabhuti and Sudharman, survived Mahavira and led his movement into its second generation.

Jains believe that Mahavira attracted 14,000 monks and 36,000 nuns to Jainism before he died. These numbers are probably exaggerated, but they accurately suggest that the movement grew rapidly at first, especially among women. Mahavira rejected the Hindu caste system, drawing his followers from any social and economic class. Under his leadership, Jainism also went from being a movement of only monastics to a movement that had many more lay members than nuns and monks.

Early Jainism saw some disagreements over monastic doctrine and practice, as we might expect in a religion that prizes individual accomplishment. The main disagreement to arise early (lasting until today) was over the degree of renunciation that monks and nuns should practice. Just how much self-denial is necessary for liberation? For example, some argued that they should wear white robes and have only minimal possessions, and others claimed that a true monk should be naked and have no possessions. (This nakedness never extended to nuns; Indian cultural attitudes permit male nudity in public, but never female.)

The results of these differences took time to assume the formal shape we know today, with Jainism split into two main groups. The **Shvetambar** ("white-clothed" monks and nuns) group wears clothing as allowed by their scriptures. The **Digambar** ("sky-clothed," a euphemism for naked) group advocates nakedness for monks as a symbol of complete denial of the world. Shvetambar monastics own only a few possessions, such as scripture books and a whisk for clearing away small beings as they walk, but Digambar monks typically own nothing. (The sight of naked monks out in public, sometimes carrying a colorful whisk of peacock feathers, is a striking reminder of this total renunciation.) Digambars believe that a soul in a female body cannot reach liberation, but Shvetambars affirm that it can. The details of this split remain unclear, because the later accounts of it

Shvetambar [shveht-AHM-bahr] "White-clothed" Jain monks and nuns

Digambar [die-GAM-bahr] "Sky-clothed" Jain group with naked monks

Seated Tirthankara in the Jain temple, Mumbai

© OSTILL/SHUTTERSTOCK.COM

were written to defend each sect and attack the other. Today, Shvetambar texts and images of Mahavira have him clothed, and Digambar texts and images have him naked.

The Shvetambar–Digambar division was probably made permanent by a series of Jain councils that formalized the new Jain scriptures, which, from earliest times, were only oral collections of teaching and monastic practice. A council held around 455 C.E. formally adopted the Shvetambar canon that is still in use today. Digambar monks refused to attend this meeting. They denounced the Shvetambar canon, and the split between the two groups was formalized.

During these early centuries, Jainism spread westward from the Ganges River valley, settling in areas where it could enjoy royal protection in the different Hindu kingdoms of northern India. During the Gupta (GOOP-tuh) dynasty in north India (320–600 C.E.), a time of Hindu revival there, many Jains left the Ganges valley area and migrated to southern, central, and western India. Jainism became stronger in these areas than it had been in its original home, and even though Jains are still

A group of Digambara monks "clothed with the sky" at a Jain temple in Rajasthan, India, where they are resting from wandering during the rainy season.

DANIEL J. RAO / ALAMY

concentrated in the north and west of India, Jainism gained a more national base throughout India, which it enjoys today.

4-2b The Next Thousand Years (600–1600)

The early part of this next period saw the flourishing of Digambar Jainism. Achieving success in the region of modern-day Karnataka, the Digambars gained the support of three Indian kingdoms. As Jain monks did earlier, Digambar monks probably influenced the succession of some kings in these dynasties, thus guaranteeing royal patronage of the new religion. Jain monks acted as spiritual teachers and counselors to many rulers and their advisors. (It might seem strange that those who have completely renounced the world would advise rulers, but this is a long Indian tradition.) For centuries rulers

Statue of Gommateshvara in Shravanabelagola, India. The scaffolding in back of the statute has been erected, and is being prepared for the ceremonies to anoint the statue.

VALERY SHANIN/SHUTTERSTOCK.COM

gave tax revenues to the Jain community, providing richly for their temples and monasteries and for the support of Jain writers and artists. Most prominently, in 981 a general paid for a colossal statue of the Jain hero Gommateshvara (go-MAHT-esh-VAR-uh) at Shravanabelagola (SHRAH-vahn-BEL-uh-GOHL-ah). Today this statue is one of the holiest and most often-visited sites in Jainism.

In the time of their greatest political influence from about 500 to 1200 C.E., Jain monks of both main groups gave up wandering asceticism and lived permanently in Jain temples or monasteries. The causes of this are disputed, but many historians point to the influence of money, power, and prestige that came from the patronage of monks by rulers. One contemporary legacy of this change is the Digambar practice of ordaining a monk to lead a Jain institution such as a temple, school, or foundation. In this practice, a new Digambar monk doesn't wander in a naked state, but rather is a settled, clothed administrator. Some Jains saw these changes as a defection from Jainism's original ideals of ending attachments to the world, but the practices persist today.

The Shvetambars in the north were not as involved in politics as the Digambars to the south, but they held their own there. On the whole, however, this period of Jainism's second millennium belonged to the Digambars. The Shvetambar community suffered under the conquest of India by Muslims in the 1100s, and the continuing Islamic power of the Mughal (MOO-guhl) Empire there. Jains in the north were persecuted and their important shrines were destroyed. Islam was not as tolerant toward Jainism as Hinduism was. The Shvetambar community was gradually reduced and marginalized, but its successful adaptation to this new status probably contributed to the long-term survival of Jainism.

4-2c Early Modern Times through Today (1600–Present)

These unhappy divisions provoked a variety of reform movements among the Shvetambar and Digambar laity. An important Digambar reform came in the early 1600s, sparked by the lay poet Banarsidas (bah-NAHR-sih-dahs). This reform stressed the traditional mystical, austere steps on the Jain path. It also attacked the Digambar temple ritual and what it saw as the corruption and worldly comforts of leading monks.

By 1850, idol-venerating Shvetambar monks had been severely reduced in numbers, and lay leaders controlled Jain temples. Shvetambar monasticism then experienced a revival led by monks such as Atmaramji (1837–1896), and the numbers of image-worshiping monks and nuns grew to around 1,500 and 4,000, respectively, by about 2000. The image-venerating Tapa sect is now the largest group of Shvetambars; the non-image-venerating Shvetambar sects are much smaller. At present, all the Shvetambar groups have about 2,500 monks and 10,000 nuns, and Digambar groups have about 550 monks and 500 nuns, according to a Jain accounting in 2006. As we saw previously, the total number of Jains in the world today is about 5 million, so the proportion of monastics is low indeed.

Today both Shvetambars and Digambars maintain their temples in India and distribute their scriptures. Modern Jains also participate in social and economic relief for the general public, such as drought relief in India. They also assist Jain widows, and maintain rescue shelters to save animals from slaughter as a part of their strict teachings on nonviolence and vegetarianism. A unifying movement within Jainism grew in the twentieth century. For example, in 1974 a committee with representatives from every sect compiled a new scripture recognized by all Jain groups, called the **Saman Suttam**, "Common Scripture." Given the divisions in Jainism, the *Saman Suttam* was a significant accomplishment and has served to unify contemporary Jains.

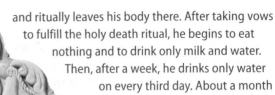

Sculpture of the Jain wheel adorns the roofline of a Jain temple in Rajasthan, India.

and ritually leaves his body there. After taking vows to fulfill the holy death ritual, he begins to eat nothing and to drink only milk and water. Then, after a week, he drinks only water on every third day. About a month after beginning this process, the monk is so physically weakened that he dies, surrounded by a large crowd of reverent witnesses. This holy death ritually affirms many key teachings of Jainism. Holy death is said to burn off the karma attached to one's soul, and allows the soul to end the cycle of continual rebirth and death.

Our survey of Jain history introduced many of the key teachings of Jainism. In this section, we'll look more closely at these important teachings.

4-3a No Gods

Strictly speaking, Jainism has no gods, and some have called it an atheistic religion. Because the world is eternal, there is no need for a divine being to create it. Also, the process of karma and reincarnation works on its own because it is a part of the universe itself and does not need a deity to preside over it. The way to salvation is shown by human "Ford Finders" and must be accomplished by one's own effort, not given by any divine being. Thus, Jainism not only *has* no gods, it also *needs* no gods. Sometimes one will hear Jains in the West say that all liberated souls together are the God of Jainism, but this is not a traditional Jain understanding.

> Jainism has no gods, and some have called it an atheistic religion.

Although most Jains believe in good and evil spirits and other heavenly beings, these are not considered gods. Jain lay followers worship some spirits of earth and heaven for daily protection and guidance, but not for eternal release. Ritual veneration of Tirthankaras is done mainly to dedicate oneself more fully to finding one's own release by moral and mental practices.

4-3 Essential Jain Teachings

Saman Suttam
[SAH-muhn SOOT-ahm]
"Common Scripture"
recognized by all Jain groups, compiled in 1974

holy death Voluntarily starving oneself to death as an act of devotion

A Jain monk, after a long and fruitful life, decides to begin the process of **holy death**, literally starving oneself to death. He has already gained the permission of his monastic order, and he has the required physical strength and soundness of mind to carry it out. He travels to a place of Jain pilgrimage

4-3b Time and the World

Time is real to Jains, who compare it to a turning wheel with twelve spokes; six spokes go up and six go down. The spokes going up signify a time of improvement. In this time, human progress in knowledge and goodness, and liberation from reincarnation is possible. In the descending direction, all human life—including religion—deteriorates, and deliverance is not possible. The two directions make one whole rotation of the wheel of time, a **kalpa** (Sanskrit for "eon"). Hindus think that a kalpa is 4.3 billion years; Jains haven't usually been that precise, but they do think that a kalpa is a very long time. Because Jains hold the universe to be eternal, without beginning or end, these kalpas repeat themselves forever, turning like an eternal wheel.

Unlike some forms of Hinduism and Buddhism, Jainism views the visible, physical world as real, not illusory. The world is eternal and uncreated. It did not come into existence, and it will not pass out of existence. The world is made up of five building blocks of reality: soul, matter, space, motion, and rest. These building blocks are eternal, and they interact constantly; this makes the cosmos and everything in it run.

Jains see the universe as having four parts. Hell is the lowest part; it has seven vertical levels, with the worst level at the bottom. Jain depictions of hell are meant to teach about the nature of evil and warn people away from it. The middle world has many concentric continents, all with life on them, separated by seas. At the center are the two continents where humans live, the only area where souls can achieve liberation. The heavenly world consists of twelve levels in two layers: one for the souls of those who are far from their deliverance and another just above it for those who are close to it. Souls become reincarnated from this heaven after a period of rest. At the top of the cosmos is the eternal home of souls that have permanently escaped the material world.

4-3c Jiva and Ajiva

According to Jains, the cosmos is made up of **jiva**, a soul made of a living substance, and **ajiva**, something not a soul, made of a substance that is not alive. Jiva is conscious of itself and the world; it is happy and energetic. Jivas, which are infinite in number, are either immobile or mobile. Immobile souls have only one sense: touch. They inhabit tiny particles of earth, water, fire, and air, and are also found in plants of all sorts. Mobile souls inhabit bodies and have between two and five sense organs.

As Jains say, just as a lamp can light up a large or small room, a jiva can fill any body it occupies. When the soul fills a body and takes on its shape, it causes the body to live. At death it keeps this shape until it is reincarnated again. Jainism is unique among many south Asian faiths in its teaching about souls: Individual souls are not parts of one cosmic soul to which they will return, but rather every soul (jiva) is eternally individual.

4-3d Karma and Liberation

Each soul in itself is pure. However, the soul is made impure through time by its contact with matter, or ajiva. When this ajiva influences the chain of birth and

Three stories of the Jain cosmos: heaven (top), earth, and hell.

COURTESY OF MR. SANJAY SURANA OF SHREE DIWAKAR PRAKASHAN

kalpa [CALL-puh] "Eon," one whole rotation of the wheel of time

jiva [JEE-vuh] Soul, a living substance

ajiva [AH-jee-vuh] Not a soul, an inanimate substance

death, it is called **karma**: deeds and the negative result of deeds. Karma is a form of matter so small that some modern Jains call it "fine," or even "atomic," dust. If the body that a soul inhabits dies, then that soul may be reborn in any of the four types of living beings: humans, animals, or plants on the earth; humans or other beings in heaven; or humans or other beings in hell.

Because of karma, a soul is confined in a series of bodies and must advance in spiritual development before becoming free from this confinement. To be free from karma and reincarnation, a Jain must stop collecting new karma and remove all previous karma. (Some Jains speak informally of "bad karma," but that is redundant, because all karma is bad.) Acquired karma can be "worn away" by many different activities: fasting, restricting one's diet to approved Jain foods, controlling taste and other senses, retreating to lonely places, strict discipline of the body, modesty, service, reading Jain scriptures, meditation, and controlling one's ego.

> Most Jains don't believe that anyone can reach liberation in the present period of cosmic decline.

Release from reincarnation, called—as in Hinduism—**moksha**, is the central teaching of Jainism. Moksha is prevented by karma that attaches to the soul, which makes it too heavy to ascend after the death of the body to the abode of the Jinas. Because it hasn't reached this permanent home, the soul must be reincarnated. This process also prevents self-realization, happiness, and freedom of the soul—all elements of Jain **nirvana**. People are called victors (*Jinas*) when they achieve spiritual freedom. This is accompanied by a great inner peace. Becoming liberated is difficult because it demands a near-perfect mental, moral, and physical observance of Jainism. Most Jains don't believe that anyone can

One step at a time to nirvana: A Jain priest praying in a Jain temple in Jaisalmer, India. He wears a cloth over his mouth to protect small flying insects.

karma [KAR-muh] Deeds and the negative result of deeds; small matter that attaches to the soul and causes it to be reborn after death

moksha [MOHK-shah] Release from reincarnation

nirvana [neer-VAH-nuh] In Jainism, the self-realization, happiness, and freedom of the soul

reach nirvana in the present period of cosmic decline. Thus, Jain nuns and monks do not seek immediate enlightenment. Instead, they practice Jainism as well as they can to pursue a reincarnation that will bring them closer to deliverance. In other words, they take one step at a time, in one life at a time, toward liberation.

4-3e Theories of Knowledge

In religions that give mediation a large role to play in the quest for deliverance, theories of knowledge can get complex, especially for nuns and monks. Jainism has theories of arising, change, and decay in a world of space and time that is real, as opposed to permanence based on a hidden spiritual reality (for many Hindus) or impermanence of all things (for

Buddhists). The Jains developed a complex theory of knowledge with four stages:

1. *Subjective knowledge* is ordinary observation, recognition, determination, and impression.
2. *Scripture knowledge* is based on one's reading and meditation on scriptures and general religious truths.
3. *Unmediated knowledge* involves supersensory perception (what we might call extrasensory perception, or ESP for short), reading the thoughts of others (clairvoyance), and knowing everything about other beings and things (omniscience).
4. *Direct, immediate knowledge* is knowledge of one's soul in its pure form; this brings freedom from reincarnation. A person with this knowledge is a **kevalin**, "possessor of omniscience."

Yoga—yoking of soul and body—is the best way to full knowledge and liberation. Yoga cultivates true knowledge and leads to faith in Jain teachings and a proper Jain lifestyle. It helps one reach the goal of Jainism: to free one's soul to reach its true nature.

4-4 Ethics: The Five Cardinal Virtues

A Jain blogger in Great Britain raises a question: Why do some people have extramarital affairs, sometimes one after the other? After discussing how common it might be among her friends and acquaintances, especially now that websites can facilitate such affairs, she goes deeper to analyze the possible causes. She invites comments on this observation from her Jain belief: Marital infidelity is caused by the attraction of evil masquerading as something positive. It leads to the loss of self-control and self-esteem, and ultimately it results in the accumulation of much karma.

Liberation from the cycle of reincarnation is the ultimate goal of Jains, but this isn't only accomplished by meditation and knowledge. Jains believe that one must first practice the following five moral principles in thought, speech, and action. They aren't "rules" as such, but ways to live according to the true nature of the soul. The principles are directed against practices that harm one's jiva, and harm others as well, by increasing its attachment to ajiva. Jain scriptures call them vows, particularly greater vows for monks and nuns and lesser vows for lay-folk. As these terms imply, the degree to which the principles are practiced is usually stricter for monastics than it is for

laity. Lay Jains are encouraged to practice them in a way that is appropriate to their life in the world, but nuns and monks must observe them rigorously.

4-4a Do No Harm; Speak the Truth

The first and fundamental moral command in Jainism is **ahimsa**: Do no harm to any other living being, whether human, animal, plant, or microscopic organism. Compassion for all life, both human and nonhuman, is central to Jainism. Ahimsa is sometimes interpreted as not physically harming another human, but it is much larger than that. One must not injure others physically or spiritually in thought, word, or deed. Jains have a strict diet (see "A Closer Look: Jainism and Food"), because all animals and many plants have souls, and to kill them causes their souls to undergo reincarnation. Mohandas Gandhi, the twentieth-century Hindu who led the struggle for Indian independence from Great Britain with nonviolent opposition, was deeply influenced by the Jain practice of ahimsa. Through Gandhi, nonviolent resistance to social evils spread to South Africa and the United States and became a part of their civil rights movements, and ahimsa found a wide, deep role in the world.

Long ago, due to ahimsa, all Jains gave up farming, which does harm to many souls in the soil. Jains went into commerce and finance instead, where they prospered. Today many Jains are also in the medical and engineering professions. Monks and nuns practice a strict form of ahimsa. They often wear a cloth over the mouth to avoid harming small insects near them, and they gently whisk away these insects as they walk along, and especially before they sit down. In sum, for monastics ahimsa entails taking no life at all. For laity, it prohibits taking life needlessly.

The second Jain virtue says that one must always speak the truth and never deceive others. This is an essential part of doing no harm. Saying and hearing the truth often depends on one's perspective, and Jains promote "not one-sidedness," the ability to see and explain all sides of an issue. So one must see that what one says is correctly understood and that true communication takes place. One must speak the truth as long as it does no harm. If speaking truth will lead to another person's harm, one should be silent. But lying to avoid harm is not an option.

kevalin [keh-VAHL-in] "Possessor of omniscience," a person who is free from reincarnation

ahimsa [ah-HIM-zuh] Doing no harm to any living being

A Closer Look

Jainism and Food

Jain vegetarianism is based on the principle of doing no harm to other living beings rather than on any principles of health and nutrition, and is more radical than Hindu vegetarianism. Monks and nuns follow these dietary practices strictly, and the laity in a basic (but still careful) way.

Jains practice a unique concept of extended vegetarianism. Not only do they eat no meat, but they also abstain from root vegetables such as potatoes, garlic, onions, mushrooms, and radishes. However, they consume rhizomes such as dried turmeric and dried ginger, and eat plantains. Root vegetables, which are grown underground, are believed to contain far more bacteria than other vegetables, and all these bacteria are living beings with souls. (Buddhists often refrain from onions, garlic, and other root vegetables, not because small beings live in them, but because the heat they cause in the body is thought to increase sexual desire.)

Jains refuse any food, whether from animals or plants, obtained with what they consider to be unnecessary cruelty. Many have a diet similar to veganism (no dairy products), in order to avoid harm to souls in processed dairy products such as cheese, although unpasteurized milk is a common drink. Observant Jains do not eat or drink between sunset and sunrise, when more harm is done to small living things because the cooking fire attracts insects that cannot be seen. Jains drink water that is gradually boiled for purification and then cooled to room temperature, to allow tiny beings to escape in the process.

CARY BATES/SHUTTERSTOCK

Root vegetables like these are forbidden in Jainism.

4-4b Do Not Steal; Do Not Be Possessive

The third and fourth commands, not to steal or be possessive, apply especially to Jain laity. Monks and nuns have only a few possessions (Shvetambars) or no possessions at all (Digambars). Jains must not take any object that is not willingly and fairly given. One must be satisfied with one's possessions, and then one will not steal. Also, one must labor, buy, and sell honestly. Any attempt to get the better of others financially is considered theft. Some particulars of do not steal are:

- Always give people a fair price for their labor or products. To use one's business power to force an unfair, harmful price is forbidden.

- Do not take things not explicitly given to you.

- Do not take things that other people leave, drop, or forget. Return these things if you can, or leave them where they are.

- Do not purchase things that are made in a way that does harm to others.

Because Jains have such strict norms for truth and honesty, they have a reputation in India for being scrupulously honest businesspeople. This in turn has contributed to their prosperity. Today, Jains are prominent in Indian businesses, and they dominate the diamond trade.

Possessiveness does not always result from owning things, but often results from emotional attachment to a possession. When that happens, one is owned by one's possessions, and a temptation to steal may arise. Nuns and monks must be nonpossessive when they enter the celibate state, having no lingering feelings for the possessions they left behind. By detaching oneself from possessions, including home and family, one takes a first step toward liberation. Householders are nonpossessive when they are not emotionally tied to the things they own. Householders are to relate to people and objects as their manager or steward, not as their owner. True nonpossessiveness also means that one can lose one's possessions without having it affect one's inner self.

4-4c Be Chaste

All sexual intercourse binds one to karma, so it is best to avoid it as much as possible. This includes thinking about it as well as doing it. For monastics, being chaste entails complete abstinence from all sexual intercourse and any other type of sexual activity. For them, chastity means celibacy. Lay Jains must be faithful within marriage. Sex outside of marriage is seen as particularly powerful in attracting karma.

To conclude this section on Jain ethics, in addition to keeping their version of these five principles, lay Jains who want a better reincarnation are urged to do a variety of things. Among them are to limit their travel, limit the number and value of their possessions, guard against avoidable evils, devote specific times to meditation, and observe periods of self-denial. Associating with monks and nuns is also urged, such as spending occasional days as a temporary nun or a monk, or giving alms in support of monastics.

4-5 Jain Ritual and Worship

Near Shravanabelagola, India, at the statue of Jain hero Gommateshvara, a variety of religious activities are taking place. At the foot of the massive statue, carved from a single piece of rock in 981 C.E., dozens of well-dressed Jains reverently place fruit and flowers as offerings to the hero. Coconuts are especially common. Devotees are sitting on mats, reading Jain scriptures, saying prayers and mantras, and meditating. At times they break out in song and dance, both celebratory and reverent. At the top of the statue, accessible by a flight of stairs, a group of Jain men prepare to pour buckets of colorful, fragrant liquids on Gommateshvara's head to venerate the statue and pay honor to the Jain ideal of finding release from reincarnation. When standing at the figure's feet, the worshipers must look up to see the inspiring vision of the Jina against the vastness of the sky. His face is designed to inspire serenity and peace in those who look on it in faith. (See the photograph in section 4-2b.)

4-5a The Life of Monks and Nuns

Monastics live lives of strong self-denial and self-control in order to liberate their souls at some point in their future lives. They have permanently left their families and spend their days in ritual activities: study of scripture, recitation of scripture, meditation, going on "begging rounds" for their main daily meal, and occasionally teaching laity. The entire life of nuns and monks is directed toward the eternal welfare and liberation of their souls. We should now look at some of the details of this life.

Monastics always walk, and always have bare feet, no matter the weather. They don't use any vehicle—such as an automobile, ship, plane, or even a cart—for traveling, because this harms more tiny beings than walking does. (No Jain monk traveled to Europe or North America until the 1890s, and when one did, his trip by ship was controversial among Jains.) By not wearing shoes, they can more easily avoid killing or injuring insects living on or in the soil. As they wander, they teach Jainism and give spiritual help to those they meet. Monks and nuns typically go around in groups of at least two. They stay only a few days in one location, except in the three months of the Indian rainy season. This constant movement is intended to inhibit personal attraction to material things and the people they meet.

Jain monastics neither cook their food nor have others cook it for them. They go once every day to Jain households and receive from each house a little uncooked food suitable for raw consumption (so householders don't have to prepare more food after the monks have departed). Unless a cook is very careful, the heat of

Mahavira plucks his hair in a fifteenth-century *Kalpa Sutra*.

the cooking process does violence to small creatures, as does vegetable chopping and water drinking; nuns and monks don't want to be a part of any violence. They don't accept any food or drink outside a house, but instead go inside where the food is cooked or kept, out of concern for small creatures more numerous outside than inside. When they return to their religious quarters, or to their temporary home if they are wandering, they eat their food in one main meal for each day, sometimes leaving a little for a smaller, unheated meal or a snack.

Jain monks and nuns don't shave their heads or even cut their hair, nor do they go to a barber. They regularly pluck out the hair on their head, or they have others do it. This plucking is a form of self-discipline and self-denial in which one bears pain calmly.

As stated previously, Digambar monks are traditionally naked at all times, but there are exceptions. Digambar nuns and all Shvetambar monastics wear unstitched white clothes. For a monk, a loincloth covers his midsection and reaches below the knee, another cloth covers the upper part of his body, and another cloth goes over his left shoulder and almost reaches his ankles. Monks also carry a bedsheet and a mat, both made of wool, to sit on. They have a piece of cloth, either in their hand or tied on their head, to cover their mouths. They use a small broom of soft woolen threads to clean away bugs before they sit or as they walk, especially outdoors. Digambar monks often have a broom and mouth cloth, but do not wear them or hang them from their bodies, because this could be considered a body covering that compromises their nakedness.

Monks and nuns give a blessing on all Jains they meet, especially the saying "May you attain spiritual prosperity." They make no distinctions between class or caste, or gender or age. Some put a little sandalwood dust on the heads of Jains as a sign of blessing. In sum, monastics teach the path of a righteous and self-controlled life to all Jains. At the end of their lives, as we saw previously, monastics and laity traditionally have the option to practice holy death. An estimated 450 holy deaths are accomplished every year among Jains in India, at times with great public celebration.

However, in August of 2015 a judge in the state of Rajasthan ruled that the practice was a form of suicide, which is illegal in India. The Indian Supreme Court then overturned this ruling, saying that holy death is a protected form of religious practice.

4-5b Life of the Laity in Worship and Devotion

Observant Jain laity have a number of daily rituals. Because Jainism arose in Hindu India and has existed mainly in India for more than two thousand years, many of these are adapted from Hinduism or formed in opposition to Hinduism. Ritual acts of compassion and ahimsa include spreading grain as food for birds and filtering or boiling water for one's drinking and cooking. Worship before Jain images kept in one's home—bowing to them and lighting a lamp in front of them—is the best way for Jains to start their day. Some Jains oppose these rituals as no better than Hindu worship, or even as superstition. Others recognize that, while the Jain idols have no spiritual power in themselves, the practice of venerating them daily promotes a reverent state of mind. Meditation is done early in the morning, and often at noon and night. It typically takes forty-eight minutes (twice the number of the twenty-four Tirthankaras) and has periods of quiet recollection and spoken prayer. It involves the letting go of all passions and negative attitudes and gaining a sense of purity and peace.

Jain woman in the Jain temple, Ranakpur, India

GARY YIM/SHUTTERSTOCK

The main prayer of Jainism is the **Namokar Mantra**. The term *mantra* correctly suggests that this prayer is brief. Jains say it in its original language of Sanskrit, in which *namokar* means "I bow." In English translation, it reads: "I bow to the Prophets. I bow to the Liberated Souls. I bow to the Spiritual Leaders. I bow to the Teachers. I bow to all the Holy Ones." This prayer, if spoken in true faith, is thought to destroy sins and obstacles and help the one who prays it to move down the road to liberation.

More elaborate worship is usually done in the temple. Jain temples in India are typically for individual worship and meditation, which can be carried out on any day at any time. In Europe and North America, the Jain community gathers for group activities. One enters a temple saying, "I bow to the Jina" and then banishes distracting thoughts about everyday affairs. Puja, which is ritual worship, involves several different activities:

- Ritual washing of the idol/image. Those present at this washing touch their heads with the fluid applied to the image.

- A series of prayers over three days in a temple to help remove karma that obstructs the rising of the soul, releasing it from reincarnation.

- Paying respect to the images of the Tirthankaras. This can take the form of bowing before them, sitting reverently in prayer or meditation in their presence, or making small offerings.

- A ritual of prayer focused on a lotus-shaped image that has the "five praiseworthy beings": a Tirthankara, a liberated soul, a religious teacher, a religious leader, and a monk. This image also depicts the "four qualities" that benefit one's soul: perception, knowledge, conduct, and austerity.

As we saw above, the members of some sects of Jainism do not worship or venerate the images found in temples. They will be found there at times, but not participating in any of these rites. Instead, they engage only in meditation and silent prayer in the temple.

Two performers participate in the annual Diwali Festival in Auckland, New Zealand.

4-5c Jain Funerals

The traditional Jain funeral ritual has these typical elements. Soon after death, the body is washed and dressed and put in a casket. A sandal-wood garland is placed on the body; flowers are not used, because they may carry small insects. A swastika, one of the symbols of Jainism, is placed near the deceased. Once the family arrives and it is time for the service, Jain songs and scriptures are recited for an hour. Eulogies are offered by family and friends. Family members then gather by the casket and apply various items to the body in a ritualized manner: a little water and rice is applied three times; then sandalwood powder; and, finally, clarified butter on the forehead, hands, and feet. Then they chant the Namokar Mantra and put more sandalwood powder on the body, a gold coin in the mouth, and a pearl under the lid of the right eye. The casket is then closed and taken to the place of cremation. In the West, this is a crematorium; in India, an outdoor location without any grass or insects is selected.

At the cremation site, the body is removed from its casket, disrobed, and washed with a wet cloth. It is then reclothed and covered entirely with a cloth. Meanwhile, a platform of wood is erected for an open-air cremation. The body is placed on the platform with logs of wood over it. Clarified butter, camphor, and sandalwood powder are sprinkled all over the body. The elder son walks around the body three times sprinkling water on it. Chanting the Namokar Mantra, he lights up the pyre. After the burning is done, milk is poured over the remains, which are then collected in bags. Then a hole is dug in the earth, the remains are placed in it, and salt is spread on it to hasten decomposition.

The Jains believe that the souls of the dead are reborn immediately. For them, death is a natural part of the cycle of life, death, and reincarnation.

Loud wailing, extended periods of mourning, and observing death anniversaries are not found in the Jain tradition.

Namokar Mantra
[NAHM-oh-kahr MAHN-truh] Main prayer of Jainism

4-5d Two Jain Festivals

Like other religions in India, Jainism has many festivals; and like other religious festivals, cultural and religious elements are mixed together in the celebrations. In what follows, we will deal briefly with the two main festivals, Paryusana and Diwali.

Paryusana (also spelled *Paryushan*) is the most important festival for Jains, an eight-day period that falls in August or September. Paryusana is a time to make amends for bad acts of the prior year; one engages in austerities to shed accumulated karma. It also helps to control the desire for sensual pleasures, preventing new karma. During this period, some people abstain from eating and drinking for all eight days, and some for three days, but it is obligatory to fast at least on the last day. Regular ceremonies are held in the temple, with readings of the *Kalpa Sutra*, the principal scripture for Shvetambars, to the congregation. On the final day of Paryusana, Jains seek forgiveness from family, friends, and foes for any wrong acts against them in the previous year. Shortly after Paryusana all Jains gather and eat dinner together, regardless of their socioeconomic status.

For Jains, **Diwali**, the Indian festival of lights, remembers Mahavira's death. Diwali falls at the end of the Indian calendar year, in October or November. The eighteen kings of northern India who, according to legend, were with Mahavira when he died, decided that the light of their master's knowledge would be best remembered by the lighting of lamps.

4-6 Jainism around the World Today

In Chicago, a thirtyish computer engineer named Churinder worships weekly at the Jain temple. Similar to other Jains around the world, Churinder offers prayers for his blessing in this world, and especially for eventual release from endless reincarnation. But there is another reason he comes to the temple, one not so spiritual: to talk to married Jain women who serve as unofficial matchmakers in his search for a suitable Jain wife. He is looking for a young woman who is educated and cultured, one who can live with him in Chicago. Even more, he wants a wife who is a faithful Jain, meditates every day, says her prayers, and observes a Jain diet. With their connections in India, the women are able to put Churinder in touch with a suitable partner there, to whom he soon becomes engaged.

Paryusana [PAR-YOO-SAHN-uh] Eight-day period of repentance and fasting

Diwali [dee-WALL-ee] Indian festival of lights; for Jains, marks the anniversary of Mahavira's death

4-6a Jainism in the West

For more than two thousand years, Jains stayed in India, faithful to their duty to minimize travel and the damage it does to other beings. It wasn't until the 1800s that Jainism became a more worldwide faith. As a result of age-old trading links, many Jains from western India settled in eastern African countries that were, similar to India, in the British Empire, especially Kenya, where the first Jain temple outside India was built, and Uganda. They pursued commerce and international trade. Political unrest in the 1960s forced many of them to relocate to the United Kingdom, where today they number about 30,000. Many Jain students came to Europe and North America for higher education, and most of them stayed there. They often distinguish themselves in their fields.

Jainism has tried to make as few accommodations as possible to life in the western world. It has not sought conversions, nor has it been interested in spreading its meditative methods among non-Jains. For instance, although Hindu forms of yoga have become widespread in the western world, Jain forms of yoga have not.

4-6b Jainism in North America

In North America, Jains have continued their traditional business and professional occupations with the same proportion of professions as in the United Kingdom: About 30 percent are engineers and 15 percent are in medicine, with others in banking, real estate, computers, and teaching. The high point of Jain immigration to the West was in the late 1970s and 1980s. In the United States, Jains number approximately 30,000, and in Canada about 10,000. Because of their prosperity, and because Jains in North America are concentrated in ten states in the United States and one province in Canada, the Jain community has been able to build and operate over sixty social centers, temples, and other organizations. These uses are often combined in one building.

Jain temples sponsor worship (often held on Sunday mornings to fit a western weekly calendar), education, and social fellowship. Although they have strong lay leadership, Jain temples in North America typically have no monks attached to them, so they function with little of the contact between monastics and laity common in India. Another distinctive feature of North American temples and social centers is that they generally accommodate all the different Jain groups to which their members belong. In this way, they further Jain unity and survival in a North American context that makes sectarian differences less important than in India.

A desire to preserve their religious identity in North America, and the increasing challenges of passing on their faith to second and third generations, has led Jains to form organizations such as the Federation of Jain Associations in North America (**JAINA**) founded in 1981. Like most local Jain temples and cultural associations, JAINA crosses the lines of regional Indian customs and the different Jaina sects. English-language publications such as the *eJain Digest* (available online) and *Jain Spirit* have presented Jain ideals such as nonviolence and vegetarianism to the faithful and the wider world. Recently, Jains have been addressing issues of environmentalism. Their religious convictions that the world is eternal and that one must do no harm to all its living beings strengthen their interest in a sustainable planet.

JAINA Federation of Jain Associations in North America, the leading Jain organization in North America

STUDY TOOLS 4

READY TO STUDY?
ONLINE ON MINDTAP, YOU CAN:

- ☐ Download the Chapter Review Card, which includes key terms and chapter summaries.
- ☐ Learn about the Jain hero Gommateshvara in a short video.
- ☐ Explore the world of Jain bloggers, and sites like the Jain Center of New York.
- ☐ Interact with figures from the text to check your understanding.
- ☐ Prepare for tests with quizzes.
- ☐ Review the key terms with Flash Cards.

BONNIE VAN VOORST © CENGAGE LEARNING

Jainism Timeline: 600s B.C.E.–1990s C.E.

1000 B.C.E.

600s B.C.E.
Parshvanatha, 23rd Tirthankara

599–527 B.C.E.
Mahavira, 24th Tirthankara, founder of Jainism

500 B.C.E.

460–360 B.C.E.
Beginning of formal Digambar–Shvetambar split

0

400s C.E.
Formation of the Shvetambar canon, the *Siddhanta*; scripture arises for Digambar communities

500

981
Carving of Gommateshvara statue at Shravanabelagola

1000

1000
Digambars migrate from south India to northwest India

1100
Shvetambar community of monks and laity concentrates in Gujarat

1500

1900
Mohandas Gandhi befriends a Jain layman and is influenced by Jainism

1971
Chitrabhanu travels to the United States, founds the Jain International Meditation Center

1983
Formal organization of Jain Associations in North America (JAINA)

1974
Saman Suttam, statement of belief common to all Jains

1990s
Jain temples built in Chicago, Cincinnati, Dayton, Detroit, and Orlando

2000

5
Encountering Buddhism: The Middle Path to Liberation

FEESNINJO/SHUTTERSTOCK.COM

LEARNING OUTCOMES

After studying this chapter, you will be able to do the following:

5-1 Explain the meaning of *Buddhism* and related terms.

5-2 Summarize how Buddhism was founded and developed into what it is today.

5-3 Outline the essential Buddhist teachings.

5-4 State the main ethical precepts of Buddhism for both monastics and laypeople.

5-5 Discuss the way Buddhists worship and meditate.

5-6 State the main features of Buddhist life around the world today, especially in North America.

"I take refuge in the Buddha; I take refuge in the Dharma; I take refuge in the Sangha." —Basic Buddhist affirmation

Your Visit to a Zen Retreat Center

Imagine that you're going on a weekend retreat to a Zen Buddhist temple and retreat center. You've read some popular books on Zen and can recite a few Zen riddles. The retreat will take you to Singapore in south Asia, but Zen centers in North America from Woodstock, New York, to San Diego, California, hold similar retreats.

As you walk into the temple, you notice a comfortable area where visitors can relax at a café near the entrance. You'll return there regularly during rest time during the retreat. It gives an impression of simplicity that is reflected in the whole retreat center. You then sign in and are required to surrender your cell phone—it will be given back when you leave, you are told. You are shown to your dormitory, where you notice about thirty woven straw mats in one large room, much like the sleeping arrangements in a Buddhist monastery.

Then you go to the main meditation hall. Meditation cushions have been neatly laid out throughout the hall, which has a white statue of the Buddha with small arrangements of flowers and small votive candles (but no incense) at one end. A drum and handbell are at the front. You begin each day with yoga and stretching exercises, so that the physical process of sitting in meditation won't distract your mind. Then come Buddhist prayers, both spoken and meditated, for thirty minutes each. The main part of each day is dedicated to several meditation sittings. They are only thirty minutes long and go quickly, with exercises such as yoga between them. The monks leading the retreat give regular lectures as well as informal talks. You learn three different ways to meditate: breath meditation, self-questioning meditation, and "silent observation of the mind" meditation. The

> Gautama Buddha, seated in meditation, is a prominent symbol of Buddhism. For Buddhists its meanings range from calmness to full Nirvana. Here Buddhists offer gifts and reverence at a shrine in a park in Anuradhapura, Sri Lanka.

A Buddhist monk meditates in a temple in Myanmar.

time at the retreat center also teaches you eight sitting positions and two sleeping positions.

The monks awaken you at 5:00 A.M., and lights-out is at 9:30 P.M. Three meals a day, all freshly prepared according to Buddhist dietary customs, are served buffet style. You are thankful that you don't have to go out begging for your food every morning as many Buddhist monks do. You are surprised how hungry you get, and how good the food tastes, but then you remember with a little guilty feeling not to develop an attachment to the food—that's not Buddhist at all! So you quietly resolve not to go up for seconds any longer.

At the end of the retreat, you have your first and only small-group session to share experiences from the past three days. When you finally leave the retreat center with a friend, you notice that your "silent observation of the mind" meditation is continuing. You take in all the sights and sounds of the city, but your mind isn't affected by it. Your friend remarks, referring to the film, "It's like living in the Matrix!"

Encountering Buddhism can be a "mind-bending" experience. As you are introduced to Buddhism in this chapter, you will notice these features:

- Buddhism has many numbered lists of teachings and practices, but Buddhism can't be known, much less lived, by the numbers.

- Because all Buddhist teaching is said to flow from the Buddha and his carefully conceived system, we might expect it to be unified. However, Buddhism grew into a diverse religion, befitting its teaching that all things are impermanent.

- Buddhists follow the teachings of the Buddha as the best model of the way to find liberation. But they also frequently quote the Buddha's saying, "Don't believe because of what your teacher says—follow your own wisdom."

- Many Buddhists have no concept of an all-powerful god, but some Buddhists view the Buddha as a supreme heavenly being.

- Buddhism has a combination of deep meditation and earnest morality, but Buddhists in Asia who aren't monks or nuns don't meditate all that regularly. Instead, they worship various buddhas and other divinities in ways that are similar to Hindu worship. (Buddhists in the western world meditate more regularly.)

- It is common for people who call themselves Buddhists—especially in China, Japan, and the West—to

> Buddhism has a combination of deep meditation and earnest morality.

also practice other religions. Moreover, they often say, "People of other religions can practice Buddhism, too."

5-1 The Name *Buddhism*

Buddhism is the religion founded by Siddhartha Gautama (sih-DAHR-tuh GOW-tah-muh), who became the Buddha. Despite the similarity of the words *Buddhism* and *Buddha*, the religion isn't named after him. **Buddhism** means the religion of enlightenment, not the religion of the Buddha. The English word *Buddhism* didn't appear until the 1830s, but it expresses accurately enough designations used by Buddhists, such as *Buddha Law, Buddha School,* or the *Teachings of the Buddha*. Today, *Buddhism* is used as the name for their religion by Buddhists in Europe and North America, and it is widely accepted in Asia as well. (For more on Buddhism as the religion of enlightenment, see the "Symbol of Buddhism" box.) The related term the **Buddha**, or Enlightened One, usually refers to Siddhartha Gautama after his enlightenment. Both words derive from the ancient Sanskrit word *buddha*, "enlightened, awakened." *Buddhism* and *Buddha* are correctly pronounced BUHD-ihz-um and BUHD-ah, respectively, with first syllables rhyming with *could*, but you will often hear BOOD-ihz-um and BOO-dah.

Buddhism teaches that anyone can become enlightened, and even become a buddha. Gautama is the model Buddha, but many Buddhists believe that he taught his followers to think for themselves and carefully examine the teachings of the religion to determine what is right for them. When anyone becomes fully enlightened that person is a buddha too. So the word *Buddha* is a term, not a personal name, as mentioned previously. We'll stay true to this by referring in this

Buddhism [BUHD-ihz-um] Religion of enlightenment

Buddha [BUH-dah] "Enlightened One"; although Gautama is "the Buddha," the term applies to all who attain enlightenment

© DARIUSH M/SHUTTERSTOCK.COM

Zen temple in Japan

A Closer Look

The Symbol of Buddhism

Buddhism is a diverse religion, and it is difficult to express in art the state of nirvana that the Buddha achieved, so Buddhism has a number of symbols. The swastika is one, seen often in temples and jewelry; the beautiful lotus blossom that grows out of the muck of the world is another; the deer is a third, especially used to symbolize Buddhist teaching; and the image of the Buddha in seated meditation is a fourth.

By far the most common Buddhist symbol, and perhaps the earliest, is the wheel. This is called the **dharmachakra**, "wheel of the teaching." It may look to you like the steering wheel of a ship, but it's really the wheel of a cart or chariot. Similar to other ancient religious symbols, it has multiple

BONNIE VAN VOORST © CENGAGE LEARNING

Figure 5.1 "Wheel of the teaching," symbol of Buddhism

STEVE ALLEN/GETTY IMAGES

Buddhist wheel with deer on the roof of Jokhang Temple, Lhasa, Tibet

layers of meaning. First, the Buddha "turned the wheel of the teaching" to get his movement going. Second, the dharmachakra's implied motion is a symbol of the spiritual change created by Buddhism. Third, the different parts of the wheel summarize Buddhism. The rim represents the endless cycle of rebirth, escaped only by following Buddhist teachings to enlightenment. The eight spokes stand for the Noble Eightfold Path taught by the Buddha. Finally, the wheel's hub symbolizes moral self-discipline, the first step to enlightenment (see Figure 5.1.)

The dharmachakra was a familiar symbol in early Buddhism. It stood for the Buddha's teachings and for the Buddha himself. Today, the dharmachakra is used in every Buddhist land. In statues of the Buddha, a wheel is sometimes seen in his palms and on the soles of his feet. It also appears when he holds his hands in the circular dharmachakra position.

---

chapter to *the Buddha*, with *the* and a capital *B*, when Gautama is meant. When another person who achieves the buddha nature is meant, we will omit *the* and use a lowercase *b*.

5-2 Buddhism Today as Shaped by Its Past

In Beijing, a two-foot tall robot monk has captivated China since 2016 by dispensing Buddhist teachings. His full name means Worthy Stupid Robot Monk, but human monks are quick to explain that "stupid" is really a term of endearment. Dressed in an orange monk's robe, the robot monk has a touch pad on his chest that allows him to receive basic questions, such as "Why am I not satisfied with my life?" He typically gives challenging, Zen-like responses

to these questions. For example, he responds to this question by saying, "If you aren't satisfied with your life, what can anybody else do about it?" Despite the popularity of this robot, which draws thousands of visitors to his temple every month, there are no plans at present to make other robot monks.

Today's Buddhism has a long and significant history behind it. Buddhists believe that Siddhartha Gautama discovered the **Middle Path** out of suffering, a new way between the extreme self-denial characteristics of Hindu renunciants and the ordinary life of the Hindu householder.

dharmachakra [DAHR-muh-CHAHK-ruh] "Wheel of the teaching," a symbol of Buddhism

Middle Path Style of life between extreme self-denial and ordinary life that can lead to enlightenment

The Buddha teaching monks, sculpture in Wat Charkyai, Thailand. This common scene in Buddhist art shows the importance of monasticism in the Buddhist religion.

story and introduce its diverse groups and teachings along the way.

5-2a Gautama's Road to Enlightenment

Buddhism is founded on the life of Siddhartha Gautama (in the Pali language, in which many Buddhist scriptures are written, *Siddhatha Gotama*). His life is known through scriptures written hundreds of years after his death. As Damien Keown has said, by the time the scriptures were written, the story of the Buddha's life "had become embellished with fanciful details, which makes it difficult to separate fact from legend."[2] Nevertheless, scholars have managed to discern in them a reliable outline of his life. This life is not what we would consider a modern biography, because Buddhist scriptures speak of only four key events in the Buddha's life: birth, enlightenment, first sermon, and death.

Gautama reached the full enlightenment that rescued him from constant reincarnation into this world. The Middle Path is built on Hindu ideas of the time and uses some similar vocabulary, but, by and large, Buddhism from the first was an alternative to Hinduism. The Buddha then taught his discovery to a monastic community that he founded. After his death, his teachings spread throughout the Indian subcontinent, and then, over the next thousand years, to the largest part of Asia. In modern times, Buddhism has come to the West and has become probably the most influential religion from Asia. With between 400 and 450 million adherents throughout the world, Buddhism is the fourth largest religion today. The 2015 Pew Center study, "The Future of World Religions," predicts that the percentage of the world's population that is Buddhist will decrease from about 7 percent in 2010 to 5 percent in 2050. In North America, however, the Buddhist population is projected to grow from 3.9 million in 2010 (or 1.1 percent of North America's population) to nearly 6.1 million in 2050 (1.4 percent).[1] This section will recount Buddhism's

> The story of the Buddha's life "had become embellished with fanciful details, which makes it difficult to separate fact from legend."
>
> —Damien Keown

Siddhartha Gautama was born into a royal family in the northern Ganges River valley, in what is today southern Nepal, and lived for eighty years. Scholars disagree on the dates of his life. The dating of his lifespan ranges from 570 B.C.E. to 300 B.C.E., but recent research based on archaeological excavations of the earliest Buddhist sites tends toward around the 500s B.C.E. His family name was Gautama and his personal name was Siddhartha, but in the custom of the times, his family name is used more than his first name. In Buddhist scriptures, his followers do not call him "Buddha," but "Lord." Another common name for the Buddha is **Shakyamuni**, "the sage of the Shakyas," referring to the clan to which Gautama belonged.

Gautama's parents were Hindus in the Kshatriya caste of warriors and rulers. An astrologer told his father, King Suddhodana, that his son would either become a powerful emperor or renounce this to become a powerful religious leader. Queen Maya dreamed one

Shakyamuni [SHAK-yah-MOO-nee] "The sage of the Shakyas" clan, another name for the Buddha

night that a baby elephant came into her womb through her side. Ten lunar months later, her son was born from her right side. The whole earth reacted to his birth, and when baby Gautama alighted by his own power on the ground, he proclaimed, "I am born for the salvation of the world; this is my last rebirth." These are probably legendary touches, but not legendary is the sad fact that Maya died a few days after Gautama's birth. Both ancient Buddhist texts and modern scholarship are divided over what role this may have played in Gautama's enlightenment.[3] Gautama's early life as a prince was affluent and comfortable, protected from the ills of the world. At age sixteen he married the Princess Yashodhara, with whom he had a son. Until he was twenty-nine Gautama had a privileged, luxurious life as he waited to become king. However, this would soon change.

The story of the Buddha's enlightenment begins with a profound experience he had during the **Four Passing Sights**. On chariot rides outside the palace, Gautama saw for the first time: (1) an old person, (2) a gravely ill person, (3) a human body on the way to cremation, and (4) a holy man who had renounced ordinary life. He was so impacted by these Four Passing Sights that he renounced his wealth, his throne, and his family in order to become a holy man and answer his religious questions. During the next seven years, he received instruction from several Hindu teachers and practiced meditation with them. With five companions who were also holy men, he practiced extreme mental and physical self-denial that reduced him to "skin and bones." Eventually he passed out from weakness, and when he regained consciousness, he knew that this extreme self-denial wouldn't lead to his goal. Instead, it weakened his mind and even threatened his life. He then devised the Middle Path that could lead to enlightenment. Hindus taught that both the householder state and the renunciant state were valid, but the Buddha forged a new path between them.

5-2b Achievement of Enlightenment

Living in this Middle Path, the prince sat in long meditation under a tree in the city of Bodh Gaya (bohd GUY-uh) and achieved his own enlightenment. He reached an understanding of life that he would soon teach to his followers. Under the tree, called in Buddhist tradition the **Bodhi Tree**, or "Bo Tree" for short, he became *the Buddha*. Not only did he gain perfect knowledge of himself and the release this brought, but he also attained full knowledge of all his past lives. He could have passed immediately from life into full release, but he postponed this in order to help others find the way to liberation. From this point on, Buddhist scriptures call him the **Tathagata**, "one who has gone" to enlightenment, and the Buddha insisted that his followers call him by this name. The Bodhi Tree that stands in Bodh Gaya today has become one of the holiest sites in all Buddhism.

The Buddha then taught publicly in a deer park in Sarnath, India, announcing his discovery of the Four Noble Truths and the Noble Eightfold Path, teachings that we'll consider next. For the next forty-five years, the Buddha taught throughout northeastern India and established an order of monks called the **sangha**, or community. In fact, Buddhism became the first of the world's religions to develop

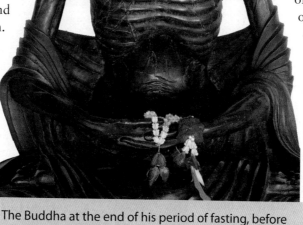

© JAVARMAN/SHUTTERSTOCK.COM

The Buddha at the end of his period of fasting, before discovering the Middle Path. Larger Buddhist temples will often have this statue.

"Decay is inherent in all things; work out your salvation with diligence!"

—last words of the Buddha

Four Passing Sights
Gautama's encounter with old age, sickness, death, and an ascetic

Bodhi Tree [BOH-dee]
Tree in Bodh Gaya under which Gautama Buddha gained enlightenment

Tathagata [tah-THAH-gah-tuh] "One who has gone" to enlightenment; honorific term for the Buddha

sangha [SAHN-guh] Community of Buddhist monastics

Traditional Thai style painting of the Buddha on a temple wall. Note that the Buddha is no longer painfully thin.

monasticism (muh-NAS-tuh-siz-uhm), a life of meditation, prayer, and self-control in a tightly regulated community of monks or nuns. (Sometimes lay Buddhists call their organizations a sangha, but this is not the original or historic use of the term.) All Buddhists are called upon to profess the **Three Refuges**: "I take refuge in the Buddha; I take refuge in the dharma; I take refuge in the Sangha." The Buddha began the practice of going into the streets every morning on begging rounds to collect food, freeing up more time for the inner life. He received the support of kings and merchants, and his movement thrived. The Buddha refused to appoint any successor to guide his movement after his death, making the community of monks his only successor instead.

At about the age of eighty, the Buddha became seriously ill in Kusinara (koo-sin-AHR-uh) and knew he would soon die. Some older scholarship suggested that he ate a bad piece of pork and got food poisoning, but many scholars now think that this is unlikely in light of his strict vegetarianism. He met with his disciples for the last time to impart his final instructions, ending with the words, "Decay is inherent in all things;

Three Refuges Basic Buddhist statement: "I take refuge in the Buddha; I take refuge in the dharma; I take refuge in the sangha."

parinirvana [PAHR-ee-neer-VAHN-uh] The Buddha's entry into full nirvana at his death

work out your salvation with diligence!" He then lay down on his right side and went into meditation. He passed through several levels of meditative trance until, when he died, he entered full nirvana, an event called his **parinirvana**. His body was cremated on an open pyre according to Indian custom. His followers decided that the small parts of his body that remained—wood-fire cremation doesn't reduce stronger bones and teeth to ash—would be distributed as relics and enshrined in monuments.

After the Buddha's funeral, hundreds of monks met in Rajagrha (rahj-AHG-ruh), India. The monastic rules and the teachings of the Buddha were finalized and formally recited. These rules, called the *Vinaya* (vihn-IGH-uh), were an oral collection for more than two centuries. The rules and teachings were recited and memorized at the council, and would soon be used in spreading the

Buddhist laity and some monks at the Bodhi ("enlightenment") Tree, Mahabodhi Temple, Bodh Gaya, India.

religion to the many peoples and languages of India. Over time they would be written down and come to form the most important part of Buddhist scripture.

5-2c India, Sri Lanka, and Theravada

Buddhism became more diverse as it spread. A significant point of diversity arose at the second Buddhist council, around 375 B.C.E. After debates between those who advocated keeping strictly to what they considered the earliest practices of Buddhism and those advocating change, the second group left and called itself the "Great Sangha." This group belittled the traditionalists as **Hinayana**, or "small vehicle" Buddhists, but the traditionalists' self-designation of **Theravada** eventually stuck. This name is usually translated as "tradition of the elders," but more accurately means "original/abiding teaching." The Theravadins themselves experienced disagreements that led to a number of splinters. Over time, eighteen different Theravadin groups developed, each with its own distinctive teachings that spread throughout India and Southeast Asia. Today, only one of these groups survives, in Sri Lankan Theravada.

The next momentous event in the development of Buddhism was the meeting of a Buddhist monk and the third-century B.C.E. Indian ruler named Ashoka (ah-SHOHK-uh). A ruler of the large Mauryan (MOHR-yuhn) Empire in India, Ashoka had expanded it until it covered modern-day India. But he had become deeply troubled by the bloodshed he caused in his conquests. Listening to the monk convinced Ashoka to devote himself to the peaceful message of Buddhism. Ashoka erected thousands of rock pillars all over his kingdom with the teachings of the Buddha carved into them—the first written evidence we have of Buddhism. He didn't make Buddhism the official religion of the Mauryan Empire, but he did support it in various ways, including building Buddhist monasteries and schools of higher learning. More importantly, Ashoka sent monks as missionaries all over India and to several foreign lands in south Asia, from which Buddhism would eventually travel to the rest of Asia and the world. Ashoka sent his son and daughter, both of them Buddhist monastics, to

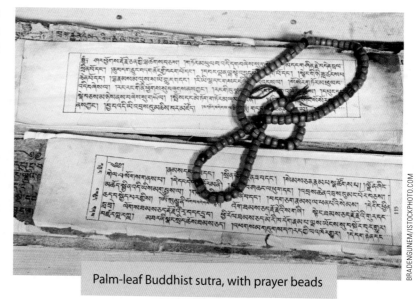

Palm-leaf Buddhist sutra, with prayer beads

> Buddhism has been a missionary religion in ways that other Indian religions haven't.

Sri Lanka (Ceylon)—an island nation just off the southern Indian coast—around the year 240 B.C.E. Its king was converted, and his kingdom went with him into Buddhism. One of the gifts for the king that Ashoka's children took with them was a cutting from the original Bodhi Tree. Trees said to have descended from this cutting can still be found in Sri Lanka. Buddhism has been a missionary religion in ways that other Indian religions haven't, a fact that is directly traceable to Ashoka.

Sri Lanka was the site of the fourth Buddhist council in the first century B.C.E. For the first time, all **sutras** (scriptures) were recorded in writing on palm leaves and in the Pali language. Much of our knowledge of Buddhism stems from this early sutra collection. It is formally known as the **Tipitaka**, or "Three Baskets." The three pitakas are the *Vinaya Pitaka* (basket of rules for monastics), the *Sutta Pitaka* (basket of the Buddha's teachings), and the *Abhidamma* (AH-bih-DAHM-uh) *Pitaka* (the higher teaching basket, for monks).

Hinayana [HIN-ah-YAHN-uh] "Small vehicle" of southern Buddhism known more commonly as Theravada

Theravada [TAIR-uh-VAH-duh] "Original/ abiding teaching," main name of southern branch of Buddhism

sutra [SOO-truh] Canonical scripture text

Tipitaka [TIH-pee-TAH-kuh] "Three Baskets," the main internal divisions of the canon (Sanskrit: *Tripitaka*)

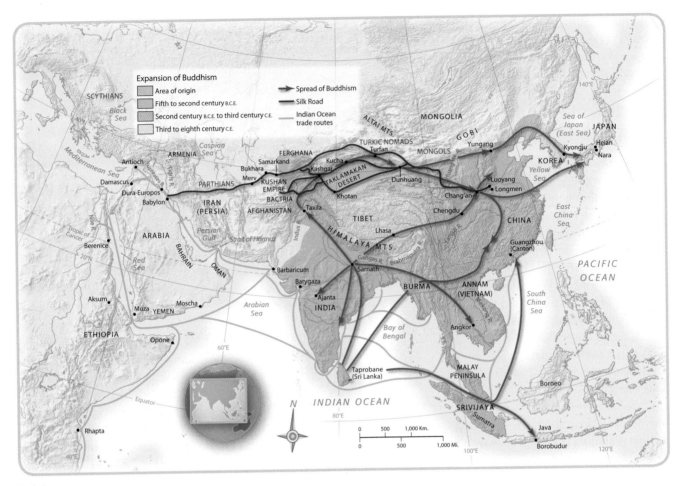

Map 5.1

Spread of Buddhism in Asia, 400 B.C.E.–800 C.E.

Buddhism originated in what is today Nepal and soon became a major religion in India. From India it spread to present-day Sri Lanka, and then to central and Southeast Asia, China, Korea, Japan, and finally Tibet.

Historians today agree that Sri Lankan monks saved the Theravada branch of Buddhism from extinction. It had spread in early years to Sri Lanka and other parts of Southeast Asia, while it declined in India. In fact, it nearly died out twice in its homeland in the northern parts of the Indian subcontinent, first when a revived Hinduism reduced its numbers, and again when India was largely taken over by Muslims in the 1500s C.E. Only Sri Lankan Buddhism survived, becoming the oldest form of Buddhism in the world. Theravada monks from Sri Lanka brought Buddhism to Myanmar (MEE-ahn-mahr, formerly called Burma), Thailand, Malaysia, Cambodia, Vietnam, and Laos (lous) (see Map 5.1).

Mahayana [MAH-hah-YAHN-uh] "Large vehicle" branch of Buddhism in northern and eastern Asia

Trikaya [TRIH-KIGH-yuh] Three bodies of the Buddha: the historical Gautama Buddha, many heavenly buddhas, and the Buddhist teaching

5-2d The Rise of Mahayana: China and Japan

Mahayana—the "large vehicle" branch of Buddhism found today in China, Japan, and Tibet—was a development of the split at the first Buddhist council. The monks of the Great Sangha held that Buddhism should be a large community, not just a vehicle for monks. They wanted to allow Buddhist layfolk to have a much greater participation in Buddhism than before. This meant that adaptation to indigenous religions was easier for Mahayanists, although Theravadins made accommodations as well. People would convert to Mahayana Buddhism more easily if some of their gods and religious practices were a part of it. So the doctrine of **Trikaya**, the three bodies of the Buddha, was developed. The historical Gautama Buddha was his first body, his second body was that of many heavenly buddhas adapted from other religions, and his abstract third body was the Buddhist teaching itself.

More significant in Mahayana was the increased importance of the **bodhisattva**, or buddha-to-be, someone who has attained enlightenment but compassionately remains in this suffering world to bring others to enlightenment. Local divinities, spirits, and heroes of other religions were often reinterpreted as bodhisattvas, and they became the objects of Buddhist worship in order to bring adherents closer to nirvana. New scriptures soon arose to explain these new teachings and practices. Mahayana Buddhists believe that they come from the Buddha himself, even though some of their leading ideas are new to Buddhism.

> ## "I preach with ever the same voice."
> —The Buddha

One of the scriptures, the *Diamond Sutra*, defends its new teaching by having the Buddha say, "I preach with ever the same voice." However, the differences between Theravada and Mahayana teachings are unmistakable. At the root of these differences is the belief in Theravada Buddhism that individuals must find the way to nirvana on their own. Mahayana Buddhists believe that others—especially the Buddha and bodhisattvas—must help the individual find nirvana, or in some Mahayana groups simply give it to them.

China already had two main religions, Confucianism and Daoism (Taoism). Both religions, but especially Daoism, had elements of folk religions reaching back to the dawn of human life in China. Folk religion consisted of local gods and nature spirits, mythologies, astrology, divination, magic, folk medicine, and so on. Over time, the Mahayana beliefs that began in India became a truly large vehicle, spreading to China and later to Korea, Japan, Nepal, and Vietnam. Many historians also consider Buddhism in Tibet to be a part of Mahayana, but it is also commonly

A Buddhist nature-spirit statue

considered a third vehicle. So what began as a small protest by monks soon after the death of the Buddha would become—after a long period of adaptation—the dominant form of Buddhism in northern and central Asia as well as the third main religion of China and the principal faith of Japan. Ultimately, it would become the branch of Buddhism best known in North America and Europe.

The different Buddhist groups in China and Japan illustrate the diversity within Mahayana. The Pure Land School of Buddhism soon became a leading Mahayana group. The Pure Land Sutra speaks of Amitabha (ah-mee-TAB-uh; in Japanese, Amida) Buddha and his "Pure Land," or heaven. If one can be reborn there, one can easily achieve nirvana. For millennia, the people of China had sacrificed to gods and goddesses; venerated their ancestors; prayed for the health of their families, animals, and crops; hoped for heaven and feared hell; and so on. The Chinese found that Mahayana Buddhism met these needs and habits. The growing conviction that this period of time was one of religious decline helped along the idea that people could not reach enlightenment by themselves, but could rely on the power of higher beings to bring them to enlightenment. Amitabha Buddha and his heavenly Western Paradise (the Pure Land) fit this idea. All one has to do, Pure Land Buddhism says, is faithfully chant the name of Buddha, and when that worshiper dies, he or she goes to the Pure Land. This is not nirvana itself, but rather a place in which the obtaining of nirvana is easy.

Another Buddhist group that arose in China was Ch'an (chahn), better known by its Japanese name, **Zen**. The Indian monk Bodhidharma came to China around 520 C.E., bringing the "silent transmission" of secret teaching about enlightenment that supposedly reached back to the Buddha. He became the founder of Zen. Zen Buddhism focuses on developing the immediate awareness of a "Buddha mind" through meditation on emptiness. One of the methods for inducing this sudden awareness has been the **koan**, a Zen riddle meant to help reach nonrational enlightenment (see "A Closer Look: Koans"). Because Zen

bodhisattva [BOHD-ee-SAHT-vuh] "Buddha-to-be," one who comes very close to achieving full buddha nature but postpones it to help others

Zen Buddhist group that aims for the immediate acquiring of a "buddha mind"

koan [KOH-an] Zen riddle meant to induce nonrational enlightenment

LIONELT/ISTOCKPHOTO.COM

Buddhism's accommodation to ancestor worship: offerings at a "spirit house."

from around 1000 C.E.; and *The Gateless Gate*, from around 1200 C.E.

Buddhist legend says that a group of Korean monks came to Japan with gifts for its emperor in 538 C.E. Among these gifts were a bronze Buddha and several sutras. After rejecting Buddhism and even throwing the gifts into the sea, the imperial court of the 600s was then drawn to the religion. Although Buddhism began in the Japanese aristocracy, in the 900s the Pure Land group became popular among the lower classes. In the 1200s, Ch'an came to Japan, where it was met with an enthusiastic response by the Samurai warrior class, among others, and renamed *Zen*. Two Japanese Buddhist monks took Zen back to Japan after having studied it in China. One introduced the Rinzai branch of Ch'an/Zen, with its koans to punish the mind and physical blows to punish the body. The other brought in the more sedate Soto (SOH-toh). Both forms of Zen have always had an artistic side, and Japanese Zen monks developed an elegant but simple style of writing, drawing, and painting. The tea ceremony, known for its sophisticated simplicity, also became expressive of Zen, as did the seventeen-syllable poems known as *haiku* (HIGH-koo). Perhaps the best-known haiku is *Old Pond*: "Old pond / a frog leaps in / water's sound." Zen became more important in Japanese Buddhism than it had been in Chinese Buddhism. From Japan, Zen would spread in the twentieth century to Europe and North America.

riddles and the process of administering them could be intellectually brutal, they were especially used in the Rinzai (RIHN-zigh) school of Zen that we will discuss next. Zen is known for rejecting the written word and for its sometimes rough physical tactics. Rinzai abbots can and do strike monks with a stick or baton if they do not like their answers, or if the monks get sleepy during the prolonged sitting meditation called **zazen**. Although a common picture from Zen history is of Bodhidharma ripping up a Buddhist scripture book, Zen Buddhists do have an appreciation for the Buddhist tradition even when they are seemingly ignoring or belittling it. Zen has contributed key books to the Mahayana canon, especially the *Platform Sutra*, written by Hui Neng, the sixth Zen patriarch, around 700 C.E.; the *Blue Cliff Record*,

> "What did your face look like before you were born?"
>
> —Zen koan (riddle)

A final Japanese innovation to be considered here was led by Nichiren (NEE-shee-rehn), a monk who lived from 1222 to 1282. He came to believe that the *Lotus Sutra* contained everything Buddhists needed. So Nichiren encouraged his students to chant the saying "I devote myself to the wonderful Law of the *Lotus Sutra*." This alone ensured enlightenment in this life. He argued that other groups of Buddhists had little value, reflecting a rare type of Buddhist intolerance that earned him opposition from other Buddhists. The Nichiren School nevertheless proved to be a highly popular form of Buddhism in Japan; even today it is the largest Buddhist group there.

5-2e Tibet and the Diamond Vehicle

Buddhism arrived in Tibet in the 700s C.E. when an Indian monk skilled in Buddhist Tantrism, named Rinpoché (RIHN-poh-shay), is said in Buddhist

zazen [ZAH-zehn] Seated meditation in Zen Buddhism

Japanese daruma dolls depicting Bodhidharma suggest his unconventionality.

© HENRY WILLIAM FU/SHUTTERSTOCK.COM

A Closer Look

Koans

In the West, koans are known as short, independent riddles employed in Rinzai Zen. Some of the more famous are these:

- What did your face look like before you were born?
- What is the sound of one hand clapping?
- Why did Bodhidharma come from the west?
- If you meet the Buddha, should you not kill him?

However, in Zen, koans typically come in the context of a short story. This story does not make gaining sudden insight from the koan any easier, but it does provide a context and an opportunity for sudden insight.

Here is one of these stories, centered on the koan "How many virtues does a cup have?"

Zen master Ummon inquired of a teaching monk, "What sutra are you talking about?"
"The *Nirvana Sutra*," the monk answered.

"The *Nirvana Sutra* speaks of the Four Virtues, doesn't it?"
"Yes, it does."
Then Ummon picked up a cup and asked, "How many virtues does this have?"
"None at all," the monk replied.
Ummon asked, "But ancient people said it has virtues, didn't they? What do you think about that?" Then he struck the cup and asked the monk, "Do you understand?"
"No," the monk replied.
Finally Ummon said, "You had better go on with your lectures on the sutra."

After a Zen master poses a koan to a monk, he carefully studies the monk's reaction and his answer. He then judges how much intuitive direct insight it shows. Answers that are rational are forbidden and will sometimes result in blows from the teacher. (For example, one could answer the first koan in the list above with "Like the face of my grandmother" if one resembles her. But this answer would be rational and incorrect, and might bring punishment.) Or the teacher may say nothing, respond in words, or simply walk away.

---

legend to have battled Tibetan demons for control of that land. Rinpoché defeated the demons and then made them protectors of Buddhism in Tibet. This story indicates well the syncretistic nature of Tibetan Buddhism—the combination of more exotic forms of Buddhism with elements of the native animistic Bön religion. Buddhism had a difficult time getting established in Tibet; during the 800s and 900s C.E., it suffered a setback there, but it eventually won over the country in the 1000s. It then developed into four main schools. In 1578, the rulers of Tibet named the head of the Gelug ("Yellow Hat") School of Tibetan Buddhism the **Dalai Lama**, a title that means "ocean of wisdom" or "oceanic teacher." The fifth Dalai Lama brought virtually all of Tibetan life under his control, and the dalai lamas were from that

PETE SOUZA/FLICKR

President Obama met four times with the Dalai Lama.

Dalai Lama [DAHL-eye (not "dolly") LAH-muh] "Ocean of wisdom," head of the Gelug School of Tibetan Buddhism

point on the nearly absolute rulers of Tibet. This made the country's government a true theocracy (rule by clergy). Tibetan Buddhism also spread to Bhutan, Nepal, and Mongolia, but the direct political rule of the Dalai Lama did not extend to these areas.

Tibetan Buddhism, also known as the Diamond Vehicle or **Vajrayana**, is the most complete blend of Buddhism and an indigenous religion. (The Diamond Vehicle is also referred to as *Lamaism* for its leaders, who are called **lamas**, meaning "gurus, teachers"; *Esoteric Buddhism* for passing its teachings secretly from guru to student; and also *Tantric Buddhism* for developing some of its doctrines from the *Tantra*.) This blending helps to explain why Vajrayana has various important features unknown in the rest of Buddhism: doctrines such as many divinities and demons, as well as the incarnation of a bodhisattva in the whole line of Dalai Lamas; organizational practices, for example, the theocratic and near-absolute rule of the Dalai Lama; ritual practices such as prayer wheels, prayer flags, religious pictures made of colored sand, and oracles for telling the future; and unusual (for Buddhism) scriptures, including the *Tibetan Book of the Dead*.

Tenzin Gyatso (TEHN-zihn gee-YAHT-soh), who was born Lhamo Dondrub in 1935, was identified as a young boy as the reincarnation of the thirteenth Dalai Lama, a bodhisattva named Avalokitesvara (AV-uh-loh-KIT-esh-VAHR-uh), the famous "Bodhisattva of Compassion." As the Dalai Lama himself tells it, he was presented with various objects, including toys, some of which had belonged to the thirteenth Dalai Lama and others not. He correctly claimed the possessions of the previous Dalai Lama, even exclaiming about some, "That's mine!" He became the fourteenth Dalai Lama in 1950. In 1951 the Communist Chinese invaded Tibet and permanently annexed it. More than 1 million Tibetans were killed in the aftermath, including

Yellow Hat order monks from India introduce the start of the 2011 Fremont Solstice Parade with a welcome chant to greet the summer in Seattle, WA.

the majority of its monks, many of them in mass executions. Six thousand monasteries were destroyed or shuttered.

The Dalai Lama fled in 1959 to exile in north India, where he leads a Tibetan government in exile. In 1989 he won the Nobel Peace Prize for spreading a message of tolerance and world peace. He has traveled around the world for speaking engagements and Tibetan Buddhist rituals. He meets regularly with national leaders to plead the cause of Tibet. Tibetan leaders in exile charge that human rights abuses continue in Tibet, including the immigration into Tibet of tens of thousands of Chinese. In 2017, United Nations officials sharply criticized China for ongoing expulsions of thousands of monks and nuns from Tibetan enclaves in China. (We will examine the current situation of Buddhism more in the last section of this chapter.)

Vajrayana [VAHJ-ruh-YAH-nuh] "Diamond Vehicle," formal name for Tibetan Buddhism

lama [LAH-muh] "Guru, teacher," leader of Tibetan Buddhism

Tibetan Buddhist prayer flags, Nepal

5-3 Essential Buddhist Teachings

A leading Buddhist authority in Thailand urges the country's 300,000 monks to join in the fight against AIDS. Chatsumarn Kabilsingh (CHAT-soo-mahrn KAHB-ihl-sing), the first woman to receive full ordination as a nun in modern Thailand, urges that monks acquire a better understanding of Buddhist teachings to be more effective in teaching the scriptural command against adultery. She says that sex outside of marriage is a primary form of suffering caused by desire, as addressed in the Four Noble Truths. Without getting into the touchy question of whether AIDS is a retribution for sexual sins, she stresses the positive: "Sex springs from the love and care shown by two individuals, and they need to be responsible to each other. With true love, there is no need to change partners, and that is the best prevention against AIDS."

> *Some in the West regard reincarnation as a ... form of eternal life, but this is not at all what Buddhists think.*

Many Indian religions in the fifth century C.E. had several basic beliefs about an unseen spiritual reality that formed a common worldview. Buddhists call their version of this worldview the **dharma**, "law, teaching" about the universe and release from it. The universe operates by **karma** (actions), the law of the cause and effect of actions done by sentient (with senses) beings. These beings have been reborn from eternity in different realms of the cosmos: in heaven, earth, and hell. This endless cycle of **samsara** (wandering) is the cause of all suffering, and the goal of Buddhism is to end that suffering. Some in the west regard reincarnation as a happy or at least neutral form of eternal life, but this is not at all what Buddhists or traditional adherents to other Asian religions think—it is a source of never-ending suffering. (See "A Closer Look: Popular Misunderstandings.")

The means of escape from samsara usually comes over millions of lifetimes, as one gains perfection and ultimately finds the way out of constant rebirth. Those who are fully enlightened are not reborn again as humans after they die, nor do they become absorbed into the world-soul Brahman, as many Hindus have taught. Rather, they go beyond suffering into **nirvana** (literally blowing out, extinction). Buddhists have been unwilling to discuss what nirvana actually is because it is indescribable, but those who come close to nirvana in this life have a deep sense of peace and calm. In short, the goal of Buddhism is a complete and definitive liberation from the painful transience of life. This can be attained through the recognition and elimination of the factors leading to endless death and rebirth.

5-3a The Four Noble Truths

A brief summary of Buddhist teaching is the **Four Noble Truths** that the Buddha taught in his first sermons. The Four Noble Truths diagnose the human problem, describe its cause, propose a cure, and prescribe a treatment.

1. *All life is suffering.* The First Noble Truth states that all thinking beings experience suffering. Suffering ranges from great physical and mental pain to mild emotional unhappiness. People suffer because they are born, get sick, age, and die. Suffering also arises from negative emotions such as anger and sadness. Even happiness is an occasion for suffering because our happiness comes and goes. Regardless of its surface quality—long or short, happy or sad, poor or rich—this life is actually one of suffering.

2. *The cause of suffering is desire.* Humans always want what they do not have and should not have. Insatiable desire, a craving for physical gratification, personal happiness, and even life itself is the cause of suffering. To put it another way, we are addicted to life; like any other addiction, this causes suffering. Due to the impermanence of the world and the fickleness of our own minds, our sensual and emotional gratifications pass, and we find ourselves once again in the grip of desire. Craving also takes the form of pursuing wealth, power, reputation, and so on, while avoiding unpleasant and undesirable things. We want to be something other

dharma [DAHR-muh] Law, teaching of Buddhism

karma [KAR-muh] Law of the cause and effect of actions done by sentient beings

samsara [sam-SAR-uh] Wandering through reincarnations, a main cause of human suffering

nirvana [neer-VAH-nuh] Blowing out, extinction of desire, attachment, and suffering

Four Noble Truths Basic teaching of Buddhism that (1) all life is suffering, (2) suffering is caused by desire, (3) to end desire is to end suffering, and (4) to end desire one must follow the Noble Eightfold Path

A Closer Look

Popular Misunderstandings of *Karma*, *Nirvana*, and *Zen*

Some key Buddhist terms are misunderstood in the West.

Karma in Buddhism isn't "fate" as we often hear today in North America and Europe. Neither is it a system of reward and punishment worked out primarily in one's present life. In fact, karma in Buddhism is the *opposite* of these ideas. In karma, each person generates her or his own reward or punishment, which comes with one's condition after reincarnation.

Today, *nirvana* is for many western people a state of personal bliss in which an individual has complete peace, fulfillment, and joy. This understanding aligns with some Mahayana groups, such as Socially Engaged Buddhism, but not with Theravada or Tibetan Buddhism. In these latter beliefs, it means to become extinct, and for Buddhists it often connotes "to cool," as a flame of desire cools when it is snuffed out. As long as individual existence continues,

samsara continues. Because Mahayana traditions of Buddhism are much more prevalent in the western world than are Theravadin traditions, westerners tend to read all of Buddhist teaching on nirvana according to Mahayana views. This leads to distortion about the variety of Buddhist thoughts on this topic. Buddhists are usually unwilling to say much about nirvana because it is indescribable, even unknowable.

Zen is the most misused in the West. It is often used to describe any ironic or profound statement, whether or not it's meant to lead to enlightenment. Zen is also linked in the popular imagination to martial arts. Popular fiction, film, and television have long drawn on the image of the otherwise peaceful Zen monk who is a master of hand-to-hand fighting. A few Ch'an/Zen groups, especially the Chinese Shaolin (shaw-LIHN) school—as shown in the well-known film *Crouching Tiger, Hidden Dragon*—use martial arts to build energy and focus the mind. But Zen groups don't typically use martial arts, and martial arts practitioners aren't usually Zen Buddhists.

---

than what we are. This constant craving, which is grounded in an erroneous view of the self, is the cause of suffering.

3. *To end desire is to end suffering.* The Third Noble Truth puts together the first and the second. The means of ending our suffering is ending the craving that causes it. This cessation of craving, which is an ending of ignorance at its root, breaks the working of negative karma, causing one not to be reborn again. This is easier to understand than to do, and this difficulty leads to the Fourth Noble Truth.

Noble Eightfold Path
Right understanding, intention, speech, conduct, livelihood, effort, mindfulness, and contemplation

4. *To end desire, one must follow the Noble Eightfold Path.* Buddhism requires this as the path toward nirvana. Following the Eightfold Path does not *cause* nirvana, but it

> { We are addicted to life; like any other addiction, this causes suffering. }

is a required aid in finding it. Nirvana is the state that is free from all suffering, because in it one is free from delusions and cravings about the nature of the self and reality.

5-3b The Noble Eightfold Path

The **Noble Eightfold Path** consists of eight aspects of thought and behavior that need to be cultivated on the path to nirvana. These eight steps on the path form the basis of Buddhist ethical teaching. Each step begins with *right*, which can be understood as full, skillful, or correct. These are as follows:

1. *Right understanding:* gaining a perspective that ends one's delusions and brings knowledge of reality.

2. *Right intention:* developing a sincere commitment to embark upon the path to liberation with determination and diligence; people must *want* to change before they *can* change.

3. *Right speech*: speaking the truth and refraining from lying, which is deceptive speech that adds to the suffering of the world.

4. *Right conduct*: following the Five Precepts of not killing, stealing, lying, drinking intoxicants, and being sexually immoral; conduct should be without ego and self-centeredness.

5. *Right livelihood*: doing work and living one's life in a way that does not injure others and is conducive to the attainment of liberation.

Impermanence performed: Monks create an intricate sand mandala only to destroy it soon after it is completed.

BESTWEB/SHUTTERSTOCK.COM

6. *Right effort*: the development of a consciousness that is free from craving; this requires a sustained effort to release consciousness from its unwholesome mental states and cultivate wholesome ones.

7. *Right **mindfulness***: the practice of meditative awareness; through mindfulness, harmful thoughts and feelings, as well as their attendant cravings and ego-boosting activities, may be discerned and dealt with.

8. *Right contemplation*: the deepening of mindfulness that leads to focused states of consciousness, akin to deep concentration, in which tranquility and penetrating insight may be obtained.

5-3c The Three Characteristics of Existence

Soon after his enlightenment, the Buddha taught that all life is marked by the **Three Characteristics of Existence** (or Reality): impermanence, suffering, and no soul. These Three Characteristics are echoed in many aspects of Buddhism, especially in its philosophical teachings:

- Impermanence, **anicca** in Sanskrit, means that the outer appearance of all things is constantly changing, but the inner essence does not. For example, when an animal dies and decomposes, the appearance of the animal ends, but the components that formed it go on to be a part of something new. The most dramatic illustration of the impermanence of all things is when Buddhist monks make a **mandala** out of colored sand and, soon after the completion of this highly symbolic picture, they sweep it up and throw the sand into moving water.

- Suffering, **dukkha**, is the Second Characteristic of Existence, in addition to being the first of the Four Noble Truths. Nothing in the physical world or even in one's mind can bring true satisfaction. Because humans are never satisfied, they form an unhealthy attachment to things, and even to life itself. This produces dukkha, of which the First Noble Truth speaks.

- "No soul/self," **anatta**, is third. In contrast to Hinduism, the Buddha taught that there is no permanent soul or self (*atman*). Impermanence thus extends even to the deepest parts of human nature, and this too produces suffering. Various elements of the human

mindfulness The practice of meditative awareness, especially of one's own state

Three Characteristics of Existence
Impermanence, suffering, and no soul

anicca [uh-NEEK-uh] Impermanence, the First Characteristic of Existence, which leads to suffering

mandala [MAHN-dah-luh] Symbolic Buddhist picture

dukkha [DUHK-uh] Suffering, the Second Characteristic of Existence, caused by desire

anatta [ah-NAHT-uh] No soul, the Third Characteristic of Existence

mind work together to create an illusion of a permanent soul, but these elements dissolve at death. (So the self is not a figment of our imagination; it is a figment of the whole mind.) The task of the Buddhist is to find enlightenment before death, because enlightenment (gaining a Buddha nature) will end the cycle of reincarnation. This teaching of anatta is still carried out in much of Theravada Buddhism, but many Mahayana schools teach that there is in fact an essential, permanent self/soul that transmigrates in this world and lives forever when it is liberated from reincarnation.

5-4 Buddhist Ethics for Monastics and Laypeople

As they visit a new Buddhist theme park in southern Vietnam, a family goes through an exhibit not found in other theme parks—a tour through hell. In paintings, surround sound, and animatronics, eight rooms depict the various tortures inflicted on sinners before they are sent back to the earth for their next lives. The mother and father occasionally chuckle nervously at the exhibits, but the children cling tightly to their parents. Similar to other depictions of punishment in the next life—and a number of religions have such teachings—this "Hell Pavilion" is meant to impress on people the dangers of doing wrong. Buddhist literary or even painted depictions of hell are not often as scary as this, and some doubt whether it is wise or even possible to scare people out of hell by scaring the hell out of them in an amusement park.

The Buddhist religious life is grounded on morality. The Eightfold Path indicates that the cultivation of meditation and wisdom is dependent on morality. Meditation and reaching release cannot be done without it. Moreover, Buddhist layfolk, in their worship of the Buddha or other buddhas, must build their worship on a foundation of solid moral goodness.

5-4a General Buddhist Morality

As in most religions, morality in Buddhism is well developed. If you asked any Buddhist what the heart of the Buddhist moral system is, he or she would probably say, "Show compassion to all beings." In the face of the suffering in the world, all sentient beings need compassion if they are to cope with their bad situation and finally gain liberation from it.

precept Buddhist moral command

Aside from this general, comprehensive command, the more detailed heart of Buddhist ethical thought is *sila* (SEE-luh). This term means virtuous behavior, morality, ethics, or **precept** (moral command). A precept is an action committed in a deed, a word, or in the mind. It involves a strong, intentional effort, because no precept comes naturally. Following the precepts leads to purity in thought, word, and deed, as well as to a proper foundation for meditative cultivation of the mind. Keeping the precepts is meritorious and brings peace of mind to the person who obeys them, and peace with others as well—for monks, nuns, and layfolk. It also prevents rebirth in hell or as an animal on the earth. Breaking the precepts will certainly mean that one will not be in a position to reach release in one's next life.

> The Eightfold Path indicates that the cultivation of meditation and wisdom is dependent on morality.

Besides the general command to all Buddhists to be nonviolent, moderate, and compassionate to all beings, Buddhists are urged to live moral, generous lives. The social outworking of Buddhist morality helped to differentiate it from Hinduism and aided in its spread throughout Asia. Two examples must suffice here. First, the Buddha didn't oppose wealth, but he also didn't make it a main goal of life as Hinduism had, and he said that wealth doesn't end suffering, but only masks it. One should develop a detachment from one's wealth and use it for the good of others. The Buddha also opposed Hinduism's caste system and the power of its priests, arguing for equality among all people. Therefore, he allowed men from all Indian castes to be monks. Today when Indian "untouchables" (Dalits) have mass conversions to other religions in order to improve their social and religious conditions, they typically turn to Buddhism or to Christianity.

5-4b The Five Precepts

The Five Precepts are ethical guidelines for a life in which one is happy, is moderately self-confident without being self-absorbed in one's ego, and can meditate well. They are necessary for morality in this life and a better rebirth in the next. The precepts are considered not only commands, but also training for life in the dharma (teaching, law). This dharma is built into the universe, governing nonsentient things just as much as it governs living beings. Following the dharma brings happiness in this life and good karma for the next; not living according to the dharma brings endless suffering in continuous rebirths. The Five Precepts call for Buddhists to keep themselves from five different errors. They are virtually universal among Buddhists, both monastic and lay. The Buddhist must not:

1. Kill sentient beings
2. Steal
3. Commit sexual immorality
4. Lie
5. Drink any intoxicants

Different Buddhist branches and groups have added to these precepts in different ways. In the Theravada branch, layfolk wishing to practice Buddhism more fully but are not able or willing to enter a monastery may adopt three precepts in addition to the Five. Some adopt them permanently, but most who take them on do so temporarily, particularly on holy days. The third of the Five Precepts is made stricter, adding the requirement of celibacy—no sexual activity at all, even within marriage. The three additional precepts command that the Buddhist must not:

6. Eat between noon and the following sunrise, as monks do
7. Dance; enjoy music, jewelry, or cosmetics; or attend artistic performances
8. Use luxurious seats and beds

As is typical of Buddhism, lay practice is based on and adapted from monastic practice. The precepts have several levels of achievement: basic morality in keeping the Five Precepts, basic morality with self-denial in keeping the Eight Precepts, novice monasticism in keeping the Ten Precepts, full-monk status with hundreds of precepts, and even more for nuns. Laypeople typically follow the Five

Precepts only. They can, at their discretion, follow eight or even ten for a short time, practicing more rigorous self-control and self-denial. Although the precepts are typically worded in the negative, Buddhists realize that much positive meaning lies behind them.

5-4c Other Precepts and Moral Rules

The complete list of the Ten Precepts is a requirement for novice monks before they have taken their final vows, especially in Theravada. The seventh precept given above is made into two precepts, and a tenth added. To keep these added precepts, the Buddhist monk must not:

1. Dance, listen to, or engage in music, singing, or shows
2. Use garlands, perfumes, lotions, or other things that beautify the body
3. Use luxurious seats and beds
4. Accept money

Young nuns shaving and washing by a stream, Nyaungshwe, Myanmar. Although shaving one's head is not a part of the Ten Precepts, it is a regular part of Buddhist monasticism.

© LITECHOICES/SHUTTERSTOCK.COM

For fully initiated monastics, more than two hundred additional precepts apply. These now take on the character of hard-and-fast rules. If they are broken, disciplinary actions are specified in the precepts. For example, in the command of celibacy, Buddhist monks and nuns are forbidden to even think about sex. Although this may strike you as extreme, for someone who is strictly celibate, to think about sex when one never carries out one's thoughts will only increase the suffering that Buddhists see as the root of all evil. Nuns have extra rules added to the rules for monks, designed in part to keep them under the supervision of nearby monks. These precepts seek to order monastic life for the purpose of promoting good morality and achievement in meditation. They are listed in the "Monastic Disciplinary Code" in the Pali canon and are broken into several groups. In the Mahayana canon, they are found in a three-volume book called the *Vinaya*. Monks must memorize these rules and follow them carefully. (For more on the life of Buddhist monastics, see "A Closer Look: Buddhist Monastic Dress.")

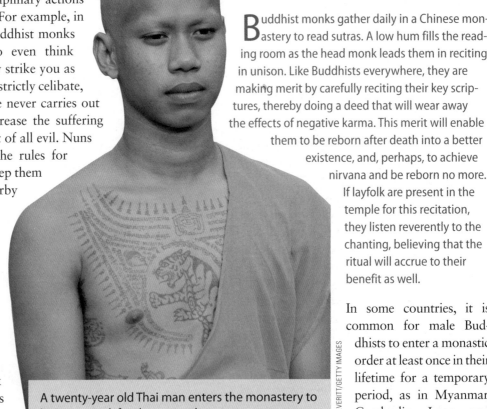

A twenty-year old Thai man enters the monastery to live as a monk for three months.

DAVE EVERITT/GETTY IMAGES

5-5 Buddhist Ritual and Meditation

Buddhist monks gather daily in a Chinese monastery to read sutras. A low hum fills the reading room as the head monk leads them in reciting in unison. Like Buddhists everywhere, they are making merit by carefully reciting their key scriptures, thereby doing a deed that will wear away the effects of negative karma. This merit will enable them to be reborn after death into a better existence, and, perhaps, to achieve nirvana and be reborn no more. If layfolk are present in the temple for this recitation, they listen reverently to the chanting, believing that the ritual will accrue to their benefit as well.

In some countries, it is common for male Buddhists to enter a monastic order at least once in their lifetime for a temporary period, as in Myanmar, Cambodia, Laos, and Thailand today. This temporary monasticism rises men in their social standing. In nearly all the Buddhist world, monks and laypeople live in a reciprocal relationship. Each group provides the other with an opportunity to gain merit, thereby making a contribution to their "karma account." For ordinary Buddhists today—monk or layperson—nirvana is far too remote and intangible a goal to be striven for immediately, so religious practice focuses on the gaining of merit. Monks recite and explain the sacred texts to laypeople, conduct protective ceremonies for them, and lead other religious rituals for them, especially funerals. The laypeople give the monks material support: food in their morning rounds outside the monastery, new monastic robes at

NINJA SS/SHUTTERSTOCK

Buddhist monk on his begging rounds. Collecting their daily food from others enables monks to spend more time in meditation and study and offers an opportunity for laity to gain merit.

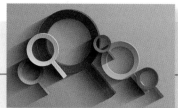

A Closer Look

Buddhist Monastic Dress

Certain kinds of clothing for monks arose in the earliest stage of Buddhism, and the basic features of this clothing have endured through today. As you might expect, Buddhism takes a middle path between the (un)dress found among Hindu renunciants and the everyday clothing of people in the householder state.

The first monks wore robes patched together from rags. This resulted in a variety of looks. Hindu renunciants could dress as they wanted, but the Buddha knew that monks living within a community needed a more uniform look. Gautama directed that robes be made of "pure cloth," that is, cloth that no one wanted. *Pure cloth* is an odd term because it included pieces of cloth chewed by animals, scorched by fire, stained by childbirth fluids or blood, or used to clothe the dead. Monks scavenged rubbish heaps and cremation grounds for discarded cloth. Any part that was unusable was cut off, and the cloth was washed and stitched together. Then it was boiled with vegetable pulp and spices, such as turmeric or saffron, giving the cloth a yellow–orange color. Theravada monks still wear spice-colored robes today in shades of curry, cumin, and paprika with the most common color being bright saffron orange. Buddhist monks and nuns no longer scavenge for cloth in unpleasant places. Instead, they wear robes made from cloth that is donated by laity.

The robes worn by Theravada monks of Southeast Asia today, from which most Buddhist monastic dress is descended, are thought by monks to be unchanged from the original robes of 2500 years ago (see Figure 5.2). Their robes have three parts:

- The most visible part of the robe is a large rectangle, approximately six by nine feet. It can be worn to cover both shoulders, but is usually wrapped to cover the left shoulder and leave the right shoulder and arm bare. It is then draped so that it is beneath the knee.

- An undergarment similar to the Indian dhoti (see Figure 3.5 in Section 3-4c) is wrapped around the waist and covers the body from the waist to the knees.

- An extra rectangle of cloth can be wrapped around the upper body for warmth. When not used, it is typically folded and draped over the left shoulder.

The original nuns' robe consisted of the same three parts as the monks' robe, with two additional pieces, making it a five-part robe (see Figure 5.3). Nuns also wear a simple bodice under the main piece of cloth, and they carry a washcloth tucked into their robe. Today, Theravada women's robes are usually in colors more muted than monks' robes, their shoulders are not bared, and their robes go down to their feet.

Of course, a good deal of variety exists in monastic robes in Asia and the west. Colors differ, but each piece of cloth is typically one color; if the pieces have different colors, they are closely matched. Perhaps the liveliest part of monastic dress is the colorful hats of Tibetan monks (see photo in Section 5-2e).

BONNIE VAN VOORST © CENGAGE LEARNING

Figure 5.2 Monk in traditional robe

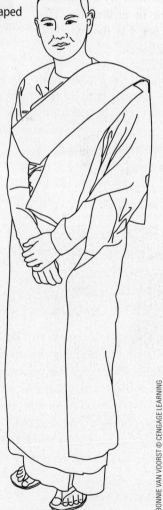

BONNIE VAN VOORST © CENGAGE LEARNING

Figure 5.3 Nun in traditional robe

an annual ceremony (for more on monastic garb, see "A Closer Look: Buddhist Monastic Dress."), and money for the maintenance and adornment of the monastery.

5-5a Temples

Inside a typical Theravada temple, you will see the following. At the front of the temple is a statue of the Buddha, most often seated and in meditation. Sometimes additional statues of the Buddha will also be present at the front. An altar on which worshipers place offerings of flowers and oil stands right in front of the statue. A place to set up burning incense sticks is on or near the altar, and larger temples will have places to burn incense in an open-air courtyard. Many temples contain pictures on the walls, showing the stages of the Buddha's life. As a rule, Mahayana and Tibetan temples are more elaborately decorated than Theravadin temples. The main hall of the temple is open space in which worshipers sit or stand in meditation. One may see mats there, but not (in a traditional Buddhist temple) chairs or pews. Buddhist temples built in Europe or North America sometimes have a different arrangement, which we will discuss in Section 5-6c on Buddhism in North America.

Woman consulting a horoscope in a Japanese Buddhist temple
CEPOLINA

5-5b Images of the Buddha

The spiritual center of any Buddhist temple, and one also found in Buddhist home altars, is a statue of the Buddha. (Paintings and printed pictures of the Buddha are also displayed, but not as prominently as the statue. Buddhists typically do not consider them as inspiring as statues of the Buddha.) The Buddha is usually depicted as seated in the lotus meditational position. His eyes are closed or mostly closed, symbolizing that he has shut out the distractions of the world to find release within himself. He often has a circular mark on his forehead, called an *urna*, showing that he has

Buddha in deep meditation, Kamakura, Japan
© SERG ZASTAVKIN/SHUTTERSTOCK.COM

mudra [MOOD-ruh]
Position in which the hands and arms are held during meditation

achieved enlightenment. His large earlobes are a traditional Indian symbol of nobility. He is dressed modestly and is physically strong and healthy, but not overfed. He holds his hands, and often his arms, in one of a variety of formal positions called **mudras**, some of which are as follows:

- Left hand resting on thigh, right hand pointing downward or touching the ground, a mudra symbolizing the attainment of enlightenment.
- Right hand held up with the palm facing forward, symbolizing a blessing of those venerating the statue.
- Right hand upward with thumb and forefinger closed (our "okay" sign), symbolizing teaching the Buddhist way.
- Forming both hands into a circle, symbolizing the wheel of dharma.

One will also see statues of the Buddha reclining on his right side, symbolizing his entry into full nirvana at death. Less often, one will see statues of a standing Buddha.

Buddha with right hand downward, symbolizing enlightenment
CLAUDIAD/ISTOCKPHOTO.COM

5-5c Prayer and Meditation

For monks, prayer has a highly meditational dimension. For layfolk, however, Buddhist prayer means expressing praise and requests to a supernatural power or being. As mentioned at the beginning of this chapter, lay Buddhists don't meditate regularly. Buddhism doesn't have a main deity on whom the religion centers and to whom worship and prayer are offered. But Buddhists do pray, which raises—at least for us—this question: To whom do Buddhists pray, and for what do they pray? Mostly, Buddhists pray for blessings from the Buddha, other buddhas, and bodhisattvas, and ask especially for help toward enlightenment. Some Tibetan Buddhists have minor gods, both male and female, to whom prayer is made for blessing and protection. They also pray for the same things people pray for in other religions: for health and healing, safety, spiritual strength, and for understanding.

Much more important than prayer for Buddhist monastics is meditation: an altered state of consciousness induced in a controlled manner. Some forms of Buddhist meditation can be intense; for example, in some Thai temples, monks meditate in front of a decaying human corpse to emphasize non-attachment to one's body and the impermanence of all things. This is a practice that is said to go all the way back to the Buddha. However, most Buddhist meditation is much more oriented to everyday life. You are used to trances that come in the form of daydreams, and we even do things such as drive a car for several minutes and suddenly realize that we haven't been paying attention to driving at all. Buddhist meditation, however, is controlled and purposeful—there is no inattentive driving in a Buddhist life! Two basic forms of meditation have been widely practiced in the Theravada tradition and have also come by way of Mahayana practice to North America.

The first form of meditation is called **trance meditation** and has several steps. First, meditators detach themselves from impure and erroneous thoughts, becoming mildly satisfied and happy. In the second stage, thinking leads to a complete inner serenity; the mind is concentrated, and the happiness from the first stage lessens. In the third stage, all feelings disappear, and the meditator becomes uninterested in everything. In the fourth stage, any tendency toward serenity is left behind, and the meditator becomes completely indifferent to self. One then begins the pursuit of higher attainments in trance meditation, reaching beyond the perception of physical and mental forms, and resting in infinite time and space. There follows a state of unlimited consciousness. Next, by fixing the mind on how everything is impermanent to the point of non-existence, the meditator reaches the nothingness suggested by nirvana. Finally, one reaches the state in which there is neither perception nor nonperception. The meditator has thought the way out of thinking!

The second type of meditation is **insight meditation**. This practice also requires intense concentration, which in insight meditation leads to a complete concentration of the mind called awareness or mindfulness. The mindfulness is not an end in itself, but enables the meditator to see that all reality is impermanent, filled with suffering, and has no self. This insight propels the meditator toward nirvana. Theravada texts recommend both trance and insight meditation. Since 1900, an emphasis on insight-meditation practices has grown, and insight movements became widespread in Mahayana and among Buddhist groups in the West. Of course, some Buddhist groups, such as Zen,

Buddha in blessing pose

PAULVINTEN/ISTOCKPHOTO.COM

Reclining Buddha, symbolizing reaching nirvana at death.

MASTERLU/ISTOCKPHOTO.COM

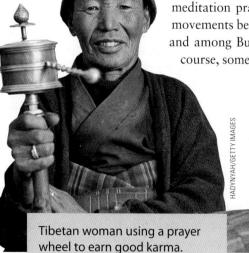
Tibetan woman using a prayer wheel to earn good karma.

HADYNYAH/GETTY IMAGES

trance meditation
Comprehensive form of meditation that goes all the way to nirvana

insight meditation
Meditation leading to awareness or mindfulness, from which nirvana can be achieved

have different patterns and practices of meditation. Other groups, for example, Nichiren, have meditation that focuses on their main chants.

5-5d Protective Rituals

Buddhism has rituals designed to protect the faithful and the whole world against danger and evil, beside the constant effort to earn good karma as a spiritual blessing. In Theravada these involve the recitation of scripture texts called **parittas**, or protections. The texts are chanted in public, often with drumming and ringing of handbells, to avert collective danger. Parittas are also used privately; for protection, a person pays for monks to recite scripture against illness and other difficulties. Most of these rituals do not speak explicitly of protections from danger; they usually comprise regular scripture texts, which are recited with the intent of using their truth and power to keep away evil.

In Mahayana and in Tibet, protective rituals are used more widely than elsewhere in Buddhism, as we might expect as these branches of Buddhism give more attention to supernatural beings and forces, including evil ones. Brief statements of Buddhist teachings are thought to share their power and are frequently used for protection, as are even shorter one- or two-word **mantras**. Protective rituals were important in the conversion of Tibet and East Asia to Buddhism; people there wanted to be assured that the new religion could deal with the spiritual forces that threatened them. Such observances are still important in these areas. Even today, the Buddhist Tibetan government in exile holds protective rituals for itself and will also consult traditional religious oracles to discern the best choices when making decisions. In Japan, worshipers in Buddhist temples can get a printed horoscope-based prediction for their life. If they tie it to a special board or a designated tree in the temple area, a good fortune will come true, but a bad fortune will be thwarted. More will be said about these in Chapter 8, on Shinto.

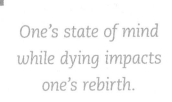

{ To whom do Buddhists pray, and for what? }

{ One's state of mind while dying impacts one's rebirth. }

paritta [puh-REET-uh] Protective ritual for an individual or community

mantra [MAHN-truh] Short formula or single word that focuses the mind and expresses great religious meaning

stupa [STOO-pah] Burial monument, often with relics of the Buddha or Buddhists

5-5e Funeral Rituals

Monks do not normally perform life-cycle rituals for laypeople. They do not lead ceremonies for newborn babies, mark passage to adulthood, or conduct weddings. These are primarily family events, and are more cultural than religious, although monks may bestow blessings on newborns and newlyweds in the monasteries.

Monks do participate in funerals, however. In fact, Buddhism has a leading role in funeral rituals in almost every country in which it has a presence. Because Buddhism has a strong interest in death, karma, and reincarnation, monks often lead services for the dead. Even before that, monks will visit the dying, because one's state of mind while dying impacts one's rebirth. Monks read sacred texts to a dying person to prepare the spirit before death. The elaborate procedures spelled out in *The Tibetan Book of the Dead* are the apex of this guidance for the dying and recently deceased. The soul, or consciousness (where Buddhists are strict on the no-soul teaching), stays in or around the body for three days after death. In general, Buddhist funeral practices for leading monks originated in India. After cremation ceremonies, the ashes and bones of leading monks were collected and **stupas**, burial mounds or monuments, built over them. The large number of stupas found near monasteries indicates that these funeral rites for leading monks were widely held in the past, but today are not carried out as often in most of Asia.

The dead bodies of ordinary monks and laypeople in Asia and the West undergo cremation. After cremation, typically carried out today in a modern crematorium, the ashes are usually buried in a cemetery. Many Buddhists will ritually honor their ancestors at their gravesites, especially in China, where the rituals are similar to those we will discuss in Chapter 7 (on Daoism and Confucianism). Some regional differences should be noted here. In Sri Lanka, whole-body burial is also common. Because wood is scarce in Tibet, cremation there is unusual. The bodies of great Tibetan lamas are reverently put in stupas in a posture of meditation. A striking Tibetan practice is one where monks cut apart the bodies of pious Tibetan Buddhists, both monastics and layfolk, and distribute them, piece by piece, to the waiting birds. Although this may seem revolting to westerners—and is not easy for mourners in Tibet to watch—this feeding of birds is seen as an act of great compassion.

5-6 Buddhism around the World Today

As U.S. president Barack Obama toured Southeast Asia in November of 2012, a monk in a famous Buddhist temple approached him to have a brief word. We can imagine that the president may have anticipated a profound spiritual comment, but what the monk said to him, with reporters standing by, became international news: "Mr. President, good luck with the fiscal cliff." He was referring, of course, to a difficult situation with the U.S. national budget, one that was causing a good deal of anxiety in the United States. People were surprised, and the press also, that a monk would make such a comment, but they shouldn't have been. Many monks are well informed about current world events. They are particularly aware of suffering, even financial suffering, in order to act against it.

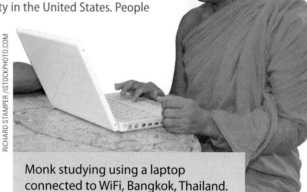

Monk studying using a laptop connected to WiFi, Bangkok, Thailand.

RICHARD STAMPER /ISTOCKPHOTO.COM

5-6a Buddhism in Modern Asia

During the nineteenth and twentieth centuries, Buddhism faced a variety of new issues. Several countries with significant Buddhist populations came under colonial rule, and many other Buddhists felt the pressure of western religions and culture. In South Korea, Christianity has converted nearly half the population from Buddhism. Even more damaging to the size and influence of Buddhism was the rise of communism in China, Mongolia, North Korea, Vietnam, Cambodia, and Tibet, as well as the rise of secularism in Japan. Around 1800, an estimated 20 to 25 percent of the world's population was Buddhist, but by 2000, it was down to 8 percent, and as stated previously, the Pew Research Center estimates that by 2050, it will be 5 percent. The number of Buddhists in the world is expected to remain steady, but it will not keep pace with growing world population.[3]

Buddhists have responded in a variety of ways to these challenges. First, Buddhism has adapted traditions it liked in Christianity. Peaceful competition between Buddhists and Christian missionaries from the West often led to Buddhist adoption of Christian practices such as Sunday schools, mission societies, and the distribution of religious literature. Some Buddhists also promoted missionary activity modeled after Christian missions in non-Buddhist parts of Asia and the West, with voluntary conversion of individuals. This differs from the historic Buddhist missionary approach of sending monks to convert kings, with the kingdoms following the ruler into Buddhism.

A second way in which Buddhism has responded to the western Christian challenge was to seek greater Buddhist unity. Three main societies were established to promote ecumenical cooperation between Buddhists: the Maha Bodhi Society (1891), which regained a Buddhist presence at the pilgrimage site at Bodh Gaya, India; the World Fellowship of Buddhists (1950); and the World Buddhist Sangha Council for monks and nuns (1966). These societies are still at work today to promote Buddhist unity and cooperation.

A third response to modernity was the development of social and political activism by monks, including a formal movement usually called Socially Engaged Buddhism, founded by the South Vietnamese Zen monk Thich Nhat Hanh (tick naught hahn) in the 1960s. He may be the most prominent leader of Buddhism today next to the Dalai Lama. Some Asian and Western Buddhists have advocated progressive political and economic changes, including ones in the areas of ecology and feminism. Although they are not a part of Socially Engaged Buddhism, Buddhist monks in Myanmar (Burma) have helped to organize peaceful protests against long-term dictatorships in that nation. At times they have been brutally suppressed and have paid a high price for their political activism.

Recent political activity by Myanmar monks has not been so peaceful. Some monks have led campaigns to stir up ethnic hatred of the Rohingya (roh-HIN-jah) peoples in Myanmar, who are Muslim. At times this opposition to the Rohingya has become brutal, with many of them confined to internment camps and denied many civil rights.

REUTERS/SOE ZEYA TUN

In Yangon, Myanmar, Buddhist monks lead a protest in February of 2015 against the right of holders of temporary identification cards to vote. Roughly two-thirds of these card holders are Rohingya Muslims, who are widely resented in the Buddhist majority nation, where many consider them illegal immigrants from Bangladesh.

time, monastic authorities in Theravadin lands typically keep women from leadership roles in the religion—something that could potentially bring reform. Until recently in Sri Lanka, monks participated in warfare against the Tamil rebels, and they are still stirring up hostilities against Tamils, Muslims, and others with an organization called the Buddhist Power Force. The number of men who enter the monastery is declining, and it may also be true (although it's hard to prove) that the quality of monks is declining. The majority of monks are not behaving badly, but problems with those who are have increased. A few scholars have even argued that rising illicit behavior by monks has caused life in general in Southeast Asia to deteriorate. But Buddhism has spiritual resources to deal with these problems, and it is in the process of doing so.

This treatment of the Rohingya in Myanmar has been strongly condemned by many other nations, and Buddhist societies have tried to correct this monastic behavior that runs counter to Buddhist values, but by the beginning of 2018 the situation had not significantly improved. In fact, in late 2016 Rohingya militants attacked the Myanmar military, which responded with continuous violent attacks on Rohingya civilians. Risking death, more than half a million Rohingya have fled the violence against them for neighboring Bangladesh through 2018.

A fourth Buddhist response to modernity involves giving laypeople more of a role in the religion. In Theravada, traditionally led by monks, lay-oriented meditation movements have been successful. In Japan, this trend has led to a founding and rapid expansion of Buddhist groups run by lay Buddhists, a novelty in the history of Buddhism. A sadder current form of lay action has been the public self-immolation of dozens of Tibetan Buddhists living in China in protest over Chinese government actions against their religion in Tibet and in areas of China with large numbers of Tibetan people.

A final pattern of Buddhist adaptation to modern life is a response to a problem too common in world religions—illicit behavior by some religious specialists. In Southeast Asia, some monks break their vows by playing violent video games in arcades, drinking alcohol, and even having sexual relations with lay women and men. At the same

5-6b Buddhism Comes to the Western World

European contact with China and Japan brought knowledge of Buddhism to the West in the 1800s, and Buddhism soon became popular here, even though the number of Buddhists was small. In England societies were organized for the promotion of Buddhism; for example, the Pali Text Society translated and published Buddhist scriptures for wide distribution. The Buddhist Society of Great Britain explained Buddhism with the expectation that this would bring converts. Books appeared recommending Buddhism—for example, Edwin Arnold's *The Light of Asia* (1879), a long poem telling of the life of the Buddha that was a best seller in England and America. In Germany and France as well, Buddhism captured serious attention and soon became the best known of the Asian religions.

Some of this interest in Buddhism bordered on exoticism. This resulted in a one-sided view of Buddhism that emphasized its other philosophy and meditation to the exclusion of its religious practices, which, unfortunately, is still typical of the western approach to Buddhism today. The first European conversions to Buddhism took place around 1880. In the twentieth century, the Buddhist Society of Great Britain won thousands of converts to Theravada. But the main story

© AREK_MALANG/SHUTTERSTOCK.COM

Lay-oriented meditation societies in the West have spread meditation widely; here an American Buddhist sits in meditation.

of Buddhism in North America and Europe begins with the emigration of Buddhists from China, Japan, and Southeast Asia, to which we now turn.

5-6c Early Buddhist Immigration to North America

Tens of thousands of Chinese immigrants with Buddhist backgrounds—usually combined with lay Daoist practices and basic Confucian social values—came to the west coasts of the United States and Canada in the late 1800s. Similar to the vast majority of immigrants to North America, they came seeking a better life, not for religious reasons. They provided labor for mining, fishing, and farming, and especially for building the railroads. The only religious objects they had were small images of the Buddha and Chinese traditional gods for their own personal use. When the railroads were finished and these immigrants settled down in "Chinatowns" in the coastal cities, Americans began noticing their forms of Buddhism, especially when temples were built.

The size of the Chinese immigrant population grew rapidly; by 1870 one-tenth of the population of California and Montana was Chinese. Their numbers provoked a backlash in the form of discriminatory laws and practices against Chinese people, some of which were aimed at cultural customs (festivals, music, and public funerals) that were grounded in Chinese religions. In 1882 the national Chinese Exclusion Act suspended further immigration, and in 1924 new quotas were set for all Asians. Many immigrants continued to practice their faiths, however. By 1900 there were hundreds of Chinese Buddhist temples and smaller shrines along the West Coast and in the Rocky Mountains. Almost all of them were founded and led by laypeople because Chinese monks did not emigrate with them. But as discrimination persisted, and with a continued absence of monks (who for thousands of years had guided lay Buddhism), many second- and third-generation Chinese began to leave Buddhist practices behind in an effort to assimilate more fully to their new culture.

Japanese immigration to North America began in the 1880s. It was much smaller in scale than Chinese immigration, and was controlled and financially supported by the Japanese government. Japanese immigrants tended to be merchants and businesspeople. Also, entire families immigrated, unlike the case with the Chinese, who were predominantly males who had to leave their families behind in China. The immigrants quickly built cultural associations and temples. By 1898, the Young Men's Buddhist Association (modeled, as its name implies, on the Young Men's Christian Association, the YMCA) had been established. By 1910 more than twenty Japanese Buddhist temples had been established on the West Coast, led by ordained Buddhist monks from Japan who had been sent by the Japanese government.

Meanwhile, on the East Coast, contact with Buddhism came from books, not immigrants. Leading intellectuals were reading about Buddhism, especially transcendentalists such as Henry Thoreau and Ralph Waldo Emerson. In 1878, the eccentric mystic Helena Blavatsky and the more conventional Henry Steel Olcott, founders of the so-called Theosophical Society, went to Sri Lanka and formally received the Five Precepts for layfolk. Olcott was committed to Buddhism. When he became aware of how little Asian Buddhist groups knew about or cooperated with each other, he worked for better relations among these groups, even publishing a *Buddhist Catechism* (CAT-uh-kihz-um) to state what he considered the main, common ideas of Buddhism.[4] (A catechism is a basic statement of

Seattle Buddhist Church with Protestantizing influences; note especially the pews and pulpit.

faith in question-and-answer form.) He was widely known as "the White Buddhist," a term not acceptable to many today but at the time considered correct and complimentary.

During World War II, the internment of all Japanese in camps set back the religious life of the Japanese in the United States. After the war, membership in Buddhist temples declined as numerous Japanese Buddhists sought to assimilate by becoming Protestant Christians at a time when Protestantism was influential in America. Many Buddhist religious institutions adapted by Protestantizing themselves, adding pews, pulpits, hymnbooks, and organs to their temples. The largest Buddhist group in the States, the Jodo Shinshu sect of Sokka Gakkai, formally changed its name to the Buddhist Churches of America, giving the Christian term *church* a Buddhist application.

A surge of interest in Zen came after World War II, when many Asian Buddhists—such as Zen expert D. T. Suzuki (1870–1966)—came to the United States to live permanently. Zen became particularly popular in the United States, even contributing to what was called at the time a "Zen boom." A number of Americans went to Japan and began a more serious, committed study of Zen. It was not uncommon for American troops based in Japan after the war to gain an appreciation for Japanese ways of life in general and Buddhism in particular. In the 1950s, Zen became a part of the countercultural "Beatnik" movement, a precursor to the more diffuse "hippie" movements of the 1960s and 1970s. It was known as *Beat Zen* and marked the first time that an Asian religion became

a part of American popular culture. In 1974 Zen would again appear in American pop culture, in the form of Robert Pirsig's perennially bestselling *Zen and the Art of Motorcycle Maintenance: An Inquiry into Values.*[5] Zen Buddhism had come to be seen in North America as a way of spiritual liberation that was suited to people of western cultures. A recent book by Jeff Wilson, *Mindful America: The Mutual Transformation of Buddhist Meditation and American Culture*, shows another aspect of Buddhism in North America that began in the 1980s. The rise of mindfulness meditation in America, Wilson argues, is a telling example of how Buddhism enters new cultures and is domesticated. Cultures take from Buddhism what they need, and in the process create new forms of Buddhism adapted to these needs. Wilson also examines the large business aspects of the mindfulness movement, typically estimated at around one billion dollars in the United States, including commercial programs, therapeutic services, and products such as books, films, CDs, and smartphone applications.[6]

Some institutional dimensions of Buddhism continued in the United States. Since the 1950s, Europeans and Americans who studied Buddhism in Asia returned home to found monasteries and societies. Also, Asian Buddhist monks came to Europe and America to found meditation centers. But Buddhist influence from the 1800s until about 1970 remained largely intellectual, cultural, and meditational. The full spectrum of Buddhism as a religion was yet to appear. Two main events in the rise of Buddhism in North America would soon occur: the arrival of Tibetan Buddhism and Vietnamese immigration into the United States after the end of the Vietnam War.

5-6d The Next Wave of Buddhist Immigration

The Tibetan Buddhist presence in North America began in the 1970s, when Tibetan meditation centers were first established by monks who had eventually settled there after fleeing Tibet. By 1990 almost every main Tibetan group had a center, especially on the East and West Coasts. These meditation centers serve Americans

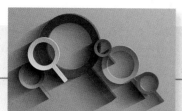

A Closer Look

Stealing Buddha's Dinner: A Memoir

In this critically praised novel, the author tells the story of her childhood as a Vietnamese Buddhist child in America. Bich Minh Nguyen (bit mihn nwin) was just eight months old when her father took her, her sister, and her grandmother out of Vietnam in 1975. They settled in Grand Rapids, Michigan, under the sponsorship of a Protestant church. Nguyen tells her story in terms of American and Vietnamese foods as she wrestled with conflicting desires for her grandmother's native cooking and American food, much of the latter the "junk food" her American friends ate. She also refers often to the pop songs she heard on the radio and sang along with, as well as the TV shows she watched, in the 1980s and early 1990s. More significantly, she traces out her complex family relationships, showing that the lives of displaced persons are often difficult for a variety of reasons.

Nguyen's short, engaging novel, published by Penguin in 2007, is a sometimes humorous coming-of-age tale that develops themes of loss, displacement, and new identity. The *San Francisco Chronicle* recommended it as "resonating with anyone who's ever felt like an outsider," but it makes a particular appeal to those who want to know what it's like to live as a young Buddhist immigrant in the United States. Although the author does not deal explicitly with her Buddhist background very often, the book itself is named from one short chapter that does deal with food offered to the Buddha in a home sacrifice: "Stealing Buddha's Dinner."

---

of non-Tibetan backgrounds, because relatively few Tibetan laypeople live in North America.

The 1990s also saw the rise of what some have called Hollywood or celebrity Buddhism. Various films about Tibet and its form of Buddhism gained much attention, especially *Seven Years in Tibet* and *Kundun.* Film stars such as Naomi Watts, Tina Turner, Steven Segal, Uma Thurman, and Richard Gere have publicly espoused Buddhism, especially Tibetan Buddhism. Gere has become a well-known spokesman for Buddhism in the world. Although golfer Tiger Woods has not openly championed his Buddhist beliefs, the disclosure of his multiple extramarital affairs in 2009 led to a public discussion of his adherence to Buddhism, and his long absence from golf tournaments due to physical ailments made some people wonder if karma was at work. In sum, celebrity Buddhism has played a role in the past twenty years in shaping the North American perception of Buddhism, in mainly positive, but sometimes superficial, ways.

In 1965, another U.S. Immigration Act resulted in a surge in emigration from Asia. Buddhists from Korea, Taiwan, Thailand, and Hong Kong filled old temples

Main worship hall with bell and drum towers at the Chuang Yen Monastery complex just north of New York City. The building of full-scale Buddhist temples in North America signals its growing presence and strength.

in the United States and established new ones. The major growth of Buddhism in the United States came in 1975 (see "A Closer Look: Stealing Buddha's Dinner"), when the Vietnam War ended as

> Celebrity Buddhism has played a role in the past twenty years in shaping the North American perception of Buddhism.

new context, where Buddhists are not numerous or socially powerful. The partly self-imposed pressure on Buddhists to secularize, convert to Christianity, or adapt elements of their wor-

Communist forces defeated the South Vietnamese army after U.S. withdrawal. The fall of South Vietnam occasioned another large wave of Buddhist immigration to the United States. When the mass-murderous Pol Pot regime in Cambodia fell in 1979, a wave of Cambodians also came. By 1990 there were approximately 1 million Vietnamese and Cambodians living in the United States. At first, these traumatized immigrants could only gather in their own homes to conduct basic forms of Buddhist worship and meditation, but by around 2000 they had made enough social and economic progress to found hundreds of temples and community centers to carry on their culture and faith for the second generation.

ship to Christianity has often been strong. The North American context fosters a level of internal Buddhist dialogue and cooperation that has never before been seen in Buddhism. At the same time, a few groups, such as Zen and Tibetan monastic orders, have become strong enough in North America to carry out their life on their own, without much interaction with other Buddhists.

5-6e Conclusion

As befits a religion that teaches that all things are impermanent, Buddhism has been constantly growing and changing. The Buddhist experience here—as for other religions in North America—has been one of adaptation and assimilation. A form of American Buddhism is growing, in which different people of different branches, countries, and sects of Asian Buddhism increasingly mix and cooperate with each other. In Asia, these different groups from Japan, Korea, Vietnam, Tibet, Thailand, and Taiwan seldom needed to work together—and indeed rarely wanted to meet. The situation that Henry Olcott found there more than a century ago is still too prevalent. In North America, however, Buddhists find themselves in a

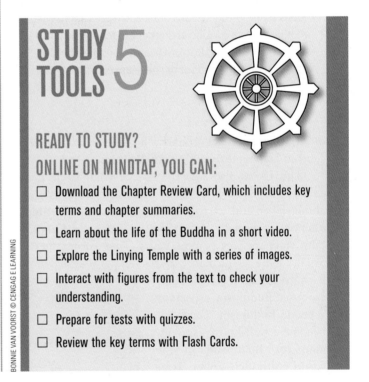

STUDY TOOLS 5

READY TO STUDY?
ONLINE ON MINDTAP, YOU CAN:

- ☐ Download the Chapter Review Card, which includes key terms and chapter summaries.
- ☐ Learn about the life of the Buddha in a short video.
- ☐ Explore the Linying Temple with a series of images.
- ☐ Interact with figures from the text to check your understanding.
- ☐ Prepare for tests with quizzes.
- ☐ Review the key terms with Flash Cards.

BONNIE VAN VOORST © CENGAGE LEARNING

Buddhism Timeline: 570 B.C.E.– Present

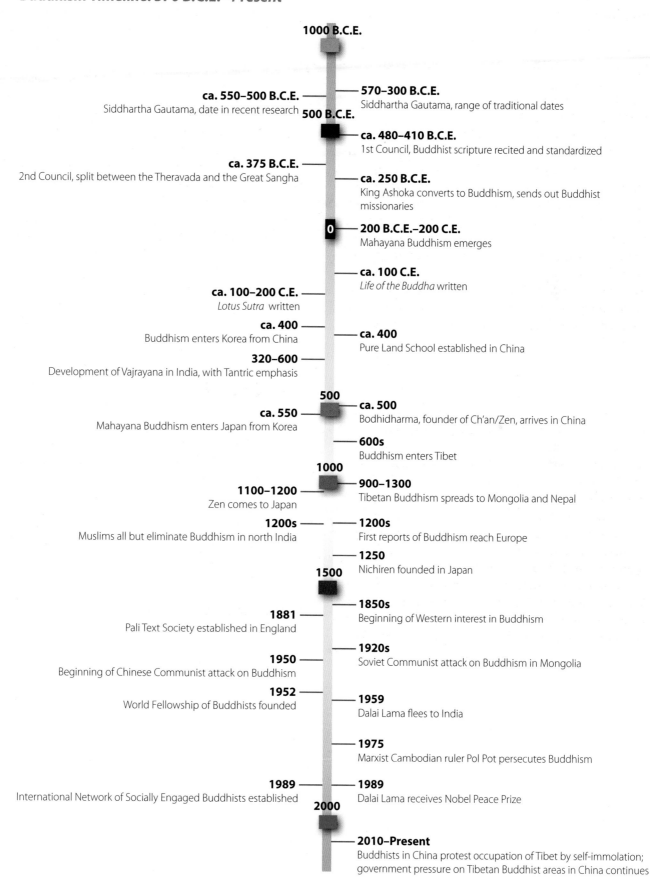

1000 B.C.E.

ca. 550–500 B.C.E.
Siddhartha Gautama, date in recent research

570–300 B.C.E.
Siddhartha Gautama, range of traditional dates

500 B.C.E.

ca. 480–410 B.C.E.
1st Council, Buddhist scripture recited and standardized

ca. 375 B.C.E.
2nd Council, split between the Theravada and the Great Sangha

ca. 250 B.C.E.
King Ashoka converts to Buddhism, sends out Buddhist missionaries

0

200 B.C.E.–200 C.E.
Mahayana Buddhism emerges

ca. 100 C.E.
Life of the Buddha written

ca. 100–200 C.E.
Lotus Sutra written

ca. 400
Buddhism enters Korea from China

ca. 400
Pure Land School established in China

320–600
Development of Vajrayana in India, with Tantric emphasis

500

ca. 550
Mahayana Buddhism enters Japan from Korea

ca. 500
Bodhidharma, founder of Ch'an/Zen, arrives in China

600s
Buddhism enters Tibet

1000

1100–1200
Zen comes to Japan

900–1300
Tibetan Buddhism spreads to Mongolia and Nepal

1200s
Muslims all but eliminate Buddhism in north India

1200s
First reports of Buddhism reach Europe

1250
Nichiren founded in Japan

1500

1850s
Beginning of Western interest in Buddhism

1881
Pali Text Society established in England

1920s
Soviet Communist attack on Buddhism in Mongolia

1950
Beginning of Chinese Communist attack on Buddhism

1952
World Fellowship of Buddhists founded

1959
Dalai Lama flees to India

1975
Marxist Cambodian ruler Pol Pot persecutes Buddhism

1989
International Network of Socially Engaged Buddhists established

1989
Dalai Lama receives Nobel Peace Prize

2000

2010–Present
Buddhists in China protest occupation of Tibet by self-immolation; government pressure on Tibetan Buddhist areas in China continues

6

Encountering Sikhism: The Way of God's Name

LEARNING OUTCOMES

After studying this chapter, you will be able to do the following:

6-1 Explain the meaning of *Sikhism* and related terms.

6-2 Summarize how Sikhism developed over time, especially its founding by the ten gurus and its life from the British Empire through the present.

6-3 Explain the essential Sikh teachings.

6-4 State and discuss the main ethical precepts of Sikhism.

6-5 Outline the way Sikhs worship and practice other rituals, especially life-cycle rituals.

6-6 Summarize the main features of Sikh life around the world today, especially in North America.

"There is only one God, whose name is true. Repeat his name!"—Sikh scripture

Your Visit to a Gurdwara

Sikhs at a service in the Gurdwara Sahib (Sikh temple) of Southwest Houston, Texas.

Visitors are welcome in any Sikh house of worship. The Sikh temple you'll visit today is the spacious new house of worship in Houston, Texas, which was established by Sikh immigrants to the Houston area from northern India.

As you go in the front door of the temple at about 10 o'clock on Sunday morning, you notice that the main hall is right in front of you. Similar to what Sikh worshipers do, you must remove your shoes; they belong to a special little shoe room just before the main hall. You must cover your head before entering the main hall. Because you didn't bring a head covering with you, a simple cloth is provided for you; many Sikhs in the main hall wear the same type of cloth. Smoking or even taking tobacco into the temple is forbidden, and if you have any alcohol on your breath you won't be admitted, even if you're completely sober.

Sikhs will bow to the big book under the canopy at the front of the main hall. This is the focal point of the temple. You also can give a slight but noticeable bow as a sign of respect, even if you don't share this religion. People then walk closer to the book and put an offering in front of it. These offerings are used to support the temple and the kitchen attached to it. If a person is too poor to offer money or food, he or she may offer a flower or a few words expressing thanks to God.

About two hundred people are attending the Sunday service. Everyone sits on the floor during the service; there are no cushions or seats. This is designed to make you humble in the presence of God, and it suggests that all are equal as they worship God. However, men and women must sit on separate sides. No one sits with their feet pointing at the book at the front; this is a sign of disrespect, so be careful where your toes point. If you walk around the book itself, you must do so in a clockwise direction, the way it's done in various Sikh ceremonies.

< A Sikh prepares to immerse himself in the waters around the Sikh golden-roofed temple in Amritsar, India.

The service consists of a few readings from the scripture book under the canopy and several songs led by musicians occupying a place to the side of the canopy. The event ends with the serving of a handful of a sweet vegetarian food. You should take this in cupped hands as a gift from God. It's not really an appetizer, but there is more food to come in about an hour; a free meal of vegetarian Indian food is offered in the adjoining hall, something Sikhs consider an important part of the service.

Sikhism is much smaller than Hinduism and Islam, but it is nonetheless important on the world stage. In 2010, the last year in which careful estimates were made, Sikhs numbered around 25 million. Most Sikhs are ethnic Punjabis (poon-JAHB-ees) living in northwest India. Sikhism is a tenacious faith that has been able to endure much pressure from Hinduism and Islam, and now from the national government of India. Sikhism has the following unique features:

- Founded between 1500 and 1700 C.E., Sikhism is one of the newest major world religions, but it isn't considered as one of the new religious movements.

- Sikhism was influenced by mystical, devotional movements in Hinduism and Islam, but Sikhs view it as God's direct revelation of a new religion.

- Sikhism began as a more-or-less pacifist religion but shifted to militancy for reasons of self-defense early in its history.

- Sikhism is one of the smaller faiths treated as a world religion, although Sikhs often say that their religion is the fifth largest in the world and rightly point out that it is widely spread around the world today.

DR. TEJENDRA GILL, SECRETARY/GURDWARA SAHIB OF SOUTHWEST HOUSTON

A Closer Look

The Symbol of Sikhism

Sikhism has several unofficial symbols: the turban; the Ek Onkar (ehk ON-kahr), or "God is One" phrase from the opening of the Sikh scriptures; and the Five Ks (all of which will be discussed in this chapter). They are dwarfed, however, by the use of the **khanda** (literally, "double-edged sword") as the main Sikh symbol. You'll see it on the Sikh flag that flies in front of and inside many gurdwaras (Sikh houses of worship). Four items, all traditional Sikh weapons, form the khanda. The Sikh symbol is unique among all the symbols of world religions for its military features.

The center is a vertical double-edged sword with a

Figure 6.1 Symbol of Sikhism

BONNIE VAN VOORST © CENGAGE LEARNING

broad blade. On the outside are two curved single-edged swords; many Sikh men carry a small one at all times, and we'll talk more about this further on. The two swords are often said to represent both the spiritual and the political power of Sikhism. At the top center is a metal ring called a *chakkar* (CHAHK-uhr). It's similar to a discus, and effective as a weapon up to about 150 feet. You may have seen a chakkar in popular film and television.

Similar to most religious symbols, the khanda has also been interpreted symbolically. The circle is often said to represent the unity and eternity of God. The vertical two-edged sword symbolizes God's concern for both truth and justice, and two crossed kirpans curved around the outside signify God's all-encompassing spiritual power.

{ *The Sikh symbol is unique among all the symbols of world religions for its military features.* }

6-1 The Name *Sikhism*

Sikh means disciple or student. Because the religion was founded by a line of gurus, or teachers, it's appropriate that those who follow it are called students. *Sikh* is usually pronounced "seek," but occasionally like "sick." *Sikhism* is the common, everyday name for the religion of the Sikhs. The early Sikh community called it the **Panth**, meaning "path." This name was too generic to last—all religions are paths, after all. The Sikhs themselves formally call their faith **Gurmat**, "the Guru's Way." *Gurmat* suggests the importance of gurus in Sikhism.

Sikhism was established by Guru Nanak (NAHN-ahk) around 1499 C.E. and then led by nine other gurus. Sikhs believe that all ten gurus had the same soul, that of Guru Nanak. The tenth guru, Gobind Singh (GOH-bind sing), led a change in Sikhism from pacifism to militarism (for Sikh militarism, see "A Closer Look: The Symbol of Sikhism"). When he died in 1708, the soul of these gurus was believed to have gone into the scripture of Sikhism, the **Guru Granth** (literally, "Guru Book"). Now this soul is believed to reside in each and every true copy of this scripture—the soul of the guru became the soul of the *Guru Granth*.

6-2 Sikhism Today as Shaped by Its Past: Two Key Periods

Regional Sikh officials in British Columbia, Canada, gathered to address the 2006 arson of the Sikh temple in Williams Lake, BC. The main hall was damaged in the fire, and much repair work would need to be done before the building could be used again. In addition to calling on police to solve this case, the gathering announced plans for the ritual cremation of the "body" of the main Sikh scripture book, the *Guru*

khanda [KAHN-duh] "Double-edged sword," the main symbol of Sikhism

Sikh [seek] "Disciple" or "student," follower of Sikhism

Panth [pahnth] "Path," an early name for Sikhism

Gurmat [GOOR-maht] "Guru's Way," Sikhs' formal name for their faith

Guru Granth [GOO-roo grahnth] "Guru Book"; the main scripture of Sikhism

Meditation on the name and being of God has always been one of the main practices of Sikhism.

Granth, which was damaged in the arson. They called the damage done to this book an "attempted murder of the living leader and teacher of the Sikhs." This startling statement reflects the long-standing Sikh devotion to their scripture as the literal embodiment of the soul of the ten founding gurus. It also reflects the long, sad history of Sikhs having to endure persecution.

6-2a The Ten Gurus

When we think of India, we tend to focus on Hinduism, but for more than a thousand years Muslims have been influential there. Sikhism arose in predominantly Hindu northern India while it was under Muslim control (see Map 6.1). During the time of the first few gurus, Muslim rulers tended to be tolerant of this new group; at the time of the later gurus, however, the rulers grew intolerant, and at times used violence.

Around 1499 C.E., Guru Nanak (1469–1539) began teachings that many saw as a new sect within Hinduism. Nanak was a Hindu and came to accept some features of the mystical **Sant** (meaning "saint") tradition of northern India, a devotional movement of both Hindus and Muslims. The Sants composed songs about the divine presence and power that they saw in all things. Several of these hymns were even incorporated later into the Sikh scriptures. The Sants promoted devotion to God as essential to obeying God (important for Muslims) and liberation from the endless cycle of reincarnation (important for Hindus). However,

Nanak also had differences with the Sant poets; for example, he started his own religious community and passed his teachings and leadership of this community to successors. Nanak preached a message of universal love and tolerance, downplaying the differences between religions and highlighting their similarities. Because of the religious situation in northern India, he particularly related his movement to Hinduism and Islam.

Nanak collected a small number of students, and it was from this first guru–student relationship that the name *Sikhism* came. He composed many mystical hymns that were eventually collected in the Sikh scripture. Nanak visited pilgrimage sites throughout India to spread his message of "remembering the name" of the one and only God by meditating on God constantly and devoting oneself to him. Moreover, Nanak had a peaceful, even pacifistic message: God's purposes could not be advanced by coercion or violence. This message, except for pacifism, has become the foundation of Sikhism through today. Beyond this, very little is known for certain about Nanak. The story of his life has been expanded at length in the *janamsakhis* (JAH-nahm SAHK-ees; "life stories"), composed in the century after his death. Today, scholars (but not pious Sikhs) see them as legendary.

Nine gurus followed Nanak. They led the Sikh community and developed its religious beliefs and practices over the next two centuries: Angad Dev (guru from 1539 to 1552), Amar Das (1552–1574), Ram Das (1574–1581), Arjan (1581–1606), Har Gobind (1606–1644), Har Rai (1644–1661), Har Krishan (1661–1664), Tegh Bahadur (1664–1675), and Gobind Singh (1675–1708). These ten gurus are greatly revered in Sikhism today, particularly because the single soul that inhabited all of them when they were gurus has now entered the Sikh scripture.

Ram Das, the fourth guru, married a daughter of the third guru. He is famous in India for founding the city of Amritsar (uhm-RIT-suhr), which would soon become the center of Sikhism. In Amritsar Sikhs built the **Darbar Sahib**, the "Sacred Court," also called the **Harmandir Sahib**, the

Sant [sahnt] Devotional movement of Hindus and Muslims in northern India

Darbar Sahib (Harmandir Sahib) [HAR-mahn-dear SAH-ihb] "House of God" temple in Amritsar, known popularly as the Golden Temple

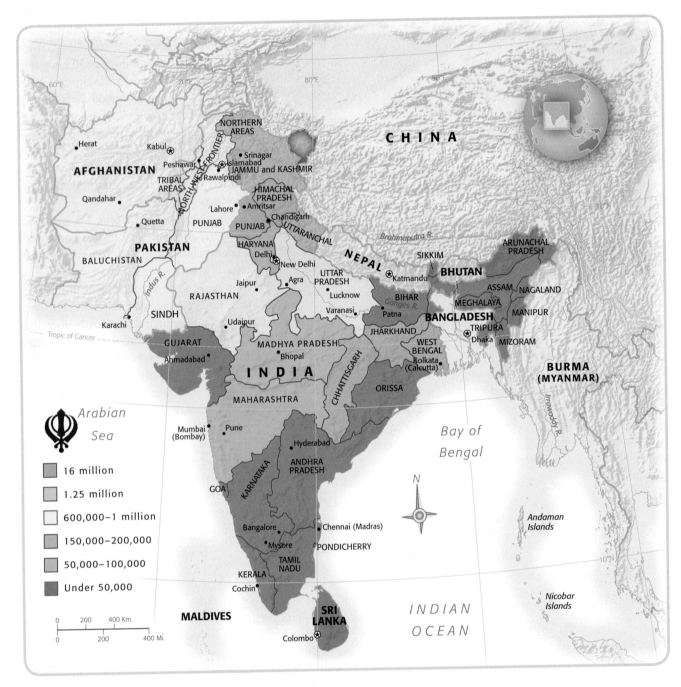

Map 6.1
Sikh Population in India and Sri Lanka, 2010

"House of God." The most common of its names, the Golden Temple, came after it was overlaid with gold in the early 1800s, but Sikhs do not typically use this name, preferring instead the Darbar/Harmandir Sahib. The Mughal (MOO-gull) emperor Akbar respected the new faith, and he granted Ram Das the land for the Darbar Sahib and permission to build it. Another lasting legacy of Ram Das is hymn singing during worship. He designated his son Arjan (AHR-juhn) to succeed him, and all the gurus after Arjan were Ram's descendants as well.

By the time of Arjan, the fifth guru, Sikhism was well established as a separate religious movement. Arjan made Amritsar the capital of the Sikh world, made it the religious center of Sikhism with the Harmandir Sahib, and began to compile the main Sikh scripture, called the *Adi Granth*, or First Book (now known more commonly as the *Guru Granth*). However, the Mughal rulers felt threatened by Arjan, and he was executed in 1606 after days of continuous torture. First the emperor's agents sat him in a tank of boiling water, the

Guru Nanak and Gobind Singh, with the other eight gurus and the richly covered *Guru Granth* at the center, in a Sikh devotional poster.

The tenth guru, Gobind Singh, who died in 1708, was the most important guru since Nanak. His portrait and that of Guru Nanak are prominently displayed in Sikh homes. The son of the ninth guru, he brought Sikhism to the basic form it is today. Gobind Singh finished the compilation of the *Adi Granth*, and it was renamed the *Guru Granth*. (Sikhs usually refer to it more honorifically as the Guru Granth Sahib, the *Revered Master Guru Granth*.) He formed the **Khalsa** ("the pure ones") as a select society within Sikhism in 1699, so that Sikhs would be soldier-saints, able and willing to defend their religion. The Khalsa has been a select and influential society within the main body of Sikhs since its inception, but not all Sikhs have belonged to it. Gobind Singh established the current Sikh rite of initiation and the distinctive dress of the Sikhs. A number of his sayings have been collected into a book called the **Dasam Granth**, commonly called the Tenth Book but better understood as the Book of the Tenth Guru. Often quoted from the *Dasam Granth* is his statement, "The temple and the mosque are one; so too are puja [Hindu worship] and prostration [Muslim worship]. All men are one though they seem to be many."

6-2b Sikhism from British Rule until Today

Sikhs lived, and on the whole prospered, in the Punjab in the 1700s. However, by 1757 Great Britain had begun its century-long conquest of India to make it the "jewel in the crown" of its empire. In 1845 to 1846, British troops defeated the Sikh armies and took over a great deal of Sikh territory in the Punjab, a prosperous region of India. The Sikhs, who, under Ranjit Singh, had founded the first and only independent Sikh nation in northern India in 1819, rebelled in an effort to regain their independence. The British quickly crushed this revolt. The Sikhs and the British then managed to build a working relationship. Soon the Sikhs were serving with honor in the British army in India and in police forces in the worldwide empire. After about 1860, Sikh migration to Africa and the west began, especially to Britain and parts of the British Empire, such as Canada.

next day on a plate of red-hot iron. On the third day they poured hot sand over his blisters. Arjan remained calm and peaceful throughout this ordeal to show that people should accept the will of God; he became the first Sikh martyr. The significance of Arjan's death was not lost on the Sikhs. The next guru, Har Gobind, began to arm the Sikh community to resist the rising persecution they encountered. Similar to his predecessors, Har Gobind exercised spiritual leadership, but he added governmental leadership as well, making the Sikhs a political community.

The Sikhs then lived in relative peace with their Muslim overlords until a less tolerant Mughal emperor tried to force his subjects to accept Islam. In the course of this persecution, he arrested and executed the ninth guru, Tegh Bahadur (tehg BAH-hah-duhr), in 1675. A Sikh stole Bahadur's body and hid it in his own house. To cremate the guru's body while avoiding detection and certain death, he burned down his house.

> "All men are one though they seem to be many."
> —Gobind Singh

Khalsa [KALL-suh] "The pure ones," Sikh society dedicated to strict observance

Dasam Granth [DAH-sum grahnth] Book of the Tenth Guru, Gobind Singh

The situation of Sikhs in the world today has largely been shaped by the partition of British India. When India became independent in 1947, its territory was divided between India and the new Muslim nation of Pakistan. This partition disadvantaged the Sikhs; the new border ran right through their home in the Punjab. Most Sikhs preferred to live in a secular state dominated by Hindus rather than in an Islamic state. Sikhs who found themselves in the new Pakistani areas of the Punjab fled to the Indian side, often displacing Muslims, who fled to Pakistan. Considerable violence ensued with loss of life on both sides. When the dust settled, the Sikhs found that they had lost much of their homeland, and were understandably embittered over this loss.

The Sikhs' continued desire for their own nation, which had persisted since the 1700s, was something that the new state of India refused to grant. As Sikh discontent grew, the political conflict suddenly became violent. Jarnail Singh Bhindranwale (BIN-drahn-wail), a Khalsa member known for his zeal for Sikhism, began around 1980 to lead the most radicalized Sikhs. In 1983, Bhindranwale and hundreds of his followers, heavily armed, captured the entire Sacred Court complex in Amritsar. They demanded that the Indian government set up an independent Sikh homeland, which they would call *Khalistan* (KALL-ih-stahn), "land of the Khalsa." In 1984, the Indian army launched an assault to crush this rebellion. The fighting to retake the Sacred Court complex was fierce. Over 1000 Sikh militants and Indian soldiers were killed, and the Sikh buildings were heavily damaged.

The assault shocked most Sikhs. They saw Prime Minister Indira Gandhi, who had ordered it, as another in the long line of Indian rulers who persecuted the Sikhs. In October 1984, Gandhi's Sikh bodyguards assassinated her in reprisal. Four days of anti-Sikh rioting followed, with mobs roaming the Indian capital of Delhi and other cities, burning Sikh shops and even setting Sikhs on fire with gasoline. Thousands of Sikhs, perhaps as many as ten thousand, were killed.

These events are a sore point for Sikhs today, but are only a part of the story of Sikhism since 1947. On the whole, Sikhs in India have enjoyed prosperity and educational opportunities for women and men. The Sikh demand for their own nation still has not been met,

©ERMESS/SHUTTERSTOCK.COM

The short knife carried by many Sikh men symbolizes resistance to oppression.

but the Punjab has been mostly peaceful despite some continuing tensions. The appointment of Manmohan (muhn-MOH-huhn) Singh, an Oxford-educated Sikh economist, as prime minister of India in 2004 created great pride and confidence for Sikhs around the world. It has given Sikhs a calming assurance that their concerns are heard—and spoken of—at the highest levels in India.

6-3 Essential Sikh Teachings

Sikhs appeal to the city council of Cardiff, United Kingdom, for permission to scatter the ashes of their deceased loved ones at a fixed site in a park along the Taff River. The scattering ceremony takes about 15 minutes and includes prayers and recitation of Sikh scripture passages as well as the actual scattering of the ashes. Sikhs had previously obtained the permission of the regional agency in charge of environmental affairs and conducted a few scatterings. But the city council took exception, and a follow-up request ran into some opposition. The issue is a sensitive one: Not only is the scattering of ashes a matter of a funeral rite, but also it touches on basic Sikh teachings on reincarnation and release from it.

As we saw previously, Sikhism is often compared with Islam and Hinduism, the main religions among which it was born and grew. Sikhism does share several key beliefs with devotional Hinduism and Sufi Islam. However, it has its own beliefs and practices that make it a distinct religion.

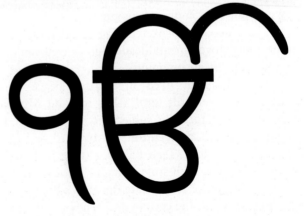

Figure 6.2   The Ek Onkar symbol

BONNIE VAN VOORST © CENGAGE LEARNING

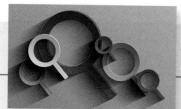

A Closer Look

Sikh Dress

A Sikh who is a member of the Khalsa wears the **Five Ks**. Other Sikhs *may* wear it, but members of the Khalsa *must*. Both men and women observe the Five Ks, the men more fully. They are as follows:

- *Kesh* (kehsh), uncut hair. Sikh men and women never cut or trim hair anywhere on their bodies. Hair on one's head is covered with a scarf for women and a turban (a single long cloth wound around the head) for men.

- *Kanga* (KAHN-guh), small comb. This is used to keep one's long hair neat.

- *Kirpan* (KEER-pahn), sword. This steel sword symbolizes one's defense of the faith and of oppressed people. It's worn at all times on the outside of the body, usually in a small form similar to a knife.

- *Kara* (KAH-ruh), bracelet. This stainless steel item is worn on the right wrist, a reminder of unity with God and the Sikh community.

- *Kachha* (KAHCH-uh), underpants. These are a reminder of the duty of purity.

©PANDORA64/SHUTTERSTOCK.COM

Five Ks of Sikhism: The turban is often thought by non-Sikhs to be one of the five Ks, but the K is what it covers: uncut hair.

6-3a The One God

Sikhs worship one universal God and hold that only one God actually exists, so they are rightly considered monotheists. God is one, holy, loving, and gracious. God does not have a body, nor does he become incarnated in human form, so God cannot and should not be pictured. This belief makes Sikhism a strongly aniconic (against images) religion. Neither do Sikhs have a specific name for God; the way that Guru Nanak spoke of God, as The True Name, has become the most common. Sikhs use the phrase **Waheguru**, meaning "Praise to the Guru," for God, especially in the context of worship. "Guru" in "Waheguru" refers, of course, to God as teacher, not any human guru. The second important symbol of Sikhism, the **Ek Onkar**, means "One God." The Ek Onkar is found in the Mul Mantar, the opening lines of the *Guru Granth*, and is repeated every day by observant

Sikhs: "There is only one God, whose name is true, the Creator who has no fear or hatred. He is immortal, unborn, self-existent; [He is known] by the favor of the guru. Repeat His Name!"

6-3b Devotion to God

Devotion to the one God in knowledge, emotion, and behavior is central to Sikhism. As in Hindu devotional movements, music has been a key way to cultivate and express this devotion. Sikh worship features extensive singing of passages from

Five Ks Five items of dress for Khalsa members: kesh (uncut hair), kanga (comb), kirpan (sword), kara (bracelet), and kachha (underpants)

Waheguru [vah-heh-GOO-roo] Name for God used especially in worship

Ek Onkar [ehk ON-kahr] "One God"; its written form is a prominent symbol of Sikhism

the *Guru Granth* to cultivate emotional and intellectual devotion to God. Salvation from the endless cycle of reincarnation comes from remembering God constantly and devoting one's life to God. Although Sikhism began as a pacifist movement, devotion to God now means a willingness to put one's life on the line for God. Devotion to God causes traditionally observant Sikhs, especially members of the Khalsa, to dress in a way that is distinctive, both in India and in the wider world (see "A Closer Look: Sikh Dress").

Let's look more closely now at some of these key teachings. Similar to other religions native to India, Sikhism teaches that all people undergo the transmigration of their soul. This cycle of reincarnation causes pain, suffering, and ignorance of God, because the world in which souls transmigrate is filled with illusion. The only way of release from this cycle is meditation on the divine **Nam** (Name). The Sikh believer undertakes the main practice of this religion: meditation on the Nam or remembering the Nam. Many Sikhs use forms of yoga adapted for their religion to help in meditation. Devoting oneself more and more to God, the believer is blessed with increasing inner peace and joy. Finally, the believer reaches the "abode of truth" and enters perfect union with God. At this point, there is no more reincarnation.

> { The main practice of Sikhism is "meditation on the Name." }

6-4 Key Sikh Ethics

In 2010, Nikki Haley became governor of South Carolina, its first governor who was not a white male. Born Nimrata Nikki Randhawa to devout Sikh parents in Bamberg, South Carolina, she converted to Christianity and has attended both the local Sikh temple and a United Methodist church. She has served in the South Carolina House of Representatives, and run a fashion business. Haley is known for her personal charm and political poise, and she is a rising star in the Republican Party. But in the sometimes-nasty arena of South Carolina politics, Haley was accused in the primary

Nam [nahm] Name of God

langar [LAHN-gar] Communal meal after every main Sikh service

Cooks preparing a meal for pilgrims at the Golden Temple, feeding up to 100,000 people a day for free. The langar is a prominent Sikh witness to social equality.

campaign of having two extramarital affairs. She sharply attacked these claims of infidelity, a conduct that both Christianity and Sikhism strongly forbid. She won the primary and general elections handily. In 2016, Haley was appointed U.S. ambassador to the United Nations, a cabinet-level post, becoming the most prominent person with a Sikh background in the United States.

Sikhs have a strong sense of ethics that is closely related to their view of one God. We'll examine in particular the Sikh social ethic that rejects traditional caste distinctions, and then we'll treat personal ethics.

6-4a Rejection of Hindu Caste

Sikhism from the first has strongly rejected Hindu caste distinctions, so there is usually no toleration of caste in a gurdwara. Sikhs from all caste backgrounds sit together, but with women on one side, and men on the other. The gurus denounced caste as irrelevant for access to God, to God's name, and to liberation from sin, ignorance, and transmigration. Another sign of the Sikhs' belief in social equality is the food after the service, which people of all social backgrounds donate, prepare, and eat together. In the **langar**, the communal meal that follows every main Sikh service, everyone sits in a straight line where no one can claim a higher status. (Men and women are usually in different lines at the langar, however, just as they sit on different sides during the main service.) We'll discuss the langar at greater length in Section 6-5b.

Although Sikhism has opposed Hindu castes, many Sikhs still have a caste. More than 60 percent of Sikhs belong to an agricultural caste. Two trading castes form a very small, albeit influential, minority within the Sikh community. Others include two Dalit castes, which are the lowest on the social scale. Sikhs have a few castes of their own in addition to Hindu castes, for example, the artisans, and they also have distinctive names for several castes shared with Hinduism. Sikhs typically marry within their caste.

6-4b Other Moral Rules

In Sikh personal ethics, the use of alcohol, drugs, and any addictive substance is forbidden. Tobacco is forbidden as well. Sikhs believe in hard work and generous charity. Members of the Khalsa are required to wear the Five Ks and to avoid four particular sins: cutting their hair, eating meat not butchered according to Sikh rules, adultery, and using tobacco and intoxicants. Sikhs who commit these sins must confess them openly and be reinitiated into the religion. If they commit these sins and don't confess, they are excluded from the faith.

Sikhs have drawn up several codes of conduct that enumerate the moral principles and behaviors by which they are to live. Here is a popular code:

- Only one God exists; remember and worship only the one God.

- Work hard and honestly and share your gains with others.

- Be truthful in all of life.

- Women are equal to men in God's sight and must be treated as equals.

- All humans are members of one human family, so distinctions based on caste or color are to be avoided.

- Do not trust in superstitions or follow empty rituals; do not use idols, magic, omens, fasts, religious body markings, sacred threads, and so on.

- Dress simply and modestly; showy or revealing clothes reflect poorly on those who wear them.

- Sikh women must not wear a veil, nor should they or Sikh men have any body piercings.

- All persons should marry and have children, and stay in the married state; asceticism and renunciation of marriage are pointless.

- Have faith in the *Guru Granth*, not in any other book or person.

- Control the Five Evils—lust, anger, greed, attachment to material things, and arrogance.

- Practice the Five Virtues—truth, contentment, compassion, humility, and love.

6-5 Sikh Rituals and Worship

Worshipers at a Sikh temple on a weekday afternoon see three life-cycle ceremonies. First, a baby is brought in for a naming ceremony. The official reader opens the *Guru Granth* at random, and the first letter on the left-hand page becomes the first letter in the child's first name. Second, a young couple comes to be married. During the ceremony, the couple circles the *Granth* several times as musicians sing verses from its marriage hymns. Third, the relatives of a recently deceased Sikh come for the conclusion of his funeral rites. A prominent feature of the funeral is the continuous reading of the entire *Granth*, a process that takes two days, and the relatives are present for the solemn end of the reading.

Similar to most mystics who value individual thought and emotion, Guru Nanak and his successors were deeply suspicious of formal ritual practices. He rejected the Hindu priesthood and all its ritual activities, and not just because it was connected to caste. Instead, Nanak taught that only with strong devotion shown in faith and love can one reach God. Nevertheless, similar to any other religion, Sikhism has a significant ritual component. We'll begin by discussing the center of Sikh life—the Sikh temples—and what happens there.

> *Guru Nanak and his successors were deeply suspicious of formal ritual practices.*

6-5a The Gurdwara

The Punjabi word **gurdwara** means "the Guru's door," which implies that the gurdwara is the residence of the Guru. The Guru is the living Sikh book, the *Guru Granth*. The gurdwara is the place of everyday worship, in the morning. It's where children learn Sikh history, morals, and sacred writings. Especially in the western world, the gurdwara is also a community and social-welfare center for Sikhs. Gurdwaras are supervised by a committee drawn from the membership.

gurdwara [guhr-DWAHR-uh] "The Guru's door," Sikh house of worship

There are four doors into a gurdwara, modeled after the four doors of the main temple in Amritsar. They are the doors of peace, livelihood, learning, and grace. Gurdwaras often fly the Sikh flag outside. Small rooms for coats and shoes can be found near the entry; shoes must be removed before worship. No statues or even religious pictures are in the gurdwara, because Sikhs regard God as having no physical form and having no incarnation that can be pictured. Nor are there any candles, incense, or bells—used prominently in Hindu and Buddhist worship. Flowers are often present, however, especially in front of the scripture book.

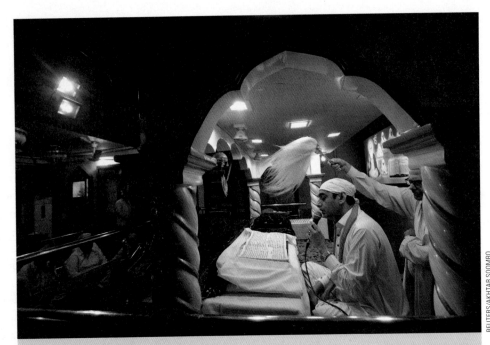

A reader in Karachi, Pakistan, recites from the Sikh scriptures as an assistant fans the book with a chaur.

The focus of attention in the gurdwara, both architecturally and in worship, is the *Guru Granth*. Sikhs give the Guru Book as much respect as a human guru—perhaps even more. It is kept in a special room at night (put to bed) and carried ceremonially to the main hall before worship begins in the morning. Then it is placed on a platform called a throne, and covered with a richly woven cloth when not being read. When Sikhs enter the main hall, they bow deeply to the book, sometimes touching their head to the floor. A man with a ceremonial fan, the **chaur**, waves it over the *Guru Granth* while it is being read. Although Sikhs revere their scripture book, this reverence is paid directly to its spiritual content and the living soul of the gurus in it, not to the book itself.

Sikh worship in a gurdwara does not follow an official form, although there is an informal order of service. Worship usually commences with the singing of "Asa Di Var" (AH-sah dee vahr), written by Guru Nanak. Instruments then accompany the singing of other hymns from the *Guru Granth*. Hymn singing, called **kirtan**, is a major element of Sikh worship. Many gurdwaras have a small group of musicians who lead the kirtan from the front. A short talk comes next, usually drawing on a teaching from Sikh tradition. Then comes the singing of "Anand Sahib," written by Guru Amar Das. After the singing, the congregation stands for prayer, keeping their eyes closed and their bodies still.

Next, the *Guru Granth* is opened at random, and a passage beginning on the left-hand page is read as the lesson of the day. This feature of Sikh scripture usage is called **vak lao**, "taking [God's] word." In the home or in the temple, the scripture is always opened at random, and the reading begins from the top of the left-hand page. This vak lao reading is thought to hold special significance for the occasion, and Sikhs believe that God guides which page falls open. This is God's word for the moment, a word that must be taken into the believer's life. Every day in the main temple in Amritsar, the *Guru Granth* is opened at random for the passage of the day, called the *hukamnama*, to be read out, and the passage is published on the Internet for all Sikhs around the world to read.

In India many Sikhs go to their gurdwara before work or during the day for private prayer and meditation. Sikhs do not observe a fixed day of the week as a holy day, but in the West they usually go to a gurdwara on Sunday morning, when services are regularly held. Services are also held there on important Sikh holy days.

chaur [chowr] Fan used to venerate the *Guru Granth* in the gurdwara

kirtan [KEER-tahn] Singing of hymns from the *Guru Granth*

vak lao [vahk low] "Taking [God's] word" by opening and reading the *Guru Granth* at random

As stated previously, Sikhs do not have ordained priests, although sometimes high officials at Sikh gurdwaras are mistaken for priests. Any male Sikh can (if he can read the language of the *Guru Granth*) lead the congregation in prayer and read the scriptures. Every gurdwara has at least one **granthi** who cares for the *Guru Granth*, reads from it during the service, and in general organizes the daily services. A granthi must be fluent in the Gurmukhi dialect in which the *Granth* is written, and must be able to care for the *Granth*. Granthis can be male or female, although women granthis are still rare and typically found only in the West. Granthis are most often Khalsa members.

Near the end of the service, food is offered to the congregation. This is **parshad**, a warm dessert-like treat made from flour, sugar, and liquefied butter. (Visitors sometimes don't appreciate its sweet, oily taste, but it should be graciously accepted, to avoid giving unintended offense. Sikhs who don't like its taste ask for a small portion.) The first five portions of parshad are offered to the Khalsa members present. Then it is served to everyone else without further social or religious distinctions.

rice pudding; water and tea are served as beverages. In Europe and North America, members of a gurdwara sign up to buy and prepare the food for the Sunday-noon langar, which is considered both a duty and an honor.

6-5c Sikh Life-Cycle Rituals from Birth to Death

Even though Sikhism is mainly nonritualistic, it does not downplay or ignore the meaning of life-cycle changes. Sikhism recognizes four major life-cycle events with formal rites of passage. The first ritual is a naming ceremony for newborns, held in a gurdwara when the mother has recovered from childbirth. A hymn is selected at random from the *Guru Granth* by an official reader, and, as mentioned previously, parents choose a traditional Sikh name for newborn children that begins with the first letter on the left-hand page. (This means that well-prepared Sikh parents have to think through possible names for all the letters of the Gurmuki alphabet.) *Singh* ("Lion") is given as a second personal name (as we say, a middle name) to all males, and *Kaur* ("Princess") to all females.

A second life-cycle ritual is marriage, called by Sikhs "blissful

Hands of a Sikh bride, decorated with henna, and groom in India

JOSHKHO/DREAMSTIME.COM

union." As a part of the ceremony, always held in a gurdwara, the bride and groom walk four times around the *Guru Granth* as one of its hymns is sung. It's likely that this circling of the holy book was introduced around 1900 to distinguish Sikh marriage from the Hindu wedding ritual of walking around a sacred fire. Whatever its time of origin, this makes a dignified recognition of the central importance of the Sikh scripture in one's marriage.

6-5b The Langar

Every gurdwara has a langar, a dining hall, attached to it. As we saw previously, this term is also used for the communal meal itself. The langar meal helps to build social and spiritual solidarity in the gurdwara. Most people in the service stay for the communal meal; observant Sikhs in the western world don't go out for Sunday brunch. The food in the langar must be uniform and plain to discourage wealthy Sikhs from using it to display their prosperity. Many Sikhs are vegetarian, so only vegetarian dishes are served in a langar. The meal typically includes dal, a variety of vegetables, and

granthi [GRAHN-thee] Official who cares for the *Guru Granth* and reads from it

parshad [PAHR-shahd] Simple food served at the end of a Sikh service

The third rite is initiation into the Khalsa, called Amrit (UHM-rith). Outsiders often call this "baptism," even though that term is of Christian origin. Five initiated Sikhs officiate at the ritual, while a sixth is positioned reverently at the *Guru Granth*. Amrit includes pouring water into an iron bowl and then dissolving sweet powder in the water. One of the officiants then stirs this with a double-edged sword. The Sikh sitting at the *Guru Granth* then recites certain portions of the Sikh scriptures, and the initiates drink five handfuls of the water, now called amrit ("nectar" of immortality). Each time this is done, the Sikh giving the water cries the main slogan

Sikhs perform traditional kirpan combat during a festival in Faenza, Italy.

of Sikhism, "Praise to the Guru's Khalsa! Praise to the Guru's victory!" Amrit is then sprinkled on the initiates' head, and they drink the rest of it. They recite the lines that begin the *Guru Granth*, and the obligations of being a Sikh are taught to them briefly. Finally, parshad is distributed, each person taking it from the same dish.

The fourth rite is the funeral ceremony, which is designed to release the soul from the body so that reincarnation can occur. Cremation and scattering of ashes into fresh, flowing water is done soon after death. When this is done in India, there is no legal problem, but scattering of ashes into flowing streams has caused occasional problems in western nations. These are not done at the gurdwara, of course, but an important part of a funeral service is in the gurdwara: the continuous reading of the entire *Guru Granth*. This is for the consolation and support of the grieving family. Relatives and friends of the deceased are expected to be present for the completion of the reading, at which time the funeral is considered finished. Musicians sing appropriate hymns, and short parts of the *Guru Granth* are read again. After the final prayer, parshad is given to the congregation.

6-5d Other Festivals

Sikhism probably seems like a serious religion to you, but it does have its festive side. In fact, Sikhism probably has more festivals than any other world religion. There are three holidays every year for each of the ten gurus—to mark their birth, their becoming a guru, and their death.

In addition to these holidays for the gurus, Sikhism has eight major festivals. Four of them mark the more important events in the lives of the gurus. The other four are the festival of the installation of the *Guru Granth*, the New Year festival of Baisakhi (buy-SAHK-ee), the all-Indian winter festival of lights known as Diwali (dee-WALL-ee), and Hola Mahalla (HOH-luh ma-HALL-uh). Festivals often have processions in the streets and visits to gurdwaras, particularly to those associated with one of the gurus or with some historical event. Speeches are commonly made to crowds of worshipers.

Hindus, Sikhs, and Jains alike observe the festival of Diwali. For Sikhs, Diwali has a historical connection with the happy release of Guru Har Gobind from imprisonment by the Mughal emperor. Gobind Singh established Hola Mahalla, which is held the day after the Hindu festival of Holi, as an alternative to the Hindu holiday. It's celebrated with parades and displays of Sikh martial arts.

6-6 Sikhism around the World Today

In a rare exception to U.S. Army regulations, Captain Simratpal Singh was temporarily allowed in 2015 to keep his neatly trimmed beard and wrap his hair in a turban. Since he was a cadet at West Point, Singh's hair had been buzzed short by the Army, and he was required to shave his face. Singh, a decorated combat engineer, remarked about this religious accommodation, "I had been living a double life, wearing a turban only at home. My two worlds have finally come back together." In 2016, this exemption was made permanent.

6-6a The Sikh Diaspora

Until well into the 1800s, Sikhs who left the Punjab, in relatively small numbers, were traders who settled in other parts of India or in closely neighboring countries. When India came under British control, Sikhs spread more widely in the unified nation. In the late 1800s, the posting of Sikh soldiers in the British army to stations in Malaya and Hong Kong prompted other Sikhs to migrate to those territories. This migration eventually spread to Australia, New Zealand, Fiji, and China as Sikhs discovered that their skills in commerce and trade—and not just those of soldiers and police—were widely valued in Asia. Many Sikhs migrated to the United Kingdom and established a strong presence there that lasts through today.

A recent book, *Sikhism in Global Context* by Pashaura Singh of the University of Michigan, carefully examines the current Sikh diaspora. Singh writes that the Sikh community has made its presence felt worldwide because of this dispersion. Although he does not specifically make this claim, his analysis shows that Sikhism has become a world religion in ways it was not earlier, when it was largely confined to India. An appreciation of the Sikh experience in various countries serves to help in understanding Sikhs from a global point of view, particularly how Sikhism is changing in the world. The author finds that the *Guru Granth* has been a constant source of shaping the Sikhs wherever they have gone—even for nonviolence, which challenges traditional Sikh ideas about militant self-defense.[1]

> By around 1910, Sikhs were widely called ragheads a term of abuse that has persisted through today.

6-6b The First Wave of Immigration to North America (1900–1940)

The first Sikhs—usually single young men, because immigration rules prevented families from entering the country—arrived in North America around 1900. Many of them sought opportunities on the West Coast. Some worked in factories, in sawmills, and building railroad lines. Others worked on farms in California, Washington, and British Columbia because they had been farmers in the Punjab. They started as migrant farmworkers, but soon many of them were so successful that they could buy their own farms and settle down. As with other immigrants from Asia, it was difficult to practice their faith here. They had left their religious institutions behind, and assimilation to North American ways of life (dress, diet, schooling, and so on) posed a direct challenge to Sikh identity.

The story of Sikh life in Canada is told well by Kamala Nayar in her book *The Sikh Diaspora in Vancouver*.[2] Most Sikh immigration to North America was to Canada, because Indian immigration within the British Empire and the British Commonwealth was easier than it was into the United States. In 2017, an observant Sikh named Jagmeet Singh became Canada's first nonwhite leader of a political party.

The first generation of Sikh migration to the United States saw the rise of a permanent feature of Sikh life here: mistreatment by other Americans, which included intolerance, discrimination, and sometimes mob violence. Immigrant Asians were often seen as unwelcome competitors by labor unions and their members, because they worked for low wages. By around 1910, Sikhs were widely called "ragheads," a term of abuse that sadly has persisted through today. In 1913 the California Alien Land Act prohibited noncitizens from owning property, which severely disadvantaged Sikh farmers, and in 1917 the U.S. Congress choked off all immigration from India and other Asian regions. The U.S. Department of Justice even went so far as to revoke the citizenship of Sikhs who had been granted it, and the Supreme Court ruled that Sikhs did not qualify for citizenship. The Court said that though they are from Indo-European stock, they are not "white" in the same way that non-Sikh "white" Americans were.

Against these forces, Sikhs persisted in the process of assimilation, all the while trying to maintain the strong Sikh identity that marked their religion from its earliest years. The first gurdwara was established in the United States in 1912, in the farming town of Stockton, California; for two generations it was the center of Sikhism in the United States. From around 1910 to the 1960s, Sikhs in the United States tried to keep moving forward against occasional opposition.

All this played out against the backdrop of a rising Indian movement for independence from the British Empire. In 1913, Hindus, Muslims, and Sikhs in

California—all from a Punjabi background—founded the Ghadar (GAHD-uhr, meaning "revolt") Movement in order to raise money for resistance to British colonial rule in India. Sikhs predominated in the Ghadar organization and gave it a militant flavor. Some Sikhs even returned to the Punjab to lead ill-fated attacks on British authorities there. Although Ghadar fortunes were set back around 1917 to 1918 during World War I, it reorganized in the 1920s and played a role in the resistance to British rule until Indian independence was established in 1947.

6-6c Second and Third Waves to North America (1965–Present)

In 1965, the Sikh situation in the United States changed for the better, with new federal legislation that lifted old prohibitions and quotas. A large number of Sikh immigrants—many of them educated professionals such as physicians, scientists, and educators—came to the United States looking for economic opportunity. Their numbers in the United States tripled in a few short years. Sikhs settled not only throughout California, but also in New York and Texas, and also near major Midwestern cities such as Detroit and Chicago. The first wave of Sikh migration had settled in the countryside, but this second wave settled directly into the suburbs.

These Sikhs also brought tensions to established gurdwaras. The newcomers were more traditionally Sikh than the more assimilated Sikhs who had been in the United States for more than three generations; some of the old-timers had married non-Sikhs and given up on distinctive Sikh dress and diet. As newcomers gradually took over, the Punjabi language was heard much more frequently in worship. Chairs were removed from the main hall so people could sit on the floor before the *Guru Granth Sahib*. Shoes were again taken off for worship, music in the service became more traditional, and the langar meal was reemphasized.

A third, smaller wave of Sikh immigrants arrived from India after the violent events of 1984 in Amritsar. They were much more politicized than the second wave and brought an urgent sense of Sikh identity. Talk about "Khalistan," at times unhappy and divisive for Sikhs, began to be heard in American gurdwaras. Despite these and other challenges, Sikhs are thriving in North America, and not just economically. Moreover, Sikhism in North America is doing something that Sikhs in the Punjab have not tried to do—they are attracting converts to the faith and healthy lifestyle of Sikhism. This movement of young American converts is now headed by an organization called the Sikh Dharma.

6-6d Sikhism in Post-9/11 America

Some events in the aftermath of the attacks on the United States on September 11, 2001, have caused collateral damage to Sikhs in the western world. Al-Qaeda, the Afghanistan-based group that launched these attacks, has a dress code for men quite similar to the way members of the Khalsa dress. For almost entirely coincidental reasons, both Afghanis aligned with Al-Qaeda and observant Sikhs do not cut their hair or beards, and they both wear turbans. Although people in south Asia have the cultural intelligence to tell them apart, many residents of the United States do not. A number of Sikhs in the United States have now been under suspicion and have sometimes experienced outright opposition and occasional violence, as so-called Muslim terrorists. Gurdwaras have been threatened with arson. Sikh children in public schools are under particular pressure by some students who don't know the difference between Sikhs and Muslims, and think all Muslims must be terrorists. For Sikhs to be identified with Muslims at all—let alone with a separatist Muslim group that carries out mass terror attacks—is a grievous thing for them. Sikhs have responded with a patient effort to educate other Americans about the differences between themselves and Muslims who engage in violence.

By far the worst incidence of violence against Sikhs in the United States occurred on Sunday, August 5, 2012, when a single gunman killed six people and wounded four others at a gurdwara in Oak Creek, Wisconsin. The victims were preparing the langar for that morning.

Young Sikhs line up for a Sikh Day parade in New York City.

A Sikh American doctor poses with a patient.

The gunman, who took his own life at the scene, was a white supremacist who had spoken about a "racial holy war." No particular reason was ever found for why he targeted Sikhs.

Despite the challenges of living in the western world, Sikhs continue to live faithful lives in North America. They struggle with issues of assimilation and discrimination. But these North American problems are much smaller than the challenges Sikhism has faced in India for the past 500 years. The Sikh community in the western world is facing its problems resolutely and decisively. By 2000 the Sikh population of the United Kingdom was more than 300,000, and there are between an estimated 78,000 to 280,000 Sikhs in both Canada and the United States. These published estimates of the number of Sikhs in the United States vary greatly, but the number of gurdwaras is certain: as of 2014, there were 246. They continue to follow the Guru, who proclaims, "There is only one God, whose name is true. Repeat his name!"

STUDY TOOLS 6

READY TO STUDY?
ONLINE ON MINDTAP, YOU CAN:

☐ Download the Chapter Review Card, which includes key terms and chapter summaries.

☐ Learn about the *Guru Granth* in a short video.

☐ Explore worship in the Fremont, California gurdwara.

☐ Interact with figures from the text to check your understanding.

☐ Prepare for tests with quizzes.

☐ Review the key terms with Flash Cards.

Sikhism Timeline: 1469–2014 C.E.

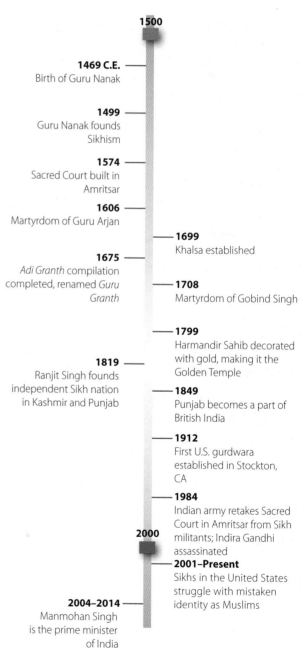

1500

1469 C.E.
Birth of Guru Nanak

1499
Guru Nanak founds Sikhism

1574
Sacred Court built in Amritsar

1606
Martyrdom of Guru Arjan

1699
Khalsa established

1675
Adi Granth compilation completed, renamed *Guru Granth*

1708
Martyrdom of Gobind Singh

1799
Harmandir Sahib decorated with gold, making it the Golden Temple

1819
Ranjit Singh founds independent Sikh nation in Kashmir and Punjab

1849
Punjab becomes a part of British India

1912
First U.S. gurdwara established in Stockton, CA

1984
Indian army retakes Sacred Court in Amritsar from Sikh militants; Indira Gandhi assassinated

2000

2001–Present
Sikhs in the United States struggle with mistaken identity as Muslims

2004–2014
Manmohan Singh is the prime minister of India

7

Encountering Daoism and Confucianism: Two Views of the Eternal Way

SHAN_SHAN/SHUTTERSTOCK.COM

LEARNING OUTCOMES

After studying this chapter, you will be able to do the following:

7-1 Explain the names *Daoism* and *Confucianism* and related terms.

7-2 Outline how Daoism and Confucianism developed over time into what they are today.

7-3 Explain the essential teachings of Daoism and Confucianism, especially their similarities and differences.

7-4 Paraphrase in your own words the main ethical principles of Daoism and Confucianism.

7-5 Outline the way Daoists and Confucianists worship and practice other rituals.

7-6 Summarize the main features of Daoism and Confucianism around the world today, especially in North America.

Your Visit to the Forbidden City in Beijing, China

A highlight of your tour of China is the Forbidden City, located in Beijing (bay-JING), the long-time capital of China. Most tourists to Beijing see at least a bit of it, but because of your interest in world religions and cultures, you are looking forward to a more in-depth view. The traditional name, Forbidden City, comes from the fact that it was formerly closed to all but the emperor, who was considered the "Son of Heaven," and his court officials. It was sacred to both Daoists and Confucianists. Now it doesn't seem at all forbidding to you, but inviting.

The complex consists of an astounding 980 surviving buildings spread out over an area one mile long and one-half mile wide. It covers 183 acres, which is the size of 166 football fields. It has two parts, both of which you can enter: the outer court, where the emperor ruled the nation, and the inner court, where he and his closest courtiers lived with their families. A wide moat and a wall thirty feet high surround the complex. As you cross into the Forbidden City through its only entrance at the Tiananmen (tee-YEN-ahn-MEN), or Heavenly Peace Gate, your guide relates the following: The Forbidden City was built in the early part of the 1400s and was home to two dynasties of China's emperors until 1912. The Ming dynasty, which ruled from 1368 to 1644, built the palace and courtyard. The Qing (ching) dynasty then governed the area until the last emperor of China left his position in

1912. Religious ceremonies in the Forbidden City ceased in that year. It was designated a World Heritage Site in 1987 by the United Nations.

Many halls in this complex have names with religious significance, because the emperor was the intermediary between Heaven and the Chinese people. The Forbidden City was made fit for tourism in the 1950s, and Tiananmen Square in front of the Gate of Heavenly Peace was developed into a huge public square. You notice, however, that the guide doesn't mention how, in the spring of 1989—the year that several Communist governments in Europe fell—a pro-democracy demonstration with thousands of people took place over several weeks in this square, complete with a small replica of the Statue of Liberty. In early June, Chinese army units brought in by the government opened fire on the protestors when they refused to disperse. Estimates of the dead range from five hundred to three thousand, with hundreds imprisoned. Your knowledge of what happened here in Tiananmen Square makes your attitude about it more somber.

> "If you google 'Confucius,' you [get] page after page of 'Confucius says' jokes . . . before you arrive at any actual quotations."
>
> —Stephen Prothero

People enter the Hall of Prayer for Good Harvests in the Temple of Heaven, Beijing, located near the Forbidden City. From 1420 to 1911 C.E., emperors of China came to this temple to pray for good crops.

The Forbidden City in Beijing

06PHOTO/GETTY IMAGES

In your study of Daoism and Confucianism, you'll be introduced to these unique, sometimes puzzling features:

- Some scholars hold that Chinese people in the world today are Confucianist in a significant sense just by virtue of being culturally Chinese, whether they self-identify as Confucianist or not. This is true, these academics say, even if they don't think of themselves as religious.

- Many Chinese who see themselves as either Daoists or Confucianists practice elements of the other religion, and a great number are Buddhists as well, in some aspects of their lives. The worldwide population of those who follow mostly Daoism is estimated by the authoritative World Religion Database at around 8 million, and the Confucianist population at around 6 million. But if we take into account those who practice major *features* of Daoism and Confucianism, their numbers rise to around 300 million each.[1]

- Confucianism is traceable with certainty to a historical founder; Daoism is not. Daoism grew out of various religious and philosophical traditions in ancient China, including shamanism and belief in the ancient gods and spirits. This difference in beginnings has proven to be one important factor in making Confucianism a more coherent system than Daoism.

- Confucianism is a thoroughly Chinese tradition, but its influence has spread widely in East Asia beyond China, especially to Taiwan, Korea, Vietnam, and Japan. The reach of formal, organized Daoism hasn't been as extensive; it is mostly contained in China and Taiwan.

- Both Daoism and Confucianism have been widely misunderstood in nonacademic popular settings in the western world, perhaps more than any other of the world religions. Daoism has been misrepresented as "just doing what comes naturally." The wisdom teaching of

Confucius in a traditional pose

Confucius is often trivialized in popular culture from fortune cookies to the Internet. For example, as Stephen Prothero remarks, "If you google 'Confucius,' you have to wade through page after page of 'Confucius says' jokes . . . before you arrive at any actual quotations from the man himself."[2]

In this chapter, we'll make a slight change in our treatment of world religions. Since Chapter 3, we've examined one religion per chapter. In this chapter, we'll consider the two main religions of China: Daoism and Confucianism.

7-1 The Names *Daoism* and *Confucianism*

Before we discuss the names of these religions, we must explain the two common systems used for rendering Chinese into English—the older Wade-Giles and the newer Pinyin (PIN-yin). Some key Chinese words in religion are spelled the same in each system, but other words are spelled differently. For instance, the Wade-Giles system spells the *d* sound in Chinese as *t*; the newer Pinyin system spells it as *d*. So the more traditional spelling is "Taoism," rather than the Pinyin system's "Daoism"; both are pronounced DOW-ihz-um. Wade-Giles spells the Chinese word for *classic book* as "ching," but Pinyin as "jing." As a result, Wade-Giles spells the name of the main Daoist scripture "Tao Te Ching," and Pinyin spells it "Daode Jing."

Popular usage in the West stays mostly with Wade-Giles, although Pinyin is growing. For example, on June 8, 2017, a Google search for "Tao" returned 254 million hits, whereas a search for "Dao" returned 161 million. Nevertheless, the Pinyin system is increasingly used in scholarship. It's usually closer to the way Chinese is pronounced, which makes it easier for beginning students of Chinese religions to pronounce Chinese terms correctly. This book uses the Pinyin spelling but occasionally refers to a significant Wade-Giles spelling the first time a word appears.

LIESKA/DREAMSTIME.COM

A Closer Look

The Symbols of Daoism and Confucianism

Daoism and Confucianism don't have official symbols of their faith. The Chinese character for *Dao*, "Way," is sometimes used as a symbol of both Daoism and Confucianism. (Each of these two religions follows its own concept of the Way.) However, for people who can't read Chinese, this symbol doesn't hold a lot of meaning, so it is not widely used as a symbol of either Daoism or Confucianism.

The most common symbol of Chinese religion is the **yin-yang**, also called the **Taiji** or "Great Ultimate." It is used often by Daoists and sometimes by Confucianists to represent their faiths, but it is also found to such an extent outside these two formal religions that it has become one of the most common symbols in the world. The circle formed by the yin and yang represents the universe, both matter and spirit, that encircles all things and holds them together. The light and dark areas inside it represent the balance of the two opposite powers in the universe. If the line between them were straight, it would suggest motionless stability between the two areas of the circle. In fact, the line is deeply curved to show that they move and that their motion and change are constants

Figure 7.1 Dao

BONNIE VAN VOORST © CENGAGE LEARNING

Figure 7.2 Yin-yang

BONNIE VAN VOORST © CENGAGE LEARNING

in the cosmos. When they move with each other, not against each other, life is peaceful and productive. When there is conflict between them, confusion and disharmony result. The ideal harmony between these two is suggested in many depictions of the symbol by a small circle of light in the dark area, and vice versa. The task of life is to live according to this balance in the symbol.

What do the two parts of the yin-yang symbolize?

- Yin represents what is feminine, soft, yielding, underneath, nurturing, cool, calm, passive, and dark.
- Yang represents what is masculine, hard, powerful, above, guiding, warm, energetic, active, and bright.

Although a purely gender-oriented understanding of yin-yang is possible— that all aspects of yang are masculine and yin feminine—this isn't necessary, nor was it the only view in Chinese history. Almost all interpretations of the yin-yang do hold that it is hierarchical, agreeing with the general Chinese cultural preference for hierarchy: The yang side and its aspects are superior to yin. One meaning it *doesn't* have is a moral dualism—it should not be understood in terms of good and evil. In the traditional Chinese view, shared by both Daoism and Confucianism, life is good. Only when the balance of natural and supernatural forces symbolized by the Taiji goes into decline does evil result.

Daoism, the religion of the natural Way, refers to diverse but related Chinese traditions that have shaped Asia for more than two thousand years and have had an influence on the western world since the nineteenth century. The word *Dao* roughly translates as "way, path, or road," and by extension "way of life." Scholars often divide Daoism into religious and philosophical branches. A leading scholar of Daoism, Livia Kohn, has more carefully divided it into three categories: (1) philosophical Daoism, the oldest branch, based on the texts *Daode Jing* and *Zhuangzi* (JWAHNG-zee; in Wade-Giles, *Chuang Tzu*); (2) religious Daoism, a collection of formal, organized religious movements originating from the Celestial Masters movement around 200 C.E.; and (3) folk Daoism, the widely diverse Chinese indigenous local religions taken up into Daoism after 200 C.E.[3]

Daoism [DOW-ihz-um]
Religion of the natural Way

yin-yang [yihn-yahng]
Symbol of opposing cosmic forces such as passivity and activity, and darkness and light

Taiji [TIGH-jee] "Great Ultimate," another name for the yin-yang symbol

Confucianism originated as a western term, not a Chinese term. Its first use was in the 1500s C.E. by Roman Catholic missionaries in China. They bypassed the common Chinese term for this tradition, the Scholarly Tradition, a name that stresses the role of official scholars in Confucianism. The missionaries added *ism* to the Latinized form of founder Kong Fuzi, *Confucius* (kon-FYOO-shuhs), to make *Confucianism*. Some scholars, Lionel Jensen among them, have argued that Kong Fuzi and Confucius as formal names are western inventions and that we should keep to what Chinese tradition calls him, *Kongzi* (KONG-zhee) or *Fuzi*.[4]

European scholars of religion in the 1800s widely spread the new name *Confucianism*. Although Confucius would probably have objected to naming his movement after himself, it has now stuck in usage. Moreover, the name *Confucianism* is accurate enough. Both Confucian and non-Confucian scholars of religion use it. More importantly, many people who follow the religion use this name. So, as in most scholarship, we will use it here.

> *The foundations of Confucianism and Daoism are as close to our time as they are to the beginnings of civilization in China.*

7-2 Daoism and Confucianism Today as Shaped by Their Past

In China, the annual celebration of Confucius's birthday has become one of the biggest holidays in the relatively short history of the Communist People's Republic of China. The festivities are televised nationwide, and thousands of socially prominent people, including many high-ranking Communist Party members, make their way to Confucius's birthplace in Shandong Province. The leaders of the party are seeking to use Confucian values to counteract social problems such as rising social unrest, lack of traditional respect for aging parents, and the growing "money first" mentality. Ironically, these were some of the same problems that prompted Confucius to begin his social and religious reforms more than 2,500 years ago. The government of China has also begun to promote the Daoist religion by reopening and even renovating temples and monasteries.

Confucianism [kun-FYOO-shuhn-ihz-um] Religion based on reforms by Confucius

In this section, we'll briefly trace the history of first Daoism and then Confucianism, from their earliest times to today. They competed with each other on an official level, especially when emperors favored one and tried to put down the other; more often they cooperated on a popular level. These two religions went with and against each other for more than two thousand years—almost like the yin and yang—and Chinese culture was deeply affected by this fluctuation. Before we discuss the founding of the two religions, we should look at their common background in Chinese culture.

7-2a China before the Rise of Daoism and Confucianism (ca. 3000–500 B.C.E.)

Daoism and Confucianism arose in a civilization that was already ancient. In fact, Chinese civilization is so old that the foundations of Confucianism and Daoism are just as close in time to us today as they are to the beginnings of civilization in China. Civilization probably began there before 3000 B.C.E., with scattered settlements along the Yellow River basin in northeast China, the "cradle of Chinese civilization." This society seems to have been highly militarized, probably because of the necessity to defend its open northern borders. Religion at this time included the worship of many gods, poetry inscribed on pottery, use of animal bones and shells in divination, and use of clay phallic statues in rituals for the fertility of crops, animals, and perhaps humans. Some of these surviving artifacts testify to religious beliefs and practices that would endure in both Confucianism and Daoism.

A golden burial mask from the Shang dynasty

The earliest period in Chinese history for which there is good evidence is the Shang (shahng) dynasty period, from about 1500 to 1122 B.C.E. This society was also based in the Yellow River valley and, similar to other early human civilizations, centered on raising crops and animals. Powerful landowning aristocrats controlled Shang society, enjoying luxurious homes and outfitting lavish tombs for their happiness in the next life. Almost everyone else in the Shang society was a peasant or a slave; there were relatively few artisans, scribes, or others to form what we would consider a middle class today. A system of writing using pictograms or ideograms as characters was developed at this time, which was the forerunner of the system that exists in China today. The demands of memorizing thousands of characters and acquiring the skills to draw them well limited literacy to the upper class and professional scribes. This would help to shape the literary aspects of Chinese religions, especially their scriptures. Animal **oracle bones** inscribed with this writing were used to foretell the future and maintain good connections with ancestral spirits and nature spirits. Other methods of divination later took

JUN MU/DREAMSTIME.COM

Oracle bone on tortoise shell from the Shang dynasty

the place of oracle bones, but divination, especially fortunetelling, is still popular in Chinese religion today.

Another practice that began during the Shang dynasty has grown widely in China and is popular in the western world today— **feng shui**, or the positioning of objects to maximize the good effects of the flow of energy. Feng shui was used at first to select the location of graves. When the dead are buried according to feng shui principles, the flow of energy in the earth brings yin power to their bones. This strengthens the spirits of the dead, and then blessing comes to their living families. Feng shui practices spread to altars and buildings, for the strengthening of the living. Especially in the western world, feng shui has now been applied to furniture and decorative items. As often happens when an ancient practice is popularized commercially in the modern world, its original meaning has been adapted.

The rulers of the Shang dynasty led the worship of the gods, as emperors of China would continue to do. The Shang practiced human sacrifice, usually of slaves, in some of their rituals. This practice was discontinued in later periods; terracotta figures took the place of slaves in burials of kings and nobles. The final contribution of the Shang period was the writing of religious books that would become scriptures—or as the

YURI YAVNIK/SHUTTERSTOCK

Great Wall of China, built on China's northern borders beginning around 200 B.C.E. to keep out nomadic invaders. That it can be seen with the naked eye from the moon is a popular but mistaken notion.

oracle bones
Inscribed animal bones used to foretell the future

feng shui [FUNG shway] Positioning of objects to maximize the good effects of the flow of energy

Terracotta army in the 210 B.C.E. tomb of Emperor Qin Shi Huang in Xian

one's life is the kind of knowledge that this book offers its users. Flux is not a negative thing, but it makes life run. The *Yi Jing* testifies clearly to a deep Chinese cultural and religious attitude that shaped Daoism and Confucianism. The universe and the natural world in which humans live are good; human life is (or can be) basically good as well, but needs guidance and correction in order for it to reach its full potential in the Way.

The Zhou (joh) dynasty that came next was the longest in Chinese history, from 1122 to 221 B.C.E. The king's duty was to lead the worship of the gods in order to insure a good harvest, and his power, and even right, to rule often depended on how those prayers were answered. The end of the Zhou dynasty is also known as the Warring States Period (481–221 B.C.E.), when the seven states of ancient China renounced their allegiance to the Zhou emperors and battled among themselves for supremacy (see Map 7.1). This prolonged period of war and social turbulence was not all destructive. By its end, China was the most populous society in the world, with between 20 and 40 million people. Many peasants had moved south to better farmland in the Yangzi (YAHNG-tsee) River area, and the merchant class grew in size and influence. This period was also a fertile time for Chinese thought and belief. Distinctive religious beliefs arose in Zhou times, especially about **Heaven**. Before the Zhou period, heaven was considered a set of gods; now it became an impersonal cosmic force working for the continuation and enrichment of life. The Zhou period also produced a number of new movements seeking to restore order to a society deeply torn by continued wars and the social troubles they brought. Two of these new movements were Daoism and Confucianism.

7-2b The Origins of Daoism (ca. 500 B.C.E.–200 C.E.)

Daoism's origins have been traced to different periods: Chinese folk religions at the beginning of the first millennium B.C.E.; the composition of the *Daode Jing* around 350–250 B.C.E.; or the founding by Zhang Daoling (jahng dow-LING) of a movement around 150 C.E. from which would come the first main Daoist group, the Celestial Masters school. Some argue that Daoism as a religious identity only arose later, by way of contrast with the newly arrived religion of Buddhism, or with

Chinese call them, **jing**, "classics." A collection of traditional poems began to take shape; it would greatly influence later Chinese culture and religion when it became known as the *Book of Poetry*. Another classic book to influence Chinese culture and religion was the **Yi Jing** (in Wade-Giles, *I Ching*), the *Classic of Changes*, a collection of sixty-four mystical symbols and their descriptions used to foretell the future. The main theme of this book is that the main forces of life are in a state of constant flux, an idea symbolized in the yin-yang. To be able to predict how flux will affect

jing "Classics," books that have scriptural standing

Yi Jing [yee jing] *Classic of Changes* also spelled *I Ching*; a diviner's manual, earliest of the Chinese classical books

Heaven Impersonal cosmic force working for the continuation and enrichment of life

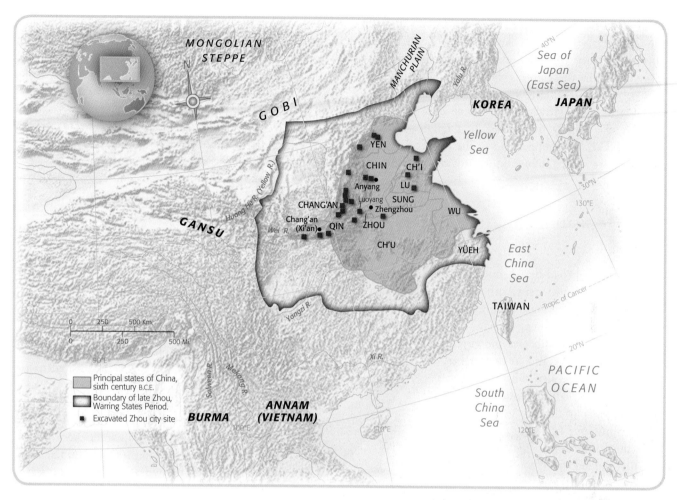

Map 7.1

China in the Sixth Century B.C.E.

During the late Zhou era, China was divided into competing, often warring states ruled only loosely by the Zhou kings. Some, such as Chiu and Wu, were large. In the third century B.C.E., the westernmost state of Qin conquered the others and formed a unified empire and the whole nation of China became known by the name of this state.

the first Daoist scripture canon in the fifth century C.E. Early religious Daoism was rooted in the religious ideas of Daoist thinkers, to which were added already ancient local rituals and beliefs. This helped to integrate Daoism into the worldviews and religious life of Chinese society, but it resulted in a religion that was not as internally consistent as Confucianism, or even Buddhism.

Laozi (low [rhymes with "how"]-DZUH; in Wade-Giles, *Lao Tzu*), whose name means "Old Master," is the traditional founder of Daoism. However, many historians conclude that we have no direct, dependable evidence that he ever existed. Some modern Daoists counter by saying that Laozi deliberately remained a shadowy figure so that others would later wonder about him. Laozi is said to be an older contemporary of Confucius and, similar to Confucius, a disappointed government official who became a wandering teacher.

Laozi riding an ox in a traditional portrait

He is also said to be the author of the *Daode Jing* and the *Zhuangzi* (in Wade-Giles, *Chuang Tzu*), but no good literary or historical evidence supports this. It's more likely that these books were written anonymously between 300 and 200 B.C.E., and later came to be associated with Laozi. However and whenever it originated, Daoism was widely recognized as a religious system by 300 B.C.E. The publication of the *Daode Jing*, and other Daoist works following it, provided a focus for Daoist thinking.

7-2c Daoism from 200 C.E. to 1664 C.E.

Daoism was a broad-based movement. In its religious aspects, it developed many different monastic orders, each with its own monasteries. Because Daoists looked to nature to show the way humans should live, they built a number of monasteries on mountain peaks and in the countryside. But they could also build monasteries near cities—the White Cloud Monastery in Beijing being the most famous of these. Each monastic order tended to write its own religious literature, eventually giving rise to a large Daoist canon, the **Daozang**.

Another product of the monasteries was martial arts. This was at first a meditational technique coupled with exercise, but it developed into a sophisticated form of fighting, usually hand to hand but sometimes with weapons. Over time, the Daoist or Buddhist meditational aspects of martial arts were downplayed or lost completely. The martial arts sought to use an enemy's force against him or her. As this method spread beyond Daoism through Asia, it assumed many different forms: judo, karate, ju-jitsu, taekwondo, and others. It was not widely known in the West until after World War II, when western armed forces began teaching it regularly as a part of basic military training. (The author's father

Two martial arts masters

learned it at that time in the U.S. Marine Corps; because he was short and slim, he was often used to demonstrate its effectiveness against other Marines who were beginning to learn it—who thought they could "take him" easily.) Daoism developed other meditational techniques and a fuller evolution of its philosophical teachings. Hundreds of commentaries were written on basic Daoist scriptures such as the *Daode Jing* and *Zhuangzi*. Daoism's popular religious aspects served to integrate thousands of local gods and cults into a Daoist pantheon.

The return of Daoism after it was suppressed in the Han dynasty is known as **Neo-Daoism**. Wang Bi and Guo Xiang wrote commentaries on the *Daode Jing* and the *Zhuangzi*, and they became important figures in this movement. The "Seven Sages of the Bamboo Grove" forged a new Daoist way of life that influenced wider culture, not just that of mountain monasteries.

This broader cultural influence of Neo-Daoism was felt in calligraphy, painting, music, and poetry. Daoist ideas on landscape painting contributed to a style that would last until modern times—the placement of human activities against a very large, imposing natural setting. The most well-known Daoist philosopher of this period was Ge Hong (283–343 C.E.). In the search for longevity and immortality, he pursued not only philosophical reflection, but alchemy as well. His main book, the *Inner Chapters of the Master Embracing Simplicity*, or *Baopuzi* (BOW-poo-tsee) for short, has been the leading scripture for those seeking longevity by meditation, alchemy, and traditional Chinese medicines.

7-2d The Near-Destruction and Revival of Daoism (1644–1980)

The Manchurians, who became rulers of China in 1644, were in the Confucian camp, and they trimmed the political and cultural power of Daoism. They removed the politically powerful Daoist head of the Dragon Tiger Mountain Monastery from his position at the imperial court. Later events would prove even more detrimental to Daoism. In the 1780s, Christian missionaries arrived in China and converted large numbers of Daoists. In 1849, the Hakka people of southern

Daozang [DOW-zhahng] Daoist canon

Neo-Daoism Rebirth and reform of Daoism after the Han dynasty

China—one of China's poorest ethnic groups—followed Hong Xiuquan (hoong shee-OH-chwahn), who claimed to be Jesus Christ's younger brother, in open rebellion against the emperor. Hong's movement was built on a combination of Daoism and Christianity, and sought to establish the "Heavenly Kingdom of Peace" (*taiping*). As the so-called Taiping Rebellion conquered southeast China, its faithful systematically destroyed Buddhist and Daoist temples and scriptures until it was finally crushed by the emperor's troops.

In the 1900s, pressure against Daoism increased. In the 1920s, the reformist New Life movement induced students to destroy Daoist sites and scriptures. By 1926, only two copies of the Daoist canon *Daozang* were left, and the Daoist heritage was in great jeopardy. But the copy of the canon kept at the White Cloud Monastery was eventually copied, and this important work was saved for posterity. There are

1,120 books in the collection, in a total of 5,305 volumes. Scholars have yet to study much of it.

Recent times have seen an even stronger pendulum swing in the fortunes of Daoism. After the Communist takeover of China in 1949, Daoism was banned and its leaders "reeducated" and forced into other occupations. All but a few temples and monasteries were closed. The number of practicing Daoists fell drastically, around 90 percent in ten years. At this time Daoism began to flourish in the greater freedom of Taiwan, as well as Hong Kong, which was a British colony then separate from China. During the Great Proletarian Cultural Revolution (1966–1976) instigated by the Chinese leader Mao Zedong (mow [rhymes with how] zuh-DOONG), strong attacks were made on the remaining vestiges of the religion. Fengyang Yang writes in his recent book, *Religion in China: Survival and Revival under Communist Rule,* that the Cultural Revolution brought the most radical suppression of religion in history.[5] Daoist monks were killed or sent to labor camps. Before 1900 there were three hundred Daoist sites in Beijing alone; in the Cultural Revolution, they were all shuttered or destroyed, and Daoism, along with all other religions in China, went underground. After the Cultural Revolution, the Chinese government began to allow a small measure of religious freedom again. Daoism began to revive in China; some temples and some monasteries were gradually reopened. Today, observant Daoists can be found throughout the country, and what, only thirty years ago, was called a dying religion is now growing again.

7-2e Confucius and the Origins of Confucianism (551–479 B.C.E.)

We now return to the sixth century B.C.E., to discuss the origins of Confucianism. The details of Confucius's life are sketchy, but we know its main outline. Confucius was born in or around 551 B.C.E. in Qufu (CHOO-foo), the capital of the small state of Lu. His real name was Kong Qiu (kong choh), but his students called him Kong Fuzi (kong foo-ZEE), Master Kong. His ancestors may have been aristocrats but perhaps were brought low during a period of social instability. This would explain how someone of a relatively low social class had such a feeling for high culture from an early age. His father, who never married Confucius's mother, died when Confucius was very young, so he was taught by his mother. Confucius distinguished himself as a passionate learner in his teens. He gained a mastery of the six traditional basic arts of the time: ritual, music,

Practicing calligraphy with a brush pen

archery, charioteering, calligraphy, and arithmetic. He also developed a strong attachment to Chinese history and traditional poetry that would be reflected in Confucianism, which would then go on to deeply affect Chinese culture.

As a young adult, Confucius began serving in minor posts in the government's ministry of agriculture, managing stables and granaries. He married a woman of similar social standing when he was nineteen, and they had children. He started his teaching career in his thirties. Confucius developed concepts about society and government that he hoped to put into practice in a political career. His loyalty to the king provoked opposition from the powerful landowning families. Also, his teaching that a ruler must set a moral example for his people did not sit well with the king's advisors, who were influencing the ruler by procuring sensuous pleasures for him. At the age of fifty-six, when he realized that his superiors in Lu had no interest in him, Confucius left to find another ruler who might listen to his ideas and make him an official. He gathered a growing number of students during the next twelve years, perhaps as many as three thousand. His reputation as a man of vision spread, and he was an occasional advisor to rulers. However, he was never able to get his teachings adopted in any Chinese state, or even find a steady position as a royal advisor. Confucius's own times were not right for implementing his ideas. When he was sixty-seven, Confucius returned home to continue teaching.

Looking back on the course of his life, Confucius summarized it this way: "At the age of fifteen, I set my heart on learning; at thirty, I firmly took my stand [for what was right]; at forty, I had no delusions [about life]; at fifty, I knew the **Mandate of Heaven**; at sixty, my ear was attuned [an obscure phrase of uncertain meaning]; at seventy, I followed my heart's desire without doing wrong" (*Analects* 2:4). Despite this remarkably positive view of himself, even to the point of knowing the Mandate of Heaven, Confucius could be a humble man. He admitted that he had not become the

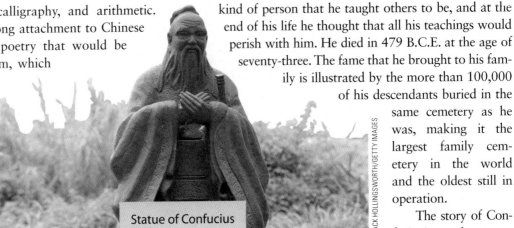
Statue of Confucius

JACK HOLLINGSWORTH/GETTY IMAGES

kind of person that he taught others to be, and at the end of his life he thought that all his teachings would perish with him. He died in 479 B.C.E. at the age of seventy-three. The fame that he brought to his family is illustrated by the more than 100,000 of his descendants buried in the same cemetery as he was, making it the largest family cemetery in the world and the oldest still in operation.

The story of Confucianism does not really begin with Confucius, nor was Confucius the founder of Confucianism in the way that others have been the founders of religions. Rather, Confucius was a transmitter of the best of the past, a reformer rather than a revolutionary. He retrieved the meaning of the past by breathing new life into it. Confucius's love of antiquity drove him to ask why certain rituals such as funeral ceremonies and reverence for Heaven had survived for centuries. He had faith in the power of culture to stabilize human life. Confucius's sense of history was so strong that he saw himself as a conservationist responsible for the continuity of the cultural values and social norms that had worked so well for the civilization of China, especially in the earlier years of the Zhou dynasty. In his system of teaching, he successfully formed a coherent system of thought and life that would shape the future of China and several other lands.

7-2f The Rise of Confucianism and Neo-Confucianism (ca. 350 B.C.E.–1200 C.E.)

Others kept Confucianism alive until it finally was recognized as a state religion. Mengzi (MUHNG-dzuh), who lived from about 372 to 289 B.C.E., is traditionally known in the West as Mencius (MEN-see-us) and, like Confucius, was a wandering advisor to rulers. His main work, the *Book of Mencius* (or *Mencius* for short), shows his positive view of the basic goodness of human nature. Heaven (*tian*) is found in the human heart; the ruler need only set a good example for his people and they will follow it. Historians generally hold that Mencius is second only to Confucius in influence on Confucianism. Confucius's beliefs were not significant in China until Dong Zhongshu (dawng ZHAWNG-shoo) effectively

Mandate of Heaven
Right to rule as king or emperor, given by Heaven by means of order and prosperity in the land

University students in Seoul, South Korea, perform during an annual ritual to honor Confucius and Confucian sages.

promoted them in the second century B.C.E. Confucianism was recognized as the official state religion in the Han dynasty (206 B.C.E.–220 C.E.). A few new religious elements, including sacrifices to Confucius, were introduced. More importantly, the four main Confucian books (see "A Closer Look: The Confucian *Four Books*") were canonized and became the core of education and culture in China.

Despite the strong influence of Daoism and Buddhism, Confucian ethics have had the strongest influence on the moral fabric of China. A revival of Confucian thought in the Song dynasty of the twelfth century produced **Neo-Confucianism**, which incorporated many Daoist and Buddhist ideas, forging a sort of compromise that enabled Confucianism to continue its role as the leading influence on Chinese culture. The philosopher Zhu Xi (JOO shee, 1130–1200), a founder of Neo-Confucianism, believed that the ideas of Confucius had been misrepresented over the centuries. He advocated what he called a return to Confucius's original teachings, which Zhu saw as moral self-improvement largely directed by reason. Despite this emphasis on a return to Confucius, he was influenced by both Daoism and Buddhism, which led to a new

{ *Confucius was a reformer, not a revolutionary.* }

and closer balance between their systems. Zhu wrote commentaries on the classics, which became required reading for the civil service exams. This exam system, which had been established in the 200s B.C.E., then grew in importance, and, until 1905, it was the only way to get an official appointment in the vast imperial government. It was also the leading way for men of the lower classes to rise in rank. In time, Neo-Confucianism replaced traditional Confucianism in the higher levels of Chinese society, especially in the universities and the government.

In 1530 C.E., a Ming emperor reformed the Confucian cult to focus more on Confucius's teachings than on the sage himself. For example, images of Confucius in Confucian temples were replaced with tablets inscribed with his name and honorific titles. The ritual veneration of Confucius declined after the founding of the Chinese Republic in 1912, but the social influence of Confucianism has continued. Neo-Confucianism was a major influence in Korea from 1392 to 1910, and it remains an important foundation of culture in South Korea. Some Confucian scholars blamed Daoism for the fall of the Ming dynasty and the subsequent establishment of the Qing dynasty (1644–1912) by the foreign Manchus. The Manchus then led a movement called National Studies that urged a return to traditional Confucianism. The Confucian classics came back into imperial favor, and Daoism was almost completely suppressed. For example, during the 1700s an imperial library was established, but excluded virtually all Daoist books. By the 1920s, as we saw previously, Daoism had fallen from favor, so much so that only two copies of the *Daozang* still remained.

Neo-Confucianism
Revival of Confucian thought in the twelfth century, incorporating Daoist and Buddhist ideas

A Closer Look

The Confucian *Four Books*

The *Four Books* of the Confucian canon are built on what Confucius and his followers saw as the main teachings of the earlier Chinese *Five Classics*. The *Analects* (*Lun yu*) of Confucius is by far the most important text in the history of Confucianism, and it gives us insight into Confucius himself. It contains sayings of Confucius, whom it calls the Master, and occasional stories about him as remembered by his disciples and recorded after his death. The *Analects* has 12,700 characters (ideograms) in twenty short books. Similar to other collections of wise sayings, the *Analects* is loosely organized. It treats, and repeatedly returns to, all the important concepts of the Confucian tradition: the virtues of humanity, propriety, and respect for parents; becoming a superior man; and proper government. Some people think that the proverbs in this book are no more helpful than proverbs that occasionally appear in fortune cookies, but they should not be atomized. In the context of the whole *Analects*, and in the living tradition of Confucianism, they are both profound and powerful.

The second of the *Four Books* is the *Mencius* (*Mengzi*), named for its author. Mencius (ca. 371–289 B.C.E.) was the most significant figure in Confucian tradition after Confucius. His disciples compiled the book of Mencius's teachings after his death. More than twice as long as the *Analects*, the *Mencius* has well-developed treatments of several important topics, especially proper government. Mencius saw filiality as the greatest of the virtues and held strongly to the teaching of innate human goodness.

Third is the *Great Learning* (*Ta xuei*), a short book that is an excerpt on virtuous government from the *Li Jing*. Its first, short chapter is held to be the work of Confucius. The next ten chapters are a commentary on the first by one of Confucius's disciples. The *Great Learning* teaches that rulers govern by example. If the ruler is morally good, his government and his subjects will be good. If the ruler is not good, his subjects will incline to evil, and his rule, along with the Mandate of Heaven to govern, will collapse.

Fourth is the *Doctrine of the Mean* (*Chung yung*). Similar to the *Great Learning*, it was originally a chapter in the *Li Jing*. *Mean* here is better translated today as moderation because of the negative connotations of *mean*. The mean is a broad concept, embracing many aspects of virtue: moderation, right conduct, decorum, and sincerity. The good Confucianist is expected to "keep to the middle" between emotional and intellectual extremes. The superior person is formed in the middle and comes into harmony with the Dao, the cosmic "Way" of life. This book was important in the Neo-Confucian movement that arose in the twelfth century. Harvard Confucian scholar Tu Wei-Ming has argued that the *Doctrine of the Mean* is the most explicitly religious of the *Four Books*.

7-2g The Modern Period of Daoism and Confucianism (1912–Present)

In 1911 to 1912, the Chinese Revolution ended the three-thousand-year-old imperial system and put a republic in its place. The Nationalist Party leaders who struggled to rule China from 1912 to 1949 embraced science, modernity, and western culture, including aspects of Christianity. They tended to view traditional Chinese religions as reactionary and parasitic. Many progressive Chinese intellectuals also rejected much of the three Chinese religions. The Nationalists confiscated some temples and monasteries for public buildings and, like the emperors of China before them, controlled traditional religious activity.

The Communist Party of China led by Mao Zedong took power in 1949. As a Communist regime, it is officially atheistic, and initially suppressed Daoism and Confucianism with even more zeal than the Nationalist Party had. ("Religion is poison," states an old Communist propaganda slogan that Mao repeated to the Dalai Lama.) Despite this suppression, most religions were still able to operate, but at a severely reduced level. Persecution of religion stopped when Mao died in 1976, and soon many Daoists and Confucianists began reviving their traditions. Since then, some of the more scenic temples and monasteries have been repaired and reopened.

The government of China now permits Daoism and Buddhism (along with Islam, Roman Catholic Christianity, and Protestant Christianity) and supervises their activities. The government considers some other religions, such as Falun Gong (which we'll discuss in

A portrait of Mao still hangs at the Gate of Heavenly Peace in Beijing. The sign reads, "Long live the People's Republic of China."

Chapter 13), to be dangerous to public order, and has fiercely cracked down on them. Sensitive areas with Chinese religions include the government's relationship to the influential Zhengyi Daoist group and their leader—who lives in Taiwan, as does the current leader of the extensive descendants of Confucius. The government occasionally suppresses various traditional temple activities such as astrology and shamanism, which it calls superstitions. It also censors films that depict popular Daoist ideas such as child vampires, ghosts, and martial-arts cults with supernatural abilities. But it has become more accommodating to religious beliefs and practices, no longer automatically seeing them as dangerous to Communist rule or the good of the people. Daoist temples and monasteries are operating more freely, and local gods have come out of hiding.

China today is even more welcoming to Confucianism. This is being done to fill a spiritual vacuum in Chinese society. The values of communism are waning as China moves toward a modified form of a free-enterprise system; social friction, crime, and corruption have arisen, which China's rulers see as inimical to China's well-being. For more on Confucianism in China today, see "A Closer Look: Confucianism Returns to China."

7-3 Essential Daoist and Confucian Teachings

At the giant Expo 2010 in Shanghai, China, people form lines to enter the dozens of new pavilions showcasing the theme of the Expo—how the Chinese past is shaping its desired future. Although the lines are long and a bit slow, people wait in a patient, orderly way. As an elderly American couple just arriving at the Expo gets in the back of a line, a security agent asks to see identification. With foreboding, they produce their drivers' licenses. To their surprise, they are shown to the front of the line and let into the exhibit immediately, because anyone who is at least seventy-five years of age doesn't have to wait in line. The woman remarks to her husband that this policy is even better than a senior citizen discount, because it means that they can see much more of the Expo than they could otherwise. This preferential treatment is based on the Chinese respect for advanced age, a leading aspect of ethics in both Confucianism and Daoism. Such practices are

Performers portraying disciples of Confucius recite passages from the *Analects* at the opening ceremonies of the 2008 Olympics in Beijing, China.

A Closer Look

Confucianism Returns to China

One of the most notable changes in China in the last 30 years has been an increasing openness to Confucianism, which has experienced a veritable return to China.

In the 1980s, when China began to move toward a more free-market economy while keeping a strong Communist Party rule, the Party noticed that Confucian values had helped to stabilize other countries in East Asia. The values of national unity and stability, important Confucian ideas, soon replaced the value of upheaval that came with communist class revolution. In 2005, the Party chief even quoted Confucius's saying that "harmony is something to be cherished." Soon, "harmony" was on billboards and in television commercials.

Some of the particular features of this growing Confucian influence include:

- Parents with means enroll their children in private Confucian academies.

- Around the country, Chinese tourists flock to the surviving Confucius temples, where they fill out prayer cards. Students asking for success in exams are very prominent.

- In 2006, government-sponsored historians unveiled what they called a standardized portrait of Confucius: a kindly old figure with a full beard, his hands crossed in friendly greeting on his chest.

- The national education ministry has set up programs of religious study in several selective Chinese universities at the graduate levels. Students are able to major in Christian, Islamic, or Chinese religion.

- The government promotes traditional Confucian values in primary and secondary schools, where students now spend a good deal of time memorizing wisdom from the *Analects*, poems from the *Classic of Poetry*, and other Confucian texts.

- Statues of Confucius are now seen in public places, especially in front of schools. The government even encourages couples to marry or renew their vows in front of these statues.

- As mentioned previously in the opening of Section 7-2, large public celebrations of Confucius's birthday and continuing influence are held every year, and several of them are televised.

---

not monoliths and can change over time, but Daoism, with its emphasis on attaining old age, and Confucianism, with its emphasis on respect for one's parents, have contributed to a cultural heritage of honoring the elderly.

In this section we'll first consider the religious teachings that predate both Confucianism and Daoism and are important for each; then we'll examine the main Daoist and Confucian teachings that build on them.

7-3a Ancient Teachings Common to Daoism and Confucianism

Many of the key teachings of both Daoism and Confucianism did not originate with them around 500 B.C.E. Rather, they go back hundreds, sometimes thousands, of years in China before these religions were recognized as separate movements. Most of the gods worshiped by Daoists and Confucianists also predate these religions. We have already considered ancient religious ideas such as yin-yang, teachings of texts such as the important *Yi Jing*, and the religious ideas behind rituals such as feng shui and divination. The other ancient teachings common to both Confucianism and Daoism are as follows:

- **Dao** is the cosmic Way of life, the Way of nature that became a Way for people to walk in. This Way brings value to human culture, it shapes better relationships, and it advances health and long life. Both Daoism and Confucianism speak about the Dao, but in different ways and to different degrees. But they share a positive view of the world and the Dao within it: The world is a good place, and humans must find the fullness of life within the Dao that guides the world.

Dao [dow] Cosmic Way of life

- The One is the essence of the Dao, the energy of life. Living in this One enables things and human beings to be truly themselves. The One is often seen as operating in dualistic form, as in the yin-yang: The circle that contains the yin and yang is the One.

- **De** is typically translated as virtue, but this implies later Confucian teaching about morality and can be confusing. Another way of looking at de is as power or working that enables a person to follow the Dao. The title of the scripture text *Daode Jing* suggests the relationship of de to the Dao, and not just for Daoists: "The Book of the Way (Dao) and its Power/ Working (De)." The Dao is not a static thing with only being; it has a working power by which it reaches out to shape every living thing.

- **Qi** is the cosmic energy that enables beings to live and links them to the universe as a whole, and it is also the basic material of all that exists. Qi gives life to the human body; its quality and movement determine human health.

> { *Tian does not suggest a god, but rather an order and principle that both transcends the world and is deeply embedded in it.* }

- **Tian** (Wade-Giles, *T'ien*) is "Heaven," an impersonal cosmic force that guides events on earth and a cosmic principle that distinguishes right from wrong. In earliest times Tian was a personal god, probably the highest deity among many, but in the Zhou dynasty it became an impersonal force guided by its own principle of what is right. In the Abrahamic monotheisms (Judaism, Christianity, and Islam), *Heaven* is closely tied to God; even for nonreligious

"The Dao that can be spoken is not the eternal Dao."
—Daode Jing

CHUCKY/DREAMSTIME.COM

Ancestor tablets with names of the dead are thought to be the dwelling places of the ancestors when they visit earth; this tablet is set up at a wedding reception, and offerings have been placed before it.

people in the western world today, it suggests a Being who lives there. In China, *Tian* does not suggest a god, but rather an order and principle that both transcends the world and is deeply embedded in it.

- *Ancestor veneration* or *worship* became a common practice in ancient China. Each family was expected to remember the names of its male ancestors and pay regular homage to them. Over time, their names were written on small rectangular tablets. This veneration made ancestors in the world of spirits happy, and they would bless—not haunt—their living descendants.

These ancient religious teachings and the ritual practices associated with them were established by about 750 B.C.E. They would endure throughout Chinese history, and all Chinese religions to come had to incorporate them in some way. Even foreign religions such as Buddhism, Christianity, and Islam had to make adjustments to this religiously shaped Chinese worldview in order to grow in China. Because Daoism and Confucianism drink deeply at this common well of ancient Chinese thought and practice, they share similar ideas that make it easy for Chinese people to combine them into daily life. Despite all the differences between these two religions at a high, official level—and despite the conflicts with each other that they have had in the past—Daoism and Confucianism can fit together for most Chinese.

7-3b Daoist Teachings on the Dao

How do Daoists understand the Dao? The first thing that Daoists say is that it cannot be described exactly in words. Human language can only sketch

de [duh] Power or working that enables a person to follow the Dao

qi [chee] Cosmic energy that gives life and connects one to the universe

Tian [tee-AHN] "Heaven," impersonal cosmic force that guides events on earth and distinguishes right from wrong

an outline of the Dao, but cannot give a full picture. The important thing to be said about the Dao is that it works to empower, structure, and guide the world; a close second in importance is how human beings choose to relate to it. So the Dao is, broadly speaking, the way of the universe and the way of human life that ideally ties into it. The Dao is not a thing, a substance, or a being. The Dao is not a god or even a spirit, and Daoists do not worship it. Daoism has many deities, but they are as dependent on the Dao as everything else in the universe. Paradoxically, the Dao gives rise to all being, but it does not have a being of its own. It is not an object of human thought or activity, but it is the hidden subject of all things. It cannot be perceived in itself, but it can be observed in the workings of the natural world.

The Dao is a Way of cosmic reality and human fulfillment. All animals and plants in the world live fully and naturally in the Dao. To some extent, humans also live naturally in the Dao, but in certain aspects humans have become distant from it. To live fully in the Dao takes knowledge and intention. Despite the Dao's deep connection to the world of nature, living in the Dao isn't naturally easy. Moreover, living in the Dao isn't a matter of achieving union with the Dao, as some people might put it, but rather being in complete conformity with the Dao. The Dao includes several concepts in its one word: the source, the ultimate, the inexpressible and indefinable, and the unnamable. It is the natural universe as a whole, as well as the principle and power within it.

7-3c Traditional Daoist Deities

Confucianists generally recognize the main Chinese deities, and Daoists recognize them all. The relationships among the vast number of Daoist gods and goddesses in China are often said to parallel, even mimic, the government bureaucracy of imperial China. Although there may be truth to this idea, some writers argue that the reverse is true: The imperial government

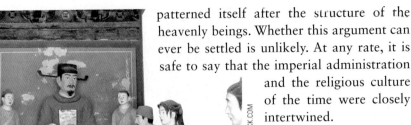

Daoist deities are arrayed in a heavenly court in the Dongyue Temple in Beijing.

©CLAUDIO ZACCHERINI/SHUTTERSTOCK.COM

patterned itself after the structure of the heavenly beings. Whether this argument can ever be settled is unlikely. At any rate, it is safe to say that the imperial administration and the religious culture of the time were closely intertwined.

Westerners who know only the philosophical side of Daoism are sometimes surprised to discover that most Daoists worship gods. To westerners, there doesn't seem to be a need for deities in Daoism. Daoism does not have a God in the way that the Abrahamic religions do, or even as the Mahayana Buddhists in China have deities. In Daoism, the universe constantly springs from the Dao, and the Dao impersonally guides things on their way. But the Dao itself is not a divine being, nor is it worshiped by Daoists. The Dao is much more important than that. Moreover, deities are within this universe and are themselves subject to the Dao just as much as humans are. This may seem surprising, as Daoists occasionally use what westerners think of as language for God—for example, when the Dao is called the Venerable Lord. Some Daoists even go so far as to occasionally revere Laozi both as the first god of Daoism and as the personification of the Dao, just as some Confucianists declared Confucius a god in the early 1900s as a last-ditch effort to prop up their place in Chinese society.

In sum, China has many gods, more than a few borrowed from other cultures. A great number of the deities are known and worshiped by their particular role rather than as personal divine beings; they have titles rather than names.

The Jade Emperor. The supreme ruler of Heaven in Chinese tradition is popularly called the **Jade Emperor**, or Yu Huang. (Note how the supreme god is called an emperor.) The Jade Emperor lives in a luxurious palace in the highest Heaven where he rules and directs all other gods. He can grant titles to the spirits of outstanding individuals and even elevate them to deities. His image, and that of the gods and goddesses under his direction, can be found in various Daoist temples. Many historians of Chinese religion conclude that *Jade Emperor* was an early Daoist title for the more ancient Chinese deity called, by various names, the Lord of Heaven.

Jade Emperor The supreme deity in Daoism

BIGBIGSHEEP/DREAMSTIME.COM

The Jade Emperor on his throne

lived on an island off the coast of China sometime during the Song dynasty (960–1279). Her legend says that she was a strong swimmer and employed her supernatural powers to cure the ill and save people on the sea from imminent danger. For this, she was deified after her death and is also known as the Sea Goddess. Mazu became the most highly venerated of all female deities in Daoism—especially after an emperor of China named her the Queen of Heaven—and she is known to Buddhists as well.

The popularity of Mazu in Taiwan is seen by the more than four hundred temples dedicated to her, and also by the processions in communities all over the island, during which her statue is carried on a chair so she can spread her blessings. Tens of thousands of worshipers join in a week-long pilgrimage in her honor, and many now make a pilgrimage across the Taiwan Strait to venerate her at her grave. Mazu is widely worshiped in the provinces of China that are on the sea, and in the Chinese diaspora as well. The oldest Daoist temple in the United States, the Tin How (Heaven's Queen) Temple—built in 1852 in the Chinatown district of San Francisco—is dedicated to Mazu.

City Gods. When we think about the gods of a religion, the first thing that comes to mind are the principal deities that everyone in a religion knows and worships, such as the three we have just discussed. However, in China there are many gods who are known and worshiped only in select locales, as are the **city gods**. The Jade Emperor has commanded them to guard particular cities against attack by enemies and protect their inhabitants from various evils. City gods were originally humans who served the people righteously during their lifetimes, had compassion for those in danger, and protected people and good spirits from being dragged into the underworld by evil ghosts. For their demonstration of classic virtues, the righteous spirits of these people were made divine at some point after their deaths.

The City God Temple in Shanghai is dedicated to three city gods, all of whom

The Earth God. We will follow the Chinese tendency in religion to think of Heaven and earth together; after discussing the supreme god of Heaven, we deal now with the main god of earth. In the countryside of Chinese lands, one can see small temples and shrines, some only a foot high, that feature a picture of a smiling, bearded old man. This is the **Earth God**, commonly called Tudi Gong or Land Elder, and more formally known as Righteous God of Good Fortune and Virtue. The Earth God has thousands of incarnated spirit forms who look after plots of land and the people residing on them. This guardian spirit is a popular divinity in Daoism, and his image is often found on family altars.

Mazu. Mazu (MAH-tsoo), or Mother Ancestor, is the spirit of Lin Moniang. Lin was a young woman who

Earth God Daoist deity who protects property

Mazu [MAHT-soo] "Mother Ancestor," the Goddess of the Sea and the Queen of Heaven

city gods Local Chinese gods, often with a protective role

ESSENTIAL DAOIST AND CONFUCIAN TEACHINGS **171**

were human beings who were deified after their deaths. Huo Guang (died 68 B.C.E.) was a famous Han dynasty chancellor. He is venerated for his role in deposing one young emperor and replacing him with another, more worthy ruler. Qin Yubo (1295–1373) was a prominent citizen of Shanghai and served in the late Yuan dynasty. When the Ming dynasty was founded, he refused two commands to serve at the court. He finally relented and served in several offices, including that of chief imperial examiner. Chen Huacheng (1776–1842) was a Qing-dynasty general who led the defense of Shanghai during the First Opium War. He vowed to defend China to the death, and was killed in battle against the British.

Lords of Pestilence. *Wang Ye* is a generic term denoting some 360 Lords of Pestilence whose lives before becoming deities are recounted in different tales. These lords are people of great merit and exemplary lives, who after death were charged by the gods with the task of protecting humans from evil spirits and epidemics. (They become Lords of Pestilence in the sense of *controlling* pestilence.) Rituals for worship of these protectors differ widely. A popular ritual for driving away disease, held twice every year, is "Burning Wang Ye's Boat." A boat made of paper and wood is burned along with its spirit-money cargo. This offering is designed to make the Lords of Pestilence more inclined to do their protective work.

Similar to most religions with many deities, Daoism can "lose" gods, add new ones, or update the portrayal of older gods. A variety of "techno-neon" portrayals of Daoist gods are popular in Chinese lands today.

7-3d Daoist Teaching of Wu Wei

The only method of following the Dao is by **wu wei**. This term is difficult to translate and has been rendered as "nonaction," "passive action," "uncontrived action," "natural nonintervention," or "not asserting." *Nonaction* wrongly implies that one does nothing at all, that one is completely passive. The *Daode Jing* might be read to support this interpretation of wu wei, as in

wu wei [woo way]
"Not asserting"; going along with the nature of the world

Mazu, goddess of the sea, the most popular goddess in Daoism

©LOONG/SHUTTERSTOCK.COM

its "When nothing is done, nothing is left undone" (Chapter 48). However, wu wei is best understood as going along with nature, letting things in one's life take their natural, Dao-determined course.

Daoists try to live balanced and harmonious lives that are attuned to the Dao as it is seen in nature—they "act naturally." They find their way through life in the same way as breezes blow in the air, as rain falls from the sky, or as a river flows through the countryside by finding its natural course. They act, even are active, but their action is carefully attuned to their perception of the Dao—therefore, easier, happier, and natural. To use a modern analogy, North Americans typically make a distinction between *work* and *pleasure*: If an activity is pleasurable, we don't think of it as work, which is supposed to be at least a little difficult. As a result, westerners can think of the expression "act naturally" as a nonsensical contradiction similar to "found

Four university students pray for blessing at the Temple of the City God, Shanghai, China.

TRAVEL PICTURES/ALAMY

7-3e Daoist Views of Qi

Daoists understand the human body to be a miniature of the universe. Similar to the universe, each human body has many parts, but it is filled with the Dao. The human body, as much as the larger universe, is also inhabited and ruled by a large number of deities.

The body also has spiritual energy that is cosmic, but not a part of the gods. Daoists believe that every living person has a normal, healthy amount of qi and that personal health results from the balance, harmony, and smooth flow of qi. This flow is seen as a complex system analogous to the movement of water, with a sea of qi in the abdomen, its main location; rivers of qi flowing through the torso and through the limbs; streams of qi flowing to the wrists and ankles; and small springs of qi in the fingers and toes. Any disruption in this system can influence the whole and require readjustment. Balance and natural smoothness in the working of qi is the general goal. Daoists want to empower their qi and be empowered by it.

All individuals receive a core of primordial qi at birth and need to sustain it during their lifetimes. They do so by drawing qi into the body from air and food, as well as from other people through social and sexual interactions. But they also lose qi by breathing bad air, eating and drinking too much, having negative emotions, and engaging in excessive sexual or social interactions. Traditional Chinese medicines drawn

A Daoist god at a 2010 festival in Taiwan

missing" or "minor catastrophe." But in the Daoist view, when work is done naturally—if a carpenter cuts wood with the grain, not against it, for example—it is a pleasure, and we do in fact "act naturally." This is wu wei in action. Wu wei doesn't forbid action in one's life, but it does command that one's activities fit into the natural pattern of the universe. After Buddhism entered China and made an impression on Daoism, wu wei was also understood as action that is not ego driven, but rather detached from individual desires. In sum, Daoism requires individuals to live and work the same way as nature naturally follows the Dao.

from nature can be used to restore the flow of qi, and acupuncture is also commonly used to unblock qi flow. Tai qi and other movement-and-meditation systems arose to maximize the flow and presence of qi in the body. Breathing properly is key to tai qi. Although it is known in the West as an exercise system especially good for older people, this is not its significance for Daoism. Nevertheless, the medical benefits of tai qi are well established. For example, a study done by Emory University's medical school concluded that training in tai qi was highly effective in improving the balance, strength, and even self-confidence of those 70 years and older.[6]

An American man practices tai qi. Tai qi is mostly known in the West as an exercise system, but this is not its main significance for Daoism.

7-3f The Daoist Quest for Immortality

Immortality doesn't mean escaping death by living forever in the present physical body. This is the stuff of western and Chinese horror stories. Daoists believe that all spirits are immortal in some sense—they survive the death of the body and go into the next world. The world of spirits is connected to the world of the gods. Spiritual immortality, a special goal of some Daoists, raises to a whole new level the practice of pursuing immortality in this life. To attain spiritual immortality, one must change all one's qi into primordial qi and then refine it. This finer qi will gradually turn into pure spirit, enabling one to become a "spirit-person" already in this life. This process requires intense training in meditation and trances, radical forms of diet, and esoteric sexual practices. The result is a bypassing of the effects of death on the spirit; the end of the body has no impact on the continuation of the spirit-person. After death, the spirit lives forever in a wonderful paradise, and the person is said to be an immortal.

7-3g Confucian Reformulations of Ancient Teachings

The Confucian reworking of ancient Chinese teachings centered on ethics—what the western tradition calls personal and social ethics. Confucianism is often called a system of social ethics, and from the western perspective that is true enough, but we should remember that this distinction between personal and social is

not often made in China. It doesn't make a great deal of sense in a culture where the personal and the social are so fully blended, and where western-style individualism is rejected. We'll consider Confucian ethics later in this chapter; here, however, we should state the Confucian take on ancient Chinese religious teachings and practices.

As stated earlier, Confucius and his followers were highly appreciative of Chinese tradition. His teaching reaffirms many aspects of Chinese religion that predated him: the role of Heaven, particularly in government; the importance of the Way (Dao); the assumption that humans are basically good and will follow the truth when they know it; and respect for the gods and traditional rituals. On respect for ritual, Confucius once defended the sacrifice of sheep by saying to someone who objected to it, "You love the sheep, but I love the ceremony" (*Analects* 3.17). Confucius's system sought to reform traditional Chinese religious and ethical ideas, not so much by changing them as by showing people their inner meaning. Confucius believed that if people knew *why* these things are important, they would follow them more fully and carefully, and life would become what it should be. (See "A Closer Look: A Famous Conversation.")

7-4 Daoist and Confucian Ethics

Throughout North America, Amy Chua's book *Battle Hymn of the Tiger Mother* (2011) raised a storm of controversy on television, on the web, and in print. In it Chua (CHEW-ah), a law professor at Yale, details how she raised two daughters with traditional tough love and Chinese mother parenting, as opposed to what she calls the lax current models of American parenting. She demanded straight As from her daughters and pushed them to excel in everything they did, often using methods that seem harsh and unloving to her readers. Many Chinese American parents do take the time to guide their children in doing homework and often give them some academic work besides what is assigned; children usually respond by taking their studies seriously. This is in line with traditional Confucian values, especially the importance of self-cultivation for one's family. Chua's approach struck a nerve, as it was designed to do (notice its provocative title), but many experts on Chinese culture wonder if she hasn't misrepresented Confucian values and thereby done these values a disservice.

A Closer Look

A Famous Conversation between Confucius and Laozi

The meeting of Confucius and Laozi probably never happened, and it appears to have been invented in later times to illustrate the differences between their systems, at least on an official level. Confucius, committed as he was to bringing proper order to social and political life, promotes to Laozi the value of ancient religious rituals and ideas of justice. He speaks positively about the way ancient kings ruled, especially Zhou rulers. Laozi is interested in acquiring peace and inner equilibrium. He urges Confucius in sharp words to seek wu wei, which leads to unity with the Dao.

> "Today I have seen Laozi, and I can only compare him to the dragon."
>
> —Confucius

Confucius asked Laozi about his opinion regarding the ancient rites and rulers. Laozi is said to have answered:

> The men about whom you talk are dead, and their bones are moldered to dust; only their words are left. When your "superior man" gets his opportunity, he succeeds; but when the time is against him, he is carried along by circumstances. I have heard that a good merchant, even if he is rich, appears as if he were poor. Likewise, the truly superior man appears outwardly unintelligent. So put away your proud airs and your many desires to change things. They are of no advantage to you; this is all I have to tell you.

In this conversation, it became clear that neither would convince the other. After their meeting, Confucius said to his disciples,

> I know how birds can fly, how fish can swim, and how animals can run. . . . But there is the dragon: I cannot tell how he mounts on the wind through the clouds and rises to Heaven. Today I have seen Laozi, and I can only compare him to the dragon.

Confucian ethics are more fully developed, and more central to Confucianism's religious system, than are Daoist ethics. For example, it is often said about Confucianism that it is a system of ethics, but this is not said about Daoism. Before we discuss Confucianism, we will consider some main moral principles from the *Daode Jing* and other early texts that have become important in Daoism.

7-4a Daoist Ethics

The basis of Daoist ethics is the *Daode Jing*. Although it is elusive in style and meaning, challenging the reader to figure out what it means, the main lines

A mind governed by yin-yang balance is filled with light and purpose.

of Daoist moral teaching are clear. The *Daode Jing* teaches that one must follow the way of the Dao in order to live a good life. Other living beings in nature—plants and animals, as well as the system of nature as a whole—follow the Dao automatically; they can't do otherwise.

But human beings do not follow the Dao naturally. The *Daode Jing* suggests that human distinctions such as good and evil, beauty and ugliness generate the troubles and problems of existence (Chapter 3). Humans impose such things on the Dao; they aren't really there. Persons following the Dao must not live according to human-made distinctions (Chapter 19).

Indeed, these distinctions emerge only when people aren't following the Dao (Chapters 18 and 38); they are a form of disease (Chapter 74). Daoists believe that the Dao unties the knots of life, blunts the sharp edges of relationships and problems, and soothes painful occurrences (Chapter 4). So it is best to practice wu wei in all endeavors, to act naturally, and not to oppose or tamper with how life is flowing.

All this can seem very abstract, but Daoism carries out these ideas in everyday practice. For example, Daoists often have a preference for vegetarianism, which they see as more natural than eating meat. This Daoist moral practice, along with the Buddhist promotion of vegetarianism, explains why Chinese restaurants have so many vegetarian dishes on their menus.

7-4b Confucian Ethics

Filial Piety. Although Confucianism has not often ranked its moral virtues, filial piety, **xiao**, is traditionally considered among the most important and has had a powerful effect on Chinese culture. As a phrase, "filial piety" is a bit unwieldy and old-fashioned as a translation of *xiao*, but no other term has taken its place. *Filial* means of a child, and *piety* means inner devotion and outward obedience. Both evoke meanings bordering on religious reverence. So *filial piety* is first of all the honor and obedience that children owe their parents.

The *Book of Filial Piety* is our main source for this topic, attributed traditionally to Confucius and one of his sons but almost certainly written anonymously in the 200s B.C.E. Filial piety must be shown toward both living parents and dead ancestors, and this leads to ancestor worship. It binds families into an eternal bond. This relationship was extended by analogy to the Five Relationships: (1) ruler and subject, (2) father and son, (3) husband and wife, (4) elder brother and younger brother, and (5) older friend and younger friend. Each person in these sets of relationships had specific duties; the first person in the relationship must lead with honor and kindness, and the second person must faithfully obey. Duties extended to the dead, who were expected to bless descendants that

xiao [show; rhymes with *now*] Filial piety; honor and obedience to parents and ancestors

> { *The family name is traditionally put first, then the personal name—family is more important than any individual member.* }

honored them and lived well, and withhold blessing from descendants who didn't. The only relationship where respect for elders did not apply was that of friend to friend. In all other relationships, high reverence was held for the older person of the two.

All this was traditional in Chinese culture by the time Confucius came onto the scene. He stressed not only the duty to perform the actions of filial piety, but much more the inner attitude of these acts. Only when inner attitude empowers and guides the outer acts will filial piety work to improve society. Confucius taught, "Filial piety nowadays means the support of one's parents. But dogs and horses are also able to do something in the way of support [for the dogs and horses that gave them birth]. Without reverence, what is there to distinguish the one support from the other?" (*Analects* 2.7).

Even for those outside the Chinese cultural and religious system, Confucius's teaching on relationships has a great deal of wisdom. For example, he said that filial piety can be illustrated by "not making your parents anxious about anything else than your being sick." To those with aging parents he said, "The [advanced] age of one's parents should always be remembered, as a reason for joy and for fear" (*Analects* 2.6, 21).

Note how family relationships are the center and key to the five relationships. When people in the West speak of family values in wider society, their ideas pale in comparison with China's emphasis on these values. The importance of one's family is shown by traditional Chinese names. The family name is traditionally put first, then the personal name—family is more important than any individual member. In general, the individual lives for the family, not vice versa. (When Chinese people in the West put their personal name first, it can get a little confusing for non-Chinese to tell the personal name from the family name. The family name typically has one syllable and the personal name has two. In the traditionally ordered name of the scholar Tu Weiming, *Tu* is the family name, *Weiming* the personal name. For a scholar who has westernized his name, Wing-tsit Chan, his two-syllable personal name is first.) Filial piety has continued to play a central role in Confucian thinking, and in Chinese culture, to the present day.

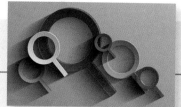

A Closer Look

Religion or Philosophy?

At this point, a common question in the study of Chinese religions should be asked: Is Confucianism a philosophy or a religion? The debate is lively, because Confucius himself—and most of his followers for the past two thousand years—had much more to say about the natural world than the supernatural, and his religion seems to westerners to center on social ethics. A recent book by Anna Sun, *Confucianism as a World Religion: Contested Histories and Contemporary Realities*, puts this debate in its historical context. Sun argues that in the late 1800s the field of religious study, also known as comparative religion, constructed Confucianism not only as a religion, but also as a world religion. At times since then, this construction has been contested by western scholars.[7] The government of China now has a divided mind about Confucianism: It does not list Confucianism as one of its five main religions, but it does recognize and support Confucian temples, rituals, and especially ethics. Scholars sharply debate the question of whether Confucianism is a religion or a philosophy. However, with China growing in influence, and with a revitalized Confucianism promoted by the communist government to fill an ethical vacuum in Maoism, Confucianism has a strong future in Asia.

Many religion scholars realize that our interest in trying to separate philosophy and religion shows a western mindset, where philosophy and religion are separate academic disciplines. The western inclination to separate these subject areas dates to the classical Greek period of philosophy and has been reinforced in early-modern and modern times. An artificial partition is often imposed between Chinese religion and philosophy. Also, the closeness of what we call philosophy and religion is suggested by the commonly used words for them, *jia* and *jiao*, respectively.

A closer study of Confucianism shows clearly that it is a religion as commonly defined in academic study, although with strong strands of what we call philosophy. Confucianists believe that human fulfillment comes from proper engagement in worldly affairs, but they also deal with matters of ultimate concern. Confucius along with Confucianists made and make room for the gods and other supernatural things but they are not the center of their religion. As a result, Confucianism is a humanistic religion strongly concerned with social ethics, but it *is* a religion as scholars generally define it.

To return to our main question: Is Confucianism a philosophy or a religion? If we must answer, perhaps the best answer is that it is *both*. Of course, this book focuses on its religious aspects.

Reciprocity. Ren—variously translated as "humaneness, reciprocity, virtue"—is a basic Confucian value, second only to filial piety in its importance. Despite the hierarchical and authoritarian structure of life that Confucianism encourages, the more powerful people in every relationship must act with humane, gentle reciprocity toward the less powerful in the relationship. Confucius himself once said that *ren* is the key moral teaching, and summarized it by saying, "What you don't want done to yourself, don't do to others."

Loyalty. Loyalty (**zhong**) is closely related to filial piety. Loyalty is an extension of one's duties to friends and family, and is carried out in the Five Relationships. Loyalty to one's father is first, then to one's spouse, one's ruler, and one's friends. Confucius's teaching on zhong has been undermined by the authoritarian

social structure of China. More emphasis is put on the ruler's power over his subjects and much less on the ruler's obligations to his subjects, whether that ruler is an emperor, a father, or a husband. Nevertheless, loyalty has always been considered one of the greater human virtues.

The "Perfect Man". The term **junzi** (Wade-Giles, *chuntzu*), literally "a prince's son," is crucial to Confucianism. More than any other Confucian concept, it expresses the process of self-cultivation and self-improvement. A succinct description of the junzi is one who,

ren "Humaneness, reciprocity, virtue"; also spelled "jen"

zhong Loyalty, duties to friends and family

junzi [JUHN-tzoo] Literally, "a prince's son"; in the teaching of Confucius, a "superior man"

Family relationships are key to Confucian ethics.

7-5 Ritual and Worship

A solitary sage studies ancient Chinese poems in Hong Kong. He pauses to reflect on their meaning, especially on how they relate to his Confucian beliefs. After reflecting, he writes out the passage calligraphically; his artistic brushstrokes of the Chinese word-characters show the inner meaning of the text and the results of his meditation. This simple ritual helps him improve his character toward becoming a "perfect man," the highest goal of the Confucian tradition, and his study of the ancient classics is a key ingredient in this self-cultivation. Daoists also use the drawing of key words and passages to promote living more deeply in the Dao.

As you study ritual and worship in Daoism and Confucianism, you will notice some important commonalities. Both religions center their worship in temples, where many of the same activities can be found: burning incense, bowing to images, sitting meditation, meditative walking, and others. Both religions have a notable lack of emphasis on life-cycle rituals, with the exception of funerals. Funeral rites also tend to be similar for Daoists and Confucianists, for two remarkable reasons: Both religions draw on ancient Chinese funeral ideas and practices, and Buddhism has strongly influenced the way the Chinese look at death. We will now look more fully at both similarities and differences in Confucian and Daoist ritual.

7-5a Daoist Temples and Worship

Daoist temples are more colorful and elaborate than those of other religions in China. They are ornately decorated both on the exterior and in the interior. Those who visit and worship there often add brightly colored flowers and streamers to decorate the temple. Color, particularly red, is seen as bringing blessing and good luck. Vendors outside most temples sell small statues for taking home, as well as incense and flowers to use in the temple. Inside is an altar at the front, on which flowers can be placed and incense burned. Worshipers may kneel in reverence in front of this altar. Behind the altar, the focal point of the temple, are statues of the gods honored in that temple.

Sometimes there are group ceremonies in the temple, such as continuous reading of a scripture text to earn merit or for monastic worship on holy days, and

in the Anglo-American expression, is a scholar and a gentleman. In ancient times, the masculine gender of the phrase was intentional—only males could become a junzi. In modern times, the masculine translation in English is still frequently used, although women are also urged (in parts of the Confucian world) toward self-cultivation.

In addition to sexism, this term has been linked with elitism. The junzi is seen as a better person than others, and he is expected to act as a moral guide for the rest of society. Indeed, *junzi* has often been translated as "exemplary person." However, becoming a junzi by education and experience was open to every class. Confucius would take on anyone as a student who could pay him even the smallest amount, and later Confucianism was in many respects a meritocracy of learning and virtue, not an aristocracy of automatic privilege for the highborn.

For Confucianists, the great example of the "perfect man" is Confucius himself. Perhaps the biggest disappointment of his life was that he was never awarded the high official position that he desired, where he would have demonstrated the social blessings that would ensue if humane, wise persons ruled and administered the state. Despite this disappointment, he continued to teach his system, even when he thought that it would die out when he did. His students carried on his teachings for hundreds of years before his system took root in Chinese life.

people in the temple are welcome to look on. But people generally come to the temples for individual experiences, to seek the favor and blessing of the god(s) for a particular need. One of their most pressing needs is to gain direction for their future. In ancient times, various divination rituals were used, going all the way back to oracle bones inscribed with writings; the bones would be put into the fire, and how they cracked would indicate the future. Other methods arose over time, and what is common today (in or just outside Daoist temples) is selecting yarrow sticks to obtain a passage from the *Yi Jing*, which a diviner will then interpret.

7-5b Confucian Temples and Worship

In China before the twentieth century C.E., every county had one official temple to Confucius. These temples were usually next to Confucian schools. The front portal of the temple was an ornamental gate. Inside, there were usually three courtyards, two in smaller temple complexes. The main building on the inner courtyard was the "Hall of Great Achievement" or "Hall of Great Perfection." This housed the ancestral tablet of Confucius and the tablets of other important masters and sages, usually the first main disciples of Confucius. A second significant

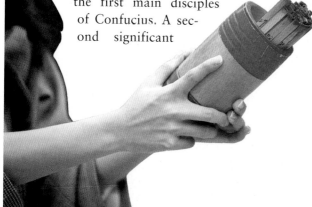

Offering incense to Daoist gods

After the bamboo cylinder is shaken, a person seeking direction selects a stick.

temple building was the "Shrine of the Great Wise Men," which honored the ancestors of Confucius.

Unlike Daoist or Buddhist temples, Confucian temples do not normally have images. In early years, Confucius and his disciples were probably represented with wall paintings and statues. However, there was rising opposition to this practice, which over time was seen as Buddhist. In the 1500s C.E., all existing images of Confucius were replaced with memorial tablets in imperial temples in the capital and other bureaucratic locations. However, statues are still found in temples controlled by Confucius's family descendants, such as that in Qufu. The point of almost all Confucian temples is to honor and promote Confucius's teachings, not Confucius himself. Confucius is a human example, not a god.

The state-mandated worship of Confucius centered upon offering sacrifices to Confucius's spirit in the Confucian temple. A dance known as the Eight-Row Dance, consisting of eight columns of eight dancers each, sometimes carrying feathers or a weapon, was also performed. Today this is performed on Confucius's birthday and is accompanied by musical performances and prayers. Animal sacrifices (the animals are killed before the service, not as a part of it) and incense are offered to the spirit of Confucius.

In addition to honoring Confucius, Confucian temples also honor other disciples and Confucian scholars throughout history. The composition and number of figures venerated have changed and have grown over time. Because temples were a statement of official Confucian teaching, the issue of which Confucianists to enshrine was often difficult. Today, a total of 162 figures are venerated in Confucian temples.

7-5c The Traditional Chinese Funeral

Life-cycle rituals are not as plentiful or as important in China as they are in some other cultures and religions. Marriage is more a social arrangement than a religious one, for example. But the traditional Chinese funeral is well developed and has great religious

The temple of Confucius in Tainan, Taiwan—the oldest on that island—shows the simplicity of Confucian temples when compared to Daoist or Buddhist temples.

and cultural significance. It still reflects some of the most ancient Chinese beliefs about life, death, and life after death.

Cremation is rare, even unthinkable, for Daoists and Confucianists, because it destroys the qi that remains in the bones of the dead. This qi is important for the spirit of the deceased in the next world. In-ground burial of the whole body is the rule. (For Chinese Buddhists, however, cremation is common.) Male heads of the family receive elaborate funerals, infants or children very simple ones, and people in between get rites on a sliding scale.

Funerals take place in the home and the cemetery, not in a temple or mortuary business. An undertaker is hired to oversee all funeral rites, especially actions involving physical contact with the corpse, because this contact is defiling to the family. When the family prepares to receive visitors who come to pay their respects, all statues of gods in the house are covered so that they will not be exposed to the body or coffin. All mirrors are removed or covered, because seeing a body in a mirror is thought to be inauspicious. When the body of the deceased is cleaned and dressed in the deceased's best clothing, it is put in the

> { Cremation is rare . . . for Daoists and Confucianists, because it destroys the qi in the bones of the dead. }

open coffin and placed inside the house or in its courtyard. Flowers, gifts, food, and a portrait of the deceased are placed near the coffin as an offering to the deceased and as a comfort to the bereaved family. The immediate family is now ready to receive visitors from among their wider family, neighbors, and friends.

Various activities take place in the home during the period of visitation. Relatives typically cry or even wail during mourning, both out of genuine emotion and as a sign of respect and loyalty to the deceased. The spirit of the dead will see this grief and be pleased by it. A small altar with burning incense and a candle is put at the foot of the coffin. This honors the dead, and helps to keep the smell of death at bay. Symbolic paper money is burned continuously outside to provide the deceased with income in the afterlife. Visitors light incense for the deceased and bow to the family out of respect. A monk reads aloud verses from Buddhist or Daoist scriptures. (Confucianists generally rely on Buddhism and Daoism for funeral rites.) Before they can enter the happier afterlife, the souls of the dead face many troubles and even torment for the sins they have committed in life. Chanting by the monks eases the passage of the deceased's soul into a happy afterlife. These prayers are accompanied by music, and the family arranges for as much scripture and music performance as it can afford.

A solemn procession then goes from the home to the cemetery. Chinese cemeteries are traditionally located on hillsides, where feng shui is best. (As we saw earlier in this chapter, feng shui began with burials, and its influence on burial is still strong.) When the coffin is removed from the hearse and lowered into the ground, the mourners look away. Then family members throw a handful of earth

BAITONG SATHITKUN/SHUTTERSTOCK.COM

Burning money for deceased ancestors, practiced by Daoists and Confucianists.

into the grave before it is filled. As they depart, the keeper of the cemetery offers other prayers for the deceased.

After the burial, the ritual continues. All clothes worn by the mourners are burned, to avoid bad fortune associated with death. Special prayers to the deceased will be offered by the family at home, especially directed at the ancestral tablet that now has the deceased's name on it. The family's mourning period continues for one hundred days, signified by a piece of colored cloth worn on their sleeves. From this time on, for as long as the family endures, the dead will be venerated in the home (and in a family temple if the family is wealthy), and money will be sent to the deceased by burning imitation paper money at their graves.

7-5d A Final Comparison of Daoism and Confucianism

Before we turn to the topic of Daoism and Confucianism in the western world, it may be helpful to sketch a final comparison of Daoism and Confucianism. Daoism shared some emphases with classical Confucianism, such as the necessity of self-cultivation and a concern for the practicalities of life, but not abstractions (the latter seen, for example, in Buddhism). Both Daoism and Confucianism are world-affirming religions, and religions that also affirm the ancient cultural and spiritual life of China. Despite these similarities, Daoism and Confucianism have been competing alternative religions—in main teachings, ethics, and ritual.

As we saw previously, Daoism teaches that human distinctions such as morality and beauty generate the troubles and problems of existence. They are imposed on the world by the human mind; they do not exist in the world itself. The person following the Dao must cease living by human distinctions. Daoists believe that the Dao naturally makes human life full and right. So it is best to practice wu wei, to act naturally, and not to oppose or tamper with how nature or even human reality is moving. Daoism teaches that it is better to be passive rather than active, yielding rather than assertive, quiet rather than vocal. In terms of the yin-yang, Daoism is the yin of China.

Confucius and his followers, on the other hand, have viewed themselves as the yang, the active and assertive side of life. They have been proactive, to use a current term, in setting human life straight. They study current life in the light of Confucian thought, plan changes, educate people to be active, and develop solutions to China's problems. A familiar Chinese saying is that Daoists "take their hands off life" and let it go its own way; Confucianists "put their hands on everything" in an effort to guide and shape people. To use another illustration, Daoists let life shape them like natural forces shape a piece of rock or wood; Confucianists carve themselves into a sculpture.

"Daoists take their hands off life, but Confucianists put their hands on everything."

—Chinese saying

7-6 Daoism and Confucianism around the World Today

For thousands of years China was an insular nation that kept to itself, and Chinese religion did the same. Daoism and Confucianism first spread into the wider world when its scriptures were translated, and then when Chinese people migrated to the West.

7-6a Daoism and Confucianism in the West

Daoism first entered the world beyond China when scholars translated its main works into European languages, beginning in the 1700s. The *Daode Jing* has been consistently popular for more than two centuries and is today one of the most translated books in the world. From 1927 to 1944, the chief advocate of Daoism for the western world was Professor Henri Maspero in Paris. More recently, Michael Saso (born 1930), an academic expert in Daoism and author of several leading books on it, has advanced Daoism in the West. He was the first westerner to become a Daoist priest. He also served as coeditor of *Taoist Resources*, a major academic journal devoted entirely to Daoism, which ceased publication in 1997. Today, many Daoist organizations have been established throughout the West.

Confucianism also came to the West by means of its writings. The *Analects* and the *Mencius* were among the first books translated in Max Müller's *Sacred Books of the East* project in the 1800s, and dozens of translations have been made since that time into every major European language. The practice of Chinese religions spread to the West not primarily from China itself, but from neighboring lands in which these religions have long been present: Taiwan and Korea in particular, and to a lesser degree Japan, Vietnam, and Indonesia. In Taiwan, despite the modernizations that have made it a thriving democracy and economic powerhouse, traditional Chinese religions remain stronger than on the mainland. Nine out of ten residents of Taiwan call themselves Buddhists, Daoists, Confucianists, or a mix of the three. In South Korea, almost half the population is Christian, but the other half is devoted to Buddhism, Confucianism, and/or the service of local gods.

7-6b Confucianism in North America

Confucianists and Daoists came to North America from the lands mentioned previously as well as from China. We will deal with Confucianism first. Because Confucianism is a moral system that is built on elements of traditional Chinese religion found in much of Daoism, and because Confucian temples in Chinese lands were state sponsored, Confucian temples couldn't be transplanted in North America as Daoist or Buddhist temples could. The temples to Confucius, and their associated schools (from primary schools in every county to the imperial university in Beijing), anchored Confucianism in Asia in a way that could not be built in North America. Indeed, they wouldn't make sense in a North American society that isn't Confucian and doesn't establish any religion as the national faith. Chinese people eventually built social and educational associations that had an appreciation for Confucianism, sometimes even with a room or two dedicated to the veneration of Confucius and his main disciples; but they couldn't, and didn't, build temples like those found in China and surrounding regions within the Chinese

This small Daoist temple was built in 1874, and is now preserved in a state park in Weaverville, California.

©ZACK FRANK/SHUTTERSTOCK.COM

cultural orbit. Confucianism is probably the only world religion to come to North America that doesn't have formal temples here. Chinese cultural centers must often host Confucian ceremonies.

> { Confucianism is probably the only world religion to come to North America that doesn't have formal temples here. }

A much more recent feature is the establishment and funding of **Confucius Institutes** in major North American cities, usually connected with universities, by the government of the People's Republic of China. More than one hundred of these institutes have been set up in the United States since about 1990; in Chicago alone, there are several. These institutes are an effort at public diplomacy by the Chinese government, an outreach especially to secondary schools and higher education. This sponsorship has made Confucius Institutes controversial at many universities, where professors fear a loss of academic freedom and independence, and several universities have recently abolished their Confucian Institutes. The main Chicago Confucius Center describes itself this way:

> The Confucius Center is a nonprofit institute aiming to enhance intercultural understanding in the world by sponsoring courses of Chinese language and culture, so as to promote a better understanding of the Chinese language and culture among the people of the world; develop friendly relationships between China and other countries; accelerate the development of multiculturalism at the international level; and help bring about global peace and harmony.

So it's clear that, despite the name Confucius Institutes or Confucius Centers, Confucianism itself isn't what they are primarily about. But there is something traditionally Chinese about this arrangement: Chinese culture and Confucian values are so deeply intertwined that to deal with the first is necessarily to deal with the second. As a result, Confucianism is found at these centers and institutes not only in the plentiful Confucian scriptures that are there, but even more in the promotion of Confucian values in Chinese life and learning.

7-6c Daoism in North America

Daoism came to North America with the first Chinese who arrived to participate in California's gold rush. The new settlers established several temples in San Francisco. One of these, the Tin How Temple mentioned in Section 7-3c, was built in 1852 and still stands today. It was built out of gratitude to Mazu, as the Queen of Heaven, for protecting the settlers on their long sea voyage. In the next decades, statues and name tablets of other gods were installed in the temple. By 1890, dozens of Chinese temples were found along the West Coast of the United States and Canada. Together they served a multitude of deities, just as their temples in China had. A trusted caretaker who acted as a janitor for the building would usually supervise the worship and sacrifices as well as organize festivals. Daoist priests were not yet to be found in the New World, and neither were monks. Despite the hard pressure on Daoism in China during the 1800s, priests and monks did not make the perilous trek to a non-Chinese culture in the West. Most of these temples disappeared over time, but some of them—such as the Tin How Temple—continue today.

Should these be considered *Daoist* temples? This depends on how one understands Daoism. To use the threefold understanding of Daoism advanced by Livia Kohn, they certainly were not temples of "philosophical Daoism." They can make a good claim for "religious Daoism," and certainly they were "folk Daoist" temples. But the majority of the gods worshiped in these temples were not the main Daoist deities, with the exception of the Jade Emperor. Rather, they were local gods that Chinese Americans could still look to for help, ones that had long ago been taken up into the vast Daoist collection of gods.

The ups and downs of Daoism in the United States varied with immigration policies, just as did all other religions of immigrants. The federal Chinese Exclusion Act of 1882 effectively stopped all new Chinese immigration, and Daoist temples suffered. When the Immigration Act of 1965 was passed, a good level of Chinese immigration resumed. Temples revived, and many Daoist organizations were founded that still exist today. The largest of these is the network of "Healing Tao" centers in the United States and Canada, a movement that combines western and Daoist healing arts. These new associations and temples typically have well-educated members from the middle and upper classes of Chinese immigrants. They have also drawn a strong following of non-Chinese and non-Daoists who are attracted to various aspects of Daoist thought and practice. Probably the greatest draw is the practice of tai qi, which is promoted as a system of physical, mental, and spiritual exercise and health.

Confucius Institutes
Educational institutes set up by the government of China in western universities

The greatest influence of Daoism on the western world continues to be its foundational teachings. The *Daode Jing* influences life and thought far beyond the lives of Daoists in the West. It continues to be the most translated book from Asia, and its elusive style and challenging wisdom have never ceased to fascinate North Americans. The appeal of this book is echoed in the titles of more than fifty recent books, such as *The Tao of [Winnie the] Pooh*, *The Tao of Parenting*, *The Tao of Love and Sex*, *The Tao of Spycraft*, *The Tao of Coaching*, *The Tao of Sales*, and even *The Tao of Jesus* and *The Tao of Islam*. Of course, many of these books include westernized adaptations of vaguely Daoist ideas and bear little resemblance to the rich Daoist understandings of the Dao. In a different category is the use of Daoism in psychology and psychotherapy, in which the late Wayne Dyer was the leading figure. All this adaptation of Daoism may raise questions in some minds, but it is probably exactly what we should expect—a wide-ranging but wu-wei attempt to tap into the elusive, all-encompassing Dao.

STUDY TOOLS 7

READY TO STUDY?

ONLINE ON MINDTAP, YOU CAN:

- ☐ Download the Chapter Review Card, which includes key terms and chapter summaries.
- ☐ Learn about the revival of Confucianism in China in a short video.
- ☐ Explore feng shui in a series of online images.
- ☐ Interact with figures from the text to check your understanding.
- ☐ Prepare for tests with quizzes.
- ☐ Review the key terms with Flash Cards.

BONNIE VAN VOORST © CENGAGE LEARNING

Daoism and Confucianism Timeline: 551 B.C.E.–Present

551–478 B.C.E.
Confucius; beginnings of *Analects*

ca. 575–525 B.C.E.
Traditional dating of Laozi

500 B.C.E.

372–289 B.C.E.
Mencius

350–250 B.C.E.
Daode Jing and *Zhuangzi* written

ca. 250 B.C.E.
Civil service exams based on Confucian classics introduced

213 B.C.E.
Emperor orders burning of Confucian books

0

226–249 C.E.
Wang Bi introduces Daoist concepts into Confucian learning

420 C.E.
Buddhism begins to enter China

500

618–626
Emperor Gaozu builds a great temple at the birthplace of Laozi

691
Daoism scaled back, Buddhist temples built

712–756
Questions from Daoist classics put on civil service examinations

1000

960–1279
Daoist canon edited

1075
Vietnam introduces Confucian civil service exam system

1130–1200
Zhu Xi, founder of Neo-Confucianism

1204
National Confucian Academy established in Korea

1500

1582–1610
Matteo Ricci translates Confucian classics into Latin

1644–1911
Manchu dynasty promotes Confucianism in its National Studies program, suppresses Daoism

1841–1897
James Legge translates Confucian and Daoist classics into English

1905
Confucian civil service examinations abolished

1912
China becomes a republic; state religious ceremonies end

1928
Republican government dismantles many Daoist and Buddhist temples

1950s
All religions controlled by the Chinese Communist government

1966–1976
All religions in China repressed in the Cultural Revolution

1976–Present
Five religions achieve toleration in China, but Tibetan Buddhism is tightly controlled; government promotes some Confucian values and ceremonies

2000

8

Encountering Shinto: The Way of the Kami

LEARNING OUTCOMES

After studying this chapter, you will be able to do the following:

8-1 Explain the meaning of *Shinto* and *Kami no michi*.

8-2 Summarize how the four main periods of Shinto's history have shaped its present.

8-3 Outline essential Shinto teachings in your own words.

8-4 Describe the main features of Shinto ethics.

8-5 Outline Shinto worship and other rituals, and explain why they play a leading role in Shinto.

8-6 Explain why Shinto religious practice has such a small role in North America.

Your Visit to the Tsubaki Shinto Shrine in Granite Falls, Washington

When you meet your guide to the Tsubaki (tsoo-BAH-kee) Shrine just outside the gate, he says, "Please remember that the shrine grounds are a sacred place, so correct behavior is very important. No food, drink, or smoking is allowed. Keep a quiet, hushed voice. You may make a formal prayer and personal prayer at any time. If you wish to talk to the priest or have him do a ceremony for you, you must not be barefoot or wearing shorts or a sleeveless shirt. And no cell phone use, please."

First you visit the hand water station to purify yourself, because purity is important in Shinto. You follow the actions of your Shinto guide, using a wooden dipper to pour water on your left hand. You lean back slightly from the basin as you pour, so water from your hands doesn't mix with the pure water. You pour water on your right hand and then into your left palm to rinse your mouth. Then you pour water again on your left hand. Last, you let the small amount of water still in the dipper run back down its handle, and you place it back in the basin.

Next, you approach the shrine building. Continuing to follow your guide's actions, you bow slightly at the inner shrine gate and then walk on. The centerline is reserved for the kami, whom you know to be the gods and spirits of Shinto, to walk on, so you carefully avoid walking on it. As you get farther in, you offer a prayer to the gods and spirits of the shrine with two bows, then two claps, then one bow. Inside the shrine, you move to the offertory box, where you drop in a few coins. Standing next to the centerline, you grip the bell rope tightly and pull it to ring the bell. You fix your gaze toward the sacred mirror in the inner shrine and then bow deeply twice. You clap twice and pray while keeping your hands together at the center of your chest. When your short, quiet prayers are done, you bow once again.

This hand-washing station outside a Shinto shrine captures a natural look.

KAZUKIED2/SHUTTERSTOCK.COM

While at a little shop in the shrine, you buy a plaque, write your wish/prayer on it, and hang it up with similar ones nearby for the gods to read. Then you randomly draw a fortune-telling slip; these slips of paper contain several predictions ranging from "great good luck" to "great bad luck." By tying your slip to a rope where others have tied theirs, good fortune will come true or bad fortune can be averted. As it happens, you drew a good fortune, making for a happy conclusion of your visit to the shrine.

Shinto is a religion of formal rituals and inner feelings more than of doctrines, ethics, and organization. Its sentiments and rituals are directed especially to the natural world of the Japanese islands and secondarily to the history of the Japanese state. Shinto connects the people of Japan and their land, as well as Japan's present and its past. In your study of Shinto, you'll encounter these unique features:

- Some scholars hold that all Japanese are Shintoists just by virtue of being culturally Japanese, whether they practice Shinto or not. Many Japanese who see themselves as Shintoists also practice elements of other religions, especially Buddhism. This makes it difficult to know how many Japanese practice Shinto.

A Shinto priest in formal robes and hat worships the kami in a Shinto shrine.

- Shinto has no founder, no creed, and (for most of its history) no central authority. It didn't even have a name until the sixth century C.E., when it was necessary to distinguish it from Buddhism, which arrived in Japan from China.

- Shinto has no scripture. In fact, Shinto is the only religion based in a literate culture that hasn't developed a scripture. It does have books of ancient Japanese mythology and history written in the eighth century, but these don't function in an authoritative way in the religion.

- Shinto has been a major part of Japanese life and culture throughout the country's history, but for more than a thousand years it has shared its spiritual, social, and political roles with Buddhism and Confucianism. This mirrors the religious situation in China, where most believers combine Daoism, Buddhism, and Confucianism in various ways.

Shinto is an indigenous religion with origins in ancient times, but it has succeeded in a starkly modern nation (at least until now—some scholars think its future is bleak). Although it could be treated with

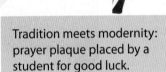

Tradition meets modernity: prayer plaque placed by a student for good luck.

other indigenous religions, Shinto's unique dual role as an indigenous religion and a faith of the modern world makes separate treatment worthwhile.

8-1 Names

Shinto means "the way of the gods." It derives from the Chinese *shen dao*, combining two words: *shin*, gods, particularly the higher gods, and *tao/dao*, the way of thought and life. After the arrival of Buddhism in Japan in the sixth century C.E., *Shinto* was invented to counter the Japanese term *but-sudo*, "the way of the Buddha." A more Japanese way to express this name, but not more prevalent in scholarship, is **Kami no michi**, "the way of the kami." *Kami no michi* is more accurate than *Shinto*, because the typical notions of gods in the religions treated in this book don't fit this religion very well. **Kami** are spirits, deities, or essences of something notable. They can be humanlike, animistic, or natural features or forces in the world (e.g., mountains, rivers, trees, rocks, lightning, and wind). Most kami are morally good, but a few are unpredictable or downright dangerous. Kami and people exist within the same world and are interrelated in it.

8-2 The Shinto Present as Shaped by Its Past

When the present emperor, Akihito (AH-kih-HEE-toh), became the 125th emperor of Japan in 1989, he spent a night with the Sun Goddess as a dinner guest, something every emperor is required to do shortly after ascending to the throne. First recorded in 712 C.E., the ritual takes place at night because the Sun Goddess is in the sky during the day; she comes down on this

Shinto [SHIN-toh] "The way of the gods"

Kami no michi [KAH-mee noh MEE-chee] "The way of the kami," another term for Shinto

Kami [KAH-mee] Spirits, deities, or essences found in both animate and inanimate objects

Masked dancers at a night festival at a Shinto shrine in Japan. Shinto has a powerful combination of serious ritual and festival revelry.

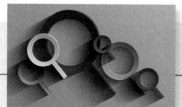

A Closer Look

The Symbol of Shinto

A **torii** is a traditional Japanese gate or portal at the entrance of, and often within, a Shinto shrine. (Its original meaning is "bird perch.") It consists of two upright wooden posts connected at the top by two horizontal crosspieces; the top one is often curved up slightly at

Figure 8.1 Torii

BONNIE VAN VOORST © CENGAGE LEARNING

the ends. The outer gate is sometimes said to separate the ordinary area from a sacred area, but in view of the strong Shinto belief that *all* Japan is sacred, it's probably more accurate to say that the outer gate marks ordinary sacred space from extraordinarily sacred space. Smaller torii are also found occasionally inside the grounds of Japanese Buddhist temples.

The first mention of torii is in 922. Torii were commonly made from wood or stone, but today they can also be made of metal, stainless steel, or other modern materials. They are usually either unpainted or painted a striking vermilion, with black tops. A person who has been successful in business often donates a torii to a shrine in gratitude. The Fushimi Inari (foo-SHEE-mee in-AHR-ee) shrine near Kyoto has some ten thousand torii, each bearing its donor's name, along paths that lead three miles up a mountainside.

©SERGII RUDIUK/SHUTTERSTOCK.COM

This torii seemingly emerging from the mountain expresses Shinto's strong orientation to nature.

---

special occasion to be present with the new emperor. After a bath for purification, the emperor carries out the ritual called the Great Food Offering. It takes place in two specially constructed log huts at the Imperial Palace in Tokyo. During the rite, the emperor receives an essence of the Sun Goddess's spirit and thus becomes, along with her, a kind of living ancestor of the entire Japanese people. The ritual reinforced the pre-World War II belief that the emperor was a living god. No one but the emperor has ever witnessed the ceremony or knows its details, and Akihito's continued participation in it was controversial among some Japanese.

Shinto history can be presented in four major periods: before the arrival of Buddhism in Japan in the 600s; Shinto and Buddhism together in Japan from 600 until about 1850; the Meiji (MAY-jee) reinterpretation of Shinto from 1850 to the end of World War II in 1945; and Shinto from 1945 to today.

8-2a Before the Arrival of Buddhism (up to 600 C.E.)

Before Buddhism came to Japan in the sixth century C.E., there probably was no religion that we would recognize as Shinto, but rather many local gods and shrines that are now grouped under Shinto. The first, aboriginal inhabitants of Japan were animists, devoted to powers of nature that they saw around them. These powers were the kami that were found in all significant natural things: plants and animals, mountains and fertile plains, rivers and seas, earthquakes, storms in the air and the seas, and even powerful human beings. Shrines began to be built in places where the kami were thought to be particularly present. At

torii [TOH-ree-ee]
Traditional Japanese gate or portal at the entrance of a Shinto shrine

SEAN PAVONE/DREAMSTIME.COM

The "Wedded Rocks" of Futami, Japan, tied together by a one-ton rope of rice straw, represent the union of Izanagi and Izanami and celebrate the marriage of male and female.

> Worship took place outdoors at sites thought to be sacred to the kami of the place.

arose at this time, telling how the husband-and-wife gods **Izanagi** and **Izanami** made Japan. Other religious groups arrived from Korea to settle in Japan in late prehistoric times; they were absorbed into Shinto. The realms of earth and the supernatural, as well as the realms of the common and the sacred, were closely related in the worldview of the early Japanese. Things that modern people regard as supernatural were just another part of the natural world, although with great power. The oldest Shinto ceremonies were oriented toward agriculture and emphasized obtaining ritual purity that would lead to the blessing of fields and flocks. Worship took place outdoors, at sites thought to be sacred to the kami of the place. In time, the ancient Japanese built permanent structures to honor their gods. Shrines were usually built on or near mountains, at the edge of forests, or in rural areas.

these shrines, simple worship would be offered to the spirits of the place, and the blessings offered to the kami would result in the kami's blessings on the people. Some of these shrines had women called **miko** who acted as shamans. With the passing of time and the coming of more patriarchal Chinese religions and culture, the miko became the shrine maidens of today—unmarried young women who assist the male priests in rituals but no longer act as shamans.

Like other indigenous peoples, the early Japanese developed myths that enabled them to make sense of life in their place, as well as rituals to bless it. For example, the myth relating the creation of the Japanese islands probably

miko [MEE-koh] Shrine maidens who assist male priests

Izanagi [EE-zah-NAH-gee (hard g)] "Male who invites"; the male deity who created the Japanese islands

Izanami [EE-zah-NAH-mee] "Female who invites"; the female deity who assisted her husband, Izanagi, in creating Japan

8-2b Shinto and Buddhism Together in Japan (600–1850)

The second stage in Shinto history is the long sweep of time from about 600 to 1850, when Shinto coexisted with Buddhism and Confucianism, religions that arrived at the beginning of this period from China. The introduction of the Buddhist religion and Confucian social values from China and Korea brought a different way of life for the Japanese, including changes to their religion. (Daoism, the third main religion of China, made little effort to enter Japan, perhaps because Shinto already had a full complement of gods and spirits.) Japan established close connections with China and Korea that would last for four hundred years, and adopted a more sophisticated culture. This new culture was essentially Chinese and included, in addition to

Confucianism and Buddhism, literature, philosophy, art, architecture, science, medicine, and government. Most important was the Chinese writing system that transformed Japan, which had no system of its own. The **Kojiki** (*Records of Ancient Matters*) and **Nihongi** (*Chronicles of Japan*), Japan's earliest histories, were written in the early 700s, soon after the introduction of Chinese writing. Ever since the time of the Kojiki and Nihongi, the relationship of Shinto with Chinese religions in Japan has been complicated—sometimes peaceful, at times conflicted. Indeed, the name *Shinto* arose then to distinguish indigenous Japanese religion from the new Buddhist beliefs coming from China. Many Shinto **shrines**, the name for Shinto houses of worship, were completely changed into Buddhist temples, made a part of Buddhist temples, or kept as Shinto shrines and led by Buddhist priests. Separate new Buddhist temples were built as well. From this time comes the distinction in names still used today: a Buddhist house of worship is called a temple, but a Shinto house of worship is called a shrine.

The rising combination of Shinto, Buddhism, and Confucianism made for religious and cultural unity—important in a relatively small land undergoing rapid change. The rulers took a role in religions by establishing a government office to oversee them, something that persisted until 1946. Shinto had a richer feeling for the natural environment than did Buddhism and Confucianism. It had a disadvantage compared with Buddhism and Confucianism in its lack of developed teachings. Unlike the other religions, Shinto had no sacred scriptures in which doctrine was formulated and by which it could be passed along. Thus, the doctrinal development of Japanese religion and philosophy inevitably drew on the comparative intellectual richness of Buddhism and Confucianism. But Shinto had found its niche in Japanese life, one that continues today.

As the Japanese nation was formed, the idea grew that humans should follow the will of the gods in political and social life. The emperor and the court had clear religious obligations, particularly the meticulous rituals that ensured that the powerful kami looked favorably on Japan and its people. These annual ceremonies for purification and blessing became a part of Japanese government. As time went on, the Japanese became more accustomed to integrating Shinto and Buddhism. For example, they accepted the Buddhist idea that the kami

were incarnations of the Buddha, manifested in Japan to save all sentient beings. During the seventh and eighth centuries, the spiritual status of the emperor as the descendant of Sun Goddess **Amaterasu**, the chief deity worshiped in Shinto, became official doctrine when it was written up in the *Kojiki* and *Nihongi*. This descent from Amaterasu was buttressed by rituals and the establishment of the important **Ise Shrine** of the imperial household.

From 800 to about 1800, Buddhist influence in government grew steadily stronger. Japan was in the hands of three power blocs: the emperor, the aristocracy, and the leaders of Buddhism and Shinto. Throughout Japanese history, up until the end of World War II, the aristocracy had more power than the emperor, despite what the creation myths implied about him.

Religion became more controversial when Roman Catholic Christian missionaries arrived in Japan in the 1500s and started making converts from Shinto and Buddhism. Over time, Christianity came to be seen as a political threat; it was a foreign religion, didn't allow converts to blend Christianity formally with other religions, and was beginning to convert the aristocracy. In 1597, dozens of Japanese Christians were crucified in a macabre imitation of the death of Jesus Christ—and more than forty thousand died in other persecutions. Surviving Christians were driven underground for hundreds of years. Buddhism dominated the seventeenth century, partly because an anti-Christian measure forced every Japanese citizen to register as a Buddhist at a Buddhist temple and pay a tax.

Popular Japanese religion is a pragmatic fusion of Shinto, Buddhism, and Confucianism. Confucianism provided social ethics to the nation; Shinto provided everyday rituals that helped to unify the nation; Buddhism provided philosophy and (because it was Mahayana Buddhism) a hope for life after death. Just as China had Three Traditions in Daoism, Confucianism,

> Annual ceremonies for purification and blessing became a part of Japanese government.

Kojiki [koh-JEE-kee] *Records of Ancient Matters,* one of Japan's earliest histories

Nihongi [nee-HAWN-gee (hard g)] *Chronicles of Japan,* one of Japan's earliest histories

shrine Shinto name for its religious sanctuaries

Amaterasu [ah-MAH-tehr-AH-soo] Sun Goddess, the chief deity worshiped in Shinto

Ise Shrine [EE-say] Leading Shinto holy place established by the imperial family

The Seven Lucky Gods are a mixed group of Shinto and other deities popular in Japan, all thought to bring good luck.

As Japan encountered East Asia in ways that it had avoided for a thousand years, it drew on its indigenous religion to buttress its national claims. A leading Shinto scholar during this period, Hirata (hih-RAH-tah), wrote in 1836, "The two foundational doctrines of Shinto are that Japan is the country of the gods, and her inhabitants are the descendants of the gods. Between the Japanese people and other peoples . . . there is a difference of kind, rather than of degree. The Emperor is the true Son of Heaven, who is entitled to reign over the four seas and the ten thousand countries. From the divine descent of the Japanese people proceeds their immeasurable superiority to the natives of other countries in courage and intelligence."[1] This growing, religiously oriented nationalism contributed to the rapid modernization of Japan in the 1800s (see Map 8.1). It would prove damaging to East Asia as Japan began to build an empire around 1900, and it would prove near-disastrous to many Pacific Rim nations from China to the United States in World War II.

and Buddhism, so too Japan had its three traditions of Shinto, Buddhism, and Confucianism.

After this long period of powerful influence of Buddhism on Shinto, Shinto pushed back. Around 1700 there was a movement toward what was considered a purer form of Shinto, with particular emphasis on the Japanese people as the descendants of the gods and, therefore, superior to other races. (This, of course, is something that Japanese Buddhists denied.) Buddhist and other influences were filtered out of institutions and rituals. Historians generally hold that this wasn't so much a return to something that had once existed as it was the creation of a more unified religion from a group of many different Shinto rituals and beliefs. During this period Shinto acquired a stronger intellectual tradition than it had previously enjoyed. A part of the Shinto revival entailed the renewed study of archaic Japanese texts. Just as Shinto myths were written down in the eighth century for national political reasons, so were they now reinterpreted for nationalistic purposes.

> "From the divine descent of the Japanese people proceeds their immeasurable superiority to the natives of other countries in courage and intelligence."
>
> —Hirata, nationalistic Shinto scholar, 1836

8-2c The Meiji Period (1850–1945)

The third major period of Shinto began with the Meiji Restoration in 1868, so called because Emperor Meiji was restored to his powers after a rebellion by warlords. (The emperor was still dominated by the aristocracy, however.) The Meiji Restoration accelerated the revival of Shinto that had been going on for two centuries and launched Japan on a path that would change its history and the history of the world. Japan had been modernizing rapidly; the Industrial Revolution that took almost two hundred years in Europe and North America was accomplished in Japan in less than a century. The aim of the new religious climate was to provide a sacred foundation and

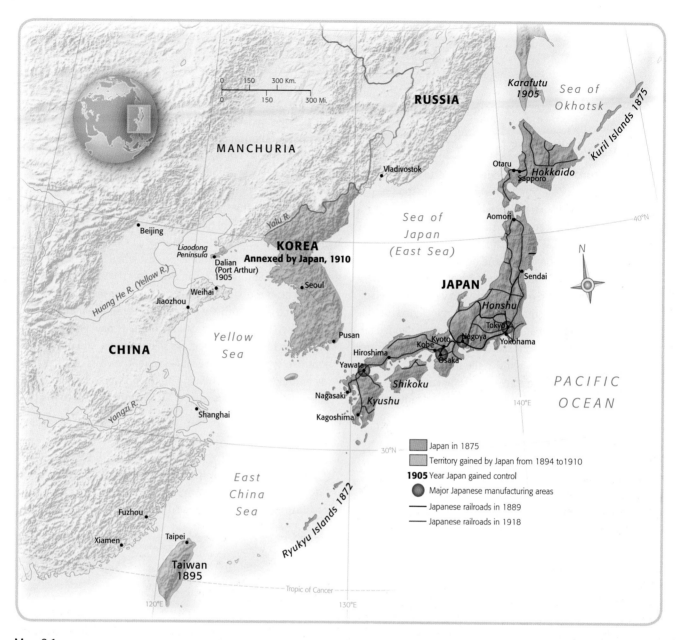

Map 8.1

Japanese Modernization and Expansion, 1868–1918

Japan undertook a crash modernization in the later 1800s. This modernization coincided with the rise of state Shinto. By 1910 its military power had increased and it had won a war with Russia and colonized Korea, Taiwan, and the Sakhalin Peninsula (then known as Karafutu).

a religious rationale for the new Japan and its national ethos. Emperor worship became a leading feature of state Shinto during this period.

In the Meiji period, Shinto was reorganized and brought under state control. The state distinguished among the new state Shinto, shrine Shinto of the traditional past, and sect Shinto comprising new movements in popular religion. Many historians of religion consider these new Shinto sects a result of the culture shock that Japan experienced after opening to the West. Between

1882 and 1908, the government recognized thirteen Shinto sects, and their number constantly increased. They are forerunners of a number of Japan's new religious movements today. The militaristic turn of the Meiji Period was already clear by 1868, when a new shrine was set up at Yasukuni to honor Japanese war dead. (See "A Closer Look: The Yasukuni Shrine Today.") Amaterasu, who until then had not been a major divinity, was brought to center stage and used to validate the role of the emperor, not only as ruler, but also as the high priest of Shinto.

A Closer Look

The Yasukuni Shrine Today

The **Yasukuni** Shrine was founded in 1869 under the orders of Emperor Meiji and is dedicated to the souls of all Japanese military personnel who have fallen in battle since that time. Most controversially to some (to Japan's enemies in World War II, at least), Yasukuni does not distinguish between honored dead and dishonorable dead. For example, it honors fourteen men, such as Prime Minister Hideki Tojo (hee-DECK-ee TOH-joh), who were convicted of the most serious war crimes—crimes that included the killing of prisoners of war and civilians—and were hanged for them after the war. All told, more than 2 million people are inscribed in the "Book of Souls" at the shrine, more than a thousand of whom were convicted of war crimes.

Within the shrine the dead are venerated rather than just remembered. They willingly sacrificed their lives for Japan, and this has made them kami. Surrounded by war banners and military regalia, they are venerated by hundreds of thousands of visitors who attend the shrine each year. Some come as tourists to this site and are not interested in venerating the dead, but others come to worship them, some even believing that the souls of the war dead live in the shrine.

Junichiro Koizumi (joo-NEE-chee-roh KOH-ee-ZOO-mee), who was the prime minister of Japan from 2001 to 2006, sparked international protest when he visited the Yasukuni Shrine in person every year. He refused to explain his reason for these visits, which caused tension with China and South Korea. Tensions flared again in late 2013 when Prime Minister Shinzo Abe (AH-bay) visited the shrine to pay his respects to the war dead, and public controversy continues in East Asia over the visits of other, lower-ranking officials. When Shinto appears today in the international news, it is frequently in connection with the Yasukuni Shrine.

Another result of Meiji rule was the separation of Buddhism from Shinto. The kami could no longer be explained as incarnations of the Buddha or various bodhisattvas. Ritual was also affected. All Shinto shrines were purged of every trace of Buddhist imagery (e.g., statues of the Buddha) and ritual (chanting scriptures). Buddhist priests were stripped of their status, and new Shinto priests were appointed to shrines. Japan's militaristic aristocracy supported Shinto, stressing that the emperor was a divine being directly descended from the gods who had given birth to the Japanese islands. Japanese children were taught at school that the emperors were descendants of Sun Goddess Amaterasu, and every classroom had a small shrine to the emperor on the wall. Shinto bound the Japanese people together with a powerful mix of devotion to kami, ancestor worship, and group loyalty to family and nation; Buddhism, with its more pacifist

Three representatives of the Emperor of Japan (at center, in traditional clothing) visit the Yasukuni Shrine in 2015 to honor the counry's war dead shortly before the Japanese prime minister made an important speech on Japan's war-time past at an international summit. Shinto priests in white garments can be seen alongside the envoys.

REUTERS/TORU HANAI

Yasukuni [YAH-soo-KOO-nee] Shrine set up in 1869 to memorialize war dead and international tendencies, was demoted. This separation of Buddhism and Shinto continues today, with both religions having different shrines, priests, and rites.

{ *Despite the religiously motivated self-sacrifice of Japanese warriors, the Divine Wind did not come.* }

Shinto played a significant role in World War II, which started in Asia with the Japanese invasion of northern China in 1937. Since the 1870s, it had been fueling a strong nationalism among the Japanese, a force that would inevitably lead to war. Service in the military was a religious as well as a civic obligation, and the spirits of those who died were honored as kami. **Kamikaze** pilots intentionally crashed their planes into American warships at the end of the war in a last-ditch effort to stave off an invasion of Japan. *Kamikaze* is often used popularly today as meaning reckless to the point of suicide, but it really means Divine (*kami*) Wind (*kaze*). The Divine Wind was a typhoon that destroyed a Chinese fleet threatening Japan in the 1200s, and the modern Divine Wind was meant to reproduce that deliverance. Another well-known feature of that war was the Japanese shout "Banzai!" (bahn-ZIGH)—"ten thousand years!"—and was understood to mean "May the emperor live ten thousand years!" This was frequently used as a cry of attack by Japanese forces. Despite the religiously motivated self-sacrifice of Japanese warriors, the Divine Wind did not come, and the emperor's rule as a god would soon end, falling far short of ten thousand years.

{ *"Banzai" . . . was understood to mean "May the emperor live ten thousand years!"* }

8-2d Shinto in Recent Times (1945–Present)

The last and current stage of Shinto history begins when the victorious Allied powers ended the status of Shinto as the state religion in 1946. Japan was allowed to keep Hirohito (HEER-oh-HEE-toh, who lived from 1901 to 1989) as emperor, but he lost his claim to divine status as part of the Allied reforms in Japan. He went on the radio to tell his people that Japan was surrendering (although such direct language was not used)—the first time that ordinary Japanese had heard an emperor's voice. He later wrote in a message to the nation,

> The ties between Us and Our people have always stood on mutual trust and affection. They do not depend upon legends and myths. They are not predicated on the false conception that the Tenno [emperor] is divine, and that the Japanese people are superior to other races and destined to rule the world.

Then he affirmed that the Japanese people still had an important role to play in the world: "By [the Japanese people's] supreme efforts . . . they will be able to make a substantial contribution to the welfare and advancement of mankind." This contribution did indeed come in the postwar revival of Japan, when Japan became a model of economic development, democracy, and peace in Asia. Since about 1990, however, Japan has been in a prolonged economic slump that has dispirited its people and lessened the appeal of Japanese ways of business to other nations. The dwindling attendance at many Shinto shrines is probably related to this economic downturn.

Japan's postwar constitution separates religion and state. Although the constitution of modern Japan had guaranteed freedom of religion since 1873, it finally came true. No religion receives support from the Japanese state. No citizen has to take part in any religious act, celebration, rite, or practice. Many (but not all) governmental ceremonies were stripped of their explicitly religious aspects. Despite the loss of its official status, Shinto retains a significant influence in Japanese spirituality and culture. Considerable Shinto religious meaning still surrounds some regular imperial ceremonies, and a few well-attended Shinto shrines honor those who died in World War II.

In sum, Japan is today both a secular and a religious society. Industrialization and urbanization have led to the declining influence of Shinto, which has accelerated since the end of World War II. Continuing controversy over the Japanese role in that war has diminished Shinto influence among the younger generation, many of whom see Shinto myths as outmoded. Most young people go to a Shinto shrine only as tourists; and some go there to pray for success in school exams. Some Japanese, especially the older generation, still frequent Shinto

Kamikaze [KAHM-ih-KAHZ-ee] "Divine Wind" of protection for Japan

shrines regularly, and all generations have a strong, even spiritual feeling for the physical beauty of Japan that is a heritage of Shinto. New religious movements have combined Buddhism, Shinto, and other religions to address contemporary Japanese issues such as family finances, environmental pollution, and family solidarity. The widespread destruction visited on northeastern Japan in the 2011 earthquake and tsunami caused many Japanese, even the younger generations, to draw upon both traditional and newer religions for comfort and strength.

However, on the whole, the Japanese people are becoming more secular. In a 2000 census, although a strong majority of Japanese called themselves Buddhists, Shintoists, or both, not even 15 percent reported a formal religious membership or regular religious practice. "The Global Religious Landscape" report by the Pew Research Center puts the number of formal Shintoists at about 3 million worldwide, with the vast majority of them in Japan. Of course, this is a very small minority of the Japanese population today.[2] Remarkably, this rising secularization hasn't had significant negative social effects, and Japan continues to be the most peaceful, law-abiding society in the developed world. (Even after the 2011 tsunami, there was virtually no increase in crime in the area it struck.) Sociologists say that this is due to a desire to honor one's living relatives or other social group and an even stronger reluctance to shame them, rather than from a connection to the spirits of one's ancestors or other aspects of Shinto or Buddhist religion. To students of Japan, the strongest religious influence today may be that of Confucianism. It has virtually no formal presence in Japan, but the system of Confucian social values that arrived in Japan 1,400 years ago still influences the lives of the majority of Japanese today.

{ *The main thing to be said about Shinto teaching is that Shinto has no developed teachings.* }

8-3 Shinto Teachings

A September 13, 2010, blog in *The New York Times* had a discussion about a writer's remarkable claim that Shinto religion explains the Japanese "love affair" with robots and robotics. He claims that Shinto's belief in kami blurs the boundaries between the animate and the inanimate, and this has shaped the positive Japanese view of robots as helpers and not as the potentially rebellious, violent machines sometimes portrayed in western stories and films. These helpers even include the recent invention of a female robotic companion for men. As one writer on the blog said of Japan, "A humanoid and sentient robot may simply not feel as creepy or threatening as it does in other cultures."[3]

The *Kojiki* and *Nihongi*, Japan's earliest histories, were compiled on the orders of the imperial family in the early 700s C.E. Although they show a political aim to unite all the regional and clan deities under the authority of the Sun Goddess Amaterasu, who was the clan deity of the emperor's family, these legends provide an explanation for the basic ideas in Shinto teachings—ideas that endure even today. We begin with three basic concepts that emerge in Shinto teachings about the kami.

8-3a The Kami

First, the kami are not gods as westerners understand them or even as Mahayana Buddhists see them, but should be understood as powerful natural forces with a spiritual dimension. No clear distinction exists between what is alive and not living, or natural and what is socially constructed, or human and divine. The kami are identified with natural features but are spirits in and beyond those features. One well-placed rock can have a kami just as much as Mount Fuji can. The whole world, including human life, is an expression of spiritual powers. Spiritual power is not found distributed evenly throughout the world, but is especially powerful in particular things, including humans.

Second, the kami are virtually countless. Shinto focuses on the kami that are important to people and influence human life directly. Kami are identified with places—especially forests, mountains, or waterfalls—that seem especially spiritual to the Japanese. They are also identified with awe-inspiring things in nature, such as wind, thunder, and lightning, and with destructive phenomena, such as the earthquakes that regularly shake Japan and tsunamis that sometimes follow them. Additionally, particular kami are identified with ordinary places and activities in human life, such as the kitchen, safety on the roads, education, and other things. Living individuals who have a special charisma or are very successful in business, politics, or life might

Food offerings to the kami in a Japanese Shinto shrine at New Year's; paper streamers call the attention of the gods.

go to a shadowy, gloomy underworld; this was probably the original Shinto thought. The living honor the dead as individuals, but they are not the individuals they were in this life.

8-4 Shinto Ethics

A follower of Shinto goes to a shrine in Kyoto. She has committed a bad act; it's weighing on her mind, and she wants to deal with it. So she goes to her local shrine and there undergoes a simple ritual of purification. She washes at the cleansing station before entering, washing more intently than she usually does, and then contacts one of the shrine priests to pray with her in front of the shrine gods. She leaves, at peace with herself and determined that she will do better.

be called kami. Other spiritual forces are recognized as kami—for example, mischievous elements such as fox spirits or tree spirits. On special occasions, a kami may possess a human medium to send a message.

Third, individuals should know and venerate the kami important to them. Not only is the kami's goodwill required, but also the spirits are said to respond to an individual's concern. They are not all-knowing, because their identity and activity are typically restricted to special objects in nature. They want to be informed about significant events that involve their activities, so prayer to the kami will sometimes contain reports about these.

8-3b Characteristics of Other Shinto Teachings

The main thing to be said about Shinto teachings is that Shinto has no developed teachings about either this world or the next. It doesn't speak about the original creation of the whole universe, only of Japan. Nor is there anything about a future end of the world. Likewise, there is no clear description of any afterlife. Some Shintoists believe that after people die, they become deeply related to their ancestral kami and have no individual soul in the afterlife. Others believe that their souls

> { The kami aren't always perfect, so they don't serve as moral examples. }

Shinto teaches that humans are born pure. Evil actions and impurity are things that come later in life and can usually be dealt with by simple cleansing or purifying rituals.

8-4a General Characteristics

To identify the distinctly Shinto elements in Japanese ethics isn't easy. Confucian values have inspired much of Japanese social ethics, supplemented by more individual ethics derived from Buddhist monastic rules. In general, Shinto ethics are based not on a set of commands or of virtues that tells one how to behave, but on following the general will of the kami, understood through myth and ritual. The way implied in the word *Shinto* is primarily a ritual way, to keep the relationship with the kami on a proper footing. Good moral practice flows from this relationship.

However, the kami aren't always perfect, so they don't serve as moral examples. Shinto texts tell many stories of kami behaving badly. As we saw earlier, some of them are mischief makers and, therefore, wouldn't serve well as role models in such an orderly, proper populace as that of Japan. This clear difference with religions whose gods are morally perfect and can serve as moral examples is probably a main reason why Shinto ethics avoids absolute moral rules.

8-4b Purity

Purity is essential to pleasing the kami, providing a happy life, and turning back disappointment or disease. A number of rituals feature the exorcism of sins in order to restore purity. Cleanliness in particular signifies a good character and freedom from bad external influences. In western societies one hears the proverb "Cleanliness is next to godliness." In traditional Japanese society, cleanliness—of body, mind, and spirit—*is* godliness. To be in harmony with the kami, one must keep one's person, home, and business clean. The Japanese emphasis on freshness and purity in food and drink brings a high quality to the diet, and practically it means that shopping for food is often done every day. (Women used to be free to shop for food during the day, but now with many of them working outside the home, they shop on the way home from work or buy food more in advance.) Purity in relationships entails being honest, sincere, and thoughtful about how other people feel; therefore, apologies for unintended affronts are very common. The kami particularly dislike blood and death. Women traditionally were excluded from shrine events during menstruation, as were people who worked with the bodies of dead animals, such as leather makers. Soldiers require special purification after battle, and people helping at funerals need to purify themselves as well.

> In western societies one hears the proverb "Cleanliness is next to godliness." In traditional Japanese society, cleanliness . . . is godliness.

The overall aims of Shinto ethics are to promote harmony and purity in all spheres of life. Purity isn't just spiritual, but also moral—having a pure and sincere heart, leading to good conduct. It has a connection with ritual purity: doing things in a certain way, in a certain state, with a certain attitude. Shinto views both human beings and the world as morally good. Evil enters from outside the world of nature and human society, usually by the agency of evil spirits. This affects humans in a manner similar to that of a physical disease. When people do wrong, they bring ritual pollution and moral fault upon themselves. This blocks the blessings of life as they flow from the kami, and must be dealt with in ceremonies of cleansing.

8-5 Shinto Ritual

Most Shinto rituals are tied to the life cycle of humans and the seasonal cycles of nature. Life-cycle rituals include naming ceremonies for children and ceremonies for blessing children as they grow. The time surrounding university entrance exams is particularly trying for Japanese young people, and going to the shrine to pray for success is important for them and their parents. We'll consider the Shinto wedding ritual later. Although Shinto does have a funeral ritual and although the emperor always receives a Shinto service, for more than a thousand years Japanese have preferred Buddhist funerals. Funeral rites will be treated later as well.

8-5a The Shinto Shrine

First, given the close connections between Shinto and Japanese Buddhism, we should consider their houses of worship. What are the differences between a Shinto shrine and a Buddhist temple? You know you are in a Shinto shrine when you see

- a *torii* gate at or near the entrance;
- a pair of guardian dogs or lions on each side of the entrance;
- a purification fountain near the entrance; and
- buildings with a "natural" look, for example, unpainted wood.

On the other hand, you know that you are at a Buddhist temple when you see

- a large incense burner at the front of a temple;
- a large image of the Buddha through the front doors;
- a pagoda on the premises; and
- buildings with a more painted and decorated look.

Incense sticks burn down in a Shinto shrine.

A Closer Look

A Shinto Prayer for the Blessing of the Crops

This Shinto prayer found in the *Yengishiki* prayer book clearly demonstrates the Shinto feeling for kami and the natural world.

I declare in the great presence of Amaterasu who sits in Ise:

Because the sovereign great goddess bestows on him [the emperor] the countries of the four quarters over which her glance extends—

As far as the limit where Heaven stands up like a wall,

As far as the bounds where the country stands up distant,

As far as the limit where the blue clouds spread flat,

As far as the bounds where the white clouds lie away fallen—

The blue sea plain as far as the limit, where come the prows of the ships,

The ships which continuously crowd on the great sea plain,

And the roads which men travel by land,

As far as the limit whither come the horses' hoofs,

With the baggage cords tied tightly,

Treading the uneven rocks and tree roots, and lining up continuously in a long path without a break.

Making the narrow countries wide and the hilly countries plain,

And drawing together the distant countries by throwing, so to speak, many ropes over them,

He will pile up his crops like a range of hills in the great presence of the sovereign great goddess, and will peacefully enjoy the remainder.

Rituals at Shinto shrines mark one's entry into a different world, the world of the kami. Even in a bustling city, shrines offer a quiet atmosphere removed from the busy noise of modern Japanese life. Surrounded by evergreen trees and approached on a gravel path, everyday conversation is hushed before one enters; the silence is broken only by ritual hand claps or the sounds of nature. Shinto ritual, including music and dance, is remarkably simple and brief, much like the Japanese tea ceremony and quite unlike complex Buddhist ritual. It has a slow, measured pace thought to be pleasing to the kami and contrasting with normal daily life outside.

However, at special festivals in and around the shrine this changes dramatically. A mass of local people will be crowded together in noisy festivity, "letting themselves go" in front of the kami in ways they would never dream of doing outside the shrine. Sometimes this includes enough consumption of alcohol to get worshipers slightly drunk. This religious carousing serves as a temporary release from a society that prizes almost-constant orderliness and properness.

Shrines are built to blend in with the environment chosen by the kami of the place. (See "A Closer Look: A Shinto Prayer for the Blessing of the Crops.")

The main sanctuary building of each shrine is the **honden**, in which symbolic sacred objects such as a mirror or a sword are kept at the center front, where they receive worship. Traditionally built from wood and usually left unpainted, the buildings need regular repair or rebuilding by the local community. This is still the tradition of one of Japan's famous shrines, the Ise Shrine, where the honden is reconstructed in time-honored style every twenty years.

The kami dwell near, not in, the shrines and must be invited politely. As we saw earlier, at least one torii marks the entrance to a shrine, and a basin is just inside to rinse one's hands and mouth. A shrine is usually dedicated to one particular kami but may host any number of smaller shrines representing other kami that local people should also venerate. Sacred places, such as particular trees and rocks, will be marked off by ropes of elaborately plaited straw or by streamers of plain paper. The kami are summoned by a series of brief actions: ringing a bell outside the shrine, making a money offering, clapping hands twice, saying a short silent prayer, and bowing twice.

honden [HAHN-den]
Main sanctuary building of a Shinto shrine

8-5b The Shinto Priesthood

The work of Shinto priests is located largely in the shrine. New Shinto priests, similar to their Japanese Buddhist monk counterparts, must now be university graduates. Women priests can be found, but they aren't nearly as numerous as men, because traditional Japanese society is still strongly patriarchal. Most priests are volunteers who have their main jobs outside the shrines. They are typically married and have families.

> The contemporary miko is typically "a university student collecting a modest wage in this part-time position."
>
> —Lisa Kuly

The Shinto priesthood exists mainly to carry out Shinto rituals and run the shrines, and duties such as teaching and religious counseling are minor activities for the priests. Traditionally, the priesthood was limited to the great shrines, and it rotated among the able men of the community. But now this has been opened up to many shrines and has also grown to about twenty thousand priests, including two thousand women. All but the smallest shrines are staffed by a team of priests of various ranks, assisted by a team of shrine maidens (the miko discussed in Section 8-2a). These miko assist with shrine functions, assist priests in ceremonies, perform ceremonial dances, sell souvenirs, and distribute omikuji (see Section 8-5c). Lisa Kuly writes that today's miko is typically "a university student collecting a modest wage in this part-time position."[4] A miko is traditionally dressed in red trousers, a white kimono jacket, and white or red hair ribbons. Shinto has no overall leader in Japan, and each shrine is self-governed and self-supporting through offerings and donations by worshipers. Most shrines are associated through a national shrine organization.

ema [AY-muhz] Wooden plaques inscribed with prayers and wishes

omikuji [oh-mee-KOO-jee] Fortunes on preprinted slips of paper

A Japanese woman ties an omikuji at Sensoji Shrine in Tokyo.

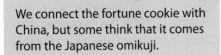

Love is in your future.

We connect the fortune cookie with China, but some think that it comes from the Japanese omikuji.

8-5c Prayer Plaques and Fortunes

In Shinto shrines, it's common to see **emas**, small wooden plaques hung in prominent places. Worshipers buy an ema, write personal wishes and hopes on the reverse, and then hang it near a sacred tree together with emas made by others. The kami then read them and help make them come true. This ritual is understood today more as asking for wishes or making hopes than as praying, although prayers can also be written on an ema.

Next, we should discuss the **omikuji**, literally "sacred drawing/lottery." They are fortunes on preprinted slips of paper. For an offering of about 100 yen (approximately one U.S. dollar), worshipers can obtain an omikuji from a person at a shrine desk, or even from a vending machine. Opening the paper allows one to see a fortune that has several items on it. The first deals with the general category of blessing and ranges from "great blessing" to "great curse." Then it gives fortunes for various aspects of life—for example, business, schooling, the stock market, falling in love, and others. (No matter the general category of blessing, in the area of schooling every omikuji advises one to study more, study harder, and the like!) If the prediction is bad, the paper is folded up and attached to a tree, to ropes, or to wires. If the prediction is favorable, one can either take it home or tie it up in the shrine; the latter is more common.

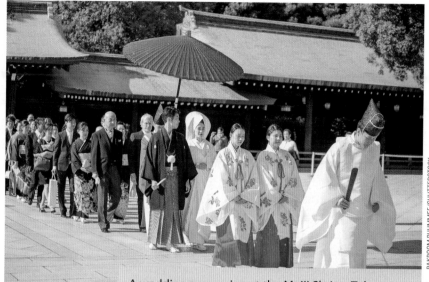

A wedding procession at the Meiji Shrine, Tokyo. The priest bows toward the shrine building before entering it; the two shrine maidens assisting in the ceremony are behind him; and the bride and groom follow with their families behind them.

> { *The Shinto priesthood exists mainly to carry out Shinto rituals and run the shrines.* }

8-5d The Wedding Ceremony

The Shinto priest (or priests) and the mikos conduct the wedding ceremony at the front of a shrine, after a formal procession. The families are present in the room. The groom and the bride typically wear formal Japanese wedding clothes. After the couple is ritually purified, the priest offers prayers for their good fortune and happiness, as well as for protection and guidance by the kami. Then the miko serves three sips of purified rice wine to the wedding couple. Brief words are spoken to the kami and rings are exchanged, followed by the offering of a small sacred evergreen branch. One more sip of rice wine is shared, and the ritual is complete. Shinto attitudes toward marriage, which as you might imagine are patriarchal, were affirmed in a late 2015 ruling by the highest court in Japan that all spouses must share the same surname, and married women may not keep their maiden names.

8-5e The Home Shrine

Traditional Japanese show respect for the kami by having a small shrine or worship space in their house or outdoors. They also have a **kamidana**, a "kami shelf" on which small statues of the kami are placed,

sometimes along with small memorial tablets containing the names of ancestors. The kamidana is typically placed so high on a wall that it is near the ceiling. It holds several different items, at the center of which is a small circular mirror, a stone, or a jewel. Worship at the kamidana includes placing flowers; offering food such as rice, fruit, and water; and saying short prayers. Family members carefully cleanse their hands with water before they perform these daily rituals.

8-5f The Shinto Funeral

As we saw earlier, Japan is a land of multiple religions, which affects how the Japanese deal with death and how they believe in an afterlife. Keeping memorial tablets with the names of one's ancestors in household shrines and offering food and drink to them is Confucian in origin. In ritual matters of entering the afterlife, such as funerals and memorial services for deceased relatives, a Buddhist priest officiates with basically Buddhist rites.

The general lines of the historic funeral rite are still discernible in villages. It particularly applies to men who are heads of households; in what follows, we will describe this sort of funeral. In towns and cities today, the rite has been adapted or lost, especially

kamidana [KAH-mee-DAH-nuh] "Kami shelf" found in traditional private homes

as the burial of cremated remains has replaced full-body burial for reasons of space and cost. The immediate family members of the deceased keep themselves in their houses. The men of the neighborhood gather near the family home to make the items required for the funeral, including paper flags containing prayers, paper processional lanterns, and a wooden candlestick. The women prepare the food required for the feast given before the burial. One woman of the neighborhood has the special honor of sewing a white pilgrim's cloak that will shroud the body for its journey to the land of the dead. Meanwhile, the men who will be pallbearers dig a grave in the cemetery.

The spirit of the dead is thought to still be present and listening, so as the relatives shroud the body, they politely describe out loud the tasks they are performing. To mask the odor of death, burning incense is kept nearby. So that the spirit may pay the ferryman for passage into eternity, a bag with a few coins is put near the body; also, meditation beads are entwined in the dead man's hand. A fan is laid in the coffin, together with a small favorite object belonging to the deceased. The Buddhist priest tells the spirit of the dead to begin its journey to the land of the dead, and other ancient formulas are recited. On completing their tasks, the family members wash their hands in saltwater.

The funeral procession reaches the cemetery with a lot of noise. For the grave, a round hole has been made, just big enough to pass the body through. The hole widens continuously as it goes deeper, until it is much wider at the usual depth of six feet. (This requires some skill at digging the grave.) At the bottom, to one side, a large compartment, approximately six feet long and four feet wide, has been excavated. The body is taken out of the coffin and laid into the grave on straw floor mats along with the objects put earlier into the coffin. The oldest son praises his father for his honorable life as the widow continues to pray for the soul of her husband.

A few days after the burial, the family holds a "feast of consecration," at which time they feed and entertain numerous guests. This feast ends with a procession in which relatives, friends, and neighbors wear sackcloth. The property of the deceased is then divided, with the oldest son receiving most of it. In older times a small memorial house was built over the grave; more commonly today, a tombstone is erected. At each of these events a Buddhist priest recites prayers before the deceased's portrait. Although the number of commemorative meals varies, they are still common in Japan today as the conclusion of the funeral ritual. Life is then expected to return to normal.

8-6 Shinto around the World Today

Shinto has a very small presence outside of Japan. Shintoists do not seek or even encourage converts, so almost all followers of Shinto are Japanese. Because the kami are tied so closely to the land of Japan, Japanese people living in the wider world often have a lessened connection with Shinto. Although the people of and in Japan combine Shinto with Buddhism, people of Japanese descent living outside Japan typically see themselves only as Buddhists if they keep to one of the traditional

Michi, a seven-month-old Chihuahua, receives a blessing with sacred bells ringing overhead at the Shinto shrine in Honolulu, Hawai'i.

Japanese religions. One estimate of Shintoists in North America has them at only two thousand people. In the recent Canadian census, fewer than 1 percent of the approximately one hundred thousand Japanese Canadians called themselves Shintoists. In the United States, most of those who practice Shinto are found on the West Coast and in Hawai'i. They are served by a small number of Shinto shrines, including the Tsubaki Shinto Shrine in Granite Falls, Washington. Of course, Shintoists in North America can and do have kamidanas in their homes, at which the simple, regular home rituals can take place.

Even though the formal presence of Shinto in the West is remarkably small, it has a certain appeal to some westerners today. Its reverence for nature, feeling for ritual, and open acknowledgment of pluralism (at least in a Buddhist and Confucian context) have attracted independent-minded religious seekers. Small movements to practice Shinto have arisen here and there in North America. Whether or not Shinto will have a larger role in North America, it will continue for the foreseeable future to be a significant feature of life in Japan.

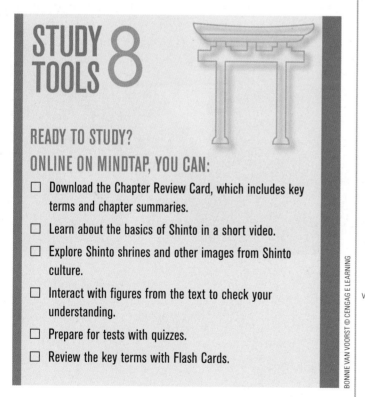

STUDY TOOLS 8

READY TO STUDY?
ONLINE ON MINDTAP, YOU CAN:

- ☐ Download the Chapter Review Card, which includes key terms and chapter summaries.
- ☐ Learn about the basics of Shinto in a short video.
- ☐ Explore Shinto shrines and other images from Shinto culture.
- ☐ Interact with figures from the text to check your understanding.
- ☐ Prepare for tests with quizzes.
- ☐ Review the key terms with Flash Cards.

BONNIE VAN VOORST © CENGAG E LEARNING

Shinto Timeline: 250–Present

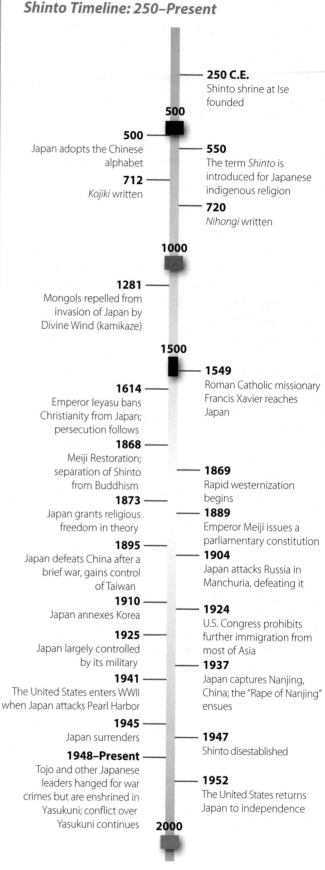

250 C.E.
Shinto shrine at Ise founded

500

500
Japan adopts the Chinese alphabet

550
The term *Shinto* is introduced for Japanese indigenous religion

712
Kojiki written

720
Nihongi written

1000

1281
Mongols repelled from invasion of Japan by Divine Wind (kamikaze)

1500

1549
Roman Catholic missionary Francis Xavier reaches Japan

1614
Emperor Ieyasu bans Christianity from Japan; persecution follows

1868
Meiji Restoration; separation of Shinto from Buddhism

1869
Rapid westernization begins

1873
Japan grants religious freedom in theory

1889
Emperor Meiji issues a parliamentary constitution

1895
Japan defeats China after a brief war, gains control of Taiwan

1904
Japan attacks Russia in Manchuria, defeating it

1910
Japan annexes Korea

1924
U.S. Congress prohibits further immigration from most of Asia

1925
Japan largely controlled by its military

1937
Japan captures Nanjing, China; the "Rape of Nanjing" ensues

1941
The United States enters WWII when Japan attacks Pearl Harbor

1945
Japan surrenders

1947
Shinto disestablished

1948–Present
Tojo and other Japanese leaders hanged for war crimes but are enshrined in Yasukuni; conflict over Yasukuni continues

1952
The United States returns Japan to independence

2000

9

Encountering Zoroastrianism: The Way of the One Wise Lord

KUNI TAKAHASHI/GETTY IMAGES

LEARNING OUTCOMES

After studying this chapter, you will be able to do the following:

9-1 Explain the meaning of *Zoroastrianism* and related terms.

9-2 Outline how Zoroastrianism developed over time into what it is today.

9-3 Explain the essential Zoroastrian teachings of monotheism and moral dualism.

9-4 State the main ethical precepts of Zoroastrianism.

9-5 Outline the way Zoroastrians worship and observe rituals.

9-6 State the main features of Zoroastrian life around the world today, especially in North America.

"I acknowledge my faith in Good Thoughts, Good Words, and Good Deeds, the Good Religion of Ahura Mazda."—Zoroastrian declaration of faith

Your Visit to Yazd, Iran

Yazd is the historic center of Zoroastrianism (ZOHR-oh-ASS-tree-uh-nihz-uhm) in present-day Iran, although many Iranian Zoroastrians now live in the capital city, Tehran. Yazd has an active Zoroastrian temple, one of the most beautiful in the world, housing a fire that the faithful believe has burned for more than a thousand years. Zoroastrians are not fire worshipers, as you may have heard some Iranians say, but use fire as a symbol of the spiritual essence of God.

You hoped to hike out into the desert to Chak-Chak, an important pilgrimage site for Zoroastrians about 110 kilometers north of Yazd, to see a four-day festival that was about to start. But then you hear that only the faithful can attend the festival and that the temple will be closed at that time to non-Zoroastrians, so you travel out there right away before the festival starts. Chak-Chak, literally "drip-drip" in Persian, is a small group of buildings constructed on the side of a mountain cliff. According to legend, a Zoroastrian princess who was fleeing the invading Muslim Arab armies escaped from Yazd into the desert. She arrived at this cliff and was cornered by the army closing in on her. She prayed to God to be spared, the cliff opened, and she disappeared inside forever. From that time on, dripping water from a spring has marked the place of her rescue. Legends such as this one have helped Iranian Zoroastrians cope with the predominantly Muslim nation in which they find themselves.

Back in Yazd the next day, you hike out of town to the round stone "towers of silence" built on the hills, used as the funeral buildings for Zoroastrians until recent times. For more than two thousand years, Zoroastrians didn't bury or cremate their dead, believing that this would contaminate the earth or the fire. Instead, they left dead bodies in these towers, to be eaten there by vultures until only clean bones remained to be bleached white by the sun. The bones were

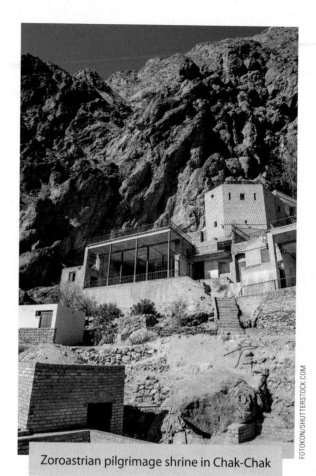

Zoroastrian pilgrimage shrine in Chak-Chak

then swept into a central depository within the tower, but you can't see them any longer. On the plains of Yazd below, you see partially ruined temples and buildings used for funeral rites. Beyond the ruins are the well-maintained, modern Zoroastrian cemeteries where the faithful now bury their dead inside concrete-lined graves. You take in the whole scene from the tower, amazed by how this site is so peaceful now. The towers are indeed silent.

Begun thousands of years ago by Zarathustra, the prophet known to the Greeks as Zoroaster, Zoroastrianism became the state religion of the ancient Persian and Sassanian empires. Some historians estimate that it had as many as 40 million followers, making it one of the largest religions in the ancient world. Today its numbers are severely reduced for reasons we will explore in this chapter. 150,000 adherents, at most the overwhelming majority of them ethnic Persians, are clustered in eastern Iran and Mumbai (Bombay), India, and about another 50,000 are scattered in twenty-three nations of the world, including 20,000 in North America. These numbers are estimates, because exact numbers are hard to come by.

> Visitors watch the fire at the main Zoroastrian fire temple in Yazd, Iran. It's said that this fire is more than 1500 years old. Opening the fire to visitors is a more modern, liberal practice; traditionalist fire temples are closed to visitors.

Despite the reduced number of followers, the study of Zoroastrianism has an appeal all its own. Any religion from so long ago that is still present today deserves to be studied carefully. But scholars also study Zoroastrianism today for a broader reason: to discern the possible influence of this religion on other western religions. Scholars generally conclude that Zoroastrianism had a direct influence on ancient Judaism as well as some indirect influence (mainly through Judaism) on Christianity and Islam. The exact extent of this influence is sharply debated. On the one hand, a leading scholar of Zoroastrianism, Mary Boyce, argues for a maximum influence: "Zoroastrianism has probably had more influence on human life, directly and indirectly, than any other single faith." She also argues that Zoroastrianism's teachings on judgment, heaven and hell, the resurrection of the body, and eternal life were borrowed by Judaism, Christianity, and Islam.[1] This position is frequently seen on the Web. On the other hand, Hebrew Bible scholar James Barr and others have argued that significant borrowing of Zoroastrian ideas, directly or indirectly, cannot be demonstrated in early Judaism, aside from a few small points of contact. Barr argues as well that later Christian and Islamic beliefs cannot be shown to have drawn from Zoroastrianism.[2] In any case, Christians and many people who aren't Christians know about the Bible's story of the "wise men from the east" visiting the newborn Jesus to honor him and bring him gifts. Two of these gifts, frankincense and myrrh, have been offered in Zoroastrian worship for more than 2,500 years now. The term the Bible uses for the wise men (which we will consider shortly) is a special Zoroastrian word for their priests.

In your study of Zoroastrianism, these unique, initially puzzling features may appear:

- Zoroastrians place a strong emphasis on morality in thought, word, and deed. But unlike many other religions that stress moral purity, Zoroastrianism deals with hundreds of ritual impurities, because these are thought to ruin the effect of moral deeds.

> "Zoroastrianism has probably had more influence on human life, directly and indirectly, than any other single faith."
>
> —Mary Boyce

- Zoroastrianism is a monotheistic religion, teaching that only one God exists. But it also features dozens of other who have large roles in human life. Sometimes they are even called divinities, as, for example, on the opening page of a matchmaking website for Zoroastrians, which invokes the power of Ava Ardvisur, the "Ahura-created Divinity of fertility and childbirth."[3]

- Zoroastrianism has a proud past, but many of its current leaders fear for its future. As stated above, it was once among the world's largest religions, but now it has been reduced to around 200,000 members. Many observers think that it may die out, at least in its traditional form, by the end of the twenty-first century.

- You might ask, Why study such a small religion? Zoroastrianism is historically important; a fascinating living religion today; and, sadly, it offers a rare thing to scholars and students of religion: studying the slow death of a religion.

9-1 Names for Zoroastrianism and Zoroastrians

Zoroastrianism is the common designation of the ancient Persian monotheistic religion. This name is built from the Greek form of the name of its founder, Zoroaster (ZOHR-oh-ass-ter). The founder is known as **Zarathustra** in the religion's most ancient writings.

Zoroastrianism was originally a European name for the faith and reflects the European tendency to name religions after their founders whether the religions themselves do so or not. Zarathustra would probably not have been pleased with this name. But *Zoroastrianism* stuck, and followers of the faith use it today.

> { *"Zoroastrianism" reflects the European tendency to name religions after their founders.* }

Zarathustra [ZAHR-uh-THOOS-truh] Founder of Zoroastrianism, now widely called Zoroaster

A Closer Look

The Symbol of Zoroastrianism

Zoroastrianism has had a few different symbols throughout its history. One ancient symbol still seen today is a sacrificial fire burning in a ritual urn. But the symbol closely associated with Zoroastrianism for more than 2,500 years is the faravahar, the figure of a human being with eagle's wings. Its origins are debated. Some think that it originally represented Ahura Mazda, because it seems to draw some elements from the symbols of gods in Assyrian religion. However, Zoroastrians have always considered God to be a spirit that cannot be depicted.

The central human figure represents the individual Zoroastrian believer. The figure is obviously a male, with the long beard that Persian men wore, but this hasn't prevented

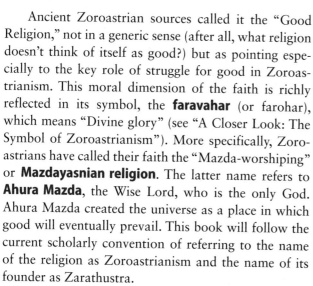

Figure 9.1 The Faravahar

BONNIE VAN VOORST
© CENGAGE LEARNING

Zoroastrian women from identifying with the symbol. He is aged in appearance, so the soul is wise. He wears a traditional Persian hat, suggesting respect for culture. One hand is open and lifted upward, symbolic of faith in and obedience to Ahura Mazda. The other hand holds a ring, which may represent loyalty and faithfulness. The circle around the center of the human figure stands for the immortality of the soul or the eternal significance of human actions in the here and now.

The two wings have three main rows of feathers, representing good thoughts, good words, and good deeds. Doing these things lifts up one's soul as on powerful wings. The tail below also has three rows of feathers, said to signify bad thoughts, bad words, and bad deeds. The two streamers below the human figure represent the spirits of good and evil. Every person must constantly choose between the two, so the figure is facing the good and turning his back on evil.

Ancient Zoroastrian sources called it the "Good Religion," not in a generic sense (after all, what religion doesn't think of itself as good?) but as pointing especially to the key role of struggle for good in Zoroastrianism. This moral dimension of the faith is richly reflected in its symbol, the **faravahar** (or farohar), which means "Divine glory" (see "A Closer Look: The Symbol of Zoroastrianism"). More specifically, Zoroastrians have called their faith the "Mazda-worshiping" or **Mazdayasnian religion**. The latter name refers to **Ahura Mazda**, the Wise Lord, who is the only God. Ahura Mazda created the universe as a place in which good will eventually prevail. This book will follow the current scholarly convention of referring to the name of the religion as Zoroastrianism and the name of its founder as Zarathustra.

One other name for Zoroastrians has become important. Zoroastrians who moved to India from Iran in the 900s C.E. are called **Parsis** (sometimes spelled Parsees), a name derived from *Persians*. The Zoroastrian communities in east Africa, Great Britain, and North America descend largely from this group, so the term has spread beyond India. *Parsis* is often used as a synonym of *Zoroastrians*.

9-2 Zoroastrianism as Shaped by Its Past

reddie Mercury (1946–1991), the lead singer in the British band Queen, was one of the most prominent Zoroastrians in the twentieth century. Born as Farrokh Bulsara to a Zoroastrian family in present-day Tanzania, he was raised as a devout Zoroastrian and was initiated into the faith as a teenager. Mercury sang many hit songs, including "Bohemian Rhapsody," "We Are the Champions," and "Crazy Little Thing Called Love." Although he hadn't formally observed his ancestral religion as an adult, his funeral in London was led (at Mercury's wishes)

faravahar [FAHR-uh-VAH-har] "Divine glory," winged symbol of Zoroastrianism

Mazdayasnian religion [MAHZ-duh-YAHZ-nee-uhn] Name of Zoroastrianism used in the past by most Zoroastrians

Ahura Mazda [ah-HOOR-uh MAHZ-duh] "Wise Lord," the single, all-powerful God worshiped by Zoroastrians

Parsis [PAR-seez] Name for Zoroastrians in India, also spelled Parsees

by Zoroastrian priests. It was conducted entirely in the Avestan language and included prayers and hymns from the Zoroastrian scriptures. After the service, his body was cremated.

The early history of Zoroastrianism is still shrouded in the mists of antiquity. We aren't certain of many key details about its beginnings, because most of its earliest writings were destroyed in persecutions. As Zoroastrianism emerged from the mists of time it became a key religion in the world. It can be divided into three main periods: birth and formation (ca. 630–550 B.C.E.); growth into the official religion of the Persian Empire, decline under Greek and Parthian rule, and revival and renewed official status in the Sassanian Empire (550 B.C.E.–650 C.E.); and slow, steady decline under Islamic rulers and in the modern world (650 C.E.–today).

{ *Zoroastrianism emerged from the mists of time and became a key religion in the world.* }

9-2a The Birth of Zoroastrianism (ca. 630–550 B.C.E.)

The question of when Zarathustra lived isn't easy to answer. A few scholars and many traditional Zoroastrians date it all the way back to 7500 B.C.E., at what they consider the dawn of human civilization; others hold to a time between 1400 and 900 B.C.E. Today, historians commonly put his birth around 630 B.C.E., at the beginning of the **Axial Age** in Europe and Asia. Modern philosopher Karl Jaspers gave this term to the period from 600 to 400 B.C.E. when many religions and value (*axial*) systems were founded. This wide chronological range, so unusual for dating the founder of a major religion, shows that firm evidence for the life of Zarathustra is lacking. The Zoroastrian scriptures that he is thought to have authored, the central chapters of the *Gathas*, do not locate him chronologically. No historical sources outside the religion give reliable information that can be used in dating his life. Moreover,

Axial Age Period from 600 to 400 B.C.E. when many religions and value (axial) systems were founded

> "No nation so readily adopts foreign customs as the Persians do."
> —Herodotus, ancient Greek historian

Zoroastrian scriptures weren't typically written down until about 400 C.E., at least a thousand years after the events they relate.

The main outline of Zarathustra's teaching, which he gave to disciples as well as at the court of the Persian kings, can be reliably traced, although the details are sketchy. The ancient Persians were polytheistic, as were all other Indo-European peoples. The basic structure of Persian polytheism was probably the same as that of Vedic Hinduism. For example, both religions worshiped many gods in nature, sacrificed animals whose souls were thought to join the gods, and used a hallucinogenic drug in occasional sacrifices.

Zarathustra saw this religion as mistaken. He had a revolutionary monotheistic vision that only one God existed, Ahura Mazda. He also had a vision of an evil figure (supernatural but not divine), named Angra Mainyu, who opposed God. Zarathustra taught that all people had to choose which of these two moral forces they would follow, a choice that would either improve the world or make it worse. This choice determined the judgment by God of a disposition toward heaven or hell when they died, but Zarathustra taught that a final restoration would come when Ahura Mazda completely defeated the forces of evil. In this restoration, even hell would come to an end, and all people would be resurrected with a re-created body to an eternal, blessed life. Despite the up-and-down fortunes of this faith, Zarathustra's powerful teaching has endured through today.

9-2b The Spread of Zoroastrianism in the Persian and Sassanian Empires (550 B.C.E.–650 C.E.)

The first certain date in Zoroastrian history is its establishment in Persia during the reign of the Persian kings, beginning in 550 B.C.E. These kings created and ruled over the largest empire the world had yet seen, and Zoroastrianism spread with it (see Map 9.1). Some Persian kings drew explicitly on the religion for the legitimacy of their empire, claiming that Ahura Mazda wanted his fame and goodness spread throughout the world.

However, the Persians never attempted to impose Zoroastrianism on subject peoples with other religions. Given the religion's monotheism and moral rigor based on individual choice—religious ideas not widely shared in the ancient Middle East—this was a wise policy. Persian rule was autocratic, but it respected and even embraced cultural and religious differences in its subjects. As the ancient Greek historian Herodotus wrote, "No nation so readily adopts foreign customs as the Persians do."[4] Herodotus did not mean this as a compliment, but many people today see the affirmation of cultural diversity as a good thing; in the ancient world, it was all the more remarkable.

The story of the Persian Empire begins with Cyrus (SIGH-ruhs) II, later called Cyrus the Great, who ruled the small Persia homeland from 550 to 530 B.C.E. He began the expansion of Persia by overthrowing the king of Media to the north, and he kept on marching. Within ten years he had conquered much of the Middle East. He was a faithful Zoroastrian, as were the emperors of Persia who came after him, but tolerant toward other religions in his empire. When he captured Babylon, he rebuilt the temple of its main God, Marduk (MAHR-dook). The **Cyrus Cylinder**, an archaeological treasure from Cyrus's time, tells how he released many captive peoples held in Babylonia, allowing them to return to their homes and pursue their religions. For example, the Cyrus Cylinder attests that Cyrus allowed the thousands of Jews taken to Babylon in 586 B.C.E. to return to Jerusalem in 539, and to rebuild their temple and land within the Persian Empire. Historians who argue for a large influence of Zoroastrianism on Judaism typically point to this "Persian period" in Jewish history as the time when it occurred.

Darius (dah-RIGH-uhs) I, called "Darius the Great," ruled from 521 to 486 B.C.E. He is known mainly for his great building projects, such as a spectacular new capital at Persepolis. He was adept at managing his empire and expanded Persian rule to its greatest extent. Darius referred to Ahura Mazda in his royal inscriptions as the source of his successes, and he had monumental faravahars carved on many walls in

Miniature relief carving of Cyrus the Great

GRAEME GILMOUR/GETTY IMAGES

Persepolis and in older cities. He attempted to conquer Greece, but wasn't successful.

Darius's son Xerxes (ZUHRK-seez), who ruled from 486 to 465 B.C.E., also tried to conquer Greece, this time with a massive effort. Similar to his father, he failed. Several relatively small Greek city-states turned back the mighty Persian Empire, marking a turning point in Persian fortunes. (This story is told in historical-fantasy form by the much-mocked 2006 film *300*, with its false depiction of the Persians and of Xerxes.) Xerxes and his successors changed their predecessors' policy of tolerating different religions and ethnic groups, betraying Zoroastrian values. Local and regional imperial officials were drawn only from Persian ranks, rather than from local national and ethnic groups as before. Over the next hundred years, the empire suffered from various revolts and struggles over the throne. It was greatly reduced in size and splendor by the time Alexander the Great of Macedon, a nation that had once been a part of the Persian Empire, easily toppled it in 334 B.C.E. Alexander, similar to the Persians, tended to be basically tolerant of other religions. But Alexander overthrew the empire to which Zoroastrianism had become closely connected, and the faith was greatly damaged in the process.

Zoroastrianism struggled under Hellenistic, Roman, and Parthian rules, which controlled parts of its homeland from 334 B.C.E. to 224 C.E. But Zoroastrian religious leaders praised the kings of the Sassanian Empire (224–651 C.E.; also known as "Sassanid") for powerfully reestablishing the religion. For the second time, Zoroastrianism was the official religion of a large empire (see Map 9.2). This was the golden age of Zoroastrianism. Several Sassanian rulers featured Zoroastrian symbols in official inscriptions and coins. Their patronage enabled the establishment of many Zoroastrian temples and the rise of a professional priesthood to staff them. The **Avesta**, the first and basic Zoroastrian scripture,

Cyrus Cylinder Artifact recording Cyrus's rule, including his release of captive peoples

Avesta [ah-VEHS-tuh] First and basic Zoroastrian scripture

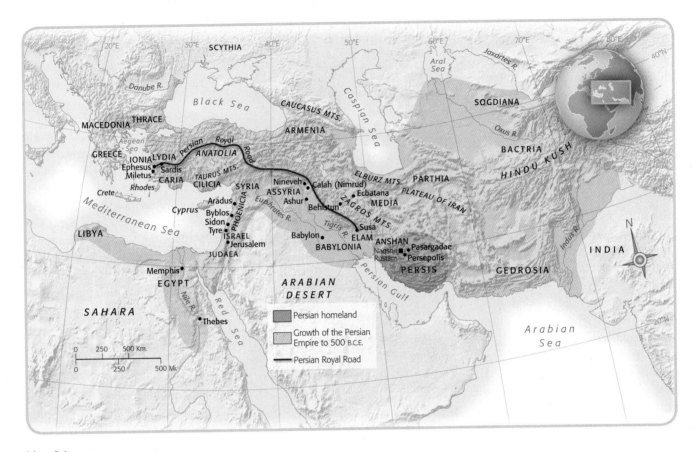

Map 9.1

The Zoroastrian Persian Empire, ca. 500 B.C.E.

At its height around 500 B.C.E., the Persian Empire controlled a huge territory that included what is today northern Greece, Egypt, and most of western Asia, from the Mediterranean coast to the Indus River in India.

was collected. **Towers of silence**, stone funeral structures for the Zoroastrian dead, were also built throughout the land. (We will discuss towers of silence in Section 9-5f.) In the Sassanian period, Zoroastrianism reached the basic form that it would keep through today.

Zoroastrians still use the date of the coronation of the last Sassanian king, Yazdgird, in 631 C.E., as the first year of their calendar (e.g., 2018 C.E. = 1387 Y). However, modern Iranian Zoroastrians blame the Sassanians for continuing the decline of their religion, saying that its misuse for political purposes led to the downfall of the empire. Arabian Muslim forces conquered the Sassanian Empire around 650 C.E. As happened earlier with Alexander's conquest of the Persian Empire, the brutal Muslim conquest of the Sassanian Empire caused great damage to the state-sponsored Zoroastrian religion. Zoroastrians found themselves in a Muslim empire that would, over time, greatly reduce their numbers and influence.

Tower of silence Stone funeral structure where the Zoroastrian dead were placed and bones stored

9-2c The Coming of Islam and the Zoroastrian Dispersion (650 C.E.–Present)

The Arabic conquest of the Sassanian Empire began a process of Islamic growth and Zoroastrian decline that would last for centuries. Muslim rulers considered Zoroastrians to be People of the Book and did not forcibly convert them, but most converted to Islam nonetheless, probably drawn by its rigorous monotheism and strict morality. Those who remained Zoroastrians had their religious liberty restricted, and they were often persecuted. Up to three-quarters of their sacred literature was destroyed. A few times, various Zoroastrian communities openly revolted against their Muslim overlords, only to be crushed and decimated. By 900 C.E. the Zoroastrians were reduced to such a small minority that they were concentrated in a few areas of Iran.

These pressures on the Iranian Zoroastrians led many to flee to the western coast of India, in the Gujarat area, in 936 C.E. In the course of time, they developed

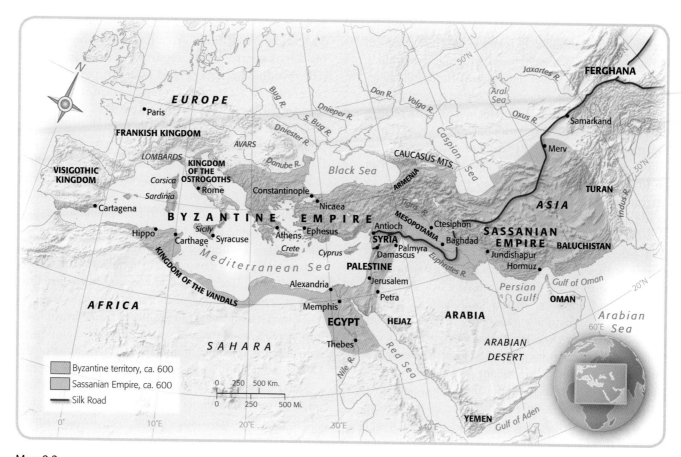

Map 9.2

The Sassanian and Byzantine Empires, 600 C.E.

By 600 C.E., the Christian Byzantine Empire controlled the eastern Mediterranean. The neighboring Zoroastrian Sassanian Empire dominated most of inland western Asia. It was centered in the older Persian homeland, which today is in southern Iran.

a specific ethnic identity with a strong sense of shared history, and even a language they named Parsi-Gujarati. The Hindu authorities tolerated Zoroastrianism, but did not allow conversions of Hindus to Zoroastrianism (which Zoroastrians prohibited as well) or even Hindu visits to Zoroastrian temples. For centuries, Zoroastrians in India had their own dress and diet codes. These have now largely disappeared in everyday life but are carefully observed on important occasions such as holidays, weddings, and funerals. Thus began the development of two different communities of Zoroastrians, Iranians and Parsis, a split that continues to this day. An effort in the early twenty-first century to found an organization for all Zoroastrians failed to overcome the old differences.

The Parsi communities blossomed during Mughal (Islamic) and British rule in India. These latter groups were more tolerant of Zoroastrianism than were the

> { *Parsis do not permit conversion to their religion.* }

rulers of Iran. Many Parsis today regard these times as a high point of their community's history—in material wealth, social prestige, cultural achievements, and political influence. Zoroastrians in India prospered economically in commerce and other professions. An unprecedented number of temples were built, most of them in urban Mumbai, which is still the modern stronghold of Zoroastrianism.

Since the late nineteenth century, the question of the permissibility of conversion to Zoroastrianism and mixed marriages has fueled an ongoing debate about Zoroastrian identity. Parsis do not permit conversion to their religion, and although intermarriage with people of other faiths happens in many Zoroastrian families, it is still regarded as taboo. The religious status of persons of other religions who marry Zoroastrians, and the children born of such marriages, is still a matter of controversy today almost everywhere Zoroastrians are found.

Indian independence in 1947 was a mixed blessing for the Parsis. It brought a greater measure of freedom, but it also brought the challenge of numerical decline. Parsis now number fewer than seventy thousand, down from more than one hundred thousand a century ago. Part of this decline is due to a reluctance to procreate—typical of modern groups with upper-class social standing such as that of the Parsis—but this is clearly at odds with the exhortations to bear children that can be found throughout Zoroastrian religious literature. Migration has also contributed to dwindling numbers in India. Starting with the late 1700s, Parsis settled in distant parts of the British Empire—including Chinese port cities, Burma, Ceylon, and parts of Africa—but mainly in Britain itself. Since the 1960s, new waves of immigration took Parsis to North America, Australia, New Zealand, and some Persian Gulf nations.

In Iran, Zoroastrianism had been reduced to a tiny minority of fewer than ten thousand by 1900. These believers had to bear a wide range of harsh discriminatory practices from the dominant Muslim population. Help from Zoroastrians in India and substantial political and legal changes improved the lot of the Iranian Zoroastrians and led to a tripling of their numbers. Many of them left agriculture, migrated to the modern capital of Tehran (which is now the main stronghold of the Iranian Zoroastrians), and went into the new middle-class professions. As the Parsis did in India, some Iranian Zoroastrians found great success in commerce.

Modern Iranian Zoroastrianism has undergone fundamental changes. When Zoroastrians were freed during secular Iranian rule from many restrictions in much of the twentieth century until 1979, the religion was reconceived as a message of moral freedom. Iranian Zoroastrians have claimed that this was the essence of Zarathustra's message. The ceremonial ritual system has been deliberately neglected, and many rules and rituals that are still carefully upheld by Indian priests have been all but abandoned in Iran. The *Yasna* (YAHZ-nuh) ceremony, for example, which the Parsis regard as an important liturgy (it takes a pair of trained priests several hours to perform it), is celebrated only rarely nowadays, and in a drastically reduced format; only a few Iranian priests can perform it. Purification rituals have largely been discarded. The professional priesthood has seen a sharp decline, and the leading priests have joined the social and intellectual elite in a crusade to uproot ancient superstition in the faith, including some rituals for women, devotion to lesser divinities such as Mithra, and animal sacrifice. The fear of being called fire worshipers led the Iranian community to emphasize the symbolic role of fire in their worship; new temples occasionally even have gas fires. Many consecrated wood fires are still kept burning but aren't tended according to past ritual.

Zoroastrianism in Iran gradually transformed itself into a religion of freedom and morality claiming to represent the splendor of ancient Iran. For most of the 1800s and 1900s, Zoroastrianism became an appealing alternative to Shi'a Islam for many Iranians, where pride in Iran's Persian heritage is widely felt. Some even converted to Zoroastrianism. This more liberal form of Zoroastrianism is also represented today by an international organization based in California called the **Zarathushtrian Assembly**. This group advocates the modernized form of their religion and accepts people willing to convert. However, the Zarathushtrian Assembly is strongly opposed by other Zoroastrian organizations, including a traditionalist organization based in

Zarathushtrian Assembly International group based in California advocating a modernized form of Zoroastrianism

The remnants of this Zoroastrian fire temple in Esfahan, Iran, show the destruction of holy places in the Arab invasions.

© ALEKSANDAR TODOROVIC/SHUTTERSTOCK.COM

A Closer Look

The Zoroastrian Creed

At key moments in a Zoroastrian's life, the Fravarane is recited. This declaration of faith is a shortened version of the full creed from the Zoroastrian scriptures.

"Come to my help, Ahura Mazda. I am a Mazdayasnian according to [the way of] Zarathustra. I firmly declare my faith. I acknowledge my faith in Good Thoughts well conceived. I acknowledge my faith in Good Words well spoken. I acknowledge my faith in Good Deeds well done. I acknowledge my acceptance of the Good Religion of Mazda, which ends strife and disarms violence, which makes us righteous and self-reliant. It is the religion of those who have been, and shall be, the noblest, the best, and most sublime. The religion of Ahura Mazda was brought to us by Zarathustra. All good derives from Ahura Mazda. This is the declaration of the Mazdayasnian religion."

Mumbai called the **Zoroastrian Studies Association**. When the Islamic Republic of Iran was established in 1979, conversion to Zoroastrianism or any other religion became nearly impossible, and Zoroastrian life in Iran became more difficult. The New Year festival, which is widely shared by Iranians who are Muslims, is among the few accepted occasions for celebration that include both Zoroastrians and Muslims.

9-3 Essential Zoroastrian Teachings: Monotheism and Moral Dualism

In 2015, the Parsi Zoroastrian Association of Kolkata, India, sued the American music star Snoop Dogg. They allege that his music video "King" defamed their religion by abusing the sacred symbol of Zoroastrianism, the faravahar. In the video, Snoop Dogg sits on a throne under the faravahar, and pictures of this symbol flash on the screen as women dance on a pole, all of which most Zoroastrians think of as demeaning to their religion. To them, it lessens the standing of their religion in India, and jeopardizes the wider understanding of the one God they serve.

The teachings of Zoroastrianism stress belief in one God and moral dualism. Zoroastrianism was probably the first faith to put these two features together, and Zoroastrian teachings are deeply connected to them.

> "Ahura Mazda is the creator, radiant, glorious and best; the most beautiful, firm, wise, perfect and bounteous Spirit!"
> —The *Avesta*

9-3a The One God, Ahura Mazda

Zoroastrianism's foundational teaching is that there is only one supreme God, Ahura Mazda, a name that means Wise Lord or Lord of Wisdom. Ahura Mazda is the source of all light, truth, goodness, and life. He is infinite, and infinitely good. Zarathustra emphasized the central importance of Ahura Mazda by portraying him as the one God, accompanied by many spirit-lords—all the other older, Indo-Aryan gods who were "demoted" in the new religion. In later Zoroastrianism, the name Ahura Mazda was compacted into a single-word form, Ormazd. As the first verse in the ancient *Avesta* scripture proclaims, "Ahura Mazda is the creator, radiant, glorious and best; the most beautiful, firm, wise, perfect and bounteous Spirit!" Zoroastrians look to Ahura Mazda as the source of all created things that are good, the one who sustains goodness and life in the present, and the one who, at the end of time, will defeat all evil and give eternal life to all people (see "A Closer Look: The Zoroastrian Creed").

For Zoroastrians, only Ahura Mazda is a true God; only he is to be worshiped. All the other lords, ahuras, and demons are beneath him and are not gods. They form an entourage of spirits that accompany the forces of either good or evil. In sum, Zoroastrianism is properly

Zoroastrian Studies Association Organization of Zoroastrian traditionalists based in Mumbai, India

called monotheistic because it teaches the existence of one God. However, it was never as assertively monotheistic against other faiths as Judaism, Islam, or Christianity tended to be. It lacks a clear denial of the existence of other gods, a characteristic of these more radical monotheisms. This may be connected to its historic tolerance toward other creeds.

9-3b The Spirit of Destruction, Angra Mainyu

Opposition to the evil and impurities in the world was also a fundamental feature of Zoroastrianism from its beginning. Because Ahura Mazda is good and made the world to be a good place, he desires the people in his creation to be morally good as well. This entails a positive effort to do what is right and a negative effort to engage in a real fight with evils of all sorts. People who think, say, and do evil on earth are deceivers and liars who turn others against the one true, good God by promoting a variety of wickedness. Evil doesn't always look like evil, nor is it always easily recognized. Instead, it disguises itself as good; hence one of the main figures of wickedness is known as the Druj (drooj), the Spirit of Deceit or the Spirit of the Lie. The supreme evil spirit, Zarathustra taught, is **Angra Mainyu**, the Spirit of Destruction. Zarathustra seems to have used this as only a title, to judge from the oldest parts of Zoroastrian scriptures, but later Angra Mainyu became a proper name and was shortened to Ahriman (AH-rih-mun).

9-3c Moral Dualism

Another foundational feature of Zoroastrianism is **dualism**, the teaching that the cosmos is composed of two competing forces. This

Dualism portrayed at the Persian palace in Persepolis: the power of the bull symbolizes the moon, and the lion symbolizes the sun.

opposition between good and evil is also found in early Vedic Hindu sources, so it probably was a part of pre-Zoroastrian Persian religion, but Zarathustra developed it significantly. From the beginning of the world, the Zoroastrian scriptures say, there have been two incompatible, antagonistic spirits in the world. One is the good God, Ahura Mazda; the other is a devil-like figure, Angra Mainyu. The **Twin Spirits** under Ahura Mazda made an ominous choice: The Bounteous Spirit chose to be truthful in thoughts, words, and deeds, but the Deceitful Spirit chose to be a follower of evil. When the Zoroastrian scriptures teach this dualism, it is always with a command to follow the good; for example, "Let those who act wisely choose correctly between these two, not as evil-doers choose" (*Yasna* 30:3).

After the Twin Spirits, it was the turn of the old gods of pre-Zoroastrian Persian religion to choose between good and evil. These gods, called **daevas**, all chose badly. Ever since, the daevas have tried to corrupt people's choices also. The two powers of good and evil are roughly equal to each other in this world, so the fight between good and evil is real. The powers draw all people into their service as they fight this cosmic moral battle, as people decide which spirit to follow. The two forces will continue to limit and challenge each other until the end of time, when evil will finally be defeated.

Zoroastrianism's form of moral dualism never claimed that good and evil are exactly equal, because its dualism was qualified by monotheism. If there is only one God, and if this God is both good and has supreme power, evil at the end of the day doesn't have much

Angra Mainyu [AHN-gruh MIGHN-yoo] Spirit of Destruction, supernatural head of all evil in the cosmos

dualism Teaching that the cosmos is composed of two competing forces

Twin Spirits The Bounteous Spirit and the Deceitful Spirit, two supernatural beings under Ahura Mazda

daevas [DIGH-vuhs] Pre-Zoroastrian gods who chose to serve evil instead of good

of a chance to win. The forces of good are assured of eventual triumph. Ahura Mazda limits the exercise of his supreme power as this struggle plays out. Humans can join the struggle because they possess free choice.

The dualism is moral, but it isn't physical—the idea that matter is evil and spirit is good. Humans serve either good or evil with both their souls and bodies, because both the human soul and the human body participate in the divine nature. For example, fasting and celibacy—important practices in many religions to control the body and its supposed impulses to do or think wrong—are almost unknown in Zoroastrianism. The fight does, however, have a ritual aspect: Humans must keep themselves pure in body and soul by treating fire with great respect and avoiding demons in their dreams. Keeping pure also means that dead human bodies must not come into contact with the earth, which led to the practice of exposing them to birds of prey. There are short but necessary rituals for cleansing oneself after cutting hair or nails, sneezing, eliminating bodily wastes, and using toothpicks. Thus, traditional Zoroastrianism has ritual aspects that are almost as all-pervading as its ethical aspects.

9-3d Supernatural Intermediaries

Zoroastrianism's strong moral dualism is buttressed by supernatural intermediaries that personify and promote what is morally good. Between Ahura Mazda and human beings there are six intermediary beings called **Amesha Spentas**, or benevolent immortals. They are Good Thoughts, Perfect Truth, Desirable Lordship, Beneficial Devotion, Plenty, and Immortality. The Amesha Spentas are the entourage of personified virtues that constantly surround Ahura Mazda. They are individual divine beings and at the same time cosmic moral virtues. Humans who choose to follow Ahura Mazda take on, one by one, the moral characteristics of these immortals, progressing from Good Thoughts to Immortality.

9-3e Judgment and the Final Victory of Ahura Mazda

In Zoroastrian belief, the soul hovers above the body for three days after death. On the fourth day, it takes a rapid journey to the next world and faces judgment on the **Chinvat Bridge**. The Requiter (Chinvat) weighs the soul's deeds during all of life. If its good deeds outweigh evil ones, the soul ascends to the stars (representing good thoughts) then to the moon (good words), to the sun (good deeds), and finally to paradise, where

eternal lights shine. There the Good Mind leads the soul to the golden throne of Ahura Mazda. However, if evil outweighs good, the soul is dragged off to hell, to be punished there until the end of time.

In a great struggle near the end of time, the armies of good and evil will battle to the death, and Ahura Mazda's soldiers will defeat their evil enemies. Then a final judgment comes at the end of the world, after all the bodies of the dead are resurrected and reunited with their souls, whether they have been in heaven or hell. A final cleansing of fire purifies the souls and bodies of evil human beings, so that all people are fit to live in paradise, and will in fact do so. This will restore the goodness of the world that existed at the time of creation. The personified Spirit of Fire and Angra Mainyu will melt the metals of the mountains and flow down as rivers of molten fire. All resurrected humans must walk through this valley of trial. The fire will burn off the sins of the wicked for three painful days, but to the righteous it will be as delicious and restorative as warm milk. Then all people will enjoy happiness and divine blessing forever. Hell will be sealed forever, and Angra Mainyu and all his forces will be annihilated.

9-4 Zoroastrian Ethics

A young Zoroastrian man in California logs onto a Zoroastrian matchmaking website. Because his religion is important to him and because it commands marriage within the faith, he is now looking for a suitable Zoroastrian who could possibly become his wife. He has tried to find a possible mate in San Francisco, but the Zoroastrian community there is too small. The website gives him worldwide possibilities, especially in India, where his family came from generations ago. Some of his friends, both male and female, have married non-Zoroastrians, and his religious community has refused to welcome them or recognize their children as Zoroastrians. The young man would like to avoid these difficult problems.

As we have seen previously, the two main doctrinal teachings of Zoroastrianism are monotheism and morality. These are deeply intertwined. In a culture that rarely thought of its gods as morally good, Zarathustra proclaimed that the one God, Ahura Mazda, was

Amesha Spentas [uh-MAY-shuh SPEN-tuhz] Six benevolent, immortal spirits who are intermediaries between Ahura Mazda and humanity

Chinvat Bridge [CHIN-vaht] Requiter Bridge, where deeds are weighed for a soul's assignment to either heaven or hell

infinitely good and was attended by six spirits who personify his righteousness and mediate it to humankind. Ahura Mazda fights a cosmic battle against evil, a force that is strong and real (*Gathas, Yasna* 44:10; 53:1).

Because Ahura Mazda does what is good, he expects all people to follow him in doing what is right and putting away evil. In this way, they join the ongoing cosmic spiritual and physical battle for righteousness, a battle that Ahura Mazda will certainly win. Zoroastrians do not simply fight against evil in themselves or in society around them, but by their good actions they fight against demons and Angra Mainyu himself. People have the freedom to know right from wrong and choose what is right, and Ahura Mazda holds them responsible for these choices. Most Zoroastrians have a lively sense of the heavenly reward for doing right and the hellish punishment for a life of doing wrong.

9-4a Zoroastrian General Morality

Zoroastrian moral teachings focus generally on the preservation of good and the destruction of evil, but this abstract ideal is carried out in very concrete ways. The oldest scriptures of Zoroastrianism relate that one must make an honest living in cattle herding and farming. This wasn't just a cultural given—it was a religious norm. Zoroastrians went into commerce and prospered in it, in part because they had a reputation for being honest with all people, not just those of their faith or ethnic group. At one time, Zoroastrians in Mumbai owned more businesses than did Hindus, who vastly outnumbered them.

Zoroastrians hold to values of speaking and acting truthfully, being faithful to Ahura Mazda, and doing what is good in the world. Goodness in one's individual life can be attained only by living a balanced, morally healthy life of good thoughts, good words, and good deeds. In the Avestan language, these three have the same beginning sound, suggesting they go together: Humata (hoo-MAHT-uh), Hukhta (HOOK-tuh), and Huvereshta (hoo-vuh-RESH-tuh). This threefold statement of morality is so important in the faith that it is a key part of the Zoroastrian confession of faith, as we saw previously. It is inscribed over many a door

kindred marriage
Requirement that Zoroastrians marry only Zoroastrians

> { At one time, Zoroastrians in Mumbai owned more businesses than did Hindus. }

to Zoroastrian temples and community centers. In the past few centuries, generous giving to Zoroastrian philanthropies has become a hallmark of the faith's moral effort. The steady work of the faithful to spread good in the world has improved the education of girls and the social status of women in India, Iran, and other countries.

Traditional Zoroastrians live their lives in this world with a view of their individual judgment after death. Their reward or punishment in the next world, at least from the time of their death to the end of the world, is decided by the total balance of their deeds, words, and thoughts. If good predominated in their life, they go to heaven; if evil predominated, they go to hell. This principle, however, is flexible enough to accommodate human failings. Zoroastrians don't believe that all their sins must be weighed on the scales. Two ways exist of erasing negative effects at one's personal judgment. The first of these is confession of one's sins, which brings forgiveness and lightens the weight of sin at the judgment. The second is the transfer of merits from the Zoroastrian saints, whose good thoughts, words, and deeds are far more than what the saints need to pass judgment and enter heaven. This is the rationale for Zoroastrian funeral prayers and rituals asking Ahura Mazda for mercy on and forgiveness of the souls of the dead.

9-4b A Current Ethical and Social Issue: Marriage and Children

Another key moral command in Zoroastrianism is the duty to marry and have children. To Zoroastrians, the world is a good place even though evil has marred it. Marriage and children are good things for every Zoroastrian; in contrast with some other religions among whom Zoroastrians have lived (for instance, Hinduism and Jainism), one won't see any form of celibacy at any stage in Zoroastrian life. Moreover, marriage must traditionally be to another within the faith, preferably a member in a clan relationship, while avoiding incest, a practice called **kindred marriage**. In other words, marriage must be close, but not too close. Zoroastrians have even called their religion the "faith of kindred marriage."

Unless more Zoroastrians marry within the faith, and Zoroastrian couples have more than one or two children on average, the faithful may all but disappear in a few centuries. Many Zoroastrians are apprehensive about the future of their faith. Other groups within the religion that call themselves reformist accept children of mixed marriages into the faith, but this is strongly rejected by the main body of Zoroastrians.

9-5 Zoroastrian Rituals

As he sits on the floor in a Zoroastrian temple in a Chicago suburb, a priest offers sacrifice for the souls of the dead. In his secular occupation, Kersey Antia is a clinical psychologist specializing in panic disorders. As a Zoroastrian priest, he officiates at fire ceremonies, feeding sandalwood and frankincense into a blazing fire in a large urn. He recites prayers that he learned to pronounce by special training in the Avestan language at a school in India. Although the faithful today understand only a few Avestan words, the Zoroastrian God Ahura Mazda speaks Avestan, so the words are still effective.

9-5a Fires in the Fire Temple

The Zoroastrian house of worship, in which all worship takes place, is the **fire temple**. In the western world an eternal flame is a symbol of honored memory; in Zoroastrianism every temple has an eternal flame for the worship of Ahura Mazda. Fire temples and their activities center on the fire within them, and they are named with reference to three types of fires.

> In the western world, an eternal flame is a symbol of honored memory; in Zoroastrianism every temple has an eternal flame for the worship of Ahura Mazda.

The Appointed Place Fire is the first classification of sacred fire. Two priests can consecrate it in two hours, with one reading scriptures out loud as the other lights and tends the fire. After it is consecrated, an approved layperson may tend the fire when no ritual is being performed with it. The smallest Zoroastrian temples have only this sort of fire.

The next level is the Fire of Fires. It requires a gathering and mingling in one sacrificial urn of fires from representatives of the four main social groups: priests, soldiers and civil servants, farmers and herders, and craftsmen and laborers. Eight priests must consecrate this fire in a ritual that takes up to three weeks.

The highest level is the Fire of Victory. Its consecration involves the gathering of sixteen different fires from sixteen different sources, including from lightning and a metal-molding furnace. Each of the sixteen fires goes through a rite of purification before its flames are put into a common fire. Thirty-two priests are needed for the consecration, which takes almost a year.

9-5b Interior Plan of the Fire Temple

When they enter a fire temple, both men and women must wear a head covering. First, one goes through a large hall where ceremonies take place. The faithful then enter an anteroom smaller than the main hall. Connected to this anteroom—but not visible from the hall, to ensure a sense of holiness and quiet—is the place of the fire where the actual fire altars stand. These fire altars are usually large urns that sit on the floor; priests sit or stand in front of them as they offer sacrifices of spices and incense into the constantly burning flame. Lay Zoroastrians stand before the fire to offer their prayers to God.

Only priests enter the inner, most sacred room, which has a double-domed roof. Each dome in this roof has vents where the smoke of the fires escapes. The outer dome's vents are offset from those of the inner dome, preventing anything but air from entering the room below and potentially desecrating the holy flame. The walls of the inner room are made of tile or marble, but there is no other decoration. The only light in the inner room is that of the fire itself, an arrangement that is powerfully symbolic to Zoroastrians.

Priests ring a bell, installed in the main room, five times every day to mark each new watch period. The fire is usually fed at this time with dried sandalwood. Non-Zoroastrians may not enter any space from which they can even glimpse the fires. This typically means no entry into a temple at all, and many Parsi temples in India have "Parsis Only" signs at their front door. If non-Zoroastrians are permitted to enter during ordinary times, the temples are closed to them during feasts and holy days. Traditionalists say that these restrictions aren't meant to offend non-Zoroastrians. Iranian and reformist Zoroastrians more often open their temples to non-Zoroastrians.

fire temple Zoroastrian house of worship centering on sacred fire

9-5c Priesthood

The **magi**, an order of non-Zoroastrian priests, learned about the prophet Zarathustra's teachings before 400 B.C.E. and converted to the faith. The priests rose to power quickly and had a monopoly on priestly power at the Persian court. Under the Sassanians, a three-level hierarchy of priests developed among the magi. Admission to the priesthood is hereditary, but all priests must go through one or more ceremonies of ordination. In 2010, a violent confrontation broke out in India when a group of more liberal Zoroastrians unsuccessfully tried to ordain to the priesthood a Russian convert to Zoroastrianism. Training for the priesthood has always centered on performing the ceremonies, especially the ritual words and actions.

Political and cosmic power of fire: coin of Sassanian King Shahpur II (309–379 C.E.), with a fire altar and priests

The main ceremony conducted by priests, the Yasna, is a sacrifice of **haoma**, the sacred liquid, to Ahura Mazda. The sacrifice is held in the presence of the sacred fire and features recitation of long portions of the Avesta. Bread and milk are also offered, substances that replace the former offerings of meat or animal fat.

The sacred fire is fed with sweet-smelling wood, at least five times a day, at the beginning of each watch. Prayers are also offered five times a day in the presence of the fire.

9-5d Worship

When a Zoroastrian enters the room where the fire burns, he or she offers wood for the fire. The person making an offering doesn't put the wood directly into the fire, but gives it to the priest. At the proper time, the priest places the offering in the fire, using silver tongs. He wears a white cloth mask over nose and mouth so his breath doesn't pollute the flame. The priest uses a special ladle to give some ashes to worshipers, who then dab the ashes on their forehead and eyelids. The Zoroastrian priest doesn't preach or teach, but offers prayer and sacrifice at the fire, which he tends. Temple attendance is especially high during festivals, particularly the New Year festival. There is no instrumental music or group singing in Zoroastrian worship, only the musical chanting of the scriptures and prayers by the priests. Social events may occur in the main hall, especially at festivals and initiations, but rarely as a part of regular worship.

9-5e Other Rituals

All young Zoroastrians must be initiated in the **navjote** ceremony when they turn seven (in India, Africa, Europe, and North America) or ten (in Iran). A priest leads the ceremony, and the young people must receive instruction before the navjote. They receive a shirt and the sacred cord called a **kusti**, which are items to be worn for the rest of their life. The kusti is tied around the waist and symbolizes a lifelong commitment to keeping the tenets of the religion.

In a religion that stresses ritual purity, Zoroastrian rituals of purification are particularly important. Three types of purification come in order of increasing importance: the ablution, ordinary washing for the smallest compromises of one's purity; the full-body bath, for medium-sized impurities; and the fullest purification ritual, the *bareshnum* (ba-RESH-num), a complicated ritual performed at special places and lasting several days. It includes a dog, whose left ear is touched by the person seeking cleansing. Evil spirits are believed to flee from the dog's threatening looks.

Penance for sins is necessary for keeping the accumulation of one's sins from resulting in condemnation after death. It entails reciting the **patet**, the firm resolve not to sin again. The patet also calls for one to confess one's sins to a priest.

Festivals are an important aspect of Zoroastrianism, and full of happy celebration. There are six seasonal festivals throughout the year, and at year's end

magi [MAY-jigh] An order of priests not originally Zoroastrian

haoma [HO-mah] Sacred liquid offered in the fire sacrifice to Ahura Mazda

navjote [nahv-JOH-tee] Initiation ceremony when young Zoroastrians reach the age of seven or ten

kusti [KOOS-tee] Sacred thread tied around a Zoroastrian's body

patet [PAH-teht] Formula expressing resolve not to sin again

Zoroastrian priests and pilgrims praying during a religious ceremony commemorating Zarathustra's birthday, at the mountain shrine at Chak-Chak, Yazd, Iran. A part of the prayers is tying on their kusti.

in. The dog's appearance frightens evil spirits into fleeing but does not threaten the soul of the dead person, which hovers above the body for three days. The ritual is repeated five times a day. On the second day after death, mourners bring fire into the room and keep it burning there for three full days after the funeral.

Placement of the body in a tower of silence must be done in the daylight. The inside of the tower has three concentric circles, one each for men, women, and children, and a large central well in the center of the tower. The body is then unclothed, and after it is exposed, the mourners leave the tower. The vultures descend from their circling flight and take only about an hour to eat the flesh from the bones. Dried by the sun for a few days, the bones are swept into a large stone box in the central well, to preserve them reverently until the resurrection. The fourth day after death is the most solemn in the funeral; the soul goes into the presence of Ahura Mazda and is judged. Special prayers are offered on this day for the souls of the dead.

a few days are dedicated to the memory of the dead. The New Year feast, **Nowruz** (also spelled **Noruz**) is the most joyous of all Zoroastrian festivals. Iranian Muslims have a similar celebration of Nowruz.

9-5f Funeral Rituals

The funeral ritual varies in the Zoroastrian world today, but here is the traditional format. After death, the body is washed and clothed in a simple white garment. A "four-eyed" dog with a spot above each eye is then brought

Zoroastrian funeral practice has changed in Iran and India. In its role as a religion in a modernizing country, Zoroastrianism in Iran replaced the towers of silence with cemeteries during the twentieth century. By the 1960s, the towers in Iran had fallen into complete disuse. In the new cemeteries, care was taken to protect the earth from direct contact with bodies of the dead, a key Zoroastrian value. The towers of silence are still used at times in Mumbai, India, despite the fact that there are few vultures there to devour the corpses. Bodies are put in the towers to decay in the sun and open air, a practice that has led to some inner Zoroastrian controversy as well as conflict with local officials over health issues. Steps are now being taken to increase the vulture population in hopes of reviving the traditional use of the towers of silence in Mumbai.

Tower of silence in Yazd, Iran

> **Nowruz or Noruz** [NOH-rooz] Iranian New Year festival celebrated by both Zoroastrians and Muslims

9-6 Zoroastrianism around the World Today

Residents of a rural area outside Washington, D.C., are upset about the construction of a Zoroastrian temple in their community. One man who lives next to the temple property worries that the temple, which will include a parking lot for fifty cars and its own water and septic system, will limit the already declining water supply for residents. Others say the worship center will bring an unwanted influx of traffic. The complaints, government officials say, have nothing to do with the religious nature of the project, but are about allowing the temple in a residentially zoned area. But the Zoroastrian community has all its permits for construction in order. The leader of the community has said, "We are a very small religion," adding that only three hundred Zoroastrians live in the Washington, D.C., area. "Our finances aren't good. We have no home for gathering together for worship."

Zoroastrians have left a rather small footprint in the world today, as one might expect from such a numerically small religion. Most Zoroastrians can be found in and around Mumbai (Bombay), India; the next largest group is found in Iran. Smaller pockets of Zoroastrians can also be found in east Africa and Great Britain. Most Zoroastrians in North America are from India; they speak English and their own dialect of Gujarati. More-recent Zoroastrian immigrants are from Iran; they speak Farsi. Because these two communities were separated in Asia for more than a thousand years, they developed some differences in their rituals and festivals that are still reflected in North America today.

Zoroastrians began to arrive in North America in the 1860s, in very small numbers, settling on the East and West Coasts. They engaged in a variety of professions, from gold prospecting to farming and commerce. The first Zoroastrian congregation, formed by seven believers in New York City in 1929, met in private homes. As with other people of Asian origin, Zoroastrians were largely prohibited by U.S. immigration laws from entering the country from about 1900 until the 1960s. Then, when the laws were liberalized, many Zoroastrians came to North America seeking a more prosperous life, and additional Zoroastrian organizations were founded. The main goal of these organizations, similar to those of almost all other Asian religions that came to North America, was to establish the faith in the New World so that it would be successfully passed down to the Zoroastrians' children. Maintaining the religious culture—language, dress, food, and festivals—through the generations is also important in North America. Many Zoroastrian temples have cultural centers attached to them where these cultural values are emphasized. One of the Zoroastrian public-relations tasks in North America today is to counter a false impression that North Americans get when they read the book *Thus Spoke Zarathustra*. It has been disavowed by almost all Zoroastrians from the time of its publication, because its theme of an individual getting beyond conventional morality, and then even beyond morality itself, contradicts one of the main beliefs of Zoroastrianism.

> { Maintaining the religious culture—language, dress, food, and festivals— ... is important in North America. }

BEHROUZ MEHRI/AFP/GETTY IMAGES

A young girl dances at a Zoroastrian cultural center; a common portrait of Zarathushtra is behind her.

220 ENCOUNTERING ZOROASTRIANISM: THE WAY OF THE ONE WISE LORD

After the 1979 Islamic Revolution in Iran toppled the more religiously tolerant regime of the Shah, many Iranian Zoroastrians no longer felt safe there. Thousands fled their ancient ancestral homeland, and a majority went to North America. The number of Zoroastrians there quickly doubled, and tensions arose between Indian and Iranian Zoroastrians. For the most part, they manage to coexist, if only because their small numbers force them to get along. In a few larger Zoroastrian communities, worship services are held separately for each group, with only some important festivals celebrated by Iranians and Indians together. In 2010, it was estimated that the entire population of Zoroastrians in North America was around twenty thousand. Zoroastrians have taken to cyberspace with many websites that promote the common faith of all Zoroastrians and also some of the distinct groups, such as the reformist Zarathushtrian Assembly and the traditionalist Mazdayasni Zoroastrian Anjuman (Society). Some observers of North American Zoroastrianism expect the differences between the groups to soften over time—especially when the second and third generations take over—and an American Zoroastrianism to be established. Zoroastrian websites often have matchmaking areas to encourage the faithful to marry each other; one pleads, "Marry inside our community, and SAVE our religion." Only time will tell if this will help to keep alive one of the world's most ancient faiths.

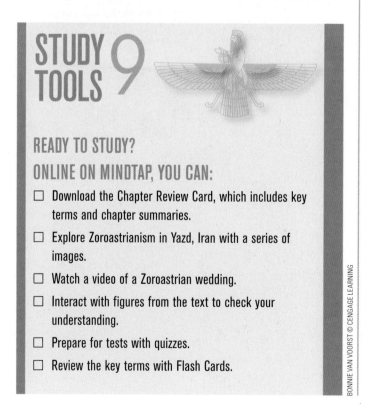

STUDY TOOLS 9

READY TO STUDY?

ONLINE ON MINDTAP, YOU CAN:

☐ Download the Chapter Review Card, which includes key terms and chapter summaries.

☐ Explore Zoroastrianism in Yazd, Iran with a series of images.

☐ Watch a video of a Zoroastrian wedding.

☐ Interact with figures from the text to check your understanding.

☐ Prepare for tests with quizzes.

☐ Review the key terms with Flash Cards.

BONNIE VAN VOORST © CENGAGE LEARNING

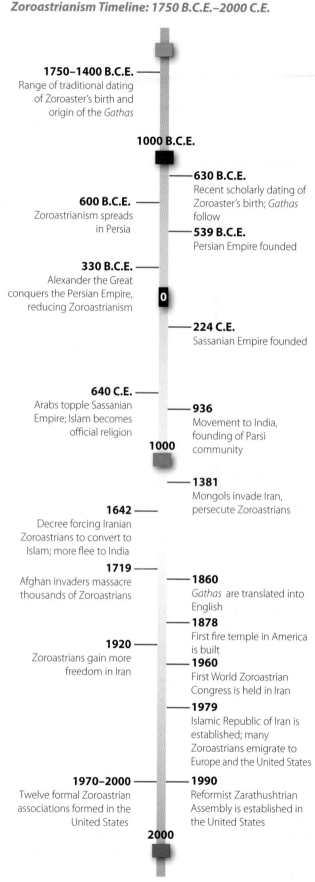

Zoroastrianism Timeline: 1750 B.C.E.–2000 C.E.

1750–1400 B.C.E. Range of traditional dating of Zoroaster's birth and origin of the *Gathas*

1000 B.C.E.

630 B.C.E. Recent scholarly dating of Zoroaster's birth; *Gathas* follow

600 B.C.E. Zoroastrianism spreads in Persia

539 B.C.E. Persian Empire founded

330 B.C.E. Alexander the Great conquers the Persian Empire, reducing Zoroastrianism

0

224 C.E. Sassanian Empire founded

640 C.E. Arabs topple Sassanian Empire; Islam becomes official religion

936 Movement to India, founding of Parsi community

1000

1381 Mongols invade Iran, persecute Zoroastrians

1642 Decree forcing Iranian Zoroastrians to convert to Islam; more flee to India

1719 Afghan invaders massacre thousands of Zoroastrians

1860 *Gathas* are translated into English

1878 First fire temple in America is built

1920 Zoroastrians gain more freedom in Iran

1960 First World Zoroastrian Congress is held in Iran

1979 Islamic Republic of Iran is established; many Zoroastrians emigrate to Europe and the United States

1970–2000 Twelve formal Zoroastrian associations formed in the United States

1990 Reformist Zarathushtrian Assembly is established in the United States

2000

10
Encountering Judaism: The Way of God's People

LEARNING OUTCOMES

After studying this chapter, you will be able to do the following:

10-1 Explain the meaning of *Judaism* and related terms.

10-2 Summarize how the main periods of Judaism's history have shaped its present.

10-3 Outline the essential teachings of Judaism in your own words.

10-4 Describe the main features of Jewish ethics.

10-5 Summarize Jewish worship, the Sabbath and major festivals, and life-cycle rituals.

10-6 Outline the main features of Judaism around the world today, especially in Israel and North America.

"Hear, O Israel: The Lord our God is One." —*Jewish statement of faith*

Your Visit to the Western Wall in Jerusalem

In your hotel the evening before you visit the Western Wall, your tour guide gives you instructions for the next day's events. "Everyone is welcome at the Wall," she says. "But you must wear modest clothing—no one in shorts, sleeveless tops, or jeans is allowed. Men must wear a hat or other head covering. Women must wear clothing that covers their shoulders and knees; they can borrow shawls at the entrance. Proper behavior is a must; be respectful of others." All this is standard stuff for holy places, you think. But there's one item that's unique to a visit to the Western Wall: People are allowed to put a paper note with a prayer written on it into a seam between the stones, where (many Jews believe) God will pay special attention to one's prayer. Today there is a long-distance option for this: people can Tweet prayers to an office in Jerusalem, and the prayers will be printed out and inserted into the Wall.

Nearly everyone in Israel calls this place simply "the Wall." But your guide gives you a warning: Don't call it "the Wailing Wall." This term is often used today, but many residents of Jerusalem find it offensive. "Wailing" is supposed to refer to mourning for the destruction of the temple at this site in 70 C.E. There is typically no wailing here.

Despite the preparation you've done for visiting the Wall, some things still surprise you during your visit. First, rules set by the most traditional form of Judaism apply here, so women and girls must go to a special section and not stand in the males-only section. In 2016, the Israeli government proposed a permanent space at the Wall where men and women of any Jewish branch could worship together, but these plans were scrapped in 2017 when political and religious opposition to this area grew powerful. Second, more than a million notes are left in the Wall each year, and

MIKHAIL/SHUTTERSTOCK.COM

A Jewish boy prays at the Western Wall; prayer notes are visible in the Wall.

you see that the cracks between the stones are jammed with papers. Twice a year the notes are collected and buried on Jerusalem's Mount of Olives. Third, and most surprising of all, is how emotionally moved you are. The closer you get to the Wall, the more it towers over you. The prayerful piety of others at the site impresses you and helps to explain why this is for Jews the holiest place in the world.

Judaism is a monotheistic religion. Jews believe that the world was created by an all-knowing, all-powerful God and that all things in the world were designed to have meaning and purpose as part of a divine order. God called the Israelites to be a chosen, special people and follow God's law, thus becoming the means by which divine blessing would flow to the world. God's law guides humans in every area of life; it is a gift from God so that people might live according to God's will.

The main influence of Judaism stems directly from its strong devotion to God over more than 2,500 years. Some of the impact of Judaism has been lost in the modern world, and Judaism itself is more fragmented in recent times than ever before. Its deep influence on everyday life and on patterns of western culture is still clearly visible, however. The belief that there is only one

The Western Wall in Jerusalem sees some of the liveliest activity in Judaism today. The main area on the left is for males, the smaller area in the center is for females, and the walkway on the far right is the only way for non-Muslims to enter the Muslim holy site on the upper level. (The Al-Aqsa Mosque, the third-holiest site in Sunni Islam, is on the left.)

YOUR VISIT TO THE WESTERN WALL IN JERUSALEM **223**

God, now self-evident for believers in all western religions, is the main gift of Judaism. The idea that the world is a real and mostly good (or at least redeemable) place has shaped western religion and thought. Our seven-day week with its rest on the weekend originates in Judaism as well. The convictions that all people are equally human before God, each other, and the law; that the human race is one family; and that each individual can fully realize the meaning of life regardless of social or economic class have also come to the western world from Judaism.

> { *Key teachings of Judaism have spread in Christianity and Islam . . . to over half the people of the world.* }

In your study of Judaism, you'll encounter and study in some depth these unique features:

- For a relatively small religion, around 14.27 million adherents today, Judaism has had a big impact. Key teachings of Judaism have spread in Christianity and Islam, which are closely related to Judaism, to over half the people of the world. However, Islam and Christianity have often been rivals of Judaism as well.

- The world has had a mixed attitude toward Judaism for more than two thousand years. Jewish monotheism and morality have been influential, but Jews have drawn near-constant opposition as well. Prejudice against them, often leading to violent persecution, has sadly been a recurrent feature in Jewish life.

- Judaism is both geographically scattered and centered. Since about 300 B.C.E., the majority of Jewish people haven't lived in the traditional Jewish area now in modern Israel. Instead, they've lived in the wider Middle East, Europe, and North America. In fact, as many Jews now live in the United States as in Israel. Still, Israel is an essential part of Judaism today.

Judaism [JOO-dee-IHZ-um] Historic religion of the Jewish people

Hebrews [HEE-brewz] Name of the ancestors of the Jews during patriarchal times through the Exodus

Israelites [IHZ-ray-EHL-ights] Name for ancestors of the Jews during the period of the Judges and during the First Temple Period

10-1 The Name *Judaism* and Related Terms

Judaism is the historic religion of the Jewish people. This name comes from the ancient tribe of Judah, one of the original twelve tribes of Israel. When the leaders of the southern kingdom of Israel came back from exile in Babylon in the 530s B.C.E., the name of their larger tribe became the name of the political area (Judah), and the people who lived there became the *Judahites* (JOO-duh-ights), or *Jews* for short. In time their religion became known as *Judaism*.

For most of the history of the Jewish people, to be Jewish was to practice Judaism in some way. But around 1800 C.E., it became possible in Europe to give up Judaism and still call oneself Jewish. Jewishness then became for many Jews a matter of ethnic status and cultural identity, not of religion. Other Jews replied that only by keeping Judaism do Jews stay Jewish. Although these two positions cannot be completely separated, this chapter will focus on Judaism as a religion.

Before 500 B.C.E., the ancestors of the Jews went by other names. The first was **Hebrews**, the name of the people during patriarchal times through the Exodus (1800–1200 B.C.E.). This name is from *Habiru* (ha-BEE-roo; also spelled "Hapiru"), a word for nomads that is found in many languages in the ancient Fertile Crescent and seems to have been attached to the descendants of Abraham while they lived in Egypt. When they settled in Palestine after the Exodus and became a nation there, they became known as **Israelites**, a name derived from the ancient patriarch Israel (whose original name was Jacob). Historians speak generically of their religions during this period as Hebrew religion and Israelite religion, not as Judaism. A more recent twist adds some confusion

Several terms name the Jewish people throughout their long history.

A Closer Look

Symbols of Judaism

Three main symbols have served Judaism over time.

Chai

Chai (chigh, with a throat-clearing initial sound; Figure 10.1), a symbol of modern origin popular and fashionable in jewelry today, is the Hebrew word for "living." Some say that it refers to God, who alone is perfectly alive; others think it comes from the common Jewish toast "Le chaim" (leh CHIGH-ihm), "To life!" More likely, it reflects Judaism's stress on the significance of life. For people who wear it, it is a symbol of their Jewish faith, but today it is the least used of the symbols treated here.

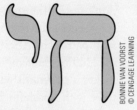

Figure 10.1 Chai

BONNIE VAN VOORST © CENGAGE LEARNING

Menorah

The oldest symbol of Judaism is the **menorah** (Figure 10.2), a large, usually seven-branched, candelabrum. It was a prominent accessory in the Jerusalem temple, and one sees it today in many Jewish homes and houses

Figure 10.2 Menorah

BONNIE VAN VOORST © CENGAGE LEARNING

of worship. It's especially prominent during the celebration of Hanukkah, when a nine-branched menorah is used for the nine days of the festival. For many Jews, the menorah symbolizes Israel's mission to be "a light to the nations" (Isaiah 42:6). It is featured on the coat of arms of the modern nation of Israel.

Star of David

The six-pointed **Star of David** (Figure 10.3) is by far the most common symbol of Judaism today, but it isn't nearly as old as the menorah. A symbol of two overlaid equilateral triangles was a common symbol of good fortune in the ancient Near East and in North Africa. It is found in early Jewish artwork as far back as the first century C.E.—in the stones of the ancient synagogue of Capernaum, Israel, for example—but not as a symbol of Judaism. In the 1600s, it began to be used to mark the exteriors of some Jewish houses of worship in Europe to identify them, and then began to be associated with the ancient King David. The Star of David reached its current status when it became the symbol of the Zionist movement to resettle Palestine in 1897 (see Section 10-2g). Today it appears on the flag of the modern nation of Israel.

Figure 10.3 Star of David

BONNIE VAN VOORST © CENGAGE LEARNING

to these names. The modern nation of Israel, founded in 1948, calls itself by the same name as that of ancient Israel, but the people of modern Israel (whether Jewish by religion or not) are called **Israelis**, not Israelites.

10-2 The Jewish Present as Shaped by Its Past

An American college professor leads his class on European religious history through the Dachau (DAHK-ow) concentration camp outside Munich, Germany. They walk through the gate, and the professor explains the macabre meaning of its inscription, *Arbeit macht frei* ("Work makes [you] free"). He explains, as they walk by, the barracks for prisoners and the other buildings around the site. They see the gas chamber disguised as a shower room and then inspect the crematorium. This is all a somber experience, but the full horror of this site doesn't really register on the students until they go into its museum, with exhibits showing what went on here. A suspicion and hatred of "alien" groups, especially the long history of hatred of the Jewish people, reached a horrific outcome in hundreds of camps such as this one. Everyone in the class is in tears as they leave, including the professor, who has been here before and isn't an emotional person. He brings his students here for this searing experience so that they'll never forget the evil humans can do and the courage it takes for persecuted groups to continue on in life.

menorah [men-OHR-uh] Large candelabrum; today a symbol of Judaism

Star of David Six-pointed star that is the most common symbol of Judaism today

Israelis [ihz-RAIL-eez] Name of people who live in the modern nation of Israel

The Jewish people have a long, storied history that includes both tragedy and triumph. In Judaism today we can see important beliefs and practices from the entire four-thousand-year sweep of Jewish experience. The periods of the history that we will consider here are these: from the creation of the world to Abraham (ca. 2000 B.C.E.); the emergence of Israel (ca. 1200–950 B.C.E.); the First Temple Period (950–586 B.C.E.); the Second Temple Period (539 B.C.E.–70 C.E.); revolts and rabbis (70 C.E.–ca. 650); Jews under Islamic and Christian rule (ca. 650–1800 C.E.); emancipation and change (1800–1932); and the Holocaust and its aftermath (1932–present).

10-2a From the Creation to Abraham (ca. 2000 B.C.E.)

Chapters 1 through 11 of the first book of the Bible, Genesis, span the creation of the universe to the time of Abraham, father of the Jewish people (ca. 2000 B.C.E.). It narrates and provides a religious perspective on the creation of the world, the rebellion of the first humans against God and their expulsion from the Garden of Eden, the wide dispersal of people, Noah and the flood, and other topics. These stories echo the earlier mythology of Mesopotamia and provide an Israelite alternative to them. The rest of Genesis (Chapters 12–50) covers just four generations of one family of the **patriarchs** and their wives: Abraham and Sarah, their son Isaac

> Scholars debate the historical accuracy of the early biblical story, but they don't doubt the role that it played in shaping Judaism.

and his wife Rebekah, their son Jacob (Israel) and his wives Rachel and Leah, and Jacob's twelve sons who founded the twelve tribes of the nation of ancient Israel. The Israelites and then the Jewish people emerged from these tribes. Scholars debate the historical accuracy of the early biblical story, but they don't doubt the role that it played in shaping Judaism.

Genesis 12 begins by narrating the migration of the first patriarch, Abraham, from Ur in Mesopotamia to the land of Canaan, a journey commanded by God. God makes a **covenant** with Abraham in which God promises to be with Abraham, be the God of his many descendants, and bless the world through these descendants. In return, God demands in the covenant that Abraham follow him faithfully. Abraham then carries out on himself and all the males in his clan the ritual of **circumcision**, cutting off the foreskin of the penis, which is the perpetual sign of the covenant. Abraham's son, Isaac, marries Rebekah; and she secures the line of succession for her younger son, Jacob. Jacob's simultaneous marriages to Leah and Rachel produce twelve sons, who are the origins of the twelve tribes. Genesis 37 to 50 tells the story of Joseph, the youngest of Jacob's twelve sons. Joseph is betrayed by his jealous brothers, who sell him to slave traders on their way to Egypt, but Joseph rises to great power under a sympathetic pharaoh. All Abraham's descendants then move to Egypt and prosper there until a later pharaoh enslaves the Israelites.

10-2b The Emergence of Ancient Israel (ca. 1200–950 B.C.E.)

The book of Exodus contains the story of Israel's enslavement in Egypt, God's call to Moses to lead his people out of Egypt, Pharaoh's stubborn resistance, and the Israelites' escape through the parted waters of the Red Sea. Moses leads the Israelites to Sinai, a mountain in the wilderness where they enter into a covenant relationship with God. The Israelites agree to live by all the teachings and commandments, the **Torah**, conveyed

patriarchs [PAY-tree-arks] Hebrew founding fathers: Abraham, Isaac, and Jacob

covenant [CUH-veh-nent] Agreement in which God promised to be with Abraham and his many descendants and Abraham promised to follow God

circumcision Ritual of the covenant, removing the foreskin of the penis

Torah [TOHR-uh] Teaching conveyed by Moses in the first five books of the Bible

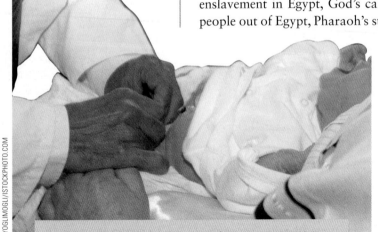
YOGLIMOGLU/ISTOCKPHOTO.COM
An eight-day-old Jewish boy undergoes circumcision.

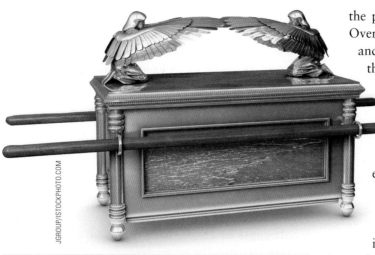

Modern depiction of the Ark of the Covenant, with its poles for transportation by priests

to them by Moses. After a forty-year journey through the wilderness, a new generation of Israelites arrives at the Jordan River, where they prepare to cross over and occupy the land promised to them. The books of Joshua and Judges relate the story of the Israelites' conquest of Palestine, its division among the tribes, and the first hundred years of settlement.

The focal center of early Israelite religion during this period was the movable tent-shrine housing the **Ark of the Covenant**, a sacred box with angels on the top containing two tablets inscribed with the Ten Commandments, Moses' staff, and a pot of manna. This tent, called the *tabernacle*, is where the first formal worship of ancient Israel took place, with sacrifice, prayer, and praise to God. Saul was anointed king of Israel around 1025 B.C.E. Israel's second monarch, David, consolidated the monarchy over all Israel. The Bible celebrates the reigns of David and his son Solomon as a golden age, but it doesn't gloss over their considerable failings.

10-2c The First Temple Period (950–586 B.C.E.)

Solomon's construction of a temple to God in Jerusalem (ca. 950) inaugurated the **First Temple Period**, which lasted until the temple was destroyed in 586. The royal court became increasingly lavish as the power and size of the state increased. Many viewed the increasing social and economic divisions, with the rich getting richer and the poor getting poorer, as a violation of God's will. Over the next centuries, a line of **prophets**, mostly men and some women who spoke for God, denounced the leaders of Israel for their greed, exploitation of the poor, and other social injustices and immoralities. The prophets also criticized the leaders' faith in alliances with other nations and lack of faith in God's power to protect the nation. Today, prophets are those who can see the future, but prophets in Israel were much more forth-tellers of God's will than foretellers of the future. The importance of prophets to Israelite and Jewish religion is indicated by the fact that the books of the prophets make up the largest section of the Bible. (We'll consider the formation and use of the Bible in Section 10-3a). As contemporary Jewish scholar Abraham Heschel wrote, the prophets portray the righteousness of God and God's anguish over Israel's disobedience.[1] The prophetic tradition that demands justice in God's name for the poor and oppressed is one of the great gifts of Judaism to the world and it endures through today.

When King Solomon died in 922 B.C.E., the people of God divided into two different nations, each with its own king: Israel, composed of ten tribes in the north, and Judah, composed of only the two tribes of Judah and Benjamin in the south (see Map 10.1). Sometimes the two kingdoms warred with each other, and at other times they cooperated against common enemies. But two centuries later, in 722, the Assyrian Empire wiped out the northern kingdom of Israel. Its ten tribes would never appear again, becoming in Jewish lore the "ten lost tribes." The southern kingdom of Judah was crippled at the same time by the Assyrians, who conquered several Judean cities and deported their citizens. Judah was finally conquered in 586 by the Babylonian Empire. The temple in Jerusalem was destroyed and the population decimated by death and exile. The First Temple Period had ended with a disaster, and Israelite religion was poised to disappear into the mists of time like the religions of so many other conquered peoples.

> Exile and return provides "the structure of all Judaism."
>
> —Jacob Neusner

Ark of the Covenant
Sacred box in the tabernacle and then the Temple

First Temple Period
Era of Israelite history from ca. 950 B.C.E. until the destruction of Jerusalem in 586 B.C.E.

prophets Those who spoke for God to ancient Israel to call them to greater obedience

This statue of the prophet Ezekiel by Carlo Chelli (1807–1877) captures Ezekiel's power and intensity as he speaks God's word.

afterward, the Israelite religion survived and emerged from the ancient world into the medieval and modern periods with a continuing religious identity now called *Judaism*. The pattern of exile and return would provide a historical and religious pattern that a leading scholar of Judaism, Jacob Neusner, called "the structure of all Judaism."[2]

10-2d The Second Temple Period (539 B.C.E.–70 C.E.)

In 539 B.C.E. the Babylonians were defeated by Cyrus (SIGH-ruhs) of Persia, a Zoroastrian whose empire covered virtually the whole Near East (see Chapter 9). Cyrus authorized the rebuilding of the Jewish temple of Jerusalem. The exiles would be allowed to return to Judea and live as a subject state within the Persian Empire. In Judea, the new leaders Ezra and Nehemiah zealously promoted a renewed commitment to the covenant made at Mount Sinai. Increasingly, community life was organized around the Torah, which was now in written form as the first five books of the Bible. The Second Temple was completed between 521 and 515, and the **Second Temple Period** would extend until 70 C.E., when the Romans destroyed the Second Temple. During this time, another abiding feature of Jewish life arose: the **Diaspora**, or dispersion, of Jews outside the ancient territory of Israel. Many, perhaps most, of the Jews in Babylon stayed there when others returned to Jerusalem in the 530s. Within a hundred years or so, there would be more Jews living outside the territory of Israel than inside it. Large Jewish communities could be found in Alexandria, Egypt, and in Antioch, Syria, with smaller ones in hundreds of cities that would eventually come into the Roman Empire. This Diaspora situation became permanent in Judaism and endures even today.

In the 330s B.C.E., Alexander of Macedon (in northern Greece) began conquering and amassing the largest empire yet seen, taking Israel in his conquest. Greek culture in Palestine extended until the rise of Islam in the 600s C.E., because many Jews in Palestine were significantly Hellenized in culture while keeping to Judaism. The two centuries after Alexander's conquests saw the formation of Jewish movements with diverse understandings of Judaism. The Sadducees were a priestly movement who accepted only the earliest books of the Bible as authoritative and cooperated with the Romans. The **Pharisees** were a lay movement of Torah teachers who later became religious leaders and developed the oral traditions of

Those carried off to Babylon in the exile were members of the Judean ruling class and skilled craftsmen. Although some exiles probably assimilated into the Babylonian religion, others viewed recent events as confirmation, rather than disproof, of the sovereignty of Israel's God. The warnings of the prophets, remembered in the exile, helped Israel interpret what had happened to them as God's punishment for repeated violations of the covenant. Despite the disaster of 586 B.C.E. and even more disasters that came

Second Temple Period Era of Jewish history from ca. 539 B.C.E. to 70 C.E.

Diaspora [dee-ASS-pohr-uh] Dispersion of Jews outside the ancient territory of Israel

Pharisees [FAIR-uh-seez] Lay movement of Torah teachers who developed the oral traditions of the Torah

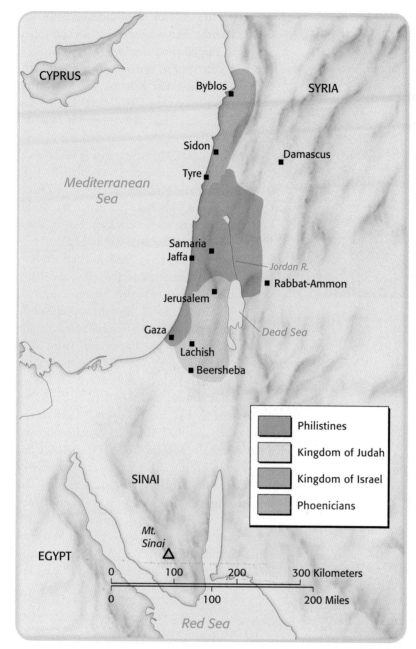

Map 10.1

The Monarchies of Israel and Judah, 922–722 B.C.E.
The northern kingdom of Israel and the southern kingdom of Judah had expanded beyond the traditional areas of the twelve tribes. The kingdom of Israel fell to the Assyrian Empire in 722–721 B.C.E.

the Torah. The **Essenes** probably began the separatist ultra-Torah-observant community at Qumran on the Dead Sea. Various prophetic or messianic movements also arose within Judaism from time to time, including one led by Jesus of Nazareth (4 B.C.E.–30 C.E.) that would later become the Christian religion.

Alexander's successors had a significant impact on Judea and Judaism. After gaining control of Judea in 198 B.C.E., the Seleucid (sell-YOO-sid) dynasty of Greek rulers that controlled the Middle East rewarded the pro-Seleucid faction of Jews. Then the Seleucid king suspected a revolt, captured Jerusalem, and plundered the Temple in 168 B.C.E. The Temple was rededicated to the Greek high god Zeus, and pagan sacrifices were made there. Many Jews were outraged, and when foundational Jewish observances such as circumcision and Sabbath observance were forbidden on pain of death, the **Maccabean Revolt** broke out. The revolt was led by Judas Maccabeus, of the Hasmonean clan, and his sons. The Seleucid armies were defeated, and the Temple was liberated and rededicated to God in December, 164 B.C.E., an event commemorated by Jews to this day in the winter festival of **Hanukkah**. Before and during the revolt, many devout Jews were tortured and killed, leading to the first written accounts of Jewish martyrs. Their example has echoed strongly through Jewish history to now. In 142 B.C.E., independence was secured, and the Hasmonean family ruled the small kingdom of Judea for several generations. The Hasmoneans ruled until the Roman general Pompey captured Jerusalem in 63 B.C.E. and took Judea into the Roman Empire.

King Herod ruled Israel by Roman appointment from 37 to 4 B.C.E. He undertook extensive and ambitious building projects, including a complete rebuilding of the Temple in Jerusalem, making it one of the most magnificent temples in the Roman Empire. However, he was hated by many Jews not only for his cruelty and his loyalty to Rome, but also because many Jews doubted if he really was Jewish by birth. Relations between the Jews and their Roman overlords steadily deteriorated, and Rome appointed its own governors to the area after Herod died.

Essenes [ESS-eenz] Separatist ultra-Torah-observant movement, probably founded the Qumran settlement

Maccabean Revolt [MAK-uh-BEE-uhn] Rebellion against Hellenistic rulers, led by Judas Maccabeus and his sons

Hanukkah [HAHN-uh-kuh] Winter festival commemorating the rededication of the Temple in 164 B.C.E.

BORIS DIAKOVSKY/SHUTTERSTOCK.COM

A modern model of the Second Temple, with an adjoining Roman fort

10-2e Revolts and Rabbis (70 C.E.–ca. 650)

In 66 C.E., a full-scale Jewish revolt broke out against Rome. Although it began well, with the Romans being chased out, it ended very differently than the Maccabean Revolt. Rome summoned all its military might to crush the revolt, slaughtering combatants and noncombatants alike. It destroyed the Temple in 70 C.E., ending the Second Temple Period, and a permanent transformation of Judaism resulted. The Temple had been the only place that represented the whole nation of God and was the location of great religious events such as Jewish festivals and the Day of Atonement. It was also the only place where sacrifices could be offered to God. The destruction of the Temple was a disaster for Judaism, and the end of the revolt against Rome brought the end of every group in Judaism except the Pharisees, who would eventually take over the religion's leadership.

rabbis [RAB-ighs] Teachers of the law and successors of the Pharisees who eventually gained authority over Judaism

synagogue [SIN-uh-gawg] Gathering of local Jews in a congregation for worship and community life

anti-Semitism [SEHM-ih-TIHZ-um] Prejudice and discrimination against the Jewish people

Jewish hopes for independence and Roman heavy-handed tactics continued in the ensuing decades, climaxing in a revolt in 130 led by messianic claimant Simon Bar Kochba. This rebellion was also crushed by Rome. The Jewish population had now been hit hard by two wars of their own making in only sixty years. However, during this period a group connected to pre-70 C.E. scribes and Pharisees preserved a Torah-centered, lay-led Judaism. It would be at least two centuries before these teachers, or **rabbis**, would begin to win broader influence and judicial authority over Judaism. In the 300s and 400s, the rabbis gradually became spiritual leaders in local Jewish communities, the **synagogues**. The influence of the rabbis was so important from 400 to 1800 C.E. that this long period is sometimes called Rabbinic Judaism. Even today, professional leaders of synagogues are called rabbis.

When Christianity became the official faith of the Roman Empire around 400 C.E., Jews were allowed to survive but not thrive. From about 100 to 400 C.E., Christianity and Judaism had been in the process of separation, and mutual hostility was often strong. The Code of Justinian in 527 C.E. contained discriminatory legislation against the Jews and Judaism that was to influence European legal systems for centuries and contribute to **anti-Semitism**, prejudice and discrimination against the Jewish people. Anti-Semitism isn't Christian

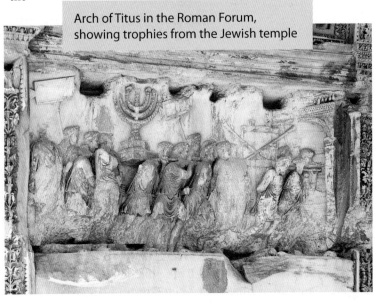
Arch of Titus in the Roman Forum, showing trophies from the Jewish temple

© MATT RAGEN/SHUTTERSTOCK.COM

or even European in origin or expression. Its oldest forms can be traced to 500 B.C.E. in Egypt, and today the strongest forms of it are found in the Muslim Middle East. Despite these hardships, or perhaps because of them, many Jews chose to form their communities around synagogues. The local synagogue became the chief organization of Jewish life in late antiquity and remained so until the modern period.

The single most important Jewish community from about 600 to 1500 C.E. was in Babylonia, outside the sphere of Greek, Roman, and Christian power. The work of the rabbinic academy in Babylon centered first on the Mishnah, a collection of primarily legal traditions based on all aspects of the Torah—what we today would call civil, criminal, and religious law—produced in Palestine and brought to Babylonia in the early third century C.E. Generations of Babylonian rabbis discussed the Mishnah and related teachings, adding to them and ultimately producing a huge legal work known as the **Babylonian Talmud**. Rabbinic Judaism is the Torah-centered way of life that finds expression in the vast sea of materials produced by Palestinian and Babylonian rabbis from 70 to 630 C.E., particularly the Babylonian Talmud. The Talmud achieved a remarkable degree of power in Jewish communities worldwide, a power that withstood serious challenges well into the early modern period. All forms of Judaism in the medieval and modern ages are built on, or react to, this foundation of Rabbinic Judaism.

All forms of Judaism in the medieval and modern ages are built on, or react to, . . . Rabbinic Judaism.

10-2f Jews under Islamic and Christian Rule (ca. 650–1800)

Jews in the medieval period lived under either Muslim or Christian rule. Muslims guaranteed religious toleration as long as the Jews recognized the supremacy of the Islamic rule. They had a second-class but protected status. On the whole, Jews adapted well to the Islamic regime and the political, economic, and social changes that it brought.

Some rabbis from these **Sephardic** Jewish communities—in the Middle East, North Africa, and Spain—were interested in the philosophical clarification of religious beliefs and the systematic presentation of their faith, just as Muslim and Christian theologians were doing. The most prominent medieval Jewish philosopher was Rabbi Moses ben Maimon (1135–1204),

known as Maimonides (my-MON-ih-dees). His *Guide for the Perplexed* is for a student whose education left him confused about his faith—a common situation even today for many students from a religious background! Maimonides was a brilliant legal scholar whose fourteen-volume work on Jewish law immediately became authoritative. In modern editions of the Talmud, his views are often cited.

The intense rationalism of medieval Jewish philosophy was undergirded by a rational system of Talmud interpretation. This emphasis on rational thought and action was countered by the rise of Jewish mysticism, emphasizing the immediate, personal, and nonrational experience of God. In twelfth-century France and thirteenth-century Spain, mystical forms of Judaism would combine with mainstream Judaism to produce **Kabbalah** (see "A Closer Look: Kabbalah"). The rabbis condemned such practices, but they grew nonetheless. They remain popular among Jews and non-Jews today.

Jews were outsiders in medieval Christian society in Western, Central, and Eastern Europe, where they called themselves **Ashkenazi**, as distinguished from Sephardic. (This distinction continues through today, where 80 percent of all Jews are Ashkenazi.) Rulers granted them permission to live in specified neighborhoods. In these neighborhoods, Jews ran their own affairs and maintained their own institutions, such as social-relief funds, schools, a synagogue led by a rabbi, a council and court for religious affairs, a bathhouse for ritual cleansing, kosher meat shops, and so on. They developed their own language, Yiddish, a combination of Hebrew and German that originated in Germany but spread widely to European Jews. Jews in Western and Central Europe typically lived in cities. Many of those in Eastern Europe (Poland and Russia) lived in small villages centered on farming, the kind of

Babylonian Talmud [TALL-mood] Jewish law code, a compilation of the "oral Torah"

Sephardic [seh-FAR-dik] Jews in medieval and modern times living in, or originating from, the Middle East, North Africa, and Spain

Kabbalah [KAHB-uh-luh] System of Jewish mysticism emphasizing a personal and emotional experience of God

Ashkenazi [ASH-kuh-NAHZ-ee] Jews living in, or originating from, Western, Central, and Eastern Europe

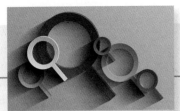

A Closer Look

Kabbalah

Kabbalah pictured God not as a simple unity, but rather as a structured Being with an inner configuration of ten attributes. Evil is believed to be provoked by human sin and set right by good deeds, fulfillment of the commandments, prayer, and mystical contemplation. More esoteric Kabbalistic beliefs have included the transmigration of souls and the practice of sexual intercourse as a mirror of the union of the divine attributes. Many of these ideas are found in *The Zohar*, the leading book on Kabbalah by Moses de Leon (1250–1305). Kabbalah spread quickly, and in the sixteenth century Rabbi Isaac Luria (1534–1572) reformulated this esoteric system to emphasize messianic redemption.

Another offshoot of Kabbalah arose around an itinerant folk healer named Israel ben Eleazar (1700–1760)—more commonly called the Baal Shem Tov (bah-AHL shehm tohv), or Master of the Good Name. This was **Hasidism**, a Jewish mystical movement

A red string worn on the left wrist is a prominent sign of Kabbalah today.

that stresses joyful emotion. Hasidism soon attracted Jews in Russia, Poland, Hungary, and Romania. The message of the Hasidic masters was that God is present and directly accessible in the world, that God is best experienced and worshiped in joy, that even the most evil persons and events are capable of redemption, and that each Jew has an essential role to play in making the world holy. The new Hasidic pietism drew on Kabbalah in a way that overcame its esoteric character.

Today, Kabbalah has popularized and spread beyond Judaism. Its psychological and social aspects are emphasized, and its Torah-related and messianic elements have been muted. Although controversial among observant Jews, today there are hundreds of Kabbalah centers, conferences, books, and other sources of information about Kabbalah practice, nearly all of them catering to non-Jews. The most prominent practitioner of Kabbalah today is the pop singer Madonna (see the beginning of Section 10-5).

---

society depicted in an 1894 collection of short stories by Sholem Aleichem (SHOH-luhm uh-LIGHK-uhm), which became the basis of the Broadway musical and 1971 film *Fiddler on the Roof*.

In the 1200s, decrees by the Roman Catholic Church after the Fourth Lateran Council altered the life of European Jews. Christians were now forbidden to lend money at interest, so Jews were free to move into banking, which they did with great success. Direct restrictions on Jews arose at this time: wearing distinctive clothing (especially hats) or a yellow badge alerting others to their presence; exclusion from the crafts and trades by guilds that controlled access to training and jobs;

Hasidism [HASS-uh-DIHZ-um] Jewish mystical movement that stresses joyful emotion

ghetto Neighborhood to which Jews were restricted

exclusion from the new universities being founded in Europe; restriction to Jewish neighborhoods called **ghettos**; and special permission required to work outside the ghetto. The rising view of Jews as dangerous was fueled by envy, irrational suspicions, and even hatred, which led to repeated expulsions and massacres. Jews were expelled from France in 1182 and 1306, and from England in 1290. Devastating massacres occurred in Germany in 1298, wiping out 140 Jewish communities, and in 1348 to 1349, when the Black Plague was falsely attributed to Jews poisoning wells. In 1492 Spain expelled all Jews, estimated to be between 100,000 and 150,000 people. Many of them fled to temporary safety in Portugal, some of whom eventually went to The Netherlands—one of the few relatively safe havens for Jews in Europe. The Protestant Reformation in the 1500s was a mixed blessing to the Jews of northern Europe. In some places, such as The Netherlands and

The Hurva Synagogue in Jerusalem is built on a medieval layout, with the reading desk and preaching area in the middle of the floor.

©ASAF ELIASON/SHUTTERSTOCK.COM

England, Protestant reformers treated them with some tolerance. But in Germany, the Protestant reformer Martin Luther eventually resumed some aspects of anti-Jewish sentiment—after a more tolerant start—in ways that would echo through later German history.

10-2g Emancipation and Diversity (1800–1932)

Around 1800, under the influence of the Enlightenment, many Western European nations began to drop their restrictions on Jews. No longer did Jews have to live in their own neighborhood, be subject to the local rabbi, or dress and talk like Jews. In less than a century, many Jews rose to become some of the leading figures in science, medicine, education, commerce, and banking. (This astonishing level of achievement continued in the twentieth century, when one-quarter of all Nobel Prize winners were Jewish.) Their **emancipation**, freedom from Christian and state control, prompted many nineteenth-century Jews to wonder why they should continue to be Jews when they could be citizens of European states. Many modern Jews chose to assimilate, which sometimes included conversion to Christianity.

> Many Jews in the early 1800s began to question why they should shoulder a "double yoke" of being both Jewish and European—why not just assimilate completely?

Many other Jews responded that Jewish identity was not primarily ethnic or national, but religious. One could be a loyal citizen of a European nation but still keep the Jewish religion. They urged not assimilation, but *acculturation*—that is, taking on the culture of one's nation while retaining Jewish religious faith. Just as Christians could practice their religion as citizens of different nations, so too should Jews. German-Jewish intellectual, Moses Mendelssohn (MEN-dul-sohn; 1729–1786), was an influential example of those who embraced modernity while staying Jewish. He urged Jews to participate in European culture and to continue in Judaism—what he called the "double yoke" placed on them by God.

However, many Jews in the early 1800s began to question why they should shoulder this "double yoke"—why not just assimilate completely? This questioning, and doubts about some elements of traditional Judaism that looked increasingly odd to many modern Jews, sparked controversies among mostly German Jews in the mid-1800s. The controversies eventually led to the three main branches of Judaism today—usually called movements: Reform, Orthodox, and Conservative. The **Reform** movement, led by Abraham Geiger (1820–1874), was the first new form of Judaism to arise. Geiger wanted to change Judaism into a modern religion with patterns of worship and devotion similar to those of German Protestant Christianity. Reform synagogues were renamed temples, as they are still known today, and services were no longer conducted in Hebrew, but German. Reform Judaism gave up kosher food regulations, Jewish dress and hair codes, the Yiddish language, and other traditional aspects. It ended beliefs and practices it considered not a part of the spiritual essence of Judaism. The Reform movement quickly spread through much of Europe and North America.

emancipation Jewish freedom from Christian and state control in Europe after 1800

Reform Movement founded by Abraham Geiger; most liberal of the three main Jewish branches

Traditionalist Jews condemned these changes as a betrayal of Judaism. (This condemnation continues today; for example, the current Israeli President Reuven Rivlin once insulted Reform Judaism by calling it "idol worship.") They viewed their form of Judaism as the only legitimate continuation of Rabbinic Judaism and biblical Israel. The leader of the modern **Orthodox** movement was Samson Raphael Hirsch (1808–1888). Hirsch urged a combination of traditional Jewish religious practices and selective appreciation of European civilization. He criticized the Reform movement for diminishing Judaism for the convenience and contentment of modern Jews. Instead, he urged the Orthodox movement to prompt Jews toward classical Judaism in a fresh and vigorous way. Because of their high birthrate and ability to keep most of their children in the faith, the Orthodox continue to grow in numbers in Europe and North America.

A third main branch of Judaism came to be known in North America as the **Conservative** movement. It was led by German-Bohemian rabbi and scholar Zecharias Frankel (FRAHN-kuhl; 1801–1875). It claimed the middle ground between Reform and Orthodox. In that sense, moderate Judaism would be a better name for it than Conservative Judaism, but the latter name stuck. (In Israel and Europe today, this movement is known as **Masorti**, "traditionalist.") It opposed Reform's sweeping changes by affirming the positive value of much of past Judaism in which the voice of God could be discerned. The Conservative movement opposed the Orthodox movement by asserting the historical evolution of the Judaic tradition, which Orthodoxy denied with its claim that the whole Law of God—the written form in the Bible and the oral form in the Talmud—was revealed to Moses on Mount Sinai.

A modern Reform synagogue

©RON ZMIRI/SHUTTERSTOCK.COM

Although many European Jews were hopeful about the future of Judaism, a wide outbreak of hostility toward the Jews in the 1870s and 1880s cast a dark shadow on their sunny optimism. Modern anti-Semitism was a backlash against Jewish success in Europe, a sign that Jews were still considered outsiders. In earlier times, anti-Semitism had a mainly religious basis, but in modern Europe it was increasingly based on ethnicity. In the light of this revived anti-Semitism, Jewish movements sprang up, emphasizing newfound Jewish nationalism. Most important was **Zionism**, so called after an ancient Hebrew name for Jerusalem, which aimed for large Jewish emigration from Europe to Palestine. In 1897, Theodor Herzl (HURT-zuhl; 1860–1904) organized the First Zionist Congress in Basel, Switzerland, which called for an internationally recognized Jewish national home in Palestine. The Zionist movement was largely secular in orientation. With continued anti-Semitism in Europe, increasing numbers of Jewish immigrants settled in Palestine and began to set up the social infrastructure of a modern nation. The quest for a Jewish nation free from the threats of anti-Semitism was well on its way.

> "A land without a people for a people without a land."
> —Zionist slogan

The Zionist slogan was "a land without a people for a people without a land," but the Jewish settlers there found that Palestine wasn't really a land without a people. Arabs in the hundreds of thousands, both Muslims and Christians, were living in Palestine when Zionist settlement began, and their ancestors had been living in that small territory for more than a thousand years. Moreover, Palestinians were culturally advanced among the various Arab groups, and still are today. As the numbers of Jewish settlers increased, friction grew with the Arab population. Freedom for European Jews would come at the expense of a future conflict between Israeli Jews and Arabs, in which they would be locked in a long struggle for a land they both considered holy. Islam had been tolerant of Judaism for 1,300 years but now became rather intolerant, largely because of long-standing Muslim resistance to non-Muslims taking their holy land. Several wars were fought between Israel and its Arab neighbors from 1948 through today, all of them won by Israel, sometimes at a high cost (see Map 10.2). A few peace treaties have been signed, but some conflict continues. Jewish settlement in Israel grew quickly after the events of World War II, especially after Germany's extermination of the majority of European Jews. We now turn to a brief examination of this horrific story.

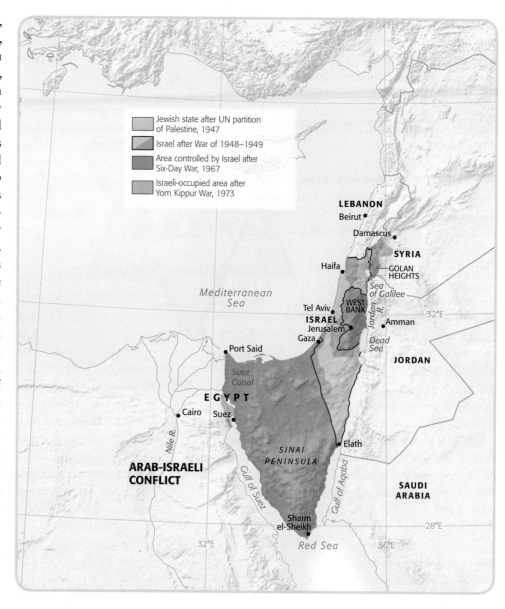

Map 10.2

Arab-Israeli Conflict, 1947–Present

By Egyptian-Israeli agreements of 1975 and 1979, Israel withdrew from the Sinai in 1982. By 1981 Israel annexed the Golan Heights in Syria. Through negotiations between Israel and the PLO, the West Bank and the Gaza Strip were placed under Palestinian self-rule, and Israeli troops were withdrawn in 1994. In 1994, Israel and Jordan signed an agreement opening their borders and normalizing their relations. In 2014, Israel and Palestinians in Gaza fought a brutal war; the United Nations has charged that both sides committed war crimes.

10-2h The Holocaust and Its Aftermath (1932–Present)

Adolf Hitler and his Nazi Party won office in the 1932 German national elections, and in 1933 Hitler quickly moved toward totalitarian power with a variety of repressive measures. Some of these pursued Nazi ideology to purify Germany through a series of anti-Semitic laws gradually introduced between 1933 and 1938. Germans who had just one grandparent who was Jewish by ethnicity—on a synagogue roll, for example, or a member of a secular Jewish organization—were deemed to be Jewish, whether or not they thought of themselves as Jewish. Jews had to wear a yellow star in public for identification. Marriage and sexual relations between Jews and so-called Aryan Germans were banned, and by 1938 all German Jews had been stripped of their citizenship and civil rights, and some from their professional jobs. Some Jews fled as these laws were passed, but the majority stayed, hoping that each new restriction would be the last.

These hopes were in vain. When World War II began in 1939, Hitler ordered a "Final Solution" of the "Jewish Question." The term **Holocaust** (a term from Jewish ritual literally meaning a completely burned sacrifice) came after the war, and was used to describe the Nazi genocide of Jews and other groups; the Hebrew term **Shoah**, "destruction," is also used. When Germany invaded Poland, special assignment groups of German troops held mass executions of hundreds of thousands of Jews who lived in villages and towns in newly conquered territory. But this soon proved inefficient. In 1942, the German government erected concentration camps in western Germany and occupied Poland, after the model of the first camp in Dachau. The purpose of these camps was not to concentrate Jews, but to kill them with all the efficiency of state-run mass murder. Jews from Germany and Poland were brought by train to be killed by poison gas or to work to death as slave laborers in adjoining factories. Then Jews from every other nation in Nazi-occupied Europe—especially Russia, Hungary, France, and The

Badge worn by Jews in Nazi Germany. "Jude" (pronounced YOO-deh) is German for "Jew."

©NACI YAVUZ/SHUTTERSTOCK.COM

Netherlands—were hunted down and brought by train to the camps. The Nazi aim of the Final Solution was to make not only Germany, but all of Europe, Jew-free. Approximately 6 million Jews perished in this Holocaust/Shoah, nearly three-quarters of Europe's Jewish population.

Relatively few Germans dared—or cared—to risk death by opposing the actions of their government. Among the famous examples of those who did are Roman Catholic industrialist Oskar Schindler, who protected 1,200 Jewish workers from death, and Protestant theologian Dietrich Bonhoeffer (BAHN-haw-fuhr), who spoke out against anti-Semitism and Nazi control of German churches. Bonhoeffer also participated in a failed plot to kill Hitler; the Nazis hanged him shortly before the war ended. When Schindler died in 1974, he was buried with great honors in Jerusalem.

The Holocaust brought a crisis of faith to Judaism like no event before it. To adapt Jacob Neusner's phrase, it was an "exile" from which "return" was extremely difficult. Orthodox Jews in general explained the Holocaust as punishment for recent Jewish sins, as a test of faith, or even as an opportunity to die for the

Holocaust [HAUL-oh-cost] Nazi genocide of Jews and other groups in World War II

Shoah [SHOW-uh] "Destruction," Hebrew term for the Holocaust

©ASAF ELIASON/SHUTTERSTOCK.COM

At a Holocaust memorial along the Danube River in Budapest, Hungary, shoes mark the area where hundreds of Hungarian Jews were ordered to remove their shoes before they were shot and put into the river.

faith. For many other Jews, it shook the foundations of Judaism. Some Jews, such as Richard Rubenstein, said that the only possible valid response to the Holocaust was the rejection of God. If God could allow the Holocaust, then there was no God. Many Jews agreed with this, and the abandonment of traditional beliefs and practices of Jewish religion that had begun in the Jewish emancipation accelerated. On the other hand, Emil Fackenheim and others insisted that the Holocaust did *not* show that God was dead. To reject Judaism's God, Fackenheim said, was to aid Hitler in the accomplishment of his evil goal to destroy Judaism. Whatever the best response to the Holocaust—not yet a settled question in Judaism—the field of religious studies has given it a large and important place in teaching and research. Around one hundred Holocaust museums, memorials, and study centers have sprung up in North American cities. Popular literature and film have also dealt extensively with the Holocaust.

10-3 Essential Teachings of Judaism

A Jewish woman enters her home in Los Angeles. Just before she goes through her front door, she looks at a small box fastened to the right frame of the door. It contains a small scroll with three short passages from the Hebrew Bible, especially the key words of Deuteronomy 6:4–9: "Take to heart these instructions. . . . Recite them when you stay at home and when you are away, when you lie down and when you get up. . . . Inscribe them on the doorposts of your house and on your gates." She touches this box reverently as a reminder to remember God and keep God's teachings within her home. This little ritual act displays a key characteristic of Judaism: It is a religion of action more than a religion of reflection.

Judaism as a whole has no official statement of its essential teachings. Unlike many other religions, it has rarely argued over doctrine to the point of division. The closest it came to a confession was the *Thirteen Articles* of Maimonides, but this was never widely accepted as a formal statement of Jewish teaching, in its time or later. Persons are Jewish whether they hold to a system of traditional Jewish teachings, have simple beliefs associated with rituals such as the Passover meal, or don't embrace any traditional Jewish teachings at all. This situation arises largely because actions in accordance with the Torah, not beliefs, are the most important aspect of Jewish religious life. Today, *Jewish* describes a people and a culture

as well as a religion, so some who call themselves Jewish have little interest in any Jewish religious practices and even less in the teachings of Judaism.

10-3a Foundation of Jewish Teachings: The Tanak

The foundation of Jewish teaching and ethics is the Jewish Bible, commonly called the **Tanak**. This name is an acronym formed from the first letters of the three divisions of the Bible: the Torah (instruction, law); the second division, called the Nevi'im (prophets); and the third, the Kethuvim (writings). The Jewish scriptures arose over a period of more than a thousand years, and the Tanak was finalized only in the first century C.E. Even before this finalization, a translation into Greek called the *Septuagint* (sep-TOO-uh-jint) had been made in second-century B.C.E. Egypt for Jews who had lived so long in the Diaspora that they had lost their knowledge of the Hebrew language. In the consolidation of Judaism that occurred after the Jewish revolt against Rome in 66–70 C.E., the status of this Greek translation fell. Soon only the Hebrew Bible was used in synagogues, even though many Jews could not understand it.

Even more important than the particular documents of the Bible is the authority that Jews have traditionally invested in the biblical canon. Traditionalist Jews view it to be the written revelation of God—containing God's very words. The Bible is especially authoritative in expressing what God expects the Jewish people to do in response to the divine self-revelation. It conveys and shapes the faith and action of Jews through all times. As Jean-Christophe Attias has shown in his recent book, *The Jews and the Bible*, Jews have debated the meaning of the Bible, have often strongly disagreed about it, have studied it with modern scholarly methods, and some have even rejected it, but a majority of Jews accept the Bible as their special book in some significant sense.[3]

Despite the lack of primary emphasis on teaching in Judaism, the Bible and Talmud contain a great deal of teaching about God, humanity, and the meaning of life. Jewish history has seen significant theological and mystical inquiry into religious concepts. We'll consider three main teachings: one God, the chosen people, and life after death. (We'll also consider other foundational teachings— the position in the Torah on obedience to God's will and the concept of *ethical monotheism*—in Section 10.4.)

Tanak [TAH-nahk] Name for the Hebrew Bible, from the first letters of Torah, Nevi'im, and Kethuvim

10-3b One God

Judaism teaches monotheism, meaning that Jews believe that only one God exists. Hebrew and Israelite religion acknowledged the possible existence of other gods, but only one God for Israel. This **henotheism**—the belief in one God while accepting that other gods may exist—seems to have been prevalent in ancient Israel. For example, Canaanite gods were worshiped at Israelite holy places shortly after Israelite settlement in their promised land, King David named some of his children after Canaanite gods, and Solomon built a shrine to a Canaanite fertility goddess outside Jerusalem.

Full, formal monotheism seems to have come during the Babylonian exile in the 500s B.C.E. As we saw earlier, the return from Babylon featured a strict enforcement of monotheism, and Judaism has continued in it ever since. Israel's God is eternal, holy, all knowing, all present, all powerful. God is a divine being, not a principle or a force. God guides not only those who know him, but also the nations and human history. God is transcendent, far above the world and human ability to comprehend God, but God is immanent as well, present in the world and in each human being. Because God is holy and just, God punishes humans for their disobedience, particularly those who know the Torah; but because God is merciful, God forgives and renews relationships.

How individual Jews choose to relate to God has varied in different times and places. Some have related to God by studying and keeping the Torah, by formal worship in the two Temples and in synagogues, with piety and emotion, and occasionally even with mysticism. An important part of Jewish piety relating to monotheism

The name for God in Hebrew, YHWH, in the Dohany Street Synagogue in Budapest, Hungary

is the **Shema**, a basic statement of faith from Deuteronomy 6 that begins "Hear, O Israel: The Lord our God is One." Some Jews today even relate to God by denying God's existence, but ironically this too has become a Jewish option.

Judaism's names for God are an important aspect of its teaching about God. The holiest name of God, as God revealed it to Moses in the book of Exodus, is YHWH. This name seems to be built on the Hebrew verb *to be* and means either "I am" or "I will be." When vowels were added to written Hebrew in the Middle Ages, this name was considered too holy to be changed, so we don't know its original pronunciation. The common word *Jehovah* (jeh-HOH-vuh), however, is incorrect as a vocalization. A more grammatically correct spelling and pronunciation, one used by scholars, is *Yahweh* (YAH-weh; one often hears YAH-way as well). Nevertheless, this discussion is irrelevant to many Jews, because they don't pronounce God's

henotheism Belief in one God while accepting that other gods may exist

Shema [sheh-MAH, or shmah] Statement of faith from Deuteronomy 6 that begins "Hear, O Israel: The Lord our God is One"

Observant Jews wear kippahs out of reverence for God.

name. When the Torah is read aloud, *Adonai* (ad-oh-NAI), meaning "Lord" is read in place of YHWH. This practice is reflected in many English translations, including in the Christian Bible, in which YHWH is rendered as "Lord." Jews demonstrate their reverence for God in a simple way, by wearing a skullcap called a *kippah* (KIHP-uh) or *yarmulke* (YAHR-muhl-kuh, sometimes YAH-mah-kuh).

Many traditionalist Jews also refer to God as *Hashem* (hah-SHEHM), "the Name," understanding that God, not just God's name, is meant. The prohibition against pronouncing God's name expresses a profound human reverence for God. Many modern Orthodox Jews and some Conservative Jews carry this reverence for God's name one step further. They refrain from writing the word *God*, replacing it instead with *G-d*. Other branches of modern Judaism do not follow them in this practice, saying that *God* is a generic noun, not a biblical name.

10-3c The Jews as God's Chosen People

The Jews believe that they are God's chosen people, that is, chosen to be in a covenant with God. They didn't choose God; God chose them. This status carries both responsibilities and blessings, as described in the biblical accounts of the covenants with God.

According to the Tanak, Israel's character as the chosen people goes all the way back to Abraham and the eternal covenant God made with him: "I will establish my covenant between me and you and your descendants after you in their generations, for an everlasting covenant, to be God to you and your descendants after you" (Genesis 17:7). Being chosen as God's people brings a call to be holy and a realization of how amazing this is: "For you are a holy people to YHWH your God, and God has chosen you to be his treasured people from all the nations that are on the face of the earth" (Deuteronomy 14:2). This choice is based on God's love, not on Israel's own qualities: "The Lord did not set his love upon you or choose you because you were more in number than any people, for you were the fewest of all people. It was because the Lord loved you, and because he would keep the oath which he had sworn to your ancestors" (Deuteronomy 7:7–8).

> Being God's chosen people is mostly a blessing, but sometimes a mixed blessing that brings trouble.

The flip side of this chosen status is demanding, even ominous at times. Alongside the positive aspects, there is the necessity of obedience: "If you will obey my voice indeed, and keep my covenant, then you shall be a peculiar treasure unto me above all people" (Exodus 19:5). The obligation, even threat, that this demand for obedience entails is emphasized by the prophet Amos: "You only have I singled out of all the families of the earth; therefore will I punish you for all your iniquities" (Amos 3:2). Despite their status as a part of the chosen people, the ten Northern Kingdom tribes of the Israelites were wiped away in 721 B.C.E. because they disobeyed God continually. Jews throughout history have found their belief in being God's chosen people mostly a blessing, but sometimes a mixed blessing that brings troubles with both God and other people. A wry reflection about this mixed blessing is in the musical *Fiddler on the Roof*, when Tevye (the main character), beset by difficulties, prays, "I know we are the chosen people. But once in a while, can't you choose someone else?"

Jewish clothing, hairstyles, and the hidden sign of circumcision have helped to define Jewish status as a chosen people. Here, a young Orthodox Jew stands behind his father in Jerusalem.

Throughout its history, Judaism has usually linked being the chosen people with a mission or purpose, such as being a "light to the nations," a "blessing to the nations," or a "kingdom of priests" between God and the world. This special duty derives from the covenant God made with Abraham, which was renewed at the giving of the Torah on Mount Sinai. Through the long history of Judaism, the idea of being God's chosen people sustained many Jews throughout military defeat and exile, discrimination, persecution, and even the Holocaust. In modern times, secular Jews have understood it to mean that their human abilities should be put to use for the good of all humankind. British historian Paul Johnson sums it up well: Historians cannot validate the religious claim that God actually chose the Jews and guided their history, but "the Jews believed that they were a special people with such unanimity and passion, and over so long a span, that they became one."[4]

10-3d Life after Death?

As the Hebrew Bible book of Job (johb) puts it, "If mortals die, will they live again?" (Job 14:14). However, the Tanak doesn't say much on this subject, and Judaism as a whole today doesn't dwell on it. This may seem surprising to non-Jews, because the sacred texts of Christianity and Islam—both of which have their foundations in Judaism—speak often about life after death. But with Judaism's focus on actions more than on beliefs, it is logical that it would not speculate about the world to come. Because many religions, including Judaism's sister faiths of Christianity and Islam, rely in part on fear of hell and the hope of heaven to motivate good conduct in their adherents, it is remarkable that Judaism, with its strong emphasis on morality, hasn't usually done the same.

An early common theme in the Bible is that death means joining one's ancestors in the land of the dead—being "gathered to one's people" (Genesis 25:8, 25:17, 35:29, 49:33; Deuteronomy 42:50). Another image emphasizes the reality of mortality. God made humans from the dust of the ground, and because of their sins they die and return to dust (Genesis 3:19). Jews take this literally: Today they regularly use wooden coffins that allow the body to rejoin the ground over time. The predominant biblical image of the afterlife is *Sheol* (SHEE-ohl), which is similar to the Greek conception of Hades. Sheol is a shadowy underworld, a land of darkness and silence (Psalms 88:13, 115:17; Job 10:21, 22). Good and evil people alike go to Sheol, and God isn't present there. These early biblical descriptions of death indicate a belief that the person continues to exist in some way after death, but not with a full or happy life. Much later in the biblical tradition the concept arises of the **resurrection** of the dead—divine raising of the dead body to eternal life—and a final judgment leading to either a blessed or a damned life. Daniel 12:2 declares, "And many of them that sleep in the dust of the earth shall awake, some to everlasting life and some to reproaches and everlasting abhorrence."

Belief in resurrection was near universal in rabbinic Judaism all the way to the time of the Jewish Enlightenment in 1800. The resurrection is one of the *Thirteen Articles* by Maimonides, and a prayer said regularly in traditionalist synagogues from medieval times through

Jewish cemetery on the Mount of Olives, facing the former site of the Temple; bodies are buried in the ground, not in the grave-covering structures.

©YOSEFER/SHUTTERSTOCK.COM

resurrection Raising of the bodies of the dead to eternal life

today affirms the resurrection. One early rabbi, Hiyya ben Joseph, suggested that the dead will travel through the ground and rise up in Jerusalem; the unrighteous will be naked and ashamed, and the righteous will be clothed and happy (Babylonian Talmud, Ketubot 111b). The hope of being raised in Jerusalem has led to large cemeteries there, especially on the Mount of Olives. Despite belief in a divine judgment that separates those whose deeds are on balance good from those whose deeds are not, some rabbis held that a middle group of people of more mixed accomplishments will go into hell for an eleven-month period of purification and then enter heaven (Babylonian Talmud, Rosh Hashanah 16b–17a, Eduyot 2.10). This belief is probably connected to the Jewish practice of eleven months of mourning deceased loved ones.

Most Jews have believed that one need not be Jewish to enter heaven. Because God judges actions and not beliefs, all those who do what God commands will be rewarded. Maimonides, for example, wrote that all good people of the world will be blessed in the next world. Those who are righteous among the Gentiles (non-Jews) by virtue of their deeds, even if they belong to a different religion, will enter heaven. Heaven is typically called the Garden of Eden, a place of joy and peace that recaptures the original home of humanity on earth. The Babylonian Talmud's imagery of heaven includes sitting at banquet tables (Taanit 25a), enjoying lavish banquets (Baba Batra 75a), and even enjoying heavenly sex with spouses (Berachot 57b). A few rabbis didn't like this imagery and held that there will be no eating, drinking, or sex in heaven—or if there is, they won't be quite so enjoyable. Instead, the blessed will enjoy heaven in a purely spiritual way (Babylonian Talmud, Berachot 17a).

As stated earlier, this Talmudic teaching on the afterlife prevailed in virtually all of Judaism from about 400 to 1800 C.E. Today, Orthodox Jewish groups still teach the resurrection of the dead, judgment by God, and life in heaven or hell. Reform Judaism, on the other hand, rejected these doctrines as binding. Instead, its members are allowed to form their own opinions on life after death. The general view in the Reform movement, drawn from Enlightenment ideas, is that even if there is existence after death, we can't know much about it here, so it shouldn't play a large role in how people live. Human immortality, Reform Jews hold, is

> "I don't believe in [an afterlife]. I believe this is it, and I believe it's the best way to live."
> —Natalie Portman

realized in one's children and the spiritual legacy one leaves behind. As a result, many Reform Jews and secular Jews have no belief in life after death. For example, when the Israeli-American actress Natalie Portman—who was raised, as she says, "Jewish but not religious"—was asked about her concept of the afterlife, she said, "I don't believe in that. I believe this is it, and I believe it's the best way to live." The Conservative movement, between Orthodoxy and Reform, holds to the continued importance of this topic, but notes its historical conditioning and interprets its more vivid imagery as symbolic.

10-4 Essential Jewish Ethics

In Grand Rapids, Michigan, a short controversy breaks out in the press over the religious implications of a museum exhibit called "Bodies Revealed." This exhibit, which has played in several other North American cities, shows fourteen full human bodies and hundreds of organs in various states of dissection. The museum's website says it has anticipated the controversy that has followed the exhibition as it travels, so it has consulted ethical and religious experts about bringing the exhibit to town. Although it is popular, with excellent ticket sales, some controversy is aired publicly. An articulate examination is in a newspaper column by a widely respected local rabbi, David Krishef. Rabbi Krishef examines the good that can come from the exhibit, but, he asks, at what cost? He raises the traditional Jewish moral command to honor the bodies of the dead, not to display them to the public for profit, entertainment, or even education.

The moral life of the Jewish people today, of all branches, rests on biblical foundations. God created the world as a good place, to reflect God's own glory and goodness, and as a place for human culture in all its fullness. When human beings rebelled against God, God went in search of them, calling Abraham to live in covenant with God. God not only searches and redeems humans, but also commands them to follow his way. For the rabbis of antiquity and the Middle Ages, and for Orthodox and a majority of Conservatives today, the moral code of the Bible is composed of laws that demand obedience—they are indeed commandments, not general moral guidelines. In their understanding, God didn't give the "Ten Suggestions."

10-4a Humans in the Image of God

Jewish morality and ethics rest on the foundation of ethical monotheism. Not only is God one and the only God, but also God is perfectly right and righteous. Holiness is at the center of God's nature; God is good, just, and compassionate. The people God put in the good world he made are created to live in conformity with God's nature and will. The Torah given by God enables people to know more exactly what God's will is, but a basic notion of God's will is written in every human heart. In contrast with other religions of the ancient Near East, evil is not built into the structure of the material universe, but rather is the product of human choices. Humans are free moral agents.

A fundamental Jewish teaching shared by nearly all Jews today (except those who reject the existence of God, of course) is that human beings are created in the "image of God." Israelites and Jews never took this to mean that humans somehow physically look like God, because God is a spirit and invisible to the human eye. Although the Bible doesn't explain the "image of God" in detail, Jews have interpreted it to mean that humans can think rationally and have a moral sense to know what is right. Because humans are created in God's image, they have the ability to know and even act like God.

The early rabbis taught that God built two moral impulses into each human being: the "good impulse" called the *yetzer hatov* (YAY-tser ha-TOHV) and the "evil impulse," the *yetzer hara* (YAY-tser ha-RAH). The good impulse is the moral conscience that reminds a person of God's law and creates an urge to follow it. The evil impulse is the urge to satisfy one's own needs and desires. Despite its name, there's nothing intrinsically evil about the evil impulse, because God created it and it's a part of human life. The evil impulse, acting with the good impulse, drives us to eat, drink, have sex, and make a living—all necessary and good things. However, it can easily lead to sin when not held in check and balanced by the good impulse, and

this is why it is called evil. Eating, drinking, having sex, and making money can be taken to extremes and can destroy human life. The competing effect of the good impulse and the evil impulse is similar to having an angel on one shoulder and a devil on the other, each urging a particular course of action. Some rabbis have been uncomfortable about talk of a created evil impulse and have preferred to speak of one impulse that can be used in two different ways.

> The competing effect of the good impulse and the evil impulse is like having an angel on one shoulder and a devil on the other.

10-4b The Torah

The Torah, the first five books of the Bible—but in a wider sense the whole teaching and law of Judaism—is Judaism's paramount text. It contains stories and commandments that teach about life and death. The rabbis enumerated 613 commandments (*mitzvot*): 248 positive commandments ("You shalls") and 365 negative commandments ("You shall nots"). Moreover, all the commandments are held to be binding and more or less equal. Some Jews in the modern age would make a distinction between the moral law, and the ceremonial and ritual law. This concept isn't found in the Bible and Talmud, but history seems to have

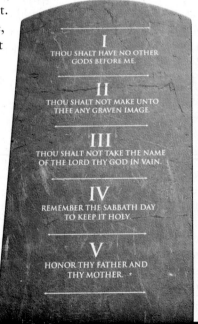

The Ten Commandments in English, in their shorter form. Writing on stone suggests the permanence and seriousness of the commandments.

ratified it, because some of the 613 commands cannot be fulfilled now that the Jewish temple is gone. All commandments come from God, the ancient and medieval rabbis said, so all of them are binding forever. Today, most Jews consider the Ten Commandments to be the leading commandments in the Torah, but not all Jews adhere to all 613; this is the basis of one of the main differences between the different branches of Judaism.

The Ten Commandments are as follows, with short explanations in brackets:

1. I am the Lord your God [not a commandment in grammatical form, but the basis of the people's relationship with God].

2. You shall not recognize any as god besides Me [the root of monotheism].

3. You shall not take the Name of the Lord your God in vain [God's name, symbolic of God's essence, must be respected].

4. Remember the day of Sabbath, to keep it holy [the Sabbath is a day of rest and rededication to God].

5. Honor your father and your mother [parents are to be respected as long as they live].

6. You shall not murder [not all killing is murder, but unlawful killing is].

7. You shall not commit adultery [breaking marriage vows breaks marriage].

8. You shall not steal [other people's property is to be respected].

9. Do not give false testimony against your neighbor [lying in legal settings undermines justice].

10. You shall not covet the possessions of others [desiring to have things that others have].

The rest of the Torah's legal material is based on these Ten Commandments. The rabbis of the ancient world compiled the Mishnah and the Gemara, finally combining them into the Talmud, expanding on these commandments and bringing them into every aspect of the life of the Jewish people.

10-4c General Jewish Ethics

Besides these Torah-based commands that originated with the Hebrew Bible, the biblical tradition also has broad legal injunctions, wisdom narratives with moral lessons, and prophetic teachings. These other teachings became important in the first millennium B.C.E., although the Torah commands remain central and foundational. In modern times, as the Torah commands became problematic for many Jews, the more general ethical principles became paramount for them.

The biblical prophets exhorted their audiences to lead a life that honored their covenant with God. They pointed primarily to obedience to the Torah, but they also spoke of more general moral duties: kindness to the needy, benevolence, faith, relief for the suffering, a peace-loving disposition, and a humble spirit. Civic loyalty and obedience, even to a foreign ruler, is urged as a duty (Jeremiah 29:7). This was also important in later times as Jews lived under non-Jewish governments.

In early rabbinic Judaism, the oral Torah both interpreted the Bible and delved afresh into many other ethical topics. Jewish morality, encompassing both commandments and general ethics, is known to Jews today as **halakhah**, literally "walk of life"—God has a way for the chosen people to walk in.

The best-loved and most influential rabbinic text on halakhah is the Mishnah tractate of Pirke Avot (PEER-kay ah-VOHT), the "Sayings of the Fathers," often translated as "Ethics of the Fathers." The Pirke Avot traces the transmission of the oral Torah from Moses to the second century C.E., when the Mishnah was compiled. Throughout this work, the word *Torah* refers especially to the oral Torah, a "fence around the [written] law," the body of legal opinions developed by the rabbis and codified in the Mishnah. The idea behind this fence is that by keeping it one would also be keeping the written Torah that it protects.

10-4d Modern Jewish Ethics

In the modern period, Jewish ethics sprouted many offshoots—due to developments in modern secular ethics and to the formation of Jewish branches—each of which required clarity on ethical teachings. The nineteenth and early twentieth-century Reform movement promoted the idea of Judaism as pure ethical monotheism. Since about 1900, liberal Reform and Reconstructionist rabbis have fostered novel approaches to Jewish ethics—in the work of Eugene Borowitz, for example. Also during this time, Orthodox rabbis have often engaged in applied ethics by interpreting the Talmud for bioethics: end-of-life issues, in vitro fertilization, genetic therapy, and other topics.

halakhah [hah-luh-KAH] "Walk of life," the way of moral obedience to God

Knowing the scriptures is an important basis of Jewish morality.

©HOWARD SANDLER/SHUTTERSTOCK.COM

"I" is. Buber taught that God is the "eternal Thou," known by both direct encounter with God, and indirect encounter with God as one develops I-Thou relationships with other people.

10-5 Jewish Worship and Ritual

In London, a prominent Jewish rabbi criticizes pop singer Madonna's ritual practice of Kabbalah. Rabbi Yitzchak Schochet of London's Mill Hill Synagogue strongly objects to Madonna's use of Kabbalah, arguing that it tarnishes Judaism when people who don't observe Jewish law engage in Jewish mysticism. Rabbi Schochet and many other traditional, observant Jews are particularly upset by the tattoo on Madonna's right shoulder of the ancient Hebrew name for God, which a majority of Jews regard as so holy that they don't use it. (They forbid permanent tattoos as well, so this is a double fault.) Madonna's interest in Kabbalah began with her 1998 *Ray of Light* album, was strengthened by her 2007 visit to the Kabbalah center in Jerusalem, and continues today. Public fascination with her use of the Kabbalah also remains strong, and she is still the leading celebrity voice of Kabbalah.

Because Judaism is a religion of practice, it has a full set of rituals for synagogue worship, home practices, and community-based religious festivals. We'll begin with synagogue worship, and then consider the Sabbath and the main festivals; finally, we'll look at the major life-cycle rituals of circumcision, bar/bat mitzvah, and funerals.

10-5a Worship in the Synagogue

The main synagogue service takes place on either Friday evening or Saturday morning, both of which fall on the Sabbath day. In Orthodox synagogues, males and females sit separately; in Conservative and Reform, they may sit together. A **minyan**, or minimum number of men necessary to have a service (usually ten), is required. We've already discussed, in Section 10-2, some of the differences between these three branches. But the three branches all share the same basic structure of service: gathering of a minyan into the main synagogue room; hymns and prayers often led by a cantor, or singer; and readings from scripture.

In synagogue worship, the readings themselves are very musical. The worship leader chants the words in Hebrew employing traditional Hebrew melodies. The place where the Torah scrolls are kept is the **ark**, a reference to the Ark of the Covenant. It is

An influential work of Jewish social ethics is *I and Thou* by Martin Buber (BOO-buhr; 1878–1965). In this profound work, which has changed the lives of many of its readers, Buber uses two pairs of words to describe two fundamentally different types of relationships between one's self and others: "I-It" and "I-Thou." For I-It relationships, the "It" refers to other people as objects. It objectifies and devalues them. In other words, the "I" looks upon others as "Its," not as people like oneself. Buber held that many human problems are caused by I-It attitudes. By contrast, the "I" in an I-Thou relationship doesn't objectify any "It" but has a living, mature relationship with others. It recognizes that the "Thou" is a whole world experience within one person, just as one's

minyan [MIHN-yahn] Minimum number of men necessary to have a service (usually ten)

ark Place in the synagogue where the Torah scrolls are kept

A Torah scroll and silver pointer

10-5b The Sabbath

One of the Ten Commandments orders that the **Sabbath** (seventh) day of the week be kept holy. This day begins at sunset on Friday and concludes on sunset on Saturday. Sabbath usually starts off at home, with a festive meal for which the whole family is present. The ritual lighting of the Sabbath candles precedes the meal. At least eighteen minutes before sundown on Friday, the mother and daughters light the candles, usually on the dining table, to welcome the Sabbath. In many modern Jewish households the candle blessing is performed together as a family. After the candles are lit, this blessing is recited over them: "Blessed are You, Eternal One our God, Ruler of the Universe, who makes us holy with mitzvot [commandments] and gives us this mitzvah [commandment] of lighting the Sabbath lights."

A Jewish mother and daughter light the Sabbath candles.

a special closet or recess in the synagogue wall on the side nearest Jerusalem and is usually the focal point of the synagogue. The scrolls themselves are typically covered with richly embroidered cloth, and the upper ends of the wooden rollers are adorned with gold and silver decorations. Their use follows a prescribed ritual:

- When a scroll is removed from the ark during the service, everyone in the synagogue stands and a special song is often sung.
- The scroll is placed on a reading desk.
- The readers use a special pointer, often made of solid silver, to keep track of their place in the text and avoid touching the scroll with their hands.
- When the reading is complete, the scroll is rolled up, its covers are put back on, and it is returned to the ark with great solemnity.

Then the rabbi sometimes preaches a short sermon based on the texts that were read, especially the Torah reading.

The Sabbath command goes on to say that no work may be done on the Sabbath. This rest from work is connected to both the creation of the world and the giving of the Torah. The Talmud interprets this strictly; this is why traditional Jews have tended to live within walking distance of the synagogue, because to walk too far is considered work.

Sabbath Seventh day of the week, from sunset on Friday to sunset on Saturday, to be kept holy

10-5c Jewish Annual Festivals

The Jewish year has several annual festivals. Most of them have both a historical reference and a contemporary meaning to build faith and obedience in those who celebrate them. We can consider them quickly here. **Rosh Hashanah** is the Jewish New Year, in September or October, depending on how the Jewish lunar calendar matches the solar calendar. It begins a ten-day solemn period of repentance and self-examination. The period ends on **Yom Kippur**, the Day of Atonement, which is the holiest day in the year. *Sukkot* (SOOK-koht) is the festival of tabernacles or booths, a seven-day harvest celebration linked to the wandering of the Hebrews after the Exodus; people often live in special outdoor huts during this time. **Passover** celebrates the escape of the Hebrews from Egyptian slavery. A special meal called the **seder**, with various foods including unleavened bread (*matzoh*), is the highlight. Hanukkah we have explained above in 10-2d. *Purim* (POOR-eem), "lots," recalls the Queen Esther story in which Persian Jews were saved from genocide when the drawing of lots exposed that evil plan. Costumes and plays, as well as special foods, are featured. Finally, *Shavuot* (SHAHV-oo-oht), meaning weeks, comes fifty days after Passover; it celebrates the giving of the Torah.

Even though its beef may be kosher, the cheese on this burger makes it nonkosher.

Rosh Hashanah [rohsh ha-SHAH-nah] Jewish New Year, in September or October, a ten-day period of repentance and self-examination

Yom Kippur [yohm kip-PUHR] Day of Atonement, the holiest day in the year

Passover Celebration of the escape of the Hebrews from Egyptian slavery

seder [SAY-duhr] Special Passover meal with various foods

kosher [KOH-sher] Jewish law dealing with what foods can be eaten, and how those foods must be prepared and consumed

Seder plate with special Passover foods

10-5d Kosher Food

Kosher means "fitting" or "proper," not (as it is often understood) "pure" or "clean." A body of ritual Jewish law deals with kosher: what foods can and cannot be eaten, and how those foods must be prepared and consumed. Contrary to popular opinion, rabbis don't bless food to make it kosher, but they do inspect it and its processing to assure kosher consumers that the food is kosher. All sorts of ethnic foods can be kosher; in fact, kosher Chinese restaurants can often be found today in Jewish neighborhoods.

Leviticus 11 gives a list of clean and unclean foods, and the Talmud treats them in detail. The types of unclean animals specified are (1) four-footed animals that don't chew the cud and have a split hoof (e.g., pigs); (2) meat-eating birds; (3) insects with wings; (4) water animals without fins and scales, for example, shrimp; and (5) small creeping (swarming) animals. To be kosher, acceptable animals must be killed humanely and prepared for sale in a clean way. Also, kosher food must be served and eaten in a kosher way (e.g., no combination of dairy products and meat in cooking or serving). In general, raw vegetables are always kosher, and so are cooked vegetables as long as they are cooked and eaten correctly.

Kosher rules are observed at all times, but additional kosher restrictions come during Passover. Some foods that are kosher for year-round use are not kosher for Passover, because they have leaven in them. A bagel, for example, can be kosher for regular use but is certainly not kosher for Passover.

Kosher food is so closely linked with Jewish identity that the misconception has arisen that it's only for Jews. Since Jews make up less than 2 percent of the American population, it's astounding that more than 40 percent of the country's new packaged food and beverage products in 2014 were labeled as kosher, making it the top label claim on food and beverages, according to market research; it even beats out gluten-free. Americans appreciate the quality of kosher food and its healthfulness compared with nonkosher. (If you like hot dogs, for example, and are concerned more about taste and health than about price, a kosher hot dog is for you.) In 2010, kosher food was served for the first time at the Super Bowl, and it nearly sold out.

10-5e Circumcision, the Sign of the Covenant

Circumcision is the most significant life-cycle ritual in Judaism and probably the one rite universally observed among Jews. Circumcision (from the Latin for "cut around") involves surgically—and carefully—removing the foreskin of the penis. Its common name among Jews is *bris milah*, Yiddish for "covenant of circumcision," and is usually called "bris" for short. Secular Jews who observe no other part of Judaism usually circumcise their male children; to be Jewish in any meaningful way is to be circumcised. Orthodox Jews affirm the Talmudic view that a person of Jewish descent who is not circumcised will not enter heaven. A few Reform and Reconstructionist leaders oppose circumcision today, but they're in the extreme minority.

As we have already seen, the commandment to circumcise is given first in Genesis 17:10–14 as an essential part of God's covenant with Abraham. According to God's command to Abraham, circumcision is performed only on males as the sign of the covenant and membership in God's people. Some Reform Jews argue that circumcision is sexist, so they have a naming ceremony for baby girls, with much of the circumcision ritual except for the actual cutting. Circumcision is often perceived by Reform and Conservative Jews to be a hygienic measure. Orthodox Jews disagree and correctly point out that this rationale isn't found in the Torah. Instead, circumcision is a religious measure: It is an outward physical sign of the eternal covenant between God and the Jewish people.

Circumcision is performed on the eighth day of a boy's life. If this falls on the Sabbath, circumcision is still done then, even though the drawing of blood is ordinarily forbidden as work. The circumcision is performed in a home or synagogue by a **mohel**, a respected Jewish man educated in the relevant Jewish laws, skilled in hygienic practices, and possessed of a steady hand. While the mohel does the cutting, an honored man holds the baby still on his lap. Blessings of God are recited, and a drop of wine is placed in the baby's mouth. He is then given a formal Hebrew name. As with most Jewish rituals, circumcision is a joyous occasion (except for the baby, of course) and is followed by refreshments or, more often, a festive meal.

10-5f Bar Mitzvah and Bat Mitzvah

A Jewish young man becomes a **bar mitzvah**, which literally means "son of the commandment," in a coming-of-age ceremony. A young woman becomes a **bat** (or **bas**) **mitzvah**, "daughter of the commandment." The singular *mitzvah* (commandment) is used here even though the Torah as a whole is meant. Although these terms literally refer only to adult standing in the Jewish community, they are also commonly taken to mean the ceremonies themselves—for example, in the expression that someone is "having a bar mitzvah." In Reform and Conservative Judaism, the ritual for females is the same as for males. In all Orthodox practice, women are not permitted to participate in rituals such as these, so a female's ceremony is usually little more than a modest party to mark her thirteenth birthday, if it is held at all.

What does it mean to become a bar/bat mitzvah? In Jewish law, children are not obligated to obey the Torah, although they are encouraged to do so. Judaism raises its children in the faith, as the Shema commands. Moreover, historic Jewish teaching knows nothing of the modern concept of teenage years between childhood and adulthood; when one reaches puberty, one is an adult. When they are at an age of understanding to know the difference between right and wrong and choose between them—traditionally thirteen—children become obligated in God's sight to obey the Torah. Now young people gradually begin to assume the privileges and responsibilities of Jewish adults. They help to lead religious services, count in a minyan, enter binding contracts, and may even marry (although marriages are not carried out until later).

The bar/bat mitzvah is an innovation of the past few centuries to mark the passage into Jewish adulthood in a ritualized way. In its earliest, basic form, it is the celebrant's first participation in leading a service. During a Sabbath service or a weekday service, the young person is called up to the Torah scroll to recite a blessing over the weekly reading. The common practice today for one becoming a bar/bat mitzvah is to do more than the blessing. The celebrant learns the entire Torah reading for the day in its chanted form and recites it during the service. He or she leads part of the service, or leads the congregation in certain important prayers. The celebrant is also generally required to make a short speech, which traditionally begins with "Today I am a man/woman." All this requires a good deal

mohel [MOI-uhl, rhymes with *oil*] Jewish man who officiates at a circumcision

bar mitzvah [bahr MITZ-vuh] "Son of the commandment," the assumption of responsibility before God for keeping the Torah

bat (bas) mitzvah [baht (bahs) MITZ-vuh] "Daughter of the commandment," the assumption of responsibility before God for keeping the Torah

At his bar mitzvah ceremony at the Western Wall in Jerusalem, a young man carries the Torah scroll with pride and joy.

ROBERT HOETINK/SHUTTERSTOCK

Jewish people. In another attempt to stem assimilation, in 2017 the governing body of Conservative Judaism in North America allowed local synagogues to accept non-Jewish persons, particularly the non-Jewish spouses of Jews, as members.

Jewish marriage has engagement (sometimes preceded by the work of matchmakers), rings, a vow or a document certifying marriage obligations, and a grand celebration. Ceremonies are often held outdoors or in hotels, not in the synagogue, as long as there is a rabbi to officiate and a canopy. But the Jewish ceremony has something unique in its ritual. As the last part of the wedding, the groom crushes under his foot a glass wrapped in a cloth, a reminder of the sorrow that came to Judaism when the Temple of Jerusalem was destroyed in 70 C.E. Then there are loud cries of "Mazel tov!" (MAH-zuhl tahv)—literally "good luck," that in celebratory situations has more of a nuance of congratulations—and the wedding reception begins.

of training by the rabbi, often over some months. The father traditionally recites a blessing thanking God that his child has become an adult. The often-elaborate post-ceremony parties that are commonplace today in North America arose around 1900 among more prosperous Jews. Today there is a growing opposition to lavish bar/bat mitzvah parties on the grounds that they distract from the spiritual meaning of the ceremony.

10-5g Marriage

Judaism strongly encourages marriage and family life. If asked what the first commandment in the Torah is, an observant Jew will reply, "Be fruitful and multiply" (Genesis 1:28), which is indeed God's first command, given to the whole human race. Among Ashkenazi Jews, monogamy has been the rule since the 900s C.E. Among Sephardic Jews, whose rules reflect the Jewish Bible and Talmud more closely on this point and have been influenced by the Muslim context, polygamy was permitted until the 1900s, but still wasn't common. For both groups, Jews married only Jews. But in the past century, intermarriage has become more common. This has posed a problem for Reform and Conservative Jews, because Jewish identity is traced through the mother, not the father, and intermarriage leads more often to assimilation of the Jewish spouse to the Gentile world than it does to the conversion of the non-Jewish spouse to Judaism. Lately, Reform Jews have urged, and sometimes instituted, either matrilineal or patrilineal descent for membership in the

10-5h Funeral Rituals

Jewish practices relating to death and mourning have had two purposes: primarily to comfort the mourners, and secondarily to help, as much as possible and appropriate, the deceased into the next world. In what follows, we will give a description of long-established Jewish practices that go back hundreds, sometimes thousands, of years. Some variations to this pattern are found among Conservative/Masorti Jews today, and more are found among the Reform.

After a person dies, burial must be carried out in less than forty-eight hours. The body is never left alone. In the past, Jewish communities had an organization to care for the dead; these societies are now making something of a comeback as a replacement for more-conventional funeral home arrangements. Autopsies are forbidden as a desecration of the body, but they are permitted where civil authorities require it. Embalming the body is also forbidden as a desecration, and organ donation is likewise not condoned. Some contemporary

Jewish ethicists have argued that organ donation is permitted, even meritorious, if the recipient's body is buried at death, but the traditional negative view of organ donation has led to a serious shortage of organs, especially kidneys, in Israel.

Both the coffin and the body's clothes are simple, so that all people are equal in death. The upper body is wrapped in a prayer shawl with its fringes cut short. People never view the body; open-casket ceremonies are forbidden by Jewish law. The body must not be cremated or put in a mausoleum, but buried in wooden coffins directly in the earth. Some Orthodox groups go so far as to poke holes in the bottom of coffins to facilitate the process of "dust to dust."

Jewish mourning practices have periods of decreasing intensity. When a person first hears of the death of a close relative, it is traditional to express the initial grief by tearing one's clothing, or sometimes a piece of cloth that is then worn on one's clothing. During the first two days after death, the family is usually left alone to allow for the full expression of their grief. The next period of mourning is known as **shiva**, the Hebrew word for seven, because it lasts seven days, beginning on the day of burial. This process is often called "sitting shiva." Shiva is observed by the entire family of the deceased in the deceased's home. The family wears the clothing they had on when they tore it in mourning. Mourners sit on low stools or on the floor. They don't wear leather shoes; shave their faces or cut their hair; wear cosmetics; work; or do things for comfort, entertainment, or pleasure.

After shiva, lighter mourning of eleven months continues for the immediate family. *Kaddish* (KAH-dish), a short prayer that praises God but does not mention death, is to be said every day. After the period is complete, the family of the deceased is not permitted to continue formal mourning. Jewish law requires that a tombstone be prepared. Many Jewish communities delay putting it up until the end of the extended mourning period. Where this custom is followed, a formal unveiling ceremony for the tombstone is usually held at the cemetery.

10-6 Judaism around the World Today

On a Friday night in Chicago, a Jewish family gathers in their home to welcome the Sabbath with a traditional ritual meal. As the sun is just about to set, the wife, assisted by her daughter, lights two Sabbath candles on the dining room table. It has been set for dinner, and on its white tablecloth are a wine cup and two loaves of challah (soft braided bread), covered with a special cloth. The father blesses each of his children and then recites a prayer of blessing over the wine, remembering how God rested on the seventh day of creation and hallowed the Sabbath day. Everyone around the table has a sip of the wine, and then all leave the table to wash their hands ritually. Gathered around the table again, they recite a blessing of God for the gift of food. Each receives a slice of the bread to eat, and the main meal begins. At the end of the meal, the family sings special Sabbath songs, and the meal is concluded with a prayer. This Sabbath ritual is so meaningful in Judaism that both Orthodox and Conservative families in North America practice it in much the same way. It is even making something of a comeback in Reform Judaism.

As stated above, in 2015 the world Jewish population was estimated at about 14.27 million, 0.2 percent of the total world population. About 42 percent of all Jews reside in Israel and about 42 percent in North America. Approximately 8 percent are in Europe, and the remainder are scattered widely in smaller communities in South America, Asia, and Africa. The Jewish Diaspora today, both inside and outside North America, has all the dynamism and diversity that Judaism has in Israel.

10-6a Judaism in Israel

The Orthodox movement is the only branch of Judaism legally recognized in Israel. Until about 2000, only Orthodox Jews could serve on religious councils. Today, only Orthodox rabbis may perform marriages, conversions, and grant divorces in Israel. Many Orthodox men were exempt from military service until 2012, when the Israeli Supreme Court struck down the law that exempted them from service, but their numbers in the military are still small. Some Orthodox scholars receive lifelong stipends from the government in order to devote themselves to full-time Torah study. Non-Orthodox Israelis increasingly bristle at this preferential treatment.

Most Israelis today don't formally identify with the three main movements. Instead, they describe themselves in terms of their degree of observance. More than half of all Israelis call themselves "secular." About 15 to 20 percent describe themselves as Orthodox. The rest in the wide middle are "traditionally observant." However, the traditionalists (Masorti) and even the secularists of Israel tend to be more observant than are their counterparts in Europe and North America.

shiva [SHIHV-uh] Period of mourning that lasts seven days, beginning on the day of burial

For example, many secular Jews in Israel observe some traditional practices, such as lighting Sabbath candles on Friday evening, limiting their activities on the Sabbath day of rest, having a Passover home ritual, or keeping some Jewish dietary laws (e.g., avoiding pork). These practices are nearly nonexistent among American Jews who call themselves secular. An Israeli quip on this combination of secularism and observance states, "Most Israelis don't belong to a synagogue, but the synagogue they don't belong to is Orthodox."

> "Most Israelis don't belong to a synagogue, but the synagogue they don't belong to is Orthodox."
>
> —Israeli quip

10-6b Judaism in North America

Jews have lived in North America from the early 1600s, with Dutch Jews of Sephardic origins settling first in New Amsterdam (modern New York City). For two hundred years, the majority of North American Jews were Sephardics. The first American synagogue was established in 1677 in Rhode Island, a colony that was a center of religious toleration. Although they usually couldn't hold office or even vote, Sephardic Jews became active in their civic communities in the 1790s.

In the mid-1800s Ashkenazi Jews from Germany started to arrive in the United States, primarily becoming merchants and shop owners. By 1880, around 250,000 Jews lived in the United States. Aviva Ben-Ur, in his recent book *Sephardic Jews in America*, tells the story of how Ashkenazis marginalized Sephardics, a practice that persists even today.[5]

Jewish immigration to North America increased sharply in the early 1880s, driven mainly by persecution in Russia and Eastern Europe. Most of the newer immigrants spoke Yiddish and were religiously observant Ashkenazis from the poor rural areas of these lands. They came to America seeking freedom and a better life. Over 2 million Jews arrived between about 1880 and 1924, when new U.S. laws all but ended immigration from Eastern Europe. Many settled in the New York metropolitan area, eventually establishing one of the world's major Jewish population centers.

Around 1900, newly arrived Jews began to build many synagogues and community associations. American Jewish leaders urged speedy integration into the wider American culture, which a large majority of Jews quickly accomplished. After World War II, in which nearly half a million American Jewish men fought against Germany and Japan, younger Jewish families joined the American trend of settling in new suburbs. There they became increasingly integrated into American culture as previous anti-Semitic discrimination lessened. For example, in the 1950s many leading universities and colleges began to drop their quota systems that held Jewish enrollment to very small levels. Enrollment in Jewish religious schools doubled between 1945 and 1955, and synagogue affiliation jumped from only 20 percent of Jews in 1930 to 60 percent in 1960. Reform and Conservative congregations experienced rapid growth. In the 1970s and 1980s, waves of Jewish immigrants from Russia largely joined the mainstream American Jewish community. However, most of these new arrivals had been secularized by generations of Soviet Communist rule and anti-Semitic pressures.

Today, approximately 5.5 million of the world's Jews live in North America. In the United States there were 5,690,000 Jews in 2010; the Pew Forum estimates that in 2050 that number will decline to

The oldest synagogue in North America, the Sephardic congregation in Newport, Rhode Island, dates to 1677; this building for their congregation is from 1763.

PETERSPIRO/ISTOCKPHOTO.COM

5,360,000. In other words, Jews will go from 1.8 percent of the U.S. population to 1.4 percent. Today 22 percent of U.S. Jews say they have no religion but consider themselves Jewish through culture and/or ancestry. Two-thirds of American Jews do not belong to a synagogue, one-fourth say they do not believe in God, and one-third have a Christmas tree in their home. The most important statistic is on the increasing speed with which American Jews are assimilating in marriage: the intermarriage rate has now reached a high of 59 percent for all Jews and 71 percent for non-Orthodox Jews. In contrast, in 1970 only 17 percent of Jews married outside their faith.[6]

Three major movements are found in North America: Reform, Conservative, and Orthodox. A fourth movement, the Reconstructionist, is more liberal than Reform and is substantially smaller than the other three. Orthodoxy consists of different groups: the modern Orthodox, who have integrated into modern North American society while strictly keeping the Jewish law from the Talmud; Hasidic Jews, who live in their own, separate neighborhoods and dress distinctively; and the Yeshiva Orthodox. They all believe that God gave Moses the whole Torah, including both the written Torah that became the first five books of the Bible and the oral Torah, an oral tradition interpreting the written Torah that became the basis of the Talmud. The Orthodox believe that the Torah contains 613 mitzvot (commands), binding upon Jews but not upon non-Jews. A recent survey of American Jews found that 10 percent identify themselves as Orthodox today. The Orthodox tend to have large families and, as mentioned previously, resist assimilation, so their overall numbers are growing, and they are becoming an ever-larger proportion of practicing Jews in North America.

Reform Judaism doesn't believe that the Torah is divinely written or inspired. It views the entire Bible as a record of Jewish religious experience. Reform Jews don't believe in the observance of many traditional commandments, but they attempt to preserve much of what they consider the spiritual essentials of Judaism, along with some selected Jewish practices and cultural aspects. A recent survey found that 35 percent of American Jews identify themselves as Reform. Approximately nine hundred Reform synagogues are found in North America today.

Conservative Judaism's efforts to mediate between the Orthodox and Reform have been well received in North America. The Conservative movement holds that the main teachings of Jewish scriptures and the Talmud come from God but have a human component. It believes that Judaism can hold true to its historic roots but can also adapt to modern life. Because Conservative Judaism occupies the large middle ground between Orthodoxy and Reform, there's a great diversity in the Conservative movement. Twenty-six percent of American Jews identify themselves as Conservative, and the approximately 750 Conservative synagogues in the world today are predominantly in North America.

All told, the varieties of Judaism in North America strive, in their widely diverse ways, to continue the mission of God's people to be a light to the nations.

STUDY TOOLS 10

READY TO STUDY?
ONLINE ON MINDTAP, YOU CAN:

- ☐ Download the Chapter Review Card, which includes key terms and chapter summaries.
- ☐ Watch the movie trailer for Ridley Scott's film "Exodus: Gods and Kings."
- ☐ Read original primary sources from Jewish tradition.
- ☐ Interact with figures from the text to check your understanding.
- ☐ Prepare for tests with quizzes.
- ☐ Review the key terms with Flash Cards.

Judaism Timeline: 2000 B.C.E.–Present

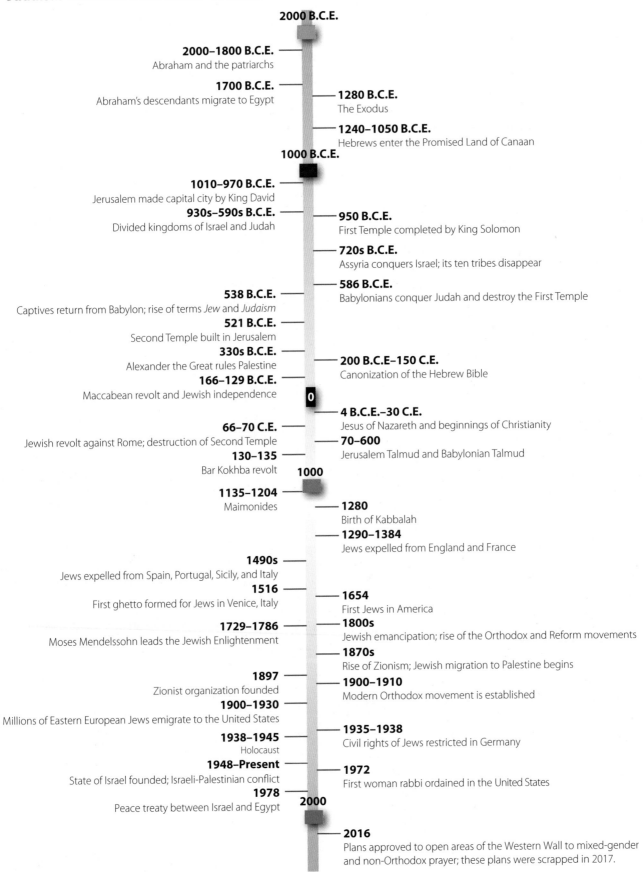

2000 B.C.E.

2000–1800 B.C.E.
Abraham and the patriarchs

1700 B.C.E.
Abraham's descendants migrate to Egypt

1280 B.C.E.
The Exodus

1240–1050 B.C.E.
Hebrews enter the Promised Land of Canaan

1000 B.C.E.

1010–970 B.C.E.
Jerusalem made capital city by King David

930s–590s B.C.E.
Divided kingdoms of Israel and Judah

950 B.C.E.
First Temple completed by King Solomon

720s B.C.E.
Assyria conquers Israel; its ten tribes disappear

586 B.C.E.
Babylonians conquer Judah and destroy the First Temple

538 B.C.E.
Captives return from Babylon; rise of terms *Jew* and *Judaism*

521 B.C.E.
Second Temple built in Jerusalem

330s B.C.E.
Alexander the Great rules Palestine

166–129 B.C.E.
Maccabean revolt and Jewish independence

200 B.C.E–150 C.E.
Canonization of the Hebrew Bible

0

4 B.C.E.–30 C.E.
Jesus of Nazareth and beginnings of Christianity

66–70 C.E.
Jewish revolt against Rome; destruction of Second Temple

70–600
Jerusalem Talmud and Babylonian Talmud

130–135
Bar Kokhba revolt

1000

1135–1204
Maimonides

1280
Birth of Kabbalah

1290–1384
Jews expelled from England and France

1490s
Jews expelled from Spain, Portugal, Sicily, and Italy

1516
First ghetto formed for Jews in Venice, Italy

1654
First Jews in America

1729–1786
Moses Mendelssohn leads the Jewish Enlightenment

1800s
Jewish emancipation; rise of the Orthodox and Reform movements

1870s
Rise of Zionism; Jewish migration to Palestine begins

1897
Zionist organization founded

1900–1910
Modern Orthodox movement is established

1900–1930
Millions of Eastern European Jews emigrate to the United States

1935–1938
Civil rights of Jews restricted in Germany

1938–1945
Holocaust

1972
First woman rabbi ordained in the United States

1948–Present
State of Israel founded; Israeli-Palestinian conflict

1978
Peace treaty between Israel and Egypt

2000

2016
Plans approved to open areas of the Western Wall to mixed-gender and non-Orthodox prayer; these plans were scrapped in 2017.

11

Encountering Christianity: The Way of Jesus Christ

LEARNING OUTCOMES

After studying this chapter, you will be able to do the following:

11-1 Explain the meaning of *Christianity* and related terms.

11-2 Trace how the main periods of Christianity's history have shaped its present.

11-3 Outline in your own words essential Christian teachings as found in the Nicene Creed.

11-4 Describe the main features of Christian ethics.

11-5 Summarize Christian worship and other rituals.

11-6 Explain the variety of Christianity around the world today, especially in the Southern Hemisphere and in North America.

"I am the Way, the Truth, and the Life." —Jesus Christ, in the Gospel of John

Your Visit to St. Peter's in Rome

As a part of a visit to Italy, you spend a day in Vatican City, the world's smallest nation, which serves as the headquarters of the Roman Catholic Church. The center of Vatican City is St. Peter's Basilica, where the pope presides. You've seen pictures of this building, and you've seen snippets on television of religious services performed there, so now you're eager to see it for yourself.

Stepping inside St. Peter's Basilica, you see that the grandness of the building itself is stunning. Seeing it from the square in front has given you no indication of how large and impressive it really is. The grandeur of this place and what it means to believers—in this case Roman Catholic Christians—brings you a deep sense of respect. Many people pause after entering the front door to take it all in. On the right you see Michelangelo's life-size sculpture of Mary the mother of Jesus holding the body of her dead son in her arms after his crucifixion. So many people want to see it that it takes several minutes to work your way to the front of the group. It shows an artistic genius that can only be marveled at, but it also shows the profound Christian faith of Michelangelo.

The natural light coming from above illuminates the church and spreads a subdued radiance all around,

especially under the dome. Looking up at the dome from as close to the main altar as you can get, you see the large letters giving, in Latin, the words of Jesus in the Gospel of Matthew (16:18–19), which the Catholic Church has always considered the foundation of its organization: "You are Peter, and on this rock I will build my church. I will give you the keys of the kingdom of heaven." You reflect on this and realize sadly that it was the way that funds were raised to build this basilica that became the spark of the Reformation, which split Western Christianity in half, into Protestant and Catholic segments that still persist today.

After you go up to the outside of the dome to take in the magnificent view of Rome, you take a guided tour of the tomb of St. Peter, led by a priest from the Vatican archaeology office. It's a few stories below the main altar of the church, what in the first century C.E. was a cemetery on Vatican Hill, outside the city of Rome. You walk down an excavated street toward the traditional grave of Peter, very simple and modest. You realize that, for all the grandeur of the building above, the foundation of it all is the grave of a humble fisherman who was killed near this spot for his faith in Jesus Christ.

Christianity is a monotheistic religion based on the first-century C.E. life, death, and resurrection of Jesus of Nazareth in Galilee. It teaches that Jesus is the Son of God and the savior of the world, and that his teaching shows how to live for God and others. Christianity began as a prophetic reform movement within Judaism, led by Jesus, in the first century C.E., but it quickly moved out into the wider world after Jesus's departure. It has been from the first a strongly missionary faith, eager to spread itself and make converts, and it has become the largest religion in the world. Geographically the most widely diffused of all faiths—the only religion to be found in every nation, for example—it has about 2.2 billion adherents today. Christianity has been a major influence in the shaping of western civilization, and since around 1500 it has increasingly shaped the rest of the world. The majority of

An aerial drone photo of St. Peter's Basilica, Vatican City, shows how large this building is, and gives an impressive overview of St. Peter's Square in front of it.

BDRONE/SHUTTERSTOCK.COM

Jesus Christ lifts his hands in blessing in this stained glass church window done in a modern, contemporary style.

Christians today live in the Southern Hemisphere. Christianity's three largest groups are the Roman Catholic Church (larger than the other two groups together), the Eastern Orthodox churches, and the Protestant churches. In your study of Christianity, you'll encounter these unique features:

- Christianity is centered on a person, Jesus Christ. But it is also strongly concerned with teaching and doctrine—more so than Judaism and Islam, the other Abrahamic monotheisms.

- Because Christianity is centered on Jesus, it takes seriously his teachings as recorded in the New Testament. But Christianity is also shaped by the church's later teaching about Jesus, which raises the question: What is the relationship of the teaching *of* Jesus to Christian teaching *about* Jesus?

- When seen from the outside, Christianity appears to be quite unified. However, when seen from the inside, it seems very diverse, even fragmented, with an estimated nine thousand different church groups.

The likeness of Jesus Christ, here from Rio de Janeiro, is the most well-known human image from the past.

which they meant the Way of Jesus; they called themselves followers of the Way. *Christians* was a name given to them by others, probably as a derogatory term that meant something like "those Christ people." But adherents transformed this putdown into an honorable name used by Christians everywhere since then.

The term *Christendom* is sometimes used in connection with Christianity. It typically refers today to those nations of the world in which Christianity is the recognized, predominant religion, whether it is the official religion of these nations or not. This term has now fallen into disuse, and in some circles even disfavor.

11-2 The Christian Present as Shaped by Its Past

In New York City, a college student who wants to train to be a priest in the Orthodox Church in North America visits his bishop, the regional leader of this church, to inquire about education and expectations for ordination. After a pleasant conversation about his background and intent, the bishop offers the requirements. The student is surprised by the first and last items mentioned: grow a beard, finish college, and get married—preferably in that order. With these things accomplished, the student can prepare for the priesthood. As the student will soon learn as he travels toward becoming a priest, these expectations are a part of the ancient tradition for almost all Eastern Orthodox clergy.

Today's Christianity has been shaped by a long and significant history. From the death and resurrection of Jesus until today, his teachings have spread throughout the world. This section will relate the high points of this story.

11-2a The Life, Death, and Resurrection of Jesus Christ (ca. 4 B.C.E.–30 C.E.)

The primary sources for knowledge of Jesus are the four **Gospels**—Matthew, Mark, Luke, and John. (When the term "gospel"—meaning "good news"—refers to an ancient book about Jesus, it will be capitalized here; when it refers to the message of Christianity, it will not

11-1 Names

The name **Christ** originated in the ancient Greek word *Christos* (KRIHS-toss), literally "anointed one." This word is in turn the Greek equivalent of the Hebrew word *messiah* (meh-SIGH-uh), one anointed as a king or prophet. The earliest Christians came to believe that Jesus was the promised messiah who would bring God's blessings to Israel. When the church moved into the Greek-speaking world, the term *Christ* was attached to the personal name *Jesus* to produce the longer name by which he is known to Christians, *Jesus Christ*.

Christianity, the religion based on Jesus Christ's life and teaching, is built from *Christians*, those who belong to the religious movement based on Christ. As related by the first-century book of early church history, the Acts of the Apostles, the first Christians themselves had called their movement within Judaism the Way, by

Christ Literally, "anointed one," or prophet

Gospel [GAHS-puhl] Early Christian book telling the "good news" of the story of Jesus

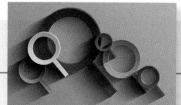

A Closer Look

Symbols of Christianity

The fish was an early informal symbol of Christianity. It was connected to one of Jesus's miracles: multiplying bread and fish to feed a crowd. Later, the five letters in the Greek word for *fish*, transliterated into English as *ichthus* (ick-THOOS), became an acronym for "Jesus Christ, God's Son, Savior." The fish (Figure 11.1) is still popular today as a symbol of Christianity, especially among Protestants; one can often see it in jewelry and on bumper stickers.

The cross on which Jesus died is the predominant symbol of Christianity, but it didn't appear as a symbol (Figure 11.2) until sometime in the 300s. It was a fearsome image of death by torture for people in the Roman Empire, which may have delayed its adoption as a symbol. The cross symbolizes the whole of the faith, but it specifically represents Jesus's death,

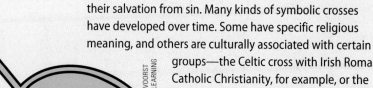

Figure 11.1 **The fish**

BONNIE VAN VOORST
© CENGAGE LEARNING

which Christians typically believe is the sacrificial basis of their salvation from sin. Many kinds of symbolic crosses have developed over time. Some have specific religious meaning, and others are culturally associated with certain groups—the Celtic cross with Irish Roman Catholic Christianity, for example, or the Russian cross with Orthodox Christianity.

The most common Christian cross is the Latin cross pictured here. The empty Latin cross, usually favored by Protestants, suggests the **resurrection** of the crucified Jesus, when his dead body was made eternally alive by the power of God. The crucifix, a Latin cross with a representation of the body of Jesus on it, favored by Catholic and Orthodox churches and some Protestants, is a reminder of Christ's sacrifice. The Greek cross, with arms of equal length, is just as ancient as the Latin cross and is found particularly in Eastern Orthodox Christianity. The ritual action of using one's right hand to make the sign of the cross on one's head and torso in prayer and formal worship is a common ritual act for a majority of Christians.

Figure 11.2 The cross

BONNIE VAN VOORST
© CENGAGE LEARNING

---

be capitalized.) These four Gospels are found in the **New Testament**. A number of other sources written in the early 100s, notably the Gospel of Thomas, contain a few stories about Jesus and many more sayings attributed to him. The material about him in ancient non-Christian sources, both Jewish and Roman, confirms the main lines of his story, but does not add substantially to our knowledge of Jesus from the New Testament.

The chronology of the life of Jesus is slightly uncertain in its details. Historians generally place Jesus's birth around 4 B.C.E. The church, following the Gospel of John, usually supposes that Jesus had a public ministry of three years, but Matthew, Mark, and Luke may portray a one-year ministry. Jesus's death during the rule of Pontius Pilate, the Roman governor of Judaea, is placed around the years 29 to 30.

When John the Baptizer, the fiery Jewish prophet who preached repentance and baptism in preparation for God's coming rule, baptized Jesus, it marked the beginning of his public ministry. Jesus taught in vivid **parables** (short stories about some aspect of life in the rule of God) and performed miraculous healings. He traveled through Galilee and became a popular

prophetic figure. He gathered twelve male Jewish followers whom he called *disciples*, or "students"; the church later called them **apostles**, those "sent out" by Christ to be missionary leaders in the church. Women, both married and unmarried, were also a prominent part of his movement, which was highly unusual for the time. Jesus's attitude toward some aspects of the observance of Jewish law generated conflict with groups such as the Pharisees. The Pharisees believed in strict Sabbath rest and not associating closely with sinners or with women. The ruling Jewish authorities also began to suspect Jesus, but he probably didn't reach the attention of the Roman rulers.

A triumphal entry into Jerusalem at Passover time was the prelude to a final crisis. After a last supper with his twelve closest disciples,

resurrection Dead body made eternally alive by the power of God

New Testament The Christian scriptural canon consisting of twenty-seven documents

parable Jesus's story about some aspect of life in the rule of God

apostles Those "sent out" by Christ to be missionary leaders in the church

and at other times when referring to his role as God's agent of judgment at the end of time. This title is derived from Daniel 7:13 in the Jewish Bible, where "one like a son of man" first represents the oppressed people of God and then ascends to heaven to be vindicated by God.

> { To Jesus, the social and religious outcasts of Jewish society . . . were the special objects of God's love. }

Jesus was critical of both Jewish and (implicitly) Greco-Roman society, saying that they fell far short of God's rule. Jesus encouraged the poor and oppressed, but rejected violent revolution. To Jesus, the social and religious outcasts of Jewish society (lepers, criminals,

Graffito of a Christian youth in Rome saluting a crucified figure with a human body and an ass's head. The Greek inscription reads, "Alexamenos worships God." This anti-Christian drawing is from about 200 C.E.

he was betrayed by one of them, Judas Iscariot. Jesus was arrested by the Jewish temple authorities and tried by the Sanhedrin (Jewish council) and then by Pilate, who condemned him to death by crucifixion, being nailed to a cross to die an agonizing death. Christians everywhere believe that three days after his death, God raised Jesus from the dead to live eternally. The earliest church believed that sometime after the resurrection—the Gospels differ on the precise timing—the risen Jesus ascended to heaven, to stay in power there until his return at the end of time.

Jesus preached the imminent coming of God's kingdom (or full rule) to the earth and said that it has both a future and a present reality. His teachings and miracles pointed to and explained this kingdom. His disciples recognized him at some point in his ministry or shortly after it as the Messiah, although the Gospels indicate that Jesus did not often call himself that. He was mainly called a prophet and teacher. Jesus characteristically used the term *Son of Man* (though mysteriously in the third person) when talking about his own suffering and death,

A pilgrim kneels at the Stone of Unction, where tradition says the body of Jesus was washed before his burial, in the Church of the Holy Sepulcher in Jerusalem. The special structure that covers the tomb of Jesus in this church received a major renovation in 2016–2017, the first in 200 years.

prostitutes, Jews who collected taxes for Rome, and others) were the special objects of God's love. He called them to repentance and faith, healed their diseases of mind and body, and restored them to membership in the people of Israel. Jesus taught that God desires the salvation of the marginalized more than the righteousness of those who constantly obey God, a teaching that has proven a continual challenge for the church. Jesus embraced some outsiders including the Samaritans, whom most other Jews regarded as terrible people.

Modern scholarship has delved fully into the Gospel accounts, and scholars have made research into the historical Jesus the largest single enterprise in religious study. What academics call "the quest for the historical Jesus" has been going strong for more than two centuries and shows no sign of lessening. In general, scholars agree on the main lines of Jesus's life and teaching as given previously. They are divided, however, over other issues:

- *Did Jesus intend to found a church?* Jesus gathered a community of followers around himself. This community continued after his time, regarding itself as God's new people. But many scholars doubt that Jesus intended to begin the organization that was later called the church.

- *Did Jesus intend his message to be addressed to Jews only?* Jesus's choice of twelve Jewish men as his closest disciples is an indication that his movement was mainly an inner-Jewish thing. Because welcoming non-Jews into the church caused such intense debate less than ten years after Jesus's departure, Jesus probably didn't address this matter.

- *How did Jesus understand his relation to the coming of the kingdom of God?* Scholars disagree about whether Jesus merely proclaimed the kingdom/rule of God or whether he inaugurated it, or something in between. To what extent did the events of his life, death, and resurrection make the kingdom/rule of God a reality for his followers?

11-2b The Earliest Church (30–100 C.E.)

The earliest church in Jerusalem was initially composed of those Jews who had followed Jesus during his ministry, perhaps one hundred people in all. They saw themselves as a continuing reform movement within Judaism. In a few days after Jesus's departure from earth, the early church experienced on the Jewish feast of Pentecost an outpouring of the Spirit of God to empower it for its continued ministry.

Saul—or as he was known when his missionary journeys began, Paul—was a Pharisee who violently persecuted the earliest church. Born at Tarsus (TAR-suhs) in southern Asia Minor (present-day Turkey), he had come to Jerusalem as a student of famous Rabbi Gamaliel and had become a persecutor of Christians. While on the road to Damascus, Paul was suddenly, dramatically converted to faith in Christ. In this conversion, or soon afterward, he came to a conviction that the Christian message must be spread among the Gentiles. Paul was a controversial figure throughout his career. Although he is criticized today by some for his conservative statements about women and slaves, in his own time Paul was criticized for being far too inclusivist, even liberal. He gained recognition in the Jerusalem church for Gentile converts. He saw clearly that the mission of the church to all humanity, implicit in the death and resurrection of Christ, meant a break with many of the Jewish traditions in which he had previously

"Garden Tomb" in Jerusalem, believed by some Protestants to be the tomb of Jesus

lived. Paul worked tirelessly as a missionary, founded dozens of churches in strategically located cities, and became known as "the Apostle to the Gentiles."

Because of the preservation of several of his letters to his churches, we know a good deal about Paul. He didn't write about Jesus's earthly life and teaching, but made the crucifixion and resurrection of Jesus the center of his proclamation. The crucifixion of Jesus was the supreme redemptive act, a self-sacrifice for the sin of humankind. Salvation is a gift of grace, and in baptism the Holy Spirit comes to transform the new Christian. Paul linked this doctrine of **justification** by faith with his strong view that Christ brings liberation from the Mosaic Law, especially for Gentiles. Justification brings freedom, not from all of the Mosaic Law, but from parts that particularly mark Jewish identity—for example, keeping Jewish food regulations, observing the last day of the week for mandatory rest, and especially being circumcised. This created difficulties in the Jerusalem church, where many followers of Jesus wanted to see the heritage of Judaism continued. Once this struggle was settled, the radical character of Paul's doctrine of justification began to be forgotten in the church, and salvation became a matter of both faith and obedience to God's law.

The four New Testament Gospels record a special commission of Jesus to Peter as the leader among the twelve disciples, but Peter's life can only be partially reconstructed. He was a key leader in the earliest Jerusalem church until James, a close relative of Jesus, became its leader. We know from Paul's letters that Peter did missionary work in the Gentile world. Two letters in the New Testament bear his name, but many scholars are doubtful about their authorship by Peter—especially the second letter. According to early tradition, Peter died in Nero's persecution in the city of Rome in 64 C.E., probably at the same time as Paul was killed. Later traditions say that he was crucified, at his request, upside down, because he wasn't worthy to die the same way that Jesus did. Rome had the bones of Peter and Paul, which helped to ensure its leading role in the Western church.

> *Although he is criticized today by some for his conservative statements about women and slaves, in his own time Paul was criticized for being inclusivist, even liberal.*

justification Salvation as being made right with God by faith, for Paul a gift of God

canon Official list of books, in Christianity the twenty-seven books of the New Testament

11-2c The Ancient Period (100–500 C.E.)

Although Christian tradition focuses on Peter and Paul, it is certain that many other missionaries also contributed to the growth of Christianity by planting churches. Some churches, prominently those in Rome, seem to have begun without any formal mission effort. By 100 C.E., Christianity had established itself in every large and midsize city in the eastern half of the Roman Empire (see Map 11.1). In the next two centuries, Christian churches were founded throughout the whole Roman Empire and even beyond it. These were all *house churches*, groups of Christians who met in private homes ("church" here refers to an association of people, not a building). Ancient Christianity experienced rapid growth for a variety of reasons:

- The struggle over whether to allow Gentiles to join the church without converting to Judaism was quickly settled in the affirmative for the majority of churches.

- Much of church life was dedicated to making converts and assimilating them into the close-knit social structure of the Christian community.

- Christianity offered things that many people in the ancient world were seeking: a deeper purpose for living, happiness in this world, the promise of eternal life, a higher standing for women and slaves, and a loving social-support network.

- Unlike other religions in the Roman world, Christianity made a broad appeal to people of all ethnicities, classes, and genders, which gave it a wide field for conversion and growth.

- A common New Testament **canon** arose rapidly. Although the official list of the entire twenty-seven-book New Testament canon was not finalized until the middle 300s, by the year 100 most Christians agreed on the four Gospels and the letters of Paul and John.

> *Judaism and Christianity are sister faiths, but like many family feuds, their conflict has been intense and sad.*

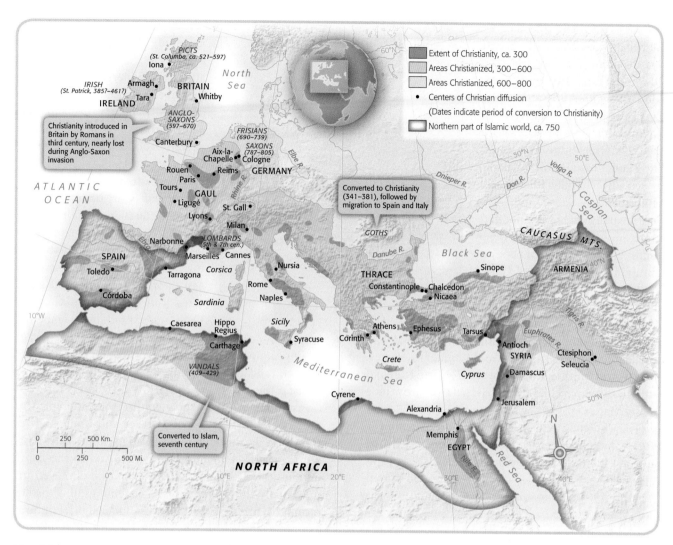

Map 11.1

The Spread of Christianity to about 800 C.E.

Christianity arose in Palestine in the first century C.E. and gradually gained footholds in parts of Western Asia, North Africa, and Southern Europe by 300 C.E. Over the next five centuries, Christianity became the dominant religion in much of Western and Central Europe, and expanded its influence in Western Asia and North Africa. By about 750, Islam had conquered much of the Middle East and all of North Africa and Spain, and many Christians in these areas converted to Islam.

As Christianity spread among Gentiles, it continued to grow out of its early status as a Jewish group. By the end of the first century, many Jewish leaders began to decree that Jews confessing Jesus to be the Messiah should be expelled from synagogues. As Christians began to outnumber Jews in some cities, Christian pressure on Jews began, and increased in 313 when the state persecution of Christianity ended. Thus began a bitter legacy of Christian anti-Semitism, prejudice against the Jewish people that has haunted the western world through our own time. Christianity did not invent anti-Semitism—it was hundreds of years old by the time Christianity was born—but it added its own twist to it. The church understood itself, and was understood by

Jews, to be Gentile. By around 400 C.E., historians generally agree today, the separation between Judaism and Christianity was complete. Judaism and Christianity are sister faiths, but similar to many family feuds, their conflict has been intense and sad. However, Christianity remains built on the foundation of Judaism. They share much of the same Bible, monotheism, a moral code, and similar patterns of worship.

As Christianity grew, it also challenged the Roman Empire. During the first century, this challenge was muted. But at the end of the first century, with the outbreak of imperial persecutions of Christians, Christianity challenged the legitimacy of the empire and the Roman religious ideology with which it was allied.

Christians believed—and acted on the belief—that Jesus, not Caesar, was the Lord of this world. This led to even more Roman persecutions and the **martyrdom** of Christians. Persecution was sporadic but often fierce, especially in the late 200s. Romans also countered Christianity in an informal, popular way by charging that Christians practiced secret cannibalism, were sexually immoral, and were intolerant of others, among other claims. However, Roman persecution didn't stem the rise of Christianity. As one church leader at this time remarked, "The blood of the martyrs is the seed of the church." This statement may still be true today; in North Korea and China, for example, where Christianity is often persecuted (North Korea) or sporadically suppressed (China), it tends to grow more rapidly than it probably would if left alone.

The church was also challenged from within by **heresy**, the church's characterization of organized internal opposition. Some alternative churches arose in the second century, and in some areas they outnumbered what was becoming mainstream Christianity. The movement known as **Gnosticism** or Gnostic Christianity believed that this material world was essentially evil and hostile toward the good. As Christianity defined itself in the second century against Judaism, Roman imperial religion, Gnosticism, and other movements, **orthodoxy** gradually arose, with its emphasis on correct teaching of the essentials of the faith. This effort to achieve and preserve correct teaching has characterized much of Christianity ever since. Gnosticism and other dissenting groups within ancient Christianity used to be viewed and studied as corruptions of

Nuns in traditional clothing

STUDIO-ANNIKA/GETTY IMAGES

orthodoxy, but today's historians study them more objectively as alternative forms of Christianity. Some heretics were given this label because they were more doctrinally conservative and morally rigorous than the mainstream church—too Christian for other Christians.

Emperor Constantine's toleration of Christianity in 312 ushered in a new era in the faith, one that many historians view as lasting until the twentieth century. This era featured the close association of church and state, often called **Constantinianism**. Constantine and later emperors saw religious unity and peace as important for their rule; there was one God, one Church, and one Emperor. By moving his capital to Constantinople in northern Asia Minor, Emperor Constantine created a new culture that attempted to preserve the best of ancient Greece and Rome and yet transform it through the Christian faith. The Eastern Orthodox branch of Christianity, with the many nations it has shaped, is the continuation of this effort.

Finally, this period saw the beginnings of Christian **monasticism** in the 200s. It was modeled on scriptural examples and ideals, including the life of Jesus, but monasticism isn't mentioned in the Bible or based on a direct Jewish precedent. Those living the monastic life are known by the generic terms *monks* and *nuns*. Monks began by living alone, at first in the Egyptian desert. As more people took on the lives of monks, they started to come together and form communities, usually living by the threefold vow of poverty, chastity, and obedience. When the great persecutions ceased with Constantine, the rigorous self-denials of monasticism, such as celibacy (no sexual activity), were seen as a substitute for martyrdom. Monks became the bearers of civilization in the western church. They preserved the Christian Bible and the literary, as well as some of the scientific heritage of Rome, which otherwise would have perished for lack of manuscript copying and study. Unlike the first Christian monks, these later monks and nuns worked in their monasteries and convents as a part of their monastic calling, and to support themselves. By the Middle Ages, many Catholic monasteries enjoyed vast properties, wealth, and social power.

martyrdom Death of Christians for their faith

heresy The church's characterization of organized internal opposition

Gnosticism Religious movement that believes this world is evil because it is material

orthodoxy Emphasis on correct teaching of the essentials of the faith

Constantinianism [CON-stan-TIN-ee-uhn-IHZ-uhm] Close association of church and state, for the promotion of religious and civil unity

monasticism Christian monks and nuns living in community

11-2d Byzantine, Medieval, and Renaissance Christianity (500–1500)

The Eastern Roman Empire, also called the Byzantine Empire, with its capital in Constantinople, lasted for more than a thousand years from its creation by Constantine in 330 to the Turkish Muslim conquest in 1453. The traditional power of Byzantine emperors over the church was curtailed after the **Iconoclastic Controversy** that began in 726. This controversy was caused by the attempt of some emperors to remove pictures of Jesus and the saints from churches, ending the veneration of these icons during worship. The emperors' iconoclasm was in part an effort to cope with Islam's attack on Christianity for its use of images. In both Eastern Orthodox and Roman Catholic Christianity, worship is offered only to God, with veneration for the saints. Muslims rejected

The head of an ancient statue of Constantine, more than four feet tall, suggests his importance in Roman history.

© ISTOCKPHOTO.COM/PIXELBARON

this distinction, thinking that offering honor to anyone other than God is idolatry. Leading monks and several empresses resisted the emperors and their allies in the church, and icons were eventually restored. The controversy over images cemented their place as an essential element of the Eastern Orthodox identity. Today, every Orthodox Church has an **iconostasis**, a screen or wall of icons, between the people and the altar. To the Orthodox, icons represent the reality of God's presence in the person of Jesus Christ, and the importance for the church of the saints in heaven. When the Iconoclastic Controversy ended in 843, the power of the church to direct its own doctrine and worship was strengthened. The controversy also strengthened the tendency of Eastern Orthodoxy to define itself by its worship and devotion rather than, as in Western Christianity (both Roman Catholicism and the Protestantism that arose later), by institution and doctrine.

Byzantine Christianity also carried out missionary activity, especially to its north. The peoples of what are now Bulgaria, Russia, and Moravia were converted to Christianity in the 800s, residents of Hungary in the 900s, and those of Poland in the 900s to the 1100s. Missionaries translated the Bible and the rituals of the church into the language of the peoples.

Slavic Orthodoxy, particularly in Russia, which thought of itself as the third Rome, was to carry on the Christian heritage of Byzantium when the Eastern Roman Empire finally fell to Muslim forces in 1453. Some of this Russian feeling for religious and cultural leadership persists today, in both the Russian Orthodox Church and the national government of Vladimir Putin.

In the Latin West, the bishop of Rome, the **pope**, set the tone for the continuing development of Christianity. By the end of the ancient period of the religion, the popes had already asserted their leadership over much of Christendom, claiming the authority of Jesus's leading disciple, Peter. When the western Roman Empire fell in the fifth century, the pope came to be the main embodiment of faith and cultural unity for Western Europe. Over time the **papacy**, the office of the pope and his authority, extended its spiritual and even political power over many of the European states. Gradually, the influence of the papacy spread across the entire western half of the European continent. At the same time, the western church's relations with the Eastern Orthodox Church worsened, until the two formally split in 1054 over doctrinal, cultural, and political issues. This division still endures today. Many Christians suppose that the Catholic-Protestant split in Western Christianity is the worse, but the split between East and West is earlier and in some ways more difficult to overcome.

Medieval Christianity in the west expressed itself not only through the papacy, bishops, and priests, but also through monks and friars. Medieval reformers within the Catholic Church, such as Bernard of Clairvaux and Pope Gregory VII, were

Iconoclastic Controversy [eye-CON-oh-CLASS-tick] Struggle in Eastern Orthodoxy over removing icons from churches

iconostasis [eye-CON-oh-STAH-sis] Screen or wall of icons at the front of Eastern Orthodox churches

pope Bishop of Rome, the head of the Roman Catholic Church

papacy [PAYP-uh-see] Office of the pope and his authority

Easter devotion using icon

friars (members of the new monastic orders that arose in the twelfth century, as opposed to the monks in the older orders). The theologians who systematized and developed Christian doctrine in the high Middle Ages, such as Anselm of Canterbury, England, and Thomas Aquinas (ah-KWIGH-nuhs), were monastics. In his major work from 1265 to 1273, Aquinas made a comprehensive overview of Christian theology, from the vantage point of the ancient Greek philosopher Aristotle's newly rediscovered thinking, and became the most influential theologian in Roman Catholicism from that point on. Some of the new movements preached the gospel to the people in churches and outdoors. Through this reform, the life of the whole Catholic Church was enriched and renewed. Another feature of the later Middle Ages was the building of cathedrals, usually one in each large city throughout Europe, in the new Gothic style that seemed to soar to heaven.

Magisterial Reformation

Mainstream Protestant reform that began with Martin Luther

A main issue in today's Christianity arose in this period: the challenge of Islam. From its beginning in 622, Islam spread rapidly in the Middle East. Soon, almost all the Middle East and North Africa were Islamic. Christian minorities lived somewhat peaceably under Islamic rule, protected by Islamic law, but they dwindled in number. Islam continued to press on the Byzantine Empire until, in 1453, Constantinople itself became a Muslim city. An important element in the confrontation of Western Christianity with Islam was to be in the long period of the Crusades (1095–1350), when Catholic forces from all over Europe retook Palestine from the Muslims, an effort that eventually failed and damaged Muslim–Christian relations through today.

At the end of the Middle Ages, around 1400, life in Western Christianity began to experience renewal in the Renaissance, the "rebirth" of classical Greco-Roman cultural ideals in art, architecture, philosophy, and literature. Some Renaissance scholars called the church back "to the foundations" of the New Testament and the ancient church. The Renaissance promoted a more human-centered view of life in place of the medieval heaven-centered view. Renaissance art, for example, more realistically portrayed saints and ordinary people on earth.

Not every aspect of the Renaissance would prove to be positive. It hastened both the rise of nationalism and the end of the medieval ideal of a Europe united by one church. Church unity had already been fractured by the split between Roman Catholicism and Eastern Orthodoxy, but it would soon be shattered completely by the Protestant Reformation, to which we now turn.

11-2e Reformation in the Western Church (1500–1600)

Movements for the reform of church teaching and practice were prevalent in the later Middle Ages. This reform usually expressed itself *through* the other traditional structures of the Catholic Church. In previous instances when reform expressed itself outside, or even against, the Catholic Church, it was declared heretical and stamped out by force, as was the case of John Wycliffe, an Oxford professor who with his followers translated the Bible into English in the 1380s, and Jan Hus, a Czech priest who led a broad reform movement in the early 1400s.

The **Magisterial Reformation**, or mainstream Protestant reform, began with Martin Luther (LOO-thur). He led an effective reform movement against the structure of the traditional church. Luther (1483–1546) was an Augustinian friar, a priest, and a professor at Wittenberg University in central Germany. Like most would-be reformers before him, Luther initially saw himself as a loyal son of the Catholic Church. In 1517, he called for a public debate over reform issues by posting his Ninety-Five Theses (propositions) on the door of the castle church in Wittenberg. The immediate complaint Luther had was the selling of indulgences to raise funds for the new St. Peter's Basilica in Rome. These were certificates securing the forgiveness of punishment in **purgatory**, the fiery place where believers' sins are burned away after death before they can enter heaven. He found the idea of buying and selling salvation unbiblical, corrupt, and even ludicrous.

Luther soon found himself so at odds with the Roman Catholic Church that he moved to create an alternative church that he called the Evangelical (characterized by the gospel of Christ) Church; after his death, others began to call it the Lutheran Church. Popes, bishops, monks, and nuns were done away with in this church, as was celibacy of the clergy. He envisioned Germany as having its own, more indigenous form of Christianity. He translated the Bible into German, put hymns and worship into the language of the people, and reformed the Mass. Evangelical Christians were urged to receive Holy Communion every week, in contrast to the once-a-year Catholic practice in the Middle Ages. Luther saw the center of Christianity in the doctrine of salvation by faith alone. He also stressed the central role of God's love and grace, the sole authority of the Bible over the Church, and the role of the individual Christian's conscience. Reformers devalued the role of the saints and denied their power to intercede with God

for Christians on earth or in purgatory. When Luther and his movement were protected and then promoted by the rulers of several German states, Protestantism gained a foothold that would enable it to endure and spread to other parts of Germany. By 1600, the Lutheran reform had taken over much of Germany and all of Scandinavia (see Map 11.2).

What historians call the **Radical Reformation** arose in tandem with the Magisterial Reformation. Conrad Grebel (GRAY-buhl) and the Swiss Brethren movement insisted that the mainstream reform of Luther and others was inconsistent and halfhearted. They argued for a radical reform to return to a pure "New Testament Christianity," including the following:

- Baptism by full-body immersion of adult believers only, after a conversion experience
- Complete separation of the church from the civil government
- Pacifism, with refusal to be drafted for warfare
- Common ownership of some property
- Strict church enforcement of Christian morality among church members

They soon became known as **Anabaptists**, "rebaptizers," but over time the name was simplified to the term we know today, *Baptists*. In the 1520s, the movement spread through Switzerland and later found a home in many Protestant lands. Eventually, the Baptists became a widespread Protestant church, even extending their influence to lands such as Russia, where other Protestant churches could not penetrate. Baptists kept their major emphasis on the baptism of believing adults only; other Anabaptist groups, which would become the Mennonites and the Amish of today, have preserved pacifism and detachment from civil authority in addition to the baptism of believers.

The Reformed (Calvinist) branch of Protestantism was, similar to the Anabaptists, born in the political world of the Swiss city-republics. (All Protestant churches were reformed from Roman Catholicism, and the movement is called the Reformation, but the churches born of the Calvinist branch of the Reformation have in

purgatory Place where believers' sins are burned away after death before they can enter heaven

Radical Reformation Branch of the Protestant Reformation that wanted radical reforms to restore "New Testament Christianity"

Anabaptists "Rebaptizers," members of the Radical Reformation group that accepted only adult baptism

Monument of Martin Luther in Wittenberg, Germany, holding his translation of the Bible into German

© CHRISTINA HANCK/DREAMSTIME.COM

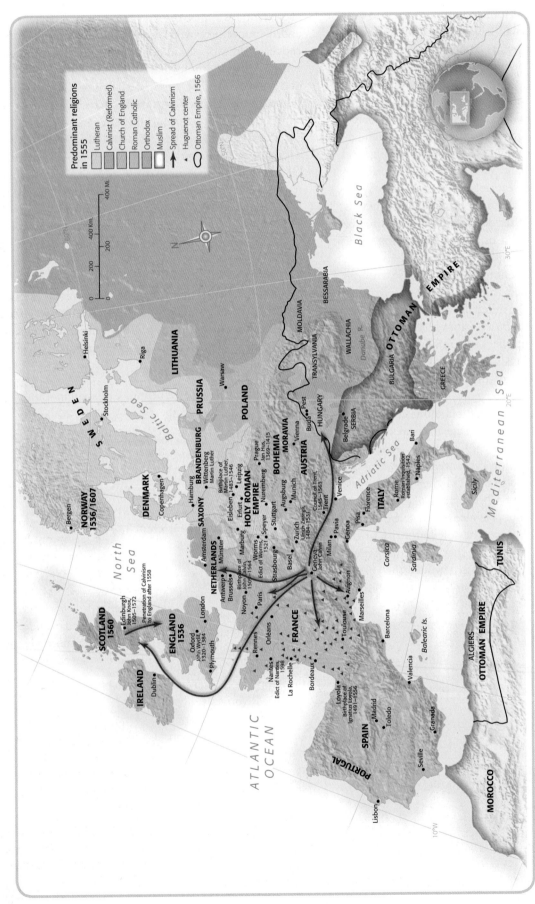

Predominant religions in 1555

- Lutheran
- Calvinist (Reformed)
- Church of England
- Roman Catholic
- Orthodox
- Muslim
- ↑ Spread of Calvinism
- ▲ Huguenot center
- ◯ Ottoman Empire, 1566

ATLANTIC OCEAN

IRELAND
Dublin

SCOTLAND 1560
Edinburgh John Knox, 1505–1572

ENGLAND 1536
Penetration of Calvinism to England after 1558
London
Oxford John Wyclif, 1320–1384
Plymouth

North Sea

NORWAY 1536/1607
Bergen

SWEDEN
Stockholm
Helsinki

DENMARK
Copenhagen

Baltic Sea

LITHUANIA
Riga

PRUSSIA
Warsaw

POLAND

BRANDENBURG
Hamburg

SAXONY
Wittenberg Martin Luther
Birthplace of Martin Luther, 1483–1546
Eisleben
Erfurt
Leipzig

HOLY ROMAN EMPIRE
Nuremberg
Speyer
Augsburg
Munich

BOHEMIA
Prague
Jan Hus, 1369–1415

MORAVIA

AUSTRIA
Vienna
Council of Trent, 1545–1563
Trent

Budapest
Buda
Pest
HUNGARY

MOLDAVIA

TRANSYLVANIA

WALLACHIA
Danube R.

BESSARABIA

Black Sea

OTTOMAN EMPIRE

BULGARIA

SERBIA
Belgrade

GREECE

NETHERLANDS
Amsterdam
Münster
Antwerp
Brussels
Birthplace of John Calvin, 1509–1564
Noyon
Marburg
Worms
Edict of Worms, 1521
Strasbourg
Basel
Zurich
Ulrich Zwingli, 1484–1531
Geneva
John Calvin
Milan
Pavia
Genoa

FRANCE
Paris
Rennes
Orléans
Nantes
Edict of Nantes, 1598
La Rochelle
Bordeaux
Toulouse
Avignon
Marseilles

Venice

ITALY
Florence
Pisa
Rome
Roman Inquisition established, 1542
Naples
Bari

Adriatic Sea

Corsica
Sardinia

Sicily

Mediterranean Sea

SPAIN
Madrid
Toledo
Loyola
Birthplace of Ignatius Loyola, 1491–1556
Barcelona
Valencia
Balearic Is.
Granada
Seville

PORTUGAL
Lisbon

MOROCCO

ALGIERS
OTTOMAN EMPIRE
TUNIS

N
400 Mi.
400 Km.
200
0

Map 11.2

Reformation Europe

The Protestant Reformation reshaped Europe's religious landscape in the 1500s and early 1600s. By the mid-1550s, some form of Protestantism had become dominant in much of northern continental Europe, England, and Scotland. Catholicism remained predominant in the southern half of Western Europe and in parts of Eastern Europe. Catholics in Europe felt pressure from the Islamic Ottoman Empire, but Muslim rulers protected Protestants under their rule in Hungary and Transylvania.

particular called themselves the Reformed Church.) Huldreich Zwingli (HUHLD-righk TSVING-lee) began the Reformed movement in Zurich, but in the next three decades it shifted to Berne, Basel, and especially French-speaking Geneva. There, Frenchman John Calvin (1509–1564), who had studied law and theology at the University of Paris, reformed the city to Protestant ideals. He stressed (in addition to Luther's main ideas) such teachings as the sovereignty of God over all life, and human responsibility to live out one's Christian calling in everyday life. Calvin carried out social reforms that became common in the western world, such as levying a tax to support free compulsory public education for all children. Geneva became a sanctuary for persecuted Protestants from many places in Europe.

Similar to Luther, Calvin wrote prolifically, and soon his ideas for reform spread widely. He was known especially as a systematizer and promoter of Protestant Christianity. His book *The Institutes [Foundations] of the Christian Religion* soon became the most influential book of Protestantism. Calvin's influence in the Reformed movement was so great that it also became known in later centuries as *Calvinism*. Calvinist churches were founded by the end of the century not only in Switzerland, but also in France (where Calvinists were called Huguenots [HYOO-guh-nots]), Scotland, The Netherlands, Germany, and Hungary.

Reformation came to England by way of politics. In the 1520s, King Henry VIII opposed the pope over the king's right to divorce and remarry. In 1529, Henry began forming a Church of England ("Anglican") under his control, which was to become a middle way between Catholics and Protestants, especially in worship and organization. Its doctrine eventually was closer to the teaching of the Reformers than to that of Rome. Henry's daughter Mary tried to bring England back to the Roman Church by a variety of means, some so violent that they earned her the name Bloody Mary, but by the reign of Henry's younger daughter, Elizabeth I, the Church of England was firmly established. English monarchs were made the head of the Church of England and "Defender of the Faith," which explains why in 2011 the wedding of Prince William (the presumptive eventual heir to the throne) and Katherine Middleton was held in formal Anglican style, and why their children have been baptized into the Anglican Church.

In 1620, the Reformed movement came to America via the English Protestants called **Puritans**—so called because they wanted to purify the Church of England from its continuing Roman Catholic elements. The name *Puritan* has come to mean "killjoy" or even "self-righteous," but Puritanism wasn't like that. Of all religious groups, the Puritans were to have the largest influence on the development of American government. As David Hall says in *A Reforming People* (2011), Puritanism was a daring and successful reform movement in the English-speaking world during early modern times.[1]

The **Catholic Reform** has been called the Counter-Reformation, and this term is still used by some. When his initial measures against Protestants didn't prove effective, the pope finally called a council of bishops and theologians in 1545 at Trent, Italy, to consider church reform. Widespread reforms of Catholic Church life emerged from Trent, and many of the more glaring abuses were removed. With the help of the new Jesuit order, these reforms were carried out

A Christian is baptized into the faith in a way that goes back to Anabaptist practice.

SCHISTRA/SHUTTERSTOCK.COM

Puritans English Protestants who wanted to purify the Church of England from its continuing Roman Catholic features

Catholic Reform Movement called the Counter-Reformation, spurred on by the 1545 Council of Trent

in nations and regions that were still predominantly Roman Catholic. Even there, the reforms of Trent were subject to national policy; for example, France rejected them as too conservative and intrusive, and Spain—which often viewed itself as more Catholic than the pope—resisted them as too liberal. For areas that had already become Protestant, about half of Europe above the Alps, the reforms of Trent were "too little, too late." Once nations became Protestant, they didn't typically return to Rome. Other parts of the Catholic Reformation were a revival of mysticism, especially in Spain, and a new focus on the system of Thomas Aquinas as a mighty fortress against Protestant thought. In all, the Roman Church emerged from the 1500s severely chastened in numbers and political influence, but strengthened in spirit.

Meanwhile, events in the New World were proving a bright spot in the fortunes of Roman Catholicism. When Spain, and later Portugal, explored and then colonized the New World in the Western Hemisphere, Roman Catholic missionaries accompanied them. They conquered together "for God and for gold." The indigenous peoples of Central and South America were quickly brought into the Christian faith. Spanish cultural, military, and religious outposts called *missions* were constructed; then thousands of churches were built for the indigenous peoples; and eventually monasteries and nunneries were established for them. A few priests and bishops protested the high cost of colonization to the indigenous peoples, even founding a Jesuit state in what is now Peru (a story told in the acclaimed film *The Mission*), but to no avail. Even today the work of these Spanish missionaries is controversial; for example, a dispute took place in 2015 over making Father Junipero Serra, a founder of several California missions, a saint. Many Native American leaders blame Father Serra for the suppression of their culture and the deaths of thousands of their ancestors. In sum,

A statue of Father Junipero Serra and a young native convert stands in the San Fernando mission he founded near Los Angeles, California.

FPI/SHUTTERSTOCK.COM

Pietism [PIGH-uh-tiz-um] Protestant movement stressing individual piety in knowledge and emotion

although the Roman Church lost many lands in Europe to Protestantism in the 1500s, it gained much in the Americas, where Catholicism is still strong.

11-2f The Early Modern Period (1600–1900)

Because of the settled and more tolerant situation after the "wars of religion" ended around 1648, each Protestant church and the Roman Catholic Church occupied its own parts of Europe, and Protestant teachings were articulated more fully. *Confessionalism*, named for the doctrinal statements called confessions issued by the various Reformation churches, brought a drive for doctrinal correctness as an important aspect of church life. *Scholasticism* stressed the rational explanation and defense of the various Protestant belief systems.

The reaction against arid confessionalism and scholasticism wasn't slow in coming. When the several dimensions of religion that we saw in Chapter 1 are reduced to just a few, reaction will set in. **Pietism** arose in the last half of the seventeenth century, born with Philip Jakob Spener's (SPAY-ner) *Pious Considerations* in 1675. Spener rebelled against the Protestant orthodoxy of his day, which he viewed as sterile and lifeless. He proposed a continuing Reformation to bring the goals of Luther to fulfillment: personal Bible study, mutual correction and encouragement in Christian living, spiritual growth for all laity, and stress on emotional dimensions of faith. Pietists formed separate churches in many Lutheran and Reformed nations. The leadership of the Lutheran churches tried to suppress Pietism, but it soon became a major movement. Similar to Anabaptist churches before them, Pietism led to *gathered churches*, not the state churches to which nearly all citizens belonged.

In the 1700s, Pietism took on the major goal of counteracting the influence on Christianity of the Enlightenment, the period of secularization of culture led by reason and not faith. The Enlightenment's rationalism and "free thinking" were easier for the church to deal with when they were aggressively atheistic, as in the French Revolution. But when the Enlightenment led to more subtle changes in the church itself, such as the introduction of modern historical sciences and their application to the Bible and theology, the effect on Christianity was profound. Especially in Protestant faculties of German universities, the acceptance of these new methods of scholarship led some to question the Christian faith. The concurrent discovery of ancient Asian religions gave rise to a questioning of the uniqueness and absoluteness of Christianity, something that continues today. The Enlightenment's effort to separate church and state, and the ideas of religious toleration and the freedom associated with it, would succeed throughout Western and Northern Europe, but would succeed most fully in the United States. Constantinianism was rapidly losing ground.

The nineteenth century saw the challenge of secular reason continue. Discoveries in natural science were particularly challenging to the old certainties of Christianity. The work of evolutionary biologist Charles Darwin called into question ancient Christian beliefs in the special creation of humanity in the image of God. Although Protestant churches were more directly and immediately affected by the Enlightenment and its heirs, which produced both secularism outside the church and doctrinal change inside, Roman Catholicism later saw its effects in the Catholic *Modernist* movement. In 1864, Pope Pius IX issued the *Syllabus of Errors* that listed eighty Modernist ideas that the Roman church had officially condemned, including the separation of church and state, recognition of Protestantism, and a purely scientific view of life. Not until the twentieth century would Catholic, Protestant, and (to a lesser extent) Eastern Orthodox churches come to grips in positive, constructive ways with the challenges of modern knowledge.

Despite these challenges, nineteenth-century Christianity was broadly optimistic about the prospects of the Christian religion. One cause for optimism was the powerful social reform movements that grew out of Christianity: the birth of the women's liberation movement; an attack on the rising rates of alcoholism in North America by the prohibition of alcoholic beverages; and especially the abolition of slavery, a story told in the film and Broadway play, *Amazing Grace*. The largest cause for optimism was the powerful missionary movement that flourished in the 1800s and continues somewhat lessened today. The Protestant and

> Discovery of the ancient religions of Asia gave rise to a questioning of the uniqueness and absoluteness of Christianity, something that continues today.

Roman Catholic churches of the west set out (in their separate ways) to evangelize the entire world, or at least the large parts of it not yet exposed to the gospel. In 1800, fewer than one in four people in the world were Christian; by 1900, one in three were Christian. Christianity finally became the global religion envisioned in the conclusion of the Gospel of Matthew, where Jesus commands his disciples to proclaim his message to all nations and peoples.

11-2g Modern Christianity (1900–Present)

The optimistic hope present in western culture and the church at the end of the 1800s went largely unfulfilled. The new era was one of severe crisis and challenge. The carnage of World War I (1914–1918), the worldwide pandemic of influenza, and then global economic depression began the movement away from cultural optimism. The rise of aggressive, totalitarian regimes, first in Russia and then in Italy and Germany, led to the horrors of World War II (1939–1945), with its massive civilian casualties and the Holocaust. Even the end of the war brought with it the new uncertainties of nuclear weapons and the Cold War. All these events were to shake Christian optimism to its roots. The result for some was a loss of faith, but for others a rethinking of the essence of Christianity. In the United States, **fundamentalism** arose to oppose liberalization of church doctrine. Fundamentalism features a strictly literal interpretation of the Bible, an insistence on the truth of certain key Christian teachings (the "fundamentals" from which the movement takes its name), and an aggressive attitude toward Christian liberalism specifically, and toward unbelief generally.

This impulse against liberalism in the 1900s was shared by others who were in no way fundamentalist. Swiss theologian Karl Barth (bart, 1886–1968), who was to become the leading Christian theologian of the century, turned away from liberal, optimistic Protestantism to

fundamentalism
Protestant movement featuring a strictly literal interpretation of the Bible and an insistence on the truth of certain "fundamental" Christian teachings

reassert the transcendent power of a faith that cannot be shaped by human culture. The movement that Barth sparked came to be called neo-orthodoxy, a new assertion in modern times of traditional Christian theology, especially in its Protestant form. (It has no formal relationship with Eastern Orthodoxy, however.) After World War II, this movement came to the English-speaking world and had a direct effect on its theology and life, as it still has today. Although liberalism has been reduced in size and chastened in spirit from its heyday around 1900, liberal, progressive theology has continued in some parts of Protestantism, especially in the mainstream denominations—Protestant churches united under a single name and organization, such as the Episcopal Church or the United Methodist Church.

While the theological reassessment occurred, a movement for greater unity among the churches came into prominence. **Ecumenism**, a movement for greater understanding and cooperation among Christian denominations, had been planted and nurtured in the mission fields of the various Protestant churches, where missionaries learned to minimize their denominational differences and cooperate in the face of a non-Christian environment. In the twentieth century, the National Council of Churches in the United States and the World Council of Churches would be the institutional bearers of this movement. Ecumenism has changed how theologians conceptualize the faith, how the different Christian churches relate to each other, and how grassroots Christians live out their faith in worship and daily life. This spirit of ecumenism also affected the Eastern Orthodox churches throughout the world; they've participated fully in the ecumenical movement from the start.

At the same time, a new movement for reform was gathering in the Roman Catholic Church that would prove to be the most important Christian event of the twentieth century.

Catholicism had been insulated from dealing with modern challenges (science, secularism, religious toleration, and so on) by its sheer size and its church structure. But when Pope John XXIII convened the **Second Vatican Council** from 1962 to 1966, fresh, strong winds of reform blew through the church. In Vatican II, the Catholic Church

- recognized the laity as essential to the church;
- reformed worship by putting the Mass in national languages and increasing lay participation;
- moved the altar from the front wall of the church and had the priest face the people as the Mass was said;
- opened ecumenical dialogue with Protestants and the Orthodox, affirming that they were in some way legitimate Christians;
- affirmed for the first time religious liberty and toleration for all people; and
- took a more balanced view of non-Christian faiths, especially Judaism.

Never before had any church changed itself so quickly and deeply as the Roman Catholic Church did after Vatican II. Many Roman Catholics today don't remember the way the Church was before Vatican II, and it's hard for them to imagine a form of Catholic Church life that had existed from the 1500s to the 1960s. The Catholic Church continues to change, recently with the resignation of Pope Benedict XVI in 2013 for reasons

A fundamentalist Christian makes a public witness to his faith outside the Lincoln Memorial in Washington, D.C., calling for national repentance.

of infirmity, the first time in more than five hundred years that a pope has resigned from his office. Only time will tell if this sets a precedent for later popes. Benedict was replaced by Jorge Bergoglio (HOHR-hay ber-GOH-lee-oh), the archbishop of Buenos Aires, Argentina, who took the name Francis, after St. Francis of Assisi. This marked three "firsts" for the Catholic Church: the first Jesuit to become pope, the first pope from the Western Hemisphere, and the first pope from the Global South. More will be said about Pope Francis in Section 11-6b.

11-3 Christian Teachings as Reflected in the Nicene Creed

Christian believers in Seoul, South Korea, gather at the Yoido Full Gospel Church, which, at 1 million members, is the largest single Christian congregation in the world. This church, which belongs to the Assemblies of God denomination, has back-to-back services held from dawn to dusk to accommodate the numbers. Protestant Christianity—both mainstream and independent—has grown so strong in South Korea that its churches have begun to send Korean missionaries to other parts of the world. The Yoido congregation's size is emblematic of the worldwide growth and power of Pentecostal, Holy Spirit–centered Christianity.

Christian teaching is founded on the doctrine of the **Trinity**, one God in three Persons—the Father, Son, and Holy Spirit. The Trinity is not found formally in the New Testament, but most of its important components are. Christians believe that Jesus was the **incarnation** (coming in human form) of the eternal Son of God. As both human and divine, Jesus suffered, died, was buried, and was resurrected from the dead to open heaven to those who believe in him. Jesus founded a community of his followers; after his bodily ascension to heaven, the church carried on Jesus's work by the power and direction of the Holy Spirit. Jesus rules and reigns with God the Father until he will return to defeat evil, judge all humans (living and dead), and grant eternal life to his followers.

The **Nicene Creed**, known by its revised form as the Nicene-Constantinopolitan Creed, completed in 381, is the leading Christian statement of belief. **Creeds** (from the Latin *credo*, "I believe") are formal statements of belief meant to be binding on the church (see "A Closer Look: The Nicene-Constantinopolitan Creed"). All Catholic and Eastern Orthodox doctrine is formally rooted in creeds, as well as that of churches originating in the Lutheran and Reformed branches of the Reformation. A precursor of the Nicene Creed, the **Apostles' Creed**, is often recited in Protestant churches. So powerful has the place of creeds been in the church that even more independent Protestant churches that reject the idea of creeds believe the doctrines taught in the Nicene Creed, such as many Baptists and Pentecostalists. In what follows, we'll discuss Christian teaching using the creeds' main headings of Father, Son, and Holy Spirit, giving the Nicene Creed something of a close reading. We'll also deal briefly in this discussion with later Christian formulation and use of these teachings.

11-3a God the Father

Thankfully for Christians and students of Christianity, its teaching about God the Father is unproblematic, and the Christian tradition has rarely had to debate it. Much of the first article of the Nicene Creed is drawn directly from Jewish belief about God that was settled long before Jesus. God is all powerful (Almighty) in heaven and on earth. God is the creator (maker) of heaven and earth, not only of all things seen on the earth, but also of all things unseen to humans (things in heaven). Nothing is outside of God's power. That God is the creator of all physical and

The Trinity Knot of Celtic Christian origin symbolizes the Father, Son, and Holy Spirit as one. The crown of thorns tied into it is a symbol of the suffering of Christ.

RICHSEARSDOTCOM/ISTOCKPHOTO.COM

Trinity Christian teaching of one God in three equal persons—the Father, Son, and Holy Spirit

incarnation The eternal Son of God becoming human in the person of Jesus Christ

Nicene Creed [nigh-SEEN] Most influential of all Christian statements of belief; completed in 381

creed Formal statement of belief meant to be binding on the church

Apostles' Creed Short creed often recited in Protestant churches

A Closer Look

The Nicene-Constantinopolitan Creed, 381 C.E.

Several English versions of the Nicene-Constantinopolitan Creed have been used in the past fifty years or so. Here is the Ecumenical Version of 1975, the form used by most Protestant churches and the Eastern Orthodox churches. (The Orthodox do not say "and the Son" in the sentence that begins "We believe in the Holy Spirit.") The Roman Catholic Church uses a slightly different version, from its recent *Third Roman Missal*, including a shift to "I believe."

> We believe in one God, the Father, the Almighty maker of heaven and earth, of all that is, seen and unseen.
>
> We believe in one Lord, Jesus Christ, the only Son of God, eternally begotten of the Father,
>
> God from God, Light from Light, true God from true God, begotten, not made, of one Being with the Father.
>
> Through him all things were made.

> For us men and for our salvation he came down from heaven: by the power of the Holy Spirit he became incarnate from the Virgin Mary, and was made man.
>
> For our sake he was crucified under Pontius Pilate; he suffered death and was buried.
>
> On the third day he rose again in accordance with the Scriptures; he ascended into heaven and is seated at the right hand of the Father.
>
> He will come again in glory to judge the living and the dead, and his kingdom will have no end.
>
> We believe in the Holy Spirit, the Lord, the giver of Life, who proceeds from the Father and the Son.
>
> With the Father and the Son he is worshiped and glorified.
>
> He has spoken through the Prophets.
>
> We believe in one holy catholic and apostolic Church.
>
> We acknowledge one baptism for the forgiveness of sins.
>
> We look for the resurrection of the dead, and the life of the world to come. Amen.

spiritual reality—and that God would become human in Jesus—strongly implies that the world is a good, or at least a redeemable, place. Behind this teaching about God lie other key Jewish ideas. God is a living being, the "I am who I am" in Exodus 3:14, not a force or a cosmic principle. Christians believe that God the Father is a personal being just as fully as Jesus is a person. The decisive aspect of creation is that God fashioned humans in God's own image. This special position of humans makes them coworkers with God in the continuation and care of creation. The incarnation of God in the human being Jesus is, for Christians, the ultimate validation of the worth of human life.

What's new in the Christian teaching about God lies in the first thing the Nicene Creed says about God: that God is *the Father*. God was known metaphorically as a father to Israel in Judaism, but this wasn't a main understanding of God. In Christianity, God is first and foremost the Christian's Father, but this relationship derives from and is built on Jesus's special relationship to God. Jesus regularly calls God "Father," especially in the prayer that he taught his disciples, known variously as the "Our Father" or the "Lord's Prayer." Jesus used the Aramaic

word *abba* (AH-bah) for God; it was usually employed by children for their earthly father and expresses childlike trust in, and intimacy with, one's father. This father–son relationship that Jesus had with God is a model for the relationship that Christians have with God.

According to the account of his baptism, Jesus understood his sonship when a voice from heaven said, "This is my beloved Son, with whom I am well pleased" (Matthew 3:17). In the Gospel of John, this sonship constitutes the basis for the self-awareness of Jesus: "I and the Father are one" (John 10:30). Although scholars disagree on whether Jesus actually said things like this, Christians believe it is an authentic insight into who Jesus really is. In Jesus Christ, God the Father was revealed more fully to humans, and worked in and through Jesus for the salvation of the world. Some Christians today dislike the term *Father* for its apparent gender reference to an ungendered God and its use of human fathers—who are often flawed and sometimes abusive—to explain God. However, the fact that Christian teaching understands the human relationship with God to be based on Jesus's relationship with God helps to ameliorate the weakness of this metaphor today.

11-3b God the Son

The fullest section of the Nicene Creed, as with Christian statements of belief in general, is the center part that deals with Jesus Christ. This, of course, is exactly what we should expect in Christianity. Teachings about Jesus go back to the faith experiences of the first disciples. The early church experienced God in the person of Jesus, although the Gospels are clear that his disciples didn't fully recognize this, much less spread this message on their own, until after Jesus's resurrection. Jesus is the crucified and exalted Lord, and the Son of God. He sits at the right hand of the Father and will return in glory to bring in the Father's rule. Jesus has become the center of belief and devotion for Christians. However, as we saw earlier, Jesus is an enigmatic figure, and the church's teaching about him can't easily be stated in a series of sentences, as much as the creeds try to do this.

From the beginning of the church, different interpretations of Jesus have existed, and it took several centuries for the church to fully articulate its understanding. The author of the Gospel of Mark, for example, seems to understand Jesus as the man upon whom the Holy Spirit descends when he is baptized in the Jordan River and about whom the voice of God declares from the heavens, "You are my beloved son" (Mark 1:11). In Matthew and Luke, Jesus's special identity begins at his conception in the womb of the Virgin Mary (see "A Closer Look: The Doctrine of the Virgin Mary"). The teaching in Mark's Gospel, and to a lesser extent in Matthew and Luke, provided the foundation for one of two early schools of thought concerning the person of Christ.

These two schools, or types of theology, dominated the ancient church's teaching on Jesus Christ. Approaches to that derived from the theological school of Antioch in Syria start from the humanity of Jesus and see his divinity as joined to him by God through the Holy Spirit. In other words, Jesus's status as God's Son is founded on his humanity. This view is common among many modern Christians—both Protestants and Roman Catholics—in the western world, who stress his humanity while also affirming that God was in him in a special way. Another view, adopted by the school of Alexandria, Egypt, is a leading theme of the Gospel of John. This Gospel regards Jesus Christ primarily as the eternal Son of God become human. Here, his divinity is first and foundational, and the humanity of Jesus is joined to it. This view is common today among traditional Roman Catholics, doctrinally conservative Protestants, and most Eastern Orthodox. Debates between Christians about the nature of Jesus, especially around the time of the Nicene Creed, got so heated that rioting broke out in major cities over it—something hard for Christians today to imagine.

The Nicene Creed affirms that Jesus Christ is "the only Son of God, eternally begotten of the Father." In other words, the divine nature in Jesus is God's eternal Son. The Creed stresses this divine nature in Jesus by poetic repetitions: Jesus Christ is "God from God, Light from Light, true God from true God." In his divine being, he is "of one Being with the Father," not a different, lesser kind of God made (created) by the Father. The Creed goes on to link the Son of God to God the Father by stating the Son's role in creation—"Through him all things were made"—just as it affirmed earlier that the Father made all things. Then the Creed talks at more length about the incarnation: "For us men [humans] and for our salvation, he came down from heaven, by the power of the Holy Spirit he became incarnate from the Virgin Mary, and was made man." Eastern Orthodoxy has stressed more than Western Christianity the meaning of the incarnation for the salvation of humankind; Western Christians stress the meaning of the death and resurrection of Jesus for salvation.

BRAINSIL/ISTOCKPHOTO.COM

Piety toward the death of Jesus is shown in different ways; here a man kisses a crucifix in devotion.

Jesus as the Good Shepherd is a common image of salvation and spiritual guidance in Christ.

Then the Creed skips to the end of Jesus's life and emphasizes the reality of his redemptive suffering. Why it should ignore the teachings of Jesus—and not even mention that he taught—is something of a mystery to modern people, but the Creed wants to emphasize the significance of Jesus's deeds, his story rather than his teaching. "For our sake he was crucified under Pontius Pilate; he suffered death and was buried. On the third day he rose again in accordance with the Scriptures." Exactly *how* Jesus's death saves humans is often debated: Is it a sacrifice, a defeat of evil (Christ as victor), a moral example, or all of these and more? Without belief that Jesus rose again in resurrection, it is clear from the New Testament accounts, his movement would have ended and Jesus would soon have disappeared into the mists of time. The final part of the Creed's section on Jesus speaks about his present and future: "He ascended into heaven and is seated on the right hand of the Father; He will come again in glory to judge the living and the dead, and his kingdom will have no end." That Jesus sits on the Father's right hand refers to his present reign with God the Father. The rest of this section of the Creed affirms the standard Christian expectation that Jesus will return "in glory" at the end of human history to bring God's eternal reign to earth.

11-3c God the Holy Spirit

The Holy Spirit is a challenging topic in Christian teaching. To begin with, the name "Holy Spirit" doesn't evoke for us meanings such as "Father" and "Son"

do. It has been harder for Christians to conceive of the Holy Spirit as a divine person in the same way as they think of the Father and the Son. (Feminists, however, hold that this is a good thing and point to the feminine aspects of the Spirit.) The foundational view of the Holy Spirit is sketched in the next section of the Nicene Creed: "We believe in the Holy Spirit, the Lord, the giver of Life, who proceeds from the Father and the Son. With the Father and the Son he is worshiped and glorified. He has spoken through the prophets."

The Creed ties the Spirit to God the Father and God the Son in a variety of ways. The Spirit is called Lord, the term Christians regularly use for the Father and the Son. Next, the Spirit is called the giver of Life, which refers not only to a role at creation, but especially to giving life to believers now and eternally. The next phrase has been problematic between the eastern and western churches. Originally, the Creed said that the Spirit "proceeds from the Father," just as Jesus (in parallel) is "begotten" by the Father, but in the Middle Ages the Catholic Church added "and the Son," which Protestant churches later shared. It might seem improbable for us today that such a small phrase could cause such big problems, but "and the Son" was a huge point of contention between the East and the West, one of the causes for their formal split in 1054. Some western churches omit it today, or put it in brackets, and it is still a bone of contention today. Next, the Creed says that the Spirit is "worshiped and glorified," a sign of certain divine status.

The last thing said about the Holy Spirit, that the Spirit "has spoken through the prophets," is a powerful and problematic statement about the Spirit. Although the Holy Spirit is said in the New Testament to mediate the presence of Jesus to the church and explain his words, essentially a conserving task, the Spirit is also powerful, uncontrollable, and unpredictable. Prophetic speech in the Spirit is challenging to the church. Every movement for change in church history has appealed to the authority and leading of the Holy Spirit. Opposition to the mainstream church—through appeal to the Spirit—was found in Montanism (MAHN-tuh-nihz-um) around 150 C.E. This movement saw itself as the fulfillment of the promise of the coming of the Spirit on the first church. Joachim of Fiore in Italy began a movement against the institutional church in the 1200s. He promised the beginning of the period of the Holy Spirit, in which the institutional church would be replaced by a community of charismatic figures, all filled with the Spirit. This was put down, but other radical movements claiming to be based on the Spirit would surface in the Protestant Reformation. In the twentieth century

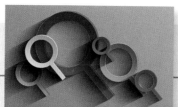
The Doctrine of the Virgin Mary

The teaching that the Virgin Mary is the "mother/bearer of God," or **Theotokos**, is closely connected to the incarnation. As the church wrestled with articulating its belief in the identity of Jesus, the mother of the Son of God gained a special place within the church as the Theotokos. To a significant degree, this was in an effort to understand the nature of Jesus, not to promote his mother.

Historians see the expansion of the veneration of the Virgin Mary as the Mother of God, and the formation of doctrines explaining this, as one of the most remarkable occurrences in the ancient church after about 100 C.E. The New Testament offers only scanty points of departure for this development. Although she has a prominent place in the narratives of the Nativity, Mary soon disappears behind the figure of Jesus. His family, including his mother—who thought he was mentally disturbed (Mark 3:21)—opposed his ministry. All the Gospels stress the fact that Jesus separated himself from his family, and only the Gospels of Matthew and Luke mention the virginal conception. The Gospel of John mentions the mother of Jesus in a positive light, but not by name. Both Roman Catholics and the Orthodox believe that Mary was a lifelong virgin; this serves as an example of dedication to God, even of celibacy. The vast majority of Protestants believe that she was virginal only until the birth of Jesus, and then had other children with Joseph by natural means.

Despite her earlier doubts, Mary was present as a believer in the earliest church, and in the early 100s the doctrine of the virginal conception of Jesus spread widely in Christianity, where it was put together with the doctrine of the incarnation. The doctrine of the virginal conception found its way into all Christian creeds, as did mention of the Virgin Mary herself. Veneration of Mary (not worship) spread widely in the West and the East, and by medieval times many churches had special chapels dedicated to the Virgin Mary. Mary became the Queen of Heaven and the chief intercessor for the church on earth. She received increasing prayer (the Hail Mary) and devotion, especially in times of great distress, such as during the Black Plague in the 1400s. Devotion to Mary was throttled back somewhat after the Catholic Reform, and it was never as strong in the Orthodox

Modern painting in Byzantine style of Mary and the child Jesus. This Mother and Child artistic theme speaks deeply to Christians about the humanity of Jesus Christ, whatever they may believe about Mary.

churches as in Roman Catholicism. A high-watermark of Marian devotion in the Roman Catholic Church was reached in 1854, when Pope Pius IX decreed that Mary was free from the consequences of Adam's fall into sin, called the Immaculate Conception. This must be distinguished carefully from the virginal conception of Jesus, with which it is often confused by non-Catholics. In recent times, veneration of Mary has been promoted by certain popes, especially John Paul II (pope from 1978 to 2005).

In sum, Christian devotion to Mary has been steady and persistent for most Roman Catholic and Eastern Orthodox Christians, and for some Anglicans as well. For Protestants, however, this devotion to the Virgin ended during the Reformation, and many liberal Protestants today no longer believe in the virginal conception of Jesus.

Theotokos [thee-AH-toh-koss] Virgin Mary as the "mother/bearer of God"

God the Father, Son, and Holy Spirit (as a dove, top) in St. Nicholas Church, Amsterdam, The Netherlands

guidance for the moral and spiritual life of the Christian. The Creed closes with an affirmation of "the resurrection of the dead, and the life of the world to come." Although the Creed doesn't mention him explicitly at this point, Jesus is the center of resurrection and life, just as he was the first to rise from the dead. He will return in glory to fully bring in God's reign, and the world to come will be present with its full life. This traditional Christian teaching about the end of the world—the return of Christ, resurrection, and judgment with eternal reward and eternal punishment—has been widely believed in the history of Christianity, but in modern times many liberal Protestants and some Roman Catholics have called it into doubt, preferring to think of an open human future.

through today, the widespread charismatic movement has centered on the recovery of the experience of the Holy Spirit.

11-3d The Conclusion of the Nicene Creed: Church, Baptism, and Christian Hope

Finally, the Nicene Creed affirms, "We believe in one holy catholic and apostolic Church. We acknowledge one baptism for the forgiveness of sins. We look for the resurrection of the dead, and the life of the world to come." Belief in the Church affirms that the Church—which is holy, catholic, and apostolic—is a divine part of God's plan for human salvation. Ancient Christians believed that it was the continuing body founded by Jesus. The Creed then mentions the importance of one baptism for salvation but makes no mention of the Eucharist or any other church ritual. Baptism has, from the first Christian generation, been the ritual of initiation into the Christian faith; the experience of baptism and the instruction that surrounds it give

Chalcedon [KAL-seh-don] Council in 451 that defined the relationship of the human and divine natures of Christ

Getting back now to the continuing controversy over Christ's nature that the Nicene Council did not fully settle, a new council at **Chalcedon** (451) finally ended the argument between Antioch and Alexandria by drawing from each. It declared, "We all unanimously teach . . . one and the same Son, our Lord Jesus Christ, perfect in deity and perfect in humanity . . . in two natures, without being mixed, transmuted, divided, or separated. . . . The identity of each nature is preserved and concurs into one person and being." At Nicea and Chalcedon, the church affirmed a paradox, and continues to do so today: First, Jesus is fully divine, the Son of God perfectly present in one person. Second, Jesus Christ is completely human, not only in his historical life, but also after his resurrection and through all eternity.

11-4 Christian Ethics: Following the Way of Jesus Christ

A new translation of the New Testament published by the American branch of Oxford University Press causes a stir around the world. Titled the *Inclusive Bible*, it features "thoroughly non-sexist" wording. Some critics deride it as the "politically correct version" and a dangerous innovation. However, students of Christianity recognize that this type of translation has a rich pedigree in America. It can trace its roots to the influential, and even more controversial, *Women's Bible* of 1898, a seminal work in the foundation of the feminist movement. The publication of the *Inclusive Bible* touches an important contemporary moral theme in Christianity: the place of women in the faith.

As an ethical monotheism, the Christian religion is based on its view of God. God's self-revelation shows God to be both radically good and radically loving. Christians must worship God but also must live their entire lives according to God's will. Jesus affirmed that the main point of this obedience is to love God and to love one's neighbor (Matthew 22:37–39).

11-4a Foundations in the Ten Commandments, the Sermon on the Mount, and the Letters of Paul

Christian ethical teaching has two main biblical foundations: the Ten Commandments (Exodus 20:1–17; Deuteronomy 5:6–21) and the Sermon on the Mount (Matthew 5–7). The Ten Commandments (see Section 10-4b) remain valid for Christians, although God's laws have been broadened by Jesus Christ. The "first table" of the Law calls on Christians to worship only God, not to worship images, and to keep the Sabbath day holy. This Sabbath was changed to Sunday, the day of the Lord's resurrection, when Christians around the world gather in the morning for worship. The "second table" of the Law tells Christians to honor parents and abstain from murder, adultery, theft, false witness, and coveting.

The Sermon on the Mount opens with the Beatitudes (or statements of blessings), which contain implicit moral directions (Matthew 5:1–12). Jesus declared that their participation in the Kingdom of God would enable his followers to witness to God in the world, even to be the "light of the world" (5:14–16). Jesus upheld the value of the Law of Moses for his followers, but radicalized it in a variety of ways. He pointed to the necessity of controlling one's thoughts and emotions, not just one's actions; Jesus called anger murderous and lust adulterous (5:21–22, 27–28). Doing what is right proceeds from the inner person, and thus is not a sham or

Christian moral virtues can often be expressed in a series of single words.

a hypocritical action. The repeated warnings against hypocrisy in the Sermon on the Mount are primarily warnings to Jesus's followers, not attacks on others. Jesus commanded his followers to "be perfect, as your heavenly Father is perfect" (5:48). Human perfection is expressed in what Christian tradition calls the Golden Rule, a summary of the ethics of the whole Jewish Bible: "In everything do to others as you would have them do to you." Christians have believed that taking the "hard way" (7:13–14) is possible by virtue of the divine gift of the Holy Spirit. Jesus knew that this hard way would not be easy for his followers and that they would fail in parts of it every day, as indicated in the daily prayer that he taught them in the Sermon on the Mount, which contains a request for divine forgiveness for one's sins (6:12).

As stated earlier, Jesus affirmed the summary of God's will given in Judaism: to "love the Lord your God" with all your being and to "love your neighbor as yourself." This love is possible because of Jesus's life, death, and resurrection. When the Christian commandment of love was connected to Christ's person and work, the demand of love for one's neighbor became a new commandment: "A new commandment I give to you, that you love one another; even as I have loved you, that you also love one another" (John 13:34). The followers of Jesus are to have this love: "By this all men will know that you are my disciples, if you have love for one another" (John 13:35). All this might imply that Christian love is given only or mostly to other Christians, but the Christian commandment of love has never been limited to fellow Christians. On the contrary, the Christian ethic crossed social and religious barriers and saw a neighbor in every suffering human being, especially the innocent and helpless. This is why, for example, Christians in the ancient world rescued infants left in remote places or garbage dumps to die. Jesus himself explicated his understanding of the commandment of love in the parable of the Good Samaritan, who followed the commandment of love and helped a person in need whom a Jewish priest and a Levite had chosen to ignore (Luke 10:29–37).

The Apostle Paul often drew on the Ten Commandments to shape the moral life of Christians. Because his churches were made up mainly of Gentiles, they needed instruction on the Jewish basis of morality. Paul's letters also stress the moral virtues of the Christian life: trust in God, hope in the future God will bring, peace in one's heart and in the church, and especially love for all people. More than any other New Testament author, Paul grounds the ethical life of the Christian in the life, death, and resurrection of Jesus. For Paul, the *indicative* (who Christians are by virtue of God's action) serves to ground the *imperatives* of moral attitude and behavior. The believer has "died with Christ" in baptism and will be "raised with Christ" at the end of time, and in the meantime must "walk in newness of life." The moral dimension of the Christian faith is a struggle; in an image drawn from clothing, one must constantly "put on Christ" and "put off" sin and self-centeredness. The presence of the Spirit in the individual and in the church gives both direction and empowerment for spiritual living. Summing up his ethic, Paul says, "I appeal to you therefore, brothers and sisters, by the mercies of God, to present your bodies as a living sacrifice, holy and acceptable to God, which is your reasonable service. Do not be conformed to this world, but be transformed by the renewal of your mind, that you may prove what is the will of God, what is good, and acceptable, and perfect" (Romans 12:1–2).

11-4b The Enactment of Moral Life in the Church

Christian social ethics are foundational for the community of the faithful. As the church took in all sorts of people, certain occupations were deemed incompatible with a Christian life of love toward others. Thieves, brothel keepers and prostitutes, workers in pagan temples, actors, charioteers, gladiators, soldiers, magicians, astrologers, and fortune-tellers could not keep their trades when they became Christians. (Slave owning, however, was still mostly tolerated, and the church often allowed slaves who were forced to engage in these forbidden trades to be church members.) Moral instruction for **catechumens**, those preparing for baptism, and many ancient sermons reveal that preachers regularly explained Christian morality and urged their audiences to keep it. In the Middle Ages and Byzantine times, moral instruction for catechumens and full Christians centered on the Ten Commandments, the Beatitudes, and the lists of virtues and vices drawn from the New Testament. The ritual of reconciliation (as it is now called), in which individuals confessed their sins in the confessional to a priest in order to receive direction and forgiveness, helped to shape individual character and conduct. At least in the West, people leaving church in the Middle Ages would typically see a painting of the Last Judgment over the doors, to remind them of the rewards of doing good and the penalty for evil.

Besides this inner-church sphere of morality, the conversion of the empire in the 300s permitted bishops to begin influencing the personal and political affairs of government and the wider life of society. Soon **canon law**—the legal system that codifies ethical, organizational, and other matters in the Roman Catholic Church—arose to guide the overall moral life of the church. Canon law is still today an important foundation of moral reflection and decision making by priests and bishops in the Church of Rome. In Protestant

catechumens [KAT-uh-ᴋʏᴏᴏ-menz] Individuals preparing for baptism by a period of instruction

canon law Legal system that codifies ethical, organizational, and other matters in the Roman Catholic Church

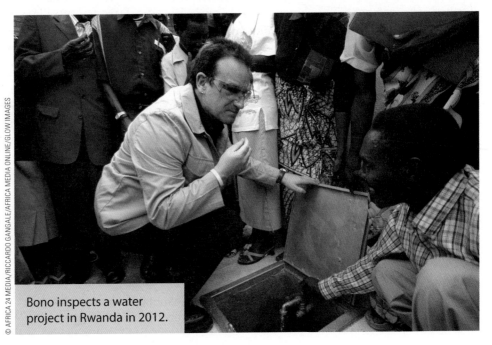

© AFRICA 24 MEDIA/RICCARDO GANGALE/AFRICA MEDIA ONLINE/GLOW IMAGES

Bono inspects a water project in Rwanda in 2012.

churches, different patterns of social ethics emerged, based more directly on the Bible. A powerful and controversial explanation of Protestant ethics is Max Weber's 1905 book *The Protestant Ethic and the Spirit of Capitalism*, which argued for a strong relationship between Protestant (specifically, Calvinist) morality and the development of modern capitalism in the West.

Modern times have seen a decline in the direct institutional role of the churches in society, as church leaders can no longer directly influence rulers. Instead, church leaders advise the shaping of public laws and policies, seeking to guide not only the members of their churches, but also the whole common life of nations. In Roman Catholicism, this has occurred at the global level through the so-called social encyclicals of popes from Leo XIII in 1891 to today. These teaching documents deal with a variety of topics in social ethics, and almost every pope has issued them. At times, they have been highly controversial, as when Pope Paul VI in 1968 used an encyclical (*Humanae Vitae*, "On Human Life") to forbid the use of all artificial birth control among Roman Catholics. Not as controversial, but still far-reaching, is the 2015 encyclical from Pope Francis on environmental concerns that calls for an "ecological conversion of the faithful" to save the earth from destruction. In Eastern Orthodoxy, the fall of Communist rule has presented particular problems and opportunities to help guide public life. Protestant denominations have typically made pronouncements and initiated programs on their own and through ecumenical agencies to which they belong.

One of these ecumenical agencies is the World Council of Churches, a fellowship of Christian churches founded in 1948. It has created "middle axioms" (the notion of a just society, for example, or the care of creation), which were intended as common ground on which Christian churches and governments could meet for discussion and action. Now, they are also common ground for cooperating with people of other religions, especially on today's environmental issues. The rise of Christian social organizations such as Church World Service, Catholic Relief Services, Bread for the World, World Vision, Habitat for Humanity, and many others is particularly notable. In the developing world, Christian organizations are among the largest nongovernmental organizations working for human and social development. Individual Christians have also had an impact here—for example, the lead singer of the rock band U2, Bono, advocates tirelessly for justice for Africa. He has become known for his advocacy of justice as well as for his music.

11-4c Moral Dimensions of Liberation Movements

Liberation movements in North American Christianity with strong moral teachings have become increasingly important in the modern period. As an example of a liberation movement, *feminism* has stressed the full emancipation of women. It recognizes that the church by its teaching and practice has held women down and tried to make second-class Christians of them. Some feminists have urged rejection of Christianity, arguing that it is hopelessly patriarchal. Most feminists in Christianity take a more moderate approach, trying to recover the biblical roots of feminism, stressing the (admittedly few) women who have played significant roles in Christian tradition, and working toward full liberation of women within the various Christian churches. This latter approach still represents the mainstream of Christian feminism, and it will continue to be a potent force for years to come, in culture in general and in the church specifically. As the movement progresses, it is widening its European-North American orientation and will likely make more of an impact in the churches of Asia, Africa, and Latin America.

The foundation of liberation movements is liberation theology, the heart of which is not theology, but moral practice. This movement stresses the active Christian mission of delivering the oppressed from evil social structures and situations. Using a combination of Marxist social analysis and Christianity, this movement was born in Roman Catholic theological circles in Latin America. Some trace its roots all the way back to the Jesuit state in Peru, mentioned earlier in Section 11-2e. But it has spread widely and been applied to several different situations: women's liberation, black liberation, Hispanic liberation, and now gay liberation. The latter has been particularly problematic in mainline Protestant churches and in the worldwide Anglican communion, which some observers think may be breaking apart over it. These new applications of liberation theology are still powerful influences in much of world Christianity, especially in the West, but the original form of political-social liberation theology in South America is waning.

11-5 Christian Worship and Ritual

In Rome, the Congregation for Divine Worship, the Roman Catholic department responsible for guiding the Church's religious services, presents to Pope John Paul II a report entitled "Authentic Liturgy." It states that language used in the Mass must avoid many of the features of inclusive language, because they obscure the meaning of the text. For example, where the original language of Scripture or the Mass book says "brothers," expressions such as "brothers and sisters" or "friends" may not be used. The document stirs up a controversy in European and North American Catholic churches, which have gotten used to more inclusive language. This controversy is an example of how issues of inclusive/exclusive language have become important in contemporary churches, both Roman Catholic and Protestant.

In this section, we'll discuss the rise of Christian worship in history. Christian worship emerged from, and then gradually separated from, the worship practices of Judaism. The Acts of the Apostles relates that the first Christian believers worshiped in the Jerusalem temple, as Jesus had; they worshiped in Jewish synagogues as well. But the earliest church also had its own meetings for worship. The Roman Catholic Church gradually built itself around seven **sacraments**, rituals believed to be a special means of grace, and the Eastern Orthodox Church made the worship in its various branches more unified. In the Protestant Reformation and Catholic Reform, and again in Vatican II, worship was reformed by being made more the work of the people, the **liturgy**. Since around 1950, the ecumenical movement has brought more of a consensus of worship style and content, and least in the churches that follow a set, formal pattern of liturgy.

11-5a Foundations of Christian Worship

Christian worship and ritual vary widely throughout the world today, but its common foundations can be traced to the first centuries of the church, and before this to the Jewish synagogues. As in the worship of the synagogue, public prayer and praise to God are a constant in the church. So too are the reading and explanation of a portion of Scripture. Christian churches, especially in the eastern half of the Roman Empire, adapted the **lectionary** system of the Jewish synagogues and added readings from the New Testament. Changes from synagogue worship were introduced as well. The weekly day for congregational worship went from the Jewish Sabbath on the last day of the week to Sunday. (Today, we commonly think of Sunday as the second day of the weekend, but of course it is the first day of the week.)

sacraments Rituals believed to be a special means of grace

liturgy Literally, "work of the people" in worship; pattern of worship in Christian churches

lectionary Systematic schedule of reading the Bible in worship

Baptism replaced circumcision as the main rite of initiation into the faith, and it was preceded by instruction and fasting. Persons about to be baptized renounced evil, and after they declared their faith, they went into the water. They then received, by anointing with oil and by the laying on of hands, the gift of the Holy Spirit, the same Spirit who had descended on Jesus at his baptism. Only the baptized were admitted to the Eucharist, and weekly participation in this ritual meal took the place of both the Passover meal and Jewish sacrifices. Baptism has been the sacrament of entry, but the Eucharist is the regular ritual of food for the body and soul.

After Christianity was permitted and then became official in the 300s, worship became more elaborate. Formal church buildings were erected, and church officials dressed for worship in special vestments modeled after Roman government garb. The church developed a liturgical calendar with seasons of self-denial, such as Advent and Lent, and seasons of celebration, such as Christmas and Easter.

Before about 350 C.E., worship was typically in private homes. (A religion almost constantly persecuted by the government isn't able to put up its own buildings.) The service was held in the largest room of the house, usually the central atrium in a middle- or upper-class house. When church buildings became common around 350, they were designed for the community. The rectangular basilica with a long nave (main area for the congregation) and an apse (semicircular area at the front), which had been used for Roman law courts, was particularly suitable for Christian worship. The basilica type of building was used by Christians for the first church buildings, and has been the most common pattern for churches since. Many Byzantine churches had mosaic pictures on their floors. Old Testament/Jewish heroes of faith also appear in the earliest Christian art in both the East and the West. The artists adapted conventional pagan art forms: the shepherd carrying a sheep, the praying person with hands uplifted, and various birds and animals. Symbols of the Eucharist and baptism were especially common. The exteriors of these churches were simple, but inside they were often richly ornamented with marble and mosaic. The decoration was designed to represent the angels and saints in heaven with whom the church on earth was joining for worship—saints whose presence was suggested by icons in the East and statues, paintings, and then stained glass in the West. The oldest church buildings to survive largely intact are from early medieval and early Byzantine times: Hagia Sophia at Constantinople (which became a mosque and is now a

Iconostasis of an Orthodox Church in Slovakia

IGOR SOKALSKI/GETTY IMAGES

museum) and San Vitale at Ravenna in Italy. Worship in churches became more impressive and formal for a greatly enlarged and now official religion, but much of the earlier intimacy that was a part of house churches was necessarily lost.

In the early Middle Ages, Catholic worship became centered on the sacraments and has stayed focused on them ever since. These are, the *Catholic Catechism* says, "efficacious signs of grace, instituted by Christ and entrusted to the Church, by which divine life is dispensed." The sacraments are necessary for salvation, because they were instituted by Christ as the means through which God communicates grace. Christ bestows a particular grace through each sacrament, such as baptism's joining one to Christ and the Church, confession/reconciliation's forgiveness of sins and amendment of life, and the Eucharist's feeding of body and soul with the mystical food of Jesus's body and blood. A sacrament works *ex opere operato* (ehks OH-puh-reh oh-puh-RAH-toh), Latin for "by the working of the work." In other words, they are effective just by being administered, regardless of the personal holiness of the one administering them. However, the holiness of the recipient *does* make a difference; lack of a proper spiritual attitude can thwart the effectiveness of the sacrament. These seven sacraments are known today as baptism, confirmation, the Eucharist, reconciliation, anointing of the sick, ordination (to holy orders), and marriage. The Eastern Orthodox Church also has seven sacraments but hasn't organized its worship so fully around them.

Other worship practices also began in post-Constantinian times. One of the more significant was the **cult of the saints**, the veneration of saints in shrines, churches, and other places. (This cult has no connection with the more modern use of the word to designate some new religious movements.) Shrines were erected in honor of local holy men and women, especially Christians who had worked miracles and those who had suffered for the faith. Usually shrines were found in churches and contained a relic or the entire body of the saint. Until modern times, many Christian saints weren't recognized by the whole church but were known and venerated regionally. The saints were recognized as intercessors with God for the faithful on earth and were thought to be vehicles for God's miraculous power. The shrines became the focus of religious pilgrimage. Many popular shrines today are dedicated to the Virgin Mary, particularly in the places where she is believed to have appeared: Lourdes, France; Medjugorje in Bosnia and Herzegovina; and Mexico City.

The pattern of the Eucharistic liturgy was basically set by the year 400, but different forms existed in different areas. The form of the Latin Mass in the 500s was basically similar to the form it has kept through today. (Most mainline Protestant forms for Holy Communion used today were adapted at the Reformation from the Roman Catholic version.) Earlier beliefs that Jesus Christ was somehow present in the celebration of Holy Communion were greatly developed in the Middle Ages. The Roman Church officially adopted the teaching of **transubstantiation**—that the bread and wine were changed in all but appearance into the substance of Christ's body. Music also became elaborate after Constantine, with chanting in Gregorian style, hymns, and service music, as well as plainsong with several voices unaccompanied by instruments. Eastern Orthodox chanting, like the liturgy in general,

cult of the saints
Veneration of saints in shrines, churches, and other places

transubstantiation
Roman Catholic teaching that the bread and wine of Holy Communion are changed in all but appearance into the substance of Christ's body

was richer, more sonorous, and more soaring than Gregorian plainsong.

The Protestant Reformation carried out an immediate reform of worship, along with theology. All Protestant churches rejected transubstantiation. In general, the Lutheran churches kept some distinctly Roman Catholic features such as crucifixes and altars, the Calvinist churches kept a few (kneeling in services, baptismal fonts), and the Anabaptist churches discarded everything they didn't find in the Bible. In general, the worship found in churches of the Baptist tradition is *nonliturgical*, not bound to a set form of worship or rituals—embracing spontaneous, informal prayer rather than written prayer, for example—but other Protestant churches tend to be *liturgical*, with set forms. Worship in the Church of England remained the most Catholic of all the breakaway churches.

All Protestant churches from the Reformation through today share a few important new features of worship. First, the Bible was restored to what the Reformers considered a more central place. Preaching the Bible in sermons was emphasized, as was private reading of the Bible in homes. Second, the sacraments were generally reduced to the two that had been founded by Jesus: baptism and Holy Communion. Many Reformers made frequent communion the rule for all laity, and denied the Roman Catholic doctrine of transubstantiation in favor of other understandings of the spiritual meaning of communion. Third, all services were put completely into the language of the people, and the liturgy again became literally the "work of the people." The Catholic Reform in the 1500s and Vatican II in the 1960s brought the Roman Church into line with many of these language changes, but its theology remained the same.

Reading the Bible regularly is a distinctive practice for many Christians.

{ Between one-fourth and one-third of all Christians today are charismatics and "speak in tongues." }

In the years since the Reformation, especially in the 1900s, Christian worship has become more diverse. The strongest impact on worship has been the **charismatic movement** stressing supernatural gifts of the Holy Spirit, a movement also known as **Pentecostalism**. These two names are a bit tricky: *Charismatic* usually refers to groups inside the Roman Catholic, Orthodox, and mainline Protestant churches. *Pentecostal* usually refers to Protestant churches such as the Assemblies of God where these practices are the norm, whether they have Pentecostal in their formal name or not. "Gifts of the Holy Spirit" are called *charismata* in Greek. These gifts are used primarily in worship. The modern Pentecostal movement began in 1906 in an African American church in Los Angeles. Over time it has moved into mainstream Protestantism and Roman Catholicism as well. Today, the charismatic movement has spread throughout the Christian world. Speaking in tongues—an emotional outpouring of prayer in human sounds but in no human language—is its primary activity, but others are often seen as well: interpretation of tongues, prophecy, healing, and so forth. The charismatic movement has often been divisive and controversial when it appears in non-Pentecostalist denominations, but it has brought new life and an emphasis on spirituality. Some observers have estimated that between one-fourth and one-third of all Christians—about 600 million people—are charismatics.

11-5b The Liturgical Year

The **liturgical year**, also known as the **church year**, is the pattern of liturgical seasons that determines when holy days are to be observed, which portions of Scripture are to be read, and the special themes of worship. Distinct liturgical colors usually mark different seasons of the year. The dates of the festivals vary somewhat between Orthodox, Roman Catholic, and Protestant churches, though the sequence and purpose are generally the same.

charismatic movement (Pentecostalism) Modern Christian movement stressing use of supernatural "gifts of the Holy Spirit"

liturgical (church) year Pattern of liturgical seasons that determines when holy days are to be observed

© CARLOS E. SANTA MARIA/SHUTTERSTOCK.COM

The extent to which the liturgical year is celebrated also varies between churches. In the Roman Catholic Church and in the Orthodox churches, the church year is rigorously observed. In general, Protestant churches observe far fewer holy days than do Catholic and Orthodox churches. The broad seasons of the year are observed in mainline Protestant churches, but many evangelical, fundamentalist, and/or Pentecostalist churches today largely ignore the main church year, celebrating only Christmas and Easter.

The church year begins with Advent, the four-week period of preparation for Christmas Day and the usually two-week Christmas period that follows Christmas Day (see Figure 11.3). The short season of Epiphany in January marks the manifestation of Christ to the world. Next is the season of Lent, a forty-day season of preparation for Easter, often with special devotions and acts of self-denial. Easter Day and the Easter season following it celebrate the resurrection of Jesus. After the feast of Pentecost, a long period of ordinary time without a specific seasonal focus extends to the beginning of Advent in December.

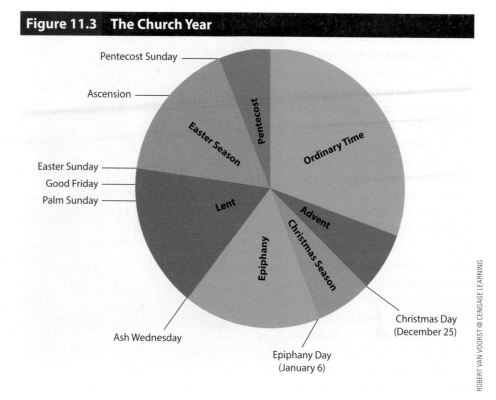

Figure 11.3 The Church Year

Pentecost Sunday
Ascension
Easter Sunday
Good Friday
Palm Sunday
Pentecost
Easter Season
Ordinary Time
Lent
Advent
Epiphany
Christmas Season
Ash Wednesday
Christmas Day (December 25)
Epiphany Day (January 6)

ROBERT VAN VOORST @ CENGAGE LEARNING

11-5c The Christian Funeral

The funeral rituals of Christianity probably have more variety than in any other religion. Nevertheless, there are some important commonalities. Most Christians believe that the soul of the deceased Christian passes from this world to the afterlife, to live in heaven, hell or (as most Roman Catholics believe) purgatory, a place where the significant sins of those eventually bound for heaven are burned away. When Christ returns at the end of time, the bodies of the dead will be resurrected and reunited with their souls. When death is near, a minister or priest is called in, and special prayers are offered, sometimes with Holy Communion.

It's most common today, even in the majority world, for a funeral home to take the body and prepare it for burial. This is more of a cultural than a religious practice; most Christians don't believe that a dead body is ritually unclean. In the Orthodox churches in Eastern Europe and Asia, preparing the body is done at home by the family. Often there is a viewing of the body, in popular Catholic terminology a "wake," a day or two after death. Prayers are often made at this viewing, and the family is comforted by those who come. The burial can take place at any time after death, but one to three days is most common; unlike many other religions, there is no set time for burial. Cremation is becoming more common in the West, but most Christian churches expect that the cremated remains be buried in a cemetery or otherwise entombed in a ritually proper way; informal scattering of ashes or keeping them at home in an urn is considered disrespectful to the deceased and a denial of the doctrine of resurrection. Cremation is prohibited in the Eastern Orthodox churches.

The funeral service is structured after regular Sunday services. The body or cremated remains are brought into the church, and prayers, hymns, scripture readings, and a sermon are made, all centered on the hope of eternal life. Sometimes eulogies are offered by family and friends in Protestant funerals, but the Catholic Church typically restricts eulogies to the wake. The Eucharist is celebrated in the Catholic funeral Mass, and often in Eastern Orthodox churches.

After the funeral service in the church, the body is taken to the cemetery, and the casket is placed over the open grave. Short prayers are offered, typically ending with the Lord's Prayer/Our Father. In the Catholic Church, the priest will first bless the grave to make it a holy place for the body to rest until the resurrection. Then the body is lowered into the grave and a small amount of ceremonial dirt is sometimes thrown on it. When the mourners depart, cemetery workers or the family complete the burial. Finally, it's common for a simple memorial meal to be held after the funeral, in which the family is comforted more informally. In contrast to other religions, Protestant and Roman Catholic Christians have no set mourning period or common mourning practices. The Eastern Orthodox churches generally hold a mourning period of forty days, during which widows and widowers wear only black clothing.

Christians in the nation of South Sudan worship with song and dance.

JOHN WOLLWERTH/SHUTTERSTOCK.COM

11-6 Christianity around the World Today

A group of Old Order Amish has met in a home for worship in Lancaster County, Pennsylvania. As their horses and buggies wait outside, they conduct a two-hour service of hymns, prayers, scripture readings, and a sermon—all in their own Pennsylvania Dutch language, which is actually a Swiss dialect of German. No cleric conducts the service, for in their religious life the men are all equal. Their worship and lifestyle continues the same pattern of "coming out from the world and being separate" that their Anabaptist ancestors practiced at the dawn of the Reformation. The Amish have been oppressed in many parts of the world, but they've found a happy haven in the United States and Canada, where they are widely respected for their consistent witness for pacifism.

Global South Christians Majority of Christians today, living in the Southern Hemisphere

11-6a Christianity in the Global South

Religion scholars today are nearly unanimous that the single most important area for the future of Christianity is outside the areas of its historic strength. In its past, Christianity has been strongest in the Northern Hemisphere, especially in Europe and North America. Now, Christianity is shifting its center of gravity to the Southern Hemisphere, where most Christians live and where Christianity is growing quickly even as the number and cultural influence of Christians in the Northern Hemisphere declines. An unmistakable sign of the increasing importance of Christianity in the Southern Hemisphere is the election of the archbishop of Buenos Aires, Argentina, as pope in 2013; he was still pope when this book was written in 2017.

These **Global South Christians**, with their more traditional interpretations of the Bible and the creeds, sometimes present a challenge to older churches. For example, the African Independent Churches, a dynamic adaptation of Christianity by European mission churches in Africa, are now spreading to North America. To cite another example, the Anglican churches in Africa—where more people in Uganda or Nigeria attend Anglican religious services on a typical Sunday than in all of Great Britain—strongly

Pope Francis greets the crowds in St. Peter's Square.

GIULIO NAPOLITANO/SHUTTERSTOCK.COM

oppose efforts by the Church of England and the Episcopal Church in the United States to approve of same-sex relationships and ordain gay and lesbian clergy. Mark Noll has written in his *The New Shape of World Christianity* that today's Global South Christians are less concerned about historic patterns of church government and doctrine (things important in the North) as they are about spiritual warfare between good and evil today and the continuing gulf between the wealthy North and the "Majority World."[2]

11-6b Changes in the Catholic Church under Pope Francis

As we have already discussed (Section 11-2g), in 2013 Argentine archbishop Jorge Bergoglio became pope, the first from the Global South. Most observers of the Catholic Church expected Francis to change the church in some ways, and the changes he has brought to the Catholic Church have been extensive. Some are controversial, and only time will tell how lasting these changes will be.

Francis's background gives some insight into the lively, independent way he has pursued his duties as pope. Before joining the Jesuit order of priests, Bergoglio was educated in chemistry and ran tests on food in a laboratory. He also was a bouncer in a bar, certainly the only pope to have such a job! When he graduated from seminary he became a Jesuit priest, but grew to disagree with much of the Marxist underpinnings he saw in the **liberation theology** of his time and place. This alienated him from the Jesuit order, and for many years he rose in the ranks of the Catholic

Church in Argentina without any deep connection to the Jesuits. Some of the changes Francis has advocated or actually started are these:

- He has appointed many cardinals who are theologically moderate and/or politically liberal, for example, welcoming immigrants and favoring universal health care.

- He has spoken extensively on the reality and danger of climate change, much more fully than previous popes. In a formal document entitled *Laudato Si* ("Praised Be"), Francis stated that "Our relationship with the environment can never be separated from our relationship with others and with God." Yet Francis is pessimistic that political actions will be effective to solve this problem.

- He has given mixed messages on same-sex relationships, saying that gays and lesbians should be accepted as they are and not be discriminated against, but he also maintains that same-sex marriage is wrong.

- He has extended hope to Roman Catholics who are divorced and remarried, saying that priests should be "more accepting" of them.

- He is for greater women's rights and responsibilities, in society and the church, but stated categorically that "women will never be priests."

- He said in 2017 that married men could perhaps serve as priests, especially in areas that have a shortage of priests. Many observers of the Vatican wonder if this will open a window to further priestly status for married men.

11-6c Christianity in North America

Christianity is the largest religion in the United States, with 78 percent of those polled identifying themselves as Christian in 2010. About 62 percent reported that they were members of a church congregation. With around 240 million Christians, the United States has the largest Christian population on earth. In Canada, the church has slightly less of a presence, but more than 60 percent of Canadians identify themselves as Christians. As a result of immigration, widespread importation of

liberation theology
Movement that stresses the active Christian mission of delivering the oppressed from evil social structures and situations

Minister and choir, important parts of the African American church

The vast majority of colonists were Christians, and over time a majority of Native Americans became Christians as well. Today, most Christian congregations are mainline Protestant, evangelical Protestant, or Roman Catholic, or they belong to the various denominations of Eastern Orthodoxy. Sociologists of religion distinguish the *mainline* Protestant churches (defined in Section 11-6d) from the *evangelical* Protestant churches. The authoritative Association of Religion Data Archives (ARDA) estimates 26 million members of mainline churches versus about 40 million members of evangelical Protestant churches. Good evidence suggests a sizable shift in membership from mainline denominations to evangelical churches since about 1960. Then, Protestant Christians tended to belong to mainline churches, and evangelical churches were comparatively smaller.

What is the likely future of Christianity in North America? Although predicting the future is an "iffy" business, the 2015 Pew study, "America's Changing Religious Landscape," provides some answers. As stated earlier in this section, there were about 240 million U.S. Christians in 2010, about 78 percent of the total population. By 2050, the number will probably grow to 261 million, but this will be only 66 percent of the U.S. population. Mainline Protestants will suffer the steepest decline in percentage; evangelicals will suffer a small decline; those of different religions will grow slightly; and the proportion of the unaffiliated, those of no formal religion, will grow the most.[3] Losses in the United States will continue to be offset by the growth of Christianity in the Global South.

11-6d The Different Churches in the United States: Roman Catholic and Protestant

At the time the United States was founded, only a small fraction of the U.S. population was Roman Catholic, generally in Maryland. As we saw previously, the number of Roman Catholics has grown dramatically in recent years. The United States now has the fourth largest Catholic population in the world. The Church's main national body is the United States Conference of Catholic Bishops, made up of all bishops and archbishops of the United States, although each bishop has independent power in his own diocese and is responsible only to the pope. Many other nations have a Roman Catholic *primate*, or lead bishop, but there is no primate for the United States.

European (and now African and Asian) churches, and new denominations springing up in the United States, Christianity is more internally diverse in North America than anywhere else in the world. This poses a challenge and an opportunity for the study of Christianity.

Protestant denominations together account for about 50 percent of North Americans, Roman Catholicism about 25 percent, and Eastern Orthodox less than 1 percent. Roman Catholics are by far the largest single church group, and the Roman Catholic Church in the United States is growing in size with Hispanic immigration. The Eastern Orthodox population is relatively tiny, making up only about 0.04 percent of North Americans—due largely to smaller immigration from Eastern Orthodox nations, recent difficulties in Americanization, and the persistence of twenty-six different ethnic-based denominations within North American Orthodoxy today.

Christianity came to the Americas when it was first colonized by Europeans, beginning in the 1500s.

Although Protestantism is divided into mainline and evangelical groups, as we saw earlier, the distinction between them is not easy to maintain. **Mainline** Protestant denominations are those brought to North America by their historic immigrant groups. The largest are the Episcopal (English, from the Anglican Church), Presbyterian (Scottish), Methodist (English and Welsh), and Lutheran (Scandinavian and German) denominations. Mainline churches are generally more open to new ideas and social changes than are evangelical Protestants and Roman Catholics. For example, they've been increasingly open to the ordination of women and to equality in church and society for gay and lesbian persons. Mainline churches belong to organizations such as the National Council of Churches and the World Council of Churches. Mainline Protestant groups were dominant in North America for more than two centuries, up until the 1960s. As stated in Section 11-6c, since the 1960s, they have lost their religious and cultural dominance to evangelical Protestantism.

Evangelicalism is the modern movement that seeks to spread the gospel of Jesus Christ, giving people an opportunity to convert. The experience of conversion that evangelicals see as necessary for salvation is called being "born again." They have a strong sense of the presence and direction of God in their lives, as explored in a recent, highly praised book by Tanya Luhrmann of Stanford University, *When God Talks Back*.[4] Although it became strong in the past two centuries, evangelicalism has roots that reach into the earliest decades of the Reformation. It arose with the Anabaptist movement in the 1500s, moved into the mainstream Reformation with Pietism in the 1700s, and became stronger in the late 1800s, especially as a result of the world mission movement of the time. A famous evangelical of the twentieth century is Southern Baptist (U.S.) evangelist Billy Graham, who held mass meetings that ended with a call to come forward to "accept Christ as your personal Lord and Savior" and be "born again." There is a good deal of variety in evangelicalism. Evangelicals tend to be politically conservative, but an increasing number today—especially younger evangelicals—are politically moderate or liberal. Probably the most influential modern voice in the evangelical movement was C. S. Lewis (1898–1963), the University of Oxford professor of medieval literature and Anglican

> The experience of conversion that evangelicals see as necessary for salvation is called being "born again."

who ironically did not call himself an evangelical but did have a powerful conversion experience as an adult. Lewis wrote popular religious works such as *Mere Christianity* and *The Screwtape Letters*, which are still best sellers for their clear, creative presentation of the faith. He also wrote the popular children's novels *The Chronicles of Narnia*, which are full of traditional Christian themes but not overtly Christian.

The black church—or, more commonly today, African American church—in North America are churches that are mainly African American in membership. Most African American congregations belong to African American denominations such as the National Baptist Convention or a variety of other Baptist or Methodist groups, although some black congregations belong to predominantly white denominations. Freed slaves in the South, especially in the North, formed the first black congregations before 1800. After slavery ended, African Americans continued in separate congregations and denominations, with communities and styles of worship that were distinct from those of their white counterparts. They continued a unique, powerful form of Christianity that adapted African religious practices in preaching, music, and congregational life. For example, matriarchal traditions from Africa have led to some women having a much higher status, even authority, in African American churches than is found in white churches. Many African American congregations have "mother boards" composed of older women who are real power brokers in their churches. Segregation of the races discouraged and, especially in the South, prevented African Americans from belonging to the same churches as whites, thus helping to preserve the distinctive patterns of African American Christianity.

African Americans continued to form separate congregations and denominations during the 1900s. This separation continues today despite the decline of segregation and the rising occurrence of integrated worship. African American churches are usually the centers of their communities, opening schools in the

mainline Protestant denominations brought to North America by their historic immigrant groups

evangelicalism The modern movement that seeks to spread the gospel of Jesus Christ, giving people an opportunity to convert

early years after the Civil War and pursuing other social welfare efforts. As a result, they have founded strong community organizations and provided spiritual and political leadership, especially during the civil rights movement, seen clearly in the leadership of African American Baptist pastor Martin Luther King Jr.

Another broad trend in North American Protestantism is **Restorationism**. This refers to the belief held by various groups that the Christianity of the first century C.E. is the purest form of the faith and that it can and should be restored. (It was a strong impulse in the United States in the 1800s.) Such groups typically claim that their group is that restoration. They teach that restoration is necessary because other Christians before them introduced defects into the Christian faith or lost a vital element of genuine Christianity. Restorationist denominations include the Christian Church (Disciples of Christ) and the Churches of Christ. Several other groups that shared the Restorationist impulse eventually became new religious movements. The Church of Jesus Christ of Latter-day Saints (LDS) founded by Joseph Smith, more commonly called the Mormons, is notable. Visitors to the Mormon headquarters in Salt Lake City, Utah, can view the hour-long movie *Joseph Smith: Prophet of the Restoration*. Another major Restorationist religion is the Jehovah's Witnesses. It's estimated that in the United States 1.9 million adults are Jehovah's Witnesses. Similar to the LDS church, the Jehovah's Witnesses church rejects many teachings of the Nicene Creed and views itself as the only true church.

In conclusion, despite the seemingly fractured life of Christianity in the world today, Christianity remains a growing, vibrant religion around the globe.

Restorationism
Protestant movement to restore first-century Christianity

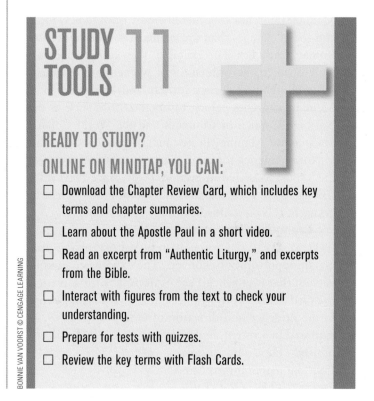

STUDY TOOLS 11

READY TO STUDY?
ONLINE ON MINDTAP, YOU CAN:

☐ Download the Chapter Review Card, which includes key terms and chapter summaries.

☐ Learn about the Apostle Paul in a short video.

☐ Read an excerpt from "Authentic Liturgy," and excerpts from the Bible.

☐ Interact with figures from the text to check your understanding.

☐ Prepare for tests with quizzes.

☐ Review the key terms with Flash Cards.

BONNIE VAN VOORST © CENGAGE LEARNING

Christianity Timeline: 27–2013 C.E.

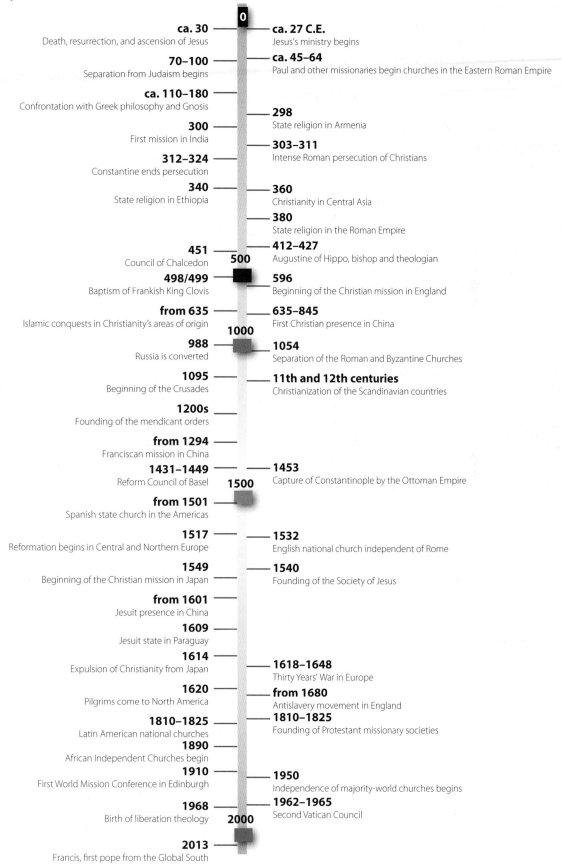

0

ca. 30 — Death, resurrection, and ascension of Jesus

ca. 27 C.E. — Jesus's ministry begins

70–100 — Separation from Judaism begins

ca. 45–64 — Paul and other missionaries begin churches in the Eastern Roman Empire

ca. 110–180 — Confrontation with Greek philosophy and Gnosis

298 — State religion in Armenia

300 — First mission in India

303–311 — Intense Roman persecution of Christians

312–324 — Constantine ends persecution

340 — State religion in Ethiopia

360 — Christianity in Central Asia

380 — State religion in the Roman Empire

451 — Council of Chalcedon

500

412–427 — Augustine of Hippo, bishop and theologian

498/499 — Baptism of Frankish King Clovis

596 — Beginning of the Christian mission in England

from 635 — Islamic conquests in Christianity's areas of origin

635–845 — First Christian presence in China

1000

988 — Russia is converted

1054 — Separation of the Roman and Byzantine Churches

1095 — Beginning of the Crusades

11th and 12th centuries — Christianization of the Scandinavian countries

1200s — Founding of the mendicant orders

from 1294 — Franciscan mission in China

1431–1449 — Reform Council of Basel

1453 — Capture of Constantinople by the Ottoman Empire

1500

from 1501 — Spanish state church in the Americas

1517 — Reformation begins in Central and Northern Europe

1532 — English national church independent of Rome

1549 — Beginning of the Christian mission in Japan

1540 — Founding of the Society of Jesus

from 1601 — Jesuit presence in China

1609 — Jesuit state in Paraguay

1614 — Expulsion of Christianity from Japan

1618–1648 — Thirty Years' War in Europe

1620 — Pilgrims come to North America

from 1680 — Antislavery movement in England

1810–1825 — Latin American national churches

1810–1825 — Founding of Protestant missionary societies

1890 — African Independent Churches begin

1910 — First World Mission Conference in Edinburgh

1950 — Independence of majority-world churches begins

1962–1965 — Second Vatican Council

1968 — Birth of liberation theology

2000

2013 — Francis, first pope from the Global South

12
Encountering Islam: The Straight Path of the One God

LEARNING OUTCOMES

After studying this chapter, you will be able to do the following:

12-1 Explain *Islam* and related terms.

12-2 Outline how the main periods of Islamic history have shaped its present, especially different Muslim groups.

12-3 Give the essential elements of Islamic teachings in your own words.

12-4 Explain Muslim ethics, especially in diet, dress, and marriage.

12-5 Explain the ways Muslims worship, especially the Five Pillars.

12-6 Explain the main aspects of Muslim life around the world today, especially in Europe and North America.

Your Visit to Mecca

Imagine, if you will, your visit to Mecca (MEHK-uh), Saudi Arabia, during the Month of Pilgrimage. (Unless you are a Muslim, you cannot actually visit Mecca, so your visit here must be done with respectful imagination.) Your emotions run high as you come within sight of Mecca. You've looked forward to this trip as long as you can remember, and now you're there, at the very center—geographically and spiritually—of Islam.

Before you enter Mecca, you must be physically and spiritually clean. If you're a man, you shave your head, take off your outer clothes, and put on over your underwear two large triangular pieces of linen. Everyone dresses in these, whether rich or poor, royal or commoner. If you're a woman, you bathe and wear a traditional Muslim full-body veil. You also stay in women's groups apart from men for your activities on the pilgrimage. From now on, until you begin the journey home, you'll strictly observe all ritual restrictions in how you dress, act, speak, and eat. These rules heighten your appreciation of how special this trip is.

Next, you walk seven times around the cube-shaped shrine at the open-air center of the Grand Mosque. This brings you closer to the shrine with each circle, so the walk isn't at all tiring for you. It ends when you touch the sacred stone, a meteorite embedded in the shrine by Abraham himself about three thousand years ago. As you circle, you notice all the different races and nationalities present.

After you touch the sacred stone, you run seven times back and forth between two hills, just as Abraham's wife, Hagar, ran between them until an angel gave her water from the Zamzam well. You know that Mecca has been the site of a few deadly stampedes in the past, most recently in 2015, but you realize that you have no fear of one as you pass through, because all is in the hands of God. Then you drink water from Zamzam before leaving this area.

Next, you move with all the other pilgrims out of the city of Mecca. You gather on the Plain of Arafat near the Mount of Mercy. From the afternoon prayer until the sunset prayer, the pilgrims stand in the presence of Allah by praying, meditating, and reading the Qur'an, the holy scripture of Islam. That evening, you walk back to the village of Mina, where all of the pilgrims live in a huge tent city for three days. Sheep and goats are slaughtered in the evening as offerings to God, then roasted and eaten in happy feasts. These sacrifices commemorate Abraham sacrificing an animal to God instead of his son Ishmael.

The next day, you throw small stones at three pillars representing the devil. Every pilgrim is supposed to do this, symbolizing your rejection of evil, a life long task. Then you go back into Mecca and walk in the Grand Mosque one more time; your pilgrimage is complete.

Islam is the world's second-most populous religion, after Christianity. It has about 1.3 billion followers, almost one of every five people. Islam is now present in virtually every part of the world. About 8 million Muslims live in North America and around 15 million in Europe. Although Islam is traditionally

HITMANSNR/SHUTTERSTOCK.COM

Pilgrims circle the shrine at the center of the Grand Mosque seven times until they get close enough to touch it.

 The facing-page photograph shows the raised walkway around the cube-shaped shrine in the Grand Mosque in Mecca built recently to accommodate handicapped and aged pilgrims.

This mosque in Singapore shows a combination of Arab and south Asian styles.

associated with the Middle East, the largest Muslim populations are in south Asia: Indonesia, Malaysia, Bangladesh, Pakistan, and India. Indonesia has the largest number of Muslims—around 200 million—of any country in the world. (It's estimated that, if present trends continue, India will have 311 million Muslims by 2050, 11 percent of the global total, making it the country with the largest number of Muslims in the world.) Large Muslim populations are also found in central Asia, including China. In the aftermath of recent events involving violence done in the name of Islam, careful and unbiased study of Islam has become more challenging for North American students than in the past. However, it is all the more necessary. As you begin your study of Islam, these particular puzzlements may emerge:

- Islam seems to be centered on Muhammad (moo-HAHM-id) and his teaching. Whenever Muslims mention his name they say, "Peace be upon him," and Muhammad is now the most common first name in the world. However, Muhammad isn't at the heart of Muslim devotion, or even near it. Muslims believe that he was only the human conduit of God's revelations.

Islam [ihz-LAHM]
"Submission" to God

Muslims [MUHZ-limz]
"Submitters," followers of Islam

- Islam is a deeply spiritual religion centered on the one God, but it is equally a religiously shaped way of life for a community of people. From its founding, Islam has preferred to function as both a religion and a state, and in twenty-five nations of the world—in the Middle East, North Africa, and south Asia—it is the official state religion.

- Some Muslims today seem to speak for all of Islam, but no one really can because of its diversity. For example, some Muslim nations enforce laws that all women wear a veil that covers their whole body when they are in public, but women in other Muslim nations are free to go out in regular clothing, with their hair covered by a scarf and their face fully visible.

- Many non-Muslims today think that Islam is a violent religion, but the vast majority of Muslims don't engage in violence for their faith or support violence—today or in the past. This misconception is especially prevalent in nations that have been the objects of recent attacks by terrorists claiming to act in the name of Islam.

> { Muslims correctly understand the name of their religion as *submission* to God, not *peace* with God. }

12-1 The Name *Islam*

Muhammad and his first followers referred to their movement as **Islam**, "submission," always understood as submission to God. They came to be known as **Muslims**, which means "submitters." (The older spelling *Moslem* is still found, and is not incorrect, but *Muslim* is now preferred.) Explanations of the word *Islam* today, even by some Muslims, sometimes imply that it comes from the Arabic word for peace, *salam* (sah-LAHM). *Salam* is indeed related to *Islam*, but it is a different word. Although Muslims see peace as coming from submission to God, the great majority of Muslims correctly understand the name of their religion as *submission* to God, not *peace* with God.

The term *Mohammedanism* for Islam came about when Christians wrongly supposed that followers of

Camel caravans were important for lucrative Meccan trade, and camels are referred to often in Islamic scripture and tradition.

Muhammad named themselves after him, just as Christians were named after Jesus Christ. It originated in the Middle Ages, and was widely used until the early 1900s; now it is hardly used at all. You may also see the current term **Islamist** for Muslim radicals, particularly those who espouse violence in the name of Islam. We'll consider this term later in this chapter, but for now you should know that it covers only a very small proportion of Muslims.

12-2 Islam Today as Shaped by Its Past

A film depicting the life of the Prophet Muhammad began production in 2009. In keeping with Muslim tradition, however, the face and voice of the Prophet won't be seen or heard on screen. *The Messenger of Peace* is a remake of *The Message* from 1977. Producer Oscar Zoghbi, who worked on *The Message*, said that his team had great respect for the original film and that this latest project will employ modern film techniques in its renewal of the original film's message. The mistaken belief that actor Anthony Quinn was portraying Muhammad in the 1977 film sparked protests by Muslims in the West, some of them violent, and harmed commercial prospects for the film. With the risk of similar misunderstandings lessened by careful publicity in the Muslim world, work on the new film goes forward, but slowly and carefully. At the beginning of 2018, its release had still not been announced, and many in Hollywood expect that this film will never be completed.

12-2a Arabia at the Time of Muhammad (500s C.E.)

Arabian religion of the sixth century C.E. had many gods, and Muslims refer to it as the age of ignorance. Mecca, the largest city in the Arabian Peninsula, was a regional center of this religion, and many pilgrims visited its shrines. Pilgrims entering Mecca first saw statues of the three beautiful daughters of Allah, one of the high gods of traditional Arab religion. They visited a cube-shaped shrine dedicated to the god Hubal and drank from a sacred well. One scholar has called pre-Islamic Arabia's way of life a "tribal humanism."[1] Arabs honored loyalty to one's kin, bravery in battle, and protection of the weak. But they had no strong religious values that could challenge tribal values and little belief in any meaningful afterlife.

In the generation before the beginning of Islam, unprecedented wealth from international commerce was pouring into Mecca, which had come to control the international trade that passed through the Arabian Peninsula, mostly by camel caravans. This new wealth produced new social divisions, and it brought more cross-cultural interaction throughout the peninsula. Jews, Christians, and Zoroastrians lived there in significant numbers along with the Arab majority, particularly in the north. A small group of Arab monotheists, the **hanifs**, or "pious ones," was devoted to the worship of Allah, the one and only God.

12-2b The Life and Work of Muhammad (ca. 570–632)

Muhammad Ibn (son of) Abdullah was the founder of Islam. He was born around 570 C.E. in Mecca, into a relatively humble family of the Quraysh (KUR-aish) tribe that controlled Mecca. He was orphaned as a boy and raised by relatives. They couldn't afford schooling for Muhammad, so he worked

Islamist Recent term for Muslim radicals

hanifs [hah-NEEFS] "Pious ones," pre-Islamic Arabian monotheists

The Symbol of Islam?

This chapter opens with a representation of the crescent and star, said by many to be a symbol of Islam. Because Islam is typically against religious images and pictures, whether worshiped or not, it hasn't officially adopted pictorial symbols for itself. The crescent-and-star symbol is featured prominently on the flags of several countries in the Islamic world. It's often thought to be an Islamic symbol from the first centuries of Islam, but it first appeared as the symbol of the Ottoman Empire, which governed much of Islam from about 1300

Figure 12.1
Crescent and star

BONNIE VAN VOORST
© CENGAGE LEARNING

to 1920, not of Islam as a whole. Thus, it's no more than five hundred years old. (The legend that the crescent roll, or croissant, was invented in Vienna to celebrate the European defeat of the Ottoman siege of that city in 1683 has no solid historical evidence behind it.)

Crescents without a star are often found at the top of mosques, where they remind Muslims of God's rule over creation, and in particular of the importance of the moon in the Muslim religious calendar, which is based on the phases of the moon, not the sun. Also, the crescent and star are carved as a symbol of Islam into the gravestones of Muslims in the U.S. armed forces buried in U.S. military cemeteries. But on the whole, Islam has no official symbol.

---

as a camel driver and then as a caravan manager. His scant financial resources meant that he wasn't able to marry at the usual age.

Eventually, he came to work for a wealthy widow engaged in trade, Khadija (kah-DEE-juh). When she suggested marriage to him, he agreed, even though she was fifteen years older than he. Muhammad and Khadija were devoted exclusively to each other; while she lived, he didn't take another wife. They had six children together, four girls and two boys, but the boys died in childhood, a situation that has influenced Islam through today, as we'll see later in this chapter. Muhammad prospered and became a wealthy merchant, and his extensive travel for business brought him into contact with Jews, Christians, and Zoroastrians as well as hanifs and believers in many gods. Much current scholarship suggests that this contact likely helped shape his own faith as he began to doubt his own inherited religion, although traditional Muslim teaching maintains that Muhammad obtained monotheism from Allah.

In 610 C.E., Muhammad was meditating continually for days and nights in a cave outside Mecca. There he saw visions that came in a dreamlike state and revealed the word of God to him. When he fell into a trance, the angel Gabriel, known to Jews and Christians from

Ramadan [RAHM-uh-dahn] Month of fasting and commemoration of the giving of the Qur'an

the Bible, spoke to him. Muhammad heard Gabriel's voice outside himself and sometimes inside. "Recite!" the angel commanded (Qur'an 96), and Muhammad submitted to this command, reciting Gabriel's words to others. In a short time, the uncertain seeker of truth became a bold prophet. He had been transformed by submitting to the one true God who spoke to him, and in his submission he found freedom and courage. According to Islamic tradition, Muhammad received his first revelation from Gabriel the night of the twenty-seventh day of the month of **Ramadan**, and the month-long fast Muslims undertake for Ramadan celebrates the giving of the revelations.

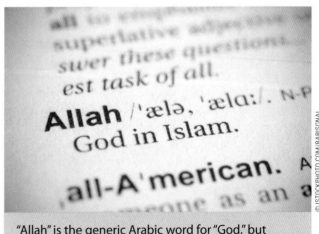

© ISTOCKPHOTO.COM/BARISONAL

"Allah" is the generic Arabic word for "God," but Muslims look upon it as God's main personal name.

Muhammad's early prophetic message to the Meccans had two main themes. First, only one God exists, **Allah** (Arabic for "the God"), who commands people to believe in this one God and to submit to God's holy will. Second, a day of judgment will certainly come, when those who have submitted to God will be rewarded forever, and those who haven't will be punished eternally. Other themes of the early revelations include generosity to the poor, widows, and orphans; the presence and goodness of God in the natural world; and the prophetic call of Muhammad himself. These themes clearly show that Islam from its beginning is in the line of the Abrahamic monotheisms, Judaism and Christianity.

> In Medinah, "Muhammad became a prophet-statesman, the founder of a political order . . . that would change the history of the world."
> —Daniel Peterson

Khadija and other members of Muhammad's immediate family believed him, but as Muhammad began his public proclamations (probably around 613), some Meccans became hostile toward him. However, Muhammad did gain some followers outside his family, and in ten years the number of Muslims numbered in the thousands. Most of them were relatively young and of lower social status. The tribal leaders in Mecca looked on Muslims as social deviants whose denial of the traditional gods and growing numbers threatened the economic foundations of the city. They ridiculed Muhammad as a lunatic, "only a poet" inventing his own revelations (Qur'an 52:30–49). They pointed out that Muhammad worked no miracles and offered no other supernatural signs of his prophetic calling, as many other prophets did before him. Muhammad responded by saying that the revelations themselves were a supernatural sign. But persecution escalated, and after the death of both his uncle and Khadija in 619, Muhammad's position in Mecca deteriorated.

In 622 C.E., the Prophet and his followers fled Mecca for Medina (then called Yathrib), about two hundred miles to the north. This relocation is called the **Hijra**, "flight," and is used to mark year 1 A.H. ("in the year of the flight") on the Islamic calendar, much as Christians traditionally use A.D., in the year of our Lord (Jesus). The Muslims were welcomed in Medina, and Muhammad was soon in charge of the fractious town. Muhammad would live in Medina for the rest of his life. There, Islam developed into a well-organized religious-political community called the **umma**, a complete way of life for its followers. As Daniel Peterson remarks about Muhammad's time in Medina, "Muhammad became a prophet-statesman, the founder of a political order and eventually of an empire that would change the history of the world. And Islam took on a political dimension that it has never abandoned."[2] Principles of a legal system came in divine revelations given at Medina, as did details about prayer, fasting, charity, and pilgrimage, key practices that would later become the pillars of Islam. Muhammad made a pact with the Jews of Medina; they didn't need to become Muslims and would have a rich measure of religious freedom.

The Muslims organized armed raids on Meccan caravans to punish Meccans for their hostility. These raids continued until the Muslim military victory over Mecca in the Battle of Badr (BAHD-er) in 624 C.E. The booty from this battle greatly increased the financial strength of the Muslims, and Muhammad gained great respect in Arabia; the battle proved to be a turning point in the fortunes of Islam. Judaism gradually declined in Medina, and hundreds of Medinan Jews were killed and the rest expelled between 624 and 627, after a failed Jewish attempt to assassinate Muhammad. This led to a more powerful dependence on Arabian religious practices reformed for Islamic use. For example, Muslims were no longer to pray facing Jerusalem, but rather toward Mecca (see Qur'an 2:142). The first Muslim pilgrimage to Mecca occurred in 629; pilgrimage to Jerusalem fell in importance. And the month-long Ramadan fast replaced the ten-day fast connected with the Jewish Day of Atonement. These changes in prayer, pilgrimage, and fasting became permanent in Islam, and are still key practices today.

Many Arab tribes in the region came into Islam while Muhammad controlled Medina, acknowledging his leadership. When the army he commanded got Mecca to surrender without a fight in 630, Muhammad immediately removed all idolatrous images from the city. He left only the sacred cubic building and its holy stone that was believed to have come directly from God. He kept Mecca as the destination for Muslim pilgrimage and maintained some of its religious sites, for example, the sacred well.

Allah [AHL-lah] "The God" in Arabic

Hijra [HIHJ-ruh] "Flight" of Muslims from Mecca to Medina in 622 C.E.

umma [OOM-uh] Organized Muslim community

Muhammad (on horseback, with an angel and soldiers behind him) receives the submission of a Jewish tribe he defeated at Medina; a manuscript painting dated to 1315. In some Muslim art from Persia and Turkey, Muhammad's face is sometimes pictured, contrary to most Muslim convention.

Muhammad raised armies to conquer the important northern regions of the Arabian Peninsula, taking on the Christian Byzantine Empire in the process. By the time Muhammad died in Medina two years later, in 632, he ruled nearly all the Arabian Peninsula. Islam had established itself permanently in this area, and it had become a rapidly growing religion (see Map 12.1).

12-2c Islam Immediately Following the Death of Muhammad (632–661)

The pressing issue at Muhammad's death was who would succeed him as leader of the Islamic movement, and how it was settled affects Islam through today. For whatever reason, Muhammad hadn't publicly designated a successor. Muslims needed to select a leader of the faith who would be the **caliph**, the "representative" or "successor" of Muhammad. This successor would not receive new revelations from Gabriel or change Islam in major ways, but would lead the community in its political and religious life. He would be the ruler of all Muslim lands. In the Arab culture

caliph [kah-LEEF] "Representative" or "successor" of Muhammad; ruler of Muslim community

Shi'as [SHEE-uhs] or **Shi'ites** [SHEE-ights] "Party" or "followers" of Ali, holding that Muhammad's true successors descended from his son-in-law Ali

Sunnis [SOON-eez] "People of the tradition," the majority of Muslims

of the times such leadership would usually stay in the family, but Muhammad had no surviving son, so the leading choice from his family was his cousin Ali (ah-LEE), who was also his son-in-law due to his marriage to Muhammad's daughter Fatima (FAH-tih-muh). Ali had always been enthusiastic for Islam, and he claimed that Muhammad had privately designated him as his successor. However, many contested Ali's fitness to rule.

A majority consensus arose among Muhammad's most powerful followers that Abu Bakr (AHB-oo BAHK-uhr), Muhammad's father-in-law, would be Muhammad's successor. He was an early believer and one of Islam's main military leaders. Abu Bakr soon took over the leadership of Islam due to three factors: his power base in the Muslim military forces; the need to squelch defections from Islam by several Arab tribes when Muhammad died; and his connection to the Prophet by way of Muhammad's favorite wife, A'isha (AH-ee-shah), who was Abu Bakr's daughter. Naturally, Ali's supporters objected to this, and the seeds of division were sown. The groups that grew from these seeds are the **Shi'as** or **Shi'ites**, "followers" or "party" (of Ali), and the **Sunnis**, the "people of the tradition," who formed the majority of Muslims. We'll discuss these two groups in more depth at the end of this history section.

> The pressing issue at Muhammad's death was who would succeed him . . ., and how it was settled affects Islam through today.

The rejection of Ali's leadership happened two more times: when Abu Bakr died and was replaced as caliph by Umar in 634, and again when Uthman became caliph in 644 when Umar was assassinated.

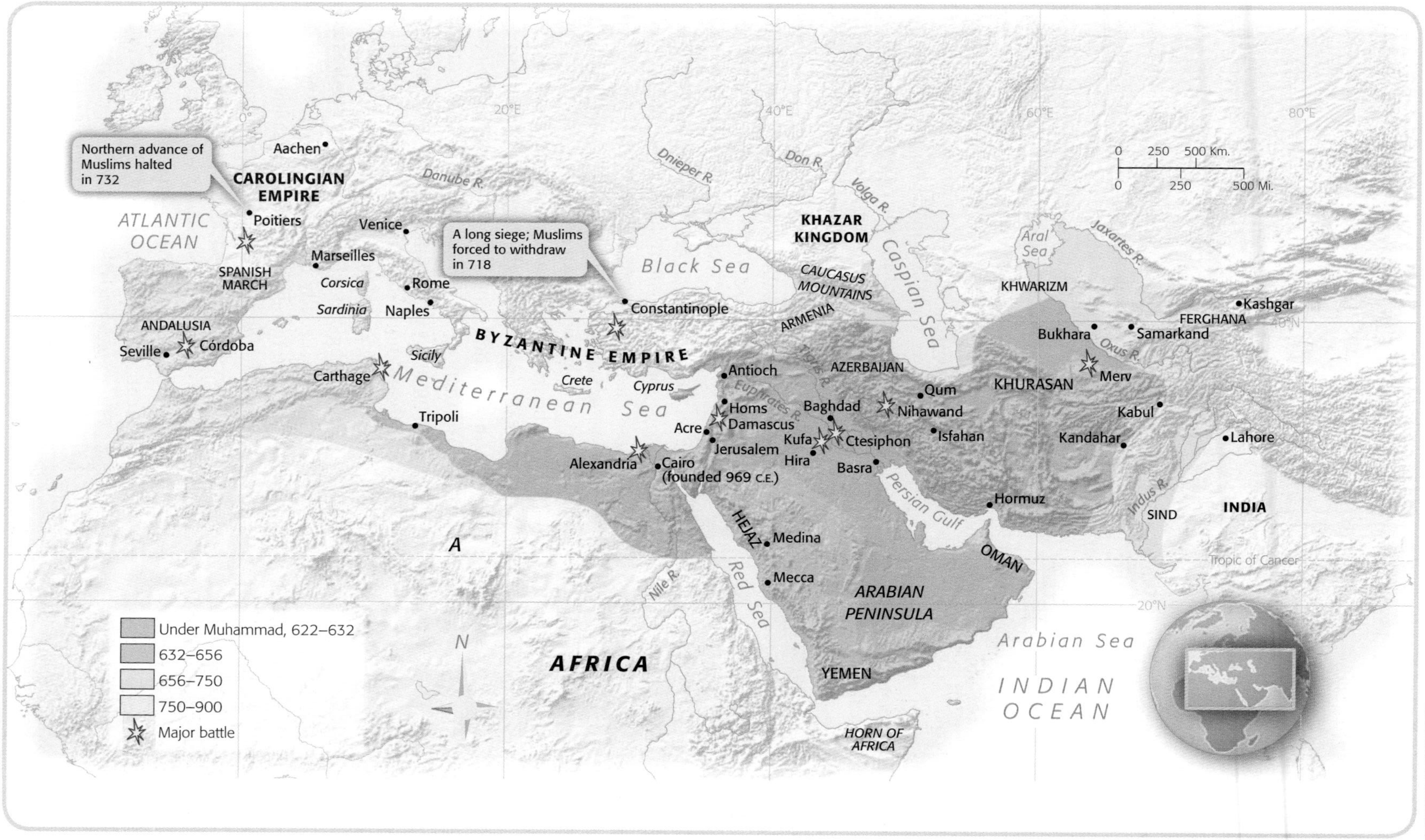

Map 12.1
Expansion of Islam to 900 C.E.

The Arabs rapidly conquered much of western Asia, North Africa, and Spain, and, in the process, expanding Islam into the conquered territories. By 900 their empire included all the Mediterranean islands, and stretched from Morocco and Spain in the west to western India and central Asia.

Legend:
- Under Muhammad, 622–632
- 632–656
- 656–750
- 750–900
- Major battle

Map labels:
Kashgar, FERGHANA, Samarkand, Bukhara, Merv, Kabul, Kandahar, Lahore, INDIA, SIND, KHURASAN, KHWARIZM, Hormuz, OMAN, Qum, Nihawand, Isfahan, Baghdad, Ctesiphon, Basra, Kufa, Hira, ARABIAN PENINSULA, YEMEN, Medina, Mecca, HEJAZ, Damascus, Homs, Antioch, Jerusalem, Acre, Cairo (founded 969 C.E.), Alexandria, AZERBAIJAN, ARMENIA, KHAZAR KINGDOM, CAUCASUS MOUNTAINS, Constantinople, BYZANTINE EMPIRE, Cyprus, Crete, Tripoli, Sicily, Naples, Rome, Venice, Marseilles, Corsica, Sardinia, Carthage, Poitiers, CAROLINGIAN EMPIRE, Aachen, SPANISH MARCH, Córdoba, Seville, ANDALUSIA

Water/geographic labels:
Jaxartes R., Oxus R., Aral Sea, Caspian Sea, Volga R., Don R., Dnieper R., Black Sea, Danube R., Mediterranean Sea, ATLANTIC OCEAN, Arabian Sea, INDIAN OCEAN, Persian Gulf, Red Sea, Nile R., Indus R., Euphrates R., Tigris R., AFRICA, HORN OF AFRICA, Tropic of Cancer, 20°N

Callouts:
A long siege; Muslims forced to withdraw in 718
Northern advance of Muslims halted in 732

© CENGAGE LEARNING 2013

500 Mi.
500 Km.

Ali's supporters grew bitter about these rejections. The caliphate seemed to be moving further and further from Muhammad's family. Despite this conflict, Islam continued to spread by Arab military conquest and follow-up Muslim missionary activity.

In an action that would influence all of Islam to come, Uthman gathered Muhammad's revelations and issued an authoritative edition of the Qur'an. Muhammad himself had not committed any of the revelations to writing, much less overseen that process. Instead, his followers had recorded his prophetic recitations on parchment, palm leaves, and even pieces of wood. Uthman gathered these, along with the collections that already existed. He kept what he knew to be authentic and destroyed the rest. The Qur'an emerged as we have it today, and Muslims believe that it perfectly reflects Gabriel's revelations to Muhammad.

After Uthman was assassinated by rebels in 656, Ali finally became caliph, the last of what Muslims call the **Rightly Guided Caliphs**—that is, the first four caliphs whom God directed to be faithful in ways other caliphs have not been. However, a leader of the Umayyad tribe soon claimed the caliphate. Hostilities between Ali and the Umayyads increased, and their armies faced off in 661. When Ali tried to compromise and avoid war, some of his followers killed him. War did break out, and the Sunnis were triumphant over the Shi'as. Sunnis had become the majority tradition of Muslims, in fact as

Rightly Guided Caliphs First four caliphs with special divine guidance

madrasas [muh-DRAH-suhz] Muslim religious schools

Crusades Christian military expeditions to take control of Palestine

Modern, idealized image of a Crusader. That Crusaders wore a cross is remembered even today by Muslims.

well as in name. The claim of a Muslim leader to be a caliph resurfaced most recently in 2014, when the leader of the so-called Islamic State made a claim to be a caliph similar to the Rightly Guided Caliphs (for more on the Islamic State movement, see Section 12-2e).

12-2d Islam from the Umayyads until Today (661–Present)

The subsequent history of Islam can be concisely traced by means of its dynasties and its geographic growth. Sunni leadership belonged to the Umayyad tribe for about one hundred years (661–750). The Umayyad Islamic Empire included nearly all the Middle East, Persia (modern-day Iran), Egypt, North Africa, and Spain. It remained largely united for two centuries after Muhammad's death. However, the Umayyad rulers and their courts were lax in devotion to Islam, and their drinking of alcohol and their marital infidelities offended pious Muslims, who often revolted.

They were replaced by the Abbasid (ah-BASS-id) dynasty, which had a long rule, from 750 to 1258. Islam spread farther into Africa and Asia; this was the second main period in the expansion of Islam. Many Muslims consider the Abbasid period to be the high point of Islamic history, particularly in such fields as art, science, philosophy, and Muslim theology. Muslim lands enjoyed a higher degree of civilization than that of most Europeans during Abbasid times. They preserved much of the science, medicine, and mathematics of the ancient Mediterranean world, and they made important contributions of their own to these fields. Abbasid rule saw Islam strengthen as a religion, with greater equality between Arab and non-Arab Muslims. Muslim belief and practices grew wider and deeper in the Arab empire. By the 900s, religious schools known as **madrasas** began to appear, usually headed by a well-known scholar of religion or religious law. Thousands of these schools can be found today all over the Muslim world.

The end of wider Abbasid rule started when the Turks took power. The Turks—a name for a wide family of tribes and peoples—had long been residents of central Asia, but around 900 C.E. some of them migrated into the northern parts of the Middle East. As they migrated, they came into contact with Islam and converted to it. The Turks took over Arab Muslim rule as they moved. They lost possession of Palestine during the **Crusades**, when Catholic military forces from Europe invaded to take control of

The Church of Holy Wisdom in Istanbul was made into a mosque in the 1400s (note the minarets at its four corners) and a state museum in the 1900s.

the Holy Land where Christianity was born. *Crusade* comes from the Latin word for cross, and Crusaders typically wore this symbol of Christianity on their clothing and shields, replacing the symbols of their own European states. The Crusader state was never large and ended by the second dynasty of Turks, the Mamluks (MAM-luhks). Because Christian nations were able to hold a key part of the Muslim homeland—including their holy city of Jerusalem—for more than a century, a negative impression toward Christianity was strengthened in Islam, one that continues today. This explains why Muslims who oppose the presence of western military personnel in Muslim lands sometimes call them "Crusaders."

In 1453, Muslims finally conquered Constantinople and renamed it Istanbul; the last Christian empire in the Middle East had finally fallen, and many of its churches were converted to mosques. For example, the former Christian Church of Holy Wisdom (Hagia Sophia) in Istanbul, Turkey, was made into a mosque. Turkish Muslim control spread eastward into India, where from 1526 until 1858 the Mughal (MOO-gahl) dynasty of Turkish Muslims ruled the largest part of the Indian subcontinent. (Our word *mogul*, meaning a powerful leader such as a Hollywood movie mogul, comes from *Mughal*.) When the early modern age began to dawn in the 1600s, Islam reached the height of its power in three main empires: the Sunni Ottoman Turks in the Middle East, North Africa, and much of southeastern Europe; the Shi'a Safavids in Iran; and the Sunni Mughals in India.

After the Mamluks lost their rule, the Ottoman Turks took over the vast empire of Islam and became the longest-lived Islamic dynasty (1300–1923). It collapsed after its defeat in World War I, when it was on the side of Germany and Austria-Hungary. For the first time, the main Muslim empire had fallen to external powers. Something new to Islam was imposed on it by the victors: Instead of one Islamic empire, there were now many Muslim nation-states, nearly all of them officially Muslim. Turkey, under its leader Mustafa Kemal (muh-STAHF-uh keh-MAHL), known as Ataturk ("Father of the Turks"), became the first and still today the only officially secular nation with a predominantly Muslim population. It remains so today not without difficulties, as some religiously conservative Muslims attempt to make it officially Muslim. Since 1923, Muslims in the nation-states have struggled to preserve Islam as an umma within their borders. They have also struggled with democratization, as European colonization after World War I held back that process. The popular uprisings in several Arab nations from 2010 through about 2012 (and still continuing today mainly in the civil war in Syria), called the **Arab Spring**, demanded an end to autocratic rule and a measure of democracy, but they have resulted in civil turmoil and increased power of radical Islamic groups. Relatively few advances toward democracy have been made in Arab nations because of the Arab Spring; for most nations, the Arab Spring has turned back into winter. Tunisia is the only exception, with a democratic movement that won its leaders the 2015 Nobel Peace Prize. Despite these challenges, Islam is firmly established today throughout North Africa, the Middle East, and both central and south Asia (see Map 12.2).

Arab Spring Uprisings in Arab nations from 2010 through 2012, demanding an end to autocratic rule and a measure of democracy

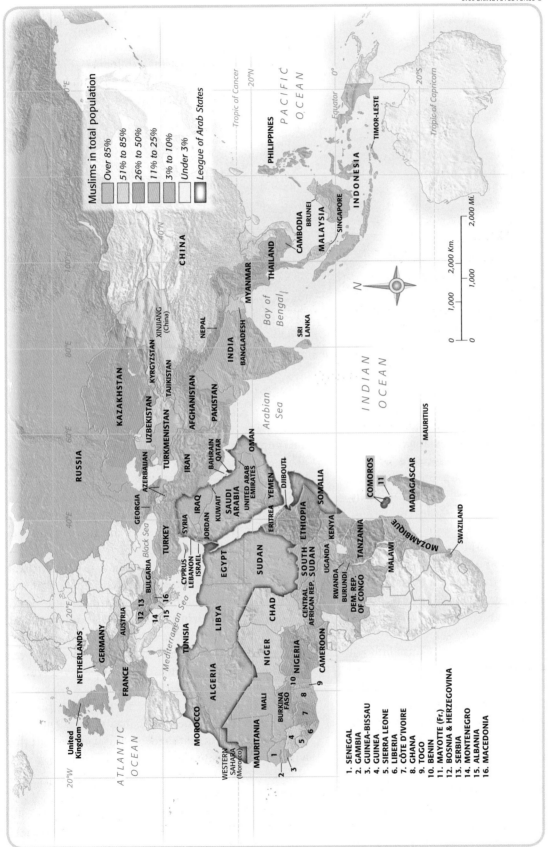

Map 12.2

The Islamic World Today

The Islamic world includes not only the Middle East—western Asia and North Africa—but also countries with Muslim majorities in sub-Saharan Africa, central Asia, and south and Southeast Asia. Sunnis predominate in most of the Islamic world; Shi'as predominate in Iran and form sizable minorities in Iraq and Lebanon. In addition, Muslims live in most other Eastern Hemisphere nations and in the Americas, where they make up under 3 percent of the population.

Muslims in total population

- Over 85%
- 51% to 85%
- 26% to 50%
- 11% to 25%
- 3% to 10%
- Under 3%
- League of Arab States

1. SENEGAL
2. GAMBIA
3. GUINEA-BISSAU
4. GUINEA
5. SIERRA LEONE
6. LIBERIA
7. CÔTE D'IVOIRE
8. GHANA
9. TOGO
10. BENIN
11. MAYOTTE (Fr.)
12. BOSNIA & HERZEGOVINA
13. SERBIA
14. MONTENEGRO
15. ALBANIA
16. MACEDONIA

12-2e Diverse Muslim Groups Today: Mainstream, Zealous, and Moderate

Now that our survey of Muslim history is complete, we should pause before proceeding to Muslim teachings to consider the diversity of Muslim groups today. Noted sociologist of religion Rodney Stark wrote in 2008, "The most persistent mistake Westerners make about Islam today is to think of it as monolithic."[3] In fact, Islam has a good deal of internal diversity, and often strongly opposing factions. We begin discussion of contemporary groups with the mainstream: Sunnis, Shi'as (two groups we've met earlier, but who are so important that they require fuller treatment here), and Sufis. Then we'll consider the more zealous groups in Sunni Islam: the Wahhabis, the Muslim Brotherhood, the Taliban, and the Islamic State. Finally, we'll consider moderate Muslim movements. Along the way, we'll take a closer look at the term *Islamic fundamentalism*.

Sunnis and Shi'as. The most important diversity within Islam is the split between Sunnis and Shi'as. As we saw earlier, the roots of this split go back to the death of Muhammad. When Caliph Ali died in 661, a lasting formal split developed between the rival Sunni and Shi'a groups. Ali had two sons, Hassan and Husain, who were of course the grandsons of Muhammad. Shi'as claimed then, and still do today, that this descent made them the rightful caliphs. Hassan gave up his claim due to illness and died soon afterward. In 680, Husain's army battled the Sunnis near the town of Karbala in present-day Iraq. But the Sunnis cut off the Shi'a army from its water supply and then destroyed the Shi'as. When Husain's severed head was thrown over the wall of Karbala, his supporters in the town put it on a lance and reverently carried it around with deep mourning. Shi'a would continue in Islam as a separate group averaging about 10 to 15 percent of all Muslims, but never again would Shi'as challenge Sunnis for control of Islam as a whole.

The day of Husain's death, the tenth of Muharram, is observed by Shi'as as a day of mourning— called **Ashura**, "the tenth." Husain's death is now viewed as martyrdom, a holy death, for the true form of Islam; commitment to martyrdom for Islam became a leading part of Shi'a. In mass processions still held today on Ashura, many Shi'a

Ruholla Khomeini, leader of the Iranian Revolution in 1979 and head Imam from 1979 to his death in 1989, pictured on Iranian currency.

men connect with Husain's martyrdom by lashing themselves with chains and whips until their blood flows. It was on Ashura in 1979 that Shi'a radicals in the capital of Iran stormed the American embassy and held its personnel hostage, in violation of international law, for more than a year— an event that still casts a dark shadow on U.S.–Iranian relations.

As we saw earlier, Shi'as believe that the line of Islamic leadership continues through Ali and Husain—that is, through the family of Muhammad. Each leader receives, as Shi'as claim Ali received from Muhammad, a direct designation of succession from his predecessor and a supernatural knowledge of Islam to be an effective leader. The Arabic term for leader is **imam**, a general term that carries different (and sometimes confusing) meanings; for example, it is also the term for the leader

> "The most persistent mistake Westerners make about Islam today is to think of it as monolithic."
> —Rodney Stark

Ashura [uh-SHOOR-uh] The tenth of Muharram, day of Husain's death, observed by Shi'as as a day of mourning

imam [IHM-ahm] Leader of prayer in a Sunni mosque, or the religious-political leader of a Shi'a community

of a Sunni mosque. Shi'as typically view their imam's interpretation of Islam as perfect and fully authoritative. Sometimes they even view the imam as unusually holy, even saintly; this is especially true for regional or local imams. All this makes for powerful religious leaders in Shi'a—more so than in Sunni groups.

Shi'as and Sunnis have typically lived and worshiped apart from each other. Shi'as have their own territories where they predominate, and beyond this they tend to be minorities in many Sunni nations. Where Sunnis and Shi'as are found in the same cities, they prefer to live in different neighborhoods. They usually don't intermarry or go into business with each other, and they have their own mosques and leaders. Shi'as have five additional pillars—besides the Five Pillars common to all Muslims that we'll consider later—stressing Shi'a doctrines and practices, and slight differences in their formal prayers. In a 2016 book, *The New Sectarianism*, Geneive Abdo shows that the Arab Spring uprisings have increased conflict between Sunnis and Shi'as over Islamic identity.[4]

Shi'a history is a story of continual internal splits. Shi'a sects are still wary of one another. (One of the features of splinter groups in religion is that they're often beset by internal splintering; in other words, splitters keep splitting.) Three main groups account for the majority of Shi'as today, but each has its own subgroups. The three groups are named by how many original imams they recognize.

- The *Twelvers*, also known as *Imamites*, recognize twelve imams in the line of succession from Muhammad. The twelfth imam vanished when he was five years old and is still living in a hidden cave. He'll return near the end of time as the **Mahdi**, "the one guided" by God, and establish worldwide Shi'a rule. Twelvers are the majority of Shi'as today; they make up most Iranian and Iraqi Shi'as, and they are present in Lebanon as well.

- The *Seveners*, or *Ismailites*, are found today in India, Pakistan, and east Africa. Some Seveners believe that the seventh imam, Ismail, was Allah in human form, a notion that all other Muslims regard as heretical. Ismailites claim that Ismail will return as the Mahdi. Also from the Seveners were the Hashishin (ha-SHEESH-een), who used hashish to induce visions before killing others for hire. (Our word *assassin* comes from this group.) The current leader of the largest group of Seveners is Prince Karim Aga Khan IV, the forty-ninth Ismaili imam, who traces his lineage to Muhammad through Fatima.

- The *Fivers*, or *Zaidites*, are a small sect of Shi'as found mostly in Yemen. Their fifth imam is Zaid, who began a different line of succession that eventually died out. He is now living in concealment. Fivers tend to be less hostile to Sunnis, but in the past decade they've engaged in armed rebellion against the Sunni government of Yemen.

> { Sufis pursue a direct, loving, and ecstatic experience of God. }

The Sunnis and Shi'as comprise the two main divisions in Islam, but other Muslim groups have brought further Muslim diversity. Despite their relatively small size, these latter groups have exerted a significant influence within Islam and are still important in Islam today. We'll consider them in chronological order.

Sufis. Islam typically emphasizes the practice of religion, not thinking or feeling it. Submitting to God's will in one's actions is most important. However, Islam developed a mystical tradition to find deeper spiritual power within its religious teachings and practices. Islamic mystics are **Sufis**, a word for the woolen garments worn by the first Muslim mystics. Sufism arose in the 700s and is still found among both Sunnis and Shi'as. It has spread Islam on the peripheries of the Muslim world. Within Islamic lands it has spread deeper religious commitment among the lower classes, particularly in folk Islam in Africa and central Asia. Sufism is also very popular today in Pakistan. In its long history, it has organized into several orders or brotherhoods, among whom are the Mevlevi (mehv-LEHV-ee) order, from which the whirling dervish dancers come. These seek ecstasy in their dance, and have attained religious and cultural fame today.

Sufis pursue a direct, loving, and ecstatic experience of God, usually to narrow the gap between God and humans. Poetry, music, and dancing are important in this mystical quest. At first Muslim authorities viewed

Mahdi [MAH-dee] "The one guided" by God, hidden Shi'a imam who will return to establish worldwide Shi'a rule

Sufis [SOO-feez] Followers of Islamic mystical movement Sufism

Sufi dancers, whirling dervishes, of the Mevlevi order

Sufism with suspicion, until it became apparent that Sufis did indeed follow key Muslim practices. Sufism was allowed to continue, but many Muslims viewed the notion of human beings becoming literally one with God as idolatrous. All Muslims expect to be close to God after the final judgment, but only the Sufis see achieving a mystical closeness—not to mention oneness—with God in this life as possible. The most influential Sufi by far was Jalal al-Din Rumi (jah-LAL al-DIHN ROO-mee), the thirteenth-century Persian poet of mystical love. Rumi has been called the most popular poet in America today, even among non-Muslims.

According to some proponents of Sufism in the western world, Sufi ideas developed prior to our modern organized religions and are universal in nature, a system of mysticism that is employable by people of many faiths. They point to verses in Rumi's poetry, such as this one from "One Song":

> All religions, all this singing, one song
> The differences are just illusion and vanity.
> Sunlight looks different on this wall than it does on
>   that wall
> and different on this other one,
> but it is still one light.

However, Sufis themselves typically reject the notion of Sufism without Islam. Despite the words of Rumi, "I am neither Christian, nor Jew, nor Zoroastrian, nor Muslim," Sufism has been, and probably will remain, an inner-Islamic movement. Moreover, recent scholarship

suggests that western translations of Rumi's poetry have deliberately downplayed, even erased, its Islamic aspects.[5]

Wahhabis. From its very beginnings, Islam has seen movements that strive for strict purity and zeal. One such group, the **Wahhabi** reform movement in Sunni Islam, was begun by Muhammad al-Wahhab (al-wah-HAHB) in the late 1700s. Wahhab was shocked by what he regarded as widespread corruption in Islam (a conviction that has shaped many radical Muslim groups since). He despised Sufism because he thought that it mixed Islam and Hindu pantheism, and he disapproved of many Shi'a popular practices as well. For example, venerating the tombs of prominent Shi'a and Sufi Muslims to gain spiritual power he considered idolatrous. His message of reform was summed up in the cry "Back to the Book [the Qur'an] and the Tradition [sunna] of the Prophet!" He adhered to a conservative method of Qur'anic interpretation that avoided all innovations.

A Wahhabi state was finally established in the 1920s, when the Sa'ud family became rulers of the new nation of Saudi Arabia. Practices that Wahhabis considered contrary to Islam were severely punished: consumption of any alcohol, veneration of saints at their tombs, playing of secular music, possession of anything deemed pornographic, or the formal presence of any other religions. Muslim religious law became the law of Saudi Arabia, and was strictly enforced. The so-called religious police (formally called the "Commission for the Promotion of Virtue and the Prevention of Vices") patrol public areas to enforce this law, particularly on women's dress and conduct, but this has been easing a bit since 2001. The western press often calls Wahhabism "puritanical," but that's a term from Protestant Christian history that ill fits this Islamic movement. Most Sunnis in the world today don't typically live under Wahhabi requirements. However, Saudi Arabia is the most influential nation in the Muslim world, for its holy

Wahhabi [wah-HAH-bee] Modern Sunni radical movement begun by Muhammad al-Wahhab

A Closer Look

"Islamic Fundamentalism"?

Deciding what to call the phenomenon commonly known as Islamic fundamentalism isn't easy. This term became popular after the Iranian Revolution in 1979 as a description of the resurgent Shi'a movement. It was used first by westerners, especially American journalists, often unaware that they were applying to Muslims a term used for certain American Protestant Christians. Sometimes other contemporary groups are labeled Islamic fundamentalists, for example, the Taliban, al-Qaeda, the Wahhabis, the Muslim Brotherhood, and the Islamic State.

The term *Islamism* is found today in the press and in scholarly writing. It avoids the weaknesses of *Islamic fundamentalism* and has the appeal of one-word simplicity. However, *Islamism* is an oddly constructed word, and the suffix *-ism* can be pejorative. Some groups labeled Islamists maintain that they are simply faithful Muslims— that they follow Islam, not Islamism—and that their political convictions are an expression of their religious belief in the Islamic way of life.

Salafi refers to the movement of Muslims who model their faith on their understanding of the *Salaf* (predecessors or ancestors), the earliest Muslims. A modern Sunni Islamic movement related to Wahhabism, Salafism is rapidly gaining popularity. Salafism is connected today with the literalist, strict practice of Islam. In Egypt, the Salafist movement is even more conservative than the Muslim Brotherhood, and has become its main political opponent.

Political Islam is occasionally used today for this movement's effort to reunite the political and the religious, but as we've seen, Islam traditionally strives to do this and has in fact done so during most of its history. In *militant Islam*, we must distinguish between those who use violence and those who don't. Even among the first group, a distinction must be drawn between those who use violence according to traditional rules of jihad and those who use it outside jihad (a term discussed in Section 12-4e).

Radical Islam is perhaps the best of these options, although it isn't without its own problems. *Radical* is vaguer than the other terms discussed, and it can have a pejorative connotation. On the positive side, it has the connotation of both going to the root and going all the way with what radicals believe God wants.

---

cities of Mecca and Medina and its vast oil wealth, so the way it practices Islam has become widely known and influential.

The Muslim Brotherhood. When the Ottoman Empire collapsed around 1920, the Muslim world was left for the first time without a caliph. This vacuum in religious leadership, coupled with new colonial control of many Middle Eastern nations by European powers under the direction of the League of Nations, led to a rise of conservative movements in several large Muslim nations. One of the earliest and most influential—the **Muslim Brotherhood**— was launched in Egypt by the charismatic Hassan al-Banna in 1929. Opposed to corruption, the lax practice of Islam, and

Salafi [suh-LAH-fee]
Sunni movement promoting strict practice of Islam

Muslim Brotherhood
Conservative religious and political movement founded in 1929

westernization in Egyptian government and life, the Brotherhood worked for purely Islamic legal systems in Egypt. Since then, the movement has spread to several other Sunni Muslim countries.

Sometimes the Brotherhood's actions are violent, and many Arab governments view the movement as undermining their rule. The Muslim Brotherhood is often said to be the beginning of organized Islamic fundamentalism, but that distinction should probably belong to Wahhabism (see "A Closer Look: 'Islamic Fundamentalism'?"). It is true, however, that Muslim Brotherhood members have taken very conservative stances; for example, in Kuwait they oppose laws giving women the right to vote. In early 2011, the Muslim Brotherhood played a key role in toppling the rule of Egyptian President Hosni Mubarak (HOHS-nee moo-BAHR-ahk). Egypt then moved toward conservative Muslim rule under President Mohamed Morsi (MOHR-see), a leader in the Muslim Brotherhood, until the Egyptian military ousted him in 2013; since then, government crackdown on the Brotherhood has been constant. Observers anticipate the Brotherhood's continued role in political change in other Middle Eastern nations.

The Taliban. Another movement important for understanding Islam today is the **Taliban**, "students" of the Qur'an. (We'll consider a related group, al-Qaeda, in Section 12-6d.) They draw members from many Sunni Islamic countries. The Taliban was influenced by the Wahhabi movement during the successful Muslim struggle to drive the Soviet Union out of the Muslim nation of Afghanistan in the 1980s. In the 1990s, the Taliban was able to gain control of Afghanistan. The first Taliban home page on the World Wide Web invited Muslims to contribute money to what they called the "first truly Islamic state in history." The Taliban gained opposition in the West for repressive measures against Afghani women, such as ending all education except homeschooling for females of any age and prohibiting women from working outside their homes. Similar to some zealous Muslims before them, the Taliban considers Muslims who don't adhere to their strict attitudes and standards of behavior to be false Muslims and enemies of Islam. Their means for bringing about their ideals have often been brutally violent, and as of this writing they continue their military struggle to regain rule in Afghanistan. Their strong belief has made them tenacious fighters.

The Islamic State. The Islamic State (IS for short) has gone by several names as it came into existence in 1999 and rose to power. It was formerly known as The Islamic State of Iraq and the Levant (ISIL) and The Islamic State of Iraq and Syria (ISIS). Occasionally, it is called DAESH (dah-ESH); this is the Arabic equivalent of ISIL, but is strongly disliked by the IS.

The IS is a radical militant group founded by former religious and military leaders in the Iraqi government of Saddam Hussein. Similar to the Taliban, IS tries to conquer and hold territory. As its name implies, it regards itself as a nation even though no other nation in the world does; even al-Qaeda has rejected it as too violent.

TERRORISM HAS NO RELIGION

The relationship between terrorism and Islam is controversial. IS's actions are clearly related to its distinctive religious beliefs.

At the end of 2017, IS had control over 10 million people in large swaths of Iraq and Syria, as well as more limited power in parts of Libya and especially Nigeria, where the Muslim militant movement known as Boko Haram (literally, "western schooling is evil") joined up with IS in 2015. IS has declared itself a worldwide caliphate, with its founder Abu Bakr al-Baghdadi its caliph. It claims religious, political, and military authority over all Muslims worldwide. IS is grounded even more than other radical Islamic movements in religious belief, fighting to induce the end of the world and the triumph of Islam. IS has been consistently ferocious in applying its extreme interpretation of Muslim law to its territories. This includes barring women from public life; enforcing dress codes for men and especially women; large-scale killings of religious minorities in Syria and Iraq who refuse to convert to Islam, especially Christians and Yazidis (yah-ZEE-dees); posting graphic videos of beheadings of prisoners of war and captured western aid workers and journalists; and forcing thousands of minority women and girls to be sex slaves for purchase by the IS military.

IS runs a social media campaign in the Arab world and the West, enticing Muslims to its territories to join the IS army or encouraging them to engage in "lone wolf" terror attacks in their own lands. In November of 2015, IS struck at multiple targets in Paris, killing 129 people and seriously injuring hundreds more. This was the second major attack outside its territory; the first was the bombing of a Russian airliner over Egypt in October of 2015, which killed 224 people. In 2015 and 2016, IS claimed responsibility for a number of high-profile terrorist attacks outside Iraq and Syria, including mass shootings, bombings, and car/truck attacks in Tunisia, Turkey, Lebanon, Belgium, Germany, and France. In 2017, a man influenced by IS carried out an attack near the British Parliament building, killing four people and injuring many more. Also in

Taliban [TAHL-ih-bahn] "Students" of the Qur'an, a radical Sunni group in Afghanistan

2017, an agent of IS struck an Ariana Grande concert in Manchester, England, killing twenty-two people and wounding at least fifty-nine others.

Moderate Muslim Movements. It might seem to you from this treatment of Muslim groups that Islam has only gotten more conservative in the past century or so. This would be a mistake. In recent times, Muslim modernism tried to revive what it considered the original form of Islam by determining the meaning of their scriptures. Some historical methods new to Islam but well known in Europe were introduced to recover the original meaning of the Qur'an. For example, Indian Muslim scholar M. Azad (1888–1958) argued that one must study Arabian culture at the time of Muhammad to understand what the Qur'an originally meant. This liberalizing movement was generally confined to the more westernized upper classes.

Since 2001, a small but vocal group of Muslims has been trying to move Islam to the center, and some even call themselves Progressives. Omid Safi, a professor at the University of North Carolina at Chapel Hill who wrote *Progressive Muslims: On Justice, Gender, and Pluralism*, opposes (along with moderates) Wahhabism, the Taliban, and all other radical Islamic groups.[6] Another example of progressive Islam is Sisters in Islam, a Malaysian group founded in the 1980s by the politically connected professor Zainab Anwar. Sisters in Islam promotes an Islamic vision of freedom, justice, and equality for women. Progressive Muslims typically claim that after Muhammad died a conservative wave swept over Islam and that his reforms were effectively frozen when they should have continued. They view themselves as carrying on in the liberating spirit and message of Muhammad.

An important part of this moderating movement is the liberation of Muslim women. The status of Muslim women has been a persistently difficult issue, both within Islam and in the wider world. Traditionally, Islam sees gender differences as given by God. The Qur'an says, "Men have authority over women because God has made the one superior to the other, and because men spend their wealth to maintain women" (4:34). It also affirms that "Women shall with justice have rights similar to those exercised against them, although men have a status above women" (2:228). Moderates and progressives struggle to give women a greater measure of freedom: to wear a head covering or not, to have an opportunity for a full education equal to that of men, to vote and participate in politics, and to attain other freedoms. Their progress is slow, and they encounter opposition in parts of the Muslim world, but they are not discouraged.

 12-3 Essential Islamic Teachings

California's Orange County has a thriving mosque. Yassir Fazaga keeps an eye on the American calendar to provide a connection for his weekly Friday sermon as the imam. Around Valentine's Day, he talks about how the Qur'an endorses romantic love within certain moral boundaries. "My main objective is to make Islam relevant," said Fazaga, who was born in east Africa, went to high school in Orange County, and attended college and a religious training school in Virginia. As the first generation of American Muslims begins to graduate from American colleges in significant numbers, some mosques are beginning to seek leaders who can teach not just about the main teachings of Islam, but also about religious and social issues that are relevant to Muslim young people here (such as dating, marriage, and drugs). One of the challenges facing Islam in North America is to obtain imams who can lead Muslim communities in the North American context.

12-3a God Is One

Muslims consider the teaching that there is only one God to be the basis and the center of their religion. The Arabic word *Allah* doesn't refer only to the God of Islam. It is the common, generic Arabic word for God—any God—and when Muslims talk in Arabic about the God of Jews, Christians, and Zoroastrians, *Allah* is the word they use.

The roots of Muhammad's understanding of Allah lie in monotheism. God is an eternal, spiritual being; God is not a force, but a divine person. The Qur'an sees Islam as carrying on this true monotheistic religion that Judaism and Christianity have mostly abandoned. Islam has a strict, absolute form of monotheism, because God is seen as one and one only. Therefore, Muslims reject all forms of polytheism as false religions, and other gods as false. Muhammad considered the "fatherhood" of Allah—which he associated with the sexual procreation of a son or the "daughters of Allah," taught in pre-Islamic Arabian religion—as idolatrous. Muslim monotheism led to opposing the Christian doctrine of Jesus as the Son of God. The Qur'an says, "God is One, the eternal God. He begot no one, nor was He begotten" (112:1–3). In Islam, idolatry (*shirk*), acknowledging other gods besides the one and only God, is considered the worst sin.

Muslims forbid idolatry so strongly that they forbid anything that may encourage it or make it possible. Therefore, they don't make images or pictures of God. If Muhammad is depicted at all, his face is omitted.

Ramadam Kareem

SAIYOOD SRIKAMON/ DREAMSTIME.COM

The cover of a Ramadan greeting card shows "Allah" written artistically. Because Muslims forbid anything that makes idolatry possible, they don't make images or pictures of God or even of Muhammad.

can be described, but not known in any comprehensive way. God is all powerful, and Muslims typically believe that all that happens in the world, good or evil, happens within the plan and control of God. Muslims use the phrase *enshallah* (en-SHAHL-ah), "if God wills it," whenever they talk about the future; in fact, it's probably the most commonly used Arabic expression.

12-3b Angels and Spirits

God created angels and spirits to serve God and the human beings created later. Muhammad received the Qur'an through the archangel Gabriel. Islam recognizes three other archangels and a large company of ordinary angels. As in Judaism and Christianity, angels are the messengers carrying divine revelation to humans. There are also many **jinn**, spirits (related to our word *genie*). In the Qur'an they say about themselves, "Some of us are Muslims and some are wrongdoers" (72:14). Evil jinn are led by the devil, a spirit who rebelled against God when humans were created.

Muslims must be on guard against the jinn, because they can cause not only physical, but also spiritual harm by luring believers away from Allah. Some westerners misunderstand jinn as spirits of deceased humans, but they are nonhuman spirits who have fallen into evil and often tempt humans to do wrong.

Many Muslim believers have a lively sense of the good and evil forces of the jinn. For example, in 2012 hundreds of Saudi teenagers raided an abandoned hospital in Riyadh to drive out evil jinn thought to haunt it, and

(A few schools of Muslim art in the past have ignored this.) Strict Muslims today object to any representational art forms as a temptation to idolatry. This has led to mosques being decorated only with colorful geometric patterns, which are said to reflect the order and beauty of the creation as a whole, not of God. These patterns can be strikingly beautiful and inspiring. When the author of this book went for the first time into the Dome of the Rock mosque in Jerusalem, the third holiest site in Islam, it impressed him as one of the most beautiful buildings he had ever seen. Verses from the Qur'an are also used in decorating mosques and homes.

God is unique in essence and attributes, infinite, and the creator and sustainer of all that exists. "His are the beautiful names," ninety-nine in all; these names are scattered throughout the Qur'an, but they were compiled in a later tradition. Moreover, God is beyond all human thought and understanding. God

Detail from a mosque ceiling painting, Istanbul, Turkey

SOPHIE MCAULAY/DREAMSTIME.COM

jinn [jihn] Spirits, both good and evil

the authorities had to intervene to stop the mayhem. Although the Qur'an and official Muslim teachings focus on belief and practices that draw the believer's focus to God alone, some Muslims practice Islam primarily to keep evil spirits at bay and bring the blessing of good spirits. Many Islamic teachers are laboring today, as Sufis did in the past, to raise all Muslims to a fuller understanding of monotheism—an understanding that the focus of one's faith should not be on spirits, but on the God who controls good and evil spirits.

12-3c The Qur'an

Muslims believe that the angel Gabriel divinely revealed to Muhammad the Qur'an, the perfect copy of an eternal, heavenly book. The name *Qur'an* means recitation, which reflects the main origin and use of this scripture, oral communication—first from Gabriel to Muhammad, and then from Muhammad to his followers.

> *Many Muslim nations televise contests of Qur'anic recitations.*

The Qur'an is divided into 114 chapters called **surahs**, and each chapter is divided into verses. Because the Qur'an is viewed by Muslims as the successor and fulfillment of the Jewish and Christian scriptures, it is legitimate to compare their relative sizes: The Qur'an is about two-thirds the size of the New Testament and half the size of the Jewish Bible. The chapters are arranged by length, from longer chapters to shorter ones. The shorter, older chapters focus on the basic themes

surah [SOO-ruhs] Chapters of the Qur'an

al-Fatihah [al-fah-TEE-huh] "The Opening," the first chapter of the Qur'an, used as a prayer in Islam

of one God and future judgment; the longer, later ones contain many detailed instructions for the Islamic community as well as references to biblical history. Unlike the Jewish and Christian Bibles, the Qur'an gives virtually no historical narratives; it's almost all teaching and commands. It begins with **al-Fatihah**, "the Opening," Chapter 1, a beautifully resonant prayer that is recited at prayer times. This chapter comes close to providing a summary of Islam:

> In the name of God, the Most Gracious, the Most Merciful. All praise and thanks be to God, the Lord of the Worlds, the Most Gracious, the Most Merciful, the only Lord of the Day of Judgment. You alone we worship, and You alone we ask for help. Guide us on the Straight Way, the Way of those on whom you have bestowed your grace, not of those who incur your anger or those who have gone astray.

The Qur'an itself is said to exist only in Arabic, the language in which it was revealed by Muhammad to others. Muslims believe that all translations of the Qur'an involve some distortion of meaning, so no translation can be the authentic, perfect Qur'an. A recent book by M. Brett Wilson, *Translating the Qur'an in an Age of Nationalism*, shows how Muslims came to accept the long-rejected idea that the Qur'an should be translated into other languages.[7] Where translations are used, many printed Qur'ans have the original Arabic text on facing pages. Muslim schoolchildren memorize large

Even mass-produced modern Qur'an covers suggest the high regard Muslims have for their scripture.

sections of the Qur'an in Arabic, even if Arabic isn't their main language. Imams are required to memorize all of it. Recitation of the Qur'an is an art form, with fame and sometimes riches going to those who are talented in the art. Many Muslim nations televise contests of Qur'anic recitations, and the level of excitement for these television shows approaches that in the United States for shows such as *America's Got Talent*.

Arab Muslim girl reads the Qur'an.

The Qur'an contains many references to people and stories in the Jewish and Christian Bibles. We meet in the Qur'an figures such as Adam and Eve, Noah, Abraham, Moses, Jesus, and Mary, all of whom are considered Muslims and prophets in the prophetic line that culminates in Muhammad. Muslims believe that Gabriel spoke these biblical references to Muhammad during the revelations of Qur'anic content, thus accounting for the differences in these accounts between the Bible and the Qur'an. However, non-Muslim scholars typically hold that Muhammad probably heard these stories first from his Jewish and Christian contacts.

Three young boys get Arabic-language Qur'an instruction in West Africa, by use of traditional wooden tablets.

12-3d Prophets

The Qur'an states that God has revealed the divine will at key points in human history through prophets. All the prophets, including Muhammad, call for the same response: submission to the will of God and preparation for an impending judgment. Most of the twenty-five prophets mentioned in the Qur'an are well-known figures in Judaism and Christianity. (The Qur'an also names three other prophets—Hud, Shu'aib, and Salih (7:66–93)—who may have been leading figures in the small Arab monotheistic tradition leading to Islam.) Although Jews and Christians claim many of the prophets as their own, Muslims view them as Islamic prophets who teach submission to God. They didn't come to found Judaism, Christianity, or the hanif tradition as different religions—Muhammad is the culmination and conclusion of the entire line of prophets.

Despite this emphasis on Muhammad as the culmination of the prophets, some Muslims look for one more prophetic figure to come: the Mahdi. As stated earlier, Shi'as expect the last in the line of imams to be the Mahdi. He will come shortly before the end of time and the final judgment; his work is to rid the world of injustice as a preparation for the end. In the early 2000s, the main Shi'a paramilitary force in Iraq was called the Mahdi Army, but without any direct implication that the powerful Shi'a imam leading it was the Mahdi.

12-3e People of the Book: Jews, Christians, and Zoroastrians

Some in the line of Muslim prophets gave books to their people: Zarathustra wrote down his message for Zoroastrians; Moses recorded the law and David composed the Psalms, for the Jews; Jesus taught the Gospels to Christians. Muslim call these groups **People of the Book**.

People of the Book Christians, Jews, and Zoroastrians, whose scriptures are related to the Qur'an

This expression doesn't refer, as is sometimes said, to all people who have sacred books in their religions—after all, many religions have sacred books—but only to people whose sacred book(s) Muslims view as in a line of religious development with *the* Book, the Qur'an. Some passages in the Qur'an even suggest that People of the Book who follow their religions carefully will enter heaven along with Muslims. (For recent treatment of inter-religious issues in the Qur'an, see Jerusha Tanner Lamptey, *Never Wholly Other: A Muslima Theology of Religious Pluralism*.[8])

Muhammad gave these People of the Book privileges not available to others under his rule. After Muslim forces conquered Christian and Zoroastrian nations—their People-of-the-Book status didn't protect these nations from attack—they weren't forced to choose between conversion to Islam and death, as people of other religions usually were. They had to pay an extra tax and were subject to greater government oversight, but they were allowed to practice their religions among themselves. As long as they respected Muslim rule in their lands, these communities were tolerated; but if they didn't obey, especially if they turned rebellious, they were subject to annihilation. They didn't have the right to seek or even accept converts from Islam, build new houses of worship, or sometimes even repair old ones. They didn't have what North Americans would call freedom of religion. Over time, most of the Jewish, Christian, and Zoroastrian communities shrank to shadows of their earlier sizes in the Middle East and North Africa, as second-class status, pressure for conversion to Islam, and migration out of the Islamic empire took their tolls. In the past sixty years or so, there has been a great migration to Israel of Jews living in Arab lands and, in the past twenty years, a steady migration of Arab Christians to the United States.

12-3f Final Judgment

On a day known only to God, a heavenly trumpet will sound, and all the dead will rise from their graves with eternal bodies to meet their Maker. Everyone will be given a book in which is recorded all the deeds he or she has done in life. Angels will put the books of the wicked in their left hand, a symbol of divine disapproval, but the righteous will receive their book in their right hand. The righteous can then enter heaven, but the wicked go straight to hell (20:100–127; 18:101–104; 23:105–115).

God will judge people by how they submitted to God's will. Saying that one is a follower of Islam won't save anyone at the judgment; living in an obedient way is the important thing. In fact, the Qur'an states that severe punishments are in store for hypocrites who claim to be Muslims but haven't lived by Islam. To other Muslims who sincerely believe in God and try to do what God has revealed, God is most gracious and most merciful. God gives special consideration to those who die in warfare or other struggle for Islam; they go to heaven, with great blessings. Literalist interpretation of this belief is used by a few radical Muslim groups today to recruit poor young men—those who seem to have little prospect for blessings on earth—for suicide missions as martyrs. Muslims trust that God will forgive the occasional sins of otherwise obedient people. For hypocrites and unbelievers, including those of other religions who know of God but haven't submitted to God, there is no forgiveness.

Islam focused from the first on heaven as an eternal reward for those who submit to God's will and on hell as an eternal punishment for those who don't. Heaven and hell are pictured in the Qur'an as places with physical and spiritual aspects (56:1–56). Heaven is a place of beautiful gardens, cool waters, plentiful food, wine that doesn't intoxicate, and the beautiful virginal women called *houris* (HOO-rees) whom God has created as rewards for righteous men. Hell is a place of physical and spiritual pain, complete with darkness, fire, and boiling filth. Although Muslims differ on how these descriptions of heaven and hell are to be interpreted—and most interpret them quite literally—all observant Muslims believe that heaven and hell are real. Muslims are motivated to submit to God by the attractive promises about heaven and fearsome warnings about hell that reach all the way back to Muhammad.

12-4 Islamic Ethics

A young married woman in Jiddah, Saudi Arabia, tuned into a twice-weekly broadcast of the *Oprah Winfrey Show* until it stopped in 2011. "I feel that Oprah truly understands me," she told an American visitor. "She gives me energy and hope for my life." This Saudi woman isn't alone; Saudi women under thirty watched *Oprah* more than any other television show. They were drawn by Oprah's welcoming personality, modest dress, and helpfulness in dealing with personal and family issues similar to some of those faced by Muslim women in Saudi Arabia. Government censors usually saw nothing subversive in the *Oprah* show, but its segments dealing with forbidden practices, such as drinking alcohol or same-sex love, were not allowed to enter the nation.

A Muslim's whole life is a matter of submitting to God's revealed way of behavior. Muslims believe that every person is born with an equal inclination toward God and doing what is good. Faith is a matter of knowing God and submitting to God's way. According to Muslim moral thought, all actions fall into one of three categories. The first are good actions that are required, such as the Five Pillars of Islam that we'll consider in the next section. The second category includes evil actions explicitly prohibited, such as idolatry, immorality, and theft. The third are neutral matters that are permitted and left up to the discretion of the believer. Here we will discuss a variety of Muslim practices: foundations in the hadith and the Shari'a; diet and other regulations; modesty in dress for both women and men; marriage and gender relations; and jihad, the struggle for the faith.

> *Muslims are obligated to commend what is good and reprimand evil.*

Muslim pilgrims praying on the hill of Arafat during the Hajj. Many pilgrims consider this "standing before God" to be a foundation of a renewed commitment to Islam.

12-4a The Hadith

The Qur'an is the main source of Muslim practices by which believers submit to God. For any issues that are undefined in the Qur'an, the Prophet's life and informal sayings are the authoritative sources. These traditions are called the **hadith,** and they were vigorously collected and evaluated in the first generations of Islam after Muhammad's death. The hadith point to Muhammad's life and teaching—as distinct from God's teaching through Muhammad as found in the Qur'an—as indications of how Muslims should act. The Qur'an itself says relatively little about the actions of Muhammad, so this further interpretive aid came to be viewed as an important context through which to understand the more difficult material in the Qur'an.

The hadith include many sayings that are attributed to Muhammad. These may be used to clarify the revelation of the Qur'an, and thus their authority comes close to that of the Qur'an itself. Among the hadith are various stories, including Muhammad's important Night Journey from Mecca to Jerusalem and back to Mecca, as well as his ascent to heaven while in Jerusalem to receive revelations.

12-4b Shari'a

If you've already heard of the **Shari'a,** traditional Islamic law enforced in many Muslim lands, it may have been in reports about the stoning of women convicted of adultery or the cutting off of thieves' hands. These reports, although based on actual events, give an incomplete and misleading impression of Muslim law. Shari'a developed to guide the implementation of Qur'anic and hadith interpretation. Shari'a deals with many aspects of day-to-day life, including politics, business, family life, sexuality, hygiene, and social issues. Many people today might consider it a civil and criminal law shaped by a religion, but Muslims don't make that distinction. They believe that Shari'a is simply God's law for the regulation of all Muslim life. Four different schools of Shari'a in Sunni Islam between 750 and 850, and still exist today. These aren't schools of theology that differ in belief or practice, because the four Sunni

hadith [huh-DEETH] "Traditions," a traditional report recording a saying or action of Muhammad

Shari'a [shah-REE-uh] "Way, path," formal system of traditional Islamic law

schools hold to the same basic Muslim beliefs and practices. Rather, they are distinct ways of defining morals and practices in precise and technical legal terms. A part of Muslim law is the **fatwa**, a religious ruling by an imam trained in Shari'a urging a particular course of action for Muslims.

Shari'a is today the most widely used religious law system in the world. It is fully implemented in only a few Muslim nations, is used more selectively in many other Muslim nations, and even seeks to make an entry in some western and Asian nations with large Muslim minorities who want to govern themselves at least partially by their own Islamic law. Informal Shari'a courts already operate in the Muslim communities of Great Britain, dealing with marital conflicts and divorce. In France, where relations between the secular government and observant French Muslims can be difficult, a nationwide political dispute broke out in 2008 when a French court upheld a Shari'a-based annulment of the marriage of two Muslims after the groom discovered on their wedding night that his bride wasn't a virgin. Debate over the role of Shari'a in both Muslim and non-Muslim countries continues today.

Muslim diversity in an African American neighborhood in New York City

JULIE FEINSTEIN/DREAMSTIME.COM

12-4c Diet and Other Regulations

Only **halal** ("permitted") foods may be eaten by Muslims. One can see restaurants and fast-food outlets in the Muslim world that advertise this concept—for example, the popular Halal Fried Chicken chain, HFC for short. Foods that are **haram**, "forbidden," may not be eaten. Consuming pork or products with even a small amount of pork mixed in them is particularly forbidden. The Qur'an also prohibits the drinking of wine (2:219); this is taken to mean that all alcoholic drinks and even food cooked with alcohol are haram.

fatwa [FAHT-wah]
Ruling by an imam urging a particular action by Muslims

halal [huh-LAHL]
"Permitted" foods and actions

haram [huh-RAHM]
"Forbidden" foods and actions

Other behaviors and practices are haram as well. Muslims must not gamble or charge interest on loans. Banks in more moderate Muslim nations don't observe this prohibition on interest; banks in stricter Muslim nations do. An interesting case on haram is the current controversy over whether smoking tobacco—a widespread practice in the Arab part of the Muslim world—should now be forbidden. Some Muslims argue that it should be forbidden because it is something that is harmful to the body that God has created. Others argue that what the Qur'an, hadith, and Shari'a don't expressly prohibit should be accepted. "Islam has so few permitted vices," some Muslims say with a smile, "so the ones it has should be kept." In general, Muslims must "commend what is good and reprimand evil," a common moral maxim says. This applies to matters of dress for both men and women (see "A Closer Look: Muslim Dress for Women and Men").

12-4d Marriage and the Status of Women

The status of women in Islam is determined by its view of marriage, not by its view of gender or gender relationships in themselves. Marriage is customary for all Muslims; parents typically arrange it while children are young, although women often can refuse engagements to men they don't like. Some Muslim parents living in North America travel back to their Middle Eastern homelands to find suitable matches for their children.

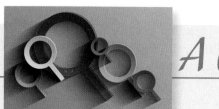

A Closer Look

Muslim Dress for Women and Men

No specific types of clothing are prescribed for Muslims. The Qur'an and hadith don't lay down requirements for dress, probably because Arab ways of dress were a given in the first decades of Islam. In line with Semitic cultures, all Muslims are required to dress modestly. You may have encountered the view of Muslim modesty most common in the West: women in head scarves with only their face visible. In some Middle Eastern cultures, a covering over the whole face and other clothes is the required Islamic mode of dress for women. For example, in the 1980s the Shi'a government of Iran required full-body veiling of Muslim women out in public. This garment, called the *chador* (shah-DOHR) in Iran, is referred to as the *burkah* (BUR-kuh) in most places. The burkah has a mesh to hide one's eyes; a similar garment called the *niqab* has an opening for the eyes. In the 1990s, the Taliban government of Afghanistan imposed it on all Muslim women there, and some Afghani women still wear it today.

Many Muslims argue correctly that the Qur'an, hadith, and Shari'a don't say that a woman must be completely shrouded, and they disagree with this added requirement. The Qur'an does require that a woman should dress in a way that conceals her physical beauty from men (24:31). Muslims typically interpret this requirement by saying that a woman's body, including her arms and legs, should be fully clothed. Her face may be visible, but her hair needs to

BONNIE VAN VOORST © CENGAGE LEARNING

Figure 12.2 Woman in burkah

be covered at least with a *hijab* (hih-JAHB), a scarf placed around the head, the most common form of modest dress in the Muslim world. These rules don't apply in the home; among her immediate family a woman is unveiled and with no hijab, but still modest. They also don't apply where only women are present, such as in all-female areas. For example, Egypt's Mediterranean coast has some all-female beaches for Muslim women who want to follow religious expectations and still wear western-style swimming suits, to "have fun and not sin." Although wearing the hijab is controversial in many nations, Leila Ahmed of Harvard University showed in her prize-winning book, *A Quiet Revolution: The Veil's Resurgence from the Middle East to America*,[9] that the surge of Muslim women wearing the hijab is not due to conservative, patriarchal forms of Islam, but is mainly a symbol of religious activism and a way for women to assert their Muslim identity.

Muslim men must dress modestly as well. As with Muslim women, their bodies must be clothed in a way that doesn't draw attention to their shape. In general, Muslim men don't expose their skin above their elbows or knees, and they're usually clothed to their ankles. (You'd rarely, if ever, see a Muslim man shirtless in public.) A head covering for men, such as a turban or cap, is a part of men's dress in many Islamic lands, but this is more cultural than religious.

BONNIE VAN VOORST © CENGAGE LEARNING

Figure 12.3 The hijab

BONNIE VAN VOORST © CENGAGE LEARNING

Figure 12.4 Muslim man in cap

The Qur'an says that a man may have up to four wives at one time as long as he provides for them equally and with separate living quarters, but the vast majority of Muslim men have only one wife.

The Qur'an also says that the limitation on the number of wives didn't apply to Muhammad (33:50–52). His multiple marriages, to nine wives after the death of Khadija, and the move to Mecca are thought to be a part of his special calling as the Prophet. Some were entered into for political reasons, but an effort to obtain a son may have figured into these multiple marriages as well. Muhammad's marriage to A'isha, Abu Bakr's nine-year-old daughter whom we have already met, was controversial because of her young age, and his marriage to Zainab, the ex-wife of Muhammad's adopted son Zaid, was controversial because of the closeness of the family relation. Because the life of Muhammad can be viewed as normative for Muslims, the Qur'an and later Muslim tradition are careful to say when these practices apply to other Muslims and when they don't.

Divorce is relatively simple for a man to obtain in most Muslim nations today; women can divorce their husbands only with difficulty. The Shari'a states that a man can divorce his wife by saying "I divorce you" in front of other male witnesses at three different times, usually over a period of three months. (You may hear that a Muslim husband can say "I divorce you" three times in one moment for a divorce to be effective, but that isn't correct.) Divorce is not to be undertaken trivially. A hadith states that divorce is "hateful in the sight of God." However, the Qur'an fully and carefully provides for it (2:228–242; 115:1–7). Of course, Muslim nations that don't follow the Shari'a fully have other procedures for divorce that follow Muslim tradition more loosely. If there are children in the marriage, they are typically in the main custody of the man after the divorce. Early Islamic law gave Muslim women significant new rights in marriage and divorce. A man must provide adequate alimony for his ex-wife as long as she lives, but there is usually no expectation that an ex-wife be supported in "the manner to which she has become accustomed," as divorce laws in the western world often say today.

12-4e Jihad

Jihad means "struggle" for God and Islam. Many people think that Islam expanded in its first centuries through methods that were mostly military struggle, not religious. Recent activities by terrorists ostensibly acting in the name of Islam have reinforced this stereotype. On the other hand, many Muslims and non-Muslims say that Islam is a religion of peace and that

Jihad [jee-HAHD]
"Struggle," both personal, inner struggle and armed struggle for Islam

jihad refers to peaceful struggle to be better Muslims. As Stephen Prothero remarks, "This crucial conversation rarely advances beyond a ping-pong match of clichés."[10] So let's go deeper into this difficult issue.

The great majority of Muslims today want to be seen as tolerant toward others. "There must be no compulsion in religion," says an often-quoted verse in the Qur'an (2:256). Muslims frequently—and correctly—point out that many Qur'anic passages about jihad refer to spiritual striving within individual Muslims. A hadith calls this the "greater jihad," and military conflict the "lesser jihad." The basic meaning of jihad for most Muslims is the struggle against one's own evil to fully submit to Allah. It also refers to groups of Muslims who struggle to improve the state of Islam. Nevertheless, jihad as military action is important in the Qur'an. Muslim scripture repeatedly commands Muslims to take up arms and fight when necessary on behalf of the Islamic community (e.g., 2:190; 8:38; 9:29; 22:39–41), and it treats jihad as military struggle more often than nonmilitary. Muhammad himself strongly criticized those who implied that spiritual struggle substituted for military struggle. Military action is commanded "even though it may be hateful to you" (2:216). This struggle is usually directed against opposing military forces, but it includes deadly action against people of other religions in Islamic lands when they resist Muslim rule. Muslim warriors in conflicts with a religious dimension are often called *mujahedeen* (moo-JAH-huh-DEEN), "those who engage in jihad." Today in the West they are frequently called "jihadists," but this is usually pejorative.

The basic principles of the military aspect of jihad were drawn up by Abu Bakr from the Qur'an and the practice of Muhammad, and expanded later by others. Although the rules for jihad vary somewhat in history and today, and are not always consistent with each other, here are the main common points:

- Jihad shouldn't be used to advance the cause of Islam. An Islamic country should not initiate conflict for religious reasons only.

- Suicide in warfare is often seen as evil. It usurps the power of God alone to determine life and death, even in battle. The Qur'an makes a blanket prohibition of suicide (4:29) but doesn't explicitly apply it to warfare, so some Muslims disagree with its application there.

> "This crucial conversation [about war and peace in Islam] rarely advances beyond a ping-pong match of clichés."
> —Stephen Prothero

- If another nation acts aggressively against an Islamic country, that country is justified in using military force to defend itself. Muslims must publicly and formally declare war in a *fatwa* (ruling by a recognized Muslim leader) before any military action can commence.

- All noncombatants—women and children, the sick and the elderly, and enemy soldiers who surrender—are to be spared and treated well.

- If a Muslim or non-Muslim country uses physical or legal force to repress the free exercise of Islam, those actions constitute hostility to Islam. It would then be appropriate, even a requirement, for Islamic nations to liberate the oppressed Muslims by force of arms.

- Jihad can be waged against other Muslim nations who are thought to have departed from the faith. For example, Ayatollah Khomeini, the Shi'a religious leader of Iran, declared its 1980s war against Sunni-ruled Iraq to be a jihad and Iranian soldiers who died in it, martyrs.

- Once a country is Islamic, it may not be allowed to go back into non-Muslim rule, as this would be an action against Islam. Jihad must be waged to bring it back to Islam. This is why most Muslims today don't recognize the nation of Israel as legitimate.

Usually there was little resistance to the spread of Islam in its first centuries, due to the strength of the Muslim forces and the cultural conditions in the lands they conquered. Whole regions welcomed the advancing Muslims, eager for them to replace the hated Byzantine rulers. Most Christians and Jews welcomed the Muslim armies, expecting and receiving basically respectful treatment. In several Muslim areas, a sizable Christian and Jewish population continued for centuries. For example, in Egypt the Coptic Christian group was a majority of the population for more than a thousand years, but over time with steady pressure, and sometimes persecution, Islam reduced the Copts to a small minority, around 10 percent today. As we saw earlier, peoples not "of the Book" were converted to Islam by force if necessary. The Muslim armies marched on, annexing an enormous amount of territory in a

Muslim engaged in armed jihad

OLEG ZABIELIN/SHUTTERSTOCK.COM

very short time. Nearly the entire Middle East came into the Islamic rule in about thirty years, and by one hundred years it stretched from the Atlantic coast of North Africa to modern Afghanistan. This was one of the fastest imperial expansions in history.

We should end our discussion of this challenging topic by saying this: Despite all the attention justifiably paid to it today in some parts of Islam and especially in the western world, jihad is not one of Islam's central practices. It isn't a pillar, nor is it one of the key doctrinal teachings. But to understand Islam in the world today, one must understand jihad well.

12-5 Worship and Ritual: The Five Pillars of Islam

In Dearborn, Michigan, home to one of the largest Muslim populations in North America, Hussein Elhaf prepares for the annual month-long fast observed by Muslims around the world. Hussein's family owns a restaurant with a mainly Muslim clientele, so he works around food during the month of Ramadan, but he will eat and drink only between sunset and sunrise, when eating and drinking are permitted. The restaurant serves food during daylight hours in Ramadan for non-Muslim customers, and it is crowded with Muslims taking their main meal of the day from sunset until 11:00 P.M. Fasting while working with food and drink all day won't be a struggle for him, he says; in fact, "it strengthens my faith and brings me closer to God."

The study and practice of religion in our time have reaffirmed the importance of core religious practices of worship: stating one's beliefs, prayer, giving of one's possessions, occasional fasting, and others. The core practices of Islam are all related to worship and ritual, and form what Muslims call the **Five Pillars of Islam**. (Shi'as generally recognize ten pillars, with particularly Shi'a additions in the second group of five.) The notion that Islam has pillars is not in the Qur'an or the hadith, although Muslims view it as faithful to what the Qur'an and hadith say about these five obligations. The pillars—of the worship of God on which Islam is built—are essential but not exhaustive. After we consider the pillars, we will look briefly at another key Muslim ritual, the funeral service.

Inside a mosque in Morocco

© POSZTOS (COLORLAB.HU)/SHUTTERSTOCK.COM

12-5a Confession of Faith

{ *Saying "Muhammad is God's prophet" entails submission to all God's commandments as given through Muhammad.* }

Five Pillars of Islam Sunni practice of confession of faith, prayer, fasting, almsgiving, and pilgrimage to Mecca

shahada [shah-hah-DAH] Fundamental confession of faith: "There is no god but God, and Muhammad is God's prophet"

salat [sah-LAHT] Ritual Muslim prayers recited five times a day

mosque [mahsk] Building for formal Muslim worship

minaret [mihn-uh-REHT] Tower on a mosque from which the call to prayer is made

The first pillar is built on the foundational rock of Islam. Although we've said that Islam is primarily a religion of action, not of belief, the first pillar is indeed a statement of belief. The **shahada** is the confession of Islam; here, confession means a formal statement of faith, not a confession of sin. It states: "There is no god but God, and Muhammad is God's prophet." Its Arabic form is resonantly poetic: *La ilaha illa Allah, Muhammad rasul Allah* (lah ih-LAH-ha ihl-lah AHL-lah, moo-HAHM-id rah-SOOL AHL-lah). This confession is among the shortest of any world

religion that has formal confessions. The shahada isn't found in the Qur'an in this exact form, but its two parts are often repeated there separately. Sometimes the shahada is translated "There is no god but Allah." But in Arabic, its second and fourth words are both *Allah*, so "There is no god but God" is a better translation.

A monotheist in any religion can sincerely recite the first part of the confession. The second part connects monotheism to Islam. Saying "Muhammad is God's prophet" entails submission to all God's commandments as given through Muhammad. He is the *rasul*, the final prophet and messenger who speaks God's words definitively. The shahada encompasses the key points of a Muslim's life. Newborn babies hear it whispered to them. Those who convert to Islam repeat this confession as their own. Those who say the formal prayers repeat it every time they pray. The last words of dying Muslims are the shahada; if they are unable to speak, someone else says it for them.

12-5b Prayer

Prayer is the main, regular form of Muslim worship, so we will treat it more fully than the other pillars. Each observant Muslim says the ritual prayers called **salat** five times a day: at sunrise, at noon, in midafternoon, at sunset, and one hour after sunset. Prayers must be performed wherever one finds oneself at the hours of prayer. A **mosque** (from *masjid*, "place of prostration") is a building for prayer. Each mosque typically has a tower, called a **minaret**. The minaret traditionally has a balcony from which the *muezzin*, or caller, summons the people to prayer. Today in Muslim lands, this task is often done through loudspeakers on the minaret. The most common pattern of the call to prayer goes like this:

> God is great. [said 4 times]
> I bear witness that there is no god but God. [2 times]
> I bear witness that Muhammad is the prophet of God. [2 times]
> Make haste to prayer. [2 times]
> Make haste to success. [2 times]
> God is great. [2 times]
> There is no god but God. [1 time]

The main part of the mosque is the prayer hall, an open room often with abstract decoration on the ceiling or walls. It has no pictures, statuary, incense, altars, or marked-off areas as are found in the sanctuaries of other world religions. To enter a prayer hall, worshipers must remove their shoes and wash. Then they get in straight lines facing a niche at the front of the prayer hall. This indicates the direction toward Mecca, or the **qiblah**, to which prayer and the whole service is oriented. The straight rows also signify to Muslims the equality of all people before God. Mosques typically have a pulpit at which the imam preaches a sermon at the Friday noon service, and one often sees a few copies of the Qur'an on wooden stands for reading.

The prayer itself then begins. The sequence of salat is tightly structured in both words and actions; personal, spontaneous prayer is not a part of salat. Just before the prayer time, the muezzin, or his recorded voice, gives the official call to prayer in a melodic chant that can be heard throughout the neighborhood. Visitors in Muslim countries often notice this public call to prayer. (When the author was studying in Amman, Jordan, as a college student, he was startled awake by the dawn call to prayer on a loudspeaker next door to the rooftop where he was sleeping.)

As stated earlier, Muslims prepare for prayer by ritual washing. Hands, feet, eyes, ears, nose, and mouth are rinsed three times with water. When women pray in the mosque, they are out of the men's sight, in back of them or in a separate room. The reason for the segregation of the sexes is said to be the preservation of the dignity of women. Because a part of the prayer ritual is to bow and prostrate oneself, it would be unseemly in traditional Muslim cultures for men to line up alongside or behind women making these movements. If a man were to touch a woman in the mosque, even accidentally, he would have to go out and ritually wash again.

Salat is a formal ritual with both postures and recitation. All the people in the prayer hall follow the words and actions together, giving a sense of unity. The imam at the front leads the process. People begin the prayer standing upright and cup their ears with their hands, showing God that they are present and listening. The first chapter of the Qur'an is spoken as a prayer, followed by other prescribed words. One's body is active in prayer: bowing, standing, kneeling, prostrating oneself while kneeling with forehead to the ground, kneeling, prostrating, and standing again. These actions remind Muslims in a physical way of their submission to God. The prayers are uttered in a quiet, humble voice, but in contrast the changes of posture are indicated by the leader's louder call of "Allah." Depending on the number of repetitions, daily prayers take approximately five to ten minutes to perform. On Friday afternoons, special prayer services in the mosque feature a sermon preached by the imam.

qiblah [KIB-luh]
Direction that Muslims face during prayer

Sermon during Friday prayers in the Ditib-Merkez mosque in Duisburg, the largest mosque in Germany

FRIEDEMANN VOGEL/GETTY IMAGES

This whole service, which is typically the best-attended service of the week, lasts between thirty and sixty minutes. It was after Friday noon prayers in the first months of 2011 that worshipers poured out into the streets to demand change from unresponsive, authoritarian governments in many Arab nations during the beginning of the Arab Spring.

12-5c Fasting

In commemoration of Muhammad receiving the Qur'an, Muslims are required to observe fasting, called in Arabic **sawm**, during daylight hours throughout the month of Ramadan. This is designed to cultivate greater submission to God. Not a bit of food or drink may be taken for the entire daylight hours. (Some particularly pious Muslims won't even swallow their own saliva.) Sexual intercourse during the daylight is also forbidden, as are some types of amusement. Eating, drinking, sex, and smoking are permissible at night. Because leap days are not inserted into the Muslim lunar calendar, Ramadan moves through the seasons. When it falls in winter, fasting is comparatively easy. But when Ramadan falls in the longer, hot days of summer—and most Muslims live in tropical or subtropical lands—it calls for much more effort.

Fasting in Ramadan is done in a humane way, as are all Muslim pillars. Infants and young children are excused from the fast at the discretion of their parents, but many students in school observe it. The hunger produced can be a challenge to learning. People who are sick, those infirm from old age, and soldiers on active duty may fast when they are better able to do so. When it is impossible to make up the fast, one may substitute a significant act of mercy or charity. When the month of Ramadan is finished, Muslims celebrate the Eid-al-Fitr festival with a special service in the mosque. Families feast together during the day and exchange gifts in decorated homes.

sawm [sahwm] Ritual fasting done during daylight hours throughout the month of Ramadan

zakat [zah-KAHT] "Almsgiving," mandatory contribution of one-fortieth of one's income to support Islam

hajj [hahj] Pilgrimage to Mecca

12-5d Almsgiving

The Qur'an urges all Muslims to give generously to the poor, such as orphans and widows (e.g., 2:43), but as with the other four items that became traditional pillars, it doesn't lay down specific requirements. The Shari'a made this generosity a formal obligation with specific rules, and it has become so important that it is the fourth pillar of Islam, called **zakat**, almsgiving or charity. Although it is an obligation, Muslims are expected to be generous from the heart, out of liberality. In most Islamic lands, it is a monetary obligation collected by a representative of the umma, often a department of the government. It is then distributed to poor families, widows and orphans, stranded travelers, and others in need. In addition, it can be used in jihad for the defense and support of Muslims under threat.

In places such as Europe and North America, zakat is based on voluntary giving to the mosque or an Islamic charity. Zakat is one-fortieth (2.5 percent) of the value of one's assets, not counting necessary personal possessions such as homes, animals, vehicles, or clothing. Because every observant Muslim gives zakat, it generates large sums of money in the international Muslim community. Zakat has provided Islamic countries with the resources for comprehensive programs of social support and development that are unique among world religions and reinforce solidarity among Muslims of different classes. It is the principal way in which Muslim lands promote a fuller measure of social justice.

> *Muslims are expected to be generous from the heart, out of liberality.*

12-5e Pilgrimage

The last of the Five Pillars of Islam is pilgrimage to Mecca. A Muslim is required to participate in the official pilgrimage to Mecca, called the **hajj**, at least once in his or her lifetime. This requirement applies to both men and women, but traditionally the great majority of pilgrims are men. As with the other pillars, it is imposed humanely: In this case, one who is unable to make the pilgrimage may designate someone else to do it on his or her behalf. The last month of the Muslim calendar, called al-Hajj, is the official period of pilgrimage. Muslims can go to Mecca at other times when it isn't so crowded, but these visits are not considered a hajj. Muhammad at first had his followers pray facing Jerusalem, and some Muslims did pilgrimages to Jerusalem as well. After his conflict with the Jews of Medina, he made Mecca, and particularly the Kaaba in the Grand Mosque there, the geographic center of Islam. (For an account of activities during the hajj, see the section that begins this chapter, "Your Visit to Mecca.")

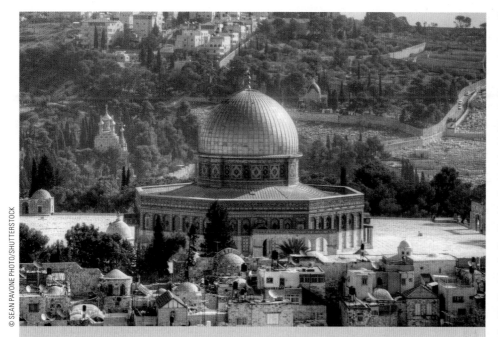

© SEAN PAVONE PHOTO/SHUTTERSTOCK

Dome of the Rock mosque in Jerusalem is a secondary pilgrimage site for Muslims.

They also make the hajj to Mecca, but sometimes violence has erupted between Sunnis and Shi'as during the hajj. Muslims have designated other centers of pilgrimage, but no other place comes close to Mecca in importance. A man who has journeyed to Mecca on the hajj receives an additional, honorary personal name, **Hajji**. The importance of the hajj for Islam and the world has been well summarized by Robert Bianchi, who, as a Muslim, made the hajj himself: "Creating a global community seems less daunting after making a pilgrimage, especially one that stirs us—physically and spiritually—in a single pot with all humanity."[11]

Other cities are centers of other pilgrimage for some Muslims. Medina is the second-holiest city in Islam, especially because it was the home of Muhammad for the second part of his prophetic career and the place where he is buried. The Dome of the Rock mosque in Jerusalem, which Muslims call the Noble Sanctuary, was built in the seventh century. Muhammad made his ascent to heaven during his lifetime from a prominent rock now inside the mosque. Shi'as have their own holy places of pilgrimage, including Qom in Iran and Karbala in Iraq.

12-5f The Muslim Funeral

Although there is some cultural variation in the Muslim funeral, here is the most common pattern in Muslim nations. At death, those present close the deceased's eyes and mouth, and cover the body with a clean sheet. Then they pray for forgiveness of the sins of the deceased. According to Shari'ah, the body should be buried as soon as possible, which means that funeral preparations begin immediately. The relatively quick burial affects many aspects of the Muslim funeral.

As in Judaism, autopsies and cremation are not acceptable in Islam; they are seen as a desecration of the body. Embalming the body is not allowed unless required by law (e.g., when a body must be transported across national lines for burial). There is no viewing of the body by anyone except family members.

To prepare the body for burial, it must be washed and shrouded. Close family members of the same sex as the deceased do the washing. The washing

AHMAD FAIZAL YAHYA/ SHUTTERSTOCK.COM

Tents for hajj pilgrims on the Plains of Mina outside Mecca

Hajji [HAHJ-ee] "Pilgrim," additional personal name given to a man who has taken the hajj

includes the practice of pressing down on the abdomen of the deceased to excrete all impure fluids. (This practice was estimated by the World Health Organization to be responsible for about 20 percent of Ebola cases in west Africa during the 2014 Ebola epidemic, and efforts were made to mitigate the danger of this practice, with only slim results.) The body is washed three times. Women's hair is washed and braided. Once clean and prepared, the body is covered in a white sheet.

To shroud the body, three large white sheets are laid on top of each other. The body is placed on top of the sheets. The deceased's left hand is placed on the chest and the right hand on the left hand, as in prayer. The sheets are then folded over the body, first the right side and then the left side, until all three sheets have wrapped the body. The shrouding is secured with ropes, one tied above the head, two around the body, and one below the feet. The body is then transported to the mosque for funeral prayers. These prayers are not held in the main hall of the mosque, but in a side prayer room or study room, or (if the crowd is large) outside the mosque.

After prayers at the mosque, the body is taken to the cemetery for burial. Traditionally, only men are allowed at the burial, though in some communities all mourners are allowed. The body is placed in the grave on its right side, facing the qiblah. A layer of wood or stones is placed on top of the body to prevent direct contact between the body and the soil that each mourner will place by handfuls into the grave. Once the grave has been filled, a small stone or marker may be placed at the grave so that it is recognizable. However, erecting a large monument on the grave or decorating the grave in an elaborate way is prohibited.

After the funeral and burial, the immediate family will gather and receive visitors for the first time. The community typically provides food for the family for the first few days of the mourning period, which customarily lasts forty days.

12-6 Islam around the World Today

In an unusual effort to reach out to the West, Iran's supreme religious leader releases a letter to young people in the United States and Europe. He urges them to learn about Islam from original sources and not, as he said in a later posting on Twitter, have it "introduced to you by prejudices" in the news media. He says he wants to address young people after the attacks on magazine offices and a Paris nightclub tarnished the image of Islam. In particular, he urges people to read the Qur'an for themselves: "Have you studied the teachings of the Prophet of Islam and his humane, ethical doctrines? Have you ever received the message of Islam from any sources other than the media? Try to find answers for yourself."

Islam has typically been spread by near-continuous, intentional movement from Arabia and other historic points to the far reaches of the world. China has a substantial Muslim population in its western and northern sections. Europe has a large Muslim population, to the extent that Islam is the second-largest religion in Europe after Christianity. Muslim Europeans have been mostly immigrants since World War II, but a native Muslim population in the Balkans has existed for centuries, because that area was under the long-term control of the Ottoman Empire. In North America, however, the picture is more mixed. Some slaves brought here from Africa were probably Muslims—estimates range widely from 5 percent to almost 50 percent—but they were unable to maintain their faith through the generations due to the harsh conditions of slavery and their owners' insistence that slaves share their masters' Christian religion. In the early twentieth century, a new Black Muslim movement grew in North America, which we will treat in Chapter 13.

12-6a Islam in Europe

Europe has around 14 million Muslim residents today. France has the largest number of Muslims in western Europe, with 6 to 7 million Muslims making up 8 to 10 percent of its population. Most French Muslims come from the former French colonies in North Africa. France is followed by Germany; most of its 4.5 million Muslims are Turkish guest workers who do unskilled labor. Great Britain has 2.7 million Muslims from its former empire, and Italy has 1.5 million from Africa. Aside from Turkey (most of which lies outside Europe geographically but which is in the process of becoming a member of the European Union), the only European nation to have a majority of Muslims is Albania in the Balkan Peninsula. Bosnia and Macedonia, also in the Balkans, have large Muslim minorities.

As indicated above in Section 12-2e, a series of violent events in Europe by radical Muslims affiliated with al-Qaeda or IS has taken place in the past decade or so. Since these events began, scrutiny of European Muslims and controversy over their place in European society has grown exponentially. Just as important for Muslim life in Europe today are matters of Muslim identity and respect, especially the wearing of the hijab. The French prohibition of Muslim head scarves in schools and other public buildings, and their 2016 banning of modest "burkini" beach wear, are particularly controversial. In general, European Muslims are not as integrated into wider national life as North American Muslims are. As if these challenges were not enough, the Muslim population in Europe grew significantly with mass migrations from North Africa and the Middle East, especially Syria, in 2015 and 2016. For example, more than a million Muslims came into Germany, leading to a sharp test of social and political tolerance there and elsewhere in western Europe.

12-6b Muslim Migration to North America

From about 1950, millions of Muslims immigrated to North America from various nations in the Middle East. Some others from British Commonwealth lands in south Asia have also moved to Canada. Some smaller immigration had occurred before 1950, but Muslims generally entered after that year. They can be found in virtually every city in North America, with more substantial numbers in large cities on the East and West Coasts. The proportion of Sunnis to Shi'as in North America is about the same as in the wider Muslim world—about 85 percent to 15 percent. Dearborn, Michigan, a suburb of Detroit, has the largest population of Muslims outside metropolitan New York City. Canada has Muslims in every major city, with larger numbers in the cities of Ontario, Alberta, and British Columbia. The majority of North American Muslims have no formal affiliation to a mosque (in lands that are officially Muslim, one doesn't belong to a mosque), but they are nonetheless practicing Muslims.

Our knowledge of Muslims in the United States is a bit imprecise, because the U.S. Census does not collect information about religious affiliation. However, scientific surveys have filled in much of this gap. A 2007 Pew Research Center survey of Muslim Americans found that about two-thirds are foreign born and have immigrated since 1980. A second generation of Muslims is now arising in the United States, facing the same sort of intergenerational issues that other immigrant groups have faced. Of the one-third of Muslim Americans born in the United States, the majority are converts and African American. In 2005, about 100,000 people from Islamic countries—most of them Muslims—became permanent residents of the United

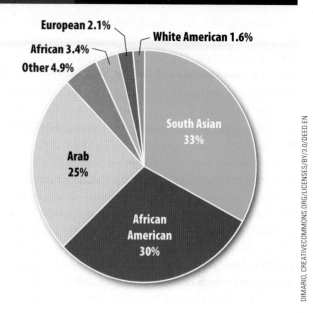

DIMARIO, CREATIVECOMMONS.ORG/LICENSES/BY/3.0/DEED.EN

Figure 12.5 Ethnicity of Muslims in the United States, 2015

- European 2.1%
- White American 1.6%
- African 3.4%
- Other 4.9%
- South Asian 33%
- Arab 25%
- African American 30%

States, more than in any single year since 1980. A majority of these are on a path to citizenship. As a result of immigration since the 1950s, Islam in North America now more closely reflects the global diversity of Islam than at any time in the past. According to the predictions of the Pew Religious Demographics report, the 2.7 million U.S. Muslims are expected to grow to about 8 million by 2050.

A recent survey by the Zogby polling company showed that Muslims are prospering in the United States. They are significantly more educated than the national average, with incomes to match. Some 60 percent of them hold at least one academic degree, and about 40 percent have an income over $75,000. As stated earlier, compared with European Muslims, North American Muslims are significantly more assimilated into wider cultural life. The United States and Canada have largely extended to Muslims the same rights to practice religion that they have extended to others. U.S. Muslims practice the pillars of Islam with little need for adaptation, although observing afternoon prayers has occasionally been problematic for Muslims working in businesses and factories. Some have worked for improved relations between Muslim and non-Muslim Americans. Many scholars have held out the hope that North American Muslims might show other Muslims how they can lead faithful religious lives in a predominantly non-Muslim environment.

12-6c Muslim Life in the United States after 9/11

On September 11, 2001, **al-Qaeda** ("the base" of jihad), an organization of radical Muslims based in Afghanistan, launched coordinated attacks on the United States. That morning, nineteen members of al-Qaeda from various Middle Eastern nations who had been living in sleeper cells in the United States hijacked four large commercial passenger airliners soon after they took off from airports in the eastern United States. The hijackers crashed two of the airplanes into the main towers of the World Trade Center in New York City, causing both towers to collapse unexpectedly about two hours later. They crashed a third airplane into the Pentagon, the U.S. military headquarters in Washington, D.C. The fourth plane crashed into a field in western Pennsylvania when its passengers and crew bravely tried to retake control of the plane as it was heading east, probably to another prominent target in Washington, D.C. Excluding the hijackers, 2,974 people died; another 24 are missing and presumed dead; and several thousand were injured. The great majority of deaths and injuries were of civilians, including citizens of more than ninety different nations who worked in the World Trade Center.

What is this al-Qaeda organization? Osama bin Laden (oh-SAM-uh bin LAHD-en; 1957–2011) founded it to oppose with violence those he saw as a threat to true Islam. A Saudi Arabian banished from his land for extremism, he took up residence with the other leaders of his movement in Afghanistan, where al-Qaeda secretly bankrolled the Taliban government. He mounted first verbal and then physical attacks against a variety of targets, with strong, religiously based opposition to the influence of western nations in Muslim nations and opposition to the presence of the Jewish state of Israel. Bin Laden typically spoke in taped addresses in the poetic cadences of the Qur'an, and he liked to be photographed living in caves as Muhammad once did while hiding from his enemies. Al-Qaeda brought something new to Islam: continual attacks on non-Muslims. Al-Qaeda and its splinter groups have carried out dozens of other attacks from the 1990s through today, on civilian targets in both western and Muslim nations especially England, Spain, Saudi Arabia, India, Indonesia, and various east African countries—attacks designed to terrorize their

al-Qaeda [al-KIGH-duh] "The base" of jihad, contemporary terrorist movement begun by Osama bin Laden

people and influence government policy. The victims have been Muslims as much as westerners, or native Christians or Jews. As a predominantly Sunni movement, however, al-Qaeda has gathered only a little support from Shi'as, and even the majority of Sunnis in the world do not approve of it.

The attacks on September 11, 2001, deeply shocked not only the United States, but also other nations of the world. The United States responded by leading a broad coalition of international military forces in invading Afghanistan to depose the Taliban and destroy the home base of the al-Qaeda network. The hunt for Osama bin Laden lasted ten years after that, ending with his 2011 death in a U.S. military raid on his hideout in Pakistan. The 2001 federal Patriot Act gave the U.S. government far greater powers than previously permitted in gathering intelligence on suspected terrorists in America and around the world. Many other nations also increased their anti-terrorism efforts and stepped up military preparations.

A Muslim soldier in a western army performs ritual prayer.

STEVE JACOBS/GETTY IMAGES

A Closer Look

Muslim Views of Islamic–Western Conflict

The largest study of public opinion in the Muslim world was completed by the Gallup organization in 2007, and was published as *Who Speaks for Islam? What a Billion Muslims Really Think*.[12] It is based on six years of research and more than fifty thousand interviews of Muslims in more than thirty-five nations that are officially Muslim, predominantly Muslim, or have sizable Muslim populations. This study carefully surveyed around 90 percent of the world's Muslim community—the billion Muslims of the title—about their attitudes to the conflict, perceived and real, between Islam and the West. It also collected comparative data from the U.S. population as a whole.

The results of this study, as outlined by the publisher, may surprise you:

- Muslims and Americans are equally likely to reject attacks on civilians as morally wrong in all circumstances.

- Large majorities of Muslims would guarantee free speech if it were up to them to write a new constitution.

- Large majorities of Muslims say that religious leaders should have no direct role in drafting laws or governing.

- Muslims state that what they least admire about the West is its perceived moral decay and breakdown of traditional values. Ironically, this is identical to what Americans themselves say when asked this question.

- Muslims say they want prosperity and security, and see conflict and violence as harming that goal.

- Muslims say that westerners can improve relations with their societies by changing their negative, stereotyped views toward Muslims and by learning to respect Islam.

The research suggests that Muslims and non-Muslim Americans have more in common than what they may think. But as authors Esposito and Mogahed caution, most Muslims do not live in democratic societies where their opinions are taken seriously, and anti-Muslim voices in the United States continue to have an outsized influence on U.S. public opinion. They conclude, "Until and unless decision makers listen directly to the people and gain an accurate understanding of this conflict, extremists on all sides will continue to gain ground."

Muslim organizations in the United States were swift to condemn the attacks on 9/11 and called upon Muslim Americans to help the victims. In addition to large donations of funds, many Islamic organizations held blood drives and provided medical assistance, food, and housing for victims of 9/11. Some Muslim groups in the United States have even worked effectively with law enforcement agencies to identify North American Muslims who may be fostering violence.

One result of 9/11 has been a rise in anti-Muslim prejudice and actions by some American citizens who suppose that most Muslims are active or potential

A Syrian woman laments the destruction of her city in 2017. Mass flight by Muslims from Syria and a few other nations has led to political conflict in the United States and Europe about whether these refugees should be welcomed, and if so, under what circumstances.

terrorists, or aid terrorists. (Other western nations—including Germany, France, and Britain—have even stronger popular prejudice against Muslims that goes far back before 9/11.) This is upsetting to American Muslims, particularly because the 9/11 attacks were the work of foreign Muslims who came to this country to carry out attacks (see "A Closer Look: Muslim Views of Islamic–Western Conflict"). Also, the latest troubling trend in Europe and North America is that some Muslims born and raised in non-Muslim nations are now launching their own terror attacks in looser connection with al-Qaeda and now especially the Islamic State. These persons are sometimes called "lone wolves." India is particularly plagued with violence from native Muslim groups, some related to al-Qaeda and some not. North America has seen a rising number of these crimes as well. In 2013, two Muslims born in the Russian area of Chechnya bombed the Boston Marathon, resulting in three deaths and dozens of serious injuries, and in 2016 a mass-shooting attack was carried out on a gay nightclub in Orlando, Florida, resulting in forty-nine dead and fifty-three wounded—at that time the deadliest shooting attack in U.S. history.

Widely troubling to many American Muslims has been the systematic monitoring of Muslim individuals and institutions. The New York City police department's active spying on mosques in New York City and even in some neighboring states from 2003 to 2014 provoked strong criticism from Muslims and many others. The last of three major lawsuits about this spying was settled in April of 2018. The U.S. government has especially investigated those Muslim charitable organizations that distribute abroad the funds raised from American Muslims, some of it from zakat. Although some funds

have indeed gone into the shadowy network of terror, the vast majority of funds do not, and many American Muslims are disturbed over this perceived interference in their exercise of a pillar of their religion. However, Muslims in the United States and Canada are increasingly working with religious and civic organizations for better Muslim relations with the wider public. They are hopeful that relations are in fact improving, although the progress isn't always steady. Another, constructive reaction to the 9/11 attacks and their aftermath has been an increase in the study of Islam in colleges and universities—of which you are now a part.

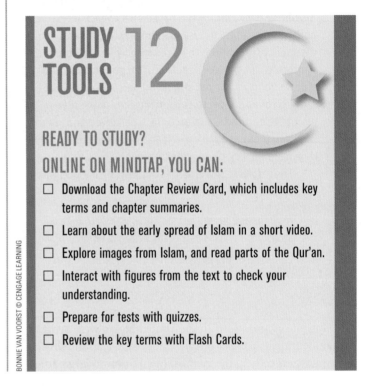

STUDY TOOLS 12

READY TO STUDY?
ONLINE ON MINDTAP, YOU CAN:

☐ Download the Chapter Review Card, which includes key terms and chapter summaries.

☐ Learn about the early spread of Islam in a short video.

☐ Explore images from Islam, and read parts of the Qur'an.

☐ Interact with figures from the text to check your understanding.

☐ Prepare for tests with quizzes.

☐ Review the key terms with Flash Cards.

BONNIE VAN VOORST © CENGAGE LEARNING

Islam Timeline: 570 C.E.–Present

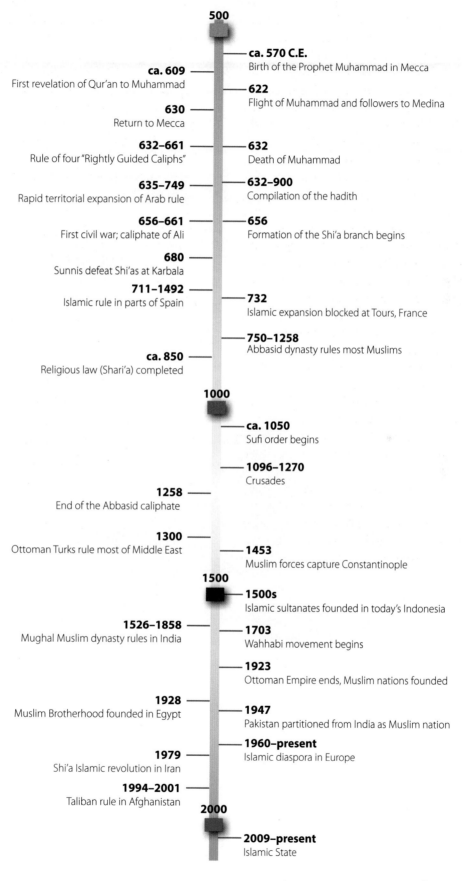

500

ca. 570 C.E.
Birth of the Prophet Muhammad in Mecca

ca. 609
First revelation of Qur'an to Muhammad

622
Flight of Muhammad and followers to Medina

630
Return to Mecca

632–661
Rule of four "Rightly Guided Caliphs"

632
Death of Muhammad

635–749
Rapid territorial expansion of Arab rule

632–900
Compilation of the hadith

656–661
First civil war; caliphate of Ali

656
Formation of the Shi'a branch begins

680
Sunnis defeat Shi'as at Karbala

711–1492
Islamic rule in parts of Spain

732
Islamic expansion blocked at Tours, France

750–1258
Abbasid dynasty rules most Muslims

ca. 850
Religious law (Shari'a) completed

1000

ca. 1050
Sufi order begins

1096–1270
Crusades

1258
End of the Abbasid caliphate

1300
Ottoman Turks rule most of Middle East

1453
Muslim forces capture Constantinople

1500

1500s
Islamic sultanates founded in today's Indonesia

1526–1858
Mughal Muslim dynasty rules in India

1703
Wahhabi movement begins

1923
Ottoman Empire ends, Muslim nations founded

1928
Muslim Brotherhood founded in Egypt

1947
Pakistan partitioned from India as Muslim nation

1960–present
Islamic diaspora in Europe

1979
Shi'a Islamic revolution in Iran

1994–2001
Taliban rule in Afghanistan

2000

2009–present
Islamic State

13

Encountering New Religious Movements: Modern Ways to Alternative Meanings

LEARNING OUTCOMES

After studying this chapter, you will be able to do the following:

13-1 Evaluate the different names for new religious movements (NRMs).

13-2 Summarize the common features of NRMs.

13-3 Survey the distribution of NRMs in the world today.

13-4 State and explain the teachings and practices of Falun Gong.

13-5 State and explain the history, teachings, and practices of the Church of Jesus Christ of Latter-day Saints.

13-6 State and explain the history, teachings and practices of the Nation of Islam.

13-7 State and explain the teachings and practices of Scientology.

Many NRMs are controversial, but several world religions today were also controversial when they were new.

Your Visit to Temple Square, Salt Lake City, Utah

The Church of Jesus Christ of Latter-day Saints (LDS), whose members are popularly called the Mormons, is headquartered in Salt Lake City. Temple Square is named for the main LDS temple that majestically stands there. The other church buildings are impressive as well, and are all near Temple Square. You notice that next to Temple Square is the billion-dollar City Creek Center mall owned by the LDS Church that opened in 2012, complete with high-end stores and restaurants, business offices, and condominiums.

The granite temple with its spires and statue of an angel blowing a trumpet soars over the downtown. Only LDS members in good standing can go inside an LDS temple (and this lends a mysterious air to it). The opportunity is the high point of any Latter-day Saint's visit to Salt Lake City, but there is still plenty to do for non-Mormons. The LDS Church has always been intent on spreading its faith, so it has built several other impressive buildings where non-Mormons can learn more about the LDS Church. There are two visitor centers where you can pick up literature and see exhibits. You can experience the LDS emphasis on sacred music at the Mormon Tabernacle building—the concert hall for the world-renowned Mormon Tabernacle Choir—or take in a concert in the Assembly Hall. You could walk around the formal gardens. Just north of Temple Square is the Conference Center, where the main representative body of the LDS Church meets twice a year.

Because you're interested in your genealogy, you've been looking forward to seeing the Family History Library near Temple Square. Even though you're only visiting, you can investigate your family tree in the genealogical collection housed there, the largest genealogical database in the world. Staff in the library can help you in your research, which is all done by computer. It's a little unnerving to you to hear that the LDS Church has collected genealogical information from every corner of the world, perhaps for every person who has ever lived and left behind a genealogical record. But you're happy for it too, because it makes for the best genealogical searching in the world.

Finally, you walk nearby to see the Beehive House dating from 1855. It's the home of Brigham Young, the second leader of the LDS Church, for whom Brigham Young University is named. Free tours are available to go through the home and see how Brigham Young and his family lived.

The academic term **new religious movements (NRMs)** denotes religious groups that arose in modern times and have sufficient size, longevity, and impact to merit academic study. (*Modern* here doesn't mean contemporary or even recent, but in the modern age of history.) These movements have been studied from the first, especially by sociologists, but the term *new religious movements* is a newcomer in the field of religious studies. Most recently published encyclopedias, handbooks, and textbooks on religion use this term and provide information about the groups to which it refers.[1] More than five hundred groups around the world today have been identified as NRMs. Each year sees the birth of dozens more religious movements, and the death of some. This chapter will first give a general description of NRMs and briefly discuss several of them to illustrate the description. Then it will focus in more detail on three NRMs that have become significant worldwide. These three are treated here to illustrate the general description offered, which students can subsequently apply to other NRMs.

Some things that students often wonder about NRMs can be listed quickly here to stir thought and imagination:

- The "new" in "new religious movements" isn't intended to imply that these groups see themselves as new. Often they don't, and some even view this term as inaccurate, even uncomplimentary. Many NRMs understand themselves as a restoration of a very old religion.

- Some of these NRMs are highly controversial. Many were persecuted or prosecuted in their early years by religious and civil authorities. However, several world religions were also controversial when they were new.

The Lotus Temple in New Delhi, India shows how the Baha'i movement adapts itself to different cultures and traditions. Opened in 1986, it is one of the most visited buildings in the world.

new religious movements (NRMs)
Religious groups that arose in modern times and have sufficient size and cultural impact to merit academic study

Temple Square in Salt Lake City, Utah, with the Temple in the center background, is filled with LDS Church buildings.

of these movements are in the news and on the Web today, and not always for complimentary reasons. Careful students of religion will want to recognize any preconceived notions that they may have about NRMs, and deal with them. You can make evaluations of NRMs, as of older religions, but you must earn the right to evaluate an NRM by studying it carefully first. In other words, before you conclude, "That's a weird group," you should learn about it and then try to think like one of its insiders: What is it about this movement that makes it appealing to some?

Because many religions are treated in this chapter, it has an organization that differs from most of the previous chapters. First, we'll discuss the variety of names that scholars have given to this type of religion, and then explain why this book calls them new religious movements. Second, we'll draw out important common characteristics of NRMs. Third, we'll examine their world distribution. Finally, we'll look in some detail at three important NRMs.

- Because the study of NRMs shows us contemporary religions as they are born and begin to grow, they are fertile fields of study for scholars and students alike. Eileen Barker, who coined the term "new religious movements," said that NRMs are "interesting because you can see a whole lot of social processes going on: conversion, leaving, bureaucratization, leadership squabbles, ways in which authority is used, [and] ways in which people can change."[2]

- Because these NRM movements are contemporary, a lot of detail is available on many of them, so much that it's sometimes overwhelming. Some of this detail will be dealt with in this chapter.

{ The study of NRMs often proves to be a strong test of a student's impartiality and objectivity. }

sect New, small group that has emerged from an established or larger religion

cult Religion or religious sect that is extremist and under the control of an authoritarian leader

But students should keep their focus on the general features of NRMs as discussed and illustrated here.

The study of NRMs often proves to be a strong test of a student's impartiality and objectivity. Some

(13-1) Names for This Type of Religion

Naming the overall type of the religions we're dealing with in this chapter has been a challenge for scholarship. The first names that were given to this type of religion were *cults* and *sects*. **Sect** derives from the Latin term for "cut off" and refers to a new, small group that has emerged from within an established religion. Many of today's world religions began as reforming sects within a larger religion and only later grew separate. **Cult** refers to a religious group that is extreme in its dedication to its beliefs, often living together under the control of an authoritarian leader. The name often carries the connotation of a dangerous religion. Although the terms have some validity, they have become so prejudicial that most religious studies scholars today don't use them to characterize new religious groups. Other, more recent terms such as **alternative religious movements** are used, sometimes in reference to more long-standing NRMs from the 1800s and early 1900s, keeping *new religious movements* for more recent groups such as Scientology and Falun Gong. However, all NRMs, whether founded in the 1800s or in 2016, present alternative religious meanings, as the subtitle of this chapter suggests. But this may prompt you to ask, *Alternative* to what? Some of these movements are so large that they can't be considered merely alternative—for example, the LDS Church, perhaps the fastest-growing religious group in the world, or Falun Gong. A final term for this type of religion is **emergent religions**, which highlights their contemporary origin and ongoing development. They are emerging in our time.

Gradually, scholars of religion and sociologists settled on the term *new religious movements*, which we have just defined. Although it is generally accepted by religion scholars, it has been criticized for three reasons. First, how does this term distinguish NRMs from reform movements in established religions (as Buddhism and Christianity started), especially before the reform movements become a separate religion? Second, even though it looks neutral, it has occasionally been used with a pejorative tone. Third, to call them religious movements may imply that they are not full-fledged religions, which they usually are.

Despite these questions, the term *new religious movements* is widely used today. "New" is ambiguous, of course, but these movements are indeed new compared with the ancient origins of other religions. A consensus among religion scholars takes "new" to mean within the past two centuries or so. *Nova Religio*, the premier scholarly journal for the study of NRMs, covers them from 1800 to the present. The term *new religious movements* holds out the nuanced understanding that in time some of today's NRMs may become regarded as established religions.

13-2 Common Features of New Religious Movements

Although there's a great deal of diversity among NRMs, they have a number of common features. First, NRMs are typically *founded by a single powerful leader*. This is true of all the NRMs named in this chapter. The founder is often believed to have extraordinary, even supernatural, powers or insights. He or she is skilled at organizing and guiding a movement. If the NRM is based in a literate culture, the leader typically writes authoritative literature that, as the group's sacred scripture, guides the movement when the founder dies.

Second, NRMs can *spring up quickly and disappear quickly*. Because they are founded by a single person, they emerge quickly, in contrast to many older religions that developed over generations, even centuries, under multiple leaders. More than thirty NRMs begin in the United States annually, but many of them don't last for more than a decade, some of them even less. At times, NRMs disappear in violent tragedy, as we'll discuss later. Those that survive often face a threat when their founder dies. When an NRM is able to last for centuries, it becomes known simply as a religion.

Third, NRMs *start small but can become international movements*. Established world religions usually started small as well, but this is the rule with all NRMs. Some NRMs from the 1800s that survived are strong in numbers today: the Church of Jesus Christ of Latter-day Saints, the Jehovah's Witness church, and others. Even more recent movements can quickly gain an international following and become worldwide religious movements. No study of world religions is complete without a consideration of NRMs.

> Although many NRMs are rooted in older traditions, they arise in the modern world and address modern concerns.

Fourth, most NRMs are *tightly organized*. Because they are controlled from the top, and because they understand themselves as countercultural movements, NRMs often make strong demands of their followers. Members live for the group and the group directs their lives. NRMs can become substitutes for one's family and friends. This emotionally intense religious life with alternative views of marriage and family life is the main reason why some NRMs are popularly known as cults. When NRMs encounter opposition, their organization becomes even tighter.

alternative religious movements One current name for NRMs, especially for the long-standing NRMs from the 1800s and early 1900s

emergent religions Another current name for NRMs, highlighting their contemporary origin

© JHDT PRODUCTIONS/SHUTTERSTOCK

Leadership by a single powerful person, usually a man, is a common feature of NRMs. Although the man in this photo holds up a Christian Bible, this feature is found in most NRMs.

Fifth, NRMs are *religious responses to the modern world*. Other world religions come from the past, often from ancient times. NRMs are not only new in the sense of recent. Although many NRMs are rooted in older traditions, they arise in the modern world and address modern concerns in new ways. NRMs are often more media-savvy than established world religions. For example, the Church of Scientology has all its scriptures in electronic form, and has probably the most sophisticated website of any religious group. Moreover, many NRMs incorporate scientific understandings, real or claimed, into their teachings and practices that older religions do not. NRMs are responses to various aspects of modern life: loss of religious meaning, religious and cultural pluralism, and the scientific worldview. Because the overall number of NRMs and the numbers of believers in them are increasing, NRMs are obviously making an effective appeal in the modern world.

Sixth, NRMs are usually *countercultural* in their response to the modern world. They move against the mainstream currents of society, especially as societies have been shaped by the dominant historic religions. This countercultural quality often makes them controversial in a whole culture, not just with established or traditional religions in that culture. To illustrate, the Unification Church and Scientology are often accused of disrupting traditional family ties of their new members. The LDS movement encountered wide cultural opposition in the 1800s for its espousal of polygamy, and pockets of polygamy among some non-LDS Mormons still make headlines—and television series such as *Big Love* and *Sister Wives*—today.

Finally, NRMs typically have *distinct patterns of gender relations*. As Laura Vance explains in her groundbreaking 2015 book, *Women in New Religions*, religious views and gender roles interact with each other in complex ways. She argues that this is especially true about NRMs: as they are formed, they typically position themselves in opposition to mainstream society, including gender roles. This may result in a more liberal stance toward women's roles (e.g., Wicca and Christian Science) or a more conservative stance (Mormonism). As NRMs change over time, these gender role expectations also shift.[3] Vance deals for the most part with four western NRMs, but her conclusions are explanatory of Asian NRMs as well.

DNY59/ISTOCKPHOTO.COM

The nearness of the end of time is a key teaching of apocalyptic.

13-3 New Religious Movements in the World Today: A Survey

Many people in the western world suppose that NRMs are primarily a western thing and aren't found in other areas of the world. Nothing could be further from the truth. As this section will show, NRMs are spread throughout the world as widely as the older, established religions are.

13-3a NRMs in the Western World

NRMs in the West are widely diverse. Most of them come from Christianity, the dominant religion in the West, but many don't. The following survey organizes this diversity into certain categories, but an NRM can often be classified into more than one category.

Some NRMs are shaped by **apocalyptic** belief that the world order will end soon and God will bring a new, perfect society in place of the old one. Many world religions also have apocalyptic features. However, modern Christian apocalypticism, especially **millenarianism**— a belief in some forms of Protestantism that Christ will establish and lead a thousand-year reign of peace on earth—has been a foundation of many NRMs in the West. Even in Asia, a millenarian impulse for a golden age on this earth occasionally surfaces, with or without Christian influence.

Two of the earliest significant NRMs in the United States were the Seventh-Day Adventists and the Jehovah's Witnesses. William Miller (1782–1849) prophesied that Christ would come to earth to establish his kingdom in 1843 or 1844. The failure of his prediction didn't deter many of his followers, who still today believe in the imminent return of Jesus. The Seventh-Day Adventist Church was started by one of Miller's followers, Ellen G. White (1827–1915). As their name implies, they keep to Saturday as their day of worship and rest, and look forward to the coming (advent) of Christ. The Jehovah's Witnesses, begun by Charles Taze Russell (1852–1916), also hold millenarian views. Members of this international movement recognize no human government and are in other ways aggressively countercultural. The Jehovah's Witnesses suffered greatly in World War II, when they were targeted in the Holocaust for refusing to recognize the authority of the Nazi government. Today they are under a great deal of pressure in Russia, where the government outlawed

them in 2017 as an extremist group. The LDS (saints living in the latter days of human history) movement begun by Joseph Smith also drew some of its energy from apocalypticism. These three NRMs have actively spread their message and are found throughout the world today.

Here we should give lengthier treatment to the Baha'i (bah-HIGH) movement, a large and widespread NRM with a strong presence in the West. It arose out of Shi'a Islam in Iran during the middle 1800s. Baha'i is founded today on: monotheism, the inner unity of religions, and the unity of humanity. According to Baha'i teachings, all humans of any religion know and love God through prayer, reflection, and service to others. Of all religions and NRMs today, Baha'i is perhaps the most fully tolerant toward other religions.

The first years of Baha'i saw a continuous struggle to define itself over against Islam, and to survive Muslim opposition. Baha'i teachings were framed at first to fulfill the teaching and practice of Islam and also to distinguish them from Islam; the inclusiveness of Baha'i was only implicit at this stage. In Baha'i, religious history unfolds through a series of divine "messengers," each of which gave a revelation that was suited to current needs and to the capacity of the people. Baha'i scripture specifically mentions figures such as Moses, Jesus, and Muhammad; later Baha'i literature speaks of Asian figures like Krishna and Buddha. In Baha'i belief, each consecutive messenger prophesied of messengers to follow, and their main messenger fulfilled the promises of all previous world scriptures, especially the Qur'an.

Baha'i calls its scriptures *Holy Writings*. The Muslim Qur'an ("Recitation") originated orally as the transmission of God's words; in contrast, the *Holy Writings* was written from the first, from the "Pen of God," a phrase often repeated in the earliest Baha'i scriptures. The *Holy Writings* of Baha'i are organized in four parts corresponding to their four authors. First are the writings of a man known as the Bab (pronounced "bob"), the "Gate" to God (1819–1850), who laid the foundation of Baha'i. Next are the writings of Baha'u'llah (bah-hah-UHL-ah, 1817–1892), the main founder of the faith. His most important writing is the *Most Holy Book*; it is the closest

apocalyptic [uh-POC-uh-LIP-tick] Belief that the world order will end soon and God will bring a new, perfect society

millenarianism [MILL-en-AIR-ee-uhn-iz-uhm] Belief in a thousand-year reign of peace on earth near the end of time

answer in Baha'i to Islam's *Qur'an*, and it imitates its style and content. Next are the writings of Abdul-Baha (1843–1921), the third leader, and finally the writings of his grandson, Shoghi Effendi (1897–1957).

Baha'i obligates its followers to perform certain practices and abstain from others, which are formed to replace Islamic pillars and other key practices. Baha'is over the age of 15 individually recite a fixed prayer once each day. They observe a fast each year during daylight hours for nineteen days in March. Baha'is make a 19 percent voluntary payment on any wealth in excess of what is necessary to live at what one considers a basic level of comfort. Gossip, a critical spirit, and any unhelpful talk are forbidden. Drinking alcohol or selling it is forbidden. Sexual intercourse is permitted only between a husband and wife; premarital, extramarital, and same-sex intercourse are forbidden.

In the twentieth century through today, Baha'i distanced itself from its relationship with Islam, and began to be an inclusive religion explained in modern terms. It was able to do this because it left its Islamic homeland to be established in the West. Shoghi Effendi was instrumental in this shift. Humanity is understood to be in a process of collective evolution, and the different world religions are all a part of this evolution. Baha'is believe that the main need of the present time is for the establishment of peace, justice, and unity among all nations. Their distinctive beliefs and practices are well-suited to empower this daunting work.

The utopian impulse in millenarianism also underlies the **New Age** movement that arose in the 1970s and 1980s outside the Christian tradition. It has touches of various Asian and indigenous religions. This is an eclectic group of beliefs and practices including: crystal

> *The aim of New Age groups is to bring the individual to a state of higher consciousness.*

The symbol of Baha'i, the nine-pointed star, is designed to replace the unofficial symbol of Islam, the crescent moon and five-pointed star.

BONNIE VAN VOORST © CENGAGE

healing, channeling spirits, shamanism, veneration of the Earth, and ritual techniques. The aim of New Age groups is to bring the individual to a state of higher consciousness. They believe that the world has entered, or is about to enter, a spiritual millennium of more fulfilling spiritual life. Scholars disagree whether New Age is a genuine movement, largely because it is so eclectic.

Apocalyptic movements can sometimes turn violent, and this happened with a prominent NRM in the 1970s. A magnetic Christian minister named Jim Jones moved many members of his large, prominent congregation called the **People's Temple** from San Francisco to Guyana, in South America. He tried to build a utopian commune on apostolic socialism, a version of Christianity inclined to liberation theology, which was strong in South America at the time. Jones became increasingly dictatorial and erratic, even naming his settlement Jonestown. In 1978, a U.S. congressman from San Francisco and some relatives of church members visited the group's settlement along with a television news crew and began to leave with an unfavorable report. Most of them were killed, and Jones then induced his followers to kill themselves by drinking a powdered drink laced with cyanide rather than see their community broken up. (This is the origin of the current expression "drink the Kool-Aid," meaning to accept something detrimental unthinkingly. In light of the tragedy from which it comes, this expression is insensitive, to say the least.) Those who didn't willingly drink the poison were forced to drink it or were killed by other means. In all, 913 persons—about equal numbers of men, women, and children—died at Jonestown.

Tragedy also befell the **Branch Davidian** (dah-VID-ee-uhn) NRM in 1993. The group, originating in the Seventh-Day Adventist Church but independent from its control, first settled in a compound near Waco, Texas, in 1935. Vernon Howell, who renamed himself David Koresh (koh-REHSH), became the leader of the group in 1987. He identified himself as an apocalyptic figure from the New Testament book of Revelation. Allegations of sexual abuse of children and the founding of a gun business in the compound attracted the suspicion

New Age Eclectic beliefs and practices that aim to bring the individual to a state of higher consciousness

People's Temple Utopian NRM led by Jones that ended in mass murder in Guyana in 1978

Branch Davidian Apocalyptic NRM led by Koresh that ended in Texas in 1993

of state and federal authorities. When federal authorities assaulted the compound to end a long standoff, a fire killed Koresh and some eighty followers, and the Branch Davidian movement died with them.

13-3b Asian NRMs in the West

As we saw in our study of Hinduism and Buddhism, the teachings of these religions appeared in Europe and the United States in the 1800s and began to influence western intellectuals. The most influential of these teachings were those of Hindu Vedantic beliefs, especially the idea that the universe participates in a single divine spiritual reality. North Americans started a few NRMs with Vedantic teachings in the 1800s, most prominently the Theosophical Society founded by Helena Petrovna Blavatsky. These groups brought Hindu concepts into a combination of traditional and nontraditional western religious teachings and practices.

By the end of the 1800s, the first Hindu groups took root in the United States when Indian gurus brought them over. Because their beliefs were presented in a language westerners appreciated, these NRMs were stronger in the West than in India, where they were often marginalized. Vivekananda (VIV-uh-kah-NAHN-duh; 1864–1902), a prominent Indian philosopher, founded the **Vedanta Society** in New York City on the doctrines of his teacher, Ramakrishna. This NRM appealed to many prominent artists of the time. With centers around the world, the Vedanta Society holds that all religions teach the same basic truth but that Vedanta articulates the truth best. Vivekananda and the Vedanta Society were instrumental in raising Hinduism to the status of a world religion.

Another teacher from India, Paramahansa Yogananda (PAR-uh-mah-HAN-suh YOH-guh-NAHN-duh; 1893–1952), established the **Self-Realization Fellowship** in Los Angeles in 1920 and was the first to teach yoga to Americans. Adapting Hindu practices of mental, physical, and spiritual self-control and self-realization, Yogananda explained yoga in scientific, not religious, terms, which helped to reach a larger audience. Like Vivekananda, Yogananda promoted an inclusive approach and said that the founders of other religions had taught the same system. More than five hundred Self-Realization Fellowship societies are found today around the world.

In 1968, the Beatles and their wives studied in India with the Maharishi Mahesh Yogi (center background). Seated left to right on the red platform are Ringo Starr and Maureen Starkey, Jane Asher and Paul McCartney, George Harrison and Patti Boyd, and Cynthia and John Lennon.

© HULTON ARCHIVE/GETTY IMAGES

Although these Hindu movements introduced Hinduism to North America, it was only in the 1960s and 1970s that Asian NRMs became popular here. In 1959, Maharishi Mahesh Yogi (MA-hah-REESH-ee MA-hesh YOH-gee; 1914–2008) began **Transcendental Meditation**, widely known as TM for short, in North America. TM was presented as a scientifically sound way to obtain both personal and world peace; like the Self-Realization Fellowship, TM promoted yoga and meditation as a nonreligious system. TM's system of so-called Vedantic science featured meditation, often with yoga, on a special mantra given to a follower by the guru. This is similar to long-standing Hindu practice. The Maharishi drew millions of practitioners to TM, even though most of them didn't formally join his movement, and he was influential in spreading yoga in North America. The fame of his movement increased when it attracted celebrities such as American film star Mia Farrow and director David Lynch, American architect R. Buckminster Fuller, and especially the Beatles and other pop music stars.

Vedanta Society
Hindu NRM founded by Vivekananda promoting Vedantic Hinduism

Self-Realization Fellowship Hindu NRM founded by Yogananda promoting Vedanta and yoga

Transcendental Meditation (TM) Hindu NRM founded by Maharishi Mahesh Yogi, promoting Vedantic science

The **Rajneesh International Foundation** is also from India. This NRM was founded by Bhagwan Shree Rajneesh (1931–1990), who developed a westernized Tantrism that stressed its psychological and sexual aspects. Also called Acharya Rajneesh, Osho, and more informally the "sex guru," Rajneesh taught a system of dynamic meditation. Unlike other meditation, which is quiet and still, dynamic meditation featured screaming and dancing, even physical violence and sexual intercourse, the latter sometimes in public. Of all Indian groups that came to North America, this one was the most widely known as a "cult," for its strongly countercultural practices and the flamboyant lifestyle of its founder.

This treatment of Hindu NRMs isn't meant to imply that the only presence of Hinduism and Buddhism in North America is by way of NRMs. As we saw in the concluding sections of the chapters on these two religions, they've been introduced into North America and Europe with little change to their traditional forms, particularly through the immigration of Hindus and Buddhists. The forms of these religions found in North American NRMs can depart significantly from their mainstream manifestations. For example, in India one would not often see the emphasis many Hindu NRMs put on leadership of a mass movement by a guru, explicit religious universalism as a key teaching, and the secular or scientific nature of religious teachings and techniques such as yoga and meditation. The modern appeal of science leads us to the next group of western NRMs.

The headquarters church of Christian Science, the First Church of Christ, Scientist, in Boston

DENISTANGNEYJR/ISTOCKPHOTO.COM

Mary Baker Eddy (1821–1910), was a prolific writer, similar to many founders of NRMs. Although NRMs sometimes consider everything their founders wrote to be scriptural, the Christian Science Church has named only one of Eddy's writings scriptural—her 1875 *Science and Health with Key to the Scriptures*. The title of the book accurately suggests its content: a "science" that uses prayer, Christian scripture, and Eddy's book itself to heal body, mind, and spirit. This science views the mind as the source of health and sickness; to cure the mind leads to cures in the body. Until around 2005 when it began to moderate its stance, the Christian Science Church had completely rejected medical science and treatment. It is still headquartered in Boston today, and its local churches spread throughout North America have reading rooms for the general public.

UFO groups, also called the contact [with space aliens] movement, represent another type of a scientific NRM, although one quite different from Christian Science. That they may look to outsiders more like science fiction than science is largely unimportant. These movements from the 1950s and 1960s came at a time when North American popular culture spread fear about space aliens coming to earth—a fear many historians believe to be related to the threat of nuclear war that was widely felt at the time. In contrast to the alarmist reports, however, UFO NRMs looked to space aliens for blessings. Adapting some religions' stories of the coming of beings from heaven, UFO groups teach about space aliens who bring scientific knowledge and spiritual wisdom. Beginning in the 1950s, groups such as Understanding, Inc.

13-3c Scientific NRMs: Christian Science and UFO Groups

Some NRMs claim to reveal scientific truths that haven't yet been acknowledged by the public or even discovered by scientists. These NRMs draw on the most powerful authority in the modern world: science.

The founder of the **Christian Science Church**,

argued that UFOs carried beings who would promote peace and happiness throughout the whole world. The Amalgamated Flying Saucer Clubs of America (certainly one of the most strikingly named U.S. NRMs!) and the yoga-employing Aetherius Society believe that space aliens will bring salvation to the world. This salvation consists of superior technical and psychological knowledge that makes possible a blessed age, not the revelation of more traditional religious truths.

The UFO groups founded in the twentieth century tend to be in decline, with one exception. The **Raëlians** is a UFO group now headquartered in Quebec, with about 55,000 members worldwide. It was established in 1973 by Raël, a French race-car driver and sports journalist whose given name was Claude Vorilhon (b. 1946). Raël states that in December of 1973 he was abducted to a flying saucer, as spaceships from other worlds were widely called at the time. There he met a four-foot tall extraterrestrial with human features, with whom Raël had conversations for one week. Raël was told that humans originated in a genetic manipulation by the Elohim—a word the Bible (according to the extraterrestrial) mistranslates as "God" and really means "those who came from the sky." Humans are descended from these beings from the sky, and knowledge of this leads to enlightenment. Raël, whose name is explained as "messenger of Elohim," has also formed a company called Clonaid to develop cloning of human beings. Clonaid created a world wide stir in 2002 when it claimed that it had successfully cloned a human being named Eve. This led to renewed debates over the ethics of human cloning, but soon the debate shifted to whether the whole announcement was a fraud.

Another UFO group was the small **Heaven's Gate** movement founded in Texas in the 1970s by Marshall Applewhite. Applewhite (who called himself Do) professed that he and his wife (Ti) were beings from another world at an "evolutionary level above human." Claiming to have already appeared on earth as Jesus, Applewhite argued that the kingdom of heaven that Jesus taught was a real place with highly evolved beings from another world. The Garden of Eden in the biblical book of Genesis was the whole earth, where human beings had been "planted" by the otherworldly beings. Applewhite organized communal living for his group of plants in a new garden. He taught that the plants could evolve into "members of the level above human," but they had to

> UFO groups teach about space aliens who bring scientific knowledge and spiritual wisdom.

discard their humanity, including sexuality. In response, some Heaven's Gate followers castrated themselves. Such self-mutilation foreshadowed worse violence to come. In 1996, the group settled near San Diego, California, where it supported itself by creating websites for Internet users. Most people who came in contact with the group thought they were harmless eccentrics, but in March of 1997 Applewhite revealed that the Hale–Bopp comet was bringing a spaceship in its tail. The mature plants would be transplanted into this spaceship before the "garden was spaded over" and the earth was destroyed. Led by Applewhite, the thirty-nine Heaven's Gate members committed suicide to free their spirits for transportation to the aliens' spaceship. The Heaven's Gate movement perished with them.

As we've seen from these examples, these UFO-oriented NRMs can express traditional religious themes in the language of science, science fiction, and biological evolution. As space-alien fervor has waned in North America with the ending of the Cold War, other types of scientific NRMs have become popular. The Church of Scientology expresses its teachings in the language of modern psychology. We'll consider the Scientology movement more fully below, but now we turn our attention to NRMs based on beliefs about nature.

13-3d Nature NRMs: Neo-Paganism, Wicca, and Druidry

Most nature NRMs are antiscientific. They oppose the alienation of humans from nature that they see in science and technology, and they advance the reenchantment of nature. They seek to return to the meaningful patterns of the natural world. Their use of magic, spells, potions, and other ritual devices to pursue their personal goals intentionally opposes modern science and technology. Neo-pagan NRMs are found particularly in Western Europe, but are present in North America as well. Some pagan groups, such as the Druids (DROO-ids), claim to be the ancient pagan religion of Europe that was suppressed by Christianity (see "A Closer Look: Druidry Gains Official Status"). Although "pagan" and "paganism" might seem pejorative to

Raëlians [rye-EHL-ee-uhnz] UFO NRM established in 1973 by Raël

Heaven's Gate UFO NRM established in the 1970s by Applewhite

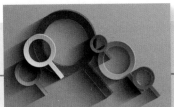
Druidry Gains Official Status

Druidry, the pagan worship that its current practitioners claim has existed for thousands of years, gained recognition by the British government as a bona fide religion in 2010 after a four-year process. The Charity Commission, established to oversee charities in England and Wales, and the body that determines whether movements qualify under British law as religions, ruled that the Druids' worship of spirits in nature is a religious activity. The Charity Commission didn't have to rule on how ancient this movement actually is, only its present status as a religion.

Current membership in the Druid Network totals about 350 dues-paying members, although the BBC claimed in 2005 that Druidry is practiced by as many as ten thousand people in the United Kingdom. Druidry has eight annual festivals, including rites on the summer solstice amid the ancient stone monoliths at Stonehenge.

Modern Druids carry out a summer solstice ceremony at Stonehenge in England.

you, these groups proudly embrace them, and they have become standard terms in scholarship. Other groups take the name **Wicca**, the NRM of modern witchcraft. Wicca draws on religious implications of ideas in today's ecology movement and in feminism. Made up predominantly of women, Wicca groups typically center on a Goddess and a female principle, which they see as the leading force of nature. Like other nature NRMs, they aim to reenchant and repersonalize the world, reclaiming it from the wrongs that science has inflicted on it.

13-3e NRMs in Asia

New religious movements in Asia today began after 1850, and they reflect the colonial impact of the West on that region. Arising in this environment, they were either in opposition to western religion and culture or in some sort of blended agreement with it. When they were against western imperialism, these NRMs reinvented older Asian traditions; when they agreed with parts of it, they blended western and Asian religions. Both types of NRMs helped Asian cultures adapt to growing westernization there, in colonial and postcolonial times.

NRMs in China arose at the end of the first Opium War in 1842. Western imperialism, poverty in southern China, and the work of the first Protestant missionaries were a part of the mix that occasioned Chinese NRMs. The most important of these NRMs was the Taiping Tianguo (tigh-PING TEE-ahn-GWOH), the Heavenly Kingdom of the Great Peace. This NRM combined evangelical Christianity, Confucianism, and various popular Daoist traditions. Guided by its powerful leader, Hong Xiuquan (hawng zyoo-KWAHN), the Heavenly Kingdom of the Great Peace established a religious state, which its follower saw as a kingdom on earth and in heaven. At first, it controlled several provinces in southern China, and then moved into the center of the country. It threatened the stability of China until it was put down in 1865.

The emperor legalized western Christian missionary work in China in 1858, and many types of Protestant messages and churches then spread through China. One effect of this was the rise of indigenous churches that were independent of foreign control. These were

Wicca [WIHK-uh]
Nature NRM of modern witchcraft

typically Pentecostal and other evangelical groups; mainline Christian denominations didn't spawn independent churches so readily.

Some of China's NRMs grew out of popular Daoism, and pre-dated the Opium Wars. New Daoist groups had been arising regularly for almost two thousand years, and the coming of westerners didn't change this. One large NRM, which evolved out of the White Lotus millenarian tradition is the eclectic Yiguan (yee-GWAHN) Dao, the Unity School. Spirit writing done in a shamanic trance provides moral direction for the group. Another spirit-writing group, the Zhihui (ZHEE-wee) Tang, the Compassion Sect, began in Taiwan in 1949.

The Yin Yang symbol stands for an invisible rolling ball in the Tai Chi exercise called Wave Hands Like Clouds.

SONGSPECKELS/ISTOCKPHOTO.COM

By far the most significant type of NRM to arise recently in China relates to **Qi Gong**, or Energy Working, an ancient practice combining physical exercise and meditation. In the 1980s and 1990s, China experienced a rebirth of traditional exercise practices with a religious basis. These encourage health by energizing the flow of cosmic qi (vital force) in one's body. Tai Qi (more commonly known by the spelling Tai Chi) is the best known of the meditational exercises. Qi Gong masters gained popularity and founded movements throughout China by displaying their extraordinary abilities. Many NRMs arose from these Qi Gong activities. The best-known Qi Gong group is Falun Gong, which began in 1992; we'll consider this movement more fully later. Religion in China today is growing rapidly, and NRMs are playing a significant part.

{ *Japan, despite its modern, increasingly secular society, has proportionally more NRMs and people in them than any other nation.* }

In Japan, the rapid changes in the 1800s saw the rise of many religious organizations, which scholars of Japan have termed **new religions**. In the wider field of international religious studies, they are usually seen as NRMs. Most Japanese new religions have their roots

in Buddhism, some in Shinto, and a few in Confucianism; they tend to be eclectic, blending these three in unique ways. The perceived empty formalism and lack of vitality in the older traditions, particularly Shinto and traditional Buddhism, has given space for new Japanese religions to arise, which are seen by many Japanese as more vital and dynamic. Similar to many NRMs worldwide, the new religions of Japan draw on lay participation, with followers spreading the faiths and running the organizations. It's safe to say that Japan, despite its modern, increasingly secular society, has proportionately more NRMs and people in them than any other nation today. Here, of course, we can mention only a few.

The earliest of the Japanese new religions include Tenrikyo (ten-REEK-yoh) and Konkokyo (kon-KOHK-yoh). Gedatsu-kai (geh-DAHT-suh-kai), a blend of Shinto, Buddhism, and Confucianism, developed before World War II. The postwar period saw many new groups appear, including the Dancing Religion and Johrei (JOH-ray), a self-help movement based on Christianity.

The most infamous of the Japanese new religions was the apocalyptic group **Aum Shinrikyo**. Founded in 1987 by Chizuo Matsumoto (chih-ZOO-oh MAHT-SOO-MOH-toh), also known as Shoko Asahara, its teachings combined Asian religions and Christianity. Aum Shinrikyo launched a 1995 nerve-gas attack on the Tokyo subway system in which twelve people died and more than fifty were seriously injured. The group later renamed itself Aleph, the first letter of the Hebrew alphabet, and tried to regroup without its founder, but it has almost completely disbanded. Two of its members evaded arrest until 2012. Five Aum Shinrikyo members are now serving life sentences for the attack and thirteen have been sentenced to death, including Matsumoto. In 2016, the supreme court of Japan

Qi Gong [chee gong]
"Energy Working," ancient Chinese traditions of spiritual and physical exercise

new religions
Characteristic name in scholarship for NRMs in Japan

rejected a final appeal, and this sentence was carried out by hanging in July of 2018.

The largest Japanese NRM is **Soka-Gakkai**, the Value Creation Society. This Buddhist group claims more than 6 million members today. Founded in 1930, it was disbanded by the Japanese government during World War II for its opposition to the war, but it was refounded in 1946. It grew rapidly in the 1950s, and in 1964 it founded the Clean Government political party. Its teachings draw from Nichiren, a thirteenth-century Japanese Buddhist, but it is independent enough from Buddhism to merit recognition as an NRM. Soka-Gakkai emphasizes beauty and goodness, and is known for its main ritual practice of chanting praise to its main scripture, the *Lotus Sutra*.

The largest NRM to emerge from Korea is the **Unification Church**, the unofficial name of the Holy Spirit Association for the Unification of World Christianity. Because of its rapid growth and now nearly worldwide reach, we will treat it more fully than the other groups in this section. The Unification Church began in South Korea with the work of Sun Myung Moon (1920–2012), formerly a Korean Presbyterian, in 1954. Moon related a vision, while a teenager, in which God commanded him to complete Jesus Christ's work. Because of Adam and Eve's failure to obey God, their selfish love has damaged human life, and God tried to save humanity in the life of Jesus. Although Jesus was the First Messiah and should have brought full salvation to humanity, he didn't marry and have children, so he failed in his mission. The Unification Church openly calls Moon the Second Messiah who completes Jesus's mission.

As the parents of an "ideal" family, Moon and his second wife Hak Ja Han expected Unification Church members to follow their example in marriage and thus bring the world to perfection. This invested special significance in the mass weddings used to unite Unification couples. The emphasis on family originates in Confucianism, where marriage and family are central to religion and life. Moon's

Sun Myung Moon, founder of the Unification Church, and his wife Hak Ja Han officiated at the 1997 mass wedding of 2,500 couples at the Kennedy Center in Washington, D.C.

© STEPHEN JAFFE/AFP/GETTY IMAGES

second marriage in 1960 marked for Unificationists the beginning of a new age. The **True Parents**, Moon and his wife, realized perfection and led humanity to a perfect state, in order to build God's ideal world on earth. Strong anticommunism and political conservatism are also found in the Unification movement.

In the late 1950s, the Unification Church came to North America. In the 1970s, it worked especially for the conversion of college students and used means that proved controversial. Some parents protested their children's membership in the communal-living groups that Unification operated, which required Unificationists to sever family ties. This controversy led to U.S. congressional hearings, and in 1982 Moon was convicted of tax evasion and spent a few years in federal prison. The Unification Church kept growing, however, and soon emerged from these troubles with a worldwide base. The church is now in more than one hundred countries, but reliable membership numbers are hard to come by. (Current estimates range from 50,000 to

Aum Shinrikyo [ohm shin-REEK-yoh] Apocalyptic Japanese NRM founded in 1987 by Matsumoto

Soka-Gakkai [SOH-kah-GAHK-kigh] Largest Japanese NRM, founded in 1930 as an offshoot of Nichiren Buddhism

Unification Church NRM from Korea founded by Moon, a blend of Christianity and Asian religions

True Parents In Unification, the late Sun Myung Moon and his wife, who led humanity to perfection

2 million.) Its influence is extended by a dozen or so church-funded organizations without its name (called "front groups" by the church's opponents)—for example, the Professor's World Peace Academy, the International Conference on the Unity of the Sciences, and the International Federation for World Peace. The church also owns media companies such as the conservative *Washington Times* newspaper and United Press International (UPI), a news-distribution company. After Sun Myung Moon died in 2012, students of NRMs have watched the Unification Church closely to see how well it turns over leadership to a new generation.

In Vietnam, Cao Dai (cow digh), a syncretistic religion, became a social force with considerable political power from 1945 to 1954. Its political power has been reduced in present-day Communist Vietnam, but as a religion it is still strong. Cao Dai attempts to create a perfect synthesis of world religions, combining Christianity, Buddhism, Islam, Confucianism, Hinduism, Daoism, and shamanism. The Cao Dai faithful must detach themselves from material possessions to cultivate their spirits. They worship one God, the most prominent

Cao Dai monks inside Holy See Temple, Tay Ninh, Vietnam

© DENIS ROZAN/SHUTTERSTOCK.COM

spirits, and their ancestors. Cao Dai also uses spiritual mediums in its worship, a practice that derives from Daoism and shamanism. These mediums offer guidance from those in the spirit world, departed family members, and other wise individuals.

13-4 An NRM from Asia: Falun Gong

Falun Gong, "Practice of the Wheel of Dharma," is a controversial NRM begun by Li Hongzhi (lee hong-ZHER) in 1992. Falun Gong is the common name in the West and in China, but its adherents usually call it Falun Dafa. The essence of this NRM is to achieve mental and spiritual renewal by way of physical and mental exercises, as well as some mystical teachings. The teachings of Falun Gong tap into Buddhism, popular and religious Daoism, Confucianism, and even New Age movements. Li teaches meditation techniques and physical exercises that encourage mental and spiritual renewal. Falun Gong exploded on the world scene in 1999 with a large, sudden demonstration in Beijing against the Chinese government, which has since denounced Falun Gong as a "falsehood" and an "evil cult." In the government's view, it does not deserve governmental toleration as a religion. As Fenggang Yang has written in his *Religion in China: Survival and Revival under Communist Rule*, the authorities claim they are justified in eradicating Falun Gong and similar groups in China.[4] The Communist government has suppressed this group through today with both prosecution and persecution, just as the emperors of China before it suppressed religious groups that were seen as a threat to their rule.

13-4a History

Qi Gong, as we saw earlier, is based on beliefs and practices that go back to the dawn of Chinese civilization. Practitioners in China have long represented these techniques as nonreligious, in an effort to evade the government prohibition of independent, unapproved religious activity. In the twentieth century, when Qi Gong appeared in China as a distinct qi school, its new practitioners taught that it was rooted in religion. Chief among them was Li Hongzhi (1951–present), who worked as a police officer and in private security before he founded Falun Gong.

Falun Gong [FAH-loon gong] "Practice of the Wheel of Dharma," a Chinese NRM founded by Li in 1992

Li, already a Qi Gong teacher with Buddhist and Daoist credentials, began promoting his own version of Qi Gong in 1992. He synthesized traditional techniques with Buddhist and Daoist concepts about self-development. His book *Zhuan Falun*, or *Turning the Wheel of the Law*, teaches a path to enlightenment and salvation through meditation and morality. After publishing *Zhuan Falun*, Li stated that he had completed his work in China. He began to travel internationally to spread his movement. Li became an American citizen in 1997 and a resident of New York City in 1998.

Falun Gong became popular in the West in the 1990s, in part because some Falun Gong followers claimed to have been healed of various diseases. Membership in the new movement grew rapidly. Li himself claimed around 100 million Falun Gong followers worldwide; this is no doubt an exaggeration, but practitioners do number in the millions.

In China, however, the government became increasingly wary of Falun Gong's continued growth. Government officials feared that Li's movement could inspire a revolutionary challenge to public order and especially to Communist Party rule. In 1999, more than ten thousand Falun Gong members protested in Beijing against being labeled a superstitious cult. This massive sit-in somehow caught the Chinese government by surprise. Three months later, the president of China declared the practitioners of Falun Gong an imminent threat to the government and a rebellious movement, and launched a harsh crackdown. He detained thousands of Falun Gong practitioners, some of whom were even officials in the Chinese Communist Party. The government confiscated and destroyed as many of Li's books and cassette tapes as possible, probably in the millions. Hundreds of Falun Gong leaders are still imprisoned in China today. Falun Gong members outside China have tried to keep up pressure on the Chinese government, and have accused prison authorities of harvesting vital organs for transplant from live or executed Falun Gong prisoners. The Chinese Communist government's actions against Falun Gong are rooted in Communist opposition to religion in general, and specifically to independent, unregulated religious activities in China. They also derive in no small measure from the Communist Party's unwillingness to give up power or share it with other groups. The actions taken against Falun Gong in China are driving it underground, but its beliefs and practices are surviving there.

Living now in the United States, Li has called for negotiation with the Chinese government to resolve the crisis over his movement. His teachings are now spread around the world by a variety of methods: books and audio recordings; a free newspaper, *The Epoch Times*, which has an online version; Chinese-language television and radio networks; and a Chinese New Year entertainment, "Shen Yun," it sponsors in major cities around the world.

13-4b Teaching and Practice

Falun Gong's scripture, *Zhuan Falun*, is the main book of its founder. It contains a series of lectures, indicating the origin of the book in Li's efforts to spread his teaching, beginning in the 1990s. It was first published in 1995, soon after the founding of the movement. The chapters in the book preserve the feel of lectures to live audiences. *Zhuan Falun* has already been translated into forty languages. Although the Falun Gong movement doesn't explicitly describe *Zhuan Falun* as scripture—for example, by calling it a "sutra" (the formal Buddhist name for a scriptural writing) or venerating it in ceremonies—it is clear nonetheless that the movement regards it as such. *Zhuan Falun* is organized into nine lectures or talks. These nine teachings discuss all the basics of Falun Gong theory and practice. A good deal of treatment is given to the relationship of Falun Gong practice with that of other traditional Buddhist teachings and with Daoism.

In Buddhism, *wheel* is the wheel of law or wheel of dharma, but in Falun Gong the wheel is the bodily center of one's energy (see Figure 13.1). Li locates this center in the abdomen and teaches that one can activate

Figure 13.1   The symbol of Falun Gong features the turning wheel

A girl examines a Chinese ceremonial dragon at a public Falun Gong festival in Moscow, Russia.

it by cultivating and practicing exercises; he also claims to be able to install his wheel in others. Most Qi Gong groups tend to be inclusive in spirit, but Falun Gong maintains that Li alone has established the correct exercises. The spiritual discipline he teaches, the "cultivation of Mind-Nature," is essential to their success.

In a twist on the teachings of UFO new religious movements, Li has said that demonic space aliens are now undermining life on earth. Since 1900, these aliens have controlled scientists and world leaders. Opponents of Falun Gong inside and outside China ridicule this as bizarre, and they regard reliance on Falun Gong as a hazard to health. Chinese medical authorities claim that 1,400 Falun Gong practitioners have died from refusing to seek modern medical care. The controversy between the Chinese government and Falun Gong appears set to continue for at least the near future, especially if this movement keeps gaining strength and stature in the world.

13-5 A North American NRM: The Church of Jesus Christ of Latter-day Saints

The Church of Jesus Christ of Latter-day Saints (LDS) is one of several churches originating in a movement begun by Joseph Smith Jr. (1805–1844) in New York State in 1830. The name **Mormon**, often used for these churches, is from the *Book of Mormon*, published by Smith in that year. Mormonism differs from the Christianity it separated from by its teachings about God,

family life, continuing revelation, and missionary work. The mission work has been largely effective in making the LDS Church the fastest-growing NRM in the world, with 14 million members. Most of them are outside North America, with about a third in Latin America.

13-5a History

Mormons believe that in 1827 an angel named Moroni (moh-ROHN-igh) appeared to Smith and told him about engraved golden plates (see Figure 13.2). Using what he called "seer stones," Smith translated them from their Reformed Egyptian language as the *Book of Mormon*. This Mormon, after whom this book is named, was an ancient American prophet who authored the book written on the plates. The *Book of Mormon* tells the story of ancient Israelites who sailed to America centuries before Jesus Christ, led by prophets. Smith's new religion originated in a setting of great fervor of competing American Protestant denominations in the early 1800s; the area of upstate New York where Smith lived was even known as the "burned-over district" for its frequent emotional revivals. Mormonism departed from them in its proclamation that, in Joseph Smith's work, God restored the true church and reestablished the true faith from which all Christianity had strayed since the first century C.E.

This new church was millennialist, and Smith hoped to establish God's kingdom in what is now the western United States. Smith received revelations of both new and traditional teachings from the *Book of Mormon*, and also received practical help from Moroni. He and his followers soon began their westward trek by moving to Kirtland, Ohio. In Jackson County, Missouri, where Zion was to be established, Smith formed his followers into a communalistic society. Growing tensions with slave-owning Missourians, who thought that the Mormons opposed slavery, resulted in armed clashes. Most Mormons fled Missouri for western Illinois in 1839. There Smith built a new city, Nauvoo. Mormon success in business and politics provoked persecution once again. Increasing rumors about secret polygamy by Smith and other top Mormon leaders began to circulate—rumors that later turned out to be true, and in 2016 were officially acknowledged by LDS leaders in their document, "Plural Marriage in Kirtland and Nauvoo," which they posted online. Smith's

Mormon [MOHR-muhn] Member of any church from the movement started by Joseph Smith

Figure 13.2 **A Statue of the Angel Moroni, found on LDS temples**

strong repression of some Mormon dissidents intensified non-Mormon hostility and led to his arrest. Joseph Smith and his brother Hyrum were jailed in Carthage, Illinois, near Nauvoo, and they were killed by a mob that took over the jail on June 27, 1844.

A **Council of the Twelve Apostles** then assumed the leadership of the church, and still leads it today. Mormons overwhelmingly favored Brigham Young as Smith's successor. When increasing violence made the Mormons' life in Nauvoo difficult, Young led a 1,100-mile trek to what is now Utah in 1846–1847. The Mormons aimed to establish a territory in Utah where they could live by themselves and practice their religion without opposition from local and state governments. (At the time, Utah was technically a part of Mexico, and out of U.S. control.) Young established more than three hundred settlements in Utah and adjacent areas. Seeking to bolster his numbers and strength, Young

Council of the Twelve Apostles In LDS, the highest ruling body

plural marriage Mormon term for polygamy

sent missionaries throughout North America and to Great Britain. They urged their converts to move to Utah. In all, about eighty thousand Mormon pioneers traveled west in wagon trains or on foot by 1869.

Despite the difficulties of life around Salt Lake, the pioneers made a prosperous life for themselves, empowered by their faith. Utah's first request for statehood in 1849 was denied; later applications for statehood were blocked by the church's announcement in 1852 of its practice of polygamy, which Mormons call **plural marriage**. As mentioned previously, it had been practiced secretly by Joseph Smith and by a few other leading Mormons during the church's time in Nauvoo (and since), but in the 1850s plural marriage became a key doctrine and practice of the LDS movement as a whole. As Young and the U.S. government argued over polygamy, and as Mormons continued to press for their own church-directed government during the 1850s, tensions boiled over. In 1857, a group of Mormons murdered all the men, women, and children of a wagon train moving through the Mountain Meadows, Utah, area. In response to this massacre and other conflicts with federal authorities, U.S. President James Buchanan threatened to dispatch the U.S. Army to suppress the Mormon rebellion and set up a non-Mormon government in the territory.

Troubles over polygamy continued until 1890, when the president of the LDS Church, Wilford Woodruff, announced with great anguish the church's abandonment of plural marriage. This and other changes led to the 1896 admission of Utah as a state, with Young as its first governor. However, Woodruff's decree applied only to the United States, and polygamy continued for decades in the LDS settlements in Mexico and illegally in remote places in the American West. Although it caused wrenching problems for Mormons at the time, the LDS Church's renunciation of polygamy is probably a main cause of its increasing strength during the 1900s; those Mormon groups that chose to keep it have had smaller growth.

The church grew rapidly through the traditionally large families that Mormons have, and after World War II the practice of sending young Mormons out as missionaries led to exponential growth. At any given moment, the LDS Church has around forty thousand missionaries active around the world. The church's appeal throughout the world was greatly enhanced when, in 1978, it dropped its racist teachings of the 1800s and allowed Africans and members of the African diaspora to become full-fledged members and priests in the LDS Church. Another step forward in the mission efforts

LINDA BAIR/DREAMSTIME.COM

The Sacred Grove outside Palmyra, New York, the traditional site of Joseph Smith, Jr.'s first vision, is for Mormons one of the holiest places in the world.

of the church came in 2012, when the LDS Church lowered its age requirement for female missionaries to 19 from 21. By 2015, the number of female missionaries had tripled, and has remained high through 2017. Fully one quarter of all Mormon missionaries are now female. Scholars of Mormonism expect that this higher level of participation in the church's key coming-of-age experience will lead over time to other changes in the role of women in the church.

In the diverging paths of Mormonism, more than 150 different independent groups have arisen. They often follow new prophets, practice polygamy, or keep various practices abandoned by the main LDS Church.

- Some Mormons rejected Brigham Young's leadership and remained in the Midwest. The largest of these groups—which Joseph Smith's widow Emma and Joseph Smith III (1860–1914) joined—formed the **Reorganized Church of Jesus Christ of Latter-day Saints** under Smith's leadership in 1852. The Reorganized Church eventually settled in Independence, Missouri, which LDS leaders had once called the location of Zion. For many decades the descendants of Joseph Smith III led the church. In the 1990s, they renamed themselves by the more Protestant-sounding name of Community of Christ. They number around 250,000 members and keep only the *Book of Mormon* as their scripture besides the Bible.

- Another Mormon group moved to Independence and purchased the Temple Lot, the site chosen by Smith for the main Mormon temple. This purchase was opposed by the Reorganized Church, whose headquarters were right next door.

- In 1847, James Strang founded a polygamous community of about three thousand Mormons on Beaver Island in northern Lake Michigan. He proclaimed himself as its prophet and king, and his following grew to as many as twelve thousand in the Upper Midwest. The movement ended in violence a few years later; King James was killed, and his followers scattered.

- Among the LDS factions to emerge in the twentieth century were groups that defiantly kept to polygamy. The first such group was established in Arizona in 1902. Other polygamist settlements were established in Mexico, Canada, and even in Salt Lake City. These groups are estimated at around thirty thousand people in all today. The largest single group committed to the continuation of plural marriage calls itself the **Fundamentalist Church of Jesus Christ of Latter-day Saints (FLDS)**. This church suffered a blow in 2011 when its leader, Warren Jeffs, was convicted for sexual assault of two underage (twelve- and fifteen-year-old) wives and sent to prison.

Despite these splits, the LDS Church has always been far larger than all other Mormon groups combined, comprising at least 90 percent of Mormons in the world.

Reorganized Church of Jesus Christ of Latter-day Saints
Historic name for the Mormon denomination now called Community of Christ

Fundamentalist Church of Jesus Christ of Latter-day Saints (FLDS) Sectarian Mormon group that still practices plural marriage

13-5b Scripture

The Church of Jesus Christ of Latter-day Saints has a four-part scripture. The *Book of Mormon* is the leading part, and it is from this title that the followers of the movement came to be known as Mormons. (At first this was a put-down name given by Smith's opponents outside his movement but was gradually accepted in the LDS Church; it is also the only instance among world religions of a faith being named from the name of its scripture.) It was first published in 1830 at Grandin Press in Palmyra, New York. A second, shorter scripture is the *Pearl of Great Price*; the third scripture is *The Doctrine and Covenants*, which contains the continuing revelation of God's word through LDS prophets, especially Joseph Smith. In addition to this second canon of scripture, the LDS Church has a first canon of the Christian Bible, the King James Version of 1611, the fourth LDS scripture.

The contents of LDS scriptures are quite complex. They record a story of ancient American peoples descended from ancient Hebrews who left Judah and sailed to North America around 600 B.C.E., and the appearance in the first century C.E. of the resurrected Jesus Christ to these Americans. This purported record ends around 400 C.E. The *Book of Mormon* has fifteen main parts, known, with one exception, as books. Similar to the Bible, these books are subdivided into chapters and verses. Mormons believe that the *Book of Mormon* is based on writings appearing on four groups of metal plates: gold plates of Nephi (NEE-figh), Mormon, and Ether and brass plates that, according to founder Joseph Smith, people fleeing Jerusalem in 600 B.C.E. brought to the Americas. In 421 C.E., Moroni, the last of the Nephite prophets, is believed to have sealed the sacred plates and hidden them by divine instruction. Smith said that in 1823 this same Moroni visited him as a resurrected prophet and directed him to the sacred plates. He reported that he translated the writing on the plates into English, and he published them in 1830. The plates themselves, Mormons believe, were returned to Moroni and then hidden away for all time.

The second LDS scripture, *Pearl of Great Price*, was first compiled in 1851 by Franklin Richards, then a member of the church's Council of the Twelve Apostles and in charge of LDS missions in Great Britain. Richards

Book of Mormon first edition (1830) with a printing plate

ANDREW RICH/RICHVINTAGE/ISTOCKPHOTO.COM

intended this book to increase circulation of Joseph Smith's testimony among Latter-day Saints. *Pearl of Great Price* quickly received wide acceptance, especially in mission fields, and became a scripture of the church by the action of its First Presidency (highest official body) in 1880.

The third LDS scripture, *Doctrine and Covenants*, has 138 sections, plus two official declarations. It contains revelations on doctrines and community life—some narrative, some theological, and some legal—from 1823 until 1978. The declarations deal with two controversial topics: the ending of polygamy and the admission of blacks to the priesthood. Although the LDS Church has an open canon, and thus could add an entirely new scriptural book if it decided to do so, its well-established practice is to add any new material to the *Doctrine and Covenants*.

Ironically, the *Book of Mormon* tends to be more similar to mainstream Protestant Christian teaching than are later official church writings and teachings. This is even true of some controversial doctrines that have set the Latter-day Saints apart from other Christians. For example, the *Book of Mormon* promotes monogamy and discourages (but does not forbid) polygamy (see Jacob 2:27, 30), but the *Doctrine and Covenants* preserves both the approval of polygamy (Section 132.37–38, 52, 61–62) and the official disapproval of it ("Official Declaration 1"). Although opponents of the church point to more than three thousand alleged changes to the *Book of Mormon* since its initial publication, the majority of these are corrections and updates of spelling and grammar. In essence, this important book remains the same today as its first edition.

13-5c Teachings

Many LDS teachings are similar to Protestant ones, but its distinctive doctrines make it an NRM in its beliefs as well as its organization. LDS members believe that their religion restores true teaching as well as organization and practices. Their official list of key doctrines, the Articles of Faith, teaches belief in God, the eternal Father; in Jesus Christ, God's Son; and in the Holy Spirit. But LDS teaches that these three are distinct divine beings rather than united in a single deity, as in mainstream Christian teaching. God was once similar to a human but became divine, as all righteous Mormons also hope to do after death. Mormons believe that Christ came to earth to bring salvation, but they maintain that salvation comes by one's own deeds as well as by the grace of God in Christ. This Mormon belief reflects cultural optimism in the 1800s as to basic human goodness and potential, even for self-salvation. Mormons also stress the importance of faith, repentance, and carrying out the key practices of the church, including baptism by immersion. They administer the Lord's Supper weekly as a memorial of Jesus's death, but use water instead of wine. They attend Sunday services regularly and **tithe**—give one-tenth of all their income to the church—faithfully. With the increasing size of the LDS Church and rising prosperity of its members, this tithe has brought in vast wealth.

As stated above, Mormons teach that the faithful may become gods themselves after death. Every human being, except for a few who reject God after coming to know him, will receive a happy afterlife. When Christ returns, he will establish a thousand-year kingdom on the earth. After this period, the earth will be a heavenly place, and the truly righteous will live on it. Others will live forever in less-significant kingdoms, happy but not so blessed.

13-5d Institutions, Practices, and Structure of the LDS Church

The LDS Church ignores the distinctions between clergy and laity that are found in most branches of Christianity. It uses Christian-clergy terms such as "priest," but this always applies in LDS to lay members. At age twelve, worthy males (a term that until 1978 did not apply to Africans and African Americans) can enter the Aaronic priesthood as deacons; they are teachers at age fourteen and priests at sixteen. At eighteen, they can enter the Melchizedek priesthood as elders and may become leaders of local churches. In general, middle-aged LDS men have local and regional authority; national and international authority goes to men of proven ability in their retirement years. (This is why pictures of top LDS leaders always feature old men.)

Many Latter-day Saints do missionary work. Single young men aged eighteen to twenty-one undertake a two-year mission. Single young women nineteen and older serve for eighteen months. This is voluntary, but many young Saints participate in it. They may serve in this country or in a foreign land. Some older married couples also serve as missionaries for eighteen months. This extensive missionary work is the main reason why the LDS Church is probably the most rapidly spreading NRM in the world. In 2015, the LDS Church had approximately 83,000 missionaries worldwide. Missionary work has also helped to give young Saints a remarkably important role in the church.

Baptism, a ritual of initiation and obedience, is considered necessary for salvation. It is administered to LDS children at age eight and to adult converts. Mormon proxy baptism is more famous for being undertaken by substitution for those who have died outside the Mormon religion. This is more widely known as **baptism for the dead**, and it is sometimes

Male LDS missionary in typical clothing; female missionaries have more latitude in dress.

LUGO/ISTOCKPHOTO.COM

tithe Giving one-tenth of all income to the church, mandatory for LDS members

baptism for the dead Ritual in which Mormons are baptized on behalf of the dead, usually their own, non-Mormon ancestors misunderstood by non-Mormons as baptism *of* the dead. The Mormons' commitment to compiling genealogies springs from their concern for bringing their ancestors who have died into the fullness of blessing. Although many people today think of this mainly as a genealogical resource, the information is used for religious purposes, to identify candidates for baptism by proxy. In 2010, after some Jewish groups protested, the LDS Church changed its policies, especially to prevent the names of Jews who had died in the Holocaust from being used in baptism.

Ceremonies of baptism, **endowment** (a ritual in which blessings and knowledge are imparted to adult Mormons in good standing), and the **sealing** of families (assuring their unity in time and eternity) all occur in the temple. In the endowment, Mormons are washed and anointed with oil. Then they see a dramatized story of creation, the fall of humanity into sin, and God's bringing of salvation to the world.

In general, Mormon moral expectations flow from the New Testament and are much the same as in mainstream Christian churches. In addition, Mormons have their own practices. The use of alcohol and tobacco is forbidden, as is drinking coffee, tea, and other drinks with caffeine. Mormons promote education and have a strong work ethic. Their outer clothing must always be modest. A **temple garment**, often called simply *garments*, is a type of white underwear worn by members of the LDS Church after they have gone through the endowment ceremony in the temple. LDS members receive their first temple garments during the washing and anointing part of this ceremony. An observant Mormon wears temple garments day and night; all endowed adults must wear them to enter an LDS temple. The undergarments remind those who wear them of the sacred covenants made in temple ceremonies. Today, the temple garment is worn as a rule by LDS members and by members of most Mormon fundamentalist churches, but optionally by more liberal Mormon groups such as the Community of Christ.

The LDS Church is structured in top-down order as follows. At the worldwide level, headquartered of course in Salt Lake City, is the First Presidency, a group of three men, including the church president (who is viewed as a prophet) and two members of the Council of the Twelve Apostles. Next is the Council of the Twelve Apostles itself, and then the First Quorum of Seventy. These men have primary spiritual and organizational leadership in the LDS Church. They also administer the church's extensive properties, businesses, and relief programs. All world church leaders are sustained in office by a vote at the twice-yearly General Conference, which is open to public observation.

Although all leadership of the LDS Church has been exclusively male, decisions in 2015 have led to the first-ever presence of women in an advisory capacity. As stated above, females are also much more welcome now in the missionary ranks of the church. At the regional level, individual churches are gathered into **stakes** of four thousand to five thousand members, under the leadership of a stake president. At the local level is the local church—called a **ward**—with no more than a few hundred members, under a bishop. Presidents and bishops are men who hold the Melchizedek priesthood, but as we said earlier, they are not clergy in the wider Christian sense, nor do they have a theological education. The religious life of the individual Mormon centers on the ward; the ward organizes weekly worship, sponsors social activities, collects tithes, and administers the local levels of the LDS Church's extensive social welfare plans. With this ward activity, individual Mormons do their part to make the Church of Jesus Christ of Latter-day Saints one of the most powerful NRMs in the world.

13-6 A North American NRM: The Nation of Islam

About one-third of North American Muslims today are African Americans who have joined either mainstream Islam or a sectarian Islamic movement. The largest sectarian group is the Black Muslim movement. In 1930, Elijah Poole, an African American living in Detroit, met W. D. Fard, a man of either Iranian or Turkish descent who preached Islam as the only true religion for African Americans. Poole converted to this movement, changing his name to Elijah Muhammad. He effectively spread Fard's teachings, and their movement grew rapidly. Fard disappeared in 1934, and Elijah Muhammad took over. The movement then became known as "The Lost-Found

endowment Mormon temple rite of adult initiation in which blessings and knowledge are imparted

sealing Mormon temple rite uniting families for time and eternity

temple garment Type of white underwear worn by Mormons

stakes Regional bodies of Mormon churches under a president

ward Local Mormon church under a bishop

Nation of Islam in the Wilderness of North America," or the **Nation of Islam** for short, and spread to many urban areas in the northern United States. Its appeal to prisoners was especially potent, and still is today. Its five main teachings are as follows:

- W. D. Fard is an incarnation of God, and Elijah Muhammad is God's prophet.

- African Americans are descended from a tribe called Shabazz, the ancient pre-Islamic inhabitants of Mecca; they are by nature good.

- White people are wicked and oppressive, the creation of an evil scientist named Yakub.

- Black people ought to recapture their African Muslim roots by submitting to the Five Pillars of Islam and opposing white oppression.

- Black people who submit to God will rule the world, and white people will get the punishment they so richly deserve.

Several obvious differences exist between these Nation of Islam teachings and the teachings of other Muslims. Other Muslims sharply reject the ideas of an incarnation of God in any human and a new prophet equal to Muhammad; they view both as idolatry. Moreover, race-based beliefs are not a legitimate part of Islam. On the other hand, the Nation of Islam appreciates Islamic practices such as the Five Pillars. Despite being largely ignored—or considered heretical—by the rest of the Islamic world, the Nation of Islam became a potent force in the African American community in the United States. It gave hope for a better life to many oppressed people, with resources to fight against drug abuse, poverty, and racism. But it had a race-based message that was problematic for fellow North Americans and for the rest of Islam.

In 1960, a Muslim led a significant change in the Nation of Islam. Malcolm X (born

Malcolm Little) went to Mecca on pilgrimage and saw a harmony between peoples of different races. This experience, along with his growing disillusionment with Elijah Muhammad, gave him a new vision for African American Muslims: God did not want one race to rule another race, but for all races to live together in harmony. He began a new organization of Muslims not based on racial hostility. Malcolm's new message was appealing to many African American Muslims, and it survived his death in 1965 at the hands of two disgruntled members of the Nation of Islam.

Warith Muhammad, Elijah's son, then led the Nation of Islam until his death in 2008, taking the Black Muslim movement in the direction that Malcolm X had begun. He brought the Black Muslim movement into mainstream Sunni Islam. He renounced all beliefs that Sunnis considered heretical, adopting authentically Muslim beliefs and practices. Muhammad began cooperating with worldwide Islam. He permitted American Muslims in his movement to participate in politics and vote, and he abolished the paramilitary wing of the Nation of Islam. This movement has had three names, currently the **American Society of Muslims**. These changes resulted in his movement receiving large amounts of Muslim financial support from Arab nations.

This reform produced an almost-immediate reaction. In 1978, Louis Farrakhan (FAIR-uh-kahn) moved some African American Muslims back to a revived Nation of Islam. Farrakhan occasionally used strong rhetoric, especially against Jews. He continued the efforts to keep African American neighborhoods free from drugs and drug-related crimes through educational and private

Malcolm X, American Muslim reformer, in 1964

LIBRARY OF CONGRESS, U.S. NEWS & WORLD REPORT MAGAZINE COLLECTION, LC-U9-11695-FRAME #5

Nation of Islam "Black Muslim" movement in North America begun by W. D. Fard and now led by Louis Farrakhan.

American Society of Muslims American Muslim reform movement founded by Malcolm X, with mainstream Sunni features

policing activities, and to free African Americans from white economic power. Farrakhan's movement is based in Chicago, but three other groups claiming to be the authentic Nation of Islam are based in Baltimore, Detroit, and Atlanta. Today, most African American Muslims belong not to these Nation of Islam groups but to the American Society of Muslims, where they are mainstream Sunnis. Despite its small size relative to the American Society of Muslims and the fact that it is much smaller now than before 1960, the Nation of Islam is an active and occasionally vocal part of American religious life today.

13-7 The Church of Scientology

Scientology was born in the 1950s from the thoughts of L. Ronald Hubbard (1911–1986). Hubbard said that he aimed to understand mental and emotional problems and propose a way to end them. His initial focus was almost completely psychological, but after a few years he broadened his thinking to a more explicitly religious approach, and called it Scientology. He established the Church of Scientology in 1954, and today it is a strong—and strongly controversial—NRM.

13-7a L. Ron Hubbard's Life and Teachings

Hubbard was an undergraduate at George Washington University from 1930 to 1932 but dropped out, as he later said, to pursue more pressing personal interests. In 1933, he married and began a successful career as a short-feature writer. His output included western fiction, horror stories, and especially science fiction. He also became interested in seafaring, and was something of an adventurer. In 1940 and 1941, he obtained licenses as a master of power and sailing vessels. Nautical themes and terms would later have a large place in Scientology.

During World War II, Hubbard entered the U.S. Navy and served in naval intelligence. At the end of the war he was treated at a naval hospital in Oakland, California. This seems to

L. Ron Hubbard

MONDADORI/GETTY IMAGES

have been the catalyst for his thinking on the human mind, and he began searching for a science of the mind. His ideas first appeared in his book *The Original Thesis* (1948) and were further developed in *Dianetics: The Modern Science of Mental Health* (1950). Although Dianetics is by far the most important of Scientology literature, all Hubbard's publications on Scientology became the official scriptures of the church.

Hubbard believed that the world is overall a good place and that the goal of human existence is survival in the world and enjoyment of it. He wrote, "Life, all life, is trying to survive." Deeds and thought habits that lead to survival are good and result in healthy pleasure. Deeds that go against survival are destructive, and they perpetuate negative mental states. Every mind in a normal state makes correct judgments for survival. However, when one's mind isn't functioning normally, what Hubbard called the "reactive mind" takes over. This mind contains memories called **engrams**, which have strong negative emotional content. Later experiences may call forth negative emotions from the stored engrams, leading to actions that hinder pleasure and survival.

To help people learn about their personal engrams and deal with them, Hubbard developed **auditing**.

This is a counseling process in which an auditor, or therapist, helps the client deal with his or her engrams. A key part of auditing is the **E-meter**, a device that measures a very small electrical current that is said to pass through a person being audited. The auditor uses E-meter readings to identify engrams, and then talks out these engrams with the person being audited. The goal of auditing is to free the mind of engrams; when that is accomplished, the individual is said to be **clear**. Much of the income of Scientology comes from the fees for these auditing sessions.

What moved Hubbard to develop Dianetics into a religion was, among other things, his experience of "exteriorization." This is when the individual consciousness senses that it has left the body. Hubbard concluded that the real spiritual self—what he called the **thetan**—is a being distinct from the body. The thetan is the true self of every person, but most people never know this. Thetans have inhabited many other bodies before coming into their present bodies, a concept similar to reincarnation. This emphasis on the thetan led to a religion that shares elements with some Asian religions, without embracing them. But it was incompatible with the teaching of Christian churches. Even though Scientology calls itself a church and has some of the trappings of Christianity such as crosses and church services (adapted for Scientology), it has never claimed to be Christian. In other words, for Hubbard and Scientologists, *church* means simply a religious organization.

Hubbard wrote that the original Cause (loosely understood as God) created thetans billions of years ago, just before the universe began. Their interaction with each other gave rise to **MEST** (matter, energy, space, and time), and thus the physical universe came into existence. In time, all thetans became trapped in MEST, and they eventually lost the knowledge of who they were. After wandering through the universe, they finally came to earth.

Scientology maintains, against some controversy, that it enables people to know how engrams inhibit them from fully living as thetans. As stated previously, Hubbard believed that freeing

the individual from mental and emotional error is the fundamental purpose of religion. The main goal of all religion, he said, has been the salvation of the human spirit, but only Scientology knows how this salvation can be realized. The most sacred and secret doctrines of Scientology are about the **Operating Thetan** (OT) levels, at which one lives as a fully conscious, well-functioning thetan freed from their engrams and MEST. In the OT, the spirit controls the body and can act independently of it.

In his habit of continually developing his teachings, Hubbard later identified more significant teachings beyond the thetan. He named these **dynamics**, or drive for survival. When auditing begins, the individual first learns the dynamic of individual survival, and then the three larger dynamics: the family, the nation, and all humans. Much of the social-betterment efforts of Scientology flow from these three larger dynamics. Four other dynamics were developed to include even larger entities—animals, the physical side of the universe in MEST, the spiritual side of the

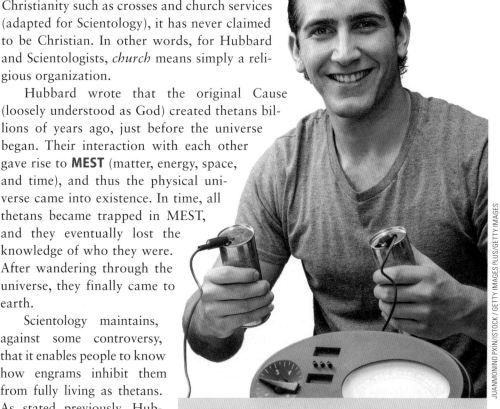

A young Scientologist holds an E-meter.

E-meter Electrical instrument used in Scientology auditing for identification of engrams

clear In Scientology, fully functioning state of the mind when it is rid of engrams

thetan [THAY-tuhn] In Scientology, spiritual entity that can exist apart from the body; the true self of every person

MEST In Scientology, matter, energy, space, and time, which form the physical universe and trap thetans

Operating Thetan Levels at which a Scientologist lives as a fully conscious, well-functioning thetan

dynamics In Scientology, the drive for survival that encompasses eight aspects

Figure 13.3 | The symbol of Scientology, an eight-pointed cross

BONNIE VAN VOORST © CENGAGE LEARNING

universe composed of thetans, and finally infinity or God. The eight-pointed cross (Figure 13.3), now the official symbol of Scientology, symbolizes these eight dynamics, with no reference to the death of Jesus Christ. Finally, we should treat more fully Scientology's beliefs about God. Individual Scientologists experience God as the highest dynamic, but Scientology asks them to reach their own conclusions about who—or what—God is. Nevertheless, what the individual Scientologist believes about God is important. As Hubbard wrote, "It is an empirical observation that men without a strong and lasting faith in a Supreme Being are less capable, less ethical and less valuable to themselves and society." Despite this affirmation of an idea that is much contested today—that one needs a God to be good—Scientology does not specify any teachings about God, but aims to realize individual potential. Scientology is a psychological, not a theological, religion.

Sea Organization
Group of full-time church workers who assist national and local Scientology organizations

13-7b Organization of the Church

Hubbard always kept a firm hand on the rudder of Scientology. Soon after its founding, he started an initiative to attract Hollywood celebrities to its ranks (see "A Closer Look: Scientology and Celebrities"). He resigned from his formal leadership of the church in 1966 in order to go to sea and discover the OT levels and write the training materials to enable members of the church to reach them. He established a society of highly dedicated church members to whom he delegated these new teachings. He called this society the Flag Service Organization. Headquartered in Clearwater, Florida, at the Fort Harrison Hotel, now owned by the church, it provides instruction for the highest OT levels. Contents of the OT training are only for church members who have paid for, and successfully completed, the basic auditing to rid themselves of engrams, thus allowing them to perfect themselves as OTs.

A well-known part of Scientology is the **Sea Organization**, (which Scientologists typically call *Sea Org* for short), established in 1968. Its approximately six thousand members work in the central offices of the Church of Scientology as well as in individual churches; they are considered the most dedicated of Scientologists. They sign agreements to serve in the Sea Org through thousands of lives and millions of years. Its members do not actually work for the Sea Org itself, but for the local church or office where they are employed, and receive a weekly allowance.

Scientology functions mainly through its local churches, but unlike local churches in Christianity, they are organized on a business model. Local churches are semi-independent corporations franchised to use Scientology materials, teach the religion, and conduct auditing and counseling. A church member who has become clear by auditing and wants to become an OT gets instruction at one of the OT training centers. As stated earlier, the majority of the church's income comes from auditing sessions, and expensive fees for instruction to reach OT levels significantly add to this. Administration of local Scientology churches and missions is carried out by the Church of Scientology International. The Religious Technology Center (RTC) of the Church of Scientology has final authority for the religion. It owns and cares for the manuscripts, recordings, and publications of L. Ron Hubbard—the Scientology scriptures. It also grants to local Scientology churches and regional organizations the legal permission to operate. The RTC also ensures that the church's

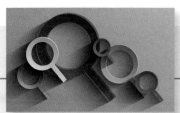

A Closer Look

Scientology and Celebrities

Scientology has always sought to attract celebrities in art, music, and especially film. Already in 1955, shortly after Scientology was founded, L. Ron Hubbard began "Project Celebrity" to work for the conversion of prominent actors and musicians. Hubbard believed that celebrities are special people who have power to shape public opinion about Scientology and attract others to it. Today Scientology operates Celebrity Centers in Los Angeles, Nashville, and Paris, luxurious facilities that cater to celebrities. This effort to bring celebrities into the church has been highly successful.

Why would celebrities be drawn to Scientology? Perhaps the best explanation comes from Hugh B. Urban, a professor of religion at Ohio State University and author of one of the few academic books on Scientology, *The Church of Scientology: A History of a New Religion*.[5] After stating on Beliefnet.com that the first reason is Scientology's targeting of celebrities, Urban goes on to say:

> [Scientology is] a religion that fits pretty well with a celebrity kind of personality. It's very individualistic. It celebrates your individual identity as ultimately divine. It claims to give you ultimate power over your own mind, self, destiny, so I think it fits well with an actor personality.... These aren't people who need more wealth, but what they do need, or often want at least, is some kind of spiritual validation for their wealth and lifestyle, and Scientology is a religion that says it's OK to be wealthy, it's OK to be famous; in fact, that's a sign of your spiritual development.[6]

Among the most well-known celebrity Scientologists are John Travolta, Kirstie Alley, Nancy Cartwright (the voice of Bart Simpson), Jason Lee, Giovanni Ribisi, Jenna Elfman, Anne Archer, and musicians Chick Corea and the late Isaac Hayes. Probably the best-known Scientology celebrity is Tom Cruise. Scientology works to convert celebrities who are at or approaching what the church considers their prime. New and rising stars in the world of music and movies, whom you may know, are not often found in its ranks.

Scientologist and film star John Travolta speaks at a new Scientology Center in St. Petersburg, Florida. A bust of L. Ron Hubbard is on his left.

WILLIE J. ALLEN JR./TIMES/ZUMA PRESS, INC / ALAM

procedures are followed, that franchises are carried out legally and faithfully, and that its "spiritual technology" (such as the E-meter) is used properly.

To meet what it described as an increasing worldwide need for Scientology, the church launched a program in 2012 to transform all local Scientology churches into what L. Ron Hubbard is said to have called Ideal Organizations. An Ideal Organization church offers all the programs of Scientology to its members and at the same time reaches out to the community where it is located with social-improvement programs. Scientologists typically see themselves as uniquely qualified and obligated to provide effective service to others. This Ideal Organization effort shows two important aspects of Scientology today: It reaches back to its deceased founder to claim guidance for new initiatives, and it shares a wider contemporary religious impulse in North America to make religion more relevant and helpful in public life.

In the 1970s, Scientology spread throughout Europe; Hubbard's writings and course materials were translated into many languages. Following the 1980s fall of Communist governments in Eastern Europe, it also spread quickly there. Today, the Church of Scientology operates in more than 150 countries, but it remains controversial. We will examine this topic next.

13-7c Controversy and Present Status

Scientology has always been controversial. When Hubbard first introduced Dianetics as a mental therapy, physicians and psychiatrists charged that it involved practicing medicine without a license. They also disputed Dianetics's understanding of the human mind. Scientologists responded that psychiatrists deny the spiritual side of human life. Thus began what would prove to be a long conflict with the American Psychiatric Association (APA). The church developed a strong opposition to medicines used to treat mental illness, claiming they did more harm than good. Conflict with the APA, including a campaign against the popular drug Prozac, has been carried on by a special organization in the church called the Citizens' Commission on Human Rights.

Another dimension of conflict is opposition to Scientology by the federal government. In 1958, the U.S. Internal Revenue Service began investigating Scientology churches for possible violations of federal tax laws. U.S. Food and Drug Administration agents searched the local church in Washington, D.C., in 1963 and took its E-meters, charging that they were unapproved medical devices. These actions by the U.S. government also led to action against the church in both Australia and the United Kingdom. In response, the church created the Guardian's Office in 1966 to vigorously defend Scientology, usually by going on the offensive against its opponents. (Scientology does not usually turn the other cheek.) The Guardian's Office filed lawsuits against publications the church considered libelous. In the 1970s, it began a worldwide operation to gather information on opposition to the church. Frustrated by the U.S. government's refusal to release information about its investigations of Scientology, some leaders in the Guardian's Office approved and carried out a plan to infiltrate or break into various federal agencies in order to obtain this information. As a result, agents of the Guardian's Office were arrested in 1979 and convicted of a variety of crimes. The church expelled those who broke the law, and the office was disbanded. However, the church still takes an active role in dealing with its opponents.

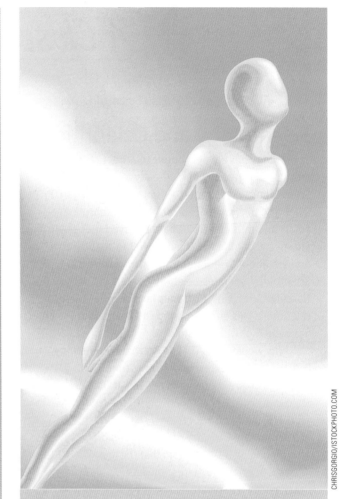

Artist's depiction of the human spirit or soul—in Scientology understood as the thetan. Hubbard's teaching on thetans is one of the several controversial aspects of Scientology.

CHRISGORGIO/ISTOCKPHOTO.COM

In 1993, the church finally gained recognition as a religious organization and the tax-exempt status that went with it. The church saw this as recognition that it is a genuine religion. Nevertheless, Scientology faces continuing controversy and challenges. Several former members have strongly criticized the church, charging it with deceiving its members financially, harrying journalists, and acting vindictively against those who try to leave the church. Scientology is under pressure in Germany and France. Some Germans hold that Scientology is a totalitarian organization, forbidden under the country's postwar constitution. The German government even proposed in the 1990s that a symbol of Scientology be put on Scientologists' identity papers, which understandably raised a storm of protest because of the use of identity marks for some groups during the Hitler era. In

2009, a French court convicted Scientology officials of fraud but did not suspend the church's activities there. Scientologists regard these actions as a violation of their religious liberty.

Opposition to Scientology continues today. An increasing number of former Scientologists, a few of them high placed in the church, have gone public to oppose it. The church responds by calling them "suppressive persons," or "suppressives" for short. Public opposition to the church has grown in recent years to probably its strongest ever. For example, "Going Clear, Scientology and the Prison of Belief," the 2015 HBO series based on the book of the same title by ex-Scientologist Lawrence Wright, was both critically and popularly acclaimed. Another blow against Scientology was struck by the actress and ex-Scientologist Leah Remini, who starred in the 2017 A&E Network documentary "Scientology and the Aftermath." Especially vexing to the church has been the Internet posting of secret, copyrighted materials for the OT levels. In recent years, hundreds of protests and demonstrations have been held at Scientology locations in North America and Europe by anti-Scientology groups.

To conclude this chapter, we can state that NRMs, for all their wide diversity, are a religious response to modern life: pluralism; the influence of science, especially the rise of psychology and psychotherapy; a rising value placed on nature and the environment; and secularization. They are also efforts to find alternatives to the mainstream religious traditions. Although a few NRMs have come to tragic ends and some have faded away quickly, many have provided meaning in life to those who have not obtained it elsewhere. A few NRMs may eventually become mainstream religions. Even now, NRMs increase the diversity and vitality of the world's religions.

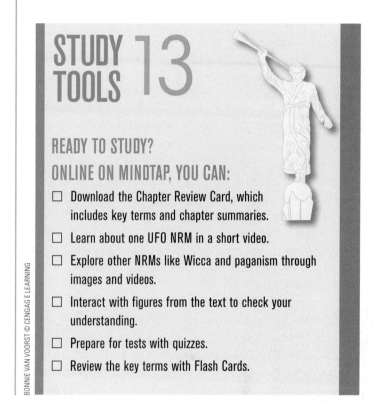

STUDY TOOLS 13

READY TO STUDY?
ONLINE ON MINDTAP, YOU CAN:

- ☐ Download the Chapter Review Card, which includes key terms and chapter summaries.
- ☐ Learn about one UFO NRM in a short video.
- ☐ Explore other NRMs like Wicca and paganism through images and videos.
- ☐ Interact with figures from the text to check your understanding.
- ☐ Prepare for tests with quizzes.
- ☐ Review the key terms with Flash Cards.

BONNIE VAN VOORST © CENGAGE LEARNING

New Religious Movements Timeline: 1782–2017

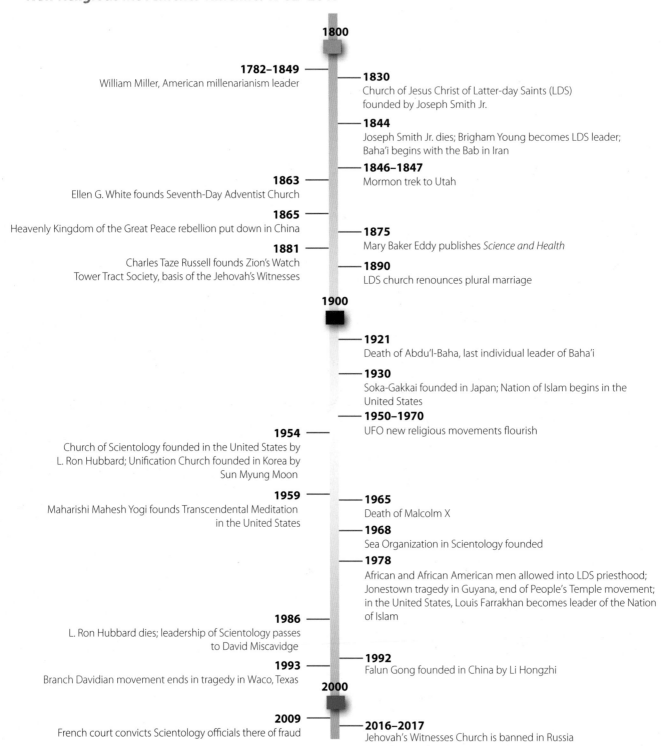

1800

1782–1849 —
William Miller, American millenarianism leader

— **1830**
Church of Jesus Christ of Latter-day Saints (LDS) founded by Joseph Smith Jr.

— **1844**
Joseph Smith Jr. dies; Brigham Young becomes LDS leader; Baha'i begins with the Bab in Iran

— **1846–1847**
Mormon trek to Utah

1863 —
Ellen G. White founds Seventh-Day Adventist Church

1865 —
Heavenly Kingdom of the Great Peace rebellion put down in China

— **1875**
Mary Baker Eddy publishes *Science and Health*

1881 —
Charles Taze Russell founds Zion's Watch Tower Tract Society, basis of the Jehovah's Witnesses

— **1890**
LDS church renounces plural marriage

1900

— **1921**
Death of Abdu'l-Baha, last individual leader of Baha'i

— **1930**
Soka-Gakkai founded in Japan; Nation of Islam begins in the United States

— **1950–1970**
UFO new religious movements flourish

1954 —
Church of Scientology founded in the United States by L. Ron Hubbard; Unification Church founded in Korea by Sun Myung Moon

1959 —
Maharishi Mahesh Yogi founds Transcendental Meditation in the United States

— **1965**
Death of Malcolm X

— **1968**
Sea Organization in Scientology founded

— **1978**
African and African American men allowed into LDS priesthood; Jonestown tragedy in Guyana, end of People's Temple movement; in the United States, Louis Farrakhan becomes leader of the Nation of Islam

1986 —
L. Ron Hubbard dies; leadership of Scientology passes to David Miscavidge

1993 —
Branch Davidian movement ends in tragedy in Waco, Texas

— **1992**
Falun Gong founded in China by Li Hongzhi

2000

2009 —
French court convicts Scientology officials there of fraud

— **2016–2017**
Jehovah's Witnesses Church is banned in Russia

Endnotes

1

1. Laurie Goodstein, "Basic Religion Test Stumps Many Americans," *New York Times*, September 28, 2010, A17, New York City edition.

2. John Bowker, ed., *Oxford Dictionary of World Religions* (New York: Oxford University Press, 1997), xv.

3. Karen Armstrong, *A History of God* (New York: Ballantine, 1994), 1.

4. P. G. W. Glare, *Oxford Latin Dictionary* (New York: Oxford University Press, 1983), 1605–06.

5. Stephen Prothero, *Religious Literacy* (San Francisco: HarperSan-Francisco, 2007), 5.

6. "American Academy of Religion Guidelines for Teaching about Religion in K–12 Public Schools in the United States," http://pluralism.org/document/guidelines-for-teaching-about-religion-in-k-12-public-schools-in-the-united-states/, accessed 8/21/17.

7. This listing of skills is adapted from "The Religion Major and Liberal Education—A White Paper," https://www.aarweb.org/sites/default/files/pdfs/About/Committees/AcademicRelations/Teagle_WhitePaper.pdf, accessed 8/21/17.

8. Rodney Stark and Charles Glock, *Patterns of Religious Commitment* (Berkeley: University of California Press, 1968).

9. Alfred North Whitehead, *Religion in the Making* (New York: World, 1960), 115.

10. Guy Stroumsa, *A New Science: The Discovery of Religion in the Age of Reason* (Cambridge: Harvard University Press, 2010).

11. Philip Jenkins, "Ancient and Modern: What the History of Religion Teaches Us about Contemporary Global Trends," ARDA Guiding Paper, http://www.thearda.com/rrh/papers/guidingpapers/jenkins.asp, accessed 7/17/10.

12. James R. Lewis and Sarah M. Lewis, *Sacred Schisms: How Religions Divide* (Cambridge, UK: Cambridge University Press, 2009).

13. Marta Trzebiatowska and Steve Bruce, *Why Are Women More Religious than Men?* (New York: Oxford University Press, 2012).

14. Bruce Malina, *The New Testament World: Insights from Cultural Anthropology*, 3rd ed. (Louisville, KY: Westminster John Knox, 2001).

15. Clifford Geertz, *Islam Observed* (New Haven: Yale University Press, 1968), 4.

16. Pew Research Center, "The Gender Gap in Religion Around the World," http://www.pewforum.org/2016/03/22/the-gender-gap-in-religion-around-the-world/, accessed 1/12/2017.

17. Dean Hamer, *The God Gene: How Faith Is Hardwired into Our Genes* (New York: Doubleday, 2004).

18. Christopher Hitchens, *God Is Not Great: How Religion Poisons Everything* (Boston: Twelve Publishing Company, 2007), 56.

19. Edward O. Wilson, *The Social Conquest of Earth* (New York: Liveright, 2012).

20. Alain de Botton, *Religion for Atheists: A Non-Believer's Guide to the Uses of Religion* (New York: Pantheon, 2012).

21. Jacques Berlinerblau, *The Secular Bible: Why Non-Believers Must Take Religion Seriously* (New York: Cambridge University Press, 2005).

22. Chris Beneke, *Beyond Toleration: The Religious Origins of American Pluralism* (New York: Oxford University Press, 2006).

23. Stephen Prothero, *God Is Not One: The Eight Rival Religions That Run the World—And Why Their Differences Matter* (New York: HarperOne, 2010).

24. Diana Eck, "What is Pluralism," at http://pluralism.org/what-is-pluralism/, accessed 8/21/17.

25. Seyyed Hossein Nasr, *Man and Nature: The Spiritual Crisis in Modern Man*, rev. ed. (Chicago: Kazi Publishers, 1997).

26. Lynn White Jr., "The Historical Roots of Our Ecologic Crisis," *Science* 155, no. 3767 (March 10, 1967).

27. Praesenjit Duara, Crisis of Global Modernity: Asian Traditions and a Sustainable Future (Cambridge, UK: Cambridge University Press, 2014).

28. Philip Jenkins, "Where Have All the Cultists Gone?" http://www.patheos.com/blogs/anxiousbench/2014/06/where-have-all-the-cultists-gone/, accessed 8/21/17.

2

1. Edward Tylor, Primitive Culture : Researches into the Development of Mythology, Philosophy, Religion, Language, Art, and Custom (London: Murray, 1871).

2. Alice Kehoe, *Shamans and Religion: An Exploration in Critical Thinking* (Long Grove, IL: Waveland Press, 2000).

3. Catherine L. Albanese, *Nature Religion in America: From the Algonkian Indians to the New Age* (Chicago: University of Chicago Press, 1991).

4. N. Scott Momaday, *The Names* (Tucson: University of Arizona Press, 1976), 25.

5. Vine Deloria Jr., *God Is Red: A Native View of Religion* (New York: Putnam, 1973), 278.

6. Mircea Eliade, *Shamanism: Archaic Techniques of Ecstasy* (New York: Random House, 1964).

7. Hiram Price, *Annual Report of the Commissioner of Indian Affairs* (Washington, D.C.: House Executive Document 1, 47th Congress), 3–4.

8. Vera L. Drysdale, *The Gift of the Sacred Pipe* (Norman, OK: University of Oklahoma Press, 1982), 6.

9. Velma E. Love, *Divining the Self: A Study in Yoruba Myth and Human Consciousness* (University Park, PA: Penn State University Press, 2012).

3

1. Andrea Jain, *Selling Yoga: From Counterculture to Pop Culture* (New York: Oxford University Press, 2014).

5

1. Damien Keown, *Buddhism* (Oxford, UK: Oxford University Press, 1996), 17.

2. Pew Research Center, "The Future of World Religions: Population Growth Projections, 2010–2050." http://www.pewforum.org/2015/04/02/religiousprojections- 2010–2050/, accessed 5/21/2015.

3. Kim Gutschow, "The Death of the Buddha's Mother," *Harvard Divinity Bulletin* 47 (2016):46-55.

4. Henry Steel Olcott, *Buddhist Catechism* (London: Truebner, 1882).

5. Robert Pirsig, *Zen and the Art of Motorcycle Maintenance* (New York: Harper, 2008; originally published in 1974).

6. Jeff Wilson, *Mindful America: The Mutual Transformaton of Buddhist Meditation and American Culture* (New York: Oxford University Press, 2014).

6

1. Pashaura Singh, *Sikhism in Global Context* (Oxford, UK: Oxford University Press, 2012).

2. Kamala Elizabeth Nayar, *Sikh Diaspora in Vancouver: Three Generations amid Tradition, Modernity, and Multiculturalism* (Toronto: Toronto University Press, 2004).

7

1. http://www.worldreligiondatabase.org/wrd_default.asp, accessed 9/12/10.

2. Stephen Prothero, *God Is Not One: The Eight Rival Religions That Run the World—And Why Their Differences Matter* (New York: HarperOne, 2010), 101.

3. Livia Kohn, ed., *Daoism Handbook* (Leiden: Brill, 2000), xi, xxix.

4. Lionel Jensen, *Manufacturing Confucianism: Chinese Traditions and Universal Civilization* (Durham: Duke University Press, 1998).

5. Fengyang Yang, *Religion in China: Survival and Revival under Communist Rule* (New York: Oxford University Press, 2012).

6. S. L. Wolf, M. O'Grady, K. A. Easley, Y. Guo, R. W. Kressig, and M. Kutner, "The Influence of Intense Tai Chi Training on Physical Performance and Hemodynamic Outcomes in Transitionally Frail, Older Adults," *Journal of Gerontology* 61, no. 2 (2006): 184–89. A summary can be found at http://www.ncbi.nlm.nih.gov/pubmed/16510864.

7. Anna Sun, *Confucianism as a World Religion: Contested Histories and Contemporary Realities* (Princeton: Princeton University Press, 2013).

8

1. *Transactions of the Asiatic Society of Japan*, vol. 3 (Yokohama, Japan: Asiatic Society Press, 1873), 36.

2. Hiroko Tabuchi, "Robot Invasion Welcomed in Japan," *The New York Times*, https://lens.blogs.nytimes.com/2010/09/13/robot-invasion-welcomed-in-japan/?mcubz=1&_r=0, accessed 8/21/2017.

3. Lisa Kuly, "Locating Transcendence in Japanese Minzoku Geino," *Ethnologies* 25 (2003): 201.

9

1. Mary Boyce, *Zoroastrians: Their Religious Beliefs and Practices* (London: Routledge and Kegan Paul, 1979), 1, 29.

2. James Barr, "The Question of Religious Influence: The Case of Zoroastrianism, Judaism, and Christianity," *Journal of the American Academy of Religion* 53 (1985): 201–35.

3. http://matrimonial.ParsiZoroastrianism.com, accessed 7/1/2015. 372 Endnotes

4. Herodotus, *Histories*, Book 1, in William Stearns Davis, "Readings in Ancient History: Illustrative Extracts from the Sources", vol. 2, *Greece and the East* (Boston: Allyn and Bacon, 1912), 60.

10

1. Abraham Heschel, *The Prophets*, study edition (Peabody, MA: Hendricksen, 2007).

2. Jacob Neusner, "Judaism," in Arvind Sharma, ed., *Our Religions* (New York: HarperOne, 1994), 314.

3. Jean-Christophe Attias, *The Jews and the Bible* (Stanford, CA: Stanford University Press, 2014).

4. Paul Johnson, *A History of the Jews* (New York: Harper and Row, 1987), 587.

5. Aviva Ben-Ur, *Sephardic Jews in America* (New York: NYU Press, 2012).

6. Pew Forum, "Religious Composition by Country, 2010-2050," www.Pewforum.org/2015/04/02/religious-projection-table, accessed 9/15/2015.

11

1. David D. Hall, *A Reforming People: Puritanism and the Transformation of Public Life in New England* (New York: Knopf, 2011).

2. Mark Noll, *The New Shape of World Christianity: How American Experience Reflects Global Faith* (Downers Grove, IL: IVP Academic, 2009).

3. "America's Changing Religious Landscape," at http://www.pewforum.org/2015/05/12/americas-changing-religious-landscape/, accessed 8/17/2015.

4. Tanya Luhrmann, *When God Talks Back: Understanding the American Evangelical Relationship with God* (New York: Vintage, 2012).

12

1. W. Montgomery Watt, *Muhammad: Prophet and Statesman* (New York: Oxford University Press, 1974), 51.

2. Daniel Peterson, *Muhammad, Prophet of God* (Grand Rapids, MI: Eerdmans, 2007), 91.

3. Rodney Stark, *Discovering God: The Origins of the Great Religions and the Evolution of Belief* (New York: HarperOne, 2008), 378.

4. Geneive Abdo, *The New Sectarianism: The Arab Uprisings and the Rebirth of the Shi'a-Sunni Divide* (New York: Oxford University Press, 2016).

5. Rozina Ali, "The Erasure of Islam from the Poetry of Rumi," *The New Yorker* (January 5, 2017), http://www.newyorker.com/books/page-turner/the-erasure-of-islam-from-the-poetry-of-rumi.

6. Omid Safi, *Progressive Muslims: On Justice, Gender, and Pluralism* (New York: OneWorld, 2003).

7. M. Brett Wilson, *Translating the Qur'an in an Age of Nationalism* (New York: Oxford University Press, 2014).

8. Jerusha Tanner Lamptey, *New Wholly Other: A Muslima Theology of Religious Pluralism* (New York: Oxford University Press, 2014).

9. Leila Ahmed, *A Quiet Revolution: The Veil's Resurgence from the Middle East to America* (New Haven: Yale University Press, 2012).

10. Stephen Prothero, *God Is Not One* (New York: HarperOne, 2010), 26.

11. Robert R. Bianchi, *Guests of God: Pilgrimage and Politics in the Islamic World* (New York: Oxford University Press, 2004), 272.

12. John Esposito and Dalia Mogahed, *Who Speaks for Islam? What a Billion Muslims Really Think* (New York: Gallup Press, 2007).

13

1. For an excellent concise overview of NRMs, see W. H., Swatus Jr., ed., *Encyclopedia of Religion and Society* (Walnut Creek, CA: AltaMira, 1998), 328–333. For an anthology, see Michael Ashcraft and Dereck Daschke, eds., *New Religious Movements: A Documentary Reader* (New York: NYU Press, 2005).

2. Quoted in Toby Lester, "Oh, Gods!" *The Atlantic* (February 2002), http://theatlantic.com/magazine/archive/2002/02/oh-gods/2412/, accessed 4/25/2011.

3. Laura Vance, *Women in New Religions* (New York: NYU Press, 2015).

4. Fenggang Yang, *Religion in China: Survival and Revival under Communist Rule* (New York: Oxford University Press, 2012), 26.

5. Hugh B. Urban, *The Church of Scientology: A History of a New Religion* (Princeton: Princeton University Press, 2013).

6. Quoted from Beliefnet.com, http://www.beliefnet.com/Faiths/Scientology/Mind-Over-Matter.aspx?p=4, accessed 1/14/2013.

Index

D

daevas, 214
Dalai Lama, 119, 120
Dalits, 77–78, 85, 124, 147
Dancing Religion, 337
Dao, 168–170, 174–176
Daode Jing, 175–176, 182, 184
Daoism (Taoism), 7, 16, 117, 154–184, 337
    around the world, 182–184
    compared with Confucianism, 181
    essential teachings, 167–174
    ethics, 175–176
    features of, 156
    history of, 158–167
    name, 156–158
    origins of, 160–162
    ritual and worship, 178–181
    symbols, 157
    timeline of, 184
    vegetarianism, 176
Daoling, Zhang, 160
Daozang, 162
Darbar Sahib, 141
Darius the Great, 209
Darwin, Charles, 269
Das, Arjan, 142
Das, Ram, 141–142
Dasam Granth, 143
David, 227, 238, 309
de, 169
death. *See also* funerals
    in Buddhism, 124, 130
    in Christianity, 283–284
    in Confucianism, 177, 180–181
    in Daoism, 173–174, 178, 180
    in feng shui, 159
    in Hinduism, 85, 87
    in Islam, 318–319
    in Jainism, 99, 104, 105
    in Judaism, 240–241, 248–249
    in Lakota religion, 47
    in Shinto, 193, 201–202
    in Sikhism, 144, 150
    in Zoroastrianism, 205, 215, 216, 218
deities. *See* gods, goddesses
denominations, 270
Devi, 72
Devotional period, in Hinduism, 68–71
dharma, 74, 80, 121
dharmachakra, 111
dhoti, 81
Diamond Sutra, 117
Diamond Vehicle, 118–120
Dianetics (Hubbard), 348, 352
diaspora, 88, 151–152, 228, 237
diet
    Daoism and, 176
    Islam and, 312
    in Jainism, 101
    Jainism and, 102

    Judaism and, 246
    Sikhism and, 149
Digambar, 96–98
divinities, Vodou, 55
divorce, 82, 249, 267, 312, 314
Diwali, 106, 150
Doctrine and Covenants, 344
Doctrine of the Mean, 166
Dogg, Snoop, 213
Dogon, 43
Dome of the Rock mosque, 319
Dong Zhongshu, 164–165
Dravidians, 63
dress
    in Islam, 313
    in Judaism, 239
    in Sikhism, 146
Druidry, 335–336
dualism, 214–215
dukkha, 123
Durkheim, Émile, 17
Dyer, Wayne, 184
dynamics, 350

E

Earth God, 171
Easter, 283
Eastern Orthodox Church, 256, 262, 263, 280, 281, 286
    ecological crisis, 25–26
    ecumenical agencies, 279
ecumenism, 270
Eddy, Mary Baker, **334**
Effendi, Shoghi, 332
Egypt, 298, 304–305
Ek Onkar, 145
elders, respect for, 168, 176
Eleazar, Israel ben, 232
Eliade, Mircea, 11
Elizabeth I, 267
ema, 200
emancipation, 233
emergent religions, 329
Emerson, Ralph Waldo, 130
emotional dimension, of religion, 12–13
endowment, 346
engrams, 348
Enlightenment, 13, 24, 233–234, 241, 268
environmentalism, 25–26
Epiphany, 283
Episcopal Church, 270
Eshu, 53
Essenes, 229
Eternal Spring Temple, 26
ethical dimension, of religion, 11
ethics
    Buddhist, 124–126
    Christian, 276–279
    Confucian, 174, 176–178
    Daoist, 176–177
    Hindu, 76–82

in Daoism, 170–172
in Hinduism, 64, 71–73, 83
in Jainism, 98
in Zoroastrianism, 214
Golden Rule, 277
Gommateshvara, 97, 103
Good Samaritan, 277
Gospels, 256, 260, 273, 275
Graham, Billy, 287
granthi, 149
Great Learning, 166
Great Spirit, 41
Grebel, Conrad, 265
Gregory VII, 263–264
gris-gris, 57
guilt, 35–36
Guo Guang, 172 (AU: Found as Huo Guang in the text)
gurdwara, 147–149, 152
Gurmat, 140
guru, 75
Guru Granth, 140, 142, 145–150
Gyatso, Tenzin, 120

H

hadith, 311
Hagia Sophia, 280, 299
Haiti, 54, 57–58
hajj, 318–319
Hajji, 319
halakhah, 243
halal, 312
Haley, Nikki, 146
Han dynasty, 165
hanifs, 293
Hanukkah, 229
haoma, 218
haram, 312
Hare Krishna movement, 27
Harijans, 77
Harmandir Sahib, 141–142
Hashem, 239
Hasidism, 232, 251
Hawaii, 41, 52
Heaven, 160, 241, 283, 310
Heavenly Kingdom of the Great Peace, 336
Heaven's Gate, 335
Hebrews, 224–225
hell, 124, 240, 241, 283, 310
henotheism, 238
Henry VIII, 267
heresy, 262
Herod, 229
Herzl, Theodor, 234
hijab, 313, 321
Hijra, 295
Hinayana, 115
Hinduism, 5, 7, 22, 27, 60–91, 116, 333, 334
around the world, 87–90
art of, 12
caste system, 67–68, 74, 76–79, 90, 146
characteristics of, 62
deities, 71–73

doctrinal concepts, 74–76
dress, 81
essential teachings, 71–76
ethics and way of life, 76–82
history of, 63–71
Jainism and, 94
name, 62–63
reform and revisionism, 69–70
rituals and meditation, 82–86
in South Asia and Africa, 87
symbols of, 64
timeline of, 91
in the West, 87–89
Hindutva, 71
Hirohito, 195
Hirsch, Samson Raphael, 234
Hispanic liberation, 279
historical anthropology, 18
historical-critical method, 14
history, 14–15, 35
history of religions school, 15
Hitchens, Christopher, 21
Hitler, Adolf, 235–236
Hola Mahalla, 150
holidays, 85
Holocaust, 23, 235–237, 240
Holy Communion, 281–282
holy death, 98, 104
Holy Spirit, 260, 271, 274–276, 280
Holy Writings, 331
home shrines, 201
honden, 199
Hong Kong, 163
Hong Xiuquan, 163, 336
honor killings, 24
house churches, 260
householder stage, 79
How God Changes Your Brain (Newberg), 17
Hsi Lai Temple, 3
Hubbard, L. Ron, 12, 348–350
Human Genome Project, 20
human migration, 40
human sacrifice, 24

I

I and Thou (Buber), 244
Iconoclastic Controversy, 263
iconostasis, 263
idols, 82, 307
ifa, 54
images
of the Buddha, 128
of Hindu deities, 82–83
of Muhammad, 306–307
imam, 301–302
Imamites, 302
Immaculate Conception, 275
immortality, 174
incarnation, 271
inclusivism, 25
India, 22
Buddhism in, 115, 116

smallpox, 53
small-scale religions, 33
Smith, Buster, 8
Smith, Joseph, 288, 341–344
Socially Engaged Buddhism, 131
sociology, 17
Soka-Gakkai, 338
Solomon, 227
souls, 99
South Asia
    Buddhism in, 115–116
    Hinduism in, 87
South Korea, 131, 182, 271, 338
Soviet Union, 9
speaking in tongues, 282
spells, 57
Spener, Philip Jakob, 268
spirits, 42, 54, 215–216, 307
Sri Lanka, 22, 87
    Buddhism in, 115–116, 132–133
    Sikhism in, 141
stained-glass ceiling, 19
stakes, 346
Star of David, 12, 225
Stealing Buddha's Dinner (Nguyen), 135, 136
Stone of Unction, 258
St. Peter's Basilica, 255
Strang, James, 343
student stage, 79
stupas, 130
subjective knowledge, 101
suffering, in Buddhism, 121–124
Sufis, 302–303
Sukkot, 246
sun dance, 48
Sunnis, 296, 301–302, 321
supernatural intermediaries, in Zoroastrianism, 215–216
surahs, 308
sutra, 115, 118, 126
suttee, 82
Suzuki, D. T., 134
swastika, 64, 95
sweat lodge, 47
symbols
    of Buddhism, 111
    of Christianity, 256
    of Confucianism, 158
    of Daoism, 158
    of Hinduism, 63
    of Islam, 293
    of Jainism, 94
    of Judaism, 224
    of Scientology, 349, 350
    of Shinto, 188
    of Sikhism, 140, 145, 146
    Zoroastrian, 207
synagogues, 230, 233, 244–245, 280

T

tabernacle, 227
Taiji, 157
Taiping Rebellion, 163

Taiping Tianguo, 336
Tai Qi (Tai Chi), 173, 174, 337
Taiwan, 41, 163, 171, 182
Taliban, 24, 305, 306, 313, 322
Talmud, 231, 234, 237, 241
Tanak, 237, 239, 240
Tantras, 69
Tantric Buddhism, 120
Tantrism, 69–70, 334
Tathagata, 113
temple garment, 346
temples
    Buddhist, 109, 128
    Confucian, 179, 182
    Daoist, 171, 178–179, 183–184
    Hindu, 83
    Jain, 104–105, 107–108
    Jewish, 234
    Sikh, 139, 143
    Zoroastrian, 217
Temple Square, 327, 328
Ten Commandments, 227, 242, 243
ten lost tribes, 227
Ten Precepts, 125
Tenrikyo, 337
terrorism, 152–153, 292, 305, 321–324
Thailand, 116, 126
theology, 13–14
Theotokos, 275
Theravada, 115, 132
thetan, 349
Thich Nhat Hanh, 131
Thoreau, Henry, 133
Three Characteristics of Existence, 123–124
Three Refuges, 114
Thus Spoke Zarathustra (Nietzsche), 220
Tian, 169
Tiananmen Square, 155–152
Tibet, 3, 41, 117–120, 130, 132
Tibetan Book of the Dead, 120, 130
Tibetan Buddhism, 134
time, in Jainism, 99
Tipitaka, 115
Tirthankaras, 94
tithe, 345
tolerance, 21–24
Torah, 226, 228, 237, 242
torii, 189
totemism, 32, 34
towers of silence, 210
traditional religion, 32
trance meditation, 129
Transcendental Meditation (TM), 89, 333
transcendentalism, 133
transubstantiation, 281, 282
tricksters, 44
Trikaya, 116–117
Trinity, 271
True Parents, 338
truth, 101
Tsubaki Shinto Shrine, 203
Turkey, 299
Turner, Victor, 19

Wovoka, 49
wu wei, 172
Wycliffe, John, 264

X

Xerxes, 209
xiao, 176

Y

Yahweh, 238
yarmulke, 239
Yasukuni, 193
Yazd, Iran, 205
Yiguan Dao, 337
Yi Jing, 160
yin-yang, 157, 160
yoga, 69, 85–86, 101, 146, 333
Yogananda, Paramahansa, 89, 333
Yogi, Maharishi Mahesh, 89, 333
Yom Kippur, 246
yoni, 73
Yoruban "spirit practices," 53
Yoruba religion, 35, 41, 50–54
  gods in, 51,–53
    religious specialists in, 53–54
    spirits of the ancestors in, 54
Young, Brigham, 327, 342, 343

Z

Zaidites, 302
zakat, 318
Zarathushtrian Assembly, 212
Zarathustra, 205–208, 212–215, 218–220, 309
zazen, 118
Zen, 24, 109, 117–118, 121, 134
Zhihui Tang, 337
zhong, 177
Zhou dynasty, 160
Zhuan Falun, 340
Zhu Xi, 165
Zionism, 234
Zionist movement, 234
zombies, 37, 55–57
Zoroastrian Creed, 213
Zoroastrianism, 204–221
  around the world, 220–221
  essential teachings, 213–215
  ethics, 215–217
  features of, 206
  history of, 207–213
  Islam and, 210–212
  names, 206–207
  rituals, 217–219
  symbol of, 206
  timeline of, 221
Zoroastrians, 309–310
Zoroastrian Studies Association, 213
Zwingli, Huldreich, 267